BUSINESS/SCIENCE/TECHNOLOGY DIVISION
CHICAGO PUBLIC LIBRARY
400 SOUTH STATE STREET
CHICAGO, IL 60605

Understanding IPv6, Second Edition

D1473580

Joseph Davies

PUBLISHED BY
Microsoft Press
A Division of Microsoft Corporation
One Microsoft Way
Redmond, Washington 98052-6399

Copyright © 2008 by Microsoft Corporation

All rights reserved. No part of the contents of this book may be reproduced or transmitted in any form or by any means without the written permission of the publisher.

Library of Congress Control Number: 2007940506

Printed and bound in the United States of America.

1 2 3 4 5 6 7 8 9 QWT 3 2 1 0 9 8

Distributed in Canada by H.B. Fenn and Company Ltd.

A CIP catalogue record for this book is available from the British Library.

Microsoft Press books are available through booksellers and distributors worldwide. For further information about international editions, contact your local Microsoft Corporation office or contact Microsoft Press International directly at fax (425) 936-7329. Visit our Web site at www.microsoft.com/mspress. Send comments to mspinput@microsoft.com.

Microsoft, Microsoft Press, Active Directory, Internet Explorer, PowerPoint, Win32, Windows, Windows Media, Windows Server, and Windows Vista are either registered trademarks or trademarks of Microsoft Corporation in the United States and/or other countries. Other product and company names mentioned herein may be the trademarks of their respective owners.

The example companies, organizations, products, domain names, e-mail addresses, logos, people, places, and events depicted herein are fictitious. No association with any real company, organization, product, domain name, e-mail address, logo, person, place, or event is intended or should be inferred.

This book expresses the author's views and opinions. The information contained in this book is provided without any express, statutory, or implied warranties. Neither the authors, Microsoft Corporation, nor its resellers, or distributors will be held liable for any damages caused or alleged to be caused either directly or indirectly by this book.

Acquisitions Editor: Martin DelRe
Developmental Editor: Karen Szall
Project Editor: Maria Gargiulo
Editorial Production: Interactive Composition Corporation
Technical Reviewer: Bob Dean; Technical Review services provided by Content Master, a member of CM Group, Ltd.
Cover: Tom Draper Design

Body Part No. X14-31167

R0421368051

CHICAGO PUBLIC LIBRARY

For Kara:
Domina mea, amata mea, vita mea.

iii

Contents at a Glance

Table of Contents

What do you think of this book? We want to hear from you!

Microsoft is interested in hearing your feedback so we can continually improve our books and learning resources for you. To participate in a brief online survey, please visit:

www.microsoft.com/learning/booksurvey/

What do you think of this book? We want to hear from you!

Microsoft is interested in hearing your feedback so we can continually improve our books and learning resources for you. To participate in a brief online survey, please visit:

www.microsoft.com/learning/booksurvey/

List of Figures

List of Tables

Foreword

Why Does Microsoft Care About IPv6?

I've been asked this question a lot over the past five years. The answer hasn't changed, and the reasons are as relevant today as they were many years ago when a few engineers in Microsoft Research started building an IPv6 stack for Microsoft Windows 2000.

We saw a connectivity imperative that began to drive new scenarios and requirements for the networking stack. Mobile users and devices using a variety of applications in a variety of locations were becoming trends. We believed Windows needed to support these trends and enable developers to build a new class of interoperable, secure, reliable, and dynamic applications.

We call these "seamless applications" because they defined a new set of capabilities that are now becoming the norm. Integrating software and services, distributing data across multiple devices, or providing a roaming experience provides users with a seamless experience from anywhere at any time.

The impact of these seamless experiences will be profound. Individuals will control their digital world in ways they cannot today. Personal computers (PCs) will give way to "personal computing" from many PCs and devices, and users will be able to access their information from anywhere at any time. In turn, IT will be revitalized and more focused on business success and employee productivity instead of building out hardware and subnets.

At Microsoft, we believe that the next generation network will be a cornerstone to enabling the continued development and deployment of these seamless applications. Windows Vista and Windows Server 2008 provide the foundation by enabling IPv6 by default with pervasive support throughout the system. I am very proud to have been a part of these releases and the milestones they represent for computing and for the Internet as a whole.

Of course IPv6 is a disruptive technology for many people. Learning how to use, manage, troubleshoot, and test for IPv6 is going to take time. This book is a great resource to prepare you for this new technology and the capabilities it offers. I hope you find it helpful in your quest to enable us all to realize seamless applications.

Chris Mitchell

Group Program Manager
Windows Networking

Preface

This book began in the spring of 1999, when I developed a set of slides and presented an "Introduction to IPv6" course at Bellevue Community College in Bellevue, Washington, to four students. Although the turnout was not what I expected, the time spent learning IPv6, creating the slide presentation, and presenting IPv6 technology to these curious students proved to be an invaluable experience and laid down a firm foundation for future endeavors.

In 2000, as a technical writer for Windows, I wrote the "Introduction to IP version 6" white paper that is published on the Microsoft Windows IPv6 Web site (*www.microsoft.com/ipv6*) and generally inserted myself in any documentation task associated with IPv6. I also developed and delivered an "IPv6 Overview" internal course, with help on Windows Sockets from Tom Fout. This one-day course was taught to Microsoft software design engineers, software test engineers, program managers, and technical writers beginning in October of 2000.

My transition to a program manager for technical content development afforded me the time, focus, and experience to turn the "IPv6 Overview" courseware and numerous other white papers and articles about IPv6 into *Understanding IPv6* (Microsoft Press, ISBN 978-0735612457), the previous version of this book. Between the publication of *Understanding IPv6* in November of 2002 and now, I continued to develop content for IPv6, supporting interim releases of IPv6 technology for Windows XP and the releases of Windows Server 2008 and Windows Vista, which have fully integrated IPv6 support for services and applications.

This second edition of *Understanding IPv6* contains the culmination of all of these efforts. It is my fervent hope that the work that I started in the spring of 1999 has culminated in a well-organized and readable text from which you can *learn and understand* the concepts, principles, and processes of IPv6.

–Joseph Davies

Acknowledgments

I would like to the thank the following people at Microsoft for participating in the technical reviews of the chapters and appendixes of the second edition of this book: Khaja Ahmed, Chris Engdahl, Lee Gibson, Parakram Khandpur, Arnaud Lheureux, Chris Mitchell, Mike Owen, Corey Plett, Jory Prather, Aaron Schrader, Ben Schultz, Amit Sehgal, Sean Siler, Jeromy Statia, Michael Surkan, Lee Walker, Jeff Westhead, Kalven Wu, and Yi Zhao. I would like to give special thanks to Chris Mitchell for the Foreword and to Ben Schultz for the "Direct from the Source" sidebar in the Introduction. I would like to give honorable mention to Dmitry Anipko, a software development engineer on the Windows Networking Core development team, who gave me very detailed feedback on both standards-based IPv6 and the implementation details of IPv6 in Windows Server 2008 and Windows Vista.

I would also like to thank Maria Gargiulo (content project manager at Microsoft Press), John Pierce (project manager), Bob Dean (technical reviewer), Roger LeBlanc (copy editor), Margaret Berson (proofreader), Lucie Haskins (indexer), and the production team at Interactive Composition Corporation (ICC).

And last, I would like to express my thanks and appreciation to my wife, Kara, and daughter, Katie, for their patience and tolerance for time away during the last weeks of writing.

Introduction

This book is a straightforward discussion of the concepts, principles, and processes of Internet Protocol version 6 (IPv6) and how it is supported by the Microsoft Windows Server 2008 and Windows Vista operating systems. Note that this book does not contain programming code-level details of the IPv6 protocol for Windows Server 2008 and Windows Vista, such as structures, tables, buffers, or coding logic. These details are highly guarded Microsoft intellectual property that is of interest only to a relative handful of software developers. However, this book does contain details of how the Microsoft implementation of IPv6 in Windows Server 2008 and Windows Vista works for described processes and how to modify default behaviors with Netsh.exe tool commands and registry values.

The purpose of this book is to provide an educational vehicle that will enable you to learn IPv6 to a fair level of technical depth—the terms, the addresses, the protocols, and the processes. This book is not intended to be a breezy marketing overview of IPv6 and how it "provides integrated and interoperable technologies to enable exciting new scenarios for personal and enterprise computing." I will leave that type of documentation to those who are much better at it than I am. The bottom line is that I am a protocols and processes person. My main concern and interest is how the protocols work and what one sees on the wire (what packets are exchanged), and these topics account for the bulk of this book.

Note The contents of this book reflect the Internet standards for IPv6 and the feature set of the IPv6 protocol for Windows Server 2008 and Windows Vista as of Release Candidate 0 (RC0) of Windows Server 2008. For information about changes in Internet standards and the IPv6 protocol for Windows Server 2008 and Windows Vista past Windows Server 2008 RC0, see the Microsoft Windows IPv6 Web site at *http://www.microsoft.com/ipv6*.

Direct from the Source: Why This Book Is Relevant

A global debate is currently in session regarding IPv6. The debate is not intense, but its frequency seems to be increasing at many technical conferences. Some are claiming that IPv6 has been under development for more than 10 years and no deployments of significance have occurred. Network Address Translator (NAT) and Classless Inter-Domain Routing (CIDR) are referenced as an indication that IPv4 will not be exhausted until some distant future date. However, the evidence at *http://www.potaroo.net/tools/ipv4* and *http://www.cisco.com/web/about/ac123/ac147/archived_issues/ipj_8-3/ipj_8-3.pdf* now suggests that the IPv4-only nature of the Internet will soon come to an end. At the time of printing this edition, recent announcements by two of the five Regional

Internet Registries (RIRs) (which you can read about at *http://lacnic.net/ipv6/en/* and *http://www.arin.net/announcements/20070521.html*) have requested that enterprises begin planning for IPv6. This is important because the Internet registries are dispassionate third parties in any technology debate. The RIRs have a problem to solve: maintain a large pool of unique addresses to meet the demand of Internet expansion. As IPv4 addresses are depleted from this reserve, IPv6 is the only viable alternative. This book should give you an understanding of IPv6 technology and the components that make it work. In light of the current trends, this will be essential knowledge for anyone who is involved in next-generation networks.

Ben Schultz

IPv6 Program Manager

Who Should Read This Book

This book is intended for the following audiences:

- **Windows Server 2008 and Windows Vista networking consultants and planners** This group includes anyone who will be planning for an eventual IPv6 migration with Windows Server 2008 and Windows Vista.

- **Microsoft Windows network administrators** This group includes anyone who manages an IPv4-based network and wants to gain technical knowledge about IPv6 and its implementation in Windows Server 2008 and Windows Vista.

- **Microsoft Certified Systems Engineers (MCSEs) and Microsoft Certified Trainers (MCTs)** Regardless of the eventual IPv6 content for Microsoft Official Curriculum (MOC) courseware for Windows Server 2008, this book can be a standard reference for MCSEs and MCTs for IPv6 technology.

- **General technical staff** Because this book is mostly about IPv6 protocols and processes, independent of its implementation in Windows Server 2008, general technical staff can use this book as an in-depth primer on IPv6 technologies.

- **Information technology students** This book originated as courseware for internal Microsoft software developers, testers, and program managers and retains its capability to be a textbook for IPv6 courses taught at an organization or educational institution.

What You Should Know Before Reading This Book

This book assumes a foundation of networking knowledge that includes basic networking concepts, widely used networking technologies, and sound knowledge of the TCP/IP suite. Wherever possible, I try to facilitate the reader's transition to IPv6 by comparing it with the corresponding feature, behavior, or component of IPv4.

For a firm foundation of knowledge of the TCP/IP protocol suite, I cannot recommend a better resource as a prerequisite for this book than *Windows Server 2008 TCP/IP Protocols and Services* by Joseph Davies (Microsoft Press, 2008). Like this book, this resource is mostly about implementation-independent protocols and processes. As the author of this resource, I may be a bit biased. However, this book was written with *Windows Server 2008 TCP/IP Protocols and Services* in mind and builds upon it. In fact, this book and *Windows Server 2008 TCP/IP Protocols and Services* are written as companion volumes. I recommend that *Windows Server 2008 TCP/IP Protocols and Services* be part of your standard TCP/IP reference library, whether you use Microsoft software or not.

Organization of This Book

Because IPv6 is a replacement for the Internet layer of the widely used TCP/IP protocol suite, there were no convenient sublayers with which to organize the material. Instead, I have ordered the chapters so that they build upon each other in a logical fashion. For example, it is difficult to understand Neighbor Discovery processes without first understanding IPv6 addressing, the IPv6 header, and Internet Control Message Protocol for IPv6 (ICMPv6), and it's almost impossible to understand IPv6 transition technologies without first understanding IPv6 addressing, Neighbor Discovery processes, name resolution, and routing.

Appendices of This Book

This book contains the following appendices:

- **Appendix A: Link-Layer Support for IPv6**   A discussion of link-layer encapsulation of IPv6 packets for typical local area network (LAN) and wide area network (WAN) technologies.

- **Appendix B: Windows Sockets Changes for IPv6**   A description of the enhancements to Windows Sockets to support both IPv6 and IPv4 at the same time.

- **Appendix C: IPv6 RFC Index**   A listing of the RFCs and Internet drafts for IPv6 that are the most relevant to the IPv6 implementation in Windows Server 2008 and Windows Vista at the time of this book's publication. This appendix is not designed to be an exhaustive list and will certainly be obsolete at some level soon after this book is printed.

- **Appendix D: Testing for Understanding Answers**   At the end of each chapter is a "Testing for Understanding" section with a series of review questions pertaining to the material in the chapter. This appendix provides answers to those review questions.

- **Appendix E: Setting Up an IPv6 Test Lab**   This appendix answers the question, "How do I get it going so that I can play with it?" By using the instructions in this appendix, you can take five computers and create an IPv6 test lab to test address autoconfiguration, routing, and name resolution. At the end, you are left with a working IPv4 and IPv6 or IPv6-only network with which you can experiment on your own.

- **Appendix F: Mobile IPv6**   An in-depth discussion of Mobile IPv6, a protocol that allows an IPv6 host to change locations and addresses while maintaining existing transport layer connections.

- **Appendix G: IPv6 Reference Tables**   A reprinting of the most relevant IPv6 tables of IPv6 protocol field values and other parameters.

About the Companion CD-ROM

The companion CD-ROM included with this book contains the following:

- **eBook form of this book**   Adobe Portable Document Format (PDF) version of this book, which allows you to view it online and perform text searches.

- **Network Monitor captures**   Throughout the book, packet structure and protocol processes are illustrated with actual IPv6 packets displayed using Microsoft Network Monitor 3.1, a frame capturing and viewing program (also known as a network sniffer) provided for free by Microsoft. The display of the frames within the capture files depends on the version of Network Monitor you are using. Some capture files cannot be viewed by versions of Network Monitor prior to version 3.1. You can install Network Monitor 3.1 from a link on the companion CD-ROM or from *http://go.microsoft.com/fwlink/ ?LinkID=92844*. For the latest information about Network Monitor, see the Network Monitor blog at *http://blogs.technet.com/netmon/*.

- **IPv6 RFCs and Internet drafts**   The Internet Engineering Task Force (IETF) Request for Comments (RFCs) and Internet drafts for IPv6 that are referenced in the chapters and appendices of the book and for understanding the IPv6 implementation in Windows Server 2008 and Windows Vista.

- **Training slides**   A set of Microsoft Office PowerPoint 2003 files that can be used to teach IPv6 using this book. For more information, see "A Special Note to Teachers and Instructors." To view the training slides, you need Microsoft Office PowerPoint 2003 or later or the PowerPoint Viewer 2003. You can install PowerPoint Viewer 2003 from *http://go.microsoft.com/fwlink/?LinkID=59771*.

> **Digital Content for Digital Book Readers**   If you bought a digital-only edition of this book, you can enjoy select content from the print edition's companion CD. Visit *http://go.microsoft.com/fwlink/?LinkId=105451* to get your downloadable content. This content is always up-to-date and available to all readers.

> **Find Additional Content Online**   As new or updated material becomes available that complements your book, it will be posted online on the Microsoft Press Online Windows Server and Client Web site. Based on the final build of Windows Server 2008, the type of material you might find includes updates to book content, articles, links to companion content, errata, sample chapters, and more. This Web site will be available soon at *www.microsoft.com/learning/books/online/serverclient* and will be updated periodically.

System Requirements

To view the eBook of this title, you need any system that is capable of running Adobe Reader, available from *http://www.adobe.com*. To view the capture files (*.cap), you must have Microsoft Network Monitor 3.1 or later. For more detailed information about system requirements, refer to the System Requirements page in the back of the book.

IPv6 Protocol and Windows Product Versions

There are different versions of the Microsoft IPv6 protocol for Windows. In this book, I have chosen to confine the discussion to the IPv6 implementation in Windows Server 2008 and Windows Vista. IPv6 in previous versions of Windows is typically not described except as a point of contrast to IPv6 in Windows Server 2008 and Windows Vista.

A Special Note to Teachers and Instructors

This book originated from courseware and retains many of the attributes of courseware, including objectives at the beginning of each chapter and review questions at the end of each chapter. If you are a teacher or instructor tasked with inculcating an understanding of IPv6 protocols and processes in others, I strongly urge you to consider using this book and the slides on the companion CD-ROM as a basis for your own IPv6 course.

The slides are included to provide a foundation for your own slide presentation. The included slides contain either bulleted text or my original PowerPoint drawings that are synchronized with their chapter content. Because the slides were completed after the final book pages were done, there are some minor differences between the slides and the chapter content. These changes were made to enhance the ability to teach an IPv6 course based on the book.

The template I have chosen for the included slides is intentionally simple so that there are minimal issues with text and drawing color translations when you switch to a different template. Please feel free to customize the slides as you see fit.

If you are designing an implementation-independent IPv6 technology course, I suggest that you skip Chapter 2, "IPv6 Protocol for Windows Server 2008 and Windows Vista," and cover Appendix A, "Link-Layer Support for IPv6," after Chapter 4, "The IPv6 Header."

As a fellow instructor, I wish you success in your efforts to teach this interesting and important new technology to others.

Disclaimers and Support

This book represents a best-effort snapshot of information available at the time of its publication for IPv6 standards and the implementation of IPv6 and related protocols in Windows Server 2008 and Windows Vista, as of the Release Candidate 0 version of Windows Server 2008. Changes to Windows Server 2008 and Windows Vista that were made after this version or to IETF standards after October 24, 2007 are not reflected in this book.

To obtain the latest information about IETF standards for IPv6, see the IETF Web site at *http://www.ietf.org*.

Technical Support

Every effort has been made to ensure the accuracy of this book and the contents of the companion CD-ROM. Microsoft Press provides corrections for books in the Microsoft Knowledge Base. If you have comments, questions, or ideas regarding this book or the companion CD, please send them to Microsoft Press by using either of the following methods:

E-mail: mspinput@microsoft.com.

Postal Mail:

Microsoft Press

Attn: Understanding IPv6, Second Edition Editor

One Microsoft Way

Redmond, WA 98052-6399

For additional support information regarding this book and the CD-ROM (including answers to commonly asked questions about installation and use), visit the Microsoft Press Technical Support Web site at *http://www.microsoft.com/learning/support/books*. To connect directly to the Microsoft Knowledge Base and enter a query, visit *http://support.microsoft.com/search*. For support information regarding Microsoft software, please visit *http://support.microsoft.com*.

Chapter 1

Introduction to IPv6

At the end of this chapter, you should be able to do the following:

- Describe the shortcomings of Internet Protocol version 4 (IPv4) and the modern-day Internet, and describe how Internet Protocol version 6 (IPv6) addresses these shortcomings.

- Describe how the address depletion problem of IPv4 leads to the use of Network Address Translators (NATs) and problems with end-to-end communication.

- List and describe the features of IPv6.

- List and describe the key differences between IPv4 and IPv6.

- State the reasons for and business value of deploying IPv6.

Limitations of IPv4

The current version of IP (known as version 4 or IPv4) has not changed substantially since Request for Comments (RFC) 791, which was published in 1981. IPv4 has proven to be robust, easily implemented, and interoperable. It has stood up to the test of scaling an internetwork to a global utility the size of today's Internet. This is a tribute to its initial design.

However, the initial design of IPv4 did not anticipate the following:

- **The recent exponential growth of the Internet and the impending exhaustion of the IPv4 address space** Although the 32-bit address space of IPv4 allows for 4,294,967,296 addresses, previous and current allocation practices limit the number of public IPv4 addresses to a few hundred million. As a result, public IPv4 addresses have become relatively scarce, forcing many users and some organizations to use a NAT to map a single public IPv4 address to multiple private IPv4 addresses. Although NATs promote reuse of the private address space, they violate the fundamental design principle of the original Internet that all nodes have a unique, globally reachable address, preventing true end-to-end connectivity for all types of networking applications.

  Additionally, the rising prominence of Internet-connected devices and appliances ensures that the public IPv4 address space will eventually be depleted.

- **The need for simpler configuration** Most current IPv4 implementations must be either manually configured or use a stateful address configuration protocol such as Dynamic Host Configuration Protocol (DHCP). With more computers and devices using IP, there is a need for a simpler and more automatic configuration of addresses and other configuration settings that do not rely on the administration of a DHCP infrastructure.

■ **The requirement for security at the Internet layer** Private communication over a public medium such as the Internet requires cryptographic services that protect the data being sent from being viewed or modified in transit. Although a standard now exists for providing security for IPv4 packets (known as Internet Protocol security, or IPsec), this standard is optional for IPv4 and additional security solutions, some of which are proprietary, are prevalent.

■ **The need for better support for prioritized and real-time delivery of data** Although standards for prioritized and real-time delivery of data—sometimes referred to as Quality of Service (QoS)—exist for IPv4, real-time traffic support relies on the 8 bits of the historical IPv4 Type of Service (TOS) field and the identification of the payload, typically using a User Datagram Protocol (UDP) or Transmission Control Protocol (TCP) port. Unfortunately, the IPv4 TOS field has limited functionality and, over time, has been redefined and has different local interpretations. The current standards for IPv4 use the TOS field to indicate a Differentiated Services Code Point (DSCP), a value set by the originating node and used by intermediate routers for prioritized delivery and handling. Additionally, payload identification that uses a TCP or UDP port is not possible when the IPv4 packet payload is encrypted.

To address these and other concerns, the Internet Engineering Task Force (IETF) has developed a suite of protocols and standards known as IP version 6 (IPv6). This new version, previously called IP-The Next Generation (IPng), incorporates the concepts of many proposed methods for updating the IPv4 protocol. IPv6 is designed intentionally to have minimal impact on upper- and lower-layer protocols and to avoid the random addition of new features.

Consequences of the Limited IPv4 Address Space

Because of the relative scarcity of public IPv4 addresses, NATs are being deployed to reuse the IPv4 private address space. In areas of the world where public IPv4 addresses are scarce, there might be multiple levels of NATs between the client computer and the Internet. Although NATs do allow more clients to connect to the Internet, they also act as traffic bottlenecks and barriers to some types of communications. Let's examine the operation of a NAT to illustrate why network address translation is a nonscalable, stopgap solution that impairs end-to-end communication.

For example, a small business uses the 192.168.0.0/24 private IPv4 address prefix for its intranet and has been assigned the public IPv4 address of 131.107.47.119 by its Internet service provider (ISP). The NAT deployed at the edge of this network maps all private addresses on 192.168.0.0/24 to the public address of 131.107.47.119. The NAT uses dynamically chosen TCP and UDP ports to map internal (intranet) data streams to external (Internet) data streams. Figure 1-1 shows this example configuration.

If a private host assigned the private IPv4 address 192.168.0.10 uses a Web browser to connect to the Web server at 157.60.13.9, the private host creates an IPv4 packet with the following:

■ Destination address: 157.60.13.9

■ Source address: 192.168.0.10

- Destination TCP port: 80
- Source TCP port: 1025

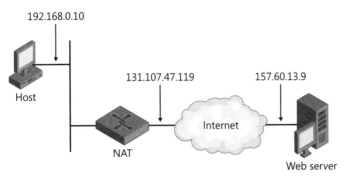

Figure 1-1   A NAT example

This IPv4 packet is then forwarded to the NAT, which typically translates the source address and source TCP port of the outgoing packet to the following:

- Destination address: 157.60.13.9
- **Source address: 131.107.47.119**
- Destination TCP port: 80
- **Source TCP port: 5000**

The NAT keeps the mapping of {192.168.0.10, TCP 1025} to {131.107.47.119, TCP 5000} in a local translation table for future reference.

The translated IPv4 packet is sent over the Internet. The response is sent back by the Web server and received by the NAT. When received, the packet contains the following:

- Destination address: 131.107.47.119
- Source address: 157.60.13.9
- Destination TCP port: 5000
- Source TCP port: 80

The NAT checks its translation table, locates the entry that was created when the initial packet was sent, translates the destination address and destination TCP port, and forwards the packet to the host at 192.168.0.10. The forwarded packet contains the following:

- **Destination address: 192.168.0.10**
- Source address: 157.60.13.9
- **Destination TCP port: 1025**
- Source TCP port: 80

For outgoing packets from the NAT, the source IPv4 address (a private address) is mapped to the ISP-assigned address (a public address), and the source TCP/UDP port numbers are mapped to different TCP/UDP port numbers. For incoming packets to the NAT, the destination IPv4 address (a public address) is mapped to the original intranet address (a private address), and the destination TCP/UDP port numbers are mapped back to their original TCP/UDP port numbers.

Normal network address translation relies on the following:

- **Address translation**   Translation of the IPv4 addresses in the IPv4 header
- **Port translation**   Translation of the TCP port numbers in the TCP header or of the UDP port numbers in the UDP header

Address and port translation lowers the forwarding performance of the NAT because of the additional operations that must be performed on each packet. As a result, NATs are typically not deployed in large-scale environments.

To make modifications to the IPv4 packet beyond address or port translation requires additional processing and software components on the NAT called *NAT editors*. HyperText Transfer Protocol (HTTP) traffic on the World Wide Web does not require a NAT editor because all HTTP traffic requires only address and TCP port translation. However, NAT editors are required in the following situations:

- **An IPv4 address, TCP port, or UDP port is stored elsewhere in the payload.**   For example, File Transfer Protocol (FTP) stores the dotted decimal representation of IPv4 addresses in the FTP header for the FTP PORT command. If the NAT does not properly translate the IPv4 address within the FTP header for the FTP PORT command and adjust the TCP sequence numbers in the data stream, connectivity and data transfer problems will occur.
- **TCP or UDP is not used to identify the data stream.**   For example, Point-to-Point Tunneling Protocol (PPTP) tunneled data does not use a TCP or UDP header. Instead, PPTP uses a Generic Routing Encapsulation (GRE) header and the Call ID field of the GRE header to identify the data stream. If the NAT does not properly translate the Call ID field within the GRE header, connectivity problems will occur.

Most traffic can traverse a NAT because either the packets require only address or port translation, or a NAT editor is present to modify the payload appropriately. However, some traffic cannot traverse a NAT. If the data requiring translation is in an encrypted part of the packet, translation is not possible. For IPsec-protected packets, address and port translation can invalidate the packet's integrity. IPsec NAT-Traversal (NAT-T) is a recent Internet standard that allows some types of IPsec-protected packets to be translated by a NAT.

An additional problem with NATs is their effect on peer-to-peer applications. In the peer-to-peer communication model, peers can act as either the client or the server and initiate communications to each other. If a peer is behind a NAT, there are two addresses associated with it, one of which is known to the peer behind the NAT (the private address) and one of which is known in front of the NAT (the public address). Let's examine a simple configuration in which NATs can cause problems for peer-to-peer applications. Figure 1-2 shows an intranet with a NAT at its edge.

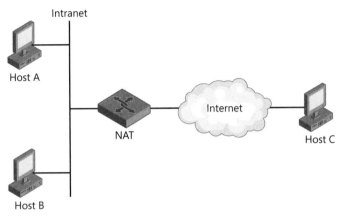

Figure 1-2   NATs and peer-to-peer applications

For a peer-to-peer application running on all hosts, Host A can initiate a session with Host B (directly reachable on its link) and with Host C. However, Host A cannot inform Host C of the public address and port number of Host B because Host A does not know it. Also, Host C cannot initiate a session with either Host A or Host B without an existing translation table entry to translate the inbound connection request packets to Host A's private address and port. Even with the table entry, Host C might not be able to initiate a session with both Host A and Host B because both hosts are known by the same public IPv4 address.

To make matters worse, it is a more common situation to have each Internet peer behind a NAT. To solve these problems, the peer-to-peer or multiple-party applications must be modified to be NAT-aware, resulting in additional complexity for the application. Additionally, some NAT-aware applications use an echo server to automatically discover their public address and port number, which adds costs for independent software vendors (ISVs) to deploy and maintain echo servers on the Internet.

NATs are a makeshift measure to extend the life of the IPv4 public address space, and they are not a solution to the IPv4 public address space problem. NATs work best for reusing the private address space for client computers and client/server-based communication when the client behind the NAT initiates the communication. Most server computers still need unambiguous public addresses. A server can be placed behind a NAT; however, the NAT must be configured manually with a static translation table entry to translate the inbound packets to the server's private address and port. In peer-to-peer communications, each end acts as both client and server and, therefore, peers separated by NATs might not operate correctly and must be modified for NAT awareness.

Features of IPv6

The following list summarizes the features of the IPv6 protocol:

- New header format
- Large address space
- Stateless and stateful address configuration
- IPsec header support required
- Better support for prioritized delivery
- New protocol for neighboring node interaction
- Extensibility

New Header Format

The IPv6 header has a new format that is designed to minimize header processing. This is achieved by moving both nonessential and optional fields to extension headers that are placed after the IPv6 header. The streamlined IPv6 header is more efficiently processed at intermediate routers.

IPv4 headers and IPv6 headers are not interoperable. IPv6 is not a superset of functionality that is backward compatible with IPv4. A host or router must use an implementation of both IPv4 and IPv6 to recognize and process both header formats. The new default IPv6 header is only twice the size of the default IPv4 header, even though the number of bits in IPv6 addresses is four times larger than IPv4 addresses.

Large Address Space

IPv6 has 128-bit (16-byte) source and destination addresses. Although 128 bits can express over 3.4×10^{38} possible combinations, the large address space of IPv6 has been designed to allow for multiple levels of subnetting and address allocation, from the Internet backbone to the individual subnets within an organization.

Even with all of the addresses currently assigned for use by hosts, plenty of addresses are available for future use. With a much larger number of available addresses, address-conservation techniques, such as the deployment of NATs, are no longer necessary.

Stateless and Stateful Address Configuration

To simplify host configuration, IPv6 supports both stateful address configuration (such as address configuration in the presence of a DHCP for IPv6, or DHCPv6, server) and stateless address configuration (such as address configuration in the absence of a DHCPv6 server). With stateless address configuration, hosts on a link automatically configure themselves with IPv6 addresses for the link (called *link-local addresses*), with IPv6 transition addresses, and with addresses derived from prefixes advertised by local routers. Even in the absence of a router, hosts on the same link can automatically configure themselves with link-local addresses and communicate without manual configuration. Link-local addresses are autoconfigured within seconds, and communication with neighboring nodes on the link is possible immediately. In comparison, some IPv4 hosts using DHCP must wait a full minute before abandoning DHCP configuration and self-configuring an IPv4 address.

IPsec Header Support Required

Support for the IPsec headers is an IPv6 protocol suite requirement. This requirement provides a standards-based solution for network protection needs and promotes interoperability between different IPv6 implementations. IPsec consists of two types of extension headers and a protocol to negotiate security settings. The Authentication header (AH) provides data integrity, data authentication, and replay protection for the entire IPv6 packet (excluding fields in the IPv6 header that must change in transit). The Encapsulating Security Payload (ESP) header and trailer provide data integrity, data authentication, data confidentiality, and replay protection for the ESP-encapsulated payload. The protocol typically used to negotiate IPsec security settings for unicast communication is the Internet Key Exchange (IKE) protocol. However, the requirement to process IPsec headers does not make IPv6 inherently more secure. IPv6 packets are not required to be protected with IPsec and IPsec is not a requirement of an IPv6 deployment. Additionally, the IPv6 standards do not require an implementation to support any specific encryption methods, hashing methods, or negotiation protocol (such as IKE).

Better Support for Prioritized Delivery

New fields in the IPv6 header define how traffic is handled and identified. Traffic is prioritized using a Traffic Class field, which specifies a DSCP value just like IPv4. A Flow Label field in the IPv6 header allows routers to identify and provide special handling for packets that belong to a flow (a series of packets between a source and destination). Because the traffic is identified in the IPv6 header, support for prioritized delivery can be achieved even when the packet payload is encrypted with IPsec and ESP.

New Protocol for Neighboring Node Interaction

The Neighbor Discovery protocol for IPv6 is a series of Internet Control Message Protocol for IPv6 (ICMPv6) messages that manages the interaction of neighboring nodes (nodes on the same link). Neighbor Discovery replaces and extends the Address Resolution Protocol (ARP) (broadcast-based), ICMPv4 Router Discovery, and ICMPv4 Redirect messages with efficient multicast and unicast Neighbor Discovery messages.

Extensibility

IPv6 can easily be extended for new features by adding extension headers after the IPv6 header. Unlike options in the IPv4 header, which can support only 40 bytes of options, the size of IPv6 extension headers is constrained only by the size of the IPv6 packet.

Comparison of IPv4 and IPv6

Table 1-1 highlights some of the key differences between IPv4 and IPv6.

Table 1-1   Differences Between IPv4 and IPv6

IPv4	IPv6
Source and destination addresses are 32 bits (4 bytes) in length.	Source and destination addresses are 128 bits (16 bytes) in length. For more information, see Chapter 3, "IPv6 Addressing."
IPsec header support is optional.	IPsec header support is required. For more information, see Chapter 4, "The IPv6 Header."
No identification of packet flow for prioritized delivery handling by routers is present within the IPv4 header.	Packet flow identification for prioritized delivery handling by routers is present within the IPv6 header using the Flow Label field. For more information, see Chapter 4.
Fragmentation is performed by the sending host and at routers, slowing router perfor- mance.	Fragmentation is performed only by the sending host. For more information, see Chapter 4.
Has no link-layer packet-size requirements, and must be able to reassemble a 576-byte packet.	Link layer must support a 1280-byte packet and be able to reassemble a 1500-byte packet. For more information, see Chapter 4.
Header includes a checksum.	Header does not include a checksum. For more information, see Chapter 4.
Header includes options.	All optional data is moved to IPv6 extension headers. For more information, see Chapter 4.
ARP uses broadcast ARP Request frames to resolve an IPv4 address to a link-layer address.	ARP Request frames are replaced with multicast Neighbor Solicitation messages. For more information, see Chapter 6, "Neighbor Discovery."
Internet Group Management Protocol (IGMP) is used to manage local subnet group mem- bership.	IGMP is replaced with Multicast Listener Discovery (MLD) messages. For more information, see Chapter 7, "Multicast Listener Discovery."
ICMP Router Discovery is used to determine the IPv4 address of the best default gateway and is optional.	ICMPv4 Router Discovery is replaced with ICMPv6 Router Solicitation and Router Advertisement messages, and it is required. For more information, see Chapter 6.
Broadcast addresses are used to send traffic to all nodes on a subnet.	There are no IPv6 broadcast addresses. Instead, a link-local scope all-nodes multicast address is used. For more information, see "Multicast IPv6 Addresses" in Chapter 3.
Must be configured either manually or through DHCP for IPv4.	Does not require manual configuration or DHCP for IPv6. For more information, see Chapter 8, "Address Autoconfiguration."
Uses host address (A) resource records in the Domain Name System (DNS) to map host names to IPv4 addresses.	Uses AAAA records in the DNS to map host names to IPv6 addresses. For more information, see Chapter 9, "IPv6 and Name Resolution."
Uses pointer (PTR) resource records in the IN-ADDR.ARPA DNS domain to map IPv4 addresses to host names.	Uses pointer (PTR) resource records in the IP6.ARPA DNS domain to map IPv6 addresses to host names. For more information, see Chapter 9.

IPv6 Terminology

The following list of common terms for network elements and concepts provides a foundation for subsequent chapters. Figure 1-3 shows an IPv6 network.

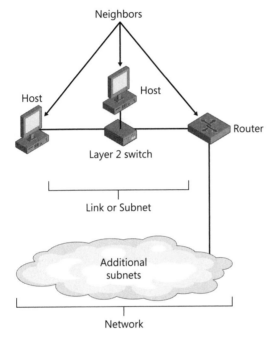

Figure 1-3   Elements of an IPv6 network

IPv6 common terms and concepts are defined as follows:

■ **Node**   Any device that runs an implementation of IPv6. This includes routers and hosts.

■ **Router**   A node that can forward IPv6 packets not explicitly addressed to itself. On an IPv6 network, a router also typically advertises its presence and host configuration information.

■ **Host**   A node that cannot forward IPv6 packets not explicitly addressed to itself (a non-router). A host is typically the source and a destination of IPv6 traffic, and it silently discards traffic received that is not explicitly addressed to itself.

■ **Upper-layer protocol**   A protocol above IPv6 that uses IPv6 as its transport. Examples include Internet layer protocols such as ICMPv6 and Transport layer protocols such as TCP and UDP (but not Application layer protocols such as FTP and DNS, which use TCP and UDP as their transport).

■ **Link**   The set of network interfaces that are bounded by routers and that use the same 64-bit IPv6 unicast address prefix. Other terms for "link" are *subnet* and *network segment*. Many link-layer technologies are already defined for IPv6, including typical LAN technologies (such as Ethernet and Institute of Electrical and Electronics Engineers [IEEE] 802.11 wireless) and wide area network (WAN) technologies (such as the Point-to-Point

Protocol [PPP] and Frame Relay). Additionally, IPv6 packets can be sent over logical links representing an IPv4 or IPv6 network, by encapsulating the IPv6 packet within an IPv4 or IPv6 header. For more information about LAN and WAN media support for IPv6, see Appendix A, "Link-Layer Support for IPv6."

- **Network**   Two or more subnets connected by routers. Another term for network is *internetwork*.

- **Neighbors**   Nodes connected to the same link. Neighbors in IPv6 have special significance because of IPv6 Neighbor Discovery, which has facilities to resolve neighbor link-layer addresses and detect and monitor neighbor reachability.

- **Interface**   The representation of a physical or logical attachment of a node to a link. An example of a physical interface is a network adapter. An example of a logical interface is a "tunnel" interface that is used to send IPv6 packets across an IPv4 network by encapsulating the IPv6 packet inside an IPv4 header.

- **Address**   An identifier that can be used as the source or destination of IPv6 packets that is assigned at the IPv6 layer to an interface or set of interfaces.

- **Packet**   The protocol data unit (PDU) that exists at the IPv6 layer and is composed of an IPv6 header and payload.

- **Link MTU**   The maximum transmission unit (MTU)—the number of bytes in the largest IPv6 packet—that can be sent on a link. Because the maximum frame size includes the link-layer medium headers and trailers, the link MTU is not the same as the maximum frame size of the link. The link MTU is the same as the maximum payload size of the link-layer technology. For example, for Ethernet using Ethernet II encapsulation, the maximum Ethernet frame payload size is 1500 bytes. Therefore, the link MTU is 1500. For a link with multiple link-layer technologies (for example, a bridged link), the link MTU is the smallest link MTU of all the link-layer technologies present on the link.

- **Path MTU**   The maximum-sized IPv6 packet that can be sent without performing host fragmentation between a source and destination over a path in an IPv6 network. The path MTU is typically the smallest link MTU of all the links in the path.

Figure 1-4 shows an IPv6-capable organization network and its relation to the IPv4 and IPv6 Internets.

A site is an autonomously operating IP-based network that is connected to the IPv6 Internet. Network architects and administrators within the site determine the addressing plan and routing policy for the organization network. An organization can have multiple sites. The actual connection to the IPv6 Internet can be either of the following types:

- **Direct**   The connection to the IPv6 Internet uses a wide area network link (such as Frame Relay or T-Carrier) and connects to an IPv6-capable ISP (shown in Figure 1-4).

- **Tunneled**   The connection to the IPv6 Internet uses an IPv6 over IPv4 tunnel and connects to an IPv6 tunneling router.

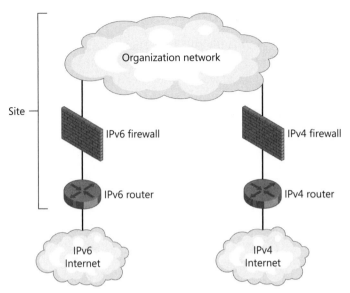

Figure 1-4   An IPv6-capable organization network and the IPv4 and IPv6 Internets

For more information about how sites use IPv6 address prefixes, see Chapter 3. For more information about how to connect an organization network to the IPv6 Internet, see Chapter 16, "Deploying IPv6."

The Case for IPv6 Deployment

Although the IPv6 protocol offers a host of technological advances and innovations, its use must still be justified from a business perspective and deployed by information technology (IT) staff in end-user organizations and ISPs. The deployment of native IPv6 support in the network infrastructure involves the planning and design of coexistence and migration strategies and the installation and maintenance of hardware and software. The resulting combination of IT staff, hardware and software resources, and time required for the transition makes the decision to deploy native IPv6 support a significant one, especially in light of other technology initiatives that might have higher visibility or better short-term benefits.

One must consider, however, that the Internet, once a pseudo-private network connecting educational institutions and United States government agencies, has become an indispensable worldwide communications medium that is an integral part of increased efficiency and productivity for commercial organizations and individuals, and a major component of the world's economic engine. *Its growth must continue.*

To continue the growth of the Internet and private intranets, IPv4 must eventually be replaced. The sooner IPv4 is replaced, the sooner the benefits of its replacement protocol are realized. The following sections present the key technological and business benefits in the case to deploy IPv6.

IPv6 Solves the Address Depletion Problem

With the explosion in the popularity of the Internet has come the introduction of commerce-related activities that can now be done over the Internet by an ever-increasing number of devices. With IPv4, the number of public addresses available to new devices is limited and shrinking. IPv4 cannot continue to scale and provide global connectivity to all of the planned Internet-capable devices to be produced and connected in the next 10 years. Although these devices can be assigned private addresses, address and port translation introduces complexity to the devices that want to perform server, listening, or peer functionality.

IPv6 solves the IPv4 public address depletion problem by providing an address space to last well into the twenty-first century. The business benefit of moving to IPv6 is that mobile cell phones, personal data assistants (PDAs), automobiles, appliances, and even people can be assigned multiple globally reachable addresses. The growth of the devices connected to the Internet and the software that these devices run can proceed without restraint and without the complexity and cost of having to operate behind NATs.

IPv6 Solves the Disjoint Address Space Problem

With IPv4, there are typically two different addressing schemes for the home and the enterprise network. In the home, an Internet gateway device (IGD) is assigned a single public IPv4 address and the IGD assigns private IPv4 addresses to the hosts on the home network. An enterprise might have multiple public IPv4 addresses or a public address range and either assign public, private, or both types of addresses within the enterprise's intranet. However, the public and private IPv4 address spaces are disjoint; they do not provide symmetric reachability at the Network layer. Symmetric reachability exists when packets can be sent to and received from an arbitrary destination. With IPv4, there is no single addressing scheme that is applied to both networks that allows seamless connectivity. Connectivity between disjoint networks requires intermediate devices such as NATs or proxy servers. With IPv6, both homes and enterprises will be assigned global address prefixes and can seamlessly connect, subject to security restrictions such as firewall filtering and authenticated communication.

IPv6 Solves the International Address Allocation Problem

The Internet was principally a creation of educational institutions and government agencies of the United States of America. In the early days of the Internet, connected sites in the United States received IPv4 address prefixes without regard to summarizability or need. The historical result of this address allocation practice is that the United States has a disproportionate number of public IPv4 addresses.

With IPv6, public address prefixes are assigned to regional Internet registries, which, in turn, assign address prefixes to other ISPs and organizations based on justified need. This new address allocation practice ensures that address prefixes will be distributed globally based on regional connectivity needs, rather than by historical origin. This makes the Internet more of a truly global resource, rather than a United States–centric one. The business benefit to organizations across the globe is that they can rely on having available public IPv6 address space, without the current cost of obtaining IPv4 public address prefixes from their ISP.

IPv6 Restores End-to-End Communication

With IPv4 NATs, there is a technical barrier for applications that rely on listening or peer-based connectivity because of the need for the communicating peers to discover and advertise their public IPv4 addresses and ports. The workarounds for the translation barrier might also require the deployment of echo or rendezvous servers on the Internet to provide public address and port configuration information.

With IPv6, NATs are no longer necessary to conserve public address space, and the problems associated with mapping addresses and ports disappear for developers of applications and gateways. More importantly, end-to-end communication is restored between hosts on the Internet by using addresses in packets that do not change in transit. This functional restoration has immense value when one considers the emergence of peer-to-peer telephony, video, and other real-time collaboration technologies for personal communications, and that the next wave of devices that are connected to the Internet include many types of peer-to-peer devices, such as mobile phones.

By restoring global addressing and end-to-end connectivity, IPv6 has no barrier to new applications that are based on ad hoc connectivity and peer-based communication. Additionally, there is no need to deploy echo servers on the Internet. The business benefit for software developers is easier development of peer-based applications to share information, music, and media or to collaborate without having to work around the NAT translation barrier. An additional benefit to global addressing and end-to-end connectivity is the ability for users to remotely access computers on their home networks, rather than having to use intermediate hosts on the Internet.

IPv6 Uses Scoped Addresses and Address Selection

Unlike IPv4 addresses, IPv6 addresses have a *scope*, or a defined area of the network over which they are unique and relevant. For example, IPv6 has a global address that is equivalent to the IPv4 public address and a unique local address that is roughly equivalent to the IPv4 private address. Typical IPv4 routers do not distinguish a public address from a private address and will forward a privately addressed packet on the Internet. An IPv6 router, on the other hand, is aware of the scope of IPv6 addresses and will never forward a packet over an interface that does not have the correct scope.

There are different types of IPv6 addresses with different scopes. When multiple IPv6 addresses are returned in a DNS name query, the sending node must be able to distinguish their types and, when initiating communication, use a pair (source address and destination address) that is matched in scope and that is the most appropriate pair to use. For example, for a source and a destination that have been assigned both global (public) and link-local addresses, a sending IPv6 host would never use a global destination with a link-local source. IPv6 sending hosts include the address selection logic that is needed to decide which pair of addresses to use in communication. Moreover, the address selection rules are configurable. This allows you to configure multiple addressing infrastructures within an organization. Regardless of how many types of addressing infrastructures are in place, the sending host always chooses the "best" set of addresses. In comparison, IPv4 nodes have no awareness of address types and can send traffic to a public address from a private address.

The benefit of scoped addresses is that by using the set of addresses of the smallest scope, your traffic does not travel beyond the scope for the address, exposing your network traffic to fewer possible malicious hosts. The benefit of standardized and built-in address selection algorithms for ISVs is that they do not have to develop and test their own address selection schemes and can rely on the sorted list of addresses, resulting in lower software development costs.

IPv6 Has More Efficient Forwarding

IPv6 is a streamlined version of IPv4. Excluding prioritized delivery traffic, IPv6 has fewer fields to process and fewer decisions to make in forwarding an IPv6 packet. Unlike IPv4, the IPv6 header is a fixed size (40 bytes), which allows routers to process IPv6 packets faster. Additionally, the hierarchical and summarizable addressing structure of IPv6 global addresses means that there are fewer routes to analyze in the routing tables of organization and Internet backbone routers. The consequence is traffic that can be forwarded at higher data rates, resulting in higher performance for tomorrow's high-bandwidth applications that use multiple data types.

IPv6 Has Support for Security and Mobility

IPv6 has been designed to support security (IPsec) (AH and ESP header support required) and mobility (Mobile IPv6) (optional). Although one could argue that these features are available for IPv4, they are available on IPv4 as extensions, and therefore they have architectural or connectivity limitations that might not have been present if they had been part of the original IPv4 design. It is always better to design features in rather than bolt them on. The result of designing IPv6 with security and mobility in mind is an implementation that is a defined standard, has fewer limitations, and is more robust and scalable to handle the current and future communication needs of the users of the Internet.

The business benefit of requiring support for IPsec and using a single, global address space is that IPv6 can protect packets from end to end across the entire IPv6 Internet. Unlike IPsec on the IPv4 Internet, which must be modified and has limited functionality when the endpoints are behind NATs, IPsec on the IPv6 Internet is fully functional between any two endpoints.

Testing for Understanding

To test your understanding of IPv6, answer the following questions. See Appendix D, "Testing for Understanding Answers," to check your answers.

1. What are the problems with IPv4 on today's Internet?

2. How does IPv6 solve these problems?

3. How does IPv6 provide better prioritized delivery support?

4. Describe at least three ways in which IPv6 is more efficient than IPv4.

5. Explain how NATs prevent peer-to-peer applications from working properly.

6. What are the key technical benefits of deploying IPv6 now?

7. What are the key business benefits of deploying IPv6 now?

Chapter 2
IPv6 Protocol for Windows Server 2008 and Windows Vista

At the end of this chapter, you should be able to do the following:

- Discuss the architecture of the IPv6 protocol for Windows Server 2008 and Windows Vista.

- List and describe the features of the IPv6 protocol for Windows Server 2008 and Windows Vista.

- Describe the applications and services provided with Windows Server 2008 and Windows Vista that are IPv6-enabled.

- List and describe the application programming interfaces (APIs) in Windows Server 2008 and Windows Vista that are IPv6-enabled.

- Describe how to manually configure the IPv6 protocol for Windows Server 2008 and Windows Vista.

- List and describe the IPv6-enabled common tools provided with Windows Server 2008 and Windows Vista.

- Describe how to display the configuration of the IPv6 protocol for Windows Server 2008 and Windows Vista.

Architecture of the IPv6 Protocol for Windows Server 2008 and Windows Vista

For Windows Server 2008 and Windows Vista, the TCP/IP protocol stack is a dual IP layer implementation, where only a single implementation of the Transport Layer protocols Transmission Control Protocol (TCP) and User Datagram Protocol (UDP) operate over both Internet layer protocols: Internet Protocol version 4 (IPv4) and Internet Protocol version 6 (IPv6). Figure 2-1 shows the architecture of the TCP/IP protocol stack for Windows Server 2008 and Windows Vista.

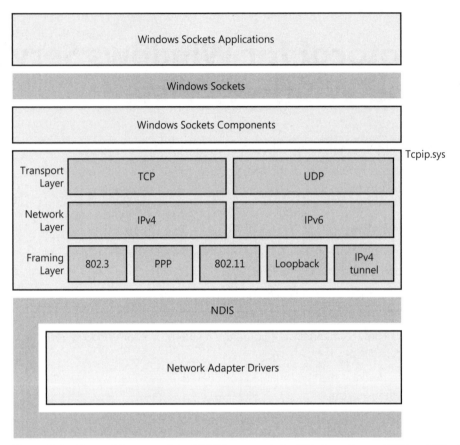

Figure 2-1   The architecture of the TCP/IP protocols for Windows Server 2008 and Windows Vista

The TCP/IP driver file, Tcpip.sys, contains both IPv4 and IPv6 Internet layers. Tcpip6.sys operates between Windows Sockets and the Network Device Interface Specification (NDIS) layers in the Windows network architecture. The architecture of Tcpip.sys consists of the following layers:

■   **Transport layer**   Contains the implementations of TCP and UDP.

■   **Network layer**   Contains implementations of both IPv4 and IPv6.

■   **Framing layer**   Contains modules that frame IPv4 or IPv6 packets. Modules exist for IEEE 802.3 (Ethernet), IEEE 802.11, and Point-to-Point Protocol (PPP) links. Modules also exist for logical interfaces such as the loopback interface and IPv4-based tunnels. IPv4-based tunnels are commonly used for IPv6 transition technologies.

The IPv4 Internet layer appears as the *Internet Protocol Version 4 (TCP/IPv4)* component in the list of protocols from the properties of a local area network (LAN) connection in the Network Connections folder. The IPv6 Internet layer appears as the *Internet Protocol Version 6 (TCP/IPv6)* component. You can enable or disable these components per connection in the Network

Connections folder, but you cannot uninstall them. You can uninstall the IPv4 Internet layer with the **netsh interface ipv4 uninstall** command, but you cannot uninstall the IPv6 Internet layer. For more information, see "Manually Configuring the IPv6 Protocol" section in this chapter.

Note   The IPv6 protocol for Windows XP and Windows Server 2003 is a separate protocol stack that contains its own implementation of TCP and UDP. This is known as a *dual stack architecture*. For more information, see Chapter 11, "IPv6 Transition Technologies."

Features of the IPv6 Protocol for Windows Server 2008 and Windows Vista

The IPv6 protocol for Windows Server 2008 and Windows Vista includes the following features:

- Installed, enabled, and preferred by default
- Basic IPv6 stack support
- IPv6 stack enhancements
- Graphical user interface (GUI) and command-line configuration
- Integrated Internet Protocol security (IPsec) support
- Windows Firewall support
- Temporary addresses
- Random Interface IDs
- Domain Name System (DNS) support
- Source and destination address selection
- Support for ipv6-literal.net names
- Link-Local Multicast Name Resolution (LLMNR)
- Peer Name Resolution Protocol (PNRP)
- Literal IPv6 addresses in URLs
- Static routing
- IPv6 over PPP
- DHCPv6
- Intra-Site Automatic Tunnel Addressing Protocol (ISATAP)
- 6to4

- Teredo
- PortProxy

Installed, Enabled, and Preferred by Default

In Windows Server 2008 and Windows Vista, IPv6 is installed and enabled by default for all connections in the Network Connections folder. In Windows Server 2008 and Windows Vista, almost all networking operating system components now support IPv6.

When both IPv4 and IPv6 are enabled, Windows Server 2008 and Windows Vista by default prefer the use of IPv6 over IPv4. For example, if a Domain Name System (DNS) Name Query Response message contains a list of both IPv6 and IPv4 addresses, Windows Server 2008 and Windows Vista will attempt to communicate over IPv6 first, subject to the address selection rules that are defined in RFC 3484. For more information, see the "Source and Destination Address Selection" section in this chapter.

The preference of IPv6 over IPv4 can provide IPv6-enabled applications better network connectivity because IPv6 connections can use IPv6 transition technologies such as Teredo, which allow peer or server applications to operate behind Network Address Translators (NATs) without requiring NAT configuration or application modification.

Enabling IPv6 by default and preferring IPv6 traffic does not impair IPv4 connectivity in most cases. For example, on networks without IPv6 records in the DNS infrastructure, communications using IPv6 addresses are not attempted unless the user or application specifies a destination IPv6 address. There are cases, however, when an application can attempt an IPv6-based connection and fail, even though IPv4 connectivity exists. For more information about deployment considerations for IPv6-capable applications, see Chapter 16, "Deploying IPv6."

To take advantage of IPv6 connectivity, networking applications might need to be updated to use networking application programming interfaces (APIs) that support IPv6. (See the section "Application Support" in this chapter.) For example, applications that use Windows Sockets might be written to use Windows Sockets functions that are IPv4-specific. You need to update these applications to use newer Windows Sockets functions that are not specific to IPv4 or IPv6. For more information, see Appendix B, "Windows Sockets Changes for IPv6," or see the "IPv6 Guide for Windows Sockets Applications" at *http://go.microsoft.com/fwlink/?LinkID=87735.*

Basic IPv6 Stack Support

The IPv6 protocol for Windows Server 2008 and Windows Vista supports Internet Engineering Task Force (IETF) standards for IPv6 protocol stack functionality, including the following:

- The IPv6 header (RFC 2460)
- Unicast, multicast, and anycast addressing (RFC 4291)

- The Internet Control Message Protocol for IPv6 (ICMPv6) (RFC 4443)

- Neighbor Discovery (ND) (RFC 4861)

- Multicast Listener Discovery (MLD) (RFC 2710) and MLD version 2 (MLD v2) (RFC 3810)

- Stateless address autoconfiguration (RFC 4862)

IPv6 Stack Enhancements

The IPv6 protocol for Windows Server 2008 and Windows Vista also supports the following enhancements:

- **Dead gateway detection through neighbor unreachability detection**   Dead gateway detection automatically switches the currently used default router to the next one in a configured list when the current default router becomes unavailable, as detected through neighbor unreachability detection. For more information about neighbor unreachability detection, see Chapter 6, "Neighbor Discovery."

- **Explicit Congestion Notification support (RFC 3168)**   When a TCP segment is lost, TCP assumes that the segment was lost due to congestion at a router and performs congestion control, which dramatically lowers the TCP sender's transmission rate. With Explicit Congestion Notification (ECN) support on both TCP peers and in the routing infrastructure, routers experiencing congestion mark the packets as they forward them. TCP peers receiving marked packets lower their transmission rate to ease congestion and prevent segment losses. Detecting congestion before packet losses are incurred increases the overall throughput between TCP peers. Windows Server 2008 and Windows Vista support ECN, but it is disabled by default. You can enable ECN support with the **netsh interface tcp set global ecncapability=enabled** command.

- **Default route preferences and Route Information options in router advertisements (RFC 4191)**   With default router preferences, you can configure the advertising routers on a subnet to indicate a preference level so that hosts use the most preferred router as their default router. With Route Information options in router advertisements, routers that do not advertise themselves as default routers can advertise directly attached routes to hosts. For more information, see Chapter 6.

- **Strong host model for both sending and receiving**   The strong host model requires that unicast traffic sent or received must be associated with the network interface on which the traffic is sent or received. For sent traffic, IPv6 can send packets on an interface only if the interface is assigned the source IPv6 address of the packet being sent. For received traffic, IPv6 can receive packets on an interface only if the interface is assigned the destination IPv6 address of the packet being received. For more information, see Chapter 10, "IPv6 Routing."

GUI and Command-Line Configuration

With Windows Server 2008 and Windows Vista, you can manually configure IPv6 settings through the following:

- The Windows GUI from the properties of the Internet Protocol version 6 (TCP/IPv6) component in the Network Connections folder

- The Windows command prompt with commands in the **netsh interface ipv6** context

For more information, see the "Manually Configuring the IPv6 Protocol" section in this chapter.

Integrated IPsec Support

IPsec support for IPv6 traffic in Windows XP and Windows Server 2003 was limited. There was no support for Internet Key Exchange (IKE) or data encryption. IPsec security policies, security associations, and keys were configured through text files and activated through a command-line tool, Ipsec6.exe.

In Windows Server 2008 and Windows Vista, IPsec support for IPv6 traffic is the same as that for IPv4. IPsec for IPv6 traffic now supports IKE and data encryption. Windows Server 2008 and Windows Vista support the configuration of IPsec policies for IPv6 traffic in the same way as IPv4 traffic using either the IP Security Policies snap-in or the new Windows Firewall with Advanced Security snap-in.

Windows Firewall Support

Windows Firewall is a built-in host-based firewall that helps protect a computer running Windows Server 2008 or Windows Vista by blocking unsolicited incoming or outgoing traffic. Windows Firewall supports IPv6 traffic and the configuration of incoming or outgoing traffic exceptions in the same way as IPv4. Both IPv4 and IPv6 share the same settings for excepted traffic. For example, if you configure an inbound rule to allow file-and-print-sharing traffic, by default unsolicited incoming file-and-print-sharing traffic over both IPv4 and IPv6 are allowed. Windows Firewall is enabled by default for both Windows Server 2008 and Windows Vista.

Temporary Addresses

To provide a level of anonymity when accessing Internet resources, the IPv6 protocol for Windows Server 2008 and Windows Vista supports the use of temporary addresses containing randomly derived interface identifiers. Temporary addresses change over time, making it difficult to track someone's Internet usage based on their IPv6 address. Temporary addresses are enabled by default for Windows Vista and disabled by default for Windows Server 2008. You can enable them with the **netsh interface ipv6 set privacy enabled** command. Temporary addresses by default have a one-day preferred lifetime and a seven-day valid lifetime, which you can configure using **netsh interface ipv6 set privacy** commands.

For more information about temporary addresses, see Chapter 3, "IPv6 Addressing."

Random Interface IDs

To prevent address scans of IPv6 addresses on a link based on the known company identifiers (IDs) of network adapter manufacturers, Windows Server 2008 and Windows Vista by default generate random interface IDs for non-temporary autoconfigured IPv6 addresses, including public and link-local addresses. A public IPv6 address is a global address that is registered in DNS and is typically used by server applications for incoming connections, such as a Web server.

Note that this new behavior is different from that for temporary IPv6 addresses. Temporary addresses also use randomly derived interface IDs. However, they are not registered in DNS and are typically used by client applications, such as a Web browser, when initiating communication.

You can disable this default behavior with the **netsh interface ipv6 set global randomizeidentifiers=disabled** command. You can enable the use of random interface IDs with the **netsh interface ipv6 set global randomizeidentifiers=enabled** command.

DNS Support

DNS support for IPv6 in Windows Server 2008 and Windows Vista consists of the following:

- The querying and processing of IPv6 host (AAAA) and corresponding pointer (PTR) records in the DNS.

- The sending of DNS traffic over IPv6. You can configure the IPv6 addresses of your IPv6-enabled DNS server manually with the **netsh interface ipv6 add dnsserver** command or with the Dynamic Host Configuration Protocol for IPv6 (DHCPv6).

- The dynamic registration of IPv6 host records in the DNS over either IPv4 or IPv6.

The DNS Server service in Windows Server 2008 supports the storage and dynamic registration of IPv6 AAAA records over both IPv4 and IPv6.

For more information about DNS support for IPv6, see Chapter 9, "IPv6 and Name Resolution."

Source and Destination Address Selection

In a DNS environment that contains both host address (A) and IPv6 host address (AAAA) records, the result of a name query for a DNS name might be multiple addresses: zero or more IPv6 addresses and zero or more IPv4 addresses. Based on the configuration of the querying host, address selection algorithms determine the pairs of source and destination addresses with which to attempt communication. The source and destination address pairs must be carefully selected to ensure that they are matched in scope and purpose. IPv6 in Windows Server 2008 and Windows Vista supports the source and destination address algorithms described in RFC 3484.

For more information about source and destination address selection, see Chapter 9.

Support for ipv6-literal.net Names

Windows Server 2008 and Windows Vista now support the use of *IPv6Address*.ipv6-literal.net names. To specify an IPv6 address within the ipv6-literal.net name, convert the colons (:) in the address to dashes (-). For example, for the IPv6 address 2001:db8:28:3:f98a:5b31:67b7:67ef, the corresponding ipv6-literal.net name is 2001-db8-28-3-f98a-5b31-67b7-67ef.ipv6-literal.net. When submitted by an application for name resolution, the 2001-db8-28-3-f98a-5b31-67b7-67ef.ipv6-literal.net name resolves to 2001:db8:28:3:f98a:5b31:67b7:67ef.

For more information, see Chapter 9.

LLMNR

Windows Server 2008 and Windows Vista support Link-Local Multicast Name Resolution (LLMNR), which allows IPv6 hosts on a single subnet without a DNS server to resolve each other's names. This capability is useful for single-subnet home networks and ad hoc wireless networks. Rather than unicasting a DNS query to a DNS server, LLMNR nodes send their DNS queries to a multicast address on which all the LLMNR-capable nodes of the subnet are listening. The owner of the queried name sends a unicast response. IPv4 nodes can also use LLMNR to perform local subnet name resolution without having to rely on NetBIOS over TCP/IP broadcasts.

For more information, see Chapter 9.

PNRP

Windows Server 2008 and Windows Vista include version 2 of the Peer Name Resolution Protocol (PNRP)—a secure, scalable, and dynamic name registration and name resolution protocol for the Windows Peer-to-Peer Networking platform. Windows Peer-to-Peer Networking applications can access PNRP name publication and resolution functions using the PNRP API. PNRP names are also integrated into the *Getaddrinfo()* Windows Sockets function. To use PNRP to resolve a name to an IPv6 address, applications can use the *Getaddrinfo()* function to resolve the fully qualified domain name (FQDN) *name*.prnp.net, in which *name* is the Windows Peer-to-Peer Networking peer name being resolved.

For more information, see Chapter 9.

Literal IPv6 Addresses in URLs

The Win32 Internet Extensions (WinInet) API in Windows Server 2008 and Windows Vista now supports RFC 3986 and the use of IPv6 literal addresses in URLs with the following syntax: http://[*IPv6Address*]:*Port*. For example, to connect to the Web server at the IPv6 address 2001:db8:100:2a5f::1, a user with a WinInet-based Web browser (such as Windows Internet Explorer) can type **http://[2001:db8:100:2a5f::1]** as the URL. Although typical users might not use IPv6 literal addresses, the ability to specify the IPv6 address in the URL is valuable to application developers, software testers, and network troubleshooters.

Static Routing

A computer running Windows Server 2008 or Windows Vista can act as a static IPv6 router that performs the following:

- Forwards IPv6 packets between interfaces based on the contents of the IPv6 routing table

  To enable an interface for forwarding, use the **netsh interface ipv6 set interface** *InterfaceNameOrIndex* **forwarding=enabled** command. You can configure static routes with the **netsh interface ipv6 add|set route** commands. Windows Server 2008 and Windows Vista do not provide support for IPv6 routing protocols.

- Sends router advertisements

  The contents of router advertisements are automatically derived from routes in the routing table. To enable the sending of router advertisements on an interface, use the **netsh interface ipv6 set interface** *InterfaceNameOrIndex* **advertise=enabled** command.

A computer running Windows Server 2008 or Windows Vista by default advertises itself as a default router (by using a router advertisement with a router lifetime other than zero) only if there is a default route that is configured to be published. To add a default route and publish it, you must use the **netsh interface ipv6 add route ::/0** *InterfaceNameorIndex* **nexthop=***Ipv6Address* **publish=yes** command.

For more information about static IPv6 routing support in Windows Server 2008 and Windows Vista, see Chapter 10.

IPv6 over PPP

The built-in remote access client of Windows Server 2008 and Windows Vista now supports the IPv6 Control Protocol (IPV6CP), as defined in RFC 5072, to configure IPv6 nodes on a Point-to-Point Protocol (PPP) link. Native IPv6 traffic can now be sent over PPP-based connections. For example, IPV6CP support allows you to connect with an IPv6-based Internet service provider (ISP) through dial-up or PPP over Ethernet (PPPoE)–based connections that might be used for broadband Internet access. Additionally, IPV6CP in the built-in remote access client supports Point-to-Point Tunneling Protocol (PPTP) and Layer Two Tunneling Protocol (L2TP)–based virtual private network (VPN) connections.

DHCPv6

The DHCP Client service in Windows Server 2008 and Windows Vista supports Dynamic Host Configuration Protocol for IPv6 (DHCPv6) defined in RFCs 3315 and 3736. A computer running Windows Server 2008 or Windows Vista can perform both DHCPv6 stateful and stateless configuration on a native IPv6 network. The DHCP Server service in Windows Server 2008 supports DHCPv6 stateful (both addresses and configuration settings) and stateless (configuration settings only) operation. The Routing and Remote Access service in Windows Server 2008 includes a DHCPv6 relay agent.

For more information, see Chapter 8, "Address Autoconfiguration."

ISATAP

Intra-Site Automatic Tunnel Addressing Protocol (ISATAP) is an IPv6 transition technology that allows IPv6/IPv4 nodes within an IPv4-only infrastructure of an intranet to use IPv6 to communicate with each other and with nodes on an IPv6-enabled portion of the intranet or the IPv6 Internet. The IPv6 protocol for Windows Server 2008 and Windows Vista supports ISATAP as an ISATAP host and an ISATAP router.

For more information, see Chapter 12, "ISATAP."

6to4

6to4 is an IPv6 transition technology that provides automatic tunneling and IPv6 connectivity between IPv6/IPv4 hosts across the IPv4 Internet. 6to4 hosts use IPv6 addresses derived from IPv4 public addresses. With 6to4, IPv6 sites and hosts can use 6to4-based addresses and the IPv4 Internet to communicate without having to obtain an IPv6 global address prefix from an ISP and then having to connect to the IPv6 Internet. The IPv6 protocol for Windows Server 2008 and Windows Vista supports 6to4 as a 6to4 host and a 6to4 router.

For more information, see Chapter 13, "6to4."

Teredo

Teredo is an IPv6 transition technology that allows automatic tunneling and IPv6 connectivity between IPv6/IPv4 hosts across the IPv4 Internet, even when the hosts are separated by IPv4 NATs. Teredo is a NAT traversal technology for IPv6 traffic designed for use in unmanaged network environments, such as small office or home office networks. IPv6 traffic tunneled using Teredo can cross one or multiple NATs and allow a Teredo client to access the hosts on the IPv6 Internet (through a Teredo relay) and other Teredo clients on the IPv4 Internet. The ability to connect to other Teredo clients that are connected to the IPv4 Internet enables communication between applications that would otherwise have problems communicating over a NAT. The IPv6 protocol for Windows Server 2008 and Windows Vista supports Teredo as a Teredo client and a Teredo host-specific relay.

For more information, see Chapter 14, "Teredo."

PortProxy

PortProxy is a component of the IPv6 protocol for Windows Server 2008 and Windows Vista that functions as a TCP proxy to facilitate the communication between nodes or applications that cannot connect using a common Internet layer protocol (IPv4 or IPv6). By using Port-Proxy, IPv6-only nodes or applications can communicate with IPv4-only nodes or applications and vice versa.

For more information, see Chapter 11.

Application Support

Windows Server 2008 includes full support for operation over IPv6 in all of its included networking applications and services, except for the File Transfer Protocol (FTP) Publishing service and the Simple Mail Transfer Protocol (SMTP) Server service in Internet Information Services (IIS). The SMTP feature of Microsoft Exchange Server 2007 with Service Pack 1 includes an IPv6-capable SMTP service. Windows Vista includes full support for operation over IPv6 in all its included networking applications and services except the File Transfer Protocol (FTP) Publishing service in Internet Information Services (IIS).

With the exception of the FTP Publishing and SMTP Server services in IIS, you can create an IPv6-only network and perform all the Windows-based infrastructure and productivity services provided with Windows Server 2008 and Windows Vista, including the following:

- Active Directory domain services
- Web services
- Certificate services
- File and printer sharing
- Windows Media Services

Application Programming Interfaces

Windows Server 2008 and Windows Vista include IPv6 support for the following application programming interfaces (APIs):

- Windows Sockets
- Winsock Kernel

- Remote Procedure Call
- Internet Protocol Helper
- Win32 Internet Extensions
- .NET Framework
- Windows Filtering Platform

Windows Sockets

Windows Sockets (Winsock) is an API based on the familiar "socket" interface from the University of California at Berkeley. It includes a set of extensions designed to take advantage of the message-driven nature of Microsoft Windows. Version 1.1 of the Windows Sockets specification was released in January 1993, and version 2.2.0 was published in May 1996.

The Microsoft Windows implementation of sockets, Winsock, is designed to run efficiently on Windows operating systems while maintaining compatibility with the Berkeley Software Distribution (BSD) standard, known as Berkeley Sockets. With Winsock, programmers can create advanced Internet, intranet, and other network-capable applications to transmit application data across the wire, independent of the network protocol being used.

Winsock for Windows Server 2008 and Windows Vista has been enhanced to include IPv6 support as specified in RFC 3493, "Basic Socket Interface Extensions for IPv6" (with some exceptions), and portions of RFC 3542, "Advanced Sockets API for IPv6." For the details of Windows Sockets support for IPv6, see Appendix B, "Windows Sockets Changes for IPv6."

Winsock Kernel

Winsock Kernel (WSK) is a new transport-independent kernel-mode API. Using WSK, kernel-mode software modules such as third-party drivers can perform network communication using socket-like programming semantics similar to those supported in user-mode Winsock. WSK was designed to provide an easy-to-use interface for kernel-mode developers. WSK supports both IPv4-based and IPv6-based connectivity for WSK-based software modules.

Remote Procedure Call

Remote procedure call (RPC) is an API that is used for creating distributed client/server programs. The RPC run-time stubs and libraries manage most of the details relating to network protocols and communication. RPC functions are used to forward application function calls to a remote system across the network. The RPC components in Windows Server 2008 and Windows Vista are IPv6-enabled. The RPC components have been modified to use the updated Winsock functions, which allows RPC to work over both IPv4 and IPv6.

IP Helper

Internet Protocol Helper (IP Helper) is an API that assists in the administration of the network configuration of the local computer. You can use IP Helper to programmatically retrieve information about the network configuration of the local computer and to modify that configuration. IP Helper also provides notification mechanisms to ensure that an application is notified when certain aspects of the network configuration change on the local computer.

IP Helper in Windows Server 2008 and Windows Vista has been extended to allow management and configuration of IPv6 and its components. Some of the areas that are IPv6-enabled are the following:

■ Retrieving information about network configuration, network adapters, interfaces, addresses, IPv6, ICMPv6, routing, TCP, and UDP

■ Receiving notification of network events

Win32 Internet Extensions

The Win32 Internet Extensions (WinInet) is an API used for creating an Internet client application. An Internet client application is a program that accesses information from a network data source (server) using Internet protocols such as gopher, FTP, or HTTP. An Internet client application might access a server to retrieve data such as weather maps, stock prices, or newspaper headlines. The Internet client can access the server through an external network (the Internet) or an internal network (an intranet).

WinInet in Windows Server 2008 and Windows Vista has been extended to support IPv6. This allows Microsoft Internet Explorer to use WinInet to access IPv6-enabled Web sites and to use literal IPv6 addresses in URLs.

.NET Framework

The .NET Framework is the programming model of the .NET platform for building, deploying, and running Extensible Markup Language (XML) Web services and applications. It manages much of the plumbing, enabling developers to focus on writing the business logic code for their applications. The .NET Framework provided with Windows Server 2008 and Windows Vista is IPv6-enabled, allowing .NET Framework applications to operate over either IPv6 or IPv4.

Windows Filtering Platform

The Windows Filtering Platform (WFP) is new to Windows Server 2008 and Windows Vista. It provides APIs so that third-party independent software vendors (ISVs) can participate in the filtering decisions that take place at several layers in the TCP/IP protocol stack and throughout the operating system. WFP also integrates and provides support for new firewall features, such as authenticated communication and dynamic firewall configuration based on applications' use of the Winsock API (application-based policy). ISVs can create firewalls, antivirus software, diagnostic software, and other types of applications and services. Windows Firewall and IPsec in Windows Server 2008 and Windows Vista use the WFP API.

For more information, see *http://go.microsoft.com/fwlink/?LinkID=90220*.

Manually Configuring the IPv6 Protocol

Unlike IPv6 in Windows XP and Windows Server 2003, the IPv6 protocol in Windows Server 2008 and Windows Vista is installed and enabled by default. The IPv6 protocol for Windows Server 2008 and Windows Vista is designed to be autoconfiguring. For example, it automatically configures link-local addresses for communication between nodes on a link. If there is an IPv6 router on the host's subnet or an ISATAP router, the host uses received router advertisements to automatically configure additional addresses, a default router, and other configuration parameters.

You can manually configure IPv6 addresses and other parameters in Windows Vista using the following:

- **The properties of Internet Protocol Version 6 (TCP/IPv6) component**   Just as you can configure IPv4 settings through the properties of the Internet Protocol Version 4 (TCP/IPv4) component in the Network Connections folder, you can now configure IPv6 settings through the properties of the Internet Protocol Version 6 (TCP/IPv6) component. The set of dialog boxes for IPv6 configuration is very similar to the corresponding dialog boxes for IPv4. However, the properties of the Internet Protocol Version 6 (TCP/IPv6) component provide only basic configuration of IPv6.

- **Commands in the netsh interface ipv6 context**   Just as you can in Windows XP and Windows Server 2003, you can configure IPv6 settings for Windows Server 2008 or Windows Vista from the **interface ipv6** context of the Netsh.exe tool. Commands in the **netsh interface ipv6** context provide complete configuration of IPv6.

Although typical IPv6 hosts do not need to be manually configured, IPv6 routers must be manually configured.

Configuring IPv6 Through the Properties of Internet Protocol Version 6 (TCP/IPv6)

To manually configure IPv6 settings through the Network Connections folder, do the following:

1. From the Network Connections folder, right-click the connection or adapter on which you want to manually configure IPv6, and then click Properties.

2. On the Networking tab for the properties of the connection or adapter, under This Connection Uses The Following Items, double-click Internet Protocol Version 6 (TCP/IPv6) in the list.

Windows Vista displays the Internet Protocol Version 6 (TCP/IPv6) Properties dialog box. Figure 2-2 shows an example.

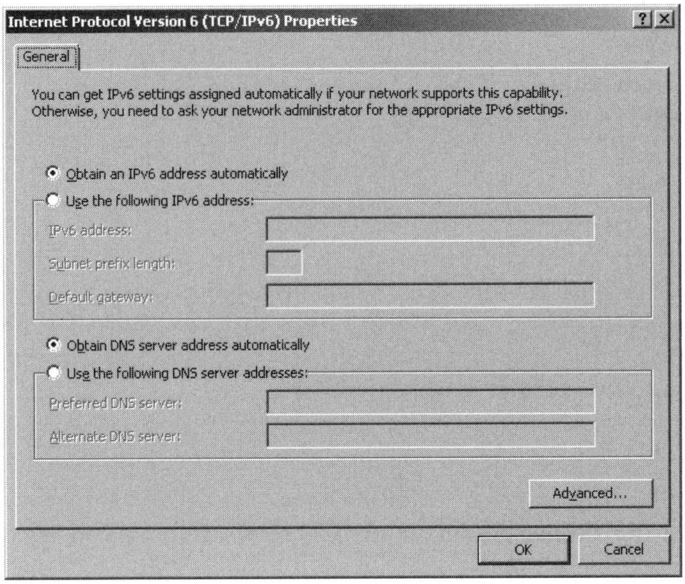

Figure 2-2   The Internet Protocol Version 6 (TCP/IPv6) Properties dialog box

General Tab

On the General tab of the Internet Protocol Version 6 (TCP/IPv6) Properties dialog box, you can configure the following:

- **Obtain an IPv6 address automatically**   Specifies that IPv6 addresses for this connection or adapter are automatically determined by stateful or stateless address autoconfiguration.

- **Use the following IPv6 address**   Specifies that an IPv6 address and default gateway for this connection or adapter are manually configured.

- **IPv6 address**   Provides a space for you to type an IPv6 unicast address. You can specify additional IPv6 addresses from the Advanced TCP/IP Settings dialog box.

- **Subnet prefix length**   Provides a space for you to type the subnet prefix length for the IPv6 address. For typical IPv6 unicast addresses, this value should be set to 64, its default value.

- **Default gateway**   Provides a space for you to type the IPv6 unicast address of the default gateway.

- **Obtain DNS server address automatically**   Specifies that the IPv6 addresses for DNS servers are automatically determined by stateful address autoconfiguration (DHCPv6).

- **Use the following DNS server addresses**   Specifies that the IPv6 addresses of the preferred and alternate DNS servers for this connection or adapter are manually configured.

- **Preferred DNS server**   Provides a space for you to type the IPv6 unicast address of the preferred DNS server.

- **Alternate DNS server**   Provides a space for you to type the IPv6 unicast address of the alternate DNS server. You can specify additional DNS servers from the Advanced TCP/IP Settings dialog box.

Advanced TCP/IP Settings

From the General tab, you can click Advanced to access the Advanced TCP/IP Settings dialog box. This dialog box is very similar to the Advanced TCP/IP Settings dialog box for the Internet Protocol Version 4 (TCP/IPv4) component except there is no WINS tab (IPv6 does not use NetBIOS and the Windows Internet Name Service [WINS]) or Options tab (TCP/IP filtering is defined only for IPv4 traffic). For IPv6, the Advanced TCP/IP Settings dialog box has IP Settings and DNS tabs. Figure 2-3 shows an example of the IP Settings tab.

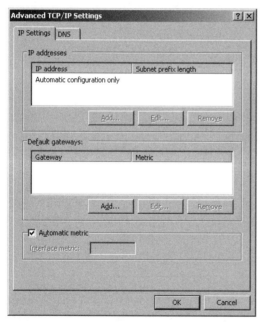

Figure 2-3   The IP Settings tab

From the IP Settings tab, you can configure the following:

- **Multiple IPv6 addresses (by clicking Add under IP Addresses)**   For each unicast IPv6 address, you must specify an IPv6 address and a subnet prefix length. The Add button is available only if Use The Following Ipv6 Address has been selected on the General tab of the Internet Protocol Version 6 (TCP/IPv6) Properties dialog box.

- **Multiple default gateways (by clicking Add under Default Gateways)**   For each default gateway, you must specify the IPv6 address of the gateway and whether you want the metric for the default route associated with this default gateway to be manually specified or based on the speed of the connection or adapter.

- **Route metrics**   You can also specify whether to use a specific metric for the routes associated with the configuration of IPv6 addresses or default gateways or a metric determined by the speed of the connection or adapter.

Figure 2-4 shows an example of the DNS tab.

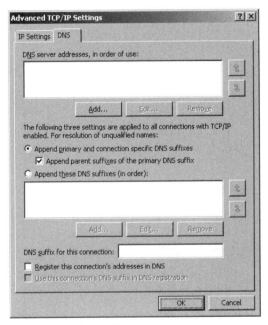

Figure 2-4   The DNS tab

From the DNS tab, you can configure the following:

- The IPv6 addresses of DNS servers, in order of use (by clicking Add under DNS Server Addresses, In Order Of Use).

- Primary and connection-specific DNS suffix and name registration and devolution behavior. These settings are the same as for IPv4.

Configuring IPv6 with the Netsh.exe Tool

You can also configure IPv6 addresses, default gateways, and DNS servers at the command line using commands in the **netsh interface ipv6** context.

Configuring Addresses

To configure IPv6 addresses, you can use the **netsh interface ipv6 add address** command with the following syntax:

netsh interface ipv6 add address [**interface=**]*InterfaceNameorIndex* [**address=**]*IPv6Address*[/*PrefixLength*] [[**type=**]unicast|anycast] [[**validlifetime=**]*Time*|infinite] [[**preferredlifetime=**]*Time*|infinite] [[**store=**]active|persistent]

- **interface**   The connection or adapter's name or interface index.
- **address**   The IPv6 address to add, optionally followed by the subnet prefix length (default of 64).
- **type**   The type of IPv6 address, either unicast (default) or anycast.
- **validlifetime**   The lifetime over which the address is valid. Time values can be expressed in days, hours, minutes, and seconds (for example, 1d2h3m4s). The default value is **infinite**.
- **preferredlifetime**   The lifetime over which the address is preferred. Time values can be expressed in days, hours, minutes, and seconds. The default value is **infinite**.
- **store**   How to store the IPv6 address—either **active** (the address is removed upon system restart) or **persistent** (address remains after system restart), which is the default.

For example, to configure the IPv6 unicast address 2001:db8:290c:1291::1 on the interface named "Local Area Connection" with infinite valid and preferred lifetimes and make the address persistent, you use the following command:

```
netsh interface ipv6 add address "Local Area Connection" 2001:db8:290c:1291::1
```

Adding Default Gateways

To configure a default gateway, you can use the **netsh interface ipv6 add route** command and add a default route (::/0) with the following syntax:

netsh interface ipv6 add route [**prefix=**]::/0 [**interface=**]*InterfaceNameorIndex* [[**nexthop=**]*IPv6Address*] [[**siteprefixlength=**]*Length*] [[**metric=**]*MetricValue*] [[**publish=**]no|yes|immortal] [[**validlifetime=**]*Time*|infinite] [[**preferredlifetime=**]*Time*|infinite] [[**store=**]active|persistent]

- **prefix**   The IPv6 address prefix and prefix length for the default route. For other routes, you can substitute ::/0 with *AddressPrefix/PrefixLength*.
- **interface**   The connection or adapter's name or interface index.
- **nexthop**   If the prefix is for destinations that are not on the local link, the next-hop IPv6 address of a neighboring router.

- **siteprefixlength**   If the prefix is for destinations on the local link, you can optionally specify the prefix length for the address prefix assigned to the site to which this IPv6 node belongs.

- **metric**   A value that specifies the preference for using the route. Lower values are preferred.

- **publish**   As an IPv6 router, this option specifies whether the subnet prefix corresponding to the route will be included in router advertisements and whether the lifetimes for the prefixes are infinite (the **immortal** option).

- **validlifetime**   The lifetime over which the route is valid. Time values can be expressed in days, hours, minutes, and seconds (for example, 1d2h3m4s). The default value is **infinite**.

- **preferredlifetime**   The lifetime over which the route is preferred. Time values can be expressed in days, hours, minutes, and seconds. The default value is **infinite**.

- **store**   How to store the route, either **active** (route is removed upon system restart) or **persistent** (route remains after restart), which is the default.

For example, to add a default route that uses the interface named "Local Area Connection" with a next-hop address of fe80::2aa:ff:fe9a:21b8, you use the following command:

```
netsh interface ipv6 add route ::/0 "Local Area Connection" fe80::2aa:ff:fe9a:21b8
```

Adding DNS Servers

To configure the IPv6 addresses of DNS servers, you can use the **netsh interface ipv6 add dnsserver** command with the following syntax:

netsh interface ipv6 add dnsserver [**name=**]*InterfaceName* [[**address=**]*IPv6Address*] [[**index=**]*PreferenceValue*]

- **name**   The connection or adapter's name.

- **address**   The IPv6 address of the DNS server.

- **index**   The preference for the DNS server address.

By default, the DNS server is added to the end of the list of DNS servers. If an index is specified, the DNS server is placed in that position in the list and the other DNS servers are moved down the list.

For example, to add a DNS server with the IPv6 address 2001:db8:99:4acd::8 that uses the interface named "Local Area Connection," you use the following command:

```
netsh interface ipv6 add dnsserver "Local Area Connection" 2001:db8:99:4acd::8
```

> **Note**   This section described only the Netsh commands for adding addresses, default gateways, and DNS servers. There are many more Netsh commands for configuring IPv6 settings and IPv6 components. For the complete list of commands and their use, see Windows Server 2008 Help and Support.

Disabling IPv6

Unlike IPv6 in Windows XP and Windows Server 2003, IPv6 in Windows Server 2008 and Windows Vista cannot be uninstalled. To disable IPv6 on a specific connection in the Network Connections folder, you can obtain properties of the connection and clear the check box next to the Internet Protocol Version 6 (TCP/IPv6) component in the list under This Connection Uses The Following Items. This method disables IPv6 on your LAN interfaces and connections, but it does not disable IPv6 on tunnel interfaces or the IPv6 loopback interface.

To selectively disable components and configure behaviors for IPv6 in Windows Vista, you must create and configure the HKEY_LOCAL_MACHINE\SYSTEM\CurrentControlSet\ Services\tcpip6\Parameters\DisabledComponents registry value (DWORD type). *Disabled-Components* does not exist by default and must be manually created with the Registry Editor tool (Regedit.exe). If the *DisabledComponents* registry value does not exist, it has a default value of 0.

The *DisabledComponents* registry value is a bit mask that controls the following series of flags, starting with the low-order bit (Bit 0):

- **Bit 0**   Set to 1 to disable all IPv6 tunnel interfaces, including ISATAP, 6to4, and Teredo tunnels. Default value is 0.

- **Bit 1**   Set to 1 to disable all 6to4-based interfaces. Default value is 0.

- **Bit 2**   Set to 1 to disable all ISATAP-based interfaces. Default value is 0.

- **Bit 3**   Set to 1 to disable all Teredo-based interfaces. Default value is 0.

- **Bit 4**   Set to 1 to disable IPv6 over all non-tunnel interfaces, including LAN interfaces and PPP-based interfaces. Default value is 0.

- **Bit 5**   Set to 1 to modify the default prefix policy table to prefer IPv4 to IPv6 when attempting connections. Default value is 0. For more information about the prefix policy table, see Chapter 9.

To determine the value of *DisabledComponents* for a specific set of bits, construct a binary number consisting of the bits and their values in their correct position and convert the resulting number to hexadecimal. For example, if you want to disable 6to4 interfaces, disable Teredo interfaces, and if you want to prefer IPv4 to IPv6, construct the following binary number: 101010. When converted to hexadecimal, the value of *DisabledComponents* is 0x2A.

Table 2-1 lists some common configuration combinations and the corresponding value of *DisabledComponents*.

Table 2-1   Configuration Combinations and the *DisabledComponents* Registry Value

Configuration Combination	*DisabledComponents* Value
Disable all tunnel interfaces	0x1
Disable 6to4	0x2
Disable ISATAP	0x4
Disable Teredo	0x8
Disable Teredo and 6to4	0xA
Disable all LAN and PPP interfaces	0x10
Disable all LAN, PPP, and tunnel interfaces	0x11
Prefer IPv4 over IPv6	0x20
Disable IPv6 over all interfaces, and prefer IPv4 to IPv6	0xFF

You must restart the computer for the changes to the *DisabledComponents* registry value to take effect.

You can set *DisabledComponents* on individual computers with the Registry Editor tool, or you can use Active Directory and Group Policy with a customized .ADM file to set *DisabledComponents* on a group of computers. If you use a customized .ADM file and then remove the *DisabledComponents* registry value from the .ADM file, the *DisabledComponents* registry value does not get automatically removed from registries of the computers to which the updated .ADM file is applied.

IPv6-Enabled Tools

Windows Server 2008 and Windows Vista include the following IPv6-enabled command-line tools that are most commonly used for network troubleshooting:

- Ipconfig
- Route
- Ping
- Tracert
- Pathping
- Netstat

Ipconfig

The Ipconfig tool displays all current TCP/IP network configuration values, and it is used to perform maintenance tasks such as refreshing DHCP and DNS settings. In Windows

Server 2008 and Windows Vista, the **ipconfig** command without options displays IPv4 and IPv6 configuration for all physical adapters and tunnel interfaces that have addresses.

The following is an example display of the **ipconfig** command on a computer running Windows Server 2008 or Windows Vista:

```
Windows IP Configuration

Ethernet adapter Local Area Connection:
    Connection-specific DNS Suffix  . : ecoast.example.com
    IPv6 Address. . . . . . . . . . . : 2001:db8:21da:7:713e:a426:d167:37ab
    Temporary IPv6 Address. . . . . . : 2001:db8:21da:7:5099:ba54:9881:2e54
    Link-local IPv6 Address . . . . . : fe80::713e:a426:d167:37ab%6
    IPv4 Address. . . . . . . . . . . : 157.60.14.11
    Subnet Mask . . . . . . . . . . . : 255.255.255.0
    Default Gateway . . . . . . . . . : fe80::20a:42ff:feb0:5400%6
                                        157.60.14.1

Tunnel adapter Local Area Connection* 6:

    Connection-specific DNS Suffix  . :
    IPv6 Address. . . . . . . . . . . : 2001:db8:908c:f70f:0:5efe:157.60.14.11
    Link-local IPv6 Address . . . . . : fe80::5efe:157.60.14.11%9
    Site-local IPv6 Address . . . . . : fec0::6ab4:0:5efe:157.60.14.11%1
    Default Gateway . . . . . . . . . : fe80::5efe:131.107.25.1%9
                                        fe80::5efe:131.107.25.2%9

Tunnel adapter Local Area Connection* 7:
    Media State . . . . . . . . . . . : Media disconnected
    Connection-specific DNS Suffix  . :
```

Ipconfig.exe displays the IPv6 addresses before the IPv4 addresses and indicates the type of IPv6 address using the following labels:

- **IPv6 Address**   A global address with a permanent interface ID

- **Temporary IPv6 Address**   A global address with a randomly derived interface ID that has a short valid lifetime

- **Link-local IPv6 Address**   A link-local address with its corresponding zone ID (the interface index)

- **Site-local IPv6 Address**   A site-local address with its corresponding zone ID (the site ID)

For more information about the different types of IPv6 addresses and the zone ID, see Chapter 3.

By default, the interface names containing an asterisk (*) are tunneling interfaces.

Route

The Route tool displays the entries in the local IPv4 and IPv6 routing tables and allows you to change them. The Route tool displays both the IPv4 and IPv6 routing table when you run the **route print** command. The following is an example of the IPv6 route table portion of the display of the **route print** command on a computer running Windows Server 2008 or Windows Vista:

```
IPv6 Route Table
===========================================================================
Active Routes:
 If Metric Network Destination        Gateway
  8    286 ::/0                        fe80::3cec:bf16:505:eae6
  1    306 ::1/128                     On-link
  8     38 2001:db8::/64               On-link
  8    286 2001:db8::4074:2dce:b313:7c65/128
                                       On-link
  8    286 2001:db8::b500:734b:fe5b:3945/128
                                       On-link
  8    286 fe80::/64                   On-link
 17    296 fe80::5efe:10.0.0.3/128     On-link
  8    286 fe80::b500:734b:fe5b:3945/128
                                       On-link
  1    306 ff00::/8                    On-link
  8    286 ff00::/8                    On-link
===========================================================================
```

You can change entries in the IPv6 routing table with the Route.exe tool with the **route add**, **route change**, and **route delete** commands.

For more information about the IPv6 routing table, see Chapter 10.

Ping

In previous versions of Windows, the Ping tool verified IPv4-level connectivity to another TCP/IP computer by sending Internet Control Message Protocol (ICMP) Echo messages. The receipt of corresponding Echo Reply messages is displayed, along with round-trip times. Ping is the primary TCP/IP tool used to troubleshoot reachability and name resolution.

The Ping tool in Windows Server 2008 and Windows Vista has been enhanced to support IPv6 in the following ways:

- Ping uses either ICMPv4 Echo or ICMPv6 Echo Request messages to verify IPv4-based or IPv6-based connectivity.

- Ping can parse both IPv4 and IPv6 address formats.

- If you specify a target host by name, the addresses returned by using Windows name resolution techniques can contain both IPv4 and IPv6 addresses—in which case, by default, an IPv6 address is preferred (subject to source and destination address selection).

The following is an example display of the Ping tool on a computer running Windows Server 2008 or Windows Vista for an IPv6 destination address:

```
F:\>ping 2001:db8:1:f282:dd48:ab34:d07c:3914

Pinging 2001:db8:1:f282:dd48:ab34:d07c:3914 from
 2001:db8:1:f282:3cec:bf16:505:eae6 with 32 bytes of data:
```

```
Reply from 2001:db8:1:f282:dd48:ab34:d07c:3914: time<1ms
Reply from 2001:db8:1:f282:dd48:ab34:d07c:3914: time<1ms
Reply from 2001:db8:1:f282:dd48:ab34:d07c:3914: time<1ms
Reply from 2001:db8:1:f282:dd48:ab34:d07c:3914: time<1ms

Ping statistics for 2001:db8:1:f282:dd48:ab34:d07c:3914:
    Packets: Sent = 4, Received = 4, Lost = 0 (0% loss),
Approximate round trip times in milli-seconds:
    Minimum = 0ms, Maximum = 0ms, Average = 0ms
```

The following command-line options support IPv6:

- **-i** *HopLimit*

  Sets the value of the Hop Limit field in the IPv6 header. The default value is 128. The **-i** option is also used to set the value of the Time-to-Live (TTL) field in the IPv4 header.

- **-R**

  Forces Ping to trace the round-trip path by sending the ICMPv6 Echo Request message to the destination and to include an IPv6 Routing extension header with the sending node as the next destination.

- **-S** *SourceAddr*

  Forces Ping to use a specified IPv6 source address.

- **-4**

  Forces Ping to use an IPv4 address when the DNS name query for a host name returns both IPv4 and IPv6 addresses.

- **-6**

  Forces Ping to use an IPv6 address when the DNS name query for a host name returns both IPv4 and IPv6 addresses.

> **Note** The Ping **-f**, **-v** *TOS*, **-r** *count*, **-s** *count*, **-j** *host-list*, and **-k** *host-list* command-line options are not supported for IPv6.

When you specify a destination IPv6 address for a Ping, Tracert, or Pathping command, you might have to specify a zone ID as part of the address. The zone ID specifies the zone of the destination for Echo Request messages. The syntax for specifying a zone ID is *IPv6Address%ZoneID*, in which *ZoneID* is an integer value. For typical link-local addresses, *ZoneID* is equal to the interface index of the sending interface, as displayed by the output of the **netsh interface ipv6 show interface** command. For site-local addresses, *ZoneID* is equal to the site number, as displayed in the output of the **netsh interface ipv6 show interface level=verbose** command (the "Zone ID for Site" property). If multiple sites are not being used, a zone ID for site-local addresses is not required. The *ZoneID* parameter is not required when the destination is a global address.

Tracert

The Tracert tool determines the path taken to a destination. For IPv4, Tracert sends ICMPv4 Echo messages to the destination with incrementally increasing TTL field values. For IPv6, Tracert sends ICMPv6 Echo Request messages to the destination with incrementally increasing Hop Limit field values. Tracert displays the path as the list of nearside router interfaces of the routers in the path between a source host and a destination node.

The Tracert tool in Windows Server 2008 and Windows Vista has been enhanced to support IPv6 in the following ways:

- Tracert can parse both IPv4 and IPv6 address formats.

- If you specify a target host by name, the addresses returned using Windows name resolution techniques can contain both IPv4 and IPv6 addresses—in which case, by default, an IPv6 address is preferred (subject to source and destination address selection).

The following is an example display of the Tracert tool on a computer running Windows Server 2008 or Windows Vista:

```
F:\>tracert 2001:db8:1:f282:dd48:ab34:d07c:3914

Tracing route to 2001:db8:1:f282:dd48:ab34:d07c:3914 over a maximum of 30 hops

  1    <1 ms    <1 ms    <1 ms   2001:db8:1:f241:2b0:d0ff:fea4:243d
  2    <1 ms    <1 ms    <1 ms   2001:db8:1:f2ac:2b0:d0ff:fea5:d347
  3    <1 ms    <1 ms    <1 ms   2001:db8:1:f282:dd48:ab34:d07c:3914

Trace complete.
```

The following Tracert command-line options support IPv6:

- **-R**

  Forces Tracert to trace the round-trip path by sending the ICMPv6 Echo Request message to the destination, including an IPv6 Routing extension header with the sending node as the next destination

- **-S** *SourceAddr*

  Forces Tracert to use a specified IPv6 source address

- **-4**

  Forces Tracert to use an IPv4 address when the DNS name query for a host name returns both IPv4 and IPv6 addresses

- **-6**

  Forces Tracert to use an IPv6 address when the DNS name query for a host name returns both IPv4 and IPv6 addresses

> **Note** The Tracert **-j** *host-list* command-line option is not supported for IPv6.

Pathping

The Pathping tool provides information about network latency and network loss at intermediate hops between a source and destination. For IPv4, Pathping sends multiple ICMPv4 Echo messages to each router between a source and destination over a period of time, and then it computes results based on the packets returned from each router. For IPv6, Pathping sends ICMPv6 Echo Request messages. Because Pathping displays the degree of packet loss at any given router or link, you can determine which routers or subnets might be having network problems. Pathping performs the equivalent of the Tracert tool by identifying which routers are in the path, and then it sends messages periodically to all the routers over a specified time period and computes statistics based on the number returned from each.

The Pathping tool in Windows Server 2008 and Windows Vista has been enhanced to support IPv6 in the following ways:

- Pathping can parse both IPv4 and IPv6 address formats.

- If you specify a target host by name, the addresses returned using Windows name resolution techniques can contain both IPv4 and IPv6 addresses—in which case, by default, an IPv6 address is preferred (subject to source and destination address selection).

The following is an example display of the Pathping tool on a computer running Windows Server 2008 or Windows Vista:

```
F:\>pathping 2001:db8:1:f282:dd48:ab34:d07c:3914

Tracing route to 2001:db8:1:f282:dd48:ab34:d07c:3914 over a maximum of 30 hops

  0  server1.example.microsoft.com [2001:db8:1:f282:204:5aff:fe56:1006]
  1  2001:db8:1:f282:dd48:ab34:d07c:3914

Computing statistics for 25 seconds...
            Source to Here   This Node/Link
Hop  RTT    Lost/Sent = Pct  Lost/Sent = Pct  Address
  0                                            server1.example.microsoft.com
[2001:db8:1:f282:204:5aff:fe56:1006]
                             0/ 100 =  0%  |
  1    0ms    0/ 100 =  0%   0/ 100 =  0% 2001:db8:1:f282:dd48:ab34:d07c:
3914
Trace complete.
```

The following Pathping command-line options support IPv6:

- **-4**

    Forces Pathping to use an IPv4 address when the DNS name query for a host name returns both IPv4 and IPv6 addresses

- **-6**

  Forces Pathping to use an IPv6 address when the DNS name query for a host name returns both IPv4 and IPv6 addresses

> **Note**   The Pathping **-g** *host-list* command-line option is not supported for IPv6.

Netstat

The Netstat tool displays active TCP connections, ports on which the computer is listening, Ethernet statistics, the IPv4 routing table, IPv4 statistics (for the IP, ICMP, TCP, and UDP protocols), the IPv6 routing table, and IPv6 statistics (for the IPv6, ICMPv6, TCP over IPv6, and UDP over IPv6 protocols).

The following is an example display of the Netstat tool on a computer running Windows Server 2008 or Windows Vista:

```
F:\>netstat -s

IPv4 Statistics

    Packets Received                    = 187107
    Received Header Errors              = 0
    Received Address Errors             = 84248
    Datagrams Forwarded                 = 0
    Unknown Protocols Received          = 0
    Received Packets Discarded          = 0
    Received Packets Delivered          = 186194
    Output Requests                     = 27767
    Routing Discards                    = 0
    Discarded Output Packets            = 0
    Output Packet No Route              = 0
    Reassembly Required                 = 0
    Reassembly Successful               = 0
    Reassembly Failures                 = 0
    Datagrams Successfully Fragmented   = 0
    Datagrams Failing Fragmentation     = 0
    Fragments Created                   = 0

IPv6 Statistics

    Packets Received                    = 53118
    Received Header Errors              = 0
    Received Address Errors             = 0
    Datagrams Forwarded                 = 0
    Unknown Protocols Received          = 0
    Received Packets Discarded          = 0
    Received Packets Delivered          = 0
    Output Requests                     = 60695
    Routing Discards                    = 0
    Discarded Output Packets            = 0
```

```
Output Packet No Route              = 0
Reassembly Required                 = 0
Reassembly Successful               = 0
Reassembly Failures                 = 0
Datagrams Successfully Fragmented   = 0
Datagrams Failing Fragmentation     = 0
Fragments Created                   = 0
```

ICMPv4 Statistics

	Received	Sent
Messages	682	881
Errors	0	0
Destination Unreachable	2	201
Time Exceeded	0	0
Parameter Problems	0	0
Source Quenches	0	0
Redirects	0	0
Echos	340	340
Echo Replies	340	340
Timestamps	0	0
Timestamp Replies	0	0
Address Masks	0	0
Address Mask Replies	0	0

ICMPv6 Statistics

	Received	Sent
Messages	309	80
Errors	0	0
Destination Unreachable	193	0
Echos	4	0
Echo Replies	0	4
MLD Reports	0	6
Router Solicitations	0	7
Router Advertisements	54	0
Neighbor Solicitations	31	32
Neighbor Advertisements	27	31

TCP Statistics for IPv4

```
Active Opens                  = 128
Passive Opens                 = 106
Failed Connection Attempts    = 0
Reset Connections             = 3
Current Connections           = 16
Segments Received             = 22708
Segments Sent                 = 26255
Segments Retransmitted        = 37
```

TCP Statistics for IPv6

```
Active Opens                  = 74
Passive Opens                 = 72
```

```
Failed Connection Attempts      = 1
Reset Connections               = 0
Current Connections             = 14
Segments Received               = 52809
Segments Sent                   = 59813
Segments Retransmitted          = 3

UDP Statistics for IPv4
  Datagrams Received     = 160982
  No Ports               = 2158
  Receive Errors         = 2
  Datagrams Sent         = 591

UDP Statistics for IPv6

  Datagrams Received     = 0
  No Ports               = 0
  Receive Errors         = 0
  Datagrams Sent         = 744
```

Displaying IPv6 Configuration with Netsh

Useful commands to display information about the IPv6 configuration of a computer running Windows Server 2008 and Windows Vista are the following:

- **Netsh interface ipv6 show interface**
- **Netsh interface ipv6 show address**
- **Netsh interface ipv6 show route**
- **Netsh interface ipv6 show neighbors**
- **Netsh interface ipv6 show destinationcache**

Netsh interface ipv6 show interface

This command displays the list of IPv6 interfaces. Here is an example:

```
Idx  Met   MTU       State        Name
---  ---  -----    -----------    -------------------
  1   50  4294967295  enabled         Loopback Pseudo-Interface 1
  9   50   1280     enabled      Local Area Connection* 6
  6   20   1500     enabled      Local Area Connection
 10   50   1280     enabled      Local Area Connection* 7
  7   10   1500     disabled     Local Area Connection 2
```

By default, the interface names containing an asterisk (*) are tunneling interfaces.

Netsh interface ipv6 show address

This command displays the list of IPv6 addresses for each interface. Here is an example:

```
Interface 1: Loopback Pseudo-Interface 1

Addr Type  DAD State    Valid Life Pref. Life Address
---------  -----------  ---------- ---------- ------------------------
Other      Preferred     infinite   infinite ::1

Interface 9: Local Area Connection* 6

Addr Type  DAD State    Valid Life Pref. Life Address
---------  -----------  ---------- ---------- ------------------------
Other      Deprecated    infinite   infinite fe80::5efe:1.0.0.127%9

Interface 6: Local Area Connection

Addr Type  DAD State    Valid Life Pref. Life Address
---------  -----------  ---------- ---------- ------------------------
Public     Preferred    29d23h59m59s 6d23h59m59s 2001:db8:21da:7:1f3e:9e51:2178:b9ob
Temporary  Preferred    5d19h59m25s 5d19h59m25s 2001:db8:21da:7:a299:85ae:21da:59cc

Other      Preferred     infinite   infinite fe80::713e:a426:d167:37ab%6

Interface 10: Local Area Connection* 7

Addr Type  DAD State    Valid Life Pref. Life Address
---------  -----------  ---------- ---------- ------------------------
Other      Deprecated    infinite   infinite fe80::5efe:1.0.0.127%10
```

Netsh interface ipv6 show route

This command displays the list of routes in the IPv6 routing table. Here is an example:

```
Publish  Type     Met  Prefix                   Idx  Gateway/Interface Name
-------  -------- ---  ------------------------ ---  ----------------------
No       Manual   256  ::/0                      8   fe80::3cec:bf16:505:eae6
No       Manual   256  ::1/128                   1   Loopback Pseudo-Interface 1
No       Manual   8    2001:db8::/64             8   Local Area Connection
No       Manual   256  2001:db8::4074:2dce:b313:7c65/128  8  Local Area Connection
No       Manual   256  2001:db8::b500:734b:fe5b:3945/128  8  Local Area Connection
No       Manual   1000 2002::/16                 11  Local Area Connection* 7
No       Manual   256  fe80::/64                 10  Local Area Connection* 9
No       Manual   256  fe80::/64                 8   Local Area Connection
No       Manual   256  fe80::100:7f:fffe/128     10  Local Area Connection* 9
No       Manual   256  fe80::5efe:10.0.0.3/128   17  Local Area Connection* 6
No       Manual   256  fe80::b500:734b:fe5b:3945/128  8   Local Area Connection
No       Manual   256  ff00::/8                  1   Loopback Pseudo-Interface 1
No       Manual   256  ff00::/8                  10  Local Area Connection* 9
No       Manual   256  ff00::/8                  8   Local Area Connection
```

Netsh interface ipv6 show neighbors

This command displays the contents of the neighbor cache, sorted by interface. The neighbor cache stores the link-layer addresses of recently resolved next-hop addresses. Here is an example:

```
Interface 1: Loopback Pseudo-Interface 1

Internet Address                            Physical Address   Type
------------------------------------------- -----------------  -----------
ff02::16                                                       Permanent
ff02::1:3                                                      Permanent

Interface 8: Local Area Connection

Internet Address                            Physical Address   Type
------------------------------------------- -----------------  -----------
2001:db8::3cec:bf16:505:eae6                00-13-72-2b-34-07  Stale (Router)
2001:db8::4074:2dce:b313:7c65               00-00-00-00-00-00  Unreachable
2001:db8::6c4b:bf6d:201a:ccbf               00-00-00-00-00-00  Unreachable
fe80::3cec:bf16:505:eae6                    00-13-72-2b-34-07  Stale (Router)
ff02::16                                    33-33-00-00-00-16  Permanent

Interface 10: Local Area Connection* 9

Internet Address                            Physical Address   Type
------------------------------------------- -----------------  -----------
fe80::b500:734b:fe5b:3945                   255.255.255.255:65535  Unreachable
ff02::16                                    255.255.255.255:65535  Permanent
```

Netsh interface ipv6 show destinationcache

This command displays the contents of the destination cache, sorted by interface. The destination cache stores the next-hop addresses for destination addresses. Here is an example:

```
Interface 8: Local Area Connection

PMTU Destination Address                         Next Hop Address
---- ------------------------------------------- -------------------------
1500 2001:db8::3cec:bf16:505:eae6                2001:db8::3cec:bf16:505:eae6
```

References

The following references were cited in this chapter:

- RFC 2460 – "Internet Protocol, Version 6 (IPv6)"
- RFC 2710 – "Multicast Listener Discovery (MLD) for IPv6"
- RFC 3168 – "The Addition of Explicit Congestion Notification (ECN) to IP"
- RFC 3315 – "Dynamic Host Configuration Protocol for IPv6 (DHCPv6)"

- RFC 3484 – "Default Address Selection for Internet Protocol version 6 (IPv6)"
- RFC 3493 – "Basic Socket Interface Extensions for IPv6"
- RFC 3542 – "Advanced Sockets Application Program Interface (API) for IPv6"
- RFC 3736 – "Stateless Dynamic Host Configuration Protocol (DHCP) Service for IPv6"
- RFC 3810 – "Multicast Listener Discovery Version 2 (MLDv2) for IPv6"
- RFC 3986 – "Uniform Resource Identifier (URI): Generic Syntax"
- RFC 4191 – "Default Router Preferences and More-Specific Routes"
- RFC 4291 – "IP Version 6 Addressing Architecture"
- RFC 4443 – "Internet Control Message Protocol (ICMPv6) for the Internet Protocol Version 6 (IPv6)"
- RFC 4861 – "Neighbor Discovery for IP Version 6 (IPv6)"
- RFC 4862 – "IPv6 Stateless Address Autoconfiguration"
- RFC 5072 – "IP Version 6 over PPP"

You can obtain these RFCs from the \RFCs_and_Drafts folder on the companion CD-ROM or from *http://www.ietf.org/rfc.html.*

Testing for Understanding

To test your understanding of the IPv6 protocol for Windows Server 2008 and Windows Vista, answer the following questions. See Appendix D, "Testing for Understanding Answers," to check your answers.

1. List and describe the features of the IPv6 protocol for IPv6 transition.

2. What are the two ways to configure the IPv6 protocol for Windows Server 2008 and Windows Vista?

3. A network administrator wants to disable all 6to4 and Teredo tunnel interfaces for computers running Windows Server 2008 or Windows Vista. What is the correct value of the *DisabledComponents* registry value?

4. Describe the purpose of LLMNR and when it is used as the primary method for name resolution for IPv6 addresses.

5. Under what circumstances will an IPv6 router running Windows Server 2008 or Windows Vista advertise itself as a default router?

6. List how the common TCP/IP troubleshooting tools have been enhanced to support IPv6 in Windows Server 2008 and Windows Vista.

7. What do the asterisks in the default interface names in the display of the Ipconfig.exe tool indicate?

8. Which Netsh command displays the interface indexes that correspond to IPv6 interfaces?

Chapter 3
IPv6 Addressing

At the end of this chapter, you should be able to do the following:

- Describe the IPv6 address space, and state why the address length of 128 bits was chosen.

- Describe IPv6 address syntax, including zero suppression and compression and prefixes.

- Enumerate and describe the function of the different types of unicast IPv6 addresses.

- Describe the format of multicast IPv6 addresses.

- Describe the function of anycast IPv6 addresses.

- Describe how IPv6 interface identifiers are determined.

- Describe how to perform bit-level subnetting on the subnet identifier portion of a unicast IPv6 address prefix.

- List and compare the different addressing concepts between IPv4 addresses and IPv6 addresses.

The IPv6 Address Space

The most obvious distinguishing feature of Internet Protocol version 6 (IPv6) is its use of much larger addresses. The size of an address in IPv6 is 128 bits, a bit-string that is four times longer than the 32-bit IPv4 address. A 32-bit address space allows for 2^{32}, or 4,294,967,296, possible addresses. A 128-bit address space allows for 2^{128}, or 340,282,366,920,938,463,463, 374,607,431,768,211,456 (3.4×10^{38} or 340 undecillion), possible addresses.

In the late 1970s, when the IPv4 address space was designed, it was unimaginable that it could ever be exhausted. However, the administrative procedures that defined address allocation did not anticipate the recent explosion of hosts on the Internet. The IPv4 address space was thus consumed to the point that, by 1992, it was clear a replacement would be necessary.

With IPv6, it is even more difficult to conceive that the IPv6 address space will ever be consumed. To help put this number in perspective, a 128-bit address space provides 6.65×10^{23} addresses for each square meter of the Earth's surface.

It is important to remember that the decision to make the IPv6 address 128 bits in length was not so that every square meter of the Earth could have 6.65×10^{23} addresses. Rather, the relatively large size of the IPv6 address is designed to be divided into hierarchical unicast routing domains that reflect the topology of the modern-day Internet. The use of 128 bits allows for multiple levels of hierarchy and flexibility in designing hierarchical unicast addressing and routing that is currently lacking on the IPv4-based Internet.

It is easy to get lost in the vastness of the IPv6 address space. As we will discover, the unthinkably large 128-bit IPv6 address that is assigned to an interface on a typical IPv6 host is composed of a 64-bit subnet prefix and a 64-bit interface identifier (a 50-50 split between subnet space and interface space). The 64 bits of subnet prefix leave enough addressing room to satisfy the addressing requirements of the levels of Internet service providers (ISPs) between your organization and the backbone of the Internet and the addressing needs of your organization. The 64 bits of interface identifier accommodate the mapping of current and future link-layer media access control (MAC) addresses.

IPv6 Address Syntax

IPv4 addresses are represented in dotted-decimal format. The 32-bit IPv4 address is divided along 8-bit boundaries. Each set of 8 bits is converted to its decimal equivalent and separated by periods. For IPv6, the 128-bit address is divided along 16-bit boundaries, and each 16-bit block is converted to a 4-digit hexadecimal number and separated by colons. The resulting representation is called *colon hexadecimal*.

The following is an IPv6 address in binary form:

```
0010000000000001000011011011100000000000000000000000000010111100111011
0000000101010101000000000011111111111111111000101000100111000101101010
```

The 128-bit address is divided along 16-bit boundaries:

```
0010000000000001   0000110110111000   0000000000000000   0010111100111011
0000001010101010   0000000011111111   1111111000101000   1001110001011010
```

Each 16-bit block is converted to hexadecimal and delimited with colons. The result is the following:

```
2001:0DB8:0000:2F3B:02AA:00FF:FE28:9C5A
```

IPv6 address representation is further simplified by suppressing the leading zeros within each 16-bit block. However, each block must have at least a single digit. With leading zero suppression, the result is the following:

```
2001:DB8:0:2F3B:2AA:FF:FE28:9C5A
```

Number System Choice for IPv6

IPv6 uses hexadecimal (the $Base_{16}$ numbering system), rather than decimal (the $Base_{10}$ numbering system), because it is easier to convert between hexadecimal and binary than it is to convert between decimal and binary. Each hexadecimal digit represents four binary digits.

With IPv4, decimal is used to make the IPv4 addresses more palatable for humans and a 32-bit address becomes 4 decimal numbers separated by the period (.) character. With IPv6, dotted-decimal representation would result in 16 decimal numbers separated by the period (.) character. IPv6 addresses are so large that there is no attempt to make them palatable to most humans. Configuration of typical end systems is automated, and end users will almost always use names rather than IPv6 addresses. Therefore, the addresses are expressed in a way to make them more palatable to computers and IPv6 network administrators who understand the semantics and relationship of hexadecimal and binary numbers.

Table 3-1 lists the conversion between binary, hexadecimal, and decimal numbers.

Table 3-1   Converting Between Binary, Hexadecimal, and Decimal Numbers

Binary	Hexadecimal	Decimal
0000	0	0
0001	1	1
0010	2	2
0011	3	3
0100	4	4
0101	5	5
0110	6	6
0111	7	7
1000	8	8
1001	9	9
1010	A	10
1011	B	11
1100	C	12
1101	D	13
1110	E	14
1111	F	15

Compressing Zeros

Some types of IPv6 addresses contain long sequences of zeros. To further simplify the representation of IPv6 addresses, a single contiguous sequence of 16-bit blocks set to 0 in the colon hexadecimal format can be compressed to ::, known as a *double colon*. For example, the link-local address of FE80:0:0:0:2AA:FF:FE9A:4CA2 can be compressed to FE80::2AA:FF:FE9A:4CA2. The multicast address FF02:0:0:0:0:0:0:2 can be compressed to FF02::2.

> **Note**   You cannot use zero compression to include part of a 16-bit block. For example, you cannot express FF02:30:0:0:0:0:0:5 as FF02:3::5, but FF02:30::5 is correct.

> ### How Many Blocks or Bits in ::?
>
> To determine how many 0 blocks are represented by the ::, you can count the number of blocks in the compressed address and subtract this number from 8. To determine how many 0 bits are represented by the ::, multiply the number of blocks the :: represents by 16. For example, in the address FF02::2, there are two blocks (the "FF02" block and the "2" block). The number of blocks expressed by the :: is 6 (8 − 2). The number of bits expressed by the :: is 96 (96 = 6 × 16). Zero compression can be used only once in a given address. Otherwise, you could not determine the number of 0 blocks or bits represented by each instance of ::.

IPv6 Prefixes

The prefix is the part of the address where the bits have fixed values or are the bits that define a route or subnet. Prefixes for IPv6 subnets and summarized routes are expressed in the same way as Classless Inter-Domain Routing (CIDR) notation for IPv4. An IPv6 prefix is written in *address/prefix-length* notation.

For example, 2001:DB8:2A0:2F3B::/64 is a subnet prefix and 2001:DB8:3F::/48 is a summarized route prefix. As described earlier in this chapter, the 64-bit prefix is used for individual subnets to which nodes are attached. All subnets have a 64-bit prefix. Any prefix that is less than 64 bits is a summarized route or an address range that is summarizing a portion of the IPv6 address space.

> **Note**   IPv4 implementations commonly use a dotted-decimal representation of the prefix length known as the *subnet mask*. A subnet mask is not used for IPv6. Only the prefix length notation is supported.

An IPv6 prefix is relevant only for routes or address ranges, not for individual unicast addresses. In IPv4, it is common to express an IPv4 address with its prefix length. For example, 192.168.29.7/24 (equivalent to 192.168.29.7 with the subnet mask 255.255.255.0) denotes the IPv4 address 192.168.29.7 with a 24-bit subnet mask. Because IPv4 addresses are no longer class-based, you cannot assume the class-based subnet mask based on the value of the leading octet. The prefix length is included so that you can determine which bits identify the subnet and which bits identify the host on the subnet. Because the number of bits used to identify the subnet in IPv4 is variable, the prefix length is needed to separate the subnet prefix from the host ID.

In common IPv6 practice, however, there is no notion of a variable-length subnet prefix. At the individual IPv6 subnet level for currently defined unicast IPv6 addresses, the number of bits used to identify the subnet is always 64 and the number of bits used to identify the host on the subnet is always 64. Therefore, while unicast IPv6 addresses written with their prefix lengths are permitted in RFC 4291, in practice their prefix lengths are always 64 and therefore do not need to be expressed. For example, there is no need to express the IPv6 unicast address 2001:DB8::2AC4:2AA:FF:FE9A:82D4 as 2001:DB8::2AC4:2AA:FF:FE9A:82D4/64. Because of the 50-50 split of subnet prefixes and interface identifiers, the unicast IPv6 address 2001:DB8::2AC4:2AA:FF:FE9A:82D4 implies that the subnet prefix is 2001:DB8:0:0:2AC4::/64.

> **Note**   Address prefixes with a prefix length longer than 64 bits can be used for point-to-point links between routers.

Types of IPv6 Addresses

There are three types of IPv6 addresses:

Unicast

A unicast address identifies a single interface within the scope of the type of address. The scope of an address is the region of the IPv6 network over which the address is unique. With the appropriate unicast routing topology, packets addressed to a unicast address are delivered to a single interface. To accommodate load-balancing systems, RFC 4291 allows for multiple interfaces to use the same address as long as they appear as a single interface to the IPv6 implementation on the host.

Multicast

A multicast address identifies zero or more interfaces on the same or different hosts. With the appropriate multicast routing topology, packets addressed to a multicast address are delivered to all interfaces identified by the address.

Anycast

An anycast address identifies multiple interfaces. With the appropriate unicast routing topology, packets addressed to an anycast address are delivered to a single interface—the nearest interface that is identified by the address. The nearest interface is defined as being the closest in terms of routing distance. A multicast address is used for one-to-many communication, with delivery to multiple interfaces. An anycast address is used for one-to-one-of-many communication, with delivery to a single interface.

In all cases, IPv6 addresses identify interfaces, not nodes. A node is identified by any unicast address assigned to any one of its interfaces.

> **Note**   RFC 4291 does not define a broadcast address. All types of IPv4 broadcast addressing are performed in IPv6 using multicast addresses. For example, the subnet and limited broadcast addresses from IPv4 are replaced with the link-local scope all-nodes multicast address of FF02::1.

Unicast IPv6 Addresses

The following types of addresses are unicast IPv6 addresses:

- Global unicast addresses
- Link-local addresses
- Site-local addresses
- Unique local addresses
- Special addresses
- Transition addresses

Global Unicast Addresses

IPv6 global addresses are equivalent to public IPv4 addresses. They are globally routable and reachable on the IPv6 Internet. Global unicast addresses are designed to be aggregated or summarized for an efficient routing infrastructure. Unlike the current IPv4-based Internet, which is a mixture of both flat and hierarchical routing, the IPv6-based Internet has been designed from its foundation to support efficient, hierarchical addressing and routing. The scope of a global address is the entire IPv6 Internet.

RFC 4291 defines global addresses as all addresses that are not the unspecified, loopback, link-local unicast, or multicast addresses (described later in this chapter). However, Figure 3-1 shows the structure of global unicast addresses defined in RFC 3587 that are currently being used on the IPv6 Internet.

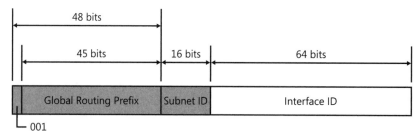

Figure 3-1   The structure of global unicast addresses defined in RFC 3587

The fields in the global unicast address are described in the following list:

- **Fixed portion set to 001**   The three high-order bits are set to 001.

- **Global Routing Prefix**   Indicates the global routing prefix for a specific organization's site. The combination of the three fixed bits and the 45-bit Global Routing Prefix is used to create a 48-bit site prefix, which is assigned to an individual site of an organization. A site is an autonomously operating IP-based network that is connected to the IPv6 Internet. Network architects and administrators within the site determine the addressing plan and routing policy for the organization network. Once assigned, routers on the IPv6 Internet forward IPv6 traffic matching the 48-bit prefix to the routers of the organization's site.

- **Subnet ID**   The Subnet ID is used within an organization's site to identify subnets within its site. The size of this field is 16 bits. The organization's site can use these 16 bits within its site to create 65,536 subnets or multiple levels of addressing hierarchy and an efficient routing infrastructure. With 16 bits of subnetting flexibility, a global unicast prefix assigned to an organization site is equivalent to a public IPv4 Class A address prefix (assuming that the last octet is used for identifying nodes on subnets). The routing structure of the organization's network is not visible to the ISP.

- **Interface ID**   Indicates the interface on a specific subnet within the site. The size of this field is 64 bits. The interface ID in IPv6 is equivalent to the node ID or host ID in IPv4.

Trillions of Sites

Another way to gauge the practical size of the IPv6 address space is to examine the number of sites that can connect to the IPv6 Internet. With the current allocation practice defined in RFC 3587 of 48-bit global address prefixes, it is possible to define 2^{45} or 35,184,372,088,832 possible 48-bit prefixes to assign to sites connected to the IPv6 Internet. There are more IPv6 sites than possible IPv4 addresses. This large number of sites is possible even when we are using only one-eighth of the entire IPv6 address space.

By comparison, using the Internet address classes originally defined for IPv4, it was possible to assign 2,113,389 address prefixes to organizations connected to the Internet. The number 2,113,389 is derived from adding up all the possible Class A, Class B, and Class C address prefixes and then subtracting the prefixes used for the private address space. Even with the adoption of CIDR to make more efficient use of unassigned Class A and Class B address prefixes, the number of possible sites connected to the Internet is not substantially increased, nor does it approach the number of possible sites that can be connected to the IPv6 Internet.

Topologies Within Global Addresses

The fields within the global address create a three-level topological structure, as shown in Figure 3-2.

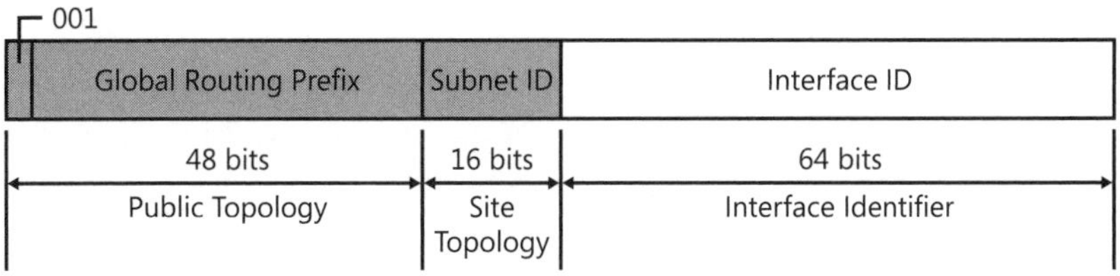

Figure 3-2   The topological structure of the global address

The public topology is the collection of larger and smaller ISPs that provide access to the IPv6 Internet. The site topology is the collection of subnets within an organization's site. The interface identifier specifies a unique interface on a subnet within an organization's site.

Local-Use Unicast Addresses

Local-use unicast addresses do not have a global scope and can be reused. There are two types of local-use unicast addresses:

1. Link-local addresses are used between on-link neighbors and for Neighbor Discovery processes.

2. Site-local addresses are used between nodes communicating with other nodes in the same organization.

Link-Local Addresses

IPv6 link-local addresses, identified by the initial 10 bits being set to 1111 1110 10 and the next 54 bits set to 0, are used by nodes when communicating with neighboring nodes on the same link. For example, on a single-link IPv6 network with no router, link-local addresses are used to communicate between hosts on the link. IPv6 link-local addresses are similar to IPv4 link-local addresses defined in RFC 3927 that use the 169.254.0.0/16 prefix. The use of IPv4 link-local addresses is known as Automatic Private IP Addressing (APIPA) in Windows Vista, Windows Server 2008, Windows Server 2003, and Windows XP. The scope of a link-local address is the local link.

Figure 3-3 shows the structure of the link-local address.

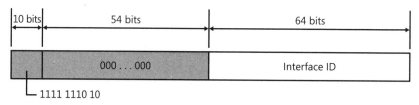

Figure 3-3 The structure of the link-local address

A link-local address is required for some Neighbor Discovery processes and is always automatically configured, even in the absence of all other unicast addresses. For more information about the address autoconfiguration process for link-local addresses, see Chapter 8, "Address Autoconfiguration."

Link-local addresses always begin with FE80. With the 64-bit interface identifier, the prefix for link-local addresses is always FE80::/64. An IPv6 router never forwards link-local traffic beyond the link.

Site-Local Addresses

Site-local addresses, identified by setting the first 10 bits to 1111 1110 11, are equivalent to the IPv4 private address space (10.0.0.0/8, 172.16.0.0/12, and 192.168.0.0/16). For example, private intranets that do not have a direct, routed connection to the IPv6 Internet can use site-local addresses without conflicting with global addresses. Site-local addresses are not reachable from other sites, and routers must not forward site-local traffic outside the site. Site-local addresses can be used in addition to global addresses. The scope of a site-local address is the site.

Figure 3-4 shows the structure of the site-local address.

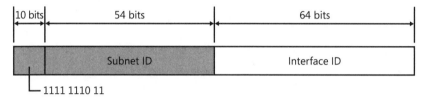

Figure 3-4   The structure of the site-local address

Unlike link-local addresses, site-local addresses are not automatically configured and must be assigned either through stateless or stateful address autoconfiguration. For more information, see Chapter 8.

The first 10 bits are always fixed for site-local addresses, beginning with FEC0::/10. After the 10 fixed bits is a 54-bit Subnet ID field that provides 54 bits with which you can create subnets within your organization. You can have a flat subnet structure, or you can divide the high-order bits of the Subnet ID field to create a hierarchical and summarizable routing infrastructure. After the Subnet ID field is a 64-bit Interface ID field that identifies a specific interface on a subnet.

Site-local addresses have been formally deprecated in RFC 3879 for future IPv6 implementations. However, existing implementations of IPv6 can continue to use site-local addresses.

Zone IDs for Local-Use Addresses

Unlike global addresses, local-use addresses (link-local and site-local addresses) can be reused. Link-local addresses are reused on each link. Site-local addresses can be reused within each site of an organization. Because of this address reuse capability, link-local and site-local addresses are ambiguous. To specify the link on which the destination is located or the site within which the destination is located, an additional identifier is needed. This additional identifier is a zone identifier (ID), also known as a scope ID, which identifies a connected portion of a network that has a specified scope.

The syntax specified in RFC 4007 for identifying the zone associated with a local-use address is *Address%zone_ID*, in which *Address* is a local-use unicast IPv6 address and *zone_ID* is an integer value representing the zone. The values of the zone ID are defined relative to the sending host. Therefore, different hosts might determine different zone ID values for the same physical zone. For example, Host A might choose 3 to represent the zone of an attached link and Host B might choose 4 to represent the same link.

For Windows-based IPv6 hosts, the zone IDs for link-local and site-local addresses are defined as follows:

- For link-local addresses, the zone ID is typically the interface index of the interface either assigned the address or to be used as the sending interface for a link-local destination. The interface index is an integer starting at 1 that is assigned to IPv6 interfaces, which include a loopback and one or multiple LAN or tunnel interfaces. Multiple interfaces can have the same link-local zone ID if they are attached to the same link. You can view the list of interface indexes from the display of the **netsh interface ipv6 show interface** command. You must include a zone ID with a link-local destination.

- For site-local addresses, the zone ID is the site ID, an integer assigned to the site of an organization. For organizations that do not reuse the site-local address prefix, the site ID is set to 1 by default and does not need to be specified. In Windows, you can view the site ID from the display of the **netsh interface ipv6 show address level=verbose** command.

The following are examples of using Windows tools and the zone ID:

- **ping fe80::2b0:d0ff:fee9:4143%3**   In this case, 3 is the interface index of the interface attached to the link containing the destination address.

- **tracert fec0::f282:2b0:d0ff:fee9:4143%2**   In this case, 2 is the site ID of the organization site containing the destination address.

In Windows Vista and Windows Server 2008, the Ipconfig.exe tool displays the zone ID of local-use IPv6 addresses. The following is an excerpt from the display of the **ipconfig** command:

```
Ethernet adapter Local Area Connection:

    Connection-specific DNS Suffix  . : ecoast.example.com
    IPv6 Address. . . . . . . . . . . : 2001:db8:21da:7:713e:a426:d167:37ab
    Temporary IPv6 Address. . . . . . : 2001:db8:21da:7:5099:ba54:9881:2e54
    Link-local IPv6 Address . . . . . : fe80::713e:a426:d167:37ab%6
    IPv4 Address. . . . . . . . . . . : 157.60.14.11
    Subnet Mask . . . . . . . . . . . : 255.255.255.0
    Default Gateway . . . . . . . . . : fe80::20a:42ff:feb0:5400%6
                                        157.60.14.1
```

For the link-local addresses in the display of the **ipconfig** command, the zone ID indicates the interface index of the interface either assigned the address (for Link-Local IPv6 Address) or the interface through which an address is reachable (for Default Gateway).

Unique Local Addresses

Site-local addresses provide a private addressing alternative to global addresses for intranet traffic. However, because the site-local address prefix can be reused to address multiple sites within an organization, a site-local address prefix can be duplicated. The ambiguity of site-local addresses in an organization adds complexity and difficulty for applications, routers, and network managers. For more information, see section 2 of RFC 3879.

To replace site-local addresses with a new type of address that is private to an organization yet unique across all the sites of the organization, RFC 4193 defines unique local IPv6 unicast addresses. Figure 3-5 shows the structure of the unique local address.

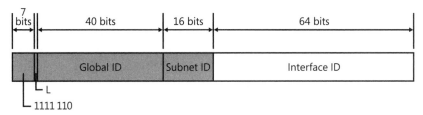

Figure 3-5   The structure of the unique local address

The first 7 bits have the fixed binary value of 1111110. All local addresses have the address prefix FC00::/7. The Local (L) flag is set 1 to indicate that the prefix is locally assigned. The L flag value set to 0 is not defined in RFC 3879. Therefore, unique local addresses within an organization with the L flag set to 1 have the address prefix of FD00::/8. The Global ID identifies a specific site within an organization and is set to a randomly derived 40-bit value. By deriving a random value for the Global ID, an organization can have statistically unique 48-bit prefixes assigned to their sites. Additionally, two organizations that use unique local addresses that merge have a low probability of duplicating a 48-bit unique local address prefix, minimizing site renumbering. Unlike the Global Routing Prefix in global addresses, the Global IDs in unique local address prefixes are not designed to be summarized.

Unique local addresses have a global scope, but their reachability is defined by routing topology and filtering policies at Internet boundaries. Organizations will not advertise their unique local address prefixes outside of their organizations or create DNS entries with unique local addresses in the Internet DNS. Organizations can easily create filtering policies at their Internet boundaries to prevent all unique local-addressed traffic from being forwarded. Because they have a global scope, unique local addresses do not need a zone ID.

The global address and unique local address share the same structure beyond the first 48 bits of the address. In both addresses, the 16-bit Subnet ID field identifies a subnet within an organization. Because of this, you can create a subnetted routing infrastructure that is used for both local and global addresses.

For example, a specific subnet of your organization can be assigned both the global prefix 2001:DB8:4D1C:221A::/64 and the local prefix FD0E:2D:BA9:221A::/64, where the subnet is identified for both types of prefixes by the Subnet ID value of *221A*. Although the subnet identifier is the same for both prefixes, routes for both prefixes must still be propagated throughout the routing infrastructure so that addresses based on both prefixes are reachable.

Special IPv6 Addresses

The following are special IPv6 addresses:

- **Unspecified address**

    The unspecified address (0:0:0:0:0:0:0:0 or ::) is used only to indicate the absence of an address. It is equivalent to the IPv4 unspecified address of 0.0.0.0. The unspecified address is typically used as a source address when a unique address has not yet been determined. The unspecified address is never assigned to an interface or used as a destination address.

- **Loopback address**

    The loopback address (0:0:0:0:0:0:0:1 or ::1) is assigned to a loopback interface, enabling a node to send packets to itself. It is equivalent to the IPv4 loopback address of 127.0.0.1. Packets addressed to the loopback address must never be sent on a link or forwarded by an IPv6 router.

Transition Addresses

To aid in the transition from IPv4 to IPv6 and the coexistence of both types of hosts, the following addresses are defined:

- **IPv4-compatible address**

    The IPv4-compatible address, 0:0:0:0:0:0:*w.x.y.z* or ::*w.x.y.z* (where *w.x.y.z* is the dotted-decimal representation of a public IPv4 address), is used by IPv6/IPv4 nodes that are communicating with IPv6 over an IPv4 infrastructure that uses public IPv4 addresses, such as the Internet. IPv4-compatible addresses are deprecated in RFC 4291 and are not supported in IPv6 for Windows Vista and Windows Server 2008.

- **IPv4-mapped address**

    The IPv4-mapped address, 0:0:0:0:0:FFFF:*w.x.y.z* or ::FFFF: *w.x.y.z*, is used to represent an IPv4 address as a 128-bit IPv6 address.

- **6to4 address**

    An address of the type 2002:*WWXX:YYZZ:Subnet ID:Interface ID*, where *WWXX:YYZZ* is the colon hexadecimal representation of *w.x.y.z* (a public IPv4 address), is assigned a node for the 6to4 IPv6 transition technology.

- **ISATAP address**

  An address of the type *64-bit prefix*:0:5EFE:*w.x.y.z*, where *w.x.y.z* is a private IPv4 address, is assigned to a node for the Intra-Site Automatic Tunnel Addressing Protocol (ISATAP) IPv6 transition technology.

- **Teredo address**

  A global address that uses the prefix 2001::/32 and is assigned to a node for the Teredo IPv6 transition technology. Beyond the first 32 bits, Teredo addresses are used to encode the IPv4 address of a Teredo server, flags, and an obscured version of a Teredo client's external address and UDP port number.

For more information about these addresses, see Chapter 11, "IPv6 Transition Technologies."

Multicast IPv6 Addresses

In IPv6, multicast traffic operates in the same way that it does in IPv4. Arbitrarily located IPv6 nodes can listen for multicast traffic on an arbitrary IPv6 multicast address. IPv6 nodes can listen to multiple multicast addresses at the same time. Nodes can join or leave a multicast group at any time.

IPv6 multicast addresses have the first 8 bits set to 1111 1111. Therefore, an IPv6 multicast address always begins with FF. Multicast addresses cannot be used as source addresses or as intermediate destinations in a Routing extension header. Beyond the first 8 bits, multicast addresses include additional structure to identify flags, their scope, and the multicast group. Figure 3-6 shows the structure of the IPv6 multicast address.

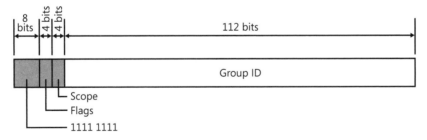

Figure 3-6   The structure of the IPv6 multicast address

The following list describes the fields in the multicast address:

- **Flags**   Indicates flags set on the multicast address. The size of this field is 4 bits, consisting of three flags in the low-order bits. The first low-order bit is the Transient (T) flag. When set to 0, the T flag indicates that the multicast address is a permanently assigned (well-known) multicast address allocated by the Internet Assigned Numbers Authority (IANA). When set to 1, the T flag indicates that the multicast address is a transient (not permanently assigned) multicast address. The second low-order bit is for the Prefix (P) flag, which indicates whether the multicast address is based on a unicast address prefix.

RFC 3306 describes the P flag. The third low-order bit is for the Rendezvous Point Address (R) flag, which indicates whether the multicast address contains an embedded rendezvous point address. RFC 3956 describes the R flag.

- **Scope**   Indicates the scope of the IPv6 network for which the multicast traffic is intended to be delivered. The size of this field is 4 bits. In addition to using information provided by multicast routing protocols, routers use the multicast scope to determine whether multicast traffic can be forwarded.

Table 3-2 lists the values for the Scope field assigned in RFC 4291. All other values are unassigned.

Table 3-2   Defined Values for the Scope Field

Scope Field Value	Scope
0	Reserved
1	Interface-local scope
2	Link-local scope
3	Reserved
4	Admin-local scope
5	Site-local scope
8	Organization-local scope
E	Global scope
F	Reserved

For example, traffic with the multicast address of FF02::2 has a link-local scope. An IPv6 router never forwards this traffic beyond the local link.

- **Group ID**   Identifies the multicast group, and is unique within the scope. The size of this field is 112 bits. Permanently assigned group IDs are independent of the scope. Transient group IDs are relevant only to a specific scope. Multicast addresses from FF01:: through FF0F:: are reserved, well-known addresses.

To identify all nodes for the interface-local and link-local scopes, the following addresses are defined:

- FF01::1 (interface-local scope all-nodes multicast address)
- FF02::1 (link-local scope all-nodes multicast address)

To identify all routers for the interface-local, link-local, and site-local scopes, the following addresses are defined:

- FF01::2 (interface-local scope all-routers multicast address)
- FF02::2 (link-local scope all-routers multicast address)
- FF05::2 (site-local scope all-routers multicast address)

For the current list of permanently assigned IPv6 multicast addresses, see *http://www.iana.org/assignments/ipv6-multicast-addresses.*

IPv6 multicast addresses replace all forms of IPv4 broadcast addresses. The IPv4 network broadcast (in which all host bits are set to 1 in a classful environment), subnet broadcast (in which all host bits are set to 1 in a non-classful environment), and limited broadcast (255.255.255.255) addresses are replaced by the link-local scope all-nodes multicast address (FF02:01) in IPv6.

Solicited-Node Address

The solicited-node address facilitates the efficient querying of network nodes during link-layer address resolution—the resolving of a link-layer address of a known IPv6 address. In IPv4, the Address Resolution Protocol (ARP) Request frame is sent to the MAC-level broadcast, disturbing all nodes on the network segment, including those that are not running IPv4. IPv6 uses the Neighbor Solicitation message to perform link-layer address resolution. However, instead of using the local-link scope all-nodes multicast address as the Neighbor Solicitation message destination, which would disturb all IPv6 nodes on the local link, the solicited-node multicast address is used. The solicited-node multicast address is constructed from the prefix FF02::1:FF00:0/104 and the last 24 bits (6 hexadecimal digits) of a unicast IPv6 address. Figure 3-7 shows the mapping of a unicast IPv6 address and its corresponding solicited-node multicast address.

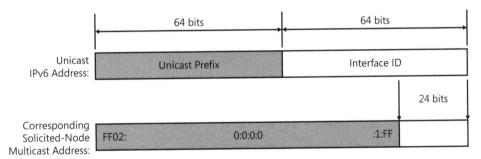

Figure 3-7   The mapping of a unicast address to its solicited-node multicast address

For example, Node A is assigned the link-local address of FE80::2AA:FF:FE28:9C5A and is also listening on the corresponding solicited-node multicast address of FF02::1:FF28:9C5A. (An underline is used to highlight the correspondence of the last six hexadecimal digits.) Node B on the local link must resolve Node A's link-local address FE80::2AA:FF:FE28:9C5A to its corresponding link-layer address. Node B sends a Neighbor Solicitation message to the solicited-node multicast address of FF02::1:FF28:9C5A. Because Node A is listening on this multicast address, it processes the Neighbor Solicitation message and sends a unicast Neighbor Advertisement message in reply.

The result of using the solicited-node multicast address is that link-layer address resolutions, a common occurrence on a link, are not using a mechanism that disturbs all network nodes. By using the solicited-node address, very few nodes are disturbed during address resolution. In practice, because of the relationship between the IPv6 interface ID and the solicited-node address, the solicited-node address acts as a pseudo-unicast address for very efficient address resolution. For more information, see the "IPv6 Interface Identifiers" section in this chapter.

Mapping IPv6 Multicast Addresses to Ethernet Addresses

When sending IPv6 multicast packets on an Ethernet link, the corresponding destination MAC address is 0x33-33-mm-mm-mm-mm, where *mm-mm-mm-mm* is a direct mapping of the last 32 bits (8 hexadecimal digits) of the IPv6 multicast address. Figure 3-8 shows the mapping of an IPv6 multicast address to an Ethernet multicast address.

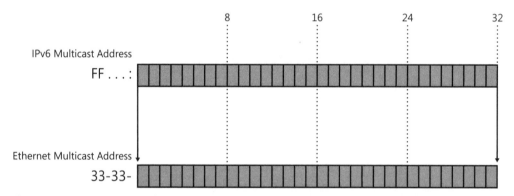

Figure 3-8   The mapping of IPv6 multicast addresses to Ethernet multicast addresses

Ethernet network adapters maintain a table of interesting destination MAC addresses. If an Ethernet frame with an interesting destination MAC address is received, it is passed to upper layers for additional processing. By default, this table contains the MAC-level broadcast address (0xFF-FF-FF-FF-FF-FF) and the unicast MAC address assigned to the adapter. To facilitate efficient delivery of multicast traffic, additional multicast destination addresses can be added or removed from the table. For every multicast address being listened to by the host, there is a corresponding entry in the table of interesting MAC addresses.

For example, an IPv6 host with the Ethernet MAC address of 00-AA-00-3F-2A-1C (link-local address of FE80::2AA:FF:FE3F:2A1C) adds the following multicast MAC addresses to the table of interesting destination MAC addresses on the Ethernet adapter:

- The address of 33-33-<u>00-00-00-01</u>, which corresponds to the link-local scope all-nodes multicast address of FF02::1 (fully expressed as FF02:0000:0000:0000:0000:0000:<u>0000:0001</u>).

- The address of 33-33-<u>FF-3F-2A-1C</u>, which corresponds to the solicited-node address of FF02::1:<u>FF3F:2A1C</u>. Remember that the solicited-node address is the prefix FF02::1:FF00:0/104 and the last 24 bits of the unicast IPv6 address.

Additional multicast addresses on which the host is listening are added and removed from the table as needed.

Anycast IPv6 Addresses

An anycast address is assigned to multiple interfaces. Packets addressed to an anycast address are forwarded by the routing infrastructure to the nearest interface to which the anycast address is assigned. To facilitate delivery, the routing infrastructure must be aware of the interfaces that have anycast addresses assigned to them and their distance in terms of routing metrics. This awareness is accomplished by the propagation of host routes throughout the routing infrastructure of the portion of the network that cannot summarize the anycast address using a route prefix.

For example, for the anycast address 3FFE:2900:D005:6187:2AA:FF:FE89:6B9A, host routes for this address are propagated within the routing infrastructure of the organization assigned the 48-bit prefix 3FFE:2900:D005::/48. Because a node assigned this anycast address can be placed anywhere on the organization's intranet, host routes for all nodes assigned this anycast address are needed in the routing tables of all routers within the organization. Outside the organization, this anycast address is summarized by the 3FFE:2900:D005::/48 prefix that is assigned to the organization. Therefore, the host routes needed to deliver IPv6 packets to the nearest anycast group member within an organization's intranet are not needed in the routing infrastructure of the IPv6 Internet.

As of RFC 4291, anycast addresses are used only as destination addresses and are assigned only to routers. Anycast addresses are assigned out of the unicast address space, and the scope of an anycast address is the scope of the type of unicast address from which the anycast address is assigned. It is not possible to determine if a given destination unicast address is also an anycast address. The only nodes that have this awareness are the routers that use host routes to forward the anycast traffic to the nearest anycast group member and the anycast group members themselves.

Subnet-Router Anycast Address

The Subnet-Router anycast address is defined in RFC 4291 and is required. It is created from the subnet prefix for a given interface. When the Subnet-Router anycast address is constructed, the bits in the subnet prefix are fixed at their appropriate values and the remaining bits are set to 0. Figure 3-9 shows the structure of the Subnet-Router anycast address.

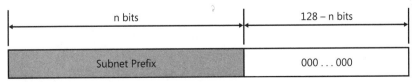

Figure 3-9   The structure of the Subnet-Router anycast address

All router interfaces attached to a subnet are assigned the Subnet-Router anycast address for that subnet. The Subnet-Router anycast address is used to communicate with the nearest router connected to a specified subnet.

IPv6 Addresses for a Host

An IPv4 host with a single network adapter typically has a single IPv4 address assigned to that adapter. An IPv6 host, however, usually has multiple IPv6 addresses assigned to each adapter. The interfaces on a typical IPv6 host are assigned the following unicast addresses:

- A link-local address for each interface
- Additional unicast addresses for each interface (which could be one or multiple unique local or global addresses)
- The loopback address (::1) for the loopback interface

Typical IPv6 hosts are always logically multihomed because they always have at least two addresses with which they can receive packets—a link-local address for local link traffic and a routable unique local or global address.

Additionally, each interface on an IPv6 host is listening for traffic on the following multicast addresses:

- The interface-local scope all-nodes multicast address (FF01::1)
- The link-local scope all-nodes multicast address (FF02::1)
- The solicited-node address for each unicast address assigned
- The multicast addresses of joined groups

IPv6 Addresses for a Router

The interfaces on an IPv6 router are assigned the following unicast addresses:

- A link-local address for each interface
- Additional unicast addresses for each interface (which could be one or multiple unique local or global addresses)
- The loopback address (::1) for the loopback interface

Additionally, the interfaces of an IPv6 router are assigned the following anycast addresses:

- A Subnet-Router anycast address for each subnet
- Additional anycast addresses (optional)

Additionally, the interfaces of an IPv6 router are listening for traffic on the following multicast addresses:

- The interface-local scope all-nodes multicast address (FF01::1)
- The interface-local scope all-routers multicast address (FF01::2)
- The link-local scope all-nodes multicast address (FF02::1)
- The link-local scope all-routers multicast address (FF02::2)
- The site-local scope all-routers multicast address (FF05::2)
- The solicited-node address for each unicast address assigned
- The multicast addresses of joined groups

Subnetting the IPv6 Address Space

Just as in IPv4, the IPv6 address space can be divided by using high-order bits that do not already have fixed values to create subnetted address prefixes. These are used either to summarize a level in the routing or addressing hierarchy (with a prefix length less than 64), or to define a specific subnet or network segment (with a prefix length of 64). IPv4 subnetting differs from IPv6 subnetting in the definition of the host ID portion of the address. In IPv4, the host ID can be of varying length, depending on the subnetting scheme. For currently defined unicast IPv6 addresses, the host ID is the interface ID portion of the IPv6 unicast address and is always a fixed size of 64 bits.

For most network administrators within an organization, subnetting the IPv6 address space consists of using subnetting techniques to divide the subnet ID portion of a global or unique local address prefix in a manner that allows for route summarization and delegation of the remaining address space to different portions of an IPv6 intranet. For both global and unique local addresses, the first 48 bits of the address are fixed. For the global address, the first 48 bits are fixed and allocated by an ISP. For the unique local address, the first 48 bits are fixed at FD00::/8 and the random 40-bit global ID assigned to a site of an organization.

Subnetting the subnet ID portion of a global or unique local address space requires a two-step procedure:

1. Determine the number of bits to be used for the subnetting.
2. Enumerate the new subnetted address prefixes.

The subnetting technique described here assumes that subnetting is done by dividing the 16-bit address space of the subnet ID using the high-order bits in the subnet ID. Although this method promotes hierarchical addressing and routing, it is not required. For example, in a small organization with a small number of subnets, you can also create a flat addressing space for the subnet ID by numbering the subnets starting at 0.

Step 1: Determining the Number of Subnetting Bits

The number of bits being used for subnetting determines the possible number of new subnetted address prefixes that can be allocated to portions of your network based on geographical or departmental divisions. In a hierarchical routing infrastructure, you need to determine how many address prefixes, and therefore how many bits, you need at each level in the hierarchy. The more bits you choose for the various levels of the hierarchy, the fewer bits you will have available to enumerate individual subnets in the last level of the hierarchy.

Depending on the needs of your organization, your subnetting scheme might be along nibble (hexadecimal digit) or bit boundaries. If you can subnet along nibble boundaries, your subnetting scheme becomes simplified and each hexadecimal digit can represent a level in the subnetting hierarchy. For example, a network administrator decides to implement a three-level hierarchy that uses the first nibble for an organization's campus, the next nibble for a building within a campus, and the last two nibbles for a subnet within a building. An example subnet ID for this scheme is 142A, which indicates campus 1, building 4, and subnet 42 (0x2A).

In some cases, bit-level subnetting is required. For example, a network administrator decides to implement a two-level hierarchy reflecting a geographical/departmental structure and uses 4 bits for the geographical level and 6 bits for the departmental level. This means that each department in each geographical location has only 6 bits of subnetting space left (16–4–6), or only 64 (= 2^6) subnets per department.

On any given level in the hierarchy, you will have a number of bits that are already fixed by the next level up in the hierarchy (f), a number of bits used for subnetting at the current level in the hierarchy (s), and a number of bits remaining for the next level down in the hierarchy (r). At all times, $f + s + r = 16$. This relationship is shown in Figure 3-10.

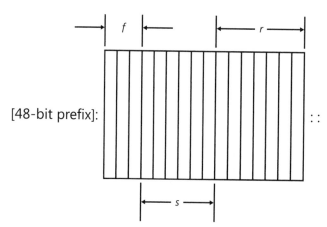

Figure 3-10   The subnetting of a subnet ID

Step 2: Enumerating Subnetted Address Prefixes

Based on the number of bits used for subnetting, you must determine the new subnetted address prefixes. There are three main approaches:

- **Binary**   Enumerate new subnetted address prefixes by using binary representations of the subnet ID and converting to hexadecimal for the subnetted address prefixes.

- **Hexadecimal**   Enumerate new subnetted address prefixes by using hexadecimal representations of the subnet ID and a calculated increment between successive subnetted address prefixes.

- **Decimal**   Enumerate new subnetted address prefixes by using decimal representations of the subnet ID and increment.

Any of these methods produces the same result: an enumerated list of subnetted address prefixes.

Using the Binary Method

In the binary method, the 16-bit subnet ID is expressed as a 16-digit binary number. The bits within the subnet ID that are being used for subnetting are incremented for all their possible values, and for each value, the 16-digit binary number is converted to hexadecimal and combined with the 48-bit site prefix, producing the subnetted address prefixes.

1. Based on s (the number of bits chosen for subnetting), m (the prefix length of the address prefix being subnetted), and f (the number of bits already subnetted), calculate the following:

   $f = m - 48$

   f is the number of bits within the subnet ID that are already fixed.

   $n = 2^s$

   n is the number of address prefixes that are obtained.

   $l = 48 + f + s$

   l is the prefix length of the new subnetted address prefixes.

2. Create a three-column table with n entries. The first column is the address prefix number (starting with 1), the second column is the binary representation of the subnet ID portion of the new address prefix, and the third column is the subnetted address prefix (in hexadecimal), which includes the 48-bit site prefix and the subnet ID.

3. In the first table entry, set all the bits being used for subnetting to 0. Convert the resulting 16-digit binary number to hexadecimal, combine it with the 48-bit site prefix, and write the subnetted address prefix. This first subnetted address prefix is just the original address prefix with the new prefix length.

4. In the next table entry, increment the value within the subnet bits. Convert the 16-digit binary number to hexadecimal, combine it with the 48-bit site prefix, and write the resulting subnetted address prefix.

5. Repeat step 4 until the table is complete.

For example, to perform a 3-bit subnetting of the global address prefix 2001:DB8:0:C000::/51, we first calculate the values for the number of prefixes and the new prefix length. Our starting values are $s = 3$, and $f = 51 - 48 = 3$. The number of prefixes is 8 ($n = 2^3$). The new prefix length is 54 ($l = 48 + 3 + 3$). The initial value for the subnet ID in binary is 1100 0000 0000 0000 (0xC000 converted to binary).

Next, we construct a table with eight entries. The entry for the address prefix 1 is 2001:DB8:0:C000::/54. Additional entries are increments of the subnet bits in the subnet ID portion of the address prefix, as shown in Table 3-3.

Table 3-3   The Binary Subnetting Technique for Address Prefix 2001:DB8:0:C000::/51

Address Prefix Number	Binary Representation of Subnet ID	Subnetted Address Prefix
1	1100 0000 0000 0000	2001:DB8:0:C000::/54
2	1100 0100 0000 0000	2001:DB8:0:C400::/54
3	1100 1000 0000 0000	2001:DB8:0:C800::/54
4	1100 1100 0000 0000	2001:DB8:0:CC00::/54
5	1101 0000 0000 0000	2001:DB8:0:D000::/54
6	1101 0100 0000 0000	2001:DB8:0:D400::/54
7	1101 1000 0000 0000	2001:DB8:0:D800::/54
8	1101 1100 0000 0000	2001:DB8:0:DC00::/54

In Table 3-3, the underline in the second column shows the bits that are being used for subnetting.

Using the Hexadecimal Method

Although the binary method allows you to see how the subnetted address prefixes are determined at their most basic level, this method is laborious and does not scale well. For example, imagine performing an 8-bit subnetting using the binary method, producing 256 subnetted prefixes. For an arbitrary subnetting scheme, a more formulaic approach is needed. The following method uses a formula for computing the hexadecimal increment between successive subnetted address prefixes:

1. Based on s (the number of bits chosen for subnetting), m (the prefix length of the address prefix being subnetted), and F (the hexadecimal value of the subnet being subnetted), calculate the following:

   $f = m - 48$

   f is the number of bits within the subnet ID that are already fixed.

   $n = 2^s$

   n is the number of address prefixes that are obtained.

   $i = 2^{16-(f+s)}$

i is the incremental value between each successive subnet ID expressed in hexadecimal form.

$$l = 48 + f + s$$

l is the prefix length of the new subnetted address prefixes.

2. Create a two-column table with *n* entries. The first column is the address prefix number (starting with 1), and the second column is the new subnetted address prefix.

3. In the first table entry, based on *F*, the hexadecimal value of the subnet ID being subnetted, set the subnetted address prefix to *48-bit prefix:F::/l*.

4. In the next table entry, increase the value within the subnet ID portion of the site address by *i*. For example, in the second table entry, set the subnetted prefix to *48-bit prefix:F + i::/l*.

5. Repeat step 4 until the table is complete.

For example, to perform a 3-bit subnetting of the global address prefix 2001:DB8:0:C000::/51, we first calculate the values of the number of prefixes, the increment, and the new prefix length. Our starting values are $F = 0xC000$, $s = 3$, and $f = 51 - 48 = 3$. The number of prefixes is 8 ($n = 2^3$). The increment is 0x400 ($i = 2^{16-(f+s)} = 1024 = 0x400$). The new prefix length is 54 ($l = 48 + 3 + 3$).

Next, we construct a table with eight entries. The entry for the address prefix 1 is 2001:DB8:0:C000::/54. Additional entries in the table are successive increments of *i* in the subnet ID portion of the address prefix, as shown in Table 3-4.

Table 3-4   The Hexadecimal Subnetting Technique for Address Prefix 2001:DB8:0:C000::/51

Address Prefix Number	Subnetted Address Prefix
1	2001:DB8:0:C000::/54
2	2001:DB8:0:C400::/54
3	2001:DB8:0:C800::/54
4	2001:DB8:0:CC00::/54
5	2001:DB8:0:D000::/54
6	2001:DB8:0:D400::/54
7	2001:DB8:0:D800::/54
8	2001:DB8:0:DC00::/54

Using the Decimal Method

If you are more comfortable working with decimal numbers, the following formulaic procedure will produce the same results. However, there are additional steps to convert to decimal and then back to hexadecimal for the representation of the subnetted address prefix.

1. Based on *s* (the number of bits chosen for subnetting), *m* (the prefix length of the address prefix being subnetted), and *F* (the hexadecimal value of the subnet ID being subnetted), calculate the following:

   `f = m - 48`

   f is the number of bits within the subnet ID that are already fixed.

   `n = 2`^{s}

   n is the number of address prefixes that are obtained.

   $i = 2^{16-(f+s)}$

   i is the incremental value between each successive subnet ID.

   `l = 48 + f + s`

   l is the prefix length of the new subnetted address prefixes.

   `D = decimal representation of F`

2. Create a three-column table with *n* entries. The first column is the address prefix number (starting with 1), the second column is the decimal representation of the subnet ID portion of the new address prefix, and the third column is the new subnetted address prefix.

3. In the first table entry, the decimal representation of the subnet ID is *D* and the subnetted address prefix is *48-bit prefix:F::/l*.

4. In the next table entry, for the second column, increase the value of the decimal representation of the subnet ID by *i*. For example, in the second table entry, the decimal representation of the subnet ID is *D* + *i*.

5. For the third column, convert the decimal representation of the subnet ID to hexadecimal and construct the prefix from *48-bit prefix:subnet ID::/l*. For example, in the second table entry, the subnetted address prefix is *48-bit prefix:D* + *i* (converted to hexadecimal)*::/l*.

6. Repeat steps 4 and 5 until the table is complete.

For example, to perform a 3-bit subnetting of the global address prefix 2001:DB8:0:C000::/51, we first calculate the values of the number of prefixes, the increment, the new prefix length, and the decimal representation of the starting subnet ID. Our starting values are *F* = 0xC000, *s* = 3, and *f* = 51 − 48 = 3. The number of prefixes is 8 (*n* = 2^3). The increment is 1024 (*i* = $2^{16-(f+s)}$). The new prefix length is 54 (*l* = 48 + 3 + 3). The decimal representation of the starting subnet ID is 49152 (*D* = 0xC000 = 49152).

Next, we construct a table with eight entries. The entry for the address prefix 1 is 49152 and 2001:DB8:0:C000::/54. Additional entries in the table are successive increments of *i* in the subnet ID portion of the address prefix, as shown in Table 3-5.

Table 3-5   The Decimal Subnetting Technique for Address Prefix 2001:DB8:0:C000::/51

Address Prefix Number	Decimal Representation of Subnet ID	Subnetted Address Prefix
1	49152	2001:DB8:0:C000::/54
2	50176	2001:DB8:0:C400::/54
3	51200	2001:DB8:0:C800::/54
4	52224	2001:DB8:0:CC00::/54
5	53248	2001:DB8:0:D000::/54
6	54272	2001:DB8:0:D400::/54
7	55296	2001:DB8:0:D800::/54
8	56320	2001:DB8:0:DC00::/54

IPv6 Interface Identifiers

The last 64 bits of a currently defined IPv6 unicast address are for the interface identifier, which is unique for a 64-bit subnet prefix of a unicast IPv6 address. In IPv4, the host or node ID portion of an IPv4 address is a logical identifier of an interface on an IPv4 subnet. IPv4 host IDs are of variable length, depending on the subnetting scheme and how many interfaces you want to allow on a given subnet. For example, with an 8-bit host ID, there were $2^8 - 2$ or 254 possible host IDs. (The all-zeros and all-ones combinations are reserved.)

In IPv6, the interface ID is of fixed length. This length was not fixed at 64 bits to allow up to 2^{64} possible hosts on the same subnet. Rather, the IPv6 interface ID is 64 bits long to accommodate the mapping of current 48-bit MAC addresses used by many local area network (LAN) technologies such as Ethernet and the mapping of 64-bit MAC addresses of IEEE 1394 (also known as FireWire) and future LAN technologies.

The ways in which an interface identifier for a LAN interface is determined are the following:

- As defined in RFC 4291, it can be derived from the Extended Unique Identifier (EUI)-64 address. The 64-bit EUI-64 address is defined by the Institute of Electrical and Electronics Engineers (IEEE). EUI-64 addresses are either assigned to a network adapter or derived from IEEE 802 addresses. This is the default behavior for IPv6 in Windows XP and Windows Server 2003.

- As defined in RFC 4941, it might have a temporarily assigned, randomly generated interface identifier to provide a level of anonymity. For more information, see the "Temporary Address Interface Identifiers" section in this chapter.

- It is assigned during stateful address autoconfiguration—for example, via Dynamic Host Configuration Protocol for IPv6 (DHCPv6).

- As defined in RFC 5072, an interface identifier can be based on link-layer addresses or serial numbers, or it can be randomly generated when configuring a Point-to-Point Protocol (PPP) interface and an EUI-64 address is not available.

- It is assigned during manual address configuration.

- It is a permanent interface identifier that is randomly generated to mitigate address scans of unicast IPv6 addresses on a subnet. This is the default behavior for LAN interfaces for IPv6 in Windows Vista and Windows Server 2008. You can disable this behavior with the **netsh interface ipv6 set global randomizeidentifiers=disabled** command. When this behavior is disabled, IPv6 for Windows Vista and Windows Server 2008 will use EUI-64–based interface identifiers.

EUI-64 Address-Based Interface Identifiers

One way to derive an IPv6 interface identifier is through the EUI-64 address, a new type of MAC address for network adapters. To gain an understanding of EUI-64 addresses, it is useful to review the current MAC address format known as *IEEE 802 addresses*.

IEEE 802 Addresses

Network adapters for common LAN technologies such as Ethernet and IEEE 802.11 use a 48-bit address called an IEEE 802 address. It consists of a 24-bit company ID (also called the *manufacturer ID*) and a 24-bit extension ID (also called the *board ID*). The combination of the company ID, which is uniquely assigned to each manufacturer of network adapters, and the extension ID, which is uniquely assigned to each network adapter at the time of manufacture, produces a globally unique 48-bit address. This 48-bit address is also called the physical, hardware, or MAC address.

Figure 3-11 shows the structure of the 48-bit IEEE 802 address for Ethernet.

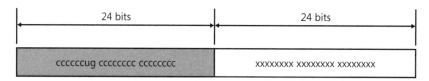

Figure 3-11   The structure of the 48-bit IEEE 802 address for Ethernet

Defined bits within the IEEE 802 address for Ethernet are as follows:

- **Universal/Local (U/L)**   The seventh bit in the first byte is used to indicate whether the address is universally or locally administered. If the U/L bit is set to 0, the IEEE (through the designation of a unique company ID) has administered the address. If the U/L bit is set to 1, the address is locally administered. In this case, the network administrator has overridden the manufactured address and specified a different address. The U/L bit is designated by the **u** in Figure 3-11.

- **Individual/Group (I/G)**   The eighth (low-order) bit of the first byte is used to indicate whether the address is an individual address (unicast) or a group address (multicast).

When set to 0, the address is a unicast address. When set to 1, the address is a multicast address. The I/G bit is designated by the **g** in Figure 3-11.

For a typical IEEE 802 address assigned to a network adapter, both the U/L and I/G bits are set to 0, corresponding to a universally administered, unicast MAC address.

IEEE EUI-64 Addresses

The IEEE EUI-64 address represents a new standard for network interface addressing. The company ID is still 24-bits long, but the extension ID is 40 bits, creating a much larger address space for a network adapter manufacturer. The EUI-64 address uses the U/L and I/G bits in the same way as the IEEE 802 address.

Figure 3-12 shows the structure of the EUI-64 address.

Figure 3-12   The structure of the EUI-64 address

Mapping IEEE 802 Addresses to EUI-64 Addresses   To create an EUI-64 address from an IEEE 802 address, the 16 bits of 11111111 11111110 (0xFFFE) are inserted into the IEEE 802 address between the company ID and the extension ID, as shown in Figure 3-13.

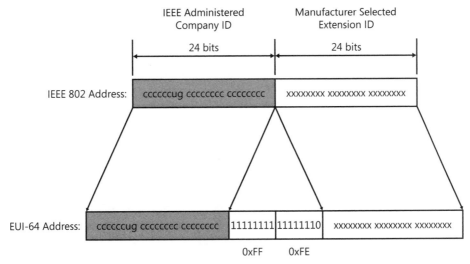

Figure 3-13   The mapping of IEEE 802 addresses to EUI-64 addresses

Obtaining Interface Identifiers for IPv6 Addresses

To obtain the 64-bit interface identifier for IPv6 unicast addresses, the U/L bit in the EUI-64 address is complemented. (If it is a 1 in the EUI-64 address, it is set to 0; and if it is a 0 in the EUI-64 address, it is set to 1.)

The main reason for complementing the U/L bit is to provide greater compressibility of locally administered EUI-64 addresses. It is common practice when assigning locally administered addresses to number them in a simple way. For example, on a point-to-point link, you can assign to one interface on the link the locally administered EUI-64 address of 02-00-00-00-00-00-00-01 and to the other interface the locally administered EUI-64 address of 02-00-00-00-00-00-00-02. If the U/L bit is not complemented, the corresponding link-local addresses for these two interfaces become FE80::200:0:0:1 and FE80::200:0:0:2. By complementing the U/L bit, the corresponding link-local addresses for these two interfaces become FE80::1 and FE80::2.

Figure 3-14 shows the conversion of an EUI-64 address to an IPv6 interface identifier.

EUI Address

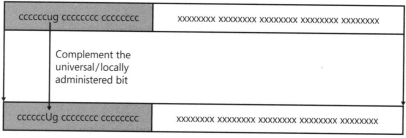

IPv6 Interface Identifier

Figure 3-14   The conversion of an EUI-64 address to an IPv6 interface identifier

> **Note**   Because the U/L bit is complemented when converting an EUI-64 address to an IPv6 interface identifier, the resulting bit in the IPv6 interface identifier has the opposite interpretation of the IEEE-defined U/L bit. If the seventh bit of the IPv6 interface identifier is set to 0, it is locally administered. If the seventh bit of the IPv6 interface identifier is set to 1, it is universally administered.

Converting IEEE 802 Addresses to IPv6 Interface Identifiers   To obtain an IPv6 interface identifier from an IEEE 802 address, you must first map the IEEE 802 address to an EUI-64 address, and then complement the U/L bit. Figure 3-15 shows this conversion process for a universally administered, unicast IEEE 802 address.

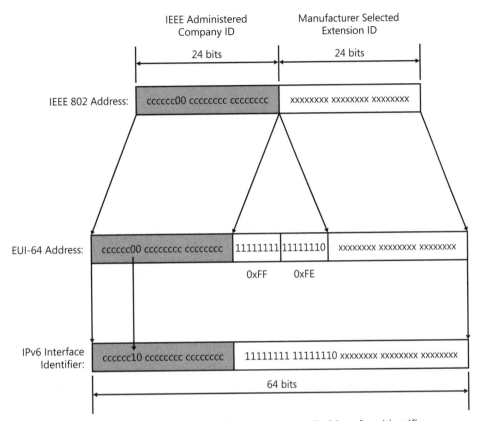

Figure 3-15   The conversion of an IEEE 802 address to an IPv6 interface identifier

IEEE 802 Address Conversion Example   Host A has the Ethernet MAC address of 00-AA-00-3F-2A-1C. First, it is converted to EUI-64 format by inserting FF-FE between the third and fourth bytes, yielding 00-AA-00-FF-FE-3F-2A-1C. Then, the U/L bit, which is the seventh bit in the first byte, is complemented. The first byte in binary form is 00000000. When the seventh bit is complemented, it becomes 00000010 (0x02). The final result is 02-AA-00-FF-FE-3F-2A-1C which, when converted to colon hexadecimal notation, becomes the interface identifier 2AA:FF:FE3F:2A1C. As a result, the link-local address that corresponds to the network adapter with the MAC address of 00-AA-00-3F-2A-1C is FE80::2AA:FF:FE3F:2A1C.

Note   When complementing the U/L bit, add 0x2 to the first byte if the EUI-64 address is universally administered, and subtract 0x2 from the first byte if the EUI-64 address is locally administered.

Temporary Address Interface Identifiers

In today's IPv4-based Internet, a typical Internet user dials an ISP and obtains an IPv4 address using PPP and the Internet Protocol Control Protocol (IPCP). Each time the user dials, a different IPv4 address might be obtained. Therefore, it is not easy to track a dial-up user's traffic on the Internet based on the user's IPv4 address.

For IPv6-based dial-up connections, the user is assigned a 64-bit prefix, at the time of connection, by using router discovery, which consists of an exchange of Router Solicitation and Router Advertisement messages. If the interface identifier is always based on the EUI-64 address (as derived from the static IEEE 802 address), it is possible to identify the traffic of a specific node regardless of the prefix assigned at the time of connection. The use of the same 64-bit interface identifier allows identification of a user's traffic whether the user is accessing the Internet from home or from work. This makes it easy for Internet merchants and malicious users to track a specific user and his or her use of the Internet.

To address this concern and provide the same level of anonymity as that provided with IPv4, RFC 4941 describes an alternative derivation of the IPv6 interface identifier that is randomly generated and changes over time.

The initial interface identifier is generated using random number techniques. For IPv6 systems that do not have the ability to store any history information for generating future values of the interface identifier, a new random interface identifier is generated each time the IPv6 protocol is initialized. For IPv6 systems that do have storage capabilities, a history value is stored and when the IPv6 protocol is initialized, a new interface identifier is created through the following process:

1. Retrieve the history value from storage, and append the interface identifier based on the EUI-64 address of the adapter.

2. Compute the Message Digest-5 (MD5) hash over the quantity in step 1. The MD5 hash computation will produce a 128-bit value.

3. Store the low-order 64 bits of the MD5 hash computed in step 2 as the history value for the next computation of the interface identifier.

4. Take the high-order 64 bits of the MD5 hash computed in step 2 and set the seventh bit to zero. The seventh bit corresponds to the U/L bit, which, when set to 0, indicates a locally administered interface identifier. The result is the interface identifier.

The resulting IPv6 address, based on this random interface identifier, is known as a *temporary address*. Temporary addresses are generated for public address prefixes that use stateless address autoconfiguration. Temporary addresses are used for the lower of the following values of the valid and preferred lifetimes:

■ The lifetimes included in the Prefix Information option in the received Router Advertisement message.

■ Local default values of 1 week for valid lifetime and 1 day for preferred lifetime.

After the temporary address valid lifetime expires, a new interface identifier and temporary address is generated. For more information about router discovery, see Chapter 6, "Neighbor Discovery." For more information about stateless address autoconfiguration and valid and preferred lifetimes, see Chapter 8.

IPv4 Addresses and IPv6 Equivalents

To summarize the relationships between IPv4 addressing and IPv6 addressing, Table 3-6 lists both IPv4 addresses and addressing concepts and their IPv6 equivalents.

Table 3-6   IPv4 Addressing Concepts and Their IPv6 Equivalents

IPv4 Address	IPv6 Address
Internet address classes	Not applicable in IPv6
Multicast addresses (224.0.0.0/4)	IPv6 multicast addresses (FF00::/8)
Broadcast addresses	Not applicable in IPv6
Unspecified address is 0.0.0.0	Unspecified address is ::
Loopback address is 127.0.0.1	Loopback address is ::1
Public IP addresses	Global unicast addresses
Private IP addresses (10.0.0.0/8, 172.16.0.0/12, and 192.168.0.0/16)	Unique local (FD00::/8) or site-local addresses (FEC0::/10) (deprecated)
APIPA addresses (169.254.0.0/16)	Link-local addresses (FE80::/64)
Text representation: Dotted-decimal notation	Text representation: Colon hexadecimal format with suppression of leading zeros and zero compression.
Prefix representation: Subnet mask in dotted-decimal notation or prefix length notation	Prefix representation: Prefix length notation only

References

The following references were cited in this chapter:

- RFC 3306 – "Unicast-Prefix-based IPv6 Multicast Addresses"
- RFC 3587 – "IPv6 Global Unicast Address Format"
- RFC 3879 – "Deprecating Site Local Addresses"
- RFC 3927 – "Dynamic Configuration of IPv4 Link-Local Addresses"
- RFC 3956 – "Embedding the Rendezvous Point (RP) Address in an IPv6 Multicast Address"
- RFC 4007 – "IPv6 Scoped Address Architecture"
- RFC 4193 – "Unique Local IPv6 Unicast Addresses"

- RFC 4291 – "IP Version 6 Addressing Architecture"
- RFC 4941 – "Privacy Extensions for Stateless Address Autoconfiguration in IPv6"
- RFC 5072 – "IP Version 6 over PPP"

You can obtain these RFCs from the \RFCs_and_Drafts folder on the companion CD-ROM or from *http://www.ietf.org/rfc.html*.

Testing for Understanding

To test your understanding of IPv6 addressing, answer the following questions. See Appendix D, "Testing for Understanding Answers," to check your answers.

1. Why is the IPv6 address length 128 bits?

2. Express FEC0:0000:0000:0001:02AA:0000:0000:0007A more efficiently.

3. How many blocks and bits are expressed by "::" in the addresses 2001:DB8::2AA:9FF:FE56:24DC and FF02::2?

4. Describe the difference between unicast, multicast, and anycast addresses in terms of a host sending packets to zero or more interfaces.

5. Why are no broadcast addresses defined for IPv6?

6. Define the structure, including field sizes, of the global unicast address.

7. Define the scope for each of the different types of unicast addresses.

8. Explain how global and unique local addressing can share the same subnetting infrastructure within an organization.

9. Define the structure, including field sizes, of the multicast address.

10. Explain how the solicited-node multicast address acts as a pseudo-unicast address.

11. How do routers know the nearest location of an anycast group member?

12. Perform a 4-bit subnetting on the unique local prefix FD1A:39C1:4BC2:3D80::/57.

13. What is the EUI-64–based IPv6 interface identifier for the universally administered, unicast IEEE 802 address of 0C-1C-09-A8-F9-CE? What is the corresponding link-local address? What is the corresponding solicited-node multicast address?

14. What is the IPv6 interface identifier for the locally administered, unicast EUI-64 address of 02-00-00-00-00-00-00-09? What is the corresponding link-local address?

15. For each type of address shown in the following table, identify how the address begins in colon hexadecimal notation.

Type of Address	Begins with...
Link-local unicast address	FE80
Site-local unicast address	
Unique local unicast address	
Global address (as defined by RFC 3587)	
Multicast address	
Link-local scope multicast address	
Site-local scope multicast address	
Solicited-node multicast address	
IPv4-mapped address	
6to4 address	
Teredo address	

Chapter 4
The IPv6 Header

At the end of this chapter, you should be able to do the following:

■ Describe the structure of an IPv6 packet.

■ List and describe the fields in the IPv4 header.

■ List and describe the fields in the IPv6 header.

■ Compare and contrast the fields in the IPv4 header with the fields in the IPv6 header.

■ List and describe each IPv6 extension header.

■ Describe the IPv6 maximum transmission unit (MTU).

■ Describe the new pseudo-header used for upper-layer checksums.

Structure of an IPv6 Packet

An Internet Protocol version 6 (IPv6) packet consists of an IPv6 header, extension headers, and an upper-layer protocol data unit. Figure 4-1 shows the structure of an IPv6 packet.

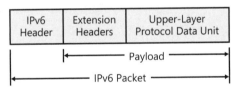

Figure 4-1   The structure of an IPv6 packet

The components of an IPv6 packet are the following:

■ **IPv6 Header**   The IPv6 header is always present and is a fixed size of 40 bytes. The fields in the IPv6 header are described in the "IPv6 Header" section in this chapter.

■ **Extension Headers**   Zero or more extension headers can be present and are of varying lengths. If extension headers are present, a Next Header field in the IPv6 header indicates the first extension header. Within each extension header is another Next Header field, indicating the next extension header. The last extension header indicates the header for the upper-layer protocol—such as Transmission Control Protocol (TCP), User Datagram Protocol (UDP), or Internet Control Message Protocol for version 6 (ICMPv6)—contained within the upper-layer protocol data unit.

The IPv6 header and extension headers replace the existing IPv4 header and its options. The new extension header format allows IPv6 to be enhanced to support future needs and capabilities. Unlike options in the IPv4 header, IPv6 extension headers have no maximum size and can expand to accommodate all the extension data needed for IPv6 communication. IPv6 extension headers are described in the "IPv6 Extension Headers" section in this chapter.

■ **Upper-Layer Protocol Data Unit**   The upper-layer protocol data unit (PDU) typically consists of an upper-layer protocol header and its payload (for example, an ICMPv6 message, a TCP segment, or a UDP message).

The IPv6 packet payload is the combination of the IPv6 extension headers and the upper-layer PDU. Normally, it can be up to 65,535 bytes long. IPv6 packets with payloads larger than 65,535 bytes in length, known as *jumbograms*, can also be sent.

IPv4 Header

Before examining the IPv6 header, you might find it helpful, for contrasting purposes, to review the IPv4 header shown in Figure 4-2.

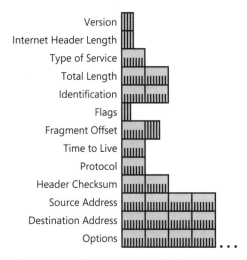

Figure 4-2   The structure of the IPv4 header

Following is a list of the fields in the IPv4 header:

■ **Version**   The Version field indicates the version of IP and is set to 4. The size of this field is 4 bits.

■ **Internet Header Length**   The Internet Header Length (IHL) field indicates the number of 4-byte blocks in the IPv4 header. The size of this field is 4 bits. Because an IPv4 header is a minimum of 20 bytes in size, the smallest value of the IHL field is 5. IPv4 options can extend the minimum IPv4 header size in increments of 4 bytes. If an IPv4 option is not an integral multiple of 4 bytes in length, the remaining bytes are padded with padding options, making the entire IPv4 header an integral multiple of 4 bytes. With a maximum IHL value of 0xF, the maximum size of the IPv4 header, including options, is 60 bytes (15 × 4).

- **Type of Service**   The Type of Service field indicates the desired service expected by this packet for delivery through routers across the IPv4 internetwork. The size of this field is 8 bits, including bits originally defined in RFC 791 for precedence, delay, throughput, reliability, and cost characteristics. RFC 2474 provides the modern definition as the Differentiated Services (DS) field. The high-order 6 bits of the DS field comprise the DS Code Point (DSCP) field. The DSCP field allows devices in a network to mark, unmark, and classify packets for forwarding. This is usually done based on the needs of an application. For example, Voice over IP and other real-time packets take precedence over e-mail in congested areas of the network. This is commonly referred to as Quality of Service (QoS). The low-order 2 bits of the Type of Service field are used for Explicit Congestion Notification (ECN), as defined in RFC 3168.

- **Total Length**   The Total Length field indicates the total length of the IPv4 packet (IPv4 header + IPv4 payload) and does not include link-layer framing. The size of this field is 16 bits, which can indicate an IPv4 packet that is up to 65,535 bytes long.

- **Identification**   The Identification field identifies this specific IPv4 packet. The size of this field is 16 bits. The Identification field is selected by the source node of the IPv4 packet. If the IPv4 packet is fragmented, all the fragments retain the Identification field value so that the destination node can group the fragments for reassembly.

- **Flags**   The Flags field identifies flags for the fragmentation process. The size of this field is 3 bits; however, only 2 bits are defined for current use. There are two flags—one to indicate whether the IPv4 packet can be fragmented and another to indicate whether more fragments follow the current fragment.

- **Fragment Offset**   The Fragment Offset field indicates the position of the fragment relative to the beginning of the original IPv4 payload. The size of this field is 13 bits.

- **Time-to-Live**   The Time-to-Live (TTL) field indicates the maximum number of links on which an IPv4 packet can travel before being discarded. The size of this field is 8 bits. The TTL field was originally defined as a time count for the number of seconds the packet could exist on the network. An IPv4 router determined the length of time required (in seconds) to forward the IPv4 packet and decremented the TTL accordingly. Modern routers almost always forward an IPv4 packet in less than a second, and they are required by RFC 791 to decrement the TTL by at least one. Therefore, the TTL becomes a maximum link count with the value set by the sending node. When the TTL equals 0, an ICMPv4 Time Exceeded-Time to Live Exceeded in Transit message is sent to the source of the packet and the packet is discarded.

- **Protocol**   The Protocol field identifies the upper-layer protocol. The size of this field is 8 bits. For example, a value of 6 in this field identifies TCP as the upper-layer protocol, a decimal value of 17 identifies UDP, and a value of 1 identifies ICMPv4. The Protocol field is used to identify the upper-layer protocol that is to receive the IPv4 packet payload.

- **Header Checksum**   The Header Checksum field provides a checksum on the IPv4 header only. The size of this field is 16 bits. The IPv4 payload is not included in the checksum calculation, as the IPv4 payload usually contains its own checksum. Each IPv4 node that receives IPv4 packets verifies the IPv4 header checksum and silently discards the IPv4 packet if checksum verification fails. When a router forwards an IPv4 packet, it must decrement the TTL. Therefore, the Header Checksum value is recomputed at each hop between source and destination.

- **Source Address**   The Source Address field stores the IPv4 address of the originating host. The size of this field is 32 bits.

- **Destination Address**   The Destination Address field stores the IPv4 address of an intermediate destination (in the case of source routing) or the destination host. The size of this field is 32 bits.

- **Options**   The Options field stores one or more IPv4 options. The size of this field is a multiple of 32 bits (4 bytes). If an IPv4 option does not use all 32 bits, padding options must be added so that the IPv4 header is an integral number of 4-byte blocks that can be indicated by the IHL field.

IPv6 Header

The IPv6 header is a streamlined version of the IPv4 header. It eliminates fields that are either unneeded or rarely used, and it adds a field that provides better support for real-time traffic. Figure 4-3 shows the structure of the IPv6 header as described in RFC 2460.

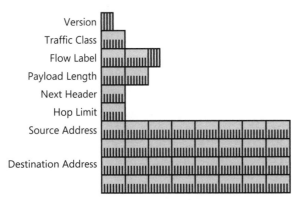

Figure 4-3   The structure of the IPv6 header

The following list describes the fields in the IPv6 header:

- **Version**   The Version field indicates the version of IP and is set to 6. The size of this field is 4 bits. While the purpose of the Version field is defined in the same way for both IPv4 and IPv6, its value is not used to pass the packet to an IPv4 or IPv6 protocol layer. This identification is done through a protocol identification field in the link-layer header. For example, a common link-layer encapsulation for Ethernet, called Ethernet II, uses a

16-bit EtherType field to identify the Ethernet frame payload. For IPv4 packets, the EtherType field is set to 0x800. For IPv6 packets, the EtherType field is set to 0x86DD. Thus, the determination of the protocol of the Ethernet payload occurs before the packet is passed to the appropriate protocol layer.

■ **Traffic Class**   The Traffic Class field indicates the IPv6 packet's class or priority. The size of this field is 8 bits. This field provides functionality similar to the IPv4 Type of Service field. Like the Type of Service field in the IPv4 header, the first 6 bits of the Traffic Class field are the DSCP field as defined in RFC 2474 and the last 2 bits are used for ECN as defined in RFC 3168.

■ **Flow Label**   The Flow Label field indicates that this packet belongs to a specific sequence of packets between a source and destination, requiring special handling by intermediate IPv6 routers. The size of this field is 20 bits. The flow label is used for prioritized delivery, such as delivery needed by real-time data (voice and video). For default router handling, the Flow Label field is set to 0. To distinguish a given flow, an intermediate router can use the packet's source address, destination address, and flow label. Therefore, there can be multiple flows between a source and destination, as distinguished by separate non-zero flow labels. The details of the use of the Flow Label field are described in RFC 3697.

■ **Payload Length**   The Payload Length field indicates the length of the IPv6 payload. The size of this field is 16 bits. The Payload Length field includes the extension headers and the upper-layer PDU. With 16 bits, an IPv6 payload of up to 65,535 bytes can be indicated. For payload lengths greater than 65,535 bytes, the Payload Length field is set to 0 and the Jumbo Payload option is used in the Hop-by-Hop Options extension header, which is described in the "Hop-by-Hop Options Header" section in this chapter.

■ **Next Header**   The Next Header field indicates either the type of the first extension header (if present) or the protocol in the upper-layer PDU (such as TCP, UDP, or ICMPv6). The size of this field is 8 bits. When indicating an upper-layer protocol, the Next Header field uses the same values that are used in the IPv4 Protocol field.

■ **Hop Limit**   The Hop Limit field indicates the maximum number of links over which the IPv6 packet can travel before being discarded. The size of this field is 8 bits. The Hop Limit field is similar to the IPv4 TTL field, except that there is no historical relation to the amount of time (in seconds) that the packet is queued at the router. When Hop Limit equals 0 at a router, the router sends an ICMPv6 Time Exceeded-Hop Limit Exceeded in Transit message to the source and discards the packet.

■ **Source Address**   The Source Address field indicates the IPv6 address of the originating host. The size of this field is 128 bits.

■ **Destination Address**   The Destination Address field indicates the IPv6 address of the current destination node. The size of this field is 128 bits. In most cases, the Destination Address field is set to the final destination address. However, if a Routing extension header is present, the Destination Address field might be set to the address of the next intermediate destination.

Network Monitor Capture

Here is an example of an IPv6 header, as displayed by Network Monitor 3.1 (capture 04_01 in the \NetworkMonitorCaptures folder on the companion CD-ROM):

```
Frame:
+ Ethernet: Etype = IPv6
- Ipv6: Next Protocol = ICMPv6, Payload Length = 40
  - Versions: IPv6, Internet Protocol, DSCP 0
    Version:   (0110..........................) IPv6, Internet Protocol, 6(0x6)
    DSCP:      (....000000.....................) Differentiated services codepoint 0
    ECT:       (..........0....................) ECN-Capable Transport not set
    CE:        (...........0...................) ECN-CE not set
    FlowLabel: (............00000000000000000000) 0
    PayloadLength: 40 (0x28)
    NextProtocol: ICMPv6, 58(0x3a)
    HopLimit: 128 (0x80)
    SourceAddress: FE80:0:0:0:260:97FF:FE02:6E8F
    DestinationAddress: FE80:0:0:0:260:97FF:FE02:6D3D
+ Icmpv6: Echo request, ID = 0x0, Seq = 0x18
```

This ICMPv6 Echo Request packet uses the default Traffic Class and Flow Label and a Hop Limit of 128, and it is sent between two hosts using link-local addresses.

Values of the Next Header Field

Table 4-1 lists typical values of the Next Header field for an IPv6 header or an IPv6 extension header. Each of the IPv6 extension headers is covered later in the chapter.

Table 4-1   Typical Values of the Next Header Field

Value (Decimal)	Header
0	Hop-by-Hop Options header
6	TCP
17	UDP
41	Encapsulated IPv6 header
43	Routing header
44	Fragment header
50	Encapsulating Security Payload header
51	Authentication header
58	ICMPv6
59	No next header
60	Destination Options header

For the most current list of the reserved values for the IPv4 Protocol and IPv6 Next Header fields, see *http://www.iana.org/assignments/protocol-numbers*.

In looking at the value of the Next Header field to indicate no next header, it would seem to make more sense to set its value to 0, rather than 59. However, the designers of IPv6 wanted to optimize the processing of IPv6 packets at intermediate routers. The only extension header that must be processed at every intermediate router is the Hop-by-Hop Options header. To optimize the test of whether the Hop-by-Hop Options header is present, its Next Header value is set to 0. In router hardware, it is easier to test for a value of 0 than to test for a value of 59.

Comparing the IPv4 and IPv6 Headers

In comparing the IPv4 and IPv6 headers, you can see the following:

- The number of fields has dropped from 12 (including options) in the IPv4 header to 8 in the IPv6 header.

- The number of fields that must be processed by an intermediate router has dropped from 6 to 4, making the forwarding of normal IPv6 packets more efficient.

- Seldom-used fields such as fields supporting fragmentation and options in the IPv4 header have been moved to extension headers in the IPv6 header.

- The size of the IPv6 header has doubled from 20 bytes for a minimum-sized IPv4 header to 40 bytes. However, the new IPv6 header contains source and destination addresses that are four times longer than IPv4 source and destination addresses.

Table 4-2 lists the individual differences between the IPv4 and IPv6 header fields.

Table 4-2   IPv4 Header Fields and Corresponding IPv6 Equivalents

IPv4 Header Field	IPv6 Header Field
Version	Same field but with a different version number.
Internet Header Length	Removed in IPv6. IPv6 does not include a Header Length field because the IPv6 header is always a fixed length of 40 bytes. Each extension header is either a fixed length or indicates its own length.
Type of Service	Replaced by the IPv6 Traffic Class field.
Total Length	Replaced by the IPv6 Payload Length field, which indicates only the size of the payload.
Identification Flags Fragment Offset	Removed in IPv6. Fragmentation information is not included in the IPv6 header. It is contained in a Fragment extension header.
Time-to-Live	Replaced by the IPv6 Hop Limit field.
Protocol	Replaced by the IPv6 Next Header field.
Header Checksum	Removed in IPv6. The link layer has a checksum that performs bit-level error detection for the entire IPv6 packet.
Source Address	The field is the same except that IPv6 addresses are 128 bits in length.
Destination Address	The field is the same except that IPv6 addresses are 128 bits in length.
Options	Removed in IPv6. IPv6 extension headers replace IPv4 options.

The one new field in the IPv6 header that is not included in the IPv4 header is the Flow Label field.

The result of the new IPv6 header is a reduction in the critical router loop, the set of instructions that must be executed to determine how to forward a packet. To forward a normal IPv4 packet, a router typically performs the following in its critical router loop:

1. Verify the Header Checksum field by performing its own checksum calculation and comparing its result with the result stored in the IPv4 header. Although this step is required by RFC 1812, modern high-speed routers commonly skip it.

2. Verify the value of the Version field. Although this step is not required by RFC 791 or 1812, performing this step saves network bandwidth, as a packet containing an invalid version number is not propagated across the IPv4 internetwork only to be discarded by the destination node.

3. Decrement the value of the TTL field. If its new value is less than 1, send an ICMPv4 Time Exceeded-Time to Live Exceeded in Transit message to the source of the packet and then discard the packet. If not, place the new value in the TTL field.

4. Check for the presence of IPv4 header options. If present, process them.

5. Use the value of the Destination Address field and the contents of the local routing table to determine a forwarding interface and a next-hop IPv4 address. If a route is not found, send an ICMPv4 Destination Unreachable-Host Unreachable message to the source of the packet and discard the packet.

6. If the IPv4 MTU of the forwarding interface is less than the value of the Total Length field and the Don't Fragment (DF) flag is set to 0, perform IPv4 fragmentation. If the MTU of the forwarding interface is less than the value of the Total Length field and the DF flag is set to 1, send an ICMPv4 Destination Unreachable-Fragmentation Needed and DF Set message to the source of the packet and discard the packet.

7. Recalculate the new header checksum, and place its new value in the Header Checksum field.

8. Forward the packet by using the appropriate forwarding interface.

 Note   This critical router loop for IPv4 routers is a simplified list of items that an IPv4 router typically performs when forwarding. This list is not meant to imply any specific implementation nor an optimized order in which to process IPv4 packets for forwarding.

To forward a normal IPv6 packet, a router typically performs the following steps in its critical router loop:

1. Verify the value of the Version field. Although this step is not required by RFC 2460, performing it saves network bandwidth, because a packet containing an invalid version number is not propagated across the IPv6 internetwork only to be discarded by the destination node.

2. Decrement the value of the Hop Limit field. If its new value is less than 1, send an ICMPv6 Time Exceeded-Hop Limit Exceeded in Transit message to the source of the packet and discard the packet. If not, place the new value in the Hop Limit field.

3. Check the Next Header field for a value of 0. If it is 0, process the Hop-by-Hop Options header.

4. Use the value of the Destination Address field and the contents of the local routing table to determine a forwarding interface and a next-hop IPv6 address. If a route is not found, send an ICMPv6 Destination Unreachable-No Route To Destination message to the source of the packet and then discard the packet.

5. If the link MTU of the forwarding interface is less than 40 plus the value of the Payload Length field, send an ICMPv6 Packet Too Big message to the source of the packet and discard the packet.

6. Forward the packet by using the appropriate forwarding interface.

Note   This critical router loop for IPv6 routers is a simplified list of items that an IPv6 router typically performs when forwarding. This list is not meant to imply any specific implementation nor an optimized order in which to process packets for forwarding.

As you can see, the process to forward an IPv6 packet is much simpler than for an IPv4 packet, as it does not have to verify and recalculate a header checksum, perform fragmentation, or process options not intended for the router.

IPv6 Extension Headers

The IPv4 header includes all options. Therefore, each intermediate router must check for their existence and process them when present. This can cause performance degradation in the forwarding of IPv4 packets. With IPv6, delivery and forwarding options are moved to extension headers. The only extension header that must be processed at each intermediate router is the Hop-by-Hop Options extension header. This increases IPv6 header processing speed and improves the performance of forwarding IPv6 packets.

RFC 2460 specifies that the following IPv6 extension headers must be supported by all IPv6 nodes:

- Hop-by-Hop Options header

- Destination Options header

- Routing header

- Fragment header

- Authentication header

- Encapsulating Security Payload header

With the exception of the Authentication header and Encapsulating Security Payload header, all the IPv6 extension headers just listed are defined in RFC 2460.

In a typical IPv6 packet, no extension headers are present. If special handling is required by either intermediate routers or the destination, the sending host adds one or more extension headers.

Each extension header must fall on a 64-bit (8-byte) boundary. Extension headers of a fixed size must be an integral multiple of 8 bytes. Extension headers of variable size contain a Header Extension Length field and must use padding as needed to ensure that their size is an integral multiple of 8 bytes.

The Next Header field in the IPv6 header and zero or more extension headers form a chain of pointers. Each pointer indicates the type of header that comes after the immediate header until the upper-layer protocol is ultimately identified. Figure 4-4 shows the chain of pointers formed by the Next Header field for various IPv6 packets.

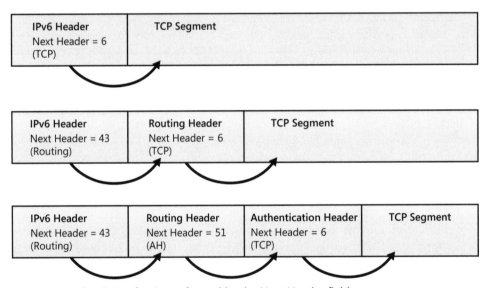

Figure 4-4   The chain of pointers formed by the Next Header field

Extension Headers Order

Extension headers are processed in the order in which they are present. Because the only extension header that is processed by every node on the path is the Hop-by-Hop Options header, it must be first. There are similar rules for other extension headers. In RFC 2460, it is recommended that extension headers be placed after the IPv6 header in the following order:

1. Hop-by-Hop Options header

2. Destination Options header (for intermediate destinations when the Routing header is present)

3. Routing header

4. Fragment header

5. Authentication header

6. Encapsulating Security Payload header

7. Destination Options header (for the final destination)

Hop-by-Hop Options Header

The Hop-by-Hop Options header is used to specify delivery parameters at each hop on the path to the destination. It is identified by the value of 0 in the IPv6 header's Next Header field. Figure 4-5 shows the structure of the Hop-by-Hop Options header.

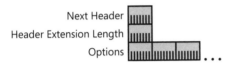

Figure 4-5   The structure of the Hop-by-Hop Options header

The Hop-by-Hop Options header consists of a Next Header field, a Header Extension Length field, and an Options field that contains one or more options. The value of the Header Extension Length field is the number of 8-byte blocks in the Hop-by-Hop Options extension header, not including the first 8 bytes. Therefore, for an 8-byte Hop-by-Hop Options header, the value of the Header Extension Length field is 0. Padding options are used to ensure 8-byte boundaries.

An IPv6 Router Optimization

The interpretation of the Header Extension Length field in the Hop-by-Hop Options header is another example of how the designers of IPv6 wanted to optimize processing of IPv6 packets at intermediate routers. For packets with a Hop-by-Hop Options header, one of the first operations is to determine the size of the header. If the Header Extension Length field were defined to be the number of 8-byte blocks in the header, its minimum value would be 1 (the minimum-sized Hop-by-Hop Options header is 8 bytes long). To ensure robustness in an IPv6 forwarding implementation, a field whose valid values begin at 1 has to be checked for the invalid value of 0 before additional processing can be done.

With the current definition of the Header Extension Length field, 0 is a valid value and no testing of invalid values needs to be done. The number of bytes in the Hop-by-Hop Options header is calculated from the following formula: (header extension length + 1) × 8.

An option is a set of fields that either describes a specific characteristic of the packet delivery or provides padding. Options are sent in the Hop-by-Hop Options header and Destination Options header (described later in this chapter). Each option is encoded in the type-length-value (TLV) format that is commonly used in TCP/IP protocols. Figure 4-6 shows the structure of an option.

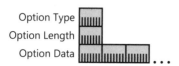

Option Type
Option Length
Option Data

Figure 4-6   The structure of an option

The Option Type field both identifies the option and determines the way it is handled by the processing node. The Option Length field indicates the number of bytes in the option, not including the Option Type and Option Length fields. The option data is the specific data associated with the option.

An option might have an alignment requirement to ensure that specific fields within the option fall on desired boundaries. For example, it is easier to process an IPv6 address if it falls on an 8-byte boundary. Alignment requirements are expressed by using the notation $xn + y$, indicating that the option must begin at a byte boundary equal to an integral multiple of x bytes plus y bytes from the start of the header. For example, the alignment requirement $4n + 2$ indicates that the option must begin at a byte boundary of (an integral multiple of 4 bytes) + 2 bytes. In other words, the option must begin at the byte boundary of 6, 10, 14, and so on, relative to the start of the Hop-by-Hop Options or Destination Options headers. To accommodate alignment requirements, padding typically appears before an option and between each option when multiple options are present.

Option Type Field

Within the Option Type field, the two high-order bits indicate how the option is handled when the node processing the option does not recognize the option type. Table 4-3 lists the defined values of these two bits and their purpose.

Table 4-3   Values of the Two High-Order Bits in the Option Type Field

Value (Binary)	Action Taken
00	Skip the option.
01	Silently discard the packet.
10	Discard the packet, and send an ICMPv6 Parameter Problem message to the sender if the Destination Address field in the IPv6 header is a unicast or multicast address.
11	Discard the packet, and send an ICMPv6 Parameter Problem message to the sender if the Destination Address field in the IPv6 header is not a multicast address.

The third-highest-order bit of the Option Type indicates whether the option data can change (= 1) or not change (= 0) in the path to the destination.

Pad1 Option

The Pad1 option is defined in RFC 2460. It is used to insert a single byte of padding so that the Hop-by-Hop Options or Destination Options headers fall on 8-byte boundaries and to accommodate the alignment requirements of options. The Pad1 option has no alignment requirements. Figure 4-7 shows the Pad1 option.

Option Type 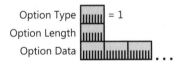 = 0

Figure 4-7   The structure of the Pad1 option

The Pad1 option consists of a single byte; Option Type is set to 0, and it has no length or value fields. With Option Type set to 0, the option is skipped if not recognized and it is not allowed to change in transit.

PadN Option

The PadN option is defined in RFC 2460. It is used to insert two or more bytes of padding so that the Hop-by-Hop Options or Destination Options headers fall on 8-byte boundaries and to accommodate the alignment requirements of options. The PadN option has no alignment requirements. Figure 4-8 shows the PadN option.

Option Type ⫿⫿⫿ = 1
Option Length ⫿⫿⫿
Option Data ⫿⫿⫿⫿⫿ . . .

Figure 4-8   The structure of the PadN option

The PadN option consists of the Option Type field (set to 1), the Length field (set to the number of padding bytes present), and 0 or more bytes of padding. With the Option Type field set to 1, the option is skipped if not recognized and it is not allowed to change in transit.

Jumbo Payload Option

The Jumbo Payload option is defined in RFC 2675. It is used to indicate a payload size that is greater than 65,535 bytes. The Jumbo Payload option has the alignment requirement of 4n + 2. Figure 4-9 shows the Jumbo Payload option.

Option Type ⫿⫿⫿ = 194
Option Length ⫿⫿⫿ = 4
Jumbo Payload Length ⫿⫿⫿⫿⫿⫿

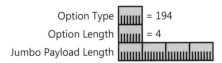

Figure 4-9   The structure of the Jumbo Payload option

With the Jumbo Payload option, the Payload Length field in the IPv6 header no longer indicates the size of the IPv6 packet payload. Instead, the Jumbo Payload Length field in the Jumbo Payload option indicates the size, in bytes, of the IPv6 packet payload. With a 32-bit Jumbo Payload Length field, payload sizes of up to 4,294,967,295 bytes can be indicated. An IPv6 packet with a payload size greater than 65,535 bytes is known as a *jumbogram*. With the Option Type field set to 194 (0xC2 hexadecimal, binary 11000010), the packet is discarded and an ICMPv6 Parameter Problem message is sent if the option is not recognized and the destination address is not a multicast address, and the option is not allowed to change in transit.

The IPv6 protocol in Windows Vista, Windows Server 2008, and Windows XP with Service Pack 2 supports incoming jumbograms at the IPv6 layer. However, there is no support in UDP or TCP for sending or receiving jumbograms.

Router Alert Option

The Router Alert option (Option Type 5) is defined in RFC 2711 and is used to indicate to a router that the contents of the packet require additional processing. The Router Alert option has the alignment requirement of 2n + 0. Figure 4-10 shows the structure of the Router Alert option.

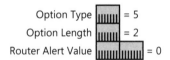

Option Type = 5
Option Length = 2
Router Alert Value = 0

Figure 4-10   The structure of the Router Alert option

The Router Alert option is used for Multicast Listener Discovery (MLD) and the Resource ReSerVation Protocol (RSVP). With the Option Type field set to 5, the option is skipped if not recognized and it is not allowed to change in transit.

Network Monitor Capture

Here is an example of a Hop-by-Hop Options header as displayed by Network Monitor 3.1 (capture 04_02 in the \NetworkMonitorCaptures folder on the companion CD-ROM):

```
Frame:
+ Ethernet: Etype = IPv6
- Ipv6: Next Protocol = ICMPv6, Payload Length = 32
  + Versions: IPv6, Internet Protocol, DSCP 0
    PayloadLength: 32 (0x20)
    NextProtocol: HOPOPT, IPv6 Hop-by-Hop Option, 0(0)
    HopLimit: 1 (0x1)
    SourceAddress: FE80:0:0:0:2B0:D0FF:FEE9:4143
    DestinationAddress: FF02:0:0:0:0:1:FFE9:4143
  - HopbyHopHeader:
    NextHeader: ICMPv6
    ExtHdrLen: 0(8 bytes)
  - OptionRouterAlert:
    - OptionType: Router Alert
      Action:      (00......) Skip over this option
```

```
   C:            (..0.....) Option Data does not change en-route
   OptionType: (...00101) Router Alert
   OptDataLen: 2 bytes
   Value: Datagram contains a Multicast Listener Discovery message, 0 (0x0)
 - OptionPadN:
  - OptionType: PadN
    Action:       (00......) Skip over this option
    C:            (..0.....) Option Data does not change en-route
    OptionType: (...00001) PadN
    OptDataLen: 0 bytes
    OptionData: 0 bytes
+ Icmpv6: Multicast Listener Report
```

Notice the use of the Router Alert option (option type 5) and the PadN option (option type 1) to pad the entire Hop-by-Hop Options header to 8 bytes (1-byte Next Header field + 1-byte Option Length field + 4-byte Router Alert option + 2-byte PadN option).

Destination Options Header

The Destination Options header is used to specify packet delivery parameters for either intermediate destinations or the final destination. This header is identified by the value of 60 in the previous header's Next Header field. The Destination Options header has the same structure as the Hop-by-Hop Options header, as shown in Figure 4-11.

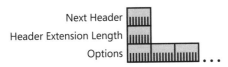

Figure 4-11   The structure of the Destination Options header

The Destination Options header is used in two ways:

1. If a Routing header is present, it specifies delivery or processing options at each intermediate destination. In this case, the Destination Options header occurs before the Routing header.

2. If no Routing header is present, or if this header occurs after the Routing header, this header specifies delivery or processing options at the final destination.

An example of a destination option is the Home Address destination option for Mobile IPv6.

Home Address Option

The Home Address destination option (Option Type 201) is defined in RFC 3775 and is used to indicate the home address of the mobile node. The home address is an address assigned to the mobile node when it is attached to the home link and through which the mobile node is always reachable, regardless of its location on an IPv6 network. For information about when the Home Address option is sent, see Appendix F, "Mobile IPv6." The Home Address option has the alignment requirement of 8n + 6. Figure 4-12 shows the structure of the Home Address option.

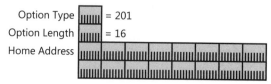

Option Type = 201
Option Length = 16
Home Address

Figure 4-12 The structure of the Home Address option

The following list describes the fields in the Home Address option:

- **Option Type** With the Option Type field set to 201 (0xC9 hexadecimal, 11001001 binary), the packet is discarded and an ICMPv6 Parameter Problem message is sent if the option is not recognized and the destination address is not a multicast address, and the option is not allowed to change in transit.

- **Option Length** The Option Length field indicates the length of the option in bytes, not including the Option Type and Option Length fields. Because the only field past the Option Length field is the Home Address field to store an IPv6 address, the Option Length field is set to 16.

- **Home Address** The Home Address field indicates the home address of the mobile node. The size of this field is 128 bits.

For an example of the Home Address option in the Destination Options header, see the Network Monitor Capture 04_03 in the \NetworkMonitorCaptures folder on the companion CD-ROM.

Summary of Option Types

Table 4-4 lists the different option types for options in Hop-by-Hop Options and Destination Options headers.

Table 4-4 Option Types

Option Type	Option and Where It Is Used	Alignment Requirement
0	Pad1 option: Hop-by-Hop and Destination Options headers	None
1	PadN option: Hop-by-Hop and Destination Options headers	None
194 (0xC2)	Jumbo Payload option: Hop-by-Hop Options header	4n + 2
5	Router Alert option: Hop-by-Hop Options header	2n + 0
201 (0xC9)	Home Address option: Destination Options header	8n + 6

Routing Header

IPv4 defines strict source routing, in which each intermediate destination must be only one hop away, and loose source routing, in which each intermediate destination can be one or more hops away. IPv6 source nodes can use the Routing header to specify a source route, which is a list of intermediate destinations for the packet to travel to on its path to the final destination. The Routing header is identified by the value of 43 in the previous header's Next Header field. Figure 4-13 shows the structure of the Routing header.

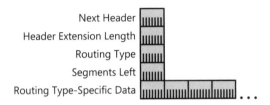

Figure 4-13   The structure of the Routing header

The Routing header consists of a Next Header field, a Header Extension Length field (defined in the same way as the Hop-by-Hop Options extension header), a Routing Type field, a Segments Left field that indicates the number of intermediate destinations that are still to be visited, and routing type-specific data.

RFC 2460 also defines Routing Type 0, used for loose source routing. Figure 4-14 shows the structure of the Routing Type 0 header.

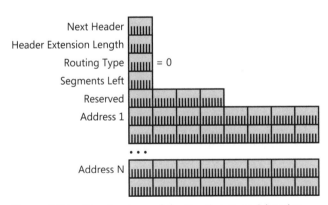

Figure 4-14   The structure of the Routing Type 0 header

For Routing Type 0, the routing type-specific data consists of a 32-bit Reserved field and a list of intermediate destination addresses, including the final destination address. When the packet is initially sent, the destination address is set to the first intermediate destination, and the routing type-specific data is the list of additional intermediate destinations and the final destination. The Segments Left field is set to the total number of addresses included in the routing type-specific data.

When the IPv6 packet reaches an intermediate destination, the Routing header is processed and the following actions are taken:

1. The current destination address and the address in the (N – Segments Left + 1) position in the list of addresses are swapped, where N is the total number of addresses in the Routing header.

2. The Segments Left field is decremented.

3. The packet is forwarded.

By the time the packet arrives at the final destination, the Segments Left field has been set to 0 and the list of intermediate addresses visited in the path to the destination is recorded in the Routing header.

IPv6 in Windows Vista will accept and process an incoming packet with a Routing Type 0 header. Because of security concerns, the Internet Engineering Task Force (IETF) is deprecating support for the Routing Type 0 header. IPv6 in Windows Server 2008 and Windows Vista Service Pack 1 will silently discard an incoming packet with a Routing Type 0 header.

Note   Mobile IPv6 uses a Type 2 Routing header. For more information, see Appendix F, "Mobile IPv6."

Network Monitor Capture

Here is an example of the Routing header as displayed by Network Monitor 3.1 (capture 04_04 in the \NetworkMonitorCaptures folder on the companion CD-ROM):

```
 Frame:
+ Ethernet: Etype = IPv6
- Ipv6: Next Protocol = ICMPv6, Payload Length = 64
  + Versions: IPv6, Internet Protocol, DSCP 0
    PayloadLength: 64 (0x40)
    NextProtocol: IPv6 Routing header, 43(0x2b)
    HopLimit: 127 (0x7F)
    SourceAddress: FEC0:0:0:2:2B0:D0FF:FEE9:4143
    DestinationAddress: FEC0:0:0:2:260:97FF:FE02:6E8F
  - RoutingHeader:
    NextHeader: ICMPv6
    ExtHdrLen: 2(24 bytes)
    RoutingType: 0 (0x0)
    SegmentsLeft: 1 (0x1)
    Reserved: 0 (0x0)
    RouteAddress: FEC0:0:0:1:260:8FF:FE52:F9D8
+ Icmpv6: Echo request, ID = 0x0, Seq = 0x3d1a
```

In this simple example of the Routing header, an ICMPv6 Echo Request message is sent from the source FEC0::2:2B0:D0FF:FEE9:4143 to the destination FEC0::1:260:8FF:FE52:F9D8 using the intermediate destination of FEC0::2:260:97FF:FE02:6E8F.

Fragment Header

The Fragment header is used for IPv6 fragmentation and reassembly services. This header is identified by the value of 44 in the previous header's Next Header field. Figure 4-15 shows the structure of the Fragment header.

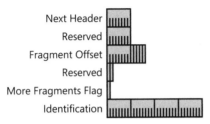

Figure 4-15   The structure of the Fragment header

The Fragment header includes a Next Header field, a 13-bit Fragment Offset field, a More Fragments flag, and a 32-bit Identification field. The Fragment Offset, More Fragments flag, and Identification fields are used in the same way as the corresponding fields in the IPv4 header. Because the use of the Fragment Offset field is defined for 8-byte fragment blocks, the Fragment header cannot be used for jumbograms. The maximum number that can be expressed with the 13-bit Fragment Offset field is 8191. Therefore, Fragment Offset can be used to indicate only a fragment data starting position of up to 8191 × 8, or 65,528.

In IPv6, only source nodes can fragment payloads. If the payload submitted by the upper-layer protocol is larger than the link or path MTU, IPv6 fragments the payload at the source and uses the Fragment header to provide reassembly information. An IPv6 router will never fragment an IPv6 packet being forwarded.

Because the IPv6 internetwork will not transparently fragment payloads, data sent from applications that do not have an awareness of the destination path MTU will not be able to sense when data needing fragmentation by the source is discarded by IPv6 routers. This can be a problem for unicast or multicast traffic sent as a UDP message or other types of message streams that do not use TCP.

Differences in Fragmentation Fields

There are some subtle differences between the fragmentation fields in IPv4 and IPv6. In IPv4, the fragmentation flags are the three high-order bits of the 16-bit quantity composed of the combination of the fragmentation flags and the Fragment Offset field. In IPv6, the bits used for fragmentation flags are the three low-order bits of the 16-bit quantity composed of the combination of the fragmentation flags and the Fragment Offset field. In IPv4, the Identification field is 16 bits rather than 32 bits in IPv6, and in IPv6 there is no Don't Fragment flag. Because IPv6 routers never perform fragmentation, the Don't Fragment flag is always set to 1 for all IPv6 packets and therefore does not need to be included.

IPv6 Fragmentation Process

When an IPv6 packet is fragmented, it is initially divided into unfragmentable and fragmentable parts:

- The unfragmentable part of the original IPv6 packet must be processed by intermediate nodes between the fragmenting node and the destination. This part consists of the IPv6 header, the Hop-by-Hop Options header, the Destination Options header for intermediate destinations, and the Routing header.

- The fragmentable part of the original IPv6 packet must be processed only at the final destination node. This part consists of the Authentication header, the Encapsulating Security Payload header, the Destination Options header for the final destination, and the upper-layer PDU.

Next, the IPv6 fragment packets are formed. Each fragment packet consists of the unfragmentable part, a fragment header, and a portion of the fragmentable part. Figure 4-16 shows the IPv6 fragmentation process for a packet fragmented into three fragments.

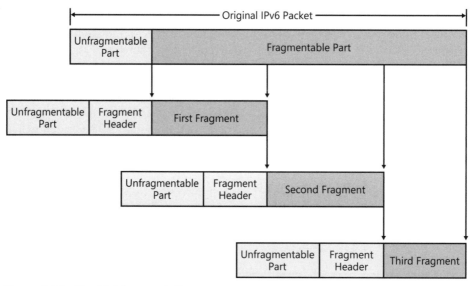

Figure 4-16   The IPv6 fragmentation process

In each fragment, the Next Header field in the Fragment header indicates the first header or the upper-layer protocol in the original fragmentable part. The Fragment Offset field in the Fragment header indicates the offset, in 8-byte units known as *fragment blocks*, of this fragment relative to the original payload. The More Fragments flag is set on all fragment packets except the last fragment packet. All fragment packets created from the same IPv6 packet must contain the same Identification field value.

Fragmentation of IPv6 packets can occur when the upper-layer protocol of the sending host submits a packet to IPv6 that is larger than the path MTU to the destination. Examples of IPv6 fragmentation are when a UDP application that is not aware of a path MTU sends large packets to a destination, or when a TCP application sends a packet before it is made aware of a path MTU update that lowers the path MTU. In this latter case, IPv6 is aware of the new path MTU, but TCP is not. TCP submits the TCP segment by using the old, larger value of the path MTU, and IPv6 fragments the TCP segment to fit the new, lower path MTU value. Once TCP is made aware of the new path MTU, subsequent TCP segments are not fragmented.

IPv6 packets sent to IPv4 destinations that undergo IPv6-to-IPv4 header translation might receive a path MTU update of less than 1280. In this case, the sending host sends IPv6 packets with a Fragment header in which the Fragment Offset field is set to 0 and the More Fragments flag is not set, and with a smaller payload size of 1272 bytes. The Fragment header is included so that the IPv6-to-IPv4 translator can use the Identification field in the Fragment header to perform IPv4 fragmentation to reach the IPv4 destination.

Network Monitor Capture

Here is an example of a Fragment header as displayed by Network Monitor 3.1 (frame 3 of capture 04_05 in the \NetworkMonitorCaptures folder on the companion CD-ROM):

```
  Frame:
+ Ethernet: Etype = IPv6
- Ipv6: Next Protocol = ICMPv6, Payload Length = 1456
  + Versions: IPv6, Internet Protocol, DSCP 0
    PayloadLength: 1456 (0x5B0)
    NextProtocol: IPv6 Fragment header, 44(0x2c)
    HopLimit: 128 (0x80)
    SourceAddress: FE80:0:0:0:210:5AFF:FEAA:20A2
    DestinationAddress: FE80:0:0:0:250:DAFF:FED8:C153
  - FragmentHeader:
    NextHeader: ICMPv6
    Reserved: 0 (0x0)
  - FragmentInfor:
    FragmentOffset: 2896(0XB50)
    Reserved: (.............00.)
    M:         (..............1) More fragments
    Identification: 5 (0x5)
    FragmentData: Binary Large Object (1448 Bytes)
```

This is a fragment of a payload that uses the identification number of 5 and starts in byte position 2896 relative to the fragmentable portion of the original IPv6 payload.

IPv6 Reassembly Process

The fragment packets are forwarded by the intermediate IPv6 router or routers to the destination IPv6 address. The fragment packets can take different paths to the destination and arrive in a different order from which they were sent. To reassemble the fragment packets into the original payload, IPv6 uses the Source Address and Destination Address fields in the IPv6 header and the Identification field in the Fragment header to group the fragments. Figure 4-17 shows the IPv6 reassembly process.

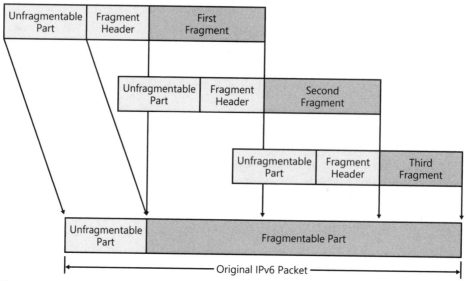

Figure 4-17   The IPv6 reassembly process

After all the fragments arrive, the original payload length is calculated and the Payload Length field in the IPv6 header for the reassembled packet is updated. Additionally, the Next Header field of the last header of the unfragmentable part is set to the Next Header field of the Fragment header of the first fragment.

RFC 2460 recommends a reassembly time of 60 seconds before abandoning reassembly and discarding the partially reassembled packet. If the first fragment has arrived and reassembly has not completed, the reassembling host sends an ICMPv6 Time Exceeded-Fragment Reassembly Time Exceeded message to the source of the fragment.

Authentication Header

The Authentication header provides data authentication (verification of the node that sent the packet), data integrity (verification that the data was not modified in transit), and antireplay protection (assurance that captured packets cannot be retransmitted and accepted as valid data) for the IPv6 packet including the fields in the IPv6 header that do not change in transit across an IPv6 internetwork. The Authentication header, described in RFC 2402, is part of the security architecture for IP, as defined in RFC 2401. The Authentication header is identified by the value of 51 in the previous header's Next Header field. Figure 4-18 shows the structure of the Authentication header.

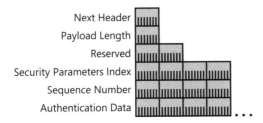

Figure 4-18   The structure of the Authentication header

The Authentication header contains a Next Header field, a Payload Length field (the number of 4-byte blocks in the Authentication header, not counting the first two), a Reserved field, a Security Parameters Index (SPI) field that helps identify a specific IP Security (IPsec) security association (SA), a Sequence Number field that provides antireplay protection, and an Authentication Data field that contains an integrity value check (ICV). The ICV provides data authentication and data integrity.

The Authentication header does not provide data confidentiality services for the upper-layer PDU by encrypting the data so that it cannot be viewed without the encryption key. To obtain data authentication and data integrity for the entire IPv6 packet and data confidentiality for the upper-layer PDU, you can use both the Authentication header and the Encapsulating Security Payload header and trailer.

Encapsulating Security Payload Header and Trailer

The Encapsulating Security Payload (ESP) header and trailer, described in RFC 2406, provide data confidentiality, data authentication, data integrity, and replay protection services to the encapsulated payload. The ESP header provides no security services for the IPv6 header or extension headers that occur before the ESP header. The ESP header and trailer are identified by the value of 50 in the previous header's Next Header field. Figure 4-19 shows the structure of the ESP header and trailer.

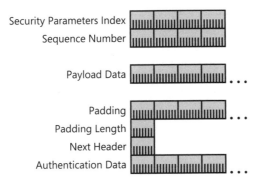

Figure 4-19   The structure of the Encapsulating Security Payload header and trailer

The ESP header contains an SPI field that helps identify the IPsec SA, and a Sequence Number field that provides antireplay protection. The ESP trailer contains the Padding, Padding Length, Next Header, and Authentication Data fields. The Padding field is used to ensure 4-byte boundaries for the ESP payload and appropriate data-block boundaries for encryption algorithms. The Padding Length field indicates the size of the Padding field in bytes. The Authentication Data field contains the ICV.

Details about how the ESP header and trailer provide data confidentiality, authentication, and integrity through cryptographic techniques are beyond the scope of this book.

IPv6 MTU

IPv6 requires that the link layer support a minimum MTU size of 1280 bytes. Link layers that do not support this MTU size must provide a link-layer fragmentation and reassembly scheme that is transparent to IPv6. For link layers that can support a configurable MTU size, RFC 2460 recommends that they be configured with an MTU size of at least 1500 bytes (the IPv6 MTU for Ethernet II encapsulation). An example of a configurable MTU is the Maximum Receive Unit (MRU) of a Point-to-Point Protocol (PPP) link.

Like IPv4, IPv6 provides a Path MTU Discovery process that uses the ICMPv6 Packet Too Big message described in the "Path MTU Discovery" section of Chapter 5, "ICMPv6." Path MTU Discovery allows the transmission of IPv6 packets that are larger than 1280 bytes.

IPv6 source hosts can fragment payloads of upper-layer protocols that are larger than the path MTU by using the process and Fragment header previously described. However, the use of IPv6 fragmentation is highly discouraged. An IPv6 node must be able to reassemble a fragmented packet that is at least 1500 bytes in size.

Table 4-5 lists commonly used local area network (LAN) and wide area network (WAN) technologies and their defined IPv6 MTUs.

Table 4-5   IPv6 MTUs for Common LAN and WAN Technologies

LAN or WAN Technology	IPv6 MTU
Ethernet (Ethernet II encapsulation)	1500
Ethernet (IEEE 802.3 SubNetwork Access Protocol [SNAP] encapsulation)	1492
IEEE 802.11	2312
Token Ring	Varies
Fiber Distributed Data Interface (FDDI)	4352
Attached Resource Computer Network (ARCNet)	9072
PPP	1500
X.25	1280
Frame Relay	1592
Asynchronous Transfer Mode (ATM) (Null or SNAP encapsulation)	9180

For more information about LAN and WAN encapsulations for IPv6 packets, see Appendix A, "Link-Layer Support for IPv6."

Upper-Layer Checksums

The current implementation of TCP, UDP, and ICMP for IPv4 incorporates into their checksum calculation a pseudo-header that includes both the IPv4 Source Address and Destination Address fields. This checksum calculation must be modified for TCP, UDP, and ICMPv6 traffic sent over IPv6 to include IPv6 addresses. Figure 4-20 shows the structure of the new IPv6 pseudo-header that must be used by TCP, UDP, and ICMPv6 checksum calculations. IPv6 uses the same algorithm as IPv4 for computing the checksum value.

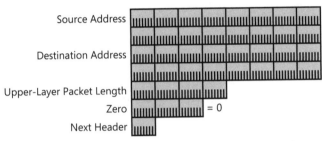

Figure 4-20   The structure of the new IPv6 pseudo-header

The IPv6 pseudo-header includes the Source Address field, the Destination Address field, an Upper Layer Packet Length field that indicates the length of the upper-layer PDU, and a Next Header field that indicates the upper-layer protocol for which the checksum is being calculated.

References

The following references were cited in this chapter:

- RFC 791 – "Internet Protocol"
- RFC 1812 – "Requirements for IP Version 4 Routers"
- RFC 2401 – "Security Architecture for the Internet Protocol"
- RFC 2402 – "IP Authentication Header"
- RFC 2406 – "IP Encapsulating Security Payload (ESP)"
- RFC 2460 – "Internet Protocol, Version 6 (IPv6)"
- RFC 2474 – "Definition of the Differentiated Services Field (DS Field)"
- RFC 2675 – "IPv6 Jumbograms"
- RFC 2711 – "IPv6 Router Alert Option"

- RFC 3168 – "The Addition of Explicit Congestion Notification (ECN) to IP"
- RFC 3697 – "IPv6 Flow Label Specification"
- RFC 3775 – "Mobility Support in IPv6"

You can obtain these RFCs from the \RFCs_and_Drafts folder on the companion CD-ROM or from *http://www.ietf.org/rfc.html.*

Testing for Understanding

To test your understanding of the IPv6 header, answer the following questions. See Appendix D, "Testing for Understanding Answers," to check your answers.

1. Why does the IPv6 header not include a checksum?

2. What is the IPv6 equivalent to the IHL field in the IPv4 header?

3. How does the combination of the Traffic Class and Flow Label fields provide better support for prioritized traffic delivery?

4. Which extension headers are fragmentable and why? Which extension headers are not fragmentable and why?

5. Describe a situation that results in an IPv6 packet that contains a Fragment Header in which the Fragment Offset field is set to 0 and the More Fragments flag is not set to 1.

6. Describe how the new upper-layer checksum calculation affects transport layer protocols such as TCP and UDP.

7. If the minimum MTU for IPv6 packets is 1280 bytes, how are 1280-byte packets sent on a link that supports only 512-byte frames?

Chapter 5
ICMPv6

At the end of this chapter, you should be able to do the following:

- Explain the purpose of ICMPv6 and the common structure of all ICMPv6 messages.
- Describe the two types of ICMPv6 messages and how to distinguish them.
- Define the four types of ICMPv6 error messages.
- Explain the two types of ICMPv6 informational messages used for diagnostics.
- Enumerate the common ICMPv4 messages, and give their ICMPv6 equivalents.
- Describe the path MTU discovery process for IPv6.

ICMPv6 Overview

Like IPv4, the specification for the Internet Protocol version 6 (IPv6) header and extension headers does not provide facilities for reporting errors. Instead, IPv6 uses an updated version of the Internet Control Message Protocol (ICMP) named ICMP version 6 (ICMPv6). ICMPv6 has the common IPv4 ICMP functions of reporting delivery and forwarding errors and providing a simple echo service for troubleshooting. ICMPv6 is defined in RFC 4443 and is required for an IPv6 implementation.

The ICMPv6 protocol also provides a packet structure framework for the following:

- **Neighbor Discovery**   Neighbor Discovery (ND) is a series of five ICMPv6 messages that manage node-to-node communication on a link. ND replaces Address Resolution Protocol (ARP), ICMPv4 Router Discovery, and the ICMPv4 Redirect message. ND is described in more detail in Chapter 6, "Neighbor Discovery."

- **Multicast Listener Discovery**   Multicast Listener Discovery (MLD) is a series of three ICMPv6 messages that are equivalent to the Internet Group Management Protocol (IGMP) for IPv4 for managing subnet multicast membership. MLD is described in more detail in Chapter 7, "Multicast Listener Discovery (MLD) and MLD Version 2 (MLDv2)."

ICMPv6 is also used by other protocols, such as Secure Neighbor Discovery (SEND). SEND is not supported by IPv6 for Windows Vista and Windows Server 2008 and is not described in this chapter.

> **Note**   RFC 4884 describes changes to ICMPv6 to support multipart messages. These changes are not supported by IPv6 for Windows Vista and Windows Server 2008 and are not described in this chapter.

Types of ICMPv6 Messages

There are two types of ICMPv6 messages:

- **Error messages**   Error messages report errors in the forwarding or delivery of IPv6 packets by either the destination node or an intermediate router. The high-order bit of the 8-bit Type field for all ICMPv6 error messages is set to 0. Therefore, valid values for the Type field for ICMPv6 error messages are in the range of 0 through 127. ICMPv6 error messages include Destination Unreachable, Packet Too Big, Time Exceeded, and Parameter Problem.

- **Informational messages**   Informational messages provide diagnostic functions and additional host functionality, such as MLD and ND. The high-order bit of the 8-bit Type field for all ICMPv6 informational messages is set to 1. Therefore, valid values for the Type field for ICMPv6 information messages are in the range of 128 through 255. ICMPv6 informational messages described in RFC 4443 include Echo Request and Echo Reply. There are additional ICMPv6 informational messages defined for Mobile IPv6. For more information, see Appendix F, "Mobile IPv6."

ICMPv6 Header

An ICMPv6 header is identified by a Next Header value of 58 in the header immediately preceding it. Figure 5-1 shows the structure of ICMPv6 messages.

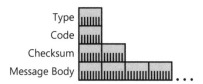

Figure 5-1   The structure of ICMPv6 messages

The following list describes the fields in the ICMPv6 header:

- **Type**   Indicates the type of ICMPv6 message. The size of this field is 8 bits. In ICMPv6 error messages, the high-order bit is set to 0. In ICMPv6 informational messages, the high-order bit is set to 1.

- **Code**   Differentiates among multiple messages within a given message type. The size of this field is 8 bits. For the first, or only, message for a given type, the value of the Code field is 0.

- **Checksum**   Stores a checksum of the ICMPv6 message. The size of this field is 16 bits. The IPv6 pseudo-header is added to the front of the ICMPv6 message when calculating the checksum. For more information about the IPv6 pseudo-header, see "Upper-Layer Checksums" in Chapter 4, "The IPv6 Header."

- **Message body**   Contains ICMPv6 message-specific data.

ICMPv6 Error Messages

ICMPv6 error messages report forwarding or delivery errors by either a router or the destination host, and they consist of the following messages:

- Destination Unreachable (ICMPv6 Type 1)

- Packet Too Big (ICMPv6 Type 2)

- Time Exceeded (ICMPv6 Type 3)

- Parameter Problem (ICMPv6 Type 4)

To conserve network bandwidth, ICMPv6 error messages are not sent for every error encountered. Instead, ICMPv6 error messages are rate limited. Although not required by RFC 4443, the recommended method for rate limiting ICMPv6 error messages is known as *token bucket*. There is an average rate of transmission of ICMPv6 error messages that cannot be exceeded. The rate of transmission can be based on a number of ICMPv6 error messages per second or a specified percentage of a link's bandwidth. However, to better handle error notification for bursty traffic, the node can send a number of messages in a burst, provided the number of messages in the burst does not exceed the overall transmission rate.

Destination Unreachable

A router or a destination host sends an ICMPv6 Destination Unreachable message when the packet cannot be forwarded to the destination node or upper-layer protocol. Figure 5-2 shows the structure of the Destination Unreachable message.

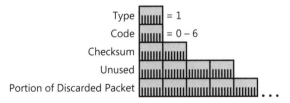

Figure 5-2   The structure of the Destination Unreachable message

In the Destination Unreachable message, the Type field is set to 1 and the Code field is set to a value in the range of 0 through 6. Following the Checksum field is a 32-bit Unused field and the leading portion of the discarded packet, sized so that the entire IPv6 packet containing the ICMPv6 message is no larger than 1280 bytes (the minimum IPv6 MTU). The number of bytes of the discarded packet included in the message varies if there are IPv6 extension headers present. For an ICMPv6 message without extension headers, up to 1232 bytes of the discarded packet are included (1280 less a 40-byte IPv6 header and an 8-byte ICMPv6 Destination Unreachable header).

Table 5-1 lists the value of the Code field for the various Destination Unreachable messages as defined in RFC 4443.

Table 5-1 ICMPv6 Destination Unreachable Messages

Code Field Value	Description
0 - No Route to Destination	No route matching the destination was found in the routing table.
1 - Communication with Destination Administratively Prohibited	The communication with the destination is prohibited by administrative policy. This is typically sent when the packet is discarded by a firewall.
2 - Beyond Scope of Source Address	The destination is beyond the scope of the source address. A router sends this when the packet must be forwarded using an interface that is not within the scoped zone of the source address.
3 - Address Unreachable	The destination address is unreachable. This is typically sent by a router because of an inability to resolve the destination's link-layer address.
4 - Port Unreachable	The destination port was unreachable. This is typically sent when an IPv6 packet containing a UDP message arrived at the destination but there were no applications listening on the destination UDP port.
5 - Source Address Failed Ingress/Egress Policy	The packet with this source address is not allowed because of inbound (ingress) or outbound (egress) packet-filtering policies.
6 - Reject Route to Destination	The packet matched a reject route and was discarded. A reject route is an address prefix configured on a router for traffic that the router must immediately discard.

Network Monitor Capture

Here is an example of a Destination Unreachable-No Route to Destination message as displayed by Network Monitor 3.1 (frame 1 of capture 05_01 in the \NetworkMonitor-Captures folder on the companion CD-ROM):

```
Frame:
+ Ethernet: Etype = IPv6
- Ipv6: Next Protocol = ICMPv6, Payload Length = 88
  + Versions: IPv6, Internet Protocol, DSCP 0
    PayloadLength: 88 (0x58)
    NextProtocol: ICMPv6, 58(0x3a)
    HopLimit: 128 (0x80)
    SourceAddress: 2001:DB8:0:2:201:2FF:FE44:87D1
    DestinationAddress: 2001:DB8:0:2:260:97FF:FE02:6E8F
- Icmpv6: Destination unreachable
    MessageType: Destination unreachable, 1(0x1)
  - DestUnreachable:
    Code: No route to destination, 0(0)
    Checksum: 6328 (0x18B8)
```

```
    Unused: 0 (0x0)
  - InvokingPacket: Next Protocol = ICMPv6, Payload Length = 40
  + Versions: IPv6, Internet Protocol, DSCP 0
    PayloadLength: 40 (0x28)
    NextProtocol: ICMPv6, 58(0x3a)
    HopLimit: 128 (0x80)
    SourceAddress: 2001:DB8:0:2:260:97FF:FE02:6E8F
    DestinationAddress: 2001:DB8:0:91:260:8FF:FE52:F9D8
    OriginalIPPayload: Binary Large Object (40 Bytes)
```

Packet Too Big

A router sends an ICMPv6 Packet Too Big message when the packet cannot be forwarded because the link MTU on the forwarding interface of the router is smaller than the size of the IPv6 packet. Figure 5-3 shows the structure of the Packet Too Big message.

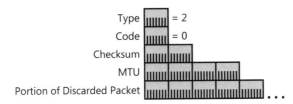

Figure 5-3   The structure of the Packet Too Big message

In the Packet Too Big message, the Type field is set to 2 and the Code field is set to 0. Following the Checksum field is a 32-bit MTU field that stores the link MTU of the interface over which the packet was being forwarded. Next is the leading portion of the discarded packet, sized so that the entire IPv6 packet containing the ICMPv6 message is no larger than 1280 bytes. The Packet Too Big message is used for the IPv6 Path MTU Discovery process described in the "Path MTU Discovery" section of this chapter.

Network Monitor Capture

Here is an example of a Packet Too Big message as displayed by Network Monitor 3.1 (frame 2 of capture 05_02 in the \NetworkMonitorCaptures folder on the companion CD-ROM):

```
  Frame:
+ Ethernet: Etype = IPv6
- Ipv6: Next Protocol = ICMPv6, Payload Length = 1240
  + Versions: IPv6, Internet Protocol, DSCP 0
    PayloadLength: 1240 (0x4D8)
    NextProtocol: ICMPv6, 58(0x3a)
    HopLimit: 64 (0x40)
    SourceAddress: FEC0:0:0:F282:201:2FF:FE44:87D1
    DestinationAddress: FEC0:0:0:F282:2B0:D0FF:FEE9:4143
- Icmpv6: Packet too big
    MessageType: Packet too big, 2(0x2)
  - PacketTooBig:
    Code: 0 (0x0)
    Checksum: 44349 (0xAD3D)
```

```
    MTU: 1280 (0x500)
  - InvokingPacket: Next Protocol = ICMPv6, Payload Length = 1460
   + Versions: IPv6, Internet Protocol, DSCP 0
     PayloadLength: 1460 (0x5B4)
     NextProtocol: ICMPv6, 58(0x3a)
     HopLimit: 63 (0x3F)
     SourceAddress: FEC0:0:0:F282:2B0:D0FF:FEE9:4143
     DestinationAddress: FEC0:0:0:0:0:0:0:1
     OriginalIPPayload: Binary Large Object (1192 Bytes)
```

This message was sent by a router attempting to forward a 1500-byte Echo Request message over an interface that supported only a 1280-byte IPv6 MTU.

Time Exceeded

A router typically sends an ICMPv6 Time Exceeded message when the Hop Limit field in the IPv6 header becomes zero after decrementing its value during the forwarding process. Figure 5-4 shows the structure of the Time Exceeded message.

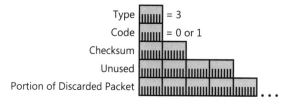

Figure 5-4   The structure of the Time Exceeded message

In the Time Exceeded message, the Type field is set to 3 and the Code field is set to the following:

■ 0 (Hop Limit Exceeded in Transit) by a router when the Hop Limit field in the IPv6 header is decremented to 0, or in the rare instance when the value of the Hop Limit field in the IPv6 header of an arriving packet is 0.

■ 1 (Fragment Reassembly Time Exceeded) by a host when the fragmentation reassembly time of the destination host expires. RFC 2460 specifies a reassembly time of 60 seconds.

Following the Checksum field is a 32-bit Unused field and the leading portion of the discarded packet, sized so that the entire IPv6 packet containing the ICMPv6 message is no larger than 1280 bytes.

The receipt of a Time Exceeded-Hop Limit Exceeded in Transit message indicates that either the value of the Hop Limit field of outgoing packets is not large enough to reach the destination or that a routing loop exists. A recommended value for the Hop Limit field set by the sending node is twice the diameter of the network, where the diameter is the maximum number of links between the farthest ends of the network. A routing loop is a condition on a network in which packets are forwarded in a loop between two or more routers.

Parameter Problem

A router or the destination sends an ICMPv6 Parameter Problem message when there is an error in the IPv6 header or an extension header that prevents IPv6 from performing additional processing. Figure 5-5 shows the structure of the Parameter Problem message.

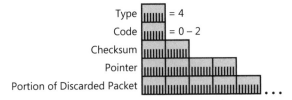

Figure 5-5   The structure of the Parameter Problem message

In the Parameter Problem message, the Type field is set to 4 and the Code field has a value in the range of 0 through 2. Following the Checksum field is the 32-bit Pointer field that indicates the byte offset (starting at 0) in the IPv6 packet at which the error was encountered. Following the Pointer field is the leading portion of the discarded packet, sized so that the entire ICMPv6 message is no larger than 1280 bytes. The Pointer field value is set to the correct offset even when the location of the error is not within the portion of the discarded packet.

Table 5-2 shows the Code field values for Parameter Problem messages.

Table 5-2   ICMPv6 Parameter Problem Messages

Code Field Value	Description
0 - Erroneous Header Field Encountered	An error in a field within the IPv6 header or an extension header was encountered.
1 - Unrecognized Next Header Type Encountered	An unrecognized Next Header field value was encountered. This is equivalent to the ICMPv4 Destination Unreachable-Protocol Unreachable message.
2 - Unrecognized IPv6 Option Encountered	An unrecognized IPv6 option was encountered.

The Parameter Problem-Unrecognized IPv6 Option Encountered message is used when both of the following are true:

- An option in a Hop-by-Hop Options header or a Destination Options header is not recognized.

- Within the option's Option Type field, the two high-order bits are set to either 10 (binary) or 11 (binary).

For more information about the Option Type field, see the "Hop-by-Hop Options Header" section in Chapter 4.

ICMPv6 Informational Messages

The ICMPv6 informational messages defined in RFC 4443 provide a simple diagnostic capability to aid in troubleshooting and consist of the following messages:

- Echo Request (ICMPv6 Type 128)
- Echo Reply (ICMPv6 Type 129)

Additional ICMPv6 informational messages are used for ND and MLD. For more information, see Chapter 6 and Chapter 7.

Echo Request

An IPv6 node sends an ICMPv6 Echo Request message to a destination to solicit an immediate Echo Reply message. The Echo Request/Echo Reply message facility provides a simple diagnostic function to aid in the troubleshooting of a variety of reachability and routing problems. Figure 5-6 shows the structure of the Echo Request message.

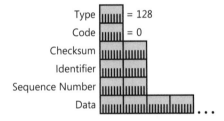

Figure 5-6   The structure of the Echo Request message

In the Echo Request message, the Type field is set to 128 and the Code field is set to 0. Following the Checksum field are the 16-bit Identifier and 16-bit Sequence Number fields. The Identifier and Sequence Number fields are set by the sending host so that they can be used to match an incoming Echo Reply message with a sent Echo Request message. The Data field is zero or more bytes of optional data that is also set by the sending host.

Network Monitor Capture

Here is an example of an Echo Request message as displayed by Network Monitor 3.1 (frame 1 of capture 05_03 in the \NetworkMonitorCaptures folder on the companion CD-ROM):

```
Frame:
+ Ethernet: Etype = IPv6
- Ipv6: Next Protocol = ICMPv6, Payload Length = 40
  + Versions: IPv6, Internet Protocol, DSCP 0
    PayloadLength: 40 (0x28)
    NextProtocol: ICMPv6, 58(0x3a)
    HopLimit: 128 (0x80)
    SourceAddress: FE80:0:0:0:260:97FF:FE02:6E8F
    DestinationAddress: FE80:0:0:0:260:97FF:FE02:6D3D
```

```
- Icmpv6: Echo request, ID = 0x0, Seq = 0x18
    MessageType: Echo request, 128(0x80)
  - EchoRequest:
    Code: 0 (0x0)
    Checksum: 52045 (0xCB4D)
    Identifier: 0 (0x0)
    SequenceNumber: 24 (0x18)
    EchoData: Binary Large Object (32 Bytes)
```

Echo Reply

An IPv6 node sends an ICMPv6 Echo Reply message in response to the receipt of an ICMPv6 Echo Request message. Figure 5-7 shows the structure of the Echo Reply message.

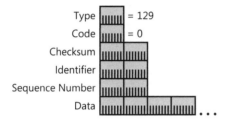

Type   = 129
Code   = 0
Checksum
Identifier
Sequence Number
Data   . . .

Figure 5-7   The structure of the Echo Reply message

In the Echo Reply message, the Type field is set to 129 and the Code field is set to 0. Following the Checksum field are the 16-bit Identifier and 16-bit Sequence Number fields. The Identifier, Sequence Number, and Data fields are set with the same values as those in the Echo Request message that prompted the Echo Reply.

Echo Request messages can be sent to a multicast address. As specified in RFC 4443, an Echo Request message sent to a multicast address should be answered with an Echo Reply message, sent from a unicast address assigned to the interface on which the Echo Request was received. The IPv6 protocol for Windows Vista and Windows Server 2008 does not respond to multicast Echo Request messages.

Network Monitor Capture

Here is an example of an Echo Reply message as displayed by Network Monitor 3.1 (frame 2 of capture 05_03 in the \NetworkMonitorCaptures folder on the companion CD-ROM):

```
  Frame:
+ Ethernet: Etype = IPv6
- Ipv6: Next Protocol = ICMPv6, Payload Length = 40
  + Versions: IPv6, Internet Protocol, DSCP 0
    PayloadLength: 40 (0x28)
    NextProtocol: ICMPv6, 58(0x3a)
    HopLimit: 128 (0x80)
    SourceAddress: FE80:0:0:0:260:97FF:FE02:6D3D
    DestinationAddress: FE80:0:0:0:260:97FF:FE02:6E8F
```

```
- Icmpv6: Echo reply, ID = 0x0, Seq = 0x18
    MessageType: Echo reply, 129(0x81)
  - EchoReply:
     Code: 0 (0x0)
     Checksum: 51789 (0xCA4D)
     Identifier: 0 (0x0)
     SequenceNumber: 24 (0x18)
     EchoData: Binary Large Object (32 Bytes)
```

This Echo Reply message was sent in response to the previously displayed Echo Request message. Notice how the Identifier, Sequence Number, and Data fields (actual contents of the Data field are not shown) match the original Echo Request message.

Comparing ICMPv4 and ICMPv6 Messages

Table 5-3 lists commonly used ICMPv4 messages and their ICMPv6 equivalents listed in order of the ICMPv4 Type and Code fields.

Table 5-3   ICMPv4 Messages and Their ICMPv6 Equivalents

ICMPv4 Message	ICMPv6 Equivalent
Destination Unreachable-Network Unreachable (Type 3, Code 0)	Destination Unreachable-No Route to Destination (Type 1, Code 0)
Destination Unreachable-Host Unreachable (Type 3, Code 1)	Destination Unreachable-Address Unreachable (Type 1, Code 3)
Destination Unreachable-Protocol Unreachable (Type 3, Code 2)	Parameter Problem-Unrecognized Next Header Type Encountered (Type 4, Code 1)
Destination Unreachable-Port Unreachable (Type 3, Code 3)	Destination Unreachable-Port Unreachable (Type 1, Code 4)
Destination Unreachable-Fragmentation Needed and DF Set (Type 3, Code 4) (as specified in RFC 1191)	Packet Too Big (Type 2, Code 0)
Destination Unreachable-Communication with Destination Host Administratively Prohibited (Type 3, Code 10)	Destination Unreachable-Communication with Destination Administratively Prohibited (Type 1, Code 1)
Source Quench (Type 4, Code 0)	This message is not present in IPv6.
Redirect (Type 5, Code 0)	Neighbor Discovery Redirect message (Type 137, Code 0). For more information, see Chapter 6.
Time Exceeded-TTL Exceeded in Transit (Type 11, Code 0)	Time Exceeded-Hop Limit Exceeded in Transit (Type 3, Code 0)
Time Exceeded-Fragment Reassembly Time Exceeded (Type 11, Code 1)	Time Exceeded-Fragment Reassembly Time Exceeded (Type 3, Code 1)
Parameter Problem (Type 12, Code 0)	Parameter Problem (Type 4, Code 0 or Code 2)

Note   The comparisons between the ICMPv4 Destination Unreachable-Network Unreachable and Destination Unreachable-Host Unreachable messages and their IPv6 equivalents are based on the historical definitions of these messages. In common practice, the ICMPv4 Destination Unreachable-Network Unreachable message is not used because in a classless addressing environment, the subnet prefix of the destination cannot be determined from the destination address. Instead, routers send the ICMPv4 Destination Unreachable-Host Unreachable message when a route is not found for the destination.

Path MTU Discovery

Sending the largest possible packets maximizes efficient use of network capacity when bulk data transfers are performed. Because IPv6 routers no longer support fragmentation, the sending host must either fragment its payload (not recommended) or discover the maximum-sized packet that can be sent to the destination and send unfragmented packets at that size.

The path maximum transmission unit (PMTU) is the smallest link MTU supported by any link in the path between a source and a destination. The link MTU is the maximum-sized link-layer payload that can be sent on the link. This corresponds to the maximum-sized packet that can be sent on the link, but it differs from the maximum-sized frame that can be sent on the link. The maximum-sized frame includes the link-layer header and trailer. For example, for Ethernet links using Ethernet II encapsulation, the link MTU is 1500 bytes and the maximum-sized frame is 1526 bytes (which includes the Ethernet preamble, source and destination addresses, the EtherType field, and the Frame Check Sequence field). For more information about the Ethernet II header and trailer, see Appendix A, "Link-Layer Support for IPv6."

IPv6 packets with a maximum size of the PMTU of the current path do not require fragmentation by the sending host and are successfully forwarded by all routers on the path. To discover the PMTU of the current path, the sending node relies on the receipt of ICMPv6 Packet Too Big messages. The PMTU is discovered through the following process:

1. The sending node assumes that the destination PMTU is the MTU of the interface on which the traffic is being forwarded.

2. The sending node sends IPv6 packets at the assumed PMTU size.

3. If a router on the path is unable to forward the packet because the forwarding interface has a link MTU that is smaller than the size of the packet, it sends an ICMPv6 Packet Too Big message back to the sending node and discards the IPv6 packet. The ICMPv6 Packet Too Big message contains the link MTU of the interface on which forwarding failed.

4. The sending node sets the new assumed PMTU for packets being sent to the destination to the value of the MTU field in the ICMPv6 Packet Too Big message.

The sending node starts again at step 2 and repeats steps 2 through 4 as many times as necessary to discover the PMTU. The PMTU is determined when either no additional ICMPv6 Packet Too Big messages are received or an acknowledgment or response packet is received from the destination.

In RFC 1981, it is recommended that IPv6 nodes support PMTU discovery. Those that do not must use the minimum link MTU of 1280 bytes as the PMTU for all destinations.

Changes in PMTU

Because of changes in routing topology, the path between source and destination might change over time. When a new path requires a lower PMTU, the PMTU process just described in the "Path MTU Discovery" section begins at step 3 and repeats steps 2 through 4 until the new PMTU is discovered.

Decreases in path MTU are immediately discovered through the receipt of ICMPv6 Packet Too Big messages. Increases in path MTU must be detected by the sending node. As described in RFC 1981, the sending node can attempt to send a larger IPv6 packet after a minimum of 5 minutes (10 minutes are recommended) upon receiving an ICMPv6 Packet Too Big message.

Figure 5-8 summarizes the PMTU discovery process of a node using the IPv6 protocol for Windows Vista and Windows Server 2008.

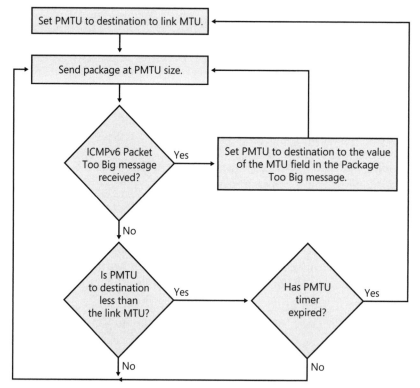

Figure 5-8   The PMTU discovery process

References

The following references were cited in this chapter:

- RFC 1191 – "Path MTU Discovery"
- RFC 1981 – "Path MTU Discovery for IP version 6"
- RFC 2460 – "Internet Protocol, Version 6 (IPv6) Specification"
- RFC 4443 – "Internet Control Message Protocol (ICMPv6) for the Internet Protocol Version 6 (IPv6)"
- RFC 4884 – "Extended ICMP to Support Multi-Part Messages"

You can obtain these RFCs from the \RFCs_and_Drafts folder on the companion CD-ROM or from *http://www.ietf.org/rfc.html*.

Testing for Understanding

To test your understanding of ICMPv6, answer the following questions. See Appendix D, "Testing for Understanding Answers," to check your answers.

1. How do you distinguish ICMPv6 error messages from ICMPv6 informational messages?

2. Which fields of the Echo Request message are echoed in the Echo Reply message?

3. For a maximum-sized IPv6 packet with a Fragment extension header sent on an Ethernet link, how many bytes of the original payload are returned in an ICMPv6 Destination Unreachable message?

4. How can you tell whether a returned packet was discarded by a firewall that is enforcing network policy or a router that could not resolve the link-layer address of the destination?

5. Why is the MTU field in the ICMPv6 Packet Too Big message 4 bytes long when the Next Hop MTU field in the ICMPv4 Destination Unreachable-Fragmentation Needed and DF Set message is only 2 bytes long?

6. Why isn't the ICMPv6 Parameter Problem-Unrecognized Option message sent when the two high-order bits of an option's Option Type field are set to either 00 (binary) or 01 (binary)?

7. Based on the IPv6 design requirement to minimize processing at IPv6 routers, why is there no equivalent to the ICMPv4 Source Quench message in IPv6?

Chapter 6
Neighbor Discovery

At the end of this chapter, you should be able to do the following:

- Describe the functions of the Neighbor Discovery (ND) protocol.
- List and describe the function and format of ND options.
- List and describe the function and format of ND messages.
- Describe which ND messages use which ND options.
- Describe the details of the address resolution, neighbor unreachability detection, duplicate address detection, router discovery, and redirect processes.
- Describe the host sending algorithm in terms of host data structures and ND messages.

Neighbor Discovery Overview

Internet Protocol version 6 (IPv6) Neighbor Discovery (ND) is a set of messages and processes defined in RFC 4861 that determine relationships between neighboring nodes. ND replaces Address Resolution Protocol (ARP), Internet Control Message Protocol (ICMP) router discovery, and the ICMP Redirect message used in IPv4. ND also provides additional functionality.

ND is used by nodes to do the following:

- Resolve the link-layer address of a neighboring node to which an IPv6 packet is being forwarded.
- Determine when the link-layer address of a neighboring node has changed.
- Determine whether a neighbor is still reachable.

ND is used by hosts to do the following:

- Discover neighboring routers.
- Autoconfigure addresses, address prefixes, routes, and other configuration parameters.

ND is used by routers to do the following:

- Advertise their presence, host configuration parameters, routes, and on-link prefixes.
- Inform hosts of a better next-hop address to forward packets for a specific destination.

IPv6 ND processes include the following:

- **Router discovery**   During router discovery, a host discovers the local routers on an attached link. This process is equivalent to ICMPv4 router discovery. For more information, see the "Router Discovery" section in this chapter.

- **Prefix discovery**   Prefix discovery is the process by which hosts discover the network prefixes for local link destinations. This is similar to the exchange of the ICMPv4 Address Mask Request and Address Mask Reply messages. For more information, see the "Router Discovery" section in this chapter.

- **Parameter discovery**   The parameter discovery process enables hosts to discover additional operating parameters, including the link maximum transmission unit (MTU) and the default hop limit for outgoing packets. For more information, see the "Router Discovery" section in this chapter.

- **Address autoconfiguration**   During address autoconfiguration, IP addresses are configured for interfaces in either the presence or absence of an address configuration server, such as a Dynamic Host Configuration Protocol for IPv6 (DHCPv6) server. For more information, see Chapter 8, "Address Autoconfiguration."

- **Address resolution**   Address resolution is the process by which nodes resolve a neighbor's IPv6 address to its link-layer address. It is equivalent to ARP in IPv4. For more information, see the "Address Resolution" section in this chapter.

- **Next-hop determination**   During next-hop determination, a node determines the IPv6 address of the neighbor to which a packet is being forwarded, based on the destination address. The next-hop address is either the destination address or the address of an on-link default router. For more information, see "Host Sending Algorithm" in this chapter.

- **Neighbor unreachability detection**   The neighbor unreachability detection process is the means by which a node determines that the IPv6 layer of a neighbor is no longer receiving packets or that an IPv6 address has moved to a different physical interface. For more information, see the "Neighbor Unreachability Detection" section in this chapter.

- **Duplicate address detection**   During duplicate address detection, a node determines that an address considered for use is not already in use by a neighboring node. This process is equivalent to using gratuitous ARP frames in IPv4. For more information, see the "Duplicate Address Detection" section in this chapter.

- **Redirect function**   The redirect function is the process of informing a host of a better first-hop IPv6 address to reach a destination. It is equivalent to the use of the ICMPv4 Redirect message. For more information, see the "Redirect Function" section in this chapter.

Neighbor Discovery Message Format

ND messages use the ICMPv6 message structure and ICMPv6 types 133 through 137. ND messages consist of an ND message header, composed of an ICMPv6 header and ND message-specific data, and zero or more ND options. Figure 6-1 shows the format of an ND message.

Figure 6-1   The format of an ND message

There are five different ND messages:

- Router Solicitation (ICMPv6 type 133)
- Router Advertisement (ICMPv6 type 134)
- Neighbor Solicitation (ICMPv6 type 135)
- Neighbor Advertisement (ICMPv6 type 136)
- Redirect (ICMPv6 type 137)

ND message options provide additional information, indicating MAC addresses, on-link network prefixes, on-link MTU information, redirection data, mobility information, and specific routes.

To ensure that ND messages that are received have originated from a node on the local link (either a physical link or a tunnel), all ND messages are sent with a hop limit of 255. When an ND message is received, the Hop Limit field in the IPv6 header is checked. If it is not set to 255, the message is silently discarded. Verifying that the ND message has a hop limit of 255 provides protection from ND-based network attacks that are launched from off-link nodes. With a hop limit of 255, a router could not have forwarded the ND message from an off-link node.

Neighbor Discovery Options

ND options are formatted in type-length-value (TLV) format. Figure 6-2 shows the TLV format.

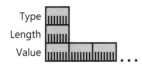

Figure 6-2   The TLV format for ND options

The 8-bit Type field indicates the type of ND option. Table 6-1 lists the ND option types defined in RFC 4861, RFC 3775, and RFC 4191.

Table 6-1   IPv6 ND Option Types

Type	Option Name	Source Document
1	Source Link-Layer Address	RFC 4861 (Neighbor Discovery for IPv6)
2	Target Link-Layer Address	RFC 4861
3	Prefix Information	RFC 4861
4	Redirected Header	RFC 4861
5	MTU	RFC 4861
7	Advertisement Interval	RFC 3775 (Mobile IPv6)
8	Home Agent Information	RFC 3775
24	Route Information	RFC 4191 (Default Router Preferences and More-Specific Routes)

The 8-bit Length field indicates the length of the entire option in 8-byte blocks. All ND options must fall on 8-byte boundaries. The variable length Value field contains the data for the option.

The Advertisement Interval and Home Agent Information options are described in Appendix F, "Mobile IPv6."

Source and Target Link-Layer Address Options

The Source Link-Layer Address option indicates the link-layer address of the ND message sender. The Source Link-Layer Address option is included in the Neighbor Solicitation, Router Solicitation, and Router Advertisement messages. The Source Link-Layer Address option is not included when the source address of the ND message is the unspecified address (::).

Figure 6-3 shows the structure of the Source Link-Layer Address option.

Figure 6-3   The structure of the Source Link-Layer Address option

The Target Link-Layer Address option indicates the link-layer address of the neighboring node to which IPv6 packets should be directed. The Target Link-Layer Address option is included in the Neighbor Advertisement and Redirect messages.

Figure 6-4 shows the structure of the Target Link-Layer Address option.

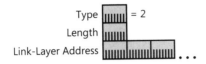

Figure 6-4   The structure of the Target Link-Layer Address option

The Source Link-Layer Address option and the Target Link-Layer Address option have the same format.

The Type field is set to 1 for a Source Link-Layer Address option and 2 for a Target Link-Layer Address option. The Length field is set to the number of 8-byte blocks in the entire option. The Link-Layer Address field is a variable-length field that contains the link-layer address of the source or target. Each link layer defined for IPv6 must specify the way in which the link-layer address is formatted in the Source and Target Link-Layer Address options.

For example, RFC 2464 defines how IPv6 packets are sent over Ethernet networks. It also includes the format of the Source and Target Link-Layer Address ND options. For Ethernet, the link-layer address is 48 bits (6 bytes) in length. Figure 6-5 shows the Target Link-Layer Address option for Ethernet.

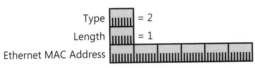

Figure 6-5   The Target Link-Layer Address option for Ethernet

Network Monitor Capture

Here is an example of a Source Link-Layer Address option used in a Neighbor Solicitation message as displayed by Network Monitor 3.1 (frame 1 of capture 06_01 in the \Network-MonitorCaptures folder on the companion CD-ROM):

```
 Frame:
+ Ethernet: Etype = IPv6
+ Ipv6: Next Protocol = ICMPv6, Payload Length = 32
- Icmpv6: Neighbor Solicitation, Target = FE80:0:0:0:260:97FF:FE02:6EA5
    MessageType: Neighbor Solicitation, 135(0x87)
  - NeighborSolicitation:
    Code: 0 (0x0)
    Checksum: 3893 (0xF35)
    Reserved: 0 (0x0)
    TargetAddress: FE80:0:0:0:260:97FF:FE02:6EA5
  - SourceLinkLayerAddress:
    Type: Source Link-Layer Address, 1(0x1)
    Length: 1, in unit of 8 octets
    Address: 00-10-5A-AA-20-A2
```

Prefix Information Option

The Prefix Information option is sent in Router Advertisement messages to indicate both address prefixes and information about address autoconfiguration. There can be multiple Prefix Information options included in a Router Advertisement message, indicating multiple address prefixes.

Figure 6-6 shows the structure of the Prefix Information option.

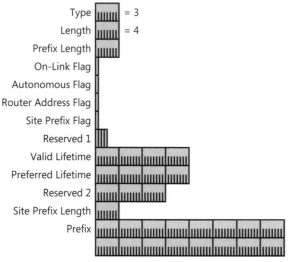

Figure 6-6   The structure of the Prefix Information option

The fields in the Prefix Information option are as follows:

- **Type**   The value of this field is 3.

- **Length**   The value of this field is 4. (The entire option is 32 bytes in length.)

- **Prefix Length**   The Prefix Length field indicates the number of leading bits in the Prefix field that make up the address prefix. The size of this field is 8 bits. The Prefix Length field has a value from 0 through 128. Because typical prefixes advertised are for subnet identifiers, the Prefix Length field is usually set to 64.

- **On-Link flag**   The On-Link flag indicates, when set to 1, that the addresses implied by the included prefix are available on the link on which this Router Advertisement message was received. When this flag is set to 0, it is not assumed that the addresses that match the prefix are available on-link. The size of this field is 1 bit.

- **Autonomous flag**   The Autonomous flag indicates, when set to 1, that the included prefix is used to create an autonomous (or stateless) address configuration. When this flag is set to 0, the included prefix is not used to create a stateless address configuration. The size of this field is 1 bit.

- **Router Address flag**   The Router Address flag is defined in RFC 3775 for Mobile IPv6. For more information, see Appendix F.

- **Site Prefix flag**   The Site Prefix flag indicates, when set to 1, that the site prefix defined by the Prefix field and the Site Prefix Length field be used to update the site prefix table. The site prefix table is maintained by the host and is utilized to prefer the use of site-local addresses when a global address matches a site prefix. This flag is described in the Internet draft titled "Site Prefixes in Neighbor Discovery."

- **Reserved1**   The Reserved1 field is a 4-bit field reserved for future use and set to 0.

- **Valid Lifetime**   The Valid Lifetime field indicates the number of seconds that an address, based on the included prefix and using stateless address configuration, remains valid. The size of this field is 32 bits. The Valid Lifetime field also indicates the number of seconds that the included prefix is valid for on-link determination. For an infinite valid lifetime, the Valid Lifetime field is set to 0xFFFFFFFF.

- **Preferred Lifetime**   The Preferred Lifetime field indicates the number of seconds that an address, based on the included prefix and using stateless address autoconfiguration, remains in a preferred state. The size of this field is 32 bits. Stateless autoconfiguration addresses that are still valid are either in a preferred or deprecated state. In the preferred state, the address can be used for unrestricted communication. In the deprecated state, the use of the address is not recommended for new communications. However, existing communications using a deprecated address can continue. An address goes from the preferred state to the deprecated state when its preferred lifetime expires. For an infinite preferred lifetime, the Preferred Lifetime field is set to 0xFFFFFFFF.

- **Reserved2**   The Reserved2 field is a 24-bit field reserved for future use and set to 0.

- **Site Prefix Length**   The Site Prefix Length field indicates the number of leading bits in the Prefix field that define a site prefix. The length of this field is 8 bits. This field is significant only if the Site Prefix flag is set to 1. This field is described in the Internet draft titled "Site Prefixes in Neighbor Discovery."

- **Prefix**   The Prefix field indicates the prefix for the IPv6 address derived through stateless autoconfiguration. The size of this field is 128 bits. Bits in the Prefix field—up to a count equaling the value of the Prefix Length field—are significant for creating the prefix. The combination of the Prefix Length field and the Prefix field unambiguously defines the prefix which, when combined with the interface identifier for the node, creates an IPv6 address. The link-local prefix should not be sent and is ignored by the receiving host.

Network Monitor Capture

Here is an example of a Prefix Information option used in a Router Advertisement message as displayed by Network Monitor 3.1 (capture 06_02 in the \NetworkMonitorCaptures folder on the companion CD-ROM):

```
Frame:
+ Ethernet: Etype = IPv6
+ Ipv6: Next Protocol = ICMPv6, Payload Length = 96
- Icmpv6: Router Advertisement
    MessageType: Router Advertisement, 134(0x86)
```

```
+ RouterAdvertisement:
- SourceLinkLayerAddress:
    Type: Source Link-Layer Address, 1(0x1)
    Length: 1, in unit of 8 octets
    Address: 00-B0-D0-23-47-33
+ MTU:
+ PrefixInformation:
- PrefixInformation:
    Type: Prefix Information, 3(0x3)
    Length: 4, in unit of 8 octets
    PrefixLength: 64 (0x40)
  - Flags: 192 (0xC0)
      L:   (1.......) On-Link determination allowed
      A:   (.1......) Autonomous address-configuration
      R:   (..0.....) Not router Address
      S:   (...0....) Not a site prefix
      P:   (....0...) Not a router prefix
      Rsv: (.....000)
    ValidLifetime: 4294967295 (0xFFFFFFFF)
    PreferredLifetime: 4294967295 (0xFFFFFFFF)
    Reserved: 0 (0x0)
    Prefix: FD43:2DA1:3FE9:2:0:0:0:0
```

Redirected Header Option

The Redirected Header option is sent in Redirect messages to specify the IPv6 packet that caused the router to send a Redirect message. It can contain all or part of the redirected IPv6 packet, depending on the size of the IPv6 packet that was initially sent.

Figure 6-7 shows the structure of the Redirected Header option.

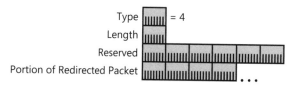

Figure 6-7   The structure of the Redirected Header option

The following list describes the fields in the Redirected Header option:

- **Type**   The value of this field is 4.

- **Length**   The value of this field is the number of 8-byte blocks in the entire option.

- **Reserved**   The Reserved field is a 48-bit field reserved for future use and set to 0.

- **Portion of redirected packet**   This field contains either the IPv6 packet or a portion of the IPv6 packet that caused the Redirect message to be sent. The amount of the original packet that is included is the leading portion of the packet so that the entire Redirect message is no more than 1280 bytes in length.

Network Monitor Capture

Here is an example of a Redirected Header option used in a Redirect message as displayed by Network Monitor 3.1 (capture 06_03 in the \NetworkMonitorCaptures folder on the companion CD-ROM):

```
 Frame:
+ Ethernet: Etype = IPv6
+ Ipv6: Next Protocol = ICMPv6, Payload Length = 128
- Icmpv6: Redirect, Target = FE80:0:0:0:2B0:D0FF:FE23:4735
    MessageType: Redirect, 137(0x89)
  - Redirect:
    Code: 0 (0x0)
    Checksum: 31003 (0x791B)
    Reserved: 0 (0x0)
    TargetAddress: FE80:0:0:0:2B0:D0FF:FE23:4735
    DestAddress: 2001:DB8:0:0:0:0:0:1
  - RedirectedHeader:
    Type: Redirected Header, 4(0x4)
    Length: 11, in unit of 8 octets
    Reserved: 0 (0x0)
  - InvokingPacket: Next Protocol = ICMPv6, Payload Length = 40
   - Versions: IPv6, Internet Protocol, DSCP 0
     Version:   (0110..........................) IPv6, Internet Protocol,
        6(0x6)
     DSCP:      (....000000....................) Differentiated services
        codepoint 0
     ECT:       (..........0...................) ECN-Capable Transport not
        set
     CE:        (...........0..................) ECN-CE not set
     FlowLabe: (............00000000000000000000) 0
     PayloadLength: 40 (0x28)
     NextProtocol: ICMPv6, 58(0x3a)
     HopLimit: 128 (0x80)
     SourceAddress: FE80:0:0:0:260:8FF:FE52:F9D8
     DestinationAddress: 3000:0:0:0:0:0:0:1
     OriginalIPPayload: Binary Large Object (40 Bytes)
```

MTU Option

The MTU option is sent in Router Advertisement messages to indicate the IPv6 MTU of the link. This option is typically used when the IPv6 MTU for a link is not well known or needs to be set because of a translational or mixed-media bridging configuration. The MTU option overrides the IPv6 MTU reported by the interface hardware.

In bridged or Layer-2 switched environments, it is possible to have different link-layer technologies with different link-layer MTUs on the same link. In this case, differences in IPv6 MTUs between nodes on the same link are not detected through Path MTU Discovery. The MTU option is used to indicate the highest IPv6 MTU supported by all link-layer technologies on the link.

Figure 6-8 shows a switched configuration where the MTU option is used to solve a mixed-media problem.

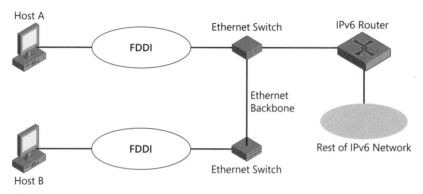

Figure 6-8   A mixed-media configuration

Two IPv6 hosts, Host A and Host B, are connected to two different Ethernet (Layer 2) switches using Fiber Distributed Data Interface (FDDI) ports. The two switches are connected by an Ethernet backbone. When Host A and Host B negotiate a TCP connection, each reports a TCP maximum segment size of 4312 (the FDDI IPv6 MTU of 4352, minus 40 bytes of the IPv6 header). However, when TCP data on the connection begins to flow, the switches silently discard IPv6 packets larger than 1500 bytes that are sent between Host A and Host B.

With the MTU option, the IPv6 router for the subnet reports an IPv6 MTU of 1500 in the Router Advertisement message for all hosts on the link. When both Host A and Host B adjust their IPv6 MTU from 4352 to 1500, maximum-sized TCP segments sent between them are not discarded by the intermediate switches.

Note   FDDI is an older technology whose use has been made obsolete by 100-Mbps Ethernet. This configuration is unlikely to be used on modern networks and serves only as an example of a mixed-media subnet.

Figure 6-9 shows the structure of the MTU option.

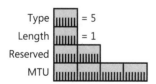

Figure 6-9   The structure of the MTU option

The following list describes the fields in the MTU option:

- **Type**   The value of this field is 5.
- **Length**   The value of this field is 1. (There are 8 bytes in the entire option.)

- **Reserved**   The Reserved field is a 16-bit field reserved for future use and set to 0.

- **MTU**   The MTU field indicates the IPv6 MTU that should be used by the host for the link on which the Router Advertisement was received. The size of this field is 32 bits. The value in the MTU field is ignored if it is larger than the link MTU.

Network Monitor Capture

Here is an example of an MTU option used in a Router Advertisement message as displayed by Network Monitor 3.1 (capture 06_02 in the \NetworkMonitorCaptures folder on the companion CD-ROM):

```
Frame:
+ Ethernet: Etype = IPv6
+ Ipv6: Next Protocol = ICMPv6, Payload Length = 96
- Icmpv6: Router Advertisement
    MessageType: Router Advertisement, 134(0x86)
  + RouterAdvertisement:
  - SourceLinkLayerAddress:
      Type: Source Link-Layer Address, 1(0x1)
      Length: 1, in unit of 8 octets
      Address: 00-B0-D0-23-47-33
  - MTU:
      Type: MTU, 5(0x5)
      Length: 1, in unit of 8 octets
      Reserved: 0 (0x0)
      MTU: 1500 (0x5DC)
  + PrefixInformation:
  + PrefixInformation:
```

Route Information Option

The Route Information option is sent in Router Advertisement messages to specify individual routes for receiving hosts to add to their local routing table. The Route Information option is described in RFC 4191.

Figure 6-10 shows the structure of the Route Information option.

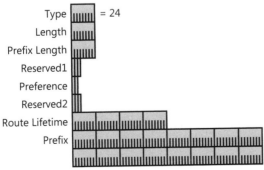

Figure 6-10   The structure of the Route Information option

The fields in the Route Information option are as follows:

- **Type** The value of this field is 24.

- **Length** The value of the Length field depends on the prefix length of the route and the corresponding size of the Prefix field. If the prefix length is 0 (and there is no Prefix field), the value of the Length field is 1. If the prefix length is greater than 0 and less than 65, the length of the Prefix field is 64 bits and the value of the Length field is 2. If the prefix length is greater than 64, the length of the Prefix field is 128 bits and the value of the Length field is 3.

- **Prefix Length** The Prefix Length field indicates the number of leading bits in the Prefix field that are significant for the route. Valid values range from 0 through 128. The size of this field is 8 bits.

- **Reserved1** The Reserved1 field is a 3-bit field reserved for future use and set to 0.

- **Preference** The Preference field indicates the level of preference for this route as sent from the advertising router. If multiple routers advertise the same prefix using a Route Information option, you can configure the routers so that they advertise the route with different preference levels. Valid values in binary are 01 (High), 00 (Medium), and 11 (Low). The size of this field is 2 bits.

- **Reserved2** The Reserved2 field is a 3-bit field reserved for future use and set to 0.

- **Route Lifetime** The Route Lifetime field indicates the amount of time in seconds that the prefix is valid for route determination. The size of this field is 32 bits. For an infinite route lifetime, the Route Lifetime field is set to 0xFFFFFFFF.

- **Prefix** The Prefix field indicates the route prefix. The size of the Prefix field can be 0, 64, or 128 bits, depending on the value of the Prefix Length field. If the prefix length is 0, the size of the Prefix field is 0. If the prefix length is greater than 0 and less than 65, the size of the Prefix field is 64 bits. If the prefix length is greater than 64, the size of the Prefix field is 128 bits. The prefix length indicates the number of high-order bits in the prefix that are relevant for route determination. All bits in the Prefix field past the prefix length must be set to 0.

A typical use of the Route Information option is to enable hosts to make better forwarding decisions when sending data. Figure 6-11 shows a simple network configuration where the Route Information option can be useful.

Without the Route Information option, you would typically configure the routers so that only Router 1 advertises itself as a default router on Subnet 1. Hosts on Subnet 1 sending traffic to hosts on Subnet 2 would have to rely on Redirect messages from Router 1 to inform them that the best next-hop address to reach hosts on Subnet 2 is actually Router 2. For more information, see the "Redirect Function" section in this chapter.

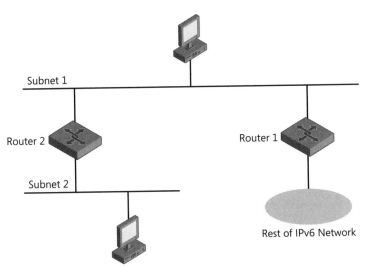

Figure 6-11   An example configuration in which the Route Information option is used

Using the Route Information option, Router 2 is configured to advertise the prefix of Subnet 2. Upon receipt of router advertisements from both routers, hosts on Subnet 1 automatically add a default route with Router 1 as its next-hop address and a specific route for the Subnet 2 prefix with Router 2 as its next-hop address. Now all the hosts on Subnet 2 are reachable by hosts on Subnet 1 without having to rely on redirects from Router 1.

A computer running Windows Server 2008, Windows Vista, Windows XP, or Windows Server 2003, acting as an IPv6 router that does not have a default route that is configured to be published, will send Route Information options in Router Advertisements to inform hosts of the subnet prefixes of the other subnets to which the IPv6 router is attached.

Neighbor Discovery Messages

All the functions of IPv6 ND are performed with the following messages:

- Router Solicitation
- Router Advertisement
- Neighbor Solicitation
- Neighbor Advertisement
- Redirect

Router Solicitation

The Router Solicitation message is sent by IPv6 hosts to discover the presence of IPv6 routers on the link. A host sends a multicast Router Solicitation message to prompt IPv6 routers to respond immediately, rather than waiting for an unsolicited Router Advertisement message.

For example, assuming that the local link is Ethernet, in the Ethernet header of the Router Solicitation message you will find these settings:

- The Source Address field is set to the MAC address of the sending network adapter.

- The Destination Address field is set to 33-33-00-00-00-02.

In the IPv6 header of the Router Solicitation message, you will find the following settings:

- The Source Address field is set to either a link-local IPv6 address assigned to the sending interface or the IPv6 unspecified address (::).

- The Destination Address field is set to the link-local scope all-routers multicast address (FF02::2).

- The Hop Limit field is set to 255.

Figure 6-12 shows the structure of the Router Solicitation message.

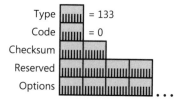

```
Type      |||||||  = 133
Code      |||||||  = 0
Checksum  ||||||||||||||
Reserved  |||||||||||||||||||||
Options   ||||||||||||||||||||||||||  . . .
```

Figure 6-12   The structure of the Router Solicitation message

The following list describes the fields in the Router Solicitation message:

- **Type**   The value of this field is 133.

- **Code**   The value of this field is 0.

- **Checksum**   The value of this field is the ICMPv6 checksum.

- **Reserved**   This is a 32-bit field reserved for future use and set to 0.

- **Source Link-Layer Address option**   When present, the Source Link-Layer Address option contains the link-layer address of the sender. For an Ethernet node, the Source Link-Layer Address option contains the Ethernet MAC address of the sending host. The address in the Source Link-Layer Address option is used by the receiving router to determine the unicast MAC address of the host to which the corresponding unicast Router Advertisement is sent.

Network Monitor Capture

Here is an example of a Router Solicitation message as displayed by Network Monitor 3.1 (capture 06_04 in the \NetworkMonitorCaptures folder on the companion CD-ROM):

```
  Frame:
+ Ethernet: Etype = IPv6
+ Ipv6: Next Protocol = ICMPv6, Payload Length = 16
- Icmpv6: Router Solicitation
    MessageType: Router Solicitation, 133(0x85)
  - RouterSolicitation:
    Code: 0 (0x0)
    Checksum: 19232 (0x4B20)
    Reserved: 0 (0x0)
  - SourceLinkLayerAddress:
    Type: Source Link-Layer Address, 1(0x1)
    Length: 1, in unit of 8 octets
    Address: 00-B0-D0-23-47-33
```

Router Advertisement

IPv6 routers send unsolicited Router Advertisement messages pseudo-periodically—that is, the interval between unsolicited advertisements is randomized to reduce synchronization issues when there are multiple advertising routers on a link—and solicited Router Advertisement messages in response to the receipt of a Router Solicitation message. The Router Advertisement message contains the information required by hosts to determine the link prefixes, the link MTU, specific routes, whether or not to use address autoconfiguration, and the duration for which addresses created through address autoconfiguration are valid and preferred.

For example, assuming that the local link is Ethernet, in the Ethernet header of the Router Advertisement message, you will find these settings:

■ The Source Address field is set to the MAC address of the sending network adapter.

■ The Destination Address field is set to either 33-33-00-00-00-01 or the unicast MAC address of the host that sent a Router Solicitation from a unicast address.

In the IPv6 header of the Router Advertisement message, you will find the following settings:

■ The Source Address field is set to the link-local address assigned to the sending interface.

■ The Destination Address field is set to either the link-local scope all-nodes multicast address (FF02::1) or the unicast IPv6 address of the host that sent the Router Solicitation message from a unicast address.

■ The Hop Limit field is set to 255.

Figure 6-13 shows the structure of the Router Advertisement message.

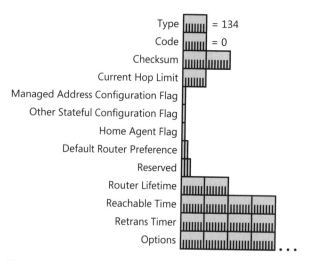

Figure 6-13   The structure of the Router Advertisement message

The fields in the Router Advertisement message are as follows:

- **Type**   The value of this field is 134.

- **Code**   The value of this field is 0.

- **Checksum**   The value of this field is the ICMPv6 checksum.

- **Current Hop Limit**   The Current Hop Limit field indicates the default value of the Hop Limit field in the IPv6 header for packets sent by hosts that receive this Router Advertisement message. The size of this field is 8 bits. A current hop limit of 0 indicates that the default value of the Hop Limit field is not specified by the router.

- **Managed Address Configuration flag**   The Managed Address Configuration flag indicates, when set to 1, that hosts receiving this Router Advertisement message must use an address configuration protocol such as DHCPv6 to obtain addresses in addition to the addresses that might be derived from stateless address autoconfiguration. The size of this field is 1 bit.

- **Other Stateful Configuration flag**   The Other Stateful Configuration flag indicates, when set to 1, that hosts receiving this Router Advertisement message must use an address configuration protocol (for example, DHCPv6) to obtain non–address configuration information. The size of this field is 1 bit.

- **Home Agent flag**   The Home Agent flag is defined in RFC 3775 for Mobile IPv6. For more information, see Appendix F.

- **Default Router Preference**   The Default Router Preference field indicates the level of preference for this router as the default router. If multiple routers advertise themselves as default routers, you can configure the routers so that they advertise with different preference levels. Valid values in binary are 01 (High), 00 (Medium), and 11 (Low). If the preference is set to 10, the receiving host should assume a value of 0 for the Router Lifetime field, effectively disabling the advertising router as a default router. The size of this field is 2 bits. This field is described in RFC 4191.

A typical configuration that can use the default router preference is a subnet that has two routers connected to the Internet or an organization intranet—one router is the primary router, and another router is a slower, secondary router intended to provide fault tolerance for the primary router. Both routers advertise themselves as default routers; however, the primary router advertises a default router preference of 01 (High) and the secondary router advertises a default router preference of 00 (Medium). If the primary router becomes unavailable, the hosts on the subnet will use the secondary router until the primary router becomes available.

- **Reserved**   This is a 3-bit field reserved for future use and set to 0.

- **Router Lifetime**   The Router Lifetime field indicates the lifetime (in seconds) of the router as the default router. The size of this field is 16 bits. The maximum Router Lifetime value is 65,535 seconds (about 18.2 hours). A value of 0 indicates that the router cannot be considered a default router; however, all other information contained in the Router Advertisement is still valid. A computer running Windows Server 2008, Windows Vista, Windows XP, or Windows Server 2003 acting as an IPv6 router that does not have a default route that is configured to be published sets the Router Lifetime field to 0.

- **Reachable Time**   The Reachable Time field indicates the amount of time (in milliseconds) that a node can consider a neighboring node reachable after receiving a reachability confirmation. The size of this field is 32 bits. A value of 0 indicates that the router does not specify the reachable time. For more information, see the "Neighbor Unreachability Detection" section in this chapter.

- **Retransmission Timer**   The Retransmission Timer field indicates the amount of time (in milliseconds) between retransmissions of Neighbor Solicitation messages. The size of this field is 32 bits. The retransmission timer is used during neighbor unreachability detection. A value of 0 indicates that the router does not specify the retransmission timer value.

The options that can be present in a Router Advertisement message are the following:

- **Source Link-Layer Address option**   When present, the Source Link-Layer Address option contains the link-layer address of the interface on which the Router Advertisement message was sent. This option can be omitted when the router is load-balancing across multiple link-layer addresses.

- **MTU option**   When present, the MTU option contains the MTU of the link. It is typically sent on links that have a variable MTU or in switched environments that have multiple link-layer technologies on the same link.

- ■ **Prefix Information options**   When present, Prefix Information options contain the on-link prefixes that are used for address autoconfiguration. The link-local prefix is never sent as a Prefix Information option.

- ■ **Advertisement Interval option**   For more information, see Appendix F.

- ■ **Home Agent Information option**   For more information, see Appendix F.

- ■ **Route Information options**   When present, Route Information options contain routes to add to the local routing table for more efficient host forwarding decisions.

Network Monitor Capture

Here is an example of a Router Advertisement message as displayed by Network Monitor 3.1 (capture 06_02 in the \NetworkMonitorCaptures folder on the companion CD-ROM):

```
Frame:
+ Ethernet: Etype = IPv6
+ Ipv6: Next Protocol = ICMPv6, Payload Length = 96
- Icmpv6: Router Advertisement
    MessageType: Router Advertisement, 134(0x86)
  - RouterAdvertisement:
    Code: 0 (0x0)
    Checksum: 8095 (0x1F9F)
    CurHopLimit: 0 (0x0)
  - RouterAdvertisementFlag:
    M:                 (0.......) Not managed address configuration
    O:                 (.0......) Not other stateful configuration
    A:                 (..0.....) Not a Mobile IP Home Agent
    RouterPreference: (...00...) Medium,0(0x0)
    Reserved:         (.....000)
    RouterLifetime: 0 (0x0)
    ReachableTime: 0 (0x0)
    RetransTimer: 0 (0x0)
  + SourceLinkLayerAddress:
  + MTU:
  + PrefixInformation:
  + PrefixInformation:
```

Neighbor Solicitation

IPv6 nodes send the Neighbor Solicitation message to discover the link-layer address of an on-link IPv6 node or to confirm a previously determined link-layer address. It typically includes the link-layer address of the sender. Typical Neighbor Solicitation messages are multicast for address resolution and unicast when the reachability of a neighboring node is being verified.

For example, assuming that the local link is Ethernet, in the Ethernet header of the Neighbor Solicitation message, you will find the following settings:

- ■ The Source Address field is set to the MAC address of the sending network adapter.

- For a multicast Neighbor Solicitation message, the Destination Address field is set to the Ethernet MAC address that corresponds to the solicited-node address of the target. For a unicast Neighbor Solicitation message, the Destination Address field is set to the unicast MAC address of the neighbor.

In the IPv6 header of the Neighbor Solicitation message, you will find these settings:

- The Source Address field is set to either a unicast IPv6 address assigned to the sending interface or, during duplicate address detection, the unspecified address (::).

- For a multicast Neighbor Solicitation, the Destination Address field is set to the solicited-node address of the target. For a unicast Neighbor Solicitation, the Destination Address field is set to the unicast address of the target.

- The Hop Limit field is set to 255.

Figure 6-14 shows the structure of the Neighbor Solicitation message.

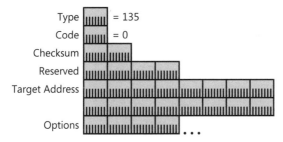

Figure 6-14   The structure of the Neighbor Solicitation message

The fields in the Neighbor Solicitation message are as follows:

- **Type**   The value of this field is 135.

- **Code**   The value of this field is 0.

- **Checksum**   The value of this field is the ICMPv6 checksum.

- **Reserved**   This is a 32-bit field reserved for future use and set to 0.

- **Target Address**   The Target Address field indicates the IP address of the target. The size of this field is 128 bits.

- **Source Link-Layer Address option**   When present, the Source Link-Layer Address option contains the link-layer address of the sender. For an Ethernet node, the Source Link-Layer Address option contains the Ethernet MAC address of the sending node. The receiving node uses the address in the Source Link-Layer Address option to determine the unicast MAC address of the node to which the corresponding Neighbor Advertisement is sent. During duplicate address detection, when the source IPv6 address is the unspecified address (::), the Source Link-Layer Address option is not included.

Network Monitor Capture

Here is an example of a Neighbor Solicitation message as displayed by Network Monitor 3.1 (frame 1 of capture 06_01 in the \NetworkMonitorCaptures folder on the companion CD-ROM):

```
Frame:
- Ethernet: Etype = IPv6
  + DestinationAddress: 3333FF 026EA5
  + SourceAddress: 00105A AA20A2
    EthernetType: IPv6, 34525(0x86dd)
- Ipv6: Next Protocol = ICMPv6, Payload Length = 32
  + Versions: IPv6, Internet Protocol, DSCP 0
    PayloadLength: 32 (0x20)
    NextProtocol: ICMPv6, 58(0x3a)
    HopLimit: 255 (0xFF)
    SourceAddress: FE80:0:0:0:210:5AFF:FEAA:20A2
    DestinationAddress: FF02:0:0:0:0:1:FF02:6EA5
- Icmpv6: Neighbor Solicitation, Target = FE80:0:0:0:260:97FF:FE02:6EA5
    MessageType: Neighbor Solicitation, 135(0x87)
  - NeighborSolicitation:
    Code: 0 (0x0)
    Checksum: 3893 (0xF35)
    Reserved: 0 (0x0)
    TargetAddress: FE80:0:0:0:260:97FF:FE02:6EA5
  - SourceLinkLayerAddress:
    Type: Source Link-Layer Address, 1(0x1)
    Length: 1, in unit of 8 octets
    Address: 00-10-5A-AA-20-A2
```

Notice how the last 24 bits of the target address (FE80::260:97FF:FE02:6EA5) correspond to the last 24 bits of the solicited-node destination address (FF02::1:FF02:6EA5) (corresponding bits underlined). Also notice how the last 32 bits of the solicited-node destination address (FF02::1:FF02:6EA5) correspond to the last 32 bits of the Ethernet destination address (3333FF026EA5) (corresponding bits underlined).

Neighbor Advertisement

An IPv6 node sends the Neighbor Advertisement message in response to a Neighbor Solicitation message. An IPv6 node also sends unsolicited Neighbor Advertisements to inform neighboring nodes of changes in link-layer addresses or the node's role. The Neighbor Advertisement contains information required by nodes to determine the type of Neighbor Advertisement message, the sender's role on the network, and typically the link-layer address of the sender.

For example, assuming that the local link is Ethernet, in the Ethernet header of the Neighbor Advertisement message, you will find the following settings:

■ The Source Address field is set to the MAC address of the sending network adapter.

■ The Destination Address field is set, for a solicited Neighbor Advertisement, to the unicast MAC address of the initial Neighbor Solicitation sender. For an unsolicited Neighbor

Advertisement, the Destination Address field is set to 33-33-00-00-00-01, which is the Ethernet MAC address corresponding to the link-local scope all-nodes multicast address.

In the IPv6 header of the Neighbor Advertisement message, you will find these settings:

■ The Source Address field is set to a unicast address assigned to the sending interface.

■ The Destination Address field is set, for a solicited Neighbor Advertisement, to the unicast IP address of the sender of the initial Neighbor Solicitation. For an unsolicited Neighbor Advertisement, the Destination Address field is set to the link-local scope all-nodes multicast address (FF02::1).

■ The Hop Limit field is set to 255.

Figure 6-15 shows the structure of the Neighbor Advertisement message.

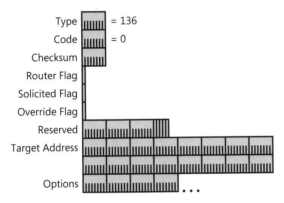

Figure 6-15   The structure of the Neighbor Advertisement message

The following list describes the fields in the Neighbor Advertisement message:

■ **Type**   The value of this field is 136.

■ **Code**   The value of this field is 0.

■ **Checksum**   The value of this field is the ICMPv6 checksum.

■ **Router flag**   The Router flag indicates the role of the sender of the Neighbor Advertisement message. The size of this field is 1 bit. The Router flag is set to 1 when the sender is a router and 0 when the sender is not. The Router flag is used by the neighbor unreachability detection process to determine when a router changes to a host.

■ **Solicited flag**   The Solicited flag indicates, when set to 1, that the Neighbor Advertisement message was sent in response to a Neighbor Solicitation message. The size of this field is 1 bit. The Solicited flag is used as a reachability confirmation during neighbor unreachability detection. The Solicited flag is set to 0 for both multicast Neighbor Advertisements and unsolicited unicast Neighbor Advertisements.

■ **Override flag**   The Override flag indicates, when set to 1, that the link-layer address in the included Target Link-Layer Address option should override the link-layer address in the existing neighbor cache entry. The size of this field is 1 bit. If the Override flag is set to 0, the enclosed link-layer address updates a neighbor cache entry only if the link-layer address is not known. The Override flag is set to 0 for a solicited anycast address or a proxied advertisement. The Override flag is set to 1 in other solicited and unsolicited advertisements. For more information about the neighbor cache, see the "Neighbor Discovery Processes" section in this chapter.

- **Reserved**   This is a 29-bit field reserved for future use and set to 0.

- **Target Address**   The Target Address field indicates the address being advertised. The size of this field is 128 bits. For solicited Neighbor Advertisement messages, the target address is set to the value of the Target Address field in the corresponding Neighbor Solicitation. For unsolicited Neighbor Advertisement messages, the target address is the address whose link-layer address or role has changed.

- **Target Link-Layer Address option**   When present, the Target Link-Layer Address option contains the link-layer address of the target, which is the sender of the Neighbor Advertisement. For an Ethernet node, the Target Link-Layer Address option contains the Ethernet MAC address of the sending node. The address in the Target Link-Layer Address option is used by receiving nodes to determine the unicast MAC address of the advertising node.

Network Monitor Capture

Here is an example of a solicited Neighbor Advertisement message as displayed by Network Monitor 3.1 (frame 2 of capture 06_01 in the \NetworkMonitorCaptures folder on the companion CD-ROM):

```
Frame:
+ Ethernet: Etype = IPv6
- Ipv6: Next Protocol = ICMPv6, Payload Length = 32
  + Versions: IPv6, Internet Protocol, DSCP 0
    PayloadLength: 32 (0x20)
    NextProtocol: ICMPv6, 58(0x3a)
    HopLimit: 255 (0xFF)
    SourceAddress: FE80:0:0:0:260:97FF:FE02:6EA5
    DestinationAddress: FE80:0:0:0:210:5AFF:FEAA:20A2
- Icmpv6: Neighbor Advertisement, Target = FE80:0:0:0:260:97FF:FE02:6EA5
    MessageType: Neighbor Advertisement, 136(0x88)
  - NeighborAdvertisement:
    Code: 0 (0x0)
    Checksum: 35244 (0x89AC)
  - NeighborAdvertisementFlag: 1610612736 (0x60000000)
    R:   (0............................) Not router
    S:   (.1...........................) Solicited
    O:   (..1..........................) Override
    Rsv: (...00000000000000000000000000000)
    TargetAddress: FE80:0:0:0:260:97FF:FE02:6EA5
  + TargetLinkLayerAddress:
```

Redirect

The Redirect message is sent by an IPv6 router to inform an originating host of a better first-hop address for a specific destination. Redirect messages are sent only by routers for unicast traffic, are unicast only to originating hosts, and are processed only by hosts.

For example, assuming that the local link is Ethernet, in the Ethernet header of the Redirect message, you will find the following settings:

- The Source Address field is set to the MAC address of the sending network adapter.
- The Destination Address field is set to the unicast MAC address of the originating sender.

In the IPv6 header of the Redirect message, you will find these settings:

- The Source Address field is set to a unicast address that is assigned to the sending interface.
- The Destination Address field is set to the unicast IP address of the originating host.
- The Hop Limit field is set to 255.

Figure 6-16 shows the structure of the Redirect message.

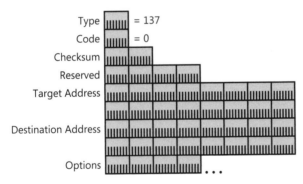

Figure 6-16   The structure of the Redirect message

The following list describes the fields in the Redirect message:

- **Type**   The value of this field is 137.
- **Code**   The value of this field is 0.
- **Checksum**   The value of this field is the ICMPv6 checksum.
- **Reserved**   This is a 32-bit field reserved for the future and set to 0.
- **Target Address**   The Target Address field indicates the better next-hop address for packets addressed to the node in the Destination Address field. The size of this field is 128 bits. For off-link traffic, the Target Address field is set to the link-local address of a

local router. For on-link traffic, the Target Address field is set to the Destination Address field in the Redirect message.

- **Destination Address**   The Destination Address field contains the destination address of the packet that caused the router to send the Redirect message. The size of this field is 128 bits. Upon receipt at the originating host, the Target Address and Destination Address fields are used to update forwarding information for the destination. Subsequent packets sent to the destination by the host are forwarded to the address in the Target Address field.

The options that can be present in a Redirect message are the following:

- **Target Link-Layer Address option**   The Target Link-Layer Address option contains the link-layer address of the target (the node to which subsequent packets should be sent). The Target Link-Layer Address option can be included when known by the router, although it is not typically sent.

- **Redirected Header option**   The Redirected Header option includes the leading portion of the original packet that caused the Redirect message to be sent, sized so that the entire IPv6 packet containing the Redirect message is no larger than 1280 bytes.

Network Monitor Capture

Here is an example of a Redirect message as displayed by Network Monitor 3.1 (capture 06_03 in the \NetworkMonitorCaptures folder on the companion CD-ROM):

```
Frame:
+ Ethernet: Etype = IPv6
+ Ipv6: Next Protocol = ICMPv6, Payload Length = 128
- Icmpv6: Redirect, Target = FE80:0:0:0:2B0:D0FF:FE23:4735
    MessageType: Redirect, 137(0x89)
  - Redirect:
    Code: 0 (0x0)
    Checksum: 31003 (0x791B)
    Reserved: 0 (0x0)
    TargetAddress: FE80:0:0:0:2B0:D0FF:FE23:4735
    DestAddress: 2001:DB8:0:0:0:0:0:1
  - RedirectedHeader:
    Type: Redirected Header, 4(0x4)
    Length: 11, in unit of 8 octets
    Reserved: 0 (0x0)
  + InvokingPacket: Next Protocol = ICMPv6, Payload Length = 40
```

Summary of Neighbor Discovery Messages and Options

Table 6-2 lists each ND message and the options that might be included with the message.

Table 6-2   **ND Messages and the Options That Might Be Included**

ND Message	ND Options That Might Be Included
Router Solicitation	Source Link-Layer Address option: Used to inform the router of the link-layer address of the host for the unicast Router Advertisement response.
Router Advertisement	Source Link-Layer Address option: Used to inform the receiving host(s) of the link-layer address of the router.
	Prefix Information option(s): Used to inform the receiving host(s) of on-link prefixes and whether to autoconfigure stateless addresses.
	MTU option: Used to inform the receiving host(s) of the IPv6 MTU of the link.
	Advertisement Interval option: Used to inform the receiving host how often the router (the home agent) is sending unsolicited multicast router advertisements.
	Home Agent Information option: Used to advertise the home agent's preference and lifetime.
	Route Information option(s): Used to inform the receiving host(s) of specific routes to add to a local routing table.
Neighbor Solicitation	Source Link-Layer Address option: Used to inform the receiving node of the link-layer address of the sender.
Neighbor Advertisement	Target Link-Layer Address option: Used to inform the receiving node(s) of the link-layer address corresponding to the Target Address field.
Redirect	Redirected Header option: Used to include all or a portion of the packet that was redirected.
	Target Link-Layer Address option: Used to inform the receiving node(s) of the link-layer address corresponding to the Target Address field.

Neighbor Discovery Processes

The ND protocol provides message exchanges for the following processes:

- Address resolution (including duplicate address detection)
- Router discovery (includes prefix and parameter discovery)
- Neighbor unreachability detection
- Redirect function

For information about address autoconfiguration, see Chapter 8. For information about next-hop determination, see the "Host Sending Algorithm" section in this chapter.

Conceptual Host Data Structures

To facilitate interactions between neighboring nodes, RFC 4861 defines the following conceptual host data structures as an example of how to store information for ND processes:

- **Neighbor cache**   The neighbor cache stores the on-link IP address of each neighbor, its corresponding link-layer address, and an indication of the neighbor's reachability state. The neighbor cache is equivalent to the ARP cache in IPv4.

- **Destination cache**   The destination cache stores information on next-hop IP addresses for destinations to which traffic has recently been sent. Each entry in the destination cache contains the destination IP address (either local or remote), the previously resolved next-hop IP address, and the path MTU for the destination.

- **Prefix list**   The prefix list contains on-link prefixes. Each entry in the prefix list defines a range of IP addresses for destinations that are directly reachable (neighbors). This list is populated from prefixes advertised by routers using the Router Advertisement message.

- **Default router list**   IP addresses corresponding to on-link routers that have sent Router Advertisement messages and are eligible to be default routers are included in the default router list.

Figure 6-17 shows the conceptual host data structures defined in RFC 4861.

Destination Cache			Neighbor Cache		
Destination	Next-Hop Address	PMTU	Next-Hop Address	Link-Layer Address	PMTU

Prefix List	Default Router List

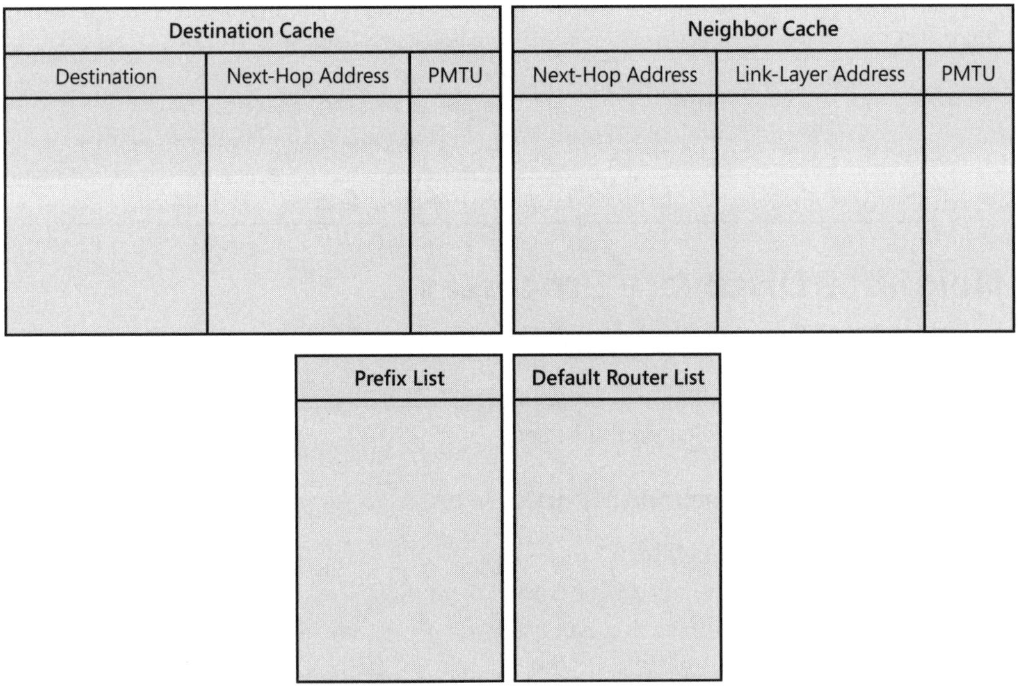

Figure 6-17   The conceptual host data structures defined in RFC 4861

RFC 4861 defines these data structures as an example of an IPv6 host conceptual model. An IPv6 implementation is not required to create these exact data structures as long as the external behavior of the host is consistent with RFC 4861. For example, the IPv6 protocol for Windows Server 2008 and Windows Vista uses a destination cache and neighbor cache. However, to determine the next-hop address for a given destination, the IPv6 protocol for Windows Server 2008 and Windows Vista uses a routing table rather than a prefix list and default router list. For more information about the IPv6 routing table, see Chapter 10, "IPv6 Routing." For more information about how IPv6 determines the next-hop address using the conceptual RFC 4861 data structures, see the "Host Sending Algorithm" section in this chapter.

To view the destination cache on a computer running Windows Server 2008 or Windows Vista, type **netsh interface ipv6 show destinationcache** at a command prompt. To view the neighbor cache, type **netsh interface ipv6 show neighbors** at a command prompt. To view the routing table, type **netsh interface ipv6 show routes** at a command prompt.

Address Resolution

The address resolution process for IPv6 nodes consists of an exchange of Neighbor Solicitation and Neighbor Advertisement messages to resolve the link-layer address of the on-link next-hop address for a given destination. The sending host sends a multicast Neighbor Solicitation message on the appropriate interface. The multicast address of the Neighbor Solicitation message is the solicited-node multicast address derived from the target IP address. The Neighbor Solicitation message includes the link-layer address of the sending host in the Source Link-Layer Address option. For information about how a host determines the next-hop address for a destination, see "Host Sending Algorithm" in this chapter.

When the target host receives the Neighbor Solicitation message, it updates its own neighbor cache based on the source address of the Neighbor Solicitation message and the link-layer address in the Source Link-Layer Address option. Next, the target node sends a unicast Neighbor Advertisement to the Neighbor Solicitation sender. The Neighbor Advertisement includes the Target Link-Layer Address option.

After receiving the Neighbor Advertisement from the target, the sending host updates its neighbor cache with an entry for the target based on the information in the Target Link-Layer Address option. At this point, unicast IPv6 traffic between the sending host and the target of the Neighbor Solicitation can be sent.

Address Resolution Example—Part 1

Host A has an Ethernet MAC address of 00-10-5A-AA-20-A2 and a corresponding link-local address of FE80::210:5AFF:FEAA:20A2. Host B has an Ethernet MAC address of 00-60-97-02-6E-A5 and a corresponding link-local address of FE80::260:97FF:FE02:6EA5. To send a packet to Host B, Host A must first use address resolution to resolve Host B's link-layer address.

Based on Host B's IP address, Host A sends a multicast Neighbor Solicitation message to the solicited-node address of FF02::1:FF02:6EA5, as shown in Figure 6-18.

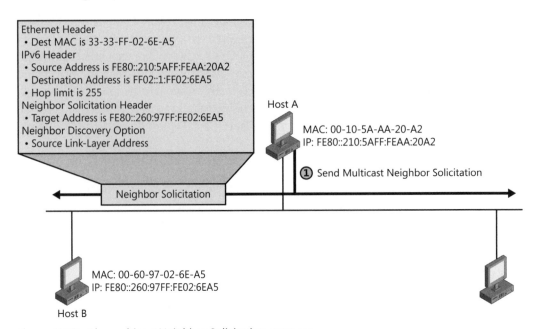

Figure 6-18 The multicast Neighbor Solicitation message

Network Monitor Capture

Here is the Neighbor Solicitation message for this example as displayed by Network Monitor 3.1 (frame 1 of capture 06_01 in the \NetworkMonitorCaptures folder on the companion CD-ROM):

```
Frame:
- Ethernet: Etype = IPv6
  + DestinationAddress: 3333FF 026EA5
  + SourceAddress: 00105A AA20A2
    EthernetType: IPv6, 34525(0x86dd)
- Ipv6: Next Protocol = ICMPv6, Payload Length = 32
  + Versions: IPv6, Internet Protocol, DSCP 0
    PayloadLength: 32 (0x20)
    NextProtocol: ICMPv6, 58(0x3a)
    HopLimit: 255 (0xFF)
    SourceAddress: FE80:0:0:0:210:5AFF:FEAA:20A2
    DestinationAddress: FF02:0:0:0:0:1:FF02:6EA5
- Icmpv6: Neighbor Solicitation, Target = FE80:0:0:0:260:97FF:FE02:6EA5
    MessageType: Neighbor Solicitation, 135(0x87)
  - NeighborSolicitation:
    Code: 0 (0x0)
    Checksum: 3893 (0xF35)
    Reserved: 0 (0x0)
    TargetAddress: FE80:0:0:0:260:97FF:FE02:6EA5
  - SourceLinkLayerAddress:
    Type: Source Link-Layer Address, 1(0x1)
    Length: 1, in unit of 8 octets
    Address: 00-10-5A-AA-20-A2
```

Address Resolution Example—Part 2

Host B, having registered the multicast MAC address of 33-33-FF-02-6E-A5 with its Ethernet adapter, receives and processes the Neighbor Solicitation message. Host B responds with a unicast Neighbor Advertisement message, as shown in Figure 6-19.

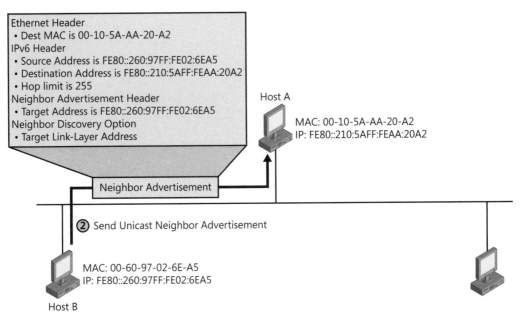

Figure 6-19   The unicast Neighbor Advertisement message

Network Monitor Capture

Here is the Neighbor Advertisement message for this example as displayed by Network Monitor 3.1 (frame 2 of capture 06_01 in the \NetworkMonitorCaptures folder on the companion CD-ROM):

```
 Frame:
- Ethernet: Etype = IPv6
  + DestinationAddress: 00105A AA20A2
  + SourceAddress: 00105A 026EA5
    EthernetType: IPv6, 34525(0x86dd)
- Ipv6: Next Protocol = ICMPv6, Payload Length = 32
  + Versions: IPv6, Internet Protocol, DSCP 0
    PayloadLength: 32 (0x20)
    NextProtocol: ICMPv6, 58(0x3a)
    HopLimit: 255 (0xFF)
    SourceAddress: FE80:0:0:0:260:97FF:FE02:6EA5
    DestinationAddress: FE80:0:0:0:210:5AFF:FEAA:20A2
- Icmpv6: Neighbor Advertisement, Target = FE80:0:0:0:260:97FF:FE02:6EA5
    MessageType: Neighbor Advertisement, 136(0x88)
  - NeighborAdvertisement:
    Code: 0 (0x0)
    Checksum: 35244 (0x89AC)
  - NeighborAdvertisementFlag: 1610612736 (0x60000000)
```

```
      R:   (0.............................) Not router
      S:   (.1............................) Solicited
      O:   (..1...........................) Override
      Rsv: (...00000000000000000000000000000)
      TargetAddress: FE80:0:0:0:0260:97FF:FE02:6EA5
   - TargetLinkLayerAddress:
      Type: Target Link-Layer Address, 2(0x2)
      Length: 1, in unit of 8 octets
      Address: 00-60-97-02-6E-A5
```

Neighbor Unreachability Detection

A neighboring node is reachable if there has been a recent confirmation that IPv6 packets sent to the neighboring node were received and processed by the neighboring node. Neighbor unreachability does not necessarily verify the end-to-end reachability of the destination. Because a neighboring node can be a host or router, the neighboring node might not be the final destination of the packet. Neighbor unreachability verifies only the reachability of the first hop to the destination.

One of the ways that reachability is confirmed is through the sending of a unicast Neighbor Solicitation message and the receipt of a solicited Neighbor Advertisement message. A solicited Neighbor Advertisement message, which has its Solicited flag set to 1, is sent only in response to a Neighbor Solicitation message. Unsolicited Neighbor Advertisement or Router Advertisement messages are not considered proof of reachability. The exchange of Neighbor Solicitation and Neighbor Advertisement messages confirms only the reachability of the node that sent the Neighbor Advertisement from the node that sent the Neighbor Solicitation. It does not confirm the reachability of the node that sent the Neighbor Solicitation from the node that sent the Neighbor Advertisement.

For example, if Host A sends a unicast Neighbor Solicitation to Host B and Host B sends a solicited unicast Neighbor Advertisement to Host A, Host A considers Host B reachable. Because there is no confirmation in this exchange that Host A actually received the Neighbor Advertisement, Host B does not consider Host A reachable. To confirm reachability of Host A from Host B, Host B must send its own unicast Neighbor Solicitation to Host A and receive a solicited unicast Neighbor Advertisement from Host A.

Here is an example of an exchange of ND messages to establish neighbor reachability by two nodes (HOST_A and HOST_B) for each other as displayed by Network Monitor 3.1 (capture 06_05 in the \NetworkMonitorCaptures folder on the companion CD-ROM):

```
1      8.356000     HOST_A      HOST_B           ICMP6
       Neighbor Solicitation; Target = fe80::210:5aff:feaa:20a2
2      8.357000     HOST_B      HOST_A           ICMP6
       Neighbor Advertisement; Target = fe80::210:5aff:feaa:20a2
3      8.527000     HOST_B      HOST_A           ICMP6
       Neighbor Solicitation; Target = fe80::250:daff:fed8:c153
4      8.527000     HOST_A      HOST_B           ICMP6
       Neighbor Advertisement; Target = fe80::250:daff:fed8:c153
```

In frames 1 and 2, HOST_A establishes the reachability of HOST_B. In frames 3 and 4, HOST_B establishes the reachability of HOST_A.

> **Note**   The Network Monitor frame summary lines have been wrapped for improved readability.

Another method of determining reachability is when upper-layer protocols indicate that the communication using the next-hop address is making forward progress. For TCP traffic, forward progress is determined when acknowledgement segments for sent data are received. The end-to-end reachability confirmed by the receipt of TCP acknowledgments implies the reachability of the first hop to the destination. The TCP module provides these indications to the IPv6 module on an ongoing basis.

Other protocols, such as UDP, might not have a method of determining or indicating the forward progress of communication. In this case, the exchange of Neighbor Solicitation and Neighbor Advertisement messages is used to confirm reachability.

Neighbor Cache Entry States

The reachability of a neighboring node is determined by monitoring the state of the neighboring node's entry in the neighbor cache.

Figure 6-20 shows the states of a neighbor cache entry.

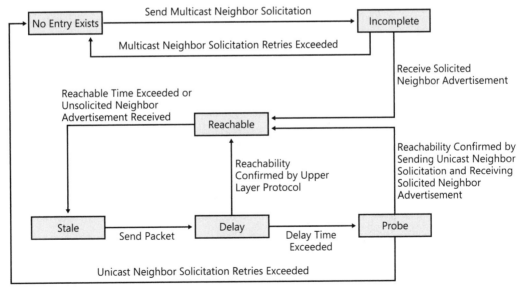

Figure 6-20   The states of a neighbor cache entry

RFC 4861 defines the following states for a neighbor cache entry:

- **INCOMPLETE** IPv6 address resolution, which uses a solicited-node multicast Neighbor Solicitation message, is in progress. The INCOMPLETE state is entered when a new neighbor cache entry is created but does not yet have the node's corresponding link-layer address. The number of multicast neighbor solicitations sent before abandoning the address resolution process and removing the neighbor cache entry is set by a configurable variable. RFC 4861 uses the variable name of MAX_MULTICAST_SOLICIT and recommends a value of 3.

- **REACHABLE** Reachability has been confirmed by receipt of a solicited unicast Neighbor Advertisement message by an indication from an upper-layer protocol. The neighbor cache entry stays in the REACHABLE state until the number of milliseconds indicated in the Reachable Time field in the Router Advertisement message (or a host default value) elapses. As long as upper-layer protocols such as TCP indicate that communication is making forward progress, the entry stays in the REACHABLE state. Each time an indication of forward progress is made, the reachable time for the entry is refreshed.

- **STALE** Reachable time (the duration since the last reachability confirmation was received) has elapsed. The neighbor cache entry goes into the STALE state after the value (milliseconds) in the Reachable Time field in the Router Advertisement message (or a host default value) elapses, and it remains in this state until a packet is sent to the neighbor. The STALE state is also entered when an unsolicited neighbor advertisement that advertises the link-layer address is received.

- **DELAY** To allow time for upper-layer protocols to provide reachability confirmation before sending Neighbor Solicitation messages, the neighbor cache entry enters the DELAY state and waits a configurable period of time. RFC 4861 uses the variable name of DELAY_FIRST_PROBE_TIME and recommends a value of 5 seconds. If no reachability confirmation is received by the delay time, the entry enters the PROBE state and a unicast Neighbor Solicitation message is sent.

- **PROBE** Reachability confirmation is in progress for a neighbor cache entry that was in either the STALE state or the DELAY state. Unicast Neighbor Solicitation messages are sent at intervals corresponding to the Retransmission Timer field in the Router Advertisement message received by this host (or a default host value). The number of Neighbor Solicitations sent before abandoning the reachability detection process and removing the neighbor cache entry is set by a configurable variable. RFC 4861 uses the variable name of MAX_UNICAST_SOLICITS and recommends a value of 3.

Depending on the IPv6 implementation, any entry can go from any state to the NO ENTRY EXISTS state at any time (not shown in Figure 6-20).

If the unreachable neighbor is a router, the host chooses another router from the default router list and performs both address resolution and neighbor unreachability detection on it.

If a router becomes a host, it should send a multicast Neighbor Advertisement message with the Router flag set to 0. If a host receives a Neighbor Advertisement message from a router where the Router flag is set to 0, the host removes that router from the default router list and, if necessary, chooses another router.

Neighbor Unreachability Detection and Dead Gateway Detection

The TCP/IP (IPv4) protocol for Windows Server 2008 and Windows Vista supports an algorithm known as *dead gateway detection*. Dead gateway detection detects the failure of the current default gateway by monitoring the number of failing TCP connections. When 25 percent of the active TCP connections have failed and have been switched to another default gateway, the default gateway of the host is switched to another default gateway.

Dead gateway detection provides some default gateway fault tolerance for hosts on subnets containing multiple default routers. However, dead gateway detection has the following limitations:

- Monitors only TCP traffic. If connectivity fails for other types of traffic, the default gateway is not switched.

- Can cause the default gateway configuration to change when a remote router fails. Remote routers in the path between the host and the destination that fail might also cause TCP connections forwarded along that path to fail and for the host to switch its default gateway. Because dead gateway detection relies on an end-to-end protocol (such as TCP), a host can switch its default gateway even when the current default gateway is fully operational.

Neighbor unreachability detection is an improvement over dead gateway detection because it does the following:

- Provides for host-based default router fault tolerance for all types of traffic, not just TCP. Although forward progress indicators are used for TCP traffic, other protocols can rely on an exchange of Neighbor Solicitation and Neighbor Advertisement messages to determine reachability.

- Detects whether the neighboring default router is operational. Neighbor unreachability detection will not cause the default router configuration to change because of a failing remote router.

Duplicate Address Detection

IPv4 nodes use ARP Request messages and a method called *gratuitous ARP* to detect a duplicate unicast IPv4 address on the local link. Similarly, IPv6 nodes use the Neighbor Solicitation message to detect duplicate address use on the local link in a process known as duplicate address detection that is described in RFC 4862.

With IPv4 gratuitous ARP, the Source Protocol Address and Target Protocol Address fields in the ARP Request message header are set to the IPv4 address for which duplication is being detected. In IPv6 duplicate address detection, the Target Address field in the Neighbor Solicitation message is set to the IPv6 address for which duplication is being detected.

Duplicate address detection differs from address resolution in the following ways:

- In the duplicate address detection Neighbor Solicitation message, the Source Address field in the IPv6 header is set to the unspecified address (::). The address being queried for duplication cannot be used until it is determined that there are no duplicates.

- In the Neighbor Advertisement reply to a duplicate address detection Neighbor Solicitation message, the Destination Address in the IPv6 header is set to the link-local scope all-nodes multicast address (FF02::1). The Solicited flag in the Neighbor Advertisement message is set to 0. Because the sender of the duplicate address detection Neighbor Solicitation message is not using the desired IP address, it cannot receive unicast Neighbor Advertisements. Therefore, the Neighbor Advertisement is multicast.

Upon receipt of the multicast Neighbor Advertisement with the Target Address field set to the IP address for which duplication is being detected, the node disables the use of the duplicate IP address on the interface. If the node does not receive a Neighbor Advertisement that defends the use of the address, it initializes the address on the interface.

An IPv6 node does not perform duplicate address detection for anycast addresses. Anycast addresses are not unique to a node.

Duplicate Address Detection Example—Part 1

Host B has a global address of 2001:DB8::2:260:8FF:FE52:F9D8. Host A is attempting to use the global address of 2001:DB8::2:260:8FF:FE52:F9D8. However, before Host A can use this address, it must verify its uniqueness through duplicate address detection.

Host A sends a Neighbor Solicitation message to the solicited-node multicast address FF02::1:FF52:F9D8, as shown in Figure 6-21.

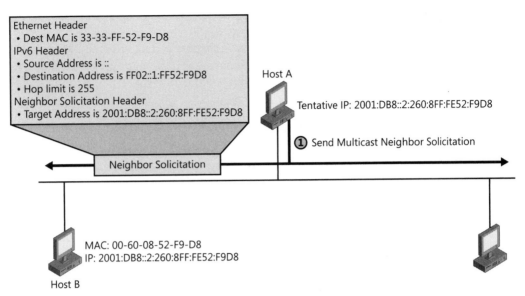

Figure 6-21   A multicast Neighbor Solicitation message for duplicate address detection

Network Monitor Capture

Here is the Neighbor Solicitation message for this example as displayed by Network Monitor 3.1 (frame 1 of capture 06_06 in the \NetworkMonitorCaptures folder on the companion CD-ROM):

```
Frame:
- Ethernet: Etype = IPv6
  + DestinationAddress: 3333FF 52F9D8
  + SourceAddress: 00B0D0 234733
    EthernetType: IPv6, 34525(0x86dd)
- Ipv6: Next Protocol = ICMPv6, Payload Length = 24
  + Versions: IPv6, Internet Protocol, DSCP 0
    PayloadLength: 24 (0x18)
    NextProtocol: ICMPv6, 58(0x3a)
    HopLimit: 255 (0xFF)
  + SourceAddress: 0:0:0:0:0:0:0:0
    DestinationAddress: FF02:0:0:0:0:1:FF52:F9D8
- Icmpv6: Neighbor Solicitation, Target = 2001:DB8:0:2:260:8FF:FE52:F9D8
    MessageType: Neighbor Solicitation, 135(0x87)
  - NeighborSolicitation:
    Code: 0 (0x0)
    Checksum: 20279 (0x4F37)
    Reserved: 0 (0x0)
    TargetAddress: 2001:DB8:0:2:260:8FF:FE52:F9D8
```

Notice the use of the unspecified address (::) in the Source Address field in the IPv6 header and the lack of the Source Link-Layer Address option.

Duplicate Address Detection Example—Part 2

Host B, having registered the multicast MAC address of 33-33-FF-52-F9-D8 with its Ethernet adapter, receives and processes the Neighbor Solicitation message. Host B notes that the source address is the unspecified address. Host B then responds with a multicast Neighbor Advertisement message, as shown in Figure 6-22.

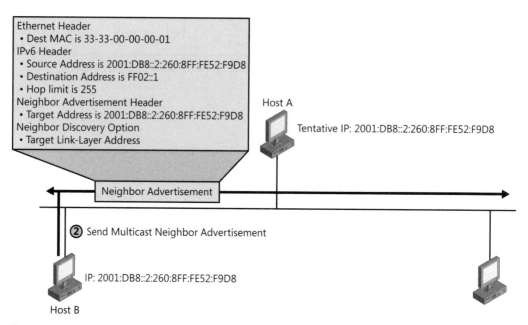

Figure 6-22   The multicast Neighbor Advertisement message

Network Monitor Capture

Here is the Neighbor Advertisement message for this example as displayed by Network Monitor 3.1 (frame 2 of capture 06_06 in the \NetworkMonitorCaptures folder on the companion CD-ROM):

```
Frame:
- Ethernet: Etype = IPv6
  + DestinationAddress: 333300 000001
  + SourceAddress: 006008 52F9D8
    EthernetType: IPv6, 34525(0x86dd)
- Ipv6: Next Protocol = ICMPv6, Payload Length = 32
  + Versions: IPv6, Internet Protocol, DSCP 0
    PayloadLength: 32 (0x20)
    NextProtocol: ICMPv6, 58(0x3a)
    HopLimit: 255 (0xFF)
    SourceAddress: 2001:DB8:0:2:260:8FF:FE52:F9D8
    DestinationAddress: FF02:0:0:0:0:0:0:1
- Icmpv6: Neighbor Advertisement, Target = 2001:DB8:0:2:260:8FF:FE52:F9D8
    MessageType: Neighbor Advertisement, 136(0x88)
  - NeighborAdvertisement:
```

```
    Code: 0 (0x0)
    Checksum: 61832 (0xF188)
  - NeighborAdvertisementFlag: 536870912 (0x20000000)
     R:   (0............................) Not router
     S:   (.0...........................) Not solicited
     O:   (..1..........................) Override
     Rsv: (...00000000000000000000000000000)
    TargetAddress: 2001:DB8:0:2:260:8FF:FE52:F9D8
  - TargetLinkLayerAddress:
    Type: Target Link-Layer Address, 2(0x2)
    Length: 1, in unit of 8 octets
    Address: 00-60-08-52-F9-D8
```

Notice the use of the link-local scope all-nodes multicast address as the destination address and the values of the Solicited and Override flags.

Router Discovery

Router discovery is the process through which nodes attempt to discover the set of routers on the local link. Router discovery in IPv6 is similar to ICMP router discovery for IPv4 described in RFC 1256. ICMP router discovery is a set of ICMP messages that allow IPv4 hosts to determine the presence of local routers, determine which local router is automatically configured as a default gateway, and automatically switch to a different router as their default gateway when the current default gateway becomes unavailable.

An important difference between ICMPv4 router discovery and IPv6 router discovery is the mechanism through which a new default router is selected when the current one becomes unavailable. In ICMPv4 router discovery, the Router Advertisement message includes an Advertisement Lifetime field. Advertisement Lifetime is the time after which the router can be considered unavailable. In the worst case, a router can become unavailable and hosts will not attempt to discover a new default router until the Router Advertisement time has elapsed.

IPv6 has a Router Lifetime field in the Router Advertisement message. This field indicates the length of time that the router can be considered a default router. However, if the current default router becomes unavailable, the condition is detected through neighbor unreachability detection instead of the Router Lifetime field in the Router Advertisement message. Because neighbor unreachability detection determines that the router is no longer reachable, a new router is chosen immediately from the default router list or the host sends a Router Solicitation message to determine if additional default routers are present on the link. For more information, see the "Neighbor Unreachability Detection" section in this chapter.

In addition to configuring a default router, IPv6 router discovery also configures the following:

- The default setting for the Hop Limit field in the IPv6 header.

- A determination of whether the node should use an address protocol, such as Dynamic Host Configuration Protocol for IPv6 (DHCPv6), for addresses and other configuration parameters.

- The timers used in neighbor unreachability detection and the retransmission of Neighbor Solicitations.

- The list of network prefixes defined for the link. Each network prefix contains both the IPv6 network prefix and its valid and preferred lifetimes. If indicated, a network prefix combined with the interface identifier creates a stateless IP address configuration for the receiving interface. A network prefix also defines the range of addresses for nodes on the local link.

- The MTU of the local link.

- Specific routes to add to the routing table.

The IPv6 router discovery processes are the following:

- IPv6 routers pseudo-periodically send a Router Advertisement message on the local link advertising their existence as routers. They also provide configuration parameters such as default hop limit, MTU, prefixes, and routes. For more information about how often routers send pseudo-periodic router advertisements, see section 6.2.4 of RFC 4861.

- Active IPv6 hosts on the local link receive the Router Advertisement messages and use the contents to maintain the default router and prefix lists, autoconfigure addresses, add routes, and configure other parameters.

- A host that is starting sends a Router Solicitation message to the link-local scope all-routers multicast address (FF02::2). If the starting host is already configured with a unicast address, the Router Solicitation is sent with a unicast source address. Otherwise, the Router Solicitation is sent with an unspecified source address (::). Upon receipt of a Router Solicitation message, all routers on the local link send a Router Advertisement message to either the unicast address of the host that sent the Router Solicitation (if the source address of the Router Solicitation is a unicast address), or to the link-local scope all-nodes multicast address (FF02::1) (if the source address of the Router Solicitation message is unspecified). The host receives the Router Advertisement messages and uses their contents to build the default router and prefix lists and set other configuration parameters. The number of Router Solicitations sent before abandoning the router discovery process is set by a configurable variable. RFC 4861 uses the variable name of MAX_RTR_SOLICITATIONS and recommends a value of 3.

Router Discovery Example—Part 1

Host A has the Ethernet MAC address of 00-B0-D0-E9-41-43. The router has an Ethernet MAC address of 00-10-FF-D6-58-C0 and a corresponding link-local address of FE80::210:FFFF:FED6:58C0. To forward packets to off-link destinations, Host A must discover the presence of the router.

As part of the startup process, Host A sends a multicast Router Solicitation message to the address FF02::2 before it has confirmed the use of its corresponding link-local address, as shown in Figure 6-23.

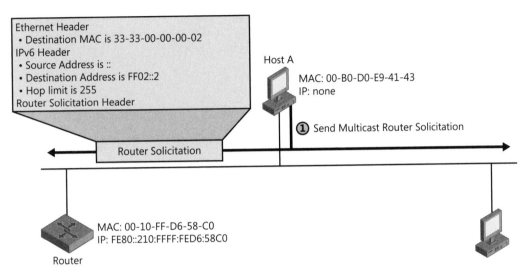

Figure 6-23   The multicast Router Solicitation message

Network Monitor Capture

Here is the Router Solicitation message for this example as displayed by Network Monitor 3.1 (frame 1 of capture 06_07 in the \NetworkMonitorCaptures folder on the companion CD-ROM):

```
Frame:
- Ethernet: Etype = IPv6
  + DestinationAddress: 333300 000002
  + SourceAddress: 00B0D0 E94143
    EthernetType: IPv6, 34525(0x86dd)
- Ipv6: Next Protocol = ICMPv6, Payload Length = 8
  + Versions: IPv6, Internet Protocol, DSCP 0
    PayloadLength: 8 (0x8)
    NextProtocol: ICMPv6, 58(0x3a)
    HopLimit: 255 (0xFF)
  + SourceAddress: 0:0:0:0:0:0:0:0
    DestinationAddress: FF02:0:0:0:0:0:0:2
- Icmpv6: Router Solicitation
    MessageType: Router Solicitation, 133(0x85)
  - RouterSolicitation:
    Code: 0 (0x0)
    Checksum: 31672 (0x7BB8)
    Reserved: 0 (0x0)
```

Notice the use of the unspecified address (::) as the source and that the Source Link-Layer Address option is not included.

Router Discovery Example—Part 2

The router, having registered the multicast MAC address of 33-33-00-00-00-02 with its Ethernet adapter, receives and processes the Router Solicitation. The router responds with a multicast Router Advertisement message containing configuration parameters and local link prefixes, as shown in Figure 6-24.

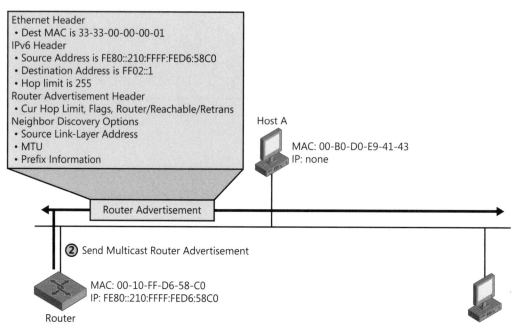

Figure 6-24   The unicast Router Advertisement message

Network Monitor Capture

Here is the Router Advertisement message for this example as displayed by Network Monitor 3.1 (frame 2 of capture 06_07 in the \NetworkMonitorCaptures folder on the companion CD-ROM):

```
Frame:
- Ethernet: Etype = IPv6
  + DestinationAddress: 333300 000001
  + SourceAddress: 0010FF D658C0
    EthernetType: IPv6, 34525(0x86dd)
- Ipv6: Next Protocol = ICMPv6, Payload Length = 88
  + Versions: IPv6, Internet Protocol, DSCP 28
    PayloadLength: 88 (0x58)
    NextProtocol: ICMPv6, 58(0x3a)
    HopLimit: 255 (0xFF)
    SourceAddress: FE80:0:0:0:210:FFFF:FED6:58C0
    DestinationAddress: FF02:0:0:0:0:0:0:1
- Icmpv6: Router Advertisement
    MessageType: Router Advertisement, 134(0x86)
```

```
- RouterAdvertisement:
    Code: 0 (0x0)
    Checksum: 24725 (0x6095)
    CurHopLimit: 64 (0x40)
  - RouterAdvertisementFlag:
    M:                  (0.......) Not managed address configuration
    O:                  (.0......) Not other stateful configuration
    A:                  (..0.....) Not a Mobile IP Home Agent
    RouterPreference: (...00...) Medium,0(0x0)
    Reserved:           (.....000)
    RouterLifetime: 1800 (0x708)
    ReachableTime: 0 (0x0)
    RetransTimer: 0 (0x0)
- SourceLinkLayerAddress:
    Type: Source Link-Layer Address, 1(0x1)
    Length: 1, in unit of 8 octets
    Address: 00-10-FF-D6-58-C0
- PrefixInformation:
    Type: Prefix Information, 3(0x3)
    Length: 4, in unit of 8 octets
    PrefixLength: 64 (0x40)
  - Flags: 192 (0xC0)
    L:  (1.......) On-Link determination allowed
    A:  (.1......) Autonomous address-configuration
    R:  (..0.....) Not router Address
    S:  (...0....) Not a site prefix
    P:  (....0...) Not a router prefix
    Rsv: (.....000)
    ValidLifetime: 2592000 (0x278D00)
    PreferredLifetime: 604800 (0x93A80)
    Reserved: 0 (0x0)
    Prefix: 2001:DB8:0:F282:0:0:0:0
- PrefixInformation:
    Type: Prefix Information, 3(0x3)
    Length: 4, in unit of 8 octets
    PrefixLength: 64 (0x40)
  - Flags: 192 (0xC0)
    L:  (1.......) On-Link determination allowed
    A:  (.1......) Autonomous address-configuration
    R:  (..0.....) Not router Address
    S:  (...0....) Not a site prefix
    P:  (....0...) Not a router prefix
    Rsv: (.....000)
    ValidLifetime: 2592000 (0x278D00)
    PreferredLifetime: 604800 (0x93A80)
    Reserved: 0 (0x0)
    Prefix: FD5A:29F1:D005:F282:0:0:0:0
```

This Router Advertisement contains two prefixes—one for 2001:DB8:0:F282::/64 and one for FD5A:29F1:D005:F282::/64. Notice how both the global prefix and the unique local prefix use the same subnet identifier (F282).

Redirect Function

Routers use the redirect function to inform originating hosts of a better first-hop neighbor to which traffic should be forwarded for a specific destination. There are two instances where redirect is used:

1. A router informs an originating host of the IP address of a router available on the local link that is "closer" to the destination. "Closer" is a routing metric function used to reach the destination network segment. This condition can occur when there are multiple routers on a network segment, and the originating host chooses a default router and it is not the better ("closer") one to use to reach the destination.

2. A router informs an originating host that the destination is a neighbor (that is, it is on the same link as the originating host). This condition can occur when the prefix list of a host does not include the prefix of the destination. Because the destination does not match a prefix in the list, the originating host forwards the packet to its default router.

The following steps occur in the IPv6 redirect process:

1. The originating host forwards a unicast packet to its default router.

2. The router processes the packet and notes that the address of the originating host is a neighbor. Additionally, it notes that both the originating host's address and the next-hop address are on the same link.

3. The router sends the originating host a Redirect message. In the Target Address field of the Redirect message is the next-hop address of the node to which the originating host should send subsequent packets addressed to the destination.

4. The router forwards the packet to the appropriate next-hop address, using address resolution if needed to obtain the link-layer address of the next hop.

    For packets redirected to a router, the Target Address field is set to the link-local address of the router. For packets redirected to a host, the Target Address field is set to the destination address of the packet originally sent.

    The Redirect message includes the Redirected Header option. It might also include the Target Link-Layer Address option.

5. Upon receipt of the Redirect message, the originating host updates the destination address entry in the destination cache with the address in the Target Address field. If the Target Link-Layer Address option is included in the Redirect message, its contents are used to create or update the corresponding neighbor cache entry.

Redirect messages are sent only by the first router in the path between the originating host and the destination. Hosts never send Redirect messages and routers never update routing tables based on the receipt of a Redirect message. Like ICMPv6 error messages, Redirect messages are rate limited.

Redirect Example—Part 1

Host A has the Ethernet MAC address of 00-AA-00-11-11-11 and a corresponding link-local address of FE80::2AA:FF:FE11:1111. Host A also has the global address of 2001:DB8::1:2AA:FF:FE11:1111. Router 2 has the Ethernet MAC address of 00-AA-00-22-22-22 and a corresponding link-local address of FE80::2AA:FF:FE22:2222. Router 2 also has the site-local address of 2001:DB8::1:2AA:FF:FE22:2222. Router 3 has the Ethernet MAC address of 00-AA-00-33-33-33 and a corresponding link-local address of FE80::2AA:FF:FE33:3333. Router 3 also has the site-local address of 2001:DB8::1:2AA:FF:FE33:3333. Host A sends a packet to an off-link host at 2001:DB8::2:2AA:FF:FE99:9999 (not shown in Figure 6-25) and uses Router 2 as its current default router. However, Router 3 is the better router to use to reach this destination.

Host A performs address resolution if needed and sends the packet destined to 2001:DB8::2:2AA:FF:FE99:9999 to Router 2, as shown in Figure 6-25.

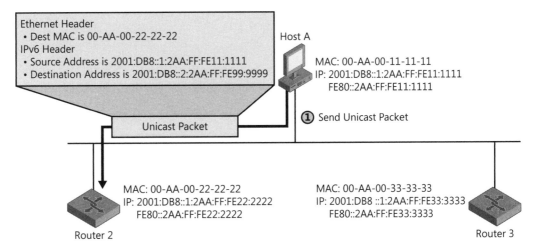

Figure 6-25   The unicast packet sent to the router

Redirect Example—Part 2

Router 2 receives the packet from Host A and notes that Host A is a neighbor. It also notes that Host A and the next-hop address for the destination are on the same link. To inform Host A that subsequent packets to the destination of 2001:DB8::2:2AA:EE:FE99:9999 should be sent to Router 3, Router 2 performs address resolution if needed and sends a Redirect message to Host A, as shown in Figure 6-26.

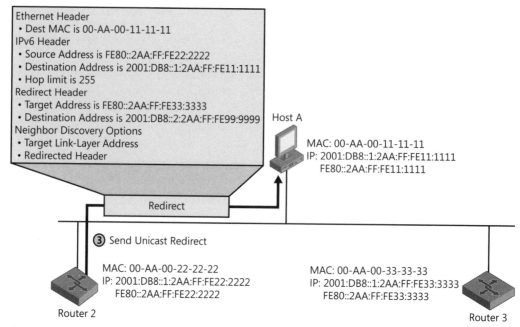

Figure 6-26 The Redirect message sent by the router

Redirect Example—Part 3

Based on the contents of its local routing table, Router 2 performs address resolution if needed and forwards the unicast packet received from Host A to Router 3, as shown in Figure 6-27.

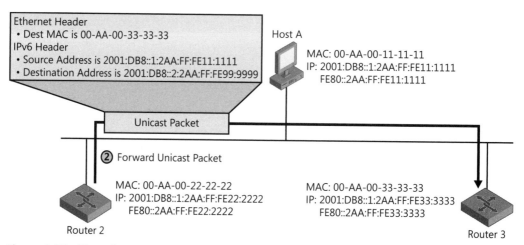

Figure 6-27 The unicast packet forwarded by the router

Host Sending Algorithm

The process by which an IPv6 host sends a unicast IPv6 packet uses a combination of the local host's conceptual data structures and the ND protocol. Based on RFC 4861, an IPv6 host uses the following algorithm when sending a unicast packet to an arbitrary destination:

1. Check the destination cache for an entry matching the destination address.

2. If an entry matching the destination address is found in the destination cache, obtain the next-hop address from the destination cache entry. If the destination is a Mobile IPv6 node, the destination cache entry might contain a pointer to a care-of destination cache entry. If so, the next-hop address is obtained from the care-of destination cache entry. For more information about Mobile IPv6, see Appendix F. Go to step 4.

    If an entry matching the destination address is not found in the destination cache, determine if the destination address matches a prefix in the prefix list:

    ❑ If the destination address matches a prefix in the prefix list, the next-hop address is set to the destination address. Go to step 3.

    ❑ If the destination address does not match a prefix in the prefix list, a default router is chosen from the default router list and the next-hop address is set to the default router address.

3. Update the destination cache.

4. Check the neighbor cache for an entry matching the next-hop address.

5. If an entry matching the next-hop address is found in the neighbor cache, use the link-layer address of the matching entry.

    If an entry matching the next-hop address is not found in the neighbor cache, use address resolution to obtain the link-layer address for the next-hop address.

    If address resolution fails, indicate an error.

6. Send the packet by using the link-layer address of the neighbor cache entry.

Figure 6-28 shows the host sending algorithm in flowchart form.

Because the IPv6 protocol for Windows Server 2008 and Windows Vista uses a routing table in place of a prefix list and default router list, the host-sending algorithm uses a different method to determine the next-hop address for the destination. For more information, see the "End-to-End IPv6 Delivery Process" section in Chapter 10.

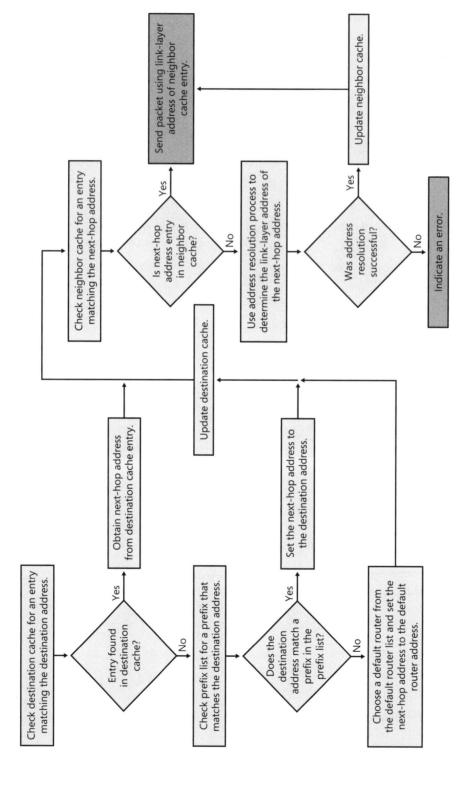

Figure 6-28 The host sending algorithm

IPv4 Neighbor Messages and Functions and IPv6 Equivalents

Table 6-3 lists IPv4 neighbor messages, components, and functions and their IPv6 equivalents.

Table 6-3   IPv4 Neighbor Messages, Components, and Functions and Their IPv6 Equivalents

IPv4	IPv6
ARP Request message	Neighbor Solicitation message
ARP Reply message	Neighbor Advertisement message
ARP cache	Neighbor cache
Gratuitous ARP	Duplicate address detection
Router Solicitation message (optional)	Router Solicitation message (required)
Router Advertisement message (optional)	Router Advertisement message (required)
Redirect message	Redirect message

References

The following references were cited in this chapter:

- RFC 1256 – "ICMP Router Discovery Messages"
- RFC 2464 – "Transmission of IPv6 Packets over Ethernet Networks"
- RFC 3775 – "Mobile IPv6"
- RFC 4191 – "Default Router Preferences and More-Specific Routes"
- RFC 4861 – "Neighbor Discovery for IP Version 6 (IPv6)"
- RFC 4862 – "IPv6 Stateless Address Autoconfiguration"
- Internet Draft – "Site Prefixes in Neighbor Discovery"

You can obtain these RFCs from the \RFCs_and_Drafts folder on the companion CD-ROM or from *http://www.ietf.org/rfc.html*.

Testing for Understanding

To test your understanding of IPv6 ND, answer the following questions. See Appendix D, "Testing for Understanding Answers," to check your answers.

1. List the IPv4 facilities that are replaced by the IPv6 ND protocol.

2. List the capabilities of the IPv6 ND protocol that are not present in IPv4.

3. List the five different ND messages and the options that can be included with them.

4. Describe the interpretation of the Length field in ND options.

5. What is the value of the Length field for a maximum-sized Redirected Header option (assuming no IPv6 extension headers are present)?

6. Describe how you would use the MTU option to provide seamless connectivity between Ethernet nodes and Asynchronous Transfer Mode (ATM) nodes on a transparently bridged link.

7. Why is the Source Link-Layer Address option not included in the Neighbor Solicitation message sent during duplicate address detection?

8. Describe the configuration parameters and their corresponding fields sent in the Router Advertisement message (not including options). Describe the configuration parameters and their corresponding fields sent in the Prefix Information option.

9. Under what circumstances is an unsolicited Neighbor Advertisement message sent?

10. What are the differences in address resolution and duplicate address detection node behavior for anycast addresses?

11. Why is the response to a duplicate address detection sent as multicast? Who sends the response, the offending or defending node?

12. Why is the value of the Hop Limit field set to 255 for all ND messages?

13. Describe the purpose of each of the host data structures described in RFC 4861.

14. What field in the Redirect message contains the next-hop address of the better router to use for packets addressed to a specific destination? Describe how the contents of that field are used to update the conceptual host data structures for subsequent data sent to the destination.

15. Under what circumstances does a router send a Router Advertisement?

16. For Host A and Host B on the same link, why is the exchange of a Neighbor Solicitation message (sent by Host A to Host B) and a Neighbor Advertisement message (sent by Host B to Host A) not considered by Host B as proof that Host A is reachable?

Chapter 7

Multicast Listener Discovery and MLD Version 2

At the end of this chapter, you should be able to do the following:

- Describe the purpose of the IPv6 Multicast Listener Discovery (MLD) and MLD version 2 (MLDv2) protocols.

- Describe how IPv6 hosts and routers support multicast communication.

- Describe the common structure of MLD and MLDv2 messages.

- Describe the structure and purpose of each type of MLD and MLDv2 message.

MLD and MLDv2 Overview

Multicast Listener Discovery (MLD) is the IPv6 equivalent of Internet Group Management Protocol version 2 (IGMPv2) defined in RFC 2236 for Internet Protocol version 4 (IPv4). MLD is a set of messages exchanged by routers and hosts, allowing routers to discover the set of multicast addresses for which there is at least one listening host for each attached subnet. Like IGMPv2, MLD does not allow routers to discover the list of individual multicast listeners for each multicast address. MLD is described in RFC 2710.

MLD version 2 (MLDv2) is the IPv6 equivalent of IGMP version 3 (IGMPv3) defined in RFC 3376 for IPv4. MLDv2 performs the same functions as MLD, but it allows IPv6 hosts to register interest in source-specific multicast traffic with their local multicast routers. An MLDv2-capable host can register interest in receiving IPv6 multicast traffic from only specific source addresses (an include list) or from any source except specific source addresses (an exclude list). MLDv2 is described in RFC 3810.

IPv6 Multicast Overview

In IPv4, multicast support is optional. In IPv6, multicast support is required. This section provides an overview of IPv6 multicast concepts.

In addition to unicast and anycast support, IPv6 also provides a mechanism to send and receive IPv6 multicast traffic. IPv6 multicast traffic is sent to a single destination address but is received and processed by multiple IPv6 hosts, regardless of their location on the network. Hosts listen to a specific IPv6 multicast address and receive all packets to that address. Multicast is more efficient than IPv6 unicast for one-to-many delivery of data. Instead of having multiple unicast packets sent, only one packet is sent.

The additional elements of IPv6 multicast include the following:

- The set of hosts listening on a specific IPv6 multicast address is called a *multicast group*.

- Multicast group membership is dynamic, and hosts can join and leave the group at any time.

- There are no limitations to the size of a multicast group.

- A multicast group can span IPv6 routers across multiple subnets. This configuration requires IPv6 multicast support on IPv6 routers and the ability for hosts to register themselves with the router. Host registration is accomplished by using MLD or MLDv2.

- A host can send traffic to a multicast address without being a member of the group.

These are the same elements that are used for IPv4 multicast.

IPv6 multicast addresses are defined by the address prefix FF00::/8 and can have different scopes. For more information about IPv6 multicast addresses, see Chapter 3, "IPv6 Addressing." In contrast, IPv4 multicast addresses use the address prefix 224.0.0.0/4.

In an IPv6 multicast-enabled network, any host can send multicast traffic to any multicast address, and any host can receive multicast traffic from any multicast address regardless of its location. To facilitate this capability, the hosts and routers of the network must support multicast traffic.

Host Support for Multicast

For a host to send IPv6 multicast packets, it must do the following:

- **Determine which IPv6 multicast destination address to use.** The IPv6 multicast address can be hard-coded by the application or obtained through a mechanism that allocates a unique multicast address.

- **Place the IPv6 multicast packet on the medium.** The sending host must construct an IPv6 packet containing the destination IPv6 multicast address and place it on the medium. In the case of Ethernet, the destination media access control (MAC) address is created from the IPv6 multicast address as described in Chapter 3.

For a host to receive IPv6 multicast packets, it must do the following:

- **Inform IPv6 to receive multicast traffic.** To determine the IPv6 multicast address to use, the application can create a multicast group or use an existing multicast group. In either case, the application can use a hard-coded multicast address or an address encoded in a Uniform Resource Locator (URL) string.

  After the multicast address is determined, an application must inform IPv6 to receive multicast packets for a specified multicast address. For example, the application can use Windows Sockets functions to notify IPv6 of the multicast groups joined. If multiple applications use the same IPv6 multicast address, IPv6 must pass a copy of the multicast packet to each application. IPv6 must track which applications use which multicast addresses, as applications join or leave multicast groups. Additionally, for a multihomed host, IPv6 must track the application membership of multicast groups for each interface.

- **Register the multicast MAC address with the network adapter.**   If the network technology supports hardware-based multicasting, the network adapter is instructed to pass up packets for a specific multicast address. In the case of shared-access technologies such as Ethernet, IPv6 instructs the network adapter to listen for and pass to higher protocol layers all frames with a multicast MAC address corresponding to the IPv6 multicast address. The IPv6 protocol for Windows Vista and Windows Server 2008 uses an NdisRequest() function to instruct the network adapter to listen for and pass to higher protocol layers all frames with a specific multicast destination MAC address.

- **Inform local routers.**   The host must inform local subnet routers that it is listening for multicast traffic at a specific multicast address. The protocol that registers multicast group information for IPv6 is MLD or MLDv2. For example, the host sends an MLDv2 Multicast Listener Report message to register membership in a specific multicast group. All multicast group membership is reported, except for the multicast group for the link-local scope, all-nodes multicast address (FF02::1).

   Even though an IPv6 multicast router would never forward traffic destined to a link-local scope multicast address beyond the local link, multicast group membership for link-local scope multicast addresses is still reported. This is done so that multicast-aware Layer 2 switches and bridges can properly forward IPv6 link-local multicast traffic to nodes on different LAN segments of a subnet.

Router Support for Multicast

To forward IPv6 multicast packets only to subnets for which there are group members, an IPv6 multicast router must be able to do the following:

- Receive all IPv6 multicast traffic.
- Forward IPv6 multicast traffic.
- Receive and process MLD or MLDv2 Multicast Listener Report and MLD Multicast Listener Done messages.
- Query attached subnets for host membership status.
- Communicate group membership to other IPv6 multicast routers.

Receive All IPv6 Multicast Traffic

For shared-access technologies, such as Ethernet, the normal listening mode for network adapters is unicast listening mode. The listening mode is the way that the network adapter analyzes the destination MAC address of incoming frames to decide to process them further. In unicast listening mode, the only frames that are considered for further processing are in a table of interesting destination MAC addresses on the network adapter. Typically, the only interesting addresses are the MAC-level broadcast address (0xFF-FF-FF-FF-FF-FF) and the unicast address of the adapter. The unicast address is also known as the MAC, physical, or hardware address.

However, for an IPv6 multicast router to receive all multicast traffic on a subnet, it must place the network adapter connected to the subnet in a special listening mode called *multicast promiscuous mode*. When an adapter is placed in multicast promiscuous mode, it analyzes the Institute of Electrical and Electronics Engineers (IEEE)–defined Individual/Group (I/G) bit to determine whether the frame requires further processing. For more information on the I/G bit in IEEE 802 addresses, see Chapter 3.

The meanings of the I/G bit are the following:

- If the I/G bit is set to 0, the address is a unicast (or individual) address.
- If the I/G bit is set to 1, the address is a multicast (or group) address. The multicast bit is also set to 1 for the MAC-level broadcast address.

When the network adapter is placed in multicast promiscuous listening mode, any frames with the I/G bit set to 1 are passed to higher protocol layers for further processing.

Multicast promiscuous mode is different from promiscuous mode. In promiscuous mode, all frames—regardless of the destination MAC address—are passed to higher protocol layers for processing. Promiscuous mode is used by protocol analyzers, also known as network sniffers, such as Microsoft Network Monitor.

Most network adapters support multicast promiscuous mode. A network adapter that supports promiscuous mode might not support multicast promiscuous mode. Consult your network adapter documentation or manufacturer for information about whether your network adapter supports multicast promiscuous mode. Network adapters of hosts are typically not placed in multicast promiscuous mode.

Forward IPv6 Multicast Traffic

The ability to forward IPv6 multicast packets is a router capability. When multicast forwarding is enabled, IPv6 multicast packets that have a scope larger than link-local are analyzed to determine over which interfaces the packet is to be forwarded. The analysis is done by comparing the source address and destination multicast address to entries in an IPv6 multicast forwarding table. Upon receipt of an IPv6 multicast packet that has a scope larger than link-local, the Hop Limit field in the IPv6 header is decremented by 1. If the hop limit is less than 1 after decrementing, the multicast packet is silently discarded. If the hop limit is greater than 0 after decrementing, the multicast forwarding table is checked. If an entry in the multicast forwarding table is found that matches the destination IPv6 multicast address, the IPv6 multicast packet is forwarded with its new hop limit over the appropriate interfaces.

The multicast forwarding process does not distinguish between hosts on locally attached subnets that are receiving multicast traffic or hosts on a subnet that is downstream from the locally attached subnet across another router. In other words, a multicast router might forward a multicast packet on a subnet for which there are no hosts listening. The multicast packet is forwarded because another router on that subnet indicated that a host in its direction is receiving the multicast traffic.

The multicast forwarding table does not record each multicast group member or the number of multicast group members. It records only that there is at least one multicast group member for a specific multicast address on a specific interface or link.

Receive and Process MLD or MLDv2 Multicast Listener Report and MLD Multicast Listener Done Messages

Multicast routers receive MLD or MLDv2 Multicast Listener Report messages from all hosts on all locally attached subnets. This information is used to track multicast group membership by placing entries in the multicast forwarding table. Because multicast routers have placed their network adapters in multicast promiscuous mode, they receive all MLD Multicast Listener Report messages sent to any multicast address.

To improve the *leave latency*, which is the time between when the last host on a subnet has left the group and when no more multicast traffic for that group is forwarded to that subnet, an IPv6 host that might be the last member of a group on a subnet sends an MLD Multicast Listener Done message. The IPv6 router then sends multicast-address-specific queries to the group reported in the MLD Multicast Listener Done message. If it receives no response, the IPv6 router determines that there are no more group members on that subnet.

Query Attached Subnets for Host Membership Status

To compensate for the loss of Multicast Listener Report and MLD Multicast Listener Done messages, IPv6 multicast routers periodically send Multicast Listener Query messages on the local subnet. A host that is still a member of a multicast group might respond to the query with a Multicast Listener Report message.

For MLD, to keep multiple hosts on a particular subnet from sending Multicast Listener Report messages for the same group, a random response timer is used on the hosts to delay the transmission of the Multicast Listener Report message. If another host sends the message on that subnet before the response timer expires, a message is not sent by the other hosts on that subnet.

Communicate Group Membership to Other IPv6 Multicast Routers

To create multicast-enabled IPv6 networks containing more than one router, multicast routers must communicate group membership information to each other so that group members can receive IPv6 multicast traffic regardless of their location on the IPv6 network. Multicast routers exchange host membership information by using a multicast routing protocol such as the Protocol Independent Multicast (PIM) protocol. Group membership is communicated either explicitly, by exchanging multicast address and subnet information, or implicitly, by informing upstream routers that no group members exist downstream from the source of the multicast traffic.

The goals of a multicast routing protocol include the following:

■ Forward traffic away from the source to prevent loops.

■ Minimize or eliminate multicast traffic to subnets that do not need the traffic.

■ Minimize CPU and memory load on the router for scalability.

■ Minimize the overhead of the routing protocol.

■ Minimize the *join latency*, which is the time it takes for the first group member on a subnet to begin receiving traffic sent to the group.

Multicast routing is more complex than unicast routing. With unicast routing, unicast traffic is forwarded to a unique destination. Unicast routes can summarize ranges of unique destinations. Unicast routes in the network are comparatively consistent and need to be updated only when the topology of the IPv6 network changes.

With multicast routing, multicast traffic is forwarded to an ambiguous group destination. Multicast addresses represent individual multicast groups, and in general, cannot be summarized in the multicast forwarding table. The location of group members is not consistent, and the multicast forwarding tables of multicast routers might need to be updated whenever a multicast group member joins or leaves a multicast group.

Just as unicast routing protocols update the unicast IPv6 routing table, multicast routing protocols update the IPv6 multicast forwarding table of a router.

MLD Packet Structure

Unlike IGMPv2, MLD uses ICMPv6 messages instead of defining a separate message structure. Figure 7-1 shows the structure of an MLD message packet.

IPv6 Header Next Header = 0 (Hop-by-Hop Options)	Hop-by-Hop Options Header IPv6 Router Alert Option Next Header = 58 (ICMPv6)	MLD Message

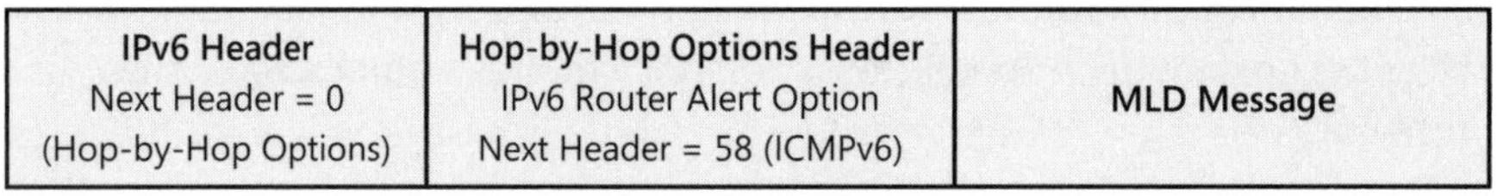

Figure 7-1   The structure of an MLD message packet

An MLD message packet consists of an IPv6 header, a Hop-by-Hop Options extension header, and the MLD message. The Hop-by-Hop Options extension header contains the IPv6 Router

Alert Option described in RFC 2711. It is used to ensure that routers process MLD messages that are sent to multicast addresses for which the router is not a group member.

MLD Messages

There are three types of MLD messages:

1. Multicast Listener Query (ICMPv6 Type 130)

2. Multicast Listener Report (ICMPv6 Type 131)

3. Multicast Listener Done (ICMPv6 Type 132)

All three MLD messages share the same message structure.

Multicast Listener Query

An IPv6 multicast-capable router uses the Multicast Listener Query message to query a subnet for multicast group membership. It is equivalent to the IGMPv2 Host Membership Query message. There are two types of Multicast Listener Query messages:

- **General query**   The general query is used to periodically query all hosts on a subnet for the presence of multicast group members of any multicast address. The only multicast addresses that are not reported are the link-local scope, all-nodes multicast address (FF02::1), and all multicast addresses with a scope of 0 (reserved) or 1 (interface-local).

- **Multicast-address-specific query**   The multicast-address-specific query is used to query all hosts on a subnet that are members of a specific multicast group.

The two message types are distinguished by the Destination Address field in the IPv6 header and the Multicast Address field within the Multicast Listener Query message.

In the IPv6 header of a Multicast Listener Query message, you will find the following information:

- The Hop Limit field is set to 1.

- The Source Address field is set to the link-local address of the interface on which the query is being sent.

- The Destination Address field is the specific multicast address being queried. For the general query, the Destination Address field is set to the link-local scope, all-nodes multicast address (FF02::1). For the multicast-address-specific query, the Destination Address field is set to the specific multicast address being queried.

Figure 7-2 shows the structure of the Multicast Listener Query message.

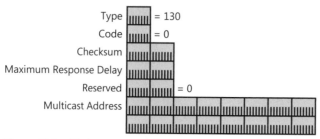

Figure 7-2 The structure of the Multicast Listener Query message

The following list describes the fields in the Multicast Listener Query message:

- **Type** The value of this field is 130.
- **Code** The value of this field is 0.
- **Checksum** The value of this field is the ICMPv6 checksum.
- **Maximum Response Delay** The Maximum Response Delay field indicates the maximum amount of time in milliseconds within which a multicast group member must report its membership by using an MLD Multicast Listener Report message. The size of this field is 16 bits.

  When a host that is a group member of a given multicast address receives a Multicast Listener Query, the host uses the value of the Maximum Response Delay field to calculate a random response time less than or equal to the current value of the field. Each host on the subnet that could report its membership sets a different random response time. The host on the subnet whose random response time expires first sends the Multicast Listener Report message. When the other hosts that could report group membership for the multicast address receive the Multicast Listener Report message, they abandon the attempt to send their own Multicast Listener Report message. This process results typically in only one host member reporting group membership for a given multicast address on each subnet.

- **Reserved** This is a 16-bit field reserved for future use and set to 0.
- **Multicast Address** For the general query, the Multicast Address field is set to the unspecified address (::). For the multicast-address-specific query, the Multicast Address field is set to the specific multicast address that is being queried. The size of this field is 128 bits.

Multicast Listener Report

The Multicast Listener Report message is used by a listening node to either immediately report its interest in receiving multicast traffic at a specific multicast address or respond to a Multicast Listener Query message (either a general or multicast-address-specific query). It is equivalent to the IGMPv2 Host Membership Report message.

In the IPv6 header of a Multicast Listener Report message, you will find the following information:

- The Hop Limit field is set to 1.

- The Source Address field is set to the link-local address of the interface on which the report is being sent. If the Multicast Listener Report message is for a solicited-node multicast address corresponding to a unicast address for which duplicate address detection is not yet complete, the source address is set to the unspecified address (::).

- The Destination Address field is the specific multicast address being reported.

Figure 7-3 shows the structure of the Multicast Listener Report message.

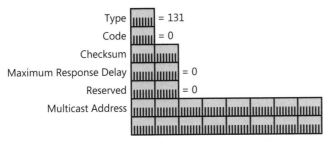

Figure 7-3   The structure of the Multicast Listener Report message

The fields in the Multicast Listener Report message are:

- **Type**   The value of this field is 131.

- **Code**   The value of this field is 0.

- **Checksum**   The value of this field is the ICMPv6 checksum.

- **Maximum Response Delay**   This field is not used in the Multicast Listener Report message and is set to 0.

- **Reserved**   This is a 16-bit field reserved for future use and set to 0.

- **Multicast Address**   The Multicast Address field is set to the specific multicast address that is being reported.

Network Monitor Capture

Here is an example of an MLD Multicast Listener Report message as displayed by Network Monitor 3.1 (capture 07_01 in the \NetworkMonitorCaptures folder on the companion CD-ROM):

```
Frame:
- Ethernet: Etype = IPv6
  + DestinationAddress: 3333FF B17480
  + SourceAddress: 009027 66C140
    EthernetType: IPv6, 34525(0x86dd)
- Ipv6: Next Protocol = ICMPv6, Payload Length = 32
```

```
 + Versions: IPv6, Internet Protocol, DSCP 0
   PayloadLength: 32 (0x20)
   NextProtocol: HOPOPT, IPv6 Hop-by-Hop Option, 0(0)
   HopLimit: 1 (0x1)
   SourceAddress: FE80:0:0:0:290:27FF:FE66:C140
   DestinationAddress: FF02:0:0:0:0:1:FFB1:7480
 - HopbyHopHeader:
    NextHeader: ICMPv6
    ExtHdrLen: 0(8 bytes)
   - OptionRouterAlert:
    - OptionType: Router Alert
      Action:        (00......) Skip over this option
      C:             (..0.....) Option Data does not change en-route
      OptionType: (...00101) Router Alert
      OptDataLen: 2 bytes
      Value: Datagram contains a Multicast Listener Discovery message, 0 (0x0)
   - OptionPadN:
    - OptionType: PadN
      Action:        (00......) Skip over this option
      C:             (..0.....) Option Data does not change en-route
      OptionType: (...00001) PadN
      OptDataLen: 0 bytes
      OptionData: 0 bytes
- Icmpv6: Multicast Listener Report
   MessageType: Multicast Listener Report, 131(0x83)
   - MulticastListener:
     Code: 0 (0x0)
     Checksum: 44424 (0xAD88)
   + MaximumResponseCode: 0
     Reserved: 0 (0x0)
     MulticastAddress: FF02:0:0:0:0:1:FFB1:7480
```

Notice the mapping of the destination IPv6 multicast address (FF02::1:<u>FFB1:7480</u>) and the destination MAC multicast address (3333<u>FFB17480</u>) (corresponding bits underlined), and note the use of the IPv6 Router Alert option (Option Type 5) and the Padding option in the Hop-by-Hop Options header.

Multicast Listener Done

The Multicast Listener Done message is equivalent to the IGMPv2 Leave Group message, and it is used to inform the local routers that there might not be any more group members of a specific multicast address on the subnet. A local router verifies that there are no more group members on the subnet.

The Multicast Listener Done message is sent when the group member that responded to the last Multicast Listener Query message for the multicast address on the subnet leaves the multicast group. Notice that the group member sending the Multicast Listener Done message might not truly be the last group member on the subnet. This is why membership for the group is verified by a local router. This simple method of reporting what might be the last group member prevents a host from having to track the presence of other multicast group members on their subnet for each multicast group for which the host is a member.

Because IPv6 multicast routers do not track how many group members are on a subnet for a given multicast group, every subnet must be treated as if there were multiple group members present. The host that sends the Multicast Listener Done message might not be the last group member. Therefore, upon receiving a Multicast Listener Done message, the multicast querying router on the subnet immediately sends a multicast-address-specific query for the multicast address being reported in the Multicast Listener Done message. If there are additional group members, one of them will send a Multicast Listener Report message.

In the IPv6 header of a Multicast Listener Done message, you will find the following settings:

- The Hop Limit field is set to 1.

- The Source Address field is set to the link-local address of the interface on which the report is being sent.

- The Destination Address field is set to the link-local scope, all-routers multicast address (FF02::2).

Figure 7-4 shows the structure of the Multicast Listener Done message.

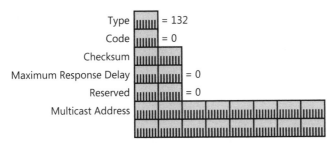

Figure 7-4   The structure of the Multicast Listener Done message

Following is a list of the fields in the Multicast Listener Done message:

- **Type**   The value of this field is 132.

- **Code**   The value of this field is 0.

- **Checksum**   The value of this field is the ICMPv6 checksum.

- **Maximum Response Delay**   This field is not used in the Multicast Listener Done message and is set to 0.

- **Reserved**   This is a 16-bit field reserved for future use and set to 0.

- **Multicast Address**   The Multicast Address field is set to the specific multicast address to which the sender is no longer listening.

Summary of MLD

Table 7-1 lists IGMPv2 messages and their corresponding MLD equivalents.

Table 7-1   IGMPv2 Messages and Their MLD Equivalents

IGMPv2 Message	MLD Equivalent
Host Membership Query (Type 17)	Multicast Listener Query
Host Membership Report (Type 22)	Multicast Listener Report
Leave Group (Type 23)	Multicast Listener Done

MLDv2 Packet Structure

Like MLD, MLDv2 uses ICMPv6 messages and has the same structure as MLD message packets, consisting of an IPv6 header, a Hop-by-Hop Options extension header with the Router Alert option, and the MLDv2 message.

MLDv2 Messages

There are two types of MLDv2 messages:

1. A modified version of the Multicast Listener Query message (ICMPv6 Type 130)

2. A version 2 Multicast Listener Report message (ICMPv6 Type 143)

To maintain compatibility with hosts that support only MLD, MLDv2 nodes also support the MLD Multicast Listener Report (ICMPv6 type 131) and MLD Multicast Listener Done (ICMPv6 Type 132) messages.

The Modified Multicast Listener Query

An MLDv2-capable IPv6 multicast router uses a modified Multicast Listener Query message to query a link for multicast group membership. There are three types of Multicast Listener Query messages for MLDv2:

1. General query

2. Multicast-address-specific query

3. Multicast-address-and-source-specific query

   The multicast-address-and-source-specific query is used to query all hosts on a subnet that are members of a specific multicast group and are listening for traffic from a specified list of multicast sources.

The message types are distinguished by the Destination Address field in the IPv6 header, the Multicast Address field within the Multicast Listener Query message, and the presence of a list of multicast sources.

In the IPv6 header of the modified Multicast Listener Query message, you will find the following settings:

- The Hop Limit field is set to 1.

- The Source Address field is set to the link-local address of the interface on which the query is being sent.

- The Destination Address field is the specific multicast address being queried. For the general query, the Destination Address field is set to the link-local scope, all-nodes multicast address (FF02::1). For the multicast-address-specific and multicast-address-and-source-specific queries, the Destination Address field is set to the specific multicast address being queried.

Figure 7-5 shows the structure of the modified Multicast Listener Query message.

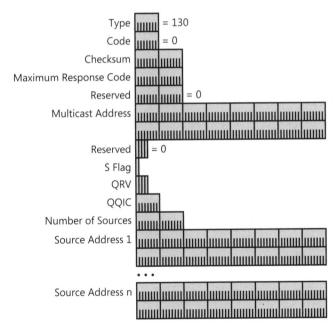

Figure 7-5   The structure of the modified Multicast Listener Query message

The following list describes the fields in the modified Multicast Listener Query message:

- **Type**   The value of this field is 130.

- **Code**   The value of this field is 0.

- **Checksum**   The value of this field is the ICMPv6 checksum.

- **Maximum Response Code**   The Maximum Response Code field indicates the maximum amount of time in milliseconds within which a multicast group member must report its membership by using an MLDv2 Multicast Listener Report message. The size of this field is 16 bits. If the value of this field is less than 32768, the value of the field is the number of milliseconds. If the value of this field is greater than 32767, the value of the field is a floating-point value for the number of milliseconds. For more details, see section 5.1.3 in RFC 3810.

- **Reserved**   This is a 16-bit field reserved for future use and set to 0.

- **Multicast Address**   For the general query, the Multicast Address field is set to the unspecified address (::). For the multicast-address-specific query, the Multicast Address field is set to the specific multicast address that is being queried. The size of this field is 128 bits.

- **S flag**   This is a 1-bit field that, when set to 1, indicates that receiving routers are to suppress normal processing when receiving a query message.

- **Reserved**   This is a 3-bit field reserved for future use and set to 0.

- **QRV**   This is a 3-bit field that indicates the Querier's Robustness Variable (QRV) of the sending router. The robustness variable is a measure of how many MLDv2 messages can be lost without recovery. MLDv2 can recover from (QRV − 1) lost MLDv2 messages.

- **QQIC**   This is an 8-bit field that indicates the Querier's Query Interval Code (QQIC), which is the number of seconds between query messages of the sending router.

- **Number of Sources**   This is a 16-bit field that indicates the number of source addresses included in the message. For general and multicast-address-specific queries, the Number of Sources field is set to 0.

- **Source Address 1 to n**   These are 128-bit fields that store the unicast IPv6 addresses of multicast sources for multicast traffic sent to the address in the Multicast Address field. The multicast-address-specific-query contains one or more Source Address fields.

MLDv2 Multicast Listener Report

The MLDv2 Multicast Listener Report message is sent by an MLDv2-capable listening node to either immediately report its interest in receiving multicast traffic at a specific multicast address or respond to a modified Multicast Listener Query message of any type. It is equivalent to the MLD Multicast Listener Report message. The MLDv2 Multicast Listener Report message is never sent for the link-local scope, all nodes multicast address and for all multicast addresses with a scope of 0 (reserved) and 1 (interface-local).

In the IPv6 header of an MLDv2 Multicast Listener Report message, you will find these settings:

- The Hop Limit field is set to 1.

- The Source Address field is set to the link-local address of the interface on which the report is being sent. If the MLDv2 Multicast Listener Report message is for a solicited-node multicast address corresponding to a unicast address for which duplicate address detection is not yet complete, the source address is set to the unspecified address (::).

- The Destination Address field is set to FF02::16, reserved by the Internet Assigned Numbers Authority as the All MLDv2-capable Routers address.

Figure 7-6 shows the structure of the MLDv2 Multicast Listener Report message.

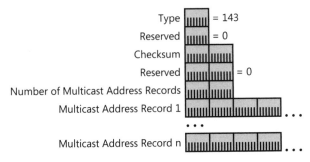

Figure 7-6   The structure of the MLDv2 Multicast Listener Report message

The following list describes the fields in the MLDv2 Multicast Listener Report message:

- **Type**   The value of this field is 143.

- **Reserved**   This is an 8-bit field that is set to 0.

- **Checksum**   The value of this field is the ICMPv6 checksum.

- **Reserved**   This is a 16-bit field that is set to 0.

- **Number of Multicast Address Records**   This is a 16-bit field that indicates the number of multicast address records in the message.

- **Multicast Address Record 1 to n**   Each variable-sized Multicast Address Record field contains a multicast address on which the sending host is listening and an optional include or exclude list of multicast sources.

With the MLD Multicast Listener Report message, a listening node can register interest in a single multicast address. With the MLDv2 Multicast Listener Report message, a listening host can register interest in multiple multicast addresses and specify an include or exclude list for each address. Each multicast address record in the MLDv2 Multicast Listener Report message contains a separate multicast address on which the reporting host is listening and an optional include or exclude source list.

Figure 7-7 shows the structure of a multicast address record for the MLDv2 Multicast Listener Report message.

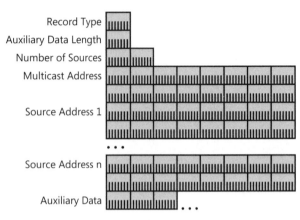

Figure 7-7   The structure of the multicast address record

The following list describes the fields in the multicast address record:

- **Record Type**   This is an 8-bit field that indicates the type of record. See Table 7-2 for a list of the defined record types.

- **Auxiliary Data Length**   This is an 8-bit field that indicates the number of bytes of auxiliary data in the record. Because RFC 3810 does not define any auxiliary data, the value of this field is 0.

- **Number of Sources**   This is a 16-bit field that indicates the number of source addresses in the record.

- **Multicast Address**   This field is set to the specific multicast address that is being reported.

- **Source Address 1 to n**   If the Number of Sources field is not zero, these fields store the unicast IPv6 address of a multicast source for multicast traffic sent to the address in the Multicast Address field.

- **Auxiliary Data**   Additional data for the record. RFC 3810 does not define the use of this field, and therefore it is not present for MLDv2 Multicast Listener Report messages. This field is reserved for future versions of MLD.

Table 7-2 lists the multicast address record types.

Table 7-2   Multicast Address Record Types

Record Type	Description
1	The list of sources for the multicast address is an include list.
2	The list of sources for the multicast address is an exclude list.
3	The list of sources for the multicast address has changed to an include list.
4	The list of sources for the multicast address has changed to an exclude list.

Table 7-2   Multicast Address Record Types

Record Type	Description
5	The source list contains additional sources from which the host will accept multicast traffic. If the existing list is an include list, the additional sources are added to the list. If the existing list is an exclude list, the additional sources are removed from the list.
6	The source list contains additional sources to block for multicast traffic. If the existing list is an include list, the additional sources are removed from the list. If the existing list is an exclude list, the additional sources are added to the list.

An MLDv2-capable host can send the following types of address records:

- **Current State Record**   A record with a Record Type of 1 or 2, providing either an include or exclude list.

- **Filter Mode Change Record**   A record with a Record Type of 3 or 4, allowing the host to change an include list to an exclude list or vice versa.

- **Source List Change Record**   A record with a Record Type of 5 or 6, allowing the host to modify the current include or exclude list.

Network Monitor Capture

Here is an example of an MLDv2 Multicast Listener Report message as displayed by Network Monitor 3.1 (capture 07_02 in the \NetworkMonitorCaptures folder on the companion CD-ROM):

```
Frame:
- Ethernet: Etype = IPv6
  + DestinationAddress: 333300 000016
  + SourceAddress: 00123F 17E0CF
    EthernetType: IPv6, 34525(0x86dd)
- Ipv6: Next Protocol = ICMPv6, Payload Length = 36
  + Versions: IPv6, Internet Protocol, DSCP 0
    PayloadLength: 36 (0x24)
    NextProtocol: HOPOPT, IPv6 Hop-by-Hop Option, 0(0)
    HopLimit: 1 (0x1)
    SourceAddress: FE80:0:0:0:B500:734B:FE5B:3945
    DestinationAddress: FF02:0:0:0:0:0:0:16
  - HopbyHopHeader:
      NextHeader: ICMPv6
      ExtHdrLen: 0(8 bytes)
    - OptionRouterAlert:
      + OptionType: Router Alert
        OptDataLen: 2 bytes
        Value: Datagram contains a Multicast Listener Discovery message, 0 (0x0)
    - OptionPadN:
      + OptionType: PadN
        OptDataLen: 0 bytes
        OptionData: 0 bytes
```

```
- Icmpv6: Version 2 Multicast Listener Report
    MessageType: Version 2 Multicast Listener Report, 143(0x8f)
  - MulticastListenerReport:
    Reserved: 0 (0x0)
    CheckSum: 4122 (0x101A)
    Reserved1: 0 (0x0)
    NrofMcastAddrRecords: 1 (0x1)
  - McastAddressRecord:
    RecordType: CHANGE_TO_EXCLUDE_MODE, 4(0x04)
    AuxDataLen: 0, in units of 4 bytes
    NumberofSources: 0 (0x0)
    MulticastAddress: FF02:0:0:0:0:0:1:3
```

Summary of MLDv2

Table 7-3 lists IGMPv3 messages and their corresponding MLDv2 equivalents.

Table 7-3   IGMPv3 Messages and Their MLDv2 Equivalents

IGMPv3 Message	MLDv2 Equivalent
Host Membership Query (Type 17)	Modified Multicast Listener Query
Host Membership Report (Type 34)	MLDv2 Multicast Listener Report

MLD and MLDv2 Support in Windows Server 2008 and Windows Vista

IPv6 in Windows Server 2008 and Windows Vista supports both MLD and MLDv2. IPv6 in Windows Server 2008 and Windows Vista uses MLDv2 by default but will use MLD if it receives an MLD message. You can configure IPv6 to use MLD with the **netsh interface ipv6 set global mldversion=version2** command. Note that the "version2" is referring to IGMPv2, the equivalent of which in IPv6 is MLD. The **mldversion** setting is common to both IPv4 and IPv6. You can configure IPv6 to use MLDv2 with the **netsh interface ipv6 set global mldversion=version3** command; however, it will use MLD if it receives an MLD message.

IPv6 in Windows Server 2008 and Windows Vista supports IPv6 multicast forwarding, which you can enable with the **netsh interface ipv6 set global multicastforwarding=enable** command. However, at the time of the publication of this book, there is no mechanism to update the IPv6 multicast forwarding table. Entries in the IPv6 multicast forwarding table allow the IPv6 protocol to determine how to forward incoming IPv6 multicast traffic. An IGMP routing protocol component for the Windows Server 2008 Routing and Remote Access service allows a computer running Windows Server 2008 to act as an IPv4-based multicast forwarding router. There is no corresponding routing protocol component for MLD that allows a Windows Server 2008–based computer to act as an IPv6-based multicast forwarding router.

References

The following references were cited in this chapter:

- RFC 2236 – "Internet Group Management Protocol, Version 2"
- RFC 2710 – "Multicast Listener Discovery (MLD) for IPv6"
- RFC 2711 – "IPv6 Router Alert Option"
- RFC 3376 – "Internet Group Management Protocol, Version 3"
- RFC 3810 – "Multicast Listener Discovery Version 2 (MLDv2) for IPv6"

You can obtain these RFCs from the \RFCs_and_Drafts folder on the companion CD-ROM or from *http://www.ietf.org/rfc.html.*

Testing for Understanding

To test your understanding of MLD and MLDv2, answer the following questions. See Appendix D, "Testing for Understanding Answers," to check your answers.

1. Why is the IPv6 Router Alert option used in the Hop-by-Hop Options header for MLD and MLDv2 messages?

2. Which addresses are used as the source address in MLD and MLDv2 messages?

3. Which addresses are used as the IPv6 destination address in MLD and MLDv2 messages?

4. How do you distinguish a general query from a multicast-address-specific query in the Multicast Listener Query message?

5. How do you distinguish a multicast-address-specific query from a multicast-address-and-source specific query in the MLDv2 Multicast Listener Query message?

6. For which multicast addresses are Multicast Listener Report messages never sent?

7. In which MLD message is the value of the Maximum Response Delay field significant?

8. Describe the use of the Multicast Address field for each MLD and MLDv2 message.

Chapter 8
Address Autoconfiguration

At the end of this chapter, you should be able to do the following:

- Describe the use of address autoconfiguration in IPv6.

- Describe the states of an autoconfigured address and their relation to preferred and valid lifetimes.

- Describe the types of autoconfiguration.

- Explain the details of the stateless address autoconfiguration process.

- Describe the Dynamic Host Configuration Protocol for IPv6 (DHCPv6), its message structure, and messages.

- Distinguish between DHCPv6 stateless and stateful operation.

- Describe the automatically configured addresses for a host using the IPv6 protocol for Windows Server 2008 and Windows Vista.

Address Autoconfiguration Overview

One of the most useful aspects of IPv6 is its ability to automatically configure itself, even without the use of an address configuration protocol such as DHCPv6. An IPv6 host can automatically configure a link-local address for each interface. By using router discovery—an exchange of Router Solicitation and Router Advertisement messages—a host can determine the addresses of neighboring routers, additional stateless addresses, on-link prefixes, and other configuration parameters. Included in the Router Advertisement message are flags that indicate whether an address configuration protocol (such as DHCPv6) should be used for additional configuration.

Types of Autoconfiguration

There are three types of autoconfiguration:

- **Stateless** Configuration of addresses and other settings is based on the receipt of Router Advertisement messages. These messages have the Managed Address Configuration and Other Stateful Configuration flags set to 0, and they include one or more Prefix Information options, each with its Autonomous flag set to 1.

- **Stateful** Configuration is based on the use of an address configuration protocol, such as DHCPv6, to obtain addresses and other configuration settings. A host uses stateful autoconfiguration when it receives a Router Advertisement message with no Prefix

Information options and either the Managed Address Configuration flag or the Other Stateful Configuration flag is set to 1. A host can also use stateful autoconfiguration when there are no routers present on the local link.

■ **Both** Configuration is based on the receipt of Router Advertisement messages that include Prefix Information options, each with its Autonomous flag set to 1, and have the Managed Address Configuration or Other Stateful Configuration flags set to 1.

For all types of autoconfiguration, a link-local address is always configured automatically.

Autoconfigured Address States

Autoconfigured addresses are in one or more of the following states:

■ **Tentative** The address is in the process of being verified as unique. Verification occurs through duplicate address detection. A node cannot receive unicast traffic to a tentative address. It can, however, receive and process multicast Neighbor Advertisement messages sent in response to the Neighbor Solicitation message that has been sent during duplicate address detection.

■ **Valid** The address can be used for sending and receiving unicast traffic. The valid state includes both the preferred and deprecated states. The sum of the times that an address remains in the tentative, preferred, and deprecated states is determined by the Valid Lifetime field in the Prefix Information option of a Router Advertisement message or the Valid-Lifetime field of a DHCPv6 IA (Identity Association) Address option.

■ **Preferred** The address is valid, its uniqueness has been verified, and it can be used for unlimited communications. A node can send and receive unicast traffic to and from a preferred address. The period of time that an address can remain in the tentative and preferred states is determined by the Preferred Lifetime field in the Prefix Information option of a Router Advertisement message or the Preferred-Lifetime field of a DHCPv6 IA Address option.

■ **Deprecated** The address is valid and its uniqueness has been verified, but its use is discouraged for new communication. Existing communication sessions can still use a deprecated address. A node can send and receive unicast traffic to and from a deprecated address.

■ **Invalid** The address can no longer be used to send or receive unicast traffic. An address enters the invalid state after the valid lifetime expires.

Figure 8-1 shows the states of an autoconfigured address and their relationship to the preferred and valid lifetimes.

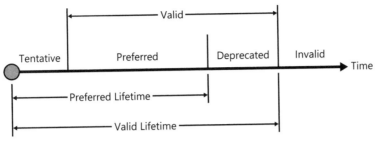

Figure 8-1   The states of an autoconfigured address

> **Note**   With the exception of autoconfiguration for link-local addresses, address autoconfiguration is specified only for hosts. Routers must obtain address and configuration parameters through another means, such as manual configuration.

Autoconfiguration Process

The address autoconfiguration process defined in RFC 4862 for the physical interface of an IPv6 node is the following:

1. A tentative link-local address is derived based on the link-local prefix of FE80::/64 and a EUI-64–derived interface identifier.

2. Using duplicate address detection to verify the uniqueness of the tentative link-local address, a Neighbor Solicitation message is sent with the Target Address field that is set to the tentative link-local address.

3. If a Neighbor Advertisement message (sent in response to the Neighbor Solicitation message) is received, this indicates that another node on the local link is using the tentative link-local address and address autoconfiguration stops. At this point, manual configuration must be performed on the node.

4. If no Neighbor Advertisement message (sent in response to the Neighbor Solicitation message) is received, the tentative link-local address is assumed to be unique and valid. The link-local address is initialized for the interface. The link-layer multicast address of the solicited-node address corresponding to the link-local address is registered with the network adapter.

For an IPv6 host, the address autoconfiguration continues as follows:

1. The host sends a Router Solicitation message. While routers periodically send router advertisements, the host sends a Router Solicitation message to request an immediate router advertisement, rather than waiting until the next router advertisement. By default, up to three Router Solicitation messages are sent.

2. If no Router Advertisement messages are received, the host uses an address configuration protocol to obtain addresses and other configuration parameters.

3. If a Router Advertisement message is received, the hop limit, reachable time, retransmission timer, and maximum transmission unit (if that option is present) are set.

4. For each Prefix Information option present, the following actions occur:

   ❑ If the On-Link flag is set to 1, the prefix is added to the prefix list.

   ❑ If the Autonomous flag is set to 1, the prefix and an appropriate interface identifier are used to derive a tentative address.

   ❑ Duplicate address detection is used to verify the uniqueness of the tentative address.

   ❑ If the tentative address is in use, the use of the address is not initialized for the interface.

   ❑ If the tentative address is not in use, the address is initialized. This includes setting the valid and preferred lifetimes based on the Valid Lifetime and Preferred Lifetime fields in the Prefix Information option. If needed, it also includes registering the link-layer multicast address of the solicited-node address corresponding to the new address with the network adapter.

5. If the Managed Address Configuration flag in the Router Advertisement message is set to 1, an address configuration protocol is used to obtain additional addresses.

6. If the Other Stateful Configuration flag in the Router Advertisement message is set to 1, an address configuration protocol is used to obtain additional configuration parameters.

Figures 8-2 and 8-3 show the address autoconfiguration process for a host.

In RFC 4862, the address configuration protocol for stateful autoconfiguration is DHCPv6.

For an example of IPv6 stateless address autoconfiguration based on an exchange of Router Solicitation and Router Advertisement messages, see Network Monitor capture 08_01 in the \NetworkMonitorCaptures folder on the companion CD-ROM.

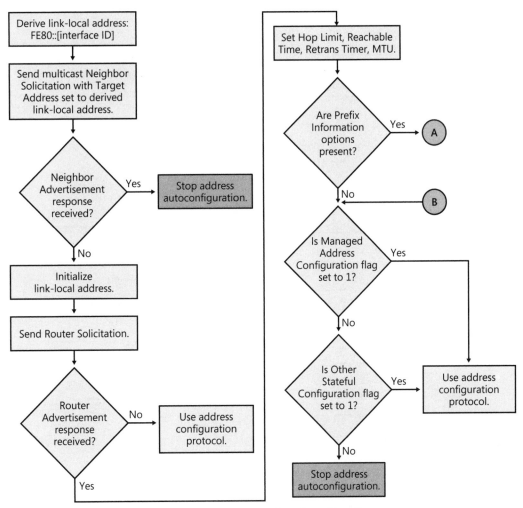

Figure 8-2   The address autoconfiguration process for a host (Part 1)

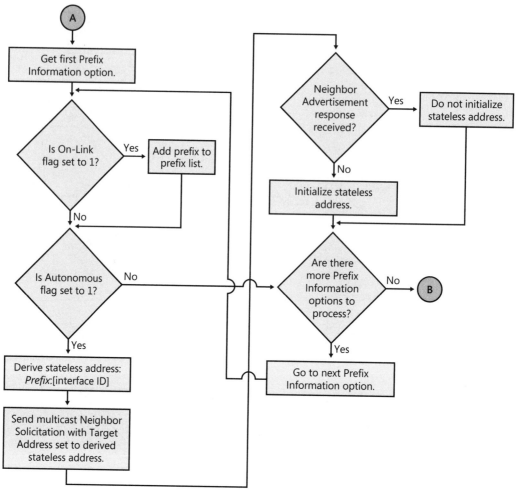

Figure 8-3 The address autoconfiguration process for a host (Part 2)

DHCPv6

DHCPv6 is defined in RFC 3315 to provide stateful address configuration or stateless configuration settings for IPv6 hosts. An IPv6 host uses a configuration protocol, such as DHCPv6, based on the following flags in the Router Advertisement message sent by a neighboring router:

- **Managed Address Configuration flag** This is also known as the *M flag*. When set to 1, this flag instructs the host to use a configuration protocol to obtain stateful addresses.

- **Other Stateful Configuration flag** This is also known as the *O flag*. When set to 1, this flag instructs the host to use a configuration protocol to obtain other configuration settings.

The combinations of the values of the M and O flags are the following:

- **Both M and O flags are set to 0**   This combination corresponds to a network without a DHCPv6 infrastructure. Hosts use router advertisements for non-link-local addresses, and they use other methods (such as manual configuration) to configure other settings.

- **Both M and O flags are set to 1**   In this combination, DHCPv6 is used for both addresses and other configuration settings. This combination is known as *DHCPv6 stateful,* in which a DHCPv6 server is assigning stateful addresses to IPv6 hosts.

- **The M flag is set to 0, and the O flag is set to 1**   In this combination, DHCPv6 is used only for other configuration settings. Neighboring routers are configured to advertise non-link-local address prefixes from which IPv6 hosts derive stateless addresses. This combination is known as *DHCPv6 stateless,* in which a DHCPv6 server is not assigning stateful addresses to IPv6 hosts, but stateless configuration settings.

- **The M flag is set to 1, and the O flag is set to 0**   In this combination, DHCPv6 is used for address configuration but not for other settings. Because IPv6 hosts typically need to be configured with other settings, such as the IPv6 addresses of Domain Name System (DNS) servers, this is an unlikely combination.

Like DHCP for IPv4, the components of a DHCPv6 infrastructure consist of DHCPv6 clients that request configuration, DHCPv6 servers that provide configuration, and DHCPv6 relay agents that relay messages between clients and servers when clients are on subnets that do not include a DHCPv6 server.

> **More Info**   You can configure an IPv6 router running Windows Server 2008 or Windows Vista to set the M flag to 1 in router advertisements with the **netsh interface ipv6 set interface** *InterfaceNameOrIndex* **managedaddress=enabled** command. Similarly, you can set the O flag to 1 in router advertisements with the **netsh interface ipv6 set interface** *InterfaceNameOrIndex* **otherstateful=enabled** command. For more information about configuring an IPv6 router running Windows Server 2008 or Windows Vista, see Chapter 10, "IPv6 Routing."

DHCPv6 Messages

As in DHCP for IPv4, DHCPv6 messages are User Datagram Protocol (UDP) messages. DHCPv6 clients listen for DHCP messages on UDP port 546. DHCPv6 servers and relay agents listen for DHCPv6 messages on UDP port 547. The structure for DHCPv6 messages is much simpler than for DHCP for IPv4, which had its historical origins in the BOOTP protocol to support diskless workstations. Figure 8-4 shows the structure of DHCPv6 messages sent between client and server.

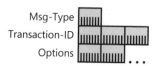

Figure 8-4   DHCPv6 messages between client and server

The following list describes the fields in a DHCPv6 message:

- **Msg-Type**   This 1-byte field indicates the type of DHCPv6 message. See Table 8-1.

- **Transaction-ID**   This 3-byte field is determined by a client and used to group the messages of a DHCPv6 message exchange together. DHCPv6 servers copy the value of the Transaction-ID field from request messages to their corresponding reply messages.

- **Options**   This variable-sized field contains one or more options that are used to contain client and server identification information, stateful IPv6 addresses, and other configuration settings.

Table 8-1 lists the DHCPv6 message types defined in RFC 3315.

Table 8-1   DHCPv6 Message Types

Msg-Type	Message	Description	Equivalent DHCP for IPv4 Message
1	Solicit	Sent by a client to locate servers.	DHCPDiscover
2	Advertise	Sent by a server in response to a Solicit message to indicate availability.	DHCPOffer
3	Request	Sent by a client to request addresses or configuration settings from a specific server.	DHCPRequest
4	Confirm	Sent by a client to all servers to determine if a client's configuration is valid for the connected link.	DHCPRequest
5	Renew	Sent by a client to a specific server to extend the lifetimes of assigned addresses and obtain updated configuration settings.	DHCPRequest
6	Rebind	Sent by a client to any server when a response to the Renew message is not received.	DHCPRequest
7	Reply	Sent by a server to a specific client in response to a Solicit, Request, Renew, Rebind, Information-Request, Confirm, Release, or Decline message.	DHCPAck

Table 8-1   DHCPv6 Message Types

Msg-Type	Message	Description	Equivalent DHCP for IPv4 Message
8	Release	Sent by a client to indicate that the client is no longer using an assigned address.	DHCPRelease
9	Decline	Sent by a client to a specific server to indicate that the assigned address is already in use.	DHCPDecline
10	Reconfigure	Sent by a server to a client to indicate that the server has new or updated configuration settings. The client then sends either a Renew or Information-Request message.	N/A
11	Information-Request	Sent by a client to request configuration settings (but not addresses).	DHCPInform
12	Relay-Forward	Sent by a relay agent to forward a message to a server. The Relay-Forward contains a client message encapsulated as the DHCPv6 Relay-Message option.	N/A
13	Relay-Reply	Sent by a server to send a message to a client through a relay agent. The Relay-Reply contains a server message encapsulated as the DHCPv6 Relay-Message option.	N/A

DHCPv6 options are formatted in type-length-value (TLV) format. Figure 8-5 shows the structure of DHCPv6 options.

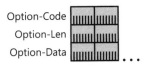

Figure 8-5   DHCPv6 options

The following list describes the fields in a DHCPv6 option:

- **Option-Code**   This 2-byte field indicates the type of DHCPv6 option.

- **Option-Len**   This 2-byte field indicates the length of the Option-Data field in bytes.

- **Option-Data**   This variable-sized field contains the data for the option.

There is a separate message structure for the messages exchanged between relay agents and servers to record additional information, such as the subnet from which the message originated so that the DHCPv6 server can determine the appropriate subnet prefix to assign to the client. Figure 8-6 shows the structure of DHCPv6 messages sent between relay agents and servers.

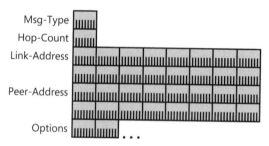

Figure 8-6   DHCPv6 messages between relay agent and server

The following list describes the additional fields in the DHCPv6 messages between relay and server:

- **Hop-Count**   This 1-byte field indicates the number of relay agents that have received the message. A receiving relay agent can discard the message if it exceeds a configured maximum hop count.

- **Link-Address**   This 16-byte field contains a non-link-local address that is assigned to an interface of the relay agent that is connected to the subnet on which the client is located. From the Link-Address field, the server can determine the correct address IPv6 scope from which to assign an address.

- **Peer-Address**   This 16-byte field contains the IPv6 address of the client that originally sent the message or the previous relay agent that relayed the message.

Beyond the Peer-Address field are DHCPv6 options that include the Relay Message option, which contains the message being relayed, and other relay options. The Relay Message option provides an encapsulation of the DHCPv6 messages being exchanged between the client and the server.

Because there are no broadcast addresses defined for IPv6, the use of the limited broadcast address for some DHCP for IPv4 messages has been replaced with the use of the All_DHCP_Relay_Agents_and_Servers address of FF02::1:2 for DHCPv6. For example, a DHCPv6 client attempting to discover the location of the DHCPv6 server on the network sends a Solicit message from its link-local address to FF02::1:2. If there is a DHCPv6 server on the host's subnet, it receives the Solicit message and sends an appropriate reply. More typically, a DHCPv6 relay agent on the host's subnet receives the Solicit message and forwards it to a DHCPv6 server.

DHCPv6 Stateful Message Exchange

A DHCPv6 stateful message exchange to obtain both IPv6 addresses and configuration settings—when both M and O flags in a received router advertisement are set to 1—typically consists of the following messages:

1. A Solicit message sent by the client to locate the servers.

2. An Advertise message sent by a server to indicate that it can provide addresses and configuration settings.

3. A Request message sent by the client to request addresses and configuration settings from a specific server.

4. A Reply message sent by the requested server that contains addresses and configuration settings.

For an example of a DHCPv6 stateful message exchange, see Network Monitor capture 08_02 in the \NetworkMonitorCaptures folder on the companion CD-ROM.

If there is a relay agent between the client and the server, the relay agent sends the server Relay-Forward messages containing the encapsulated Solicit and Request messages from the client. The server sends the relay agent Relay-Reply messages containing the encapsulated Advertise and Reply messages for the client.

DHCPv6 Stateless Message Exchange

A DHCPv6 stateless message exchange to obtain only configuration settings—when the M flag is set to 0 and the O flag is set to 1 in a received router advertisement—typically consists of the following messages:

1. An Information-Request message sent by the client to request configuration settings from a server.

2. A Reply message sent by a server that contains the requested configuration settings.

For an IPv6 network that has routers configured to assign stateless address prefixes to IPv6 hosts, the two-message DHCPv6 exchange can be used to assign DNS servers, DNS domain names, and other configuration settings that are not included in the router advertisement message.

For an example of a DHCPv6 stateless message exchange, see Network Monitor capture 08_03 in the \NetworkMonitorCaptures folder on the companion CD-ROM.

DHCPv6 Support in Windows

DHCPv6 support in Windows Server 2008 and Windows Vista includes the following:

■ DHCPv6 client

- DHCPv6 relay agent
- DHCPv6 stateless and stateful server

DHCPv6 Client

Windows Server 2008 and Windows Vista include a DHCPv6 client. The DHCPv6 client attempts DHCPv6-based configuration based on the values of the M and O flags in received Router Advertisement messages. Therefore, to use DHCPv6, you must configure DHCPv6 servers and relay agents to service each IPv6 subnet and then configure your advertising IPv6 routers to set these two flags to their appropriate values. If there are multiple advertising routers for a given subnet, they should be configured to advertise the same stateless address prefixes and values of the M and O flags. IPv6 hosts running Windows XP or Windows Server 2003 do not include a DHCPv6 client and ignore the values of the M and O flags in received router advertisements.

DHCPv6 Relay Agent

Windows Server 2008 supports a DCHPv6 relay agent as a component of Routing and Remote Access. To install and configure the DHCPv6 relay agent component, do the following:

1. Use the Server Manager administrative tool to add the Routing and Remote Access Services role service of the Network Policy and Access Services role.

2. Click Start, point to Administrative Tools, and then click Routing and Remote Access.

3. If needed, run the Routing And Remote Access Server Setup Wizard to perform the initial setup of Routing And Remote Access. In the console tree of the Routing and Remote Access snap-in, right-click the server name, and then click Configure And Enable Routing And Remote Access.

4. On the Welcome To The Routing And Remote Access Server Setup Wizard page, click Next. On the Configuration page, click Custom Configuration, and then click Next. On the Custom Configuration page, click LAN Routing, and then click Next. On the Completing The Routing And Remote Access Server Setup Wizard page, click Finish.

5. In the console tree of the Routing And Remote Access snap-in, expand the IPv6 node.

6. Right-click General, and then click New Routing Protocol. In the New Routing Protocol dialog box, click DHCPv6 Relay Agent and then click OK.

7. In the console tree of the Routing And Remote Access snap-in, right-click DHCPv6 Relay Agent, and then click Interface. In the New Interface For DHCPv6 Relay Agent dialog box, click the interface on which the Routing and Remote Access server will be listening for DHCPv6 messages sent by DHCPv6 clients, and then click OK. Modify settings on the DHCPv6 Relay Properties dialog box as needed, and then click OK. Repeat this step for all the appropriate interfaces of the Routing and Remote Access server.

8. In the console tree of the Routing And Remote Access snap-in, right-click DHCPv6 Relay Agent, and then click Properties. In the DHCPv6 Relay Agent Properties dialog box, click the Servers tab. Figure 8-7 shows an example.

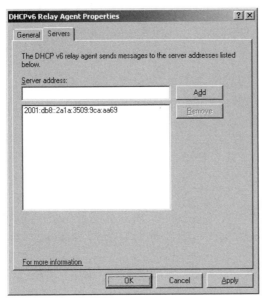

Figure 8-7 The DHCPv6 Relay Agent Properties dialog box

9. Type the non-link-local address of a DHCPv6 server on your network, and then click Add. Repeat this step as needed for additional DHCPv6 servers.

10. Click OK.

DHCPv6 Stateless and Stateful Server

The DHCP Server service in Windows Server 2008 supports DHCPv6 stateful and stateless configuration as a DHCPv6 server.

To configure DHCPv6 options for DHCPv6 stateless operation with the DHCP Server service, do the following:

1. Use the Server Manager administrative tool to add the DHCP Server role.

2. Click Start, point to Administrative Tools, and then click DHCP.

3. In the console tree of the DHCP snap-in, right-click DHCP, and then click Add Server. In the Add Server dialog box, click This Authorized DHCP Server, click the name of the server, and then click OK.

4. In the console tree of the DHCP snap-in, expand the IPv6 node.

5. Right-click Server Options, and then click Configure Options.

6. On the General tab, enable the appropriate DHCPv6 options and configure their settings as needed. Typical options for DHCPv6 stateless include option 23 (DNS Recursive Name Server IPv6 Address List) and option 24 (Domain Search List), as defined in RFC 3646.

7. Click OK.

To configure DHCPv6 scopes and options for DHCPv6 stateful operation with the DHCP Server service, do the following:

1. In the console tree of the DHCP snap-in, expand the IPv6 node.

2. To configure IPv6 configuration settings that apply to all IPv6 scopes, right-click Server Options, and then click Configure Options.

3. On the General tab, enable the appropriate DHCPv6 options and configure their settings as needed.

4. To create an IPv6 scope, right-click IPv6, and then click New Scope.

5. On the Welcome To The New Scope Wizard page of the New Scope Wizard, click Next.

6. On the Scope Name page, type the name and description of the scope and then click Next.

7. On the Scope Prefix page, type the subnet prefix for the scope. For example, type **2001:db8:23aa:1414::** for the 2001:db8:23aa:1414::/64 subnet prefix. Specify a preference value if needed. Figure 8-8 shows an example.

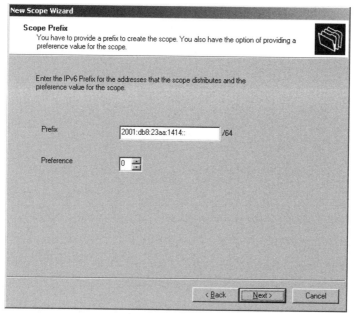

Figure 8-8   The Scope Prefix page

8. Click Next. On the Add Exclusions page, type the list of starting and ending interface IDs to exclude from the range as needed. Click Next.

9. On the Scope Lease page, specify the non-temporary and temporary address preferred and valid lifetimes as needed. Click Next.

10. On the Completing The New Scope Wizard page, click Finish.

When the scope is created, you can configure scope-specific DHCPv6 options by right-clicking Scope Options within the scope, and then clicking Configure Options.

IPv6 Protocol for Windows Server 2008 and Windows Vista Autoconfiguration Specifics

The following are the specific autoconfiguration behaviors of IPv6 in Windows Server 2008 and Windows Vista:

■ Computers running Windows Server 2008 or Windows Vista by default generate random interface IDs for non-temporary autoconfigured IPv6 addresses, including public and link-local addresses, rather than using EUI-64–based interface IDs. A public IPv6 address is a global address that is registered in DNS and is typically used by server applications for incoming connections, such as a Web server. You can disable this default behavior with the **netsh interface ipv6 set global randomizeidentifiers=disabled** command. You can enable the default behavior with the **netsh interface ipv6 set global randomizeidentifiers=enabled** command.

■ With a randomly derived interface ID, the chance of duplicating the link-local address is very small. Therefore, computers running Windows Server 2008 or Windows Vista do not wait for duplicate address detection (DAD) to complete before sending router solicitations or multicast listener discovery reports using their derived link-local addresses. This is known as optimistic DAD.

■ Computers running Windows Server 2008 or Windows Vista do not attempt stateful address autoconfiguration with DHCPv6 if no router advertisements are received.

■ RFC 4862 does not require a specific order for sending the initial router solicitation and performing duplicate address detection for the derived link-local address. The IPv6 protocol for Windows Server 2008 and Windows Vista sends the Router Solicitation message before performing duplicate address detection on the link-local address. In this way, duplicate address detection and router discovery are done in parallel to save time during the interface initialization process.

■ If the derived link-local address is a duplicate, stateless address autoconfiguration for the IPv6 protocol for Windows Server 2008 and Windows Vista can continue with the receipt of a multicast Router Advertisement message containing site-local, unique local, or global prefixes. The attempted link-local address is shown with a "Duplicate" state in the display of the **netsh interface ipv6 show address** command and a site-local, unique local, or global address—rather than the duplicate link-local address—is used for neighbor discovery processes.

Autoconfigured Addresses for the IPv6 Protocol for Windows Server 2008 and Windows Vista

By default, the following IPv6 addresses are automatically configured for the IPv6 protocol for Windows Server 2008 and Windows Vista:

■ Link-local addresses using randomly derived interface identifiers are assigned to all local area network (LAN) interfaces.

■ If included as a site-local prefix in a Prefix Information option of a router advertisement with the Autonomous flag set to 1, a site-local address using a randomly derived interface identifier is assigned to the LAN interface that received the router advertisement.

■ If included as a global or unique local prefix in a Prefix Information option of a router advertisement with the Autonomous flag set to 1, a global or unique local address using a randomly derived permanent interface identifier is assigned to the LAN interface that received the router advertisement.

■ If included as a global or unique local prefix in a Prefix Information option of a router advertisement with the Autonomous flag set to 1, a temporary global or unique local address using a randomly derived temporary interface identifier is assigned to the LAN interface that received the router advertisement. This is the default behavior for Windows Vista. Window Server 2008 does not create temporary addresses by default. You can enable temporary addresses with the **netsh interface ipv6 set privacy enabled** command.

■ If the M flag is set to 1 in a received Router Advertisement message, a stateful IPv6 address based on DHCPv6 scope for the subnet is assigned to the LAN interface that received the DHCPv6 Reply message.

■ If public IPv4 addresses are assigned to interfaces of the computer and there are no global or unique local autoconfiguration prefixes received in Router Advertisement messages, corresponding 6to4 addresses using 6to4-derived interface identifiers are assigned to the 6to4 tunneling interface. 6to4 is described in RFC 3056.

■ For computers running Windows Vista, for all IPv4 addresses that are assigned to interfaces of the computer, corresponding link-local addresses using Intra-Site Automatic Tunnel Addressing Protocol (ISATAP)–derived interface identifiers (::0:5EFE:*w.x.y.z* or ::200:5EFE:*w.x.y.z*) are assigned to the ISATAP tunneling interface. ISATAP is described in RFC 4214.

■ If included as a global, unique local, or site-local prefix in a Prefix Information option of a router advertisement received on the ISATAP interface, a global, unique local, or site-local address using the ISATAP-derived interface identifier corresponding to the IPv4 address that is the best source to use to reach the ISATAP router is assigned to the ISATAP interface.

■ The loopback address (::1) is assigned to the Loopback Pseudo-Interface 1.

> **Note**   To receive a Router Advertisement message from an ISATAP router, by default the host must be able to resolve the name "isatap" to an IPv4 address. This is done through normal name resolution mechanisms, including DNS and NetBIOS over TCP/IP name queries. Once resolved, the host sends a Router Solicitation message encapsulated in an IPv4 header to the ISATAP router. The ISATAP router then sends a Router Advertisement message encapsulated in an IPv4 header to the host. Computers running Windows Server 2008 or Windows Vista with Service Pack 1 will not automatically create an ISATAP tunneling interface or assign it link-local ISATAP addresses unless the name "isatap" is resolved to an IPv4 address.

For more information about ISATAP, see Chapter 12, "ISATAP." For more information about 6to4, see Chapter 13, "6to4."

The following is an example of the display of the **netsh interface ipv6 show address** command for a host running Windows Vista that received a Router Advertisement message containing the prefixes fd4a:3a9:27a1:f282::/64 and 2001:db8:d005:f282::/64 with both the M and O flags set to 0 on its LAN interface (interface index 8):

```
Interface 1: Loopback Pseudo-Interface 1

Addr Type  DAD State    Valid Life Pref. Life Address
---------  -----------  ---------- ---------- ------------------------
Other      Preferred      infinite   infinite ::1


Interface 8: Local Area Connection

Addr Type  DAD State    Valid Life Pref. Life Address
---------  -----------  ---------- ---------- ------------------------
Temporary  Preferred    6d19h37m21s 6d19h37m21s 2001:db8:d005:f282:ed46:5dd4:5439:2e1c
Public     Preferred      infinite   infinite 2001:db8:d005:f282:3521:12fa:2c44:87d1
Temporary  Preferred    6d19h37m21s 6d19h37m21s fd4a:3a9:27a1:f282:ed46:5dd4:5439:2e1c
Public     Preferred      infinite   infinite fd4a:3a9:27a1:f282:3521:12fa:2c44:87d1
Other      Preferred      infinite   infinite fe80::3521:12fa:2c44:87d1%8


Interface 17: Local Area Connection* 9

Addr Type  DAD State    Valid Life Pref. Life Address
---------  -----------  ---------- ---------- ------------------------
Other      Preferred      infinite   infinite fe80::5efe:10.47.181.92%17
```

> **Note**   In this example display, the ISATAP interface is named "Local Area Connection* 9."

In addition to autoconfigured addresses, the IPv6 protocol for Windows Server 2008 and Windows Vista also supports manual configuration of IPv6 addresses through the properties of the Internet Protocol Version 6 (TCP/IPv6) component in the Network Connections folder and with the **netsh interface ipv6 add address** command. For more information, see Chapter 2, "IPv6 Protocol for Windows Server 2008 and Windows Vista ."

References

The following references were cited in this chapter:

- RFC 3056 – "Connection of IPv6 Domains via IPv4 Clouds"
- RFC 3315 – "Dynamic Host Configuration Protocol for IPv6 (DHCPv6)"
- RFC 3646 – "DNS Configuration Options for Dynamic Host Configuration Protocol for IPv6 (DHCPv6)"
- RFC 4214 – "Intra-Site Automatic Tunnel Addressing Protocol (ISATAP)"
- RFC 4862 – "IPv6 Stateless Address Autoconfiguration"

You can obtain these RFCs from the \RFCs_and_Drafts folder on the companion CD-ROM or from *http://www.ietf.org/rfc.html*.

Testing for Understanding

To test your understanding of IPv6 address autoconfiguration, answer the following questions. See Appendix D, "Testing for Understanding Answers," to check your answers.

1. List and describe the states of an IPv6 autoconfigured address.

2. What is the formula for calculating the amount of time an autoconfigured address remains in the deprecated state?

3. How does a router obtain addresses other than link-local addresses?

4. According to RFC 4862, what addresses are autoconfigured for LAN interfaces on hosts when duplicate address detection for the EUI-64–derived link-local address fails? What is the behavior for the IPv6 protocol for Windows Server 2008 and Windows Vista?

5. A host computer is running Windows Vista and is assigned the IPv4 address 172.30.90.65 on its single LAN interface. IPv6 on this computer starts up and receives a Router Advertisement message on its LAN interface that contains both a unique local prefix (FD0D:3A41:21D:29D8::/64) and a global prefix (2001:DB8:A3:29D8::/64), and both M and O flags are set to 0. List and describe the autoconfigured addresses for all the interfaces on this host.

6. Describe the difference between IPv6 stateful and stateless autoconfiguration. Describe the difference between DHCPv6 stateful and stateless operation.

7. List all the different ways that an IPv6 host running Windows Vista can be configured with IPv6 addresses.

Chapter 9
IPv6 and Name Resolution

At the end of this chapter, you should be able to do the following:

- Describe the Domain Name System (DNS) support for IPv6 name-to-address and address-to-name resolution.
- Describe the Link-Local Multicast Name Resolution Protocol (LLMNR).
- Describe source and destination address selection.
- Describe the name resolution support for IPv6 provided by Windows Server 2008 and Windows Vista.

Name Resolution for IPv6

For Internet Protocol version 6 (IPv6), it is more important than ever that names, rather than addresses, be used to reference network resources. With IPv4, it is hard enough to remember an IPv4 address as a series of four decimal numbers. An IPv6 address can have up to 32 hexadecimal digits. It is unreasonable to expect end users to remember or reliably type an IPv6 address when attempting to access a resource. Additionally, with a mixture of both IPv4 and IPv6 addresses, specifying a name allows the operating system to choose the best set of addresses with which to communicate. Therefore, name resolution support for IPv6 addresses is a critically important part of an IPv6 deployment.

Two protocols for providing name resolution support for IPv6 are DNS and LLMNR.

DNS Enhancements for IPv6

RFC 1886 defines a new DNS resource record type, AAAA (also known as "quad A"), for resolving a fully qualified domain name to an IPv6 address. AAAA records are comparable to the host address (A) resource records used for IPv4 name resolution and use the DNS record type of 28. The resource record type is named AAAA because 128-bit IPv6 addresses are four times longer than 32-bit IPv4 addresses.

The AAAA resource record in a typical DNS database file has the following structure:

```
Name    IN    AAAA    Address
```

Name is the fully qualified domain name, and *Address* is the IPv6 address associated with the name. The following is an example of an AAAA resource record:

```
host1.microsoft.com    IN    AAAA    2001:DB8::1:DD48:AB34:D07C:3914
```

To receive IPv6 address resolution data in the DNS query answer sections of the DNS query response, a host must specify either an AAAA query (by setting the Question Type field in a DNS query question entry to 0x1C, or 28 in decimal) or a query of type Any (by setting the Question Type field in a DNS query question entry to 0xFF, or 255 in decimal).

The IP6.ARPA domain has been created for IPv6 reverse queries. Also called *pointer queries*, reverse queries determine a host name based on the address. To create the namespace for reverse queries, each hexadecimal digit in the fully expressed 32-digit IPv6 address becomes a separate level in the reverse domain hierarchy in inverse order.

For example, the reverse lookup domain name for the address 2001:DB8::1:DD48:AB34:D07C:3914 (fully expressed as 2001:0DB8:0000:0001:DD48:AB34:D07C:3914) is 4.1.9.3.C.7.0.D.4.3.B.A.8.4.D.D.1.0.0.0.0.0.0.0.8.B.D.0.1.0.0.2.IP6.ARPA.

An example pointer (PTR) record is the following (folded for readability):

```
4.1.9.3.C.7.0.D.4.3.B.A.8.4.D.D.1.0.0.0.0.0.0.0.8.B.D.0.1.0.0.2.IP6.ARPA.
    IN  PTR   host1.microsoft.com
```

The DNS support for IPv6 is a simple way to both map host names to IPv6 addresses and provide reverse name resolution. It is a direct translation of IPv4 name and reverse name resolution techniques to IPv6.

LLMNR

LLMNR is a new protocol defined in RFC 4795 that provides an additional method to resolve the names of neighboring computers for networks that do not have a DNS server. LLMNR allows both IPv6 and IPv4 hosts to perform name resolution for the computer names of neighboring computers with a simple exchange of request and reply messages without requiring a DNS server or DNS client configuration.

IPv4 hosts can use NetBIOS over TCP/IP (NetBT) to resolve computer names to IPv4 addresses for neighboring hosts by broadcasting a NetBIOS Name Query Request message to the subnet broadcast IPv4 address. The node that owns the queried name sends back a unicast NetBIOS Name Query Response message to the requestor and the name is resolved. However, NetBT only resolves IPv4 addresses, not IPv6 addresses. Additionally, network administrators can disable NetBT in an environment in which DNS is exclusively used for name resolution. With NetBT disabled on a network without DNS servers, you must add entries to the Hosts file to resolve names.

LLMNR allows name resolution on networks where a DNS server is not present or practical. A good example is the temporary subnet formed by a group of computers that form an ad hoc IEEE 802.11 wireless network. With LLMNR, hosts in the ad hoc wireless network can resolve each other's computer names without having to configure one of the computers as a DNS server and the other computers with the IPv4 or IPv6 address of the computer acting as the DNS server.

LLMNR messages use a similar format as DNS messages that are defined in RFC 1035, and they use a different port than DNS messages. LLMNR hosts send LLMNR Name Query Request messages to UDP port 5355, and they send LLMNR Name Query Response messages from UDP port 5355. The LLMNR resolver cache is separate from the DNS resolver cache.

> **Note**   RFC 4795 also describes how LLMNR messages can be sent and received over TCP. However, TCP-based LLMNR messages are not supported in Windows Server 2008 or Windows Vista.

For LLMNR messages sent over IPv6, a querying host (a requestor) sends an LLMNR Name Query Request message to the link-local scope IPv6 multicast address of FF02::1:3. All IPv6-based LLMNR hosts listen on the IPv6 multicast address FF02::1:3, and they instruct their Ethernet network adapters to listen for Ethernet frames with the destination multicast address of 33-33-00-01-00-03.

The typical LLMNR message exchange for a name query consists of a multicast query and, if a host on the subnet is authoritative for the requested name, a unicast response to the requestor. Windows Server 2008 and Windows Vista–based LLMNR hosts neither send nor respond to unicast queries.

In contrast to DNS servers, LLMNR hosts are authoritative for specific names that have been assigned to them, rather than for a portion of the DNS namespace beginning at the assigned name. Using DNS terminology, LLMNR hosts are authoritative only for the zone apexes corresponding to their assigned names. (The term *zone* is used loosely here because LLMNR hosts are not DNS servers that store zones.) For example, an LLMNR node that has been assigned the name office.example.com is not also authoritative for all names that end with office.example.com.

LLMNR Message Structure

LLMNR uses a similar format as DNS messages, which Figure 9-1 shows.

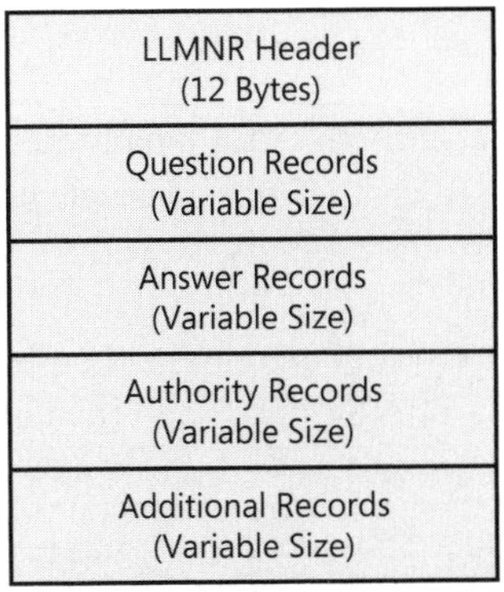

LLMNR Header (12 Bytes)
Question Records (Variable Size)
Answer Records (Variable Size)
Authority Records (Variable Size)
Additional Records (Variable Size)

Figure 9-1   The LLMNR message format

Similar to DNS messages, LLMNR uses a 12-byte header and a series of sections containing zero or more question records, answer records, authority records, and additional records.

Figure 9-2 shows the structure of the LLMNR header.

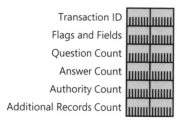

Figure 9-2   The LLMNR header

Similar to DNS messages, LLMNR uses a 2-byte Transaction Identifier (ID) field to match queries with their responses, a 2-byte field for flags and indicators (described later in this chapter), and a series of 2-byte fields that indicate how many question records, answer records, authority records, and additional records are contained in the message past the LLMNR header.

A maximum-sized LLMNR message can be 65,527 bytes long (corresponding to the maximum size of a UDP message for IPv6) or 65,507 bytes long (corresponding to the maximum size of a UDP message for IPv4). LLMNR messages that exceed the maximum transmission unit (MTU) of the link are fragmented by the sending host.

Figure 9-3 shows the structure of the 2-byte field for flags and indicators in the LLMNR header.

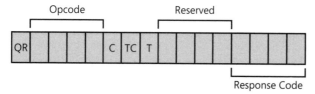

Figure 9-3   The flags and indicators in the LLMNR header

Within these two bytes, the following fields and flags are defined for LLMNR:

- **QR flag**   Similar to DNS, the Query/Response (QR) flag indicates whether the message is a query (QR=0) or a response (QR=1).

- **Opcode field**   Similar to DNS, the 4-bit Operation Code (Opcode) field indicates the type of query. For LLMNR, the Opcode is set to 0 for both queries and responses.

- **C flag**   The Conflict (C) flag indicates name conflicts. If a name is considered to be unique on the subnet, the responder sets the C flag to 0. If a requestor has previously received multiple responses for the name being queried, it sets the C flag to 1. Responders do not send a response to a query with the C flag set to 1, but potential responders that have previously determined the name to be unique need to verify that the names for which they are authoritative are unique.

■ **TC flag**   Similar to DNS, the Truncation (TC) flag is set to 1 only in a response to indicate that the message was truncated because it was larger than the maximum payload size allowed on the link. If a requestor receives a response with the TC flag set to 1, it can send a new TCP-based request message to the unicast address of the responder. Because LLMNR messages have such a large maximum size, LLMNR in Windows Server 2008 and Windows Vista never sets the TC flag in queries or responses. If the message exceeds the maximum size, the response will carry truncated information with the TC flag set to 0.

■ **T flag**   The Tentative (T) flag is set to 1 in a response if the responder is authoritative for the name but has not verified the name's uniqueness.

■ **RCODE field**   Similar to DNS, the 4-bit Return Code (RCODE) field indicates the success of the response. For LLMNR, the RCODE field is set to 0 by requestors and responders. Unlike DNS servers, LLMNR responders that are not authoritative for a queried name do not respond to the query with an RCODE set to 3, indicating that the name was not found. LLMNR responders that are not authoritative for the queried name send no response. The requestor interprets the lack of a response to a query in the same way as a DNS client that receives a name query response from a DNS server with an RCODE set to 3.

Source and Destination Address Selection

Unlike typical IPv4 hosts, typical IPv6 hosts can have multiple addresses assigned to local area network (LAN) or tunneling interfaces that correspond to the following:

■ **Different scopes**   For example, a LAN interface on an IPv6 host always has a link-local address (scoped for the local subnet), and it typically has either a global address (scoped for the entire Internet) or a unique local address (scoped for the site of an organization). In some cases, a LAN interface might be configured with all three types of addresses (a link-local, global, and unique local address).

■ **Different states**   Autoconfigured stateless addresses can be in a nondeprecated (also known as *preferred*) state or deprecated state. For more information, see Chapter 8, "Address Autoconfiguration."

■ **Different uses**   For global address prefixes, it is possible to have temporary addresses (with a short lifetime and a randomly determined interface ID) and public addresses (with a long lifetime and an interface ID based on a random number or the IEEE 802 address of the LAN adapter). For mobile IPv6 nodes, it is possible to have a home address and one or multiple care-of addresses.

Additionally, an IPv6/IPv4 host typically has one or more tunnel interfaces that could have link-local, global, and unique local addresses assigned.

For a typical IPv4-only host that has a single interface assigned one IPv4 address and resolves names using DNS, the choice of which IPv4 addresses to use as the source and destination when initiating communication is straightforward. The source IPv4 address is the address assigned to the interface of the host. The destination addresses to which connections are attempted are the IPv4 addresses returned in the DNS Name Query Response message.

For a typical IPv6 host that has multiple IPv6 addresses assigned to multiple interfaces and multiple IPv6 addresses are returned in the DNS Name Query Response message, the choice of the source and destination IPv6 address is more complex. The source and destination IPv6 addresses should be matched in scope and purpose. For example, an IPv6 host should not choose a link-local source address when communicating with a global destination address. Additionally, the possible destination addresses should be sorted by preference.

To provide a standardized method to choose source and destination IPv6 addresses with which to attempt communications, RFC 3484 defines the following required algorithms:

- A source address selection algorithm to choose the best source address to use with a destination address
- A destination address selection algorithm to sort the list of possible destination addresses in order of preference

Because RFC 3484 defines a standard method of determining source and destination addresses, applications do not need to include their own address selection algorithms, reducing the development burden on IPv6-capable applications. Applications should use standard Windows Sockets functions such as WSAConnectByName() and not manipulate the set of addresses returned from a DNS name query.

The source address selection algorithm is not used when the application specifies the source address. The destination address selection algorithm is not used when the application specifies the destination address rather than a name. Additionally, the application can override the order of the destination addresses determined by the destination address selection algorithm.

To allow administrative control over the preference of source or destination addresses based on address prefixes, RFC 3484 defines the use of a local policy table. The table consists of a series of entries containing the following:

- **An address prefix** Used to determine the best entry in the table for a given source or destination address. Just like the IPv6 route determination process, the best entry is based on the longest matching prefix.
- **A precedence value** Used to specify preference of one destination address over another. For example, when comparing two destination addresses (D1 and D2), if the precedence value for D1 is greater than the precedence value for D2, D1 will be preferred over D2.

■ **A label value**   Used to prefer a specific source address if the label of the source address matches the label of the destination address. For example, when comparing two source addresses (S1 and S2) against a destination address (D), if the label for S1 is the same as the label for D and the label for S2 is not same as the label for D, S1 is preferred for use over S2.

The following sections describe the source address selection and destination address selection algorithms in detail and provide an example of their use.

Source Address Selection Algorithm

The purpose of the source address selection algorithm is to identify a source IPv6 address of maximum preference for a given destination IPv6 address from a list of candidate source addresses. For hosts, the list of candidate source addresses depends on whether the host is using strong host or weak host behavior. For strong host send behavior, the list of candidate source addresses consists of the unicast addresses assigned to the sending interface for the destination. For weak host send behavior, the list of candidates can include addresses assigned to any interface that has weak host sends enabled. For more information about strong and weak host behavior, see Chapter 10, "IPv6 Routing." For routers, the list of candidates can include addresses assigned to any forwarding interface of the router.

The source address selection algorithm compares two source addresses against the destination address and determines which of the two has a higher preference. By iteratively comparing the list of candidate source addresses, the algorithm determines the most preferred source address.

When comparing two possible source addresses S1 and S2 against a destination address D, the source address selection algorithm performs the following analysis:

1. Prefer the source address that equals the destination address.

    If S1 = D, prefer S1.

    If S2 = D, prefer S2.

    If neither S1 nor S2 equal D, S1 and S2 are at the same level of preference.

2. Prefer the source address that has a scope appropriate for the destination address.

    If the scope of S1 is smaller than the scope of S2, the following determination is made:

    ❑   If the scope of S1 is smaller than the scope of the destination, prefer S2.

    ❑   Otherwise, prefer S1.

    If the scope of S2 is smaller than the scope of S1, the following determination is made:

    ❑   If the scope of S2 is smaller than the scope of the destination, prefer S1.

    ❑   Otherwise, prefer S2.

If both S1 and S2 have the same appropriate scope for D or a smaller scope than D, S1 and S2 are at the same level of preference.

3. Prefer an address that is not deprecated over one that is deprecated.

   If S2 is deprecated and S1 is not deprecated, prefer S1.

   If S1 is deprecated and S2 is not deprecated, prefer S2.

   If both S1 and S2 are not deprecated or both S1 and S2 are deprecated, S1 and S2 are at the same level of preference.

4. Prefer the use of a home address (for mobile IPv6 nodes).

   If S1 is both a home address and a care-of address and S2 is not, prefer S1.

   If S1 is a home address and S2 is a care-of address, prefer S1.

   If S2 is both a home address and a care-of address and S1 is not, prefer S2.

   If S2 is a home address and S1 is a care-of address, prefer S2.

   If neither S1 nor S2 are home addresses, S1 and S2 are at the same level of preference.

   For more information about home and care-of addresses, see Appendix F, "Mobile IPv6."

5. For weak host send behavior or for routers, prefer the source address that is assigned to the next-hop interface for the destination.

   If S1 is assigned to the interface that will be used to send packets to D, prefer S1.

   If S2 is assigned to the interface that will be used to send packets to D, prefer S2.

   If neither S1 nor S2 are assigned to the outgoing interface for D or if both S1 and S2 are assigned to the outgoing interface for D, S1 and S2 are at the same level of preference.

6. Prefer the source address that has the same label in the prefix policy table as the destination address.

   If the label of S1 matches the label of D and the label of S2 does not match the label of D, prefer S1.

   If the label of S2 matches the label of D and the label of S1 does not match the label of D, prefer S2.

   If neither S1 nor S2 have the same label as D or if both S1 and S2 have the same label as D, S1 and S2 are at the same level of preference.

7. Prefer the source address that is a public address over the source address that is a temporary address.

   If S1 is a public address and S2 is a temporary address, prefer S1.

   If S2 is a public address and S1 is a temporary address, prefer S2.

   If both S1 and S2 are public addresses or if both S1 and S2 are temporary addresses, S1 and S2 are at the same level of preference.

8. Prefer the source address that has the longest matching prefix with the destination.

    If the matching prefix length of S1 and D is greater than the matching prefix length of S2 and D, prefer S1.

    If the matching prefix length of S2 and D is greater than the matching prefix length of S1 and D, prefer S2.

    If both S1 and S2 have the same longest matching prefix length, S1 and S2 are at the same level of preference.

Destination Address Selection Algorithm

The purpose of the destination address selection algorithm is to sort the list of possible IPv4 and IPv6 destination addresses in order of highest to lowest preference. Destination IPv4 addresses are expressed as IPv4-mapped addresses (::ffff:*w.x.y.z*) and are scoped as global for public IPv4 addresses, site-local for private IPv4 addresses, and link-local for IPv4 link-local addresses (169.254.0.0/16).

The destination address selection algorithm compares two destination addresses and determines which of the two has a higher preference. The algorithm sorts the list of destination addresses by iteratively comparing the list of candidate destination addresses.

When comparing two possible destination addresses D1 and D2, the destination address selection algorithm performs the following analysis:

1. Prefer the destination that is reachable to the one that is not.

    If D2 is known to be unreachable or if the source address for D2 is not defined, prefer D1.

    If D1 is known to be unreachable or if the source address for D1 is not defined, prefer D2.

    If D1 and D2 are both reachable or are both unreachable, D1 and D2 are at the same level of preference.

2. Prefer the destination that matches the scope of its source address.

    If the scope of D1 is the same as the scope of its source address and the scope of D2 is not the same as the scope of its source address, prefer D1.

    If the scope of D2 is the same as the scope of its source address and the scope of D1 is not the same as the scope of its source address, prefer D2.

    If both D1 and D2 are at the same or at different scopes for their respective source addresses, D1 and D2 are at the same level of preference.

3. Prefer destination addresses with source addresses that are not deprecated.

If the source address for D1 is not deprecated and the source address for D2 is deprecated, prefer D1.

If the source address for D2 is not deprecated and the source address for D1 is deprecated, prefer D2.

If D1 and D2 are either both deprecated or both not deprecated, D1 and D2 are at the same level of preference.

4. Prefer destinations with source addresses that are home addresses.

   If the source address for D1 is both a home address and a care-of address and the source address for D2 is not, prefer D1.

   If the source address for D1 is a home address and the source address for D2 is a care-of address, prefer D1.

   If the source address for D2 is both a home address and a care-of address and the source address for D1 is not, prefer D2.

   If the source address for D2 is a home address and the source address for D1 is a care-of address, prefer D2.

   If neither D1 nor D2 are home addresses or care-of addresses, D1 and D2 are at the same level of preference.

5. Prefer the destination address that has the same label from the prefix policy table as its source address.

   If the label of the source address for D1 matches the label of D1 and the label of the source address for D2 does not match the label of D2, prefer D1.

   If the label of the source address for D2 matches the label of D2 and the label of the source address for D1 does not match the label of D1, prefer D2.

   If both D1 and D2 match the labels of their respective source addresses or do not match the labels of their respective source addresses, D1 and D2 are at the same level of preference.

6. Prefer the destination address that has the highest precedence from the prefix policy table.

   If the precedence of D1 is higher than the precedence of D2, prefer D1.

   If the precedence of D2 is higher than the precedence of D1, prefer D2.

   If D1 and D2 have the same precedence, D1 and D2 are at the same level of preference.

7. Prefer a native IPv6 destination to an IPv6 transition technology destination.

   If D2 is reached over an IPv6 transition technology and D1 is not, prefer D1.

   If D1 is reached over an IPv6 transition technology and D2 is not, prefer D2.

   If D1 and D2 are both native IPv6 addresses or are both IPv6 transition addresses, D1 and D2 are at the same level of preference.

8. Prefer the destination address with the smallest scope.

   If the scope for D1 is smaller than D2, prefer D1.

   If the scope for D2 is smaller than D1, prefer D2.

   If D1 and D2 have the same scope, D1 and D2 are at the same level of preference.

9. Prefer the destination address that has the longest matching prefix length with its source address.

   If the matching prefix length of D1 and its source address is longer than the matching prefix length of D2 and its source address, prefer D1.

   If the matching prefix length of D2 and its source address is longer than the matching prefix length of D1 and its source address, prefer D2.

   If both D1 and D2 have the same longest matching prefix length with their respective source addresses, D1 and D2 are at the same level of preference.

10. Leave the order of destination addresses unchanged.

Example of Using Address Selection

Host A is an IPv6/IPv4 host that has multiple interfaces and multiple addresses for each interface. Host A constructs and sends a DNS Name Query Request message for any resource records corresponding to the name web.example.com. The DNS Name Query Response message received by Host A contains a single IPv4 address record and multiple IPv6 address records.

Based on the contents of the DNS Name Query Response message, IPv6 on Host A does the following:

1. Uses the source address selection algorithm to determine the most preferred source address to use with each destination IPv6 address.

2. Uses the destination address selection algorithm to determine the preference order of the destination IPv4 and IPv6 addresses.

The ordered set of destination addresses with their corresponding source addresses is provided to the application. The application can then try communicating using each destination and source address combination until communications are established.

For example, Host A is configured with the following addresses.

- LAN interface:
  - 2001:db8:21a5:a454:3cec:bf16:505:eae6 (global address, nondeprecated state, public use)
  - 2001:db8:21a5:a454:20da:3198:2c50:1a57 (global address, nondeprecated state, temporary use)

- ❑ 2001:db8:21a5:a454:1d15:9c:8e4c:902b (global address, deprecated state, temporary use)

- ❑ fec0:3a4f:78ea:a454:3cec:bf16:505:eae6 (site-local address, nondeprecated state)

- ❑ fe80::3cec:bf16:505:eae6 (link-local address, nondeprecated state)

- ❑ 157.60.17.211 (public IPv4 address [global scope], nondeprecated state)

- ■ Intra-Site Automatic Tunnel Addressing Protocol (ISATAP) tunnel interface:

  - ❑ 2001:db8:21a5:a499::5efe:157.60.17.211 (global ISATAP address, nondeprecated state)

  - ❑ fe80::5efe:157.60.17.211 (link-local address, nondeprecated state)

The DNS Name Query Response message for the name web.example.com returns the following addresses:

- ■ 207.73.118.98 (public IPv4 address [global scope])

- ■ 2001:db8:21a5:a4ca:2aa:ff:fe35:2c1a (global address)

- ■ 2001:db8:21a5:a499::5efe:207.73.118.98 (ISATAP global address)

- ■ fec0:3a4f:2a34:1aa7:2aa:ff:fe35:2c1a (site-local address)

The result of the source address selection algorithm is the following:

- ■ For destination address 2001:db8:21a5:a4ca:2aa:ff:fe35:2c1a, the preferred source address to use is 2001:db8:21a5:a454:3cec:bf16:505:eae6 (global address, non-deprecated state, public use) because it has a matching scope, it is a public address, and has the longest prefix match with the destination.

- ■ For destination address 2001:db8:21a5:a499::5efe:207.73.118.98, the preferred source address to use is 2001:db8:21a5:a499::5efe:157.60.17.211 (global ISATAP address, nondeprecated state) because it has a matching scope and the longest prefix match with the destination.

- ■ For destination address fec0:3a4f:2a34:1aa7:2aa:ff:fe35:2c1a, the preferred source address to use is fec0:3a4f:78ea:a454:3cec:bf16:505:eae6 (site-local address, non-deprecated state) because it has a matching scope and the longest prefix match with the destination.

The result of the destination address selection algorithm is the following destination addresses in preferred order:

1. fec0:3a4f:2a34:1aa7:2aa:ff:fe35:2c1a (smallest scope)

2. 2001:db8:21a5:a4ca:2aa:ff:fe35:2c1a (native addresses preferred over ISATAP addresses)

3. 2001:db8:21a5:a499::5efe:207.73.118.98 (ISATAP addresses preferred over IPv4-mapped addresses)

4. 207.73.118.98

Therefore, Host A attempts to establish communications with the web.example.com server using the following sets of source and destination addresses:

1. Source address fec0:3a4f:78ea:a454:3cec:bf16:505:eae6, destination address fec0:3a4f:2a34:1aa7:2aa:ff:fe35:2c1a

2. Source address 2001:db8:21a5:a454:3cec:bf16:505:eae6 with destination address 2001:db8:21a5:a4ca:2aa:ff:fe35:2c1a

3. Source address 2001:db8:21a5:a499::5efe:157.60.17.211, destination address 2001:db8:21a5:a499::5efe:207.73.118.98

4. Source address 157.60.17.211, destination address 207.73.118.98

IPv6 addresses are preferred over IPv4 addresses because the entry in the default prefix policy table for IPv4 addresses (the address prefix ::ffff:0:0/96) has a low precedence value.

 Note   An application can skip address selection and begin using the addresses as they are returned in the DNS Name Query Response message.

Name Resolution Support in Windows Server 2008 and Windows Vista

Name resolution support for the IPv6 protocol for Windows Server 2008 and Windows Vista consists of the following:

- Entries in the Hosts file
- DNS resolver support
- DNS Server service support
- DNS dynamic update
- Source and destination address selection
- LLMNR support
- Support for ipv6-literal.net names
- Peer Name Resolution Protocol

Unlike the IPv4 protocol, IPv6 does not support the Network Basic Input Output System (NetBIOS). Therefore, all the methods associated with NetBIOS name resolution (the NetBIOS name cache, Windows Internet Name Service [WINS], NetBIOS name broadcasts, and entries in the Lmhosts file) result only in IPv4 addresses.

Hosts File

The Hosts file stored in the *%SystemRoot%\System32\Drivers\Etc* folder supports static entries for IPv6 addresses. Each entry must be of the following form:

Address   *Name*

Address is an IPv6 address, and *Name* is a name associated with the address. The address and name are not case sensitive and must be separated by at least one space or tab character.

The following is an example entry:

```
2001:db8:6c2b:f282:DD48:AB34:D07C:3914      ipv6test
```

The entries in the Hosts file are automatically loaded into the DNS resolver cache. You cannot specify a zone ID (also known as a *scope ID*) as part of the address. If you put entries for link-local addresses in the Hosts file, the IPv6 protocol will select a zone ID for the destination traffic to the resolved link-local address.

DNS Resolver

The DNS resolver, which is part of the DNS Client service in Windows Server 2008 and Windows Vista that queries for DNS names and processes the results, supports the processing of both A and AAAA records in DNS query responses.

The DNS resolver supports queries and responses over IPv6 when the IPv6 addresses of DNS servers have been configured. By default, DNS resolvers are configured with the well-known site-local IPv6 addresses of FEC0:0:0:FFFF::1, FEC0:0:0:FFFF::2, and FEC0:0:0:FFFF::3 as DNS server IPv6 addresses. If you have deployed DNS servers at these addresses and provided reachability to these servers in your routing infrastructure, no other configuration of DNS resolvers is needed. However, in many cases, network administrators will want to place DNS servers in strategic locations on the network and configure the DNS resolvers with their global or unique local addresses.

You can configure Windows Server 2008 and Windows Vista for the addresses of IPv6-enabled DNS servers with the following methods:

- Through the Dynamic Host Configuration Protocol for IPv6 (DHCPv6) and the DNS Recursive Name Server option that is defined in RFC 3646. For more information about DHCPv6, see Chapter 8.

- From the DNS tab for the properties of the Internet Protocol Version 6 (TCP/IPv6) component from the properties of a connection in the Network Connections folder.

- With the **netsh interface ipv6 add dnsserver** command.

DNS Server Service

The DNS Server service in Windows Server 2008 supports the manual creation and DNS dynamic update of AAAA and PTR records. To manually create an AAAA record for the Windows Server 2008 DNS Server service, do the following:

1. Run the DNS snap-in from the Administrative Tools folder.

2. Right-click the zone in which the record is to be stored, and click New Host (A Or AAAA).

3. In the New Host dialog box, type the host name and the IPv6 address, and then click Add Host.

    Figure 9-4 shows an example of adding an AAAA record with the New Host dialog box.

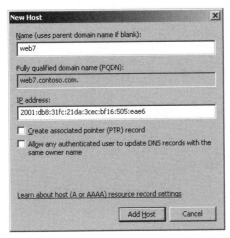

Figure 9-4   The New Host dialog box for AAAA records

For DNS dynamic update, the zones in which records are dynamically updated by DNS clients must be configured to allow dynamic updates. For the Windows Server 2008 DNS Server service, you can enable dynamic updates when the zone file is created with the New Zone Wizard or from the General tab for the properties of the zone.

Reverse lookup zones for IPv6-based PRT records can be automatically created when a computer running Windows Server 2008 uses DNS dynamic update to register its PTR record. You can also manually create reverse lookup zones for IPv6-based PRT records with the following:

1. From the console tree of the DNS snap-in, right-click Reverse Name Lookup Zones, and then click New Zone.

2. On the Welcome To The New Zone Wizard page of the New Zone Wizard, click Next.

3. On the Zone Type page, select the appropriate zone type (primary, secondary, or stub) and then click Next.

4. If you have not installed and configured Active Directory proceed to step 5; otherwise, on the Active Directory Zone Replication page, select the appropriate zone replication behavior and then click Next.

5. On the Reverse Lookup Zone Name page, click IPv6 Reverse Lookup Zone and then click Next.

6. On the Reverse Lookup Zone Name page, type the IPv6 address prefix of the zone (including the prefix length) and then click Next. The following figure shows an example:

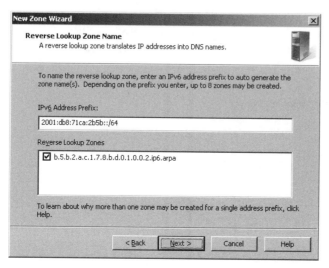

7. If the new primary zone is not integrated into Active Directory, on the Zone File page, select the appropriate method to create a new zone file or use an existing file, specify the file name, and then click Next.

8. On the Dynamic Update page, select the appropriate dynamic update behavior and then click Next.

9. On the Completing The New Zone Wizard page, click Finish.

The Windows Server 2008 DNS Server service by default supports DNS traffic over IPv6, including name queries and dynamic updates.

DNS Dynamic Update

Windows Server 2008 and Windows Vista support DNS dynamic update to automatically register AAAA records over either IPv4 or IPv6 for the following addresses:

- Global addresses with random or EUI-64 IDs (public addresses), and global addresses with ISATAP-derived interface IDs.

- Unique local addresses with random, EUI-64, and ISATAP-derived interface IDs.

- Site-local addresses with random, EUI-64, and ISATAP-derived interface IDs.

Temporary addresses (short-lived global addresses with randomly derived interface IDs), 6to4 addresses assigned to the 6to4 tunnel interface (by default), Teredo addresses (by default), the loopback address, and link-local addresses are not registered with DNS.

DNS dynamic update for IPv6 for connections in the Network Connections folder is controlled by the Register This Connection's Address In DNS check box on the DNS tab from the advanced settings of the Internet Protocol Version 6 (TCP/IPv6) protocol. This check box is enabled by default.

Computers running Windows Server 2008 register PTR records for host names in the IP6.ARPA reverse domain. Computers running Windows Vista register PTR records for host names in the IP6.ARPA reverse domain for stateless addresses. You can configure PRT records manually for the Windows Server 2008 DNS Server service by adding PTR records to the appropriate zone files using the DNS snap-in.

Source and Destination Address Selection

IPv6 in Windows Server 2008 and Windows Vista support the source and destination address selection algorithms described in RFC 2874 with the following exceptions:

- Windows Vista prefers the use of temporary addresses over public addresses.

- Windows Vista uses a global scope for both public and private IPv4 addresses.

You can modify the default preference behavior for IPv6 address prefixes by changing the entries in the prefix policy table. You can view the prefix policy table with the **netsh interface ipv6 show prefixpolicies** command. The following is an example of the default prefix policy table:

```
Precedence  Label  Prefix
----------  -----  -------------------------------
        50      0  ::1/128
        40      1  ::/0
        30      2  2002::/16
        20      3  ::/96
        10      4  ::ffff:0:0/96
         5      5  2001::/32
```

The entries in this table correspond to the following types of IPv6 traffic:

- Prefix ::1/128 is for the loopback address.

- Prefix ::/0 is for all IPv6 traffic.

- Prefix 2002::/16 is for 6to4 traffic.

- Prefix ::/96 is for IPv4-compatible traffic (deprecated).

- Prefix ::ffff:0:0/96 is for IPv4-mapped traffic.

- Prefix 2001::/32 is for Teredo traffic.

Based on this default prefix policy table, computers running Windows Server 2008 or Windows Vista prefer the use of IPv6 addresses over IPv4 addresses, and therefore prefer IPv6 traffic over IPv4 traffic. The entry that matches all IPv6 addresses (with the prefix ::/0) has a higher precedence than the entry that matches all IPv4 addresses (with the prefix ::ffff:0:0/96 for IPv4-mapped addresses).

You can manage the prefix policy table in the following ways:

- Add entries with the **netsh interface ipv6 add prefixpolicy** command.

- Modify existing entries with the **netsh interface ipv6 set prefixpolicy** command.

- Remove entries with **netsh interface ipv6 delete prefixpolicy** command.

LLMNR Support

Windows Server 2008 and Windows Vista support LLMNR for both IPv4 and IPv6. LLMNR query messages sent over IPv6 use the following fields in the IPv6 header:

- The Destination Address field is set to FF02::1:3.

- The Source Address field is set to a link-local or other unicast address of the sending interface.

- The Hop Limit field is set to 1.

For LLMNR queries, a requestor sets the UDP Destination Port field to 5355 and the UDP Source Port field to a dynamically allocated port number. For LLMNR responses, the responder sets the UDP Destination Port field to the dynamically allocated port of the matching query and the UDP Source Port field to 5355.

When a host running Windows Server 2008 or Windows Vista starts, the DNS Client service verifies name uniqueness by sending LLMNR Name Query Request messages for its authoritative name, which is its computer name as a single-label name.

For example, a computer named client1 with the primary DNS suffix of wcoast.example.com is authoritative for LLMNR for the name client1, but not also authoritative for client1. wcoast.example.com. If there is a response to any of the initial requests for its own name with the C flag set to 0, there is a name conflict. The LLMNR host notes the conflict and does not respond to LLMNR requests for its name. However, the host that detected the conflict sends a new query for its name every 15 minutes to determine if the computer with the conflicting name is no longer on the link. If there are no responses to a subsequent query for its own name, the host begins responding to queries.

As a convenience to users who are accustomed to querying names of the form *hostname*.local, the LLMNR component in Windows Server 2008 and Windows Vista will convert the *hostname*.local name to *hostname* and use LLMNR to attempt to resolve the single-label name. A computer running Windows Server 2008 or Windows Vista is not also authoritative for the *hostname*.local name.

When a single-label, unqualified name needs to be resolved, a computer running Windows Server 2008 or Windows Vista that is using both IPv6 and IPv4 (the default configuration) will do the following:

1. Perform normal DNS resolution by combining the single-label name with the primary DNS suffix of the computer and sending a DNS Name Query Request message to its DNS server. Windows Server 2008 and Windows Vista perform additional DNS queries as needed based on name devolution or additional search suffixes that have been configured.

2. If DNS name resolution is not successful, send up to two sets of multicast LLMNR Name Query Request messages over both IPv6 and IPv4.

3. If LLMNR name resolution is not successful and NetBT is enabled, broadcast up to three NetBIOS Name Query Request messages.

If the name being resolved is not a single-label name (or a *hostname*.local name), LLMNR and NetBT are not used. Notice that LLMNR is used regardless of whether the host has been configured to use a DNS server. This allows a computer running Windows Server 2008 or Windows Vista to resolve the computer names of neighboring LLMNR hosts that do not have corresponding address records stored in DNS.

Neighboring LLMNR hosts that receive the LLMNR Name Query Request message check to see if they are authoritative for the name in the Question section of the message. If authoritative, the LLMNR host constructs and sends a unicast LLMNR Name Query Response message containing the original Question section and an Answer section containing one or more IP addresses that can be used to reach the responder. The responder must include only those addresses that are reachable to the requestor. For example, the addresses must be assigned to the interface that received the query.

Support for ipv6-literal.net Names

Windows Server 2008 and Windows Vista support the use of *IPv6Address*.ipv6-literal.net names. The *IPv6Address*.ipv6-literal.net name resolves to *IPv6Address*. To specify an IPv6 address within the ipv6-literal.net name, convert the colons (:) in the address to dashes (-). For example, for the IPv6 address 2001:db8:28:3:f98a:5b31:67b7:67ef, the corresponding ipv6-literal.net name is 2001-db8-28-3-f98a-5b31-67b7-67ef.ipv6-literal.net. When submitted by an application for name resolution, the 2001-db8-28-3-f98a-5b31-67b7-67ef.ipv6-literal.net name resolves to 2001:db8:28:3:f98a:5b31:67b7:67ef.

The IPv6 address in the name can be global, unique local, or link local (with or without a zone ID). To specify a zone ID (also known as a *scope ID*), replace the "%" used to separate the IPv6 address from the zone ID with an "s". For example, to specify the destination fe80::218:8bff:fe17:a226%4, the name is fe80--218-8bff-fe17-a226s4.ipv6-literal.net.

An ipv6-literal.net name can be used in services or applications that do not recognize the syntax of normal IPv6 addresses. It is always preferable to use a DNS name that corresponds to a destination, such as filesrv1.example.com. However, the ipv6-literal.net name can be used for connectivity when the DNS name for the destination is not registered and the IPv6 address is known.

You can use an ipv6-literal.net name in the computer name part of a Universal Naming Convention (UNC) path. For example, to specify the Docs share of the computer with the IPv6 address of 2001:db8:28:3:f98a:5b31:67b7:67ef, use the UNC path \\2001-db8-28-3-f98a-5b31-67b7-67ef.ipv6-literal.net\docs. The ipv6-literal.net name is an alias for the name of the file server. See Knowledge Base article 281308 at *http://support.microsoft.com/ default.aspx?scid=kb;en-us;281308* for information about how to configure a Windows-based file server to accept alias names in a UNC.

Peer Name Resolution Protocol

In peer-to-peer environments, peers rely on name resolution systems to resolve each other's network locations (addresses, protocols, and ports) from names or other types of identifiers. Peer-to-peer name resolution has been complicated by transient connectivity and shortcomings in DNS.

The Windows Peer-to-Peer Networking platform built into Windows Server 2008 and Windows Vista solves this problem with the Peer Name Resolution Protocol (PNRP), a secure, scalable, and dynamic name-registration and name-resolution protocol. PNRP has the following properties:

- **Distributed and serverless for incredible scalability and reliability**   PNRP is almost entirely serverless (servers are required only for bootstrapping). PNRP easily scales to billions of names. The system is fault tolerant, and there are no bottlenecks.

- **Effortless name publication without third parties**   DNS name publication requires updates to DNS servers. Most people must contact a server administrator. This takes time and incurs costs. PNRP name publication is instantaneous, effortless, and free.

- **Real time updates**   DNS relies heavily on caching to improve performance. Unfortunately, this means names cannot be reliably updated in real time. PNRP is much more efficient than DNS and can process updates almost instantaneously. Name resolutions will never return stale addresses, making PNRP an excellent solution for finding mobile users.

- **Name more than just computers**   A PNRP resolution includes an address, port, and possibly an extended payload. With PNRP, you can name more than just computers. You can also name services.

- **Protected name publication**   Names can be published as secured (protected) or unsecured (unprotected) with PNRP. PNRP uses public key cryptography to protect secure peer names against spoofing.

PNRP uses multiple clouds, in which a cloud is a grouping of computers that are able to find each other. PNRP provides two clouds:

- The global cloud corresponds to the global IPv6 address scope and global addresses and represents all the computers on the entire IPv6 Internet. There is only a single global cloud.

- The link-local cloud corresponds to the link-local IPv6 address scope and link-local addresses. A link-local cloud is for a specific link, which is typically the same as the locally attached subnet. There can be multiple link-local clouds.

In Windows Server 2008 and Windows Vista, Windows Peer-to-Peer Networking applications can access PNRP name publication and resolution functions through a simplified PNRP application programming interface (API). With the simplified PNRP publication API, you do not have to specify the clouds with which to register the name and addresses. The PNRP component will automatically determine the appropriate clouds to join and the addresses to publish within the clouds.

For highly simplified PNRP name resolution, PNRP names are now integrated into the Getaddrinfo() Windows Sockets function. To use PNRP to resolve a name to an IPv6 address, applications can use the Getaddrinfo() function to resolve the FQDN *name*.prnp.net, in which *name* is the peer name being resolved. The pnrp.net domain is a reserved domain in Windows Server 2008 and Windows Vista for PNRP name resolution.

The details of how PNRP works to resolve names is beyond the scope of this book. For more information, see the Peer Name Resolution Protocol article at *http://technet.microsoft.com/en-us/library/bb726971.aspx*.

References

The following references were cited in this chapter:

- RFC 1035 – "Domain Names - Implementation and Specification"
- RFC 1886 – "DNS Extensions to support IP version 6"
- RFC 3484 – "Default Address Selection for Internet Protocol version 6 (IPv6)"
- RFC 3646 – "DNS Configuration options for Dynamic Host Configuration Protocol for IPv6 (DHCPv6)"
- RFC 4795 – "Link-local Multicast Name Resolution (LLMNR)"

You can obtain these RFCs from the \RFCs_and_Drafts folder on the companion CD-ROM or from *http://www.ietf.org/rfc.html*.

Testing for Understanding

To test your understanding of IPv6 name resolution, answer the following questions. See Appendix D, "Testing for Understanding Answers," to check your answers.

1. Why is the DNS record for IPv6 name resolution named the "AAAA" record?

2. A host computer running Windows Vista is assigned the IPv4 address 172.30.90.65 on its single LAN interface. IPv6 on this computer receives a Router Advertisement message on its ISATAP tunneling interface that contains both a unique local prefix (FD3A:47A1:2CB9:C140::/64) and a global prefix (2001:DB8:A3:C140::/64). List the IPv6 addresses for the AAAA records registered with DNS by this host.

3. Describe the importance of address selection rules for a node running both IPv4 and IPv6 that is using a DNS infrastructure containing both A and AAAA records.

4. Describe how LLMNR messages are the same as and different from DNS messages.

Chapter 10
IPv6 Routing

At the end of this chapter, you should be able to do the following:

- Describe the contents of the IPv6 routing table.
- Explain the end-to-end IPv6 packet delivery process.
- Understand dynamic routing and the routing protocols used on IPv6 networks.
- Describe the routing support for IPv6 in Windows Server 2008 and Windows Vista.

Routing in IPv6

Similar to IPv4 nodes, typical Internet Protocol version 6 (IPv6) nodes use a local IPv6 routing table to determine how to forward packets. IPv6 creates default routing table entries when initializing, and it adds entries based on its static configuration, based on the receipt of Router Advertisement messages containing on-link prefixes and routes, or with the Dynamic Host Configuration Protocol for IPv6 (DHCPv6).

A *routing table* is present on all nodes running the IPv6 protocol for Windows Server 2008 and Windows Vista. The routing table stores information about IPv6 address prefixes and how they can be reached (either directly or indirectly). Before checking the IPv6 routing table, IPv6 checks the destination cache for an entry matching the destination address in the IPv6 packet being forwarded. If an entry for the destination address is not in the destination cache, IPv6 uses the routing table to determine the following:

- **The next-hop address**   For a direct delivery (in which the destination is on a local link), the next-hop address is the destination address in the IPv6 header of the packet. For an indirect delivery (in which the destination is not on a local link), the next-hop address is typically the link-local address of a neighboring router.

- **The interface to be used for the forwarding (the next-hop interface)**   The next-hop interface identifies the physical or logical interface that is used to forward the packet to either its destination (for a direct delivery) or a neighboring router (for an indirect delivery).

After IPv6 determines the next-hop address and interface, it adds an entry to the destination cache. If the contents of the routing table do not change, IPv6 uses the destination cache entry for subsequent packets to the destination, rather than having to check the routing table.

IPv6 Routing Table Entry Types

IPv6 routing table entries store the following types of routes:

- **Directly attached subnet or network routes**   Routes for subnets or address prefixes that are directly attached. Subnet routes have a 64-bit prefix length. Network routes that summarize a unicast address space have a prefix length less than 64 bits.

- **Remote subnet or network routes**   Address prefixes for subnets or address prefixes that are not directly attached but are available across neighboring routers. Remote subnet routes have a 64-bit prefix length. Remote network routes typically summarize an IPv6 address space and have a prefix length less than 64. An example of a remote network route is fd9c:31f1:2a59::/48, which is a route for a unique local address prefix that summarizes all of the address space within a site of an organization.

- **Host routes**   A route to a specific IPv6 address. Host routes allow routing to occur on a per-IPv6-address basis. For host routes, the address prefix is a specific IPv6 address with a 128-bit prefix length.

- **Default routes**   A route that summarizes all IPv6 traffic and is used when a more specific host, subnet, or network route is not found. The default route address prefix is ::/0.

Route Determination Process

To determine which routing table entry is used for the forwarding decision, an IPv6 router uses the following process:

1. For each entry in a routing table, compare the bits in the address prefix of the route to the same bits in the destination address for the number of bits indicated in the prefix length of the route. If all the bits in the address prefix match all the bits in the destination IPv6 address for the number of bits in the prefix length for the route, the route is a match for the destination.

2. Compile the list of matching routes, and choose the route that is usable and has the longest prefix length, which is the route that matched the most high-order bits with the destination address. The longest matching route is the most specific route to the destination. If there are multiple longest matching routes (for example, multiple routes to the same remote network prefix), select the route with the lowest metric. If there are multiple usable routes that are the longest match and the lowest metric, IPv6 can choose which routing table entry to use. RFC 4191 describes how IPv6 can choose among multiple matching routes with the same lowest metric.

> **Note**   This is the same process that an IPv4 router uses to determine the closest matching route.

For any given destination, this process finds matching routes in the following order:

1. A host route that matches the destination (all 128 bits match).

2. A subnet route that matches the destination (the first 64 bits match).

3. A network route with the longest prefix length that matches the destination (the first n bits match, where n is less than 64).

4. The default route (the address prefix ::/0).

The route determination process selects a single route in the routing table. The selected route yields a next-hop address and interface. If the route determination process on a router fails to find a route, IPv6 sends an ICMPv6 Destination Unreachable–No Route to Destination message to the sending host and discards the packet. In contrast, if the route determination process on the sending host fails to find a route, IPv6 indicates an error.

Strong and Weak Host Behaviors

In the weak host model, an IPv6 host can send packets on an interface that is not assigned the source IPv6 address of the packet being sent. This is known as *weak host send behavior*. An IPv6 host can also receive packets on an interface that is not assigned the destination IP address of the packet being received. This is known as *weak host receive behavior*.

In the strong host model, the send and receive behaviors are different. With strong host sends, the host can send packets on an interface only if the interface is assigned the source IPv6 address of the packet being sent. With strong host receives, the host can receive packets on an interface only if the interface is assigned the destination IPv6 address of the packet being received. The sending process works differently on a host than on a router when you allow strong host sends and receives to be enabled or disabled on a per-interface basis.

For packets being sent, IPv6 first checks whether a source address has already been specified. If it has not, IPv6 performs an unconstrained lookup of the destination address of the packet in the routing table. In an unconstrained lookup, all the routes in the routing table are considered. Based on the selected route for the destination, IPv6 determines the next-hop interface (the interface used for placing the packet on the link layer) and the next-hop address. Based on the next-hop interface, IPv6 uses the address selection process defined in RFC 3484 as needed to determine the best source address. At this point, IPv6 has everything it needs to send the packet: the source and destination addresses, the next-hop interface, and the next-hop address.

If the source address has been specified, the source interface is known. The source interface is assigned the source address. IPv6 then determines whether strong host sends are enabled on the source interface. If they are disabled, IPv6 performs an unconstrained lookup of the packet's destination address in the routing table. Based on the best matching route for the destination, IPv6 determines the next-hop interface and the next-hop address. IPv6 has the source and destination addresses, the next-hop interface, and the next-hop address. Note that with strong host send behavior disabled on the source interface, the next-hop interface might not be the same as the source interface.

If strong host sends are enabled on the source interface, IPv6 performs a constrained lookup of the destination address of the packet in the routing table. In a constrained lookup, only those routes with a next-hop interface of the source interface are considered. Based on the selected route for the destination, IPv6 determines the next-hop address. IPv6 has the source and destination addresses, the next-hop interface, and the next-hop address. Note that with strong host send behavior enabled on the source interface, the next-hop interface is always the same as the source interface. When the source address has been specified, the constrained route lookup can select a route with a higher metric among multiple routes in the routing table that are the closest match to the destination.

Computers running Windows Server 2008 or Windows Vista support the strong host model for sent IPv6 packets by default. You can enable the weak host model for sent IPv6 packets with the **netsh interface ipv6 set interface** *InterfaceNameOrIndex* **weakhostsend=enabled** command.

Example IPv6 Routing Table for Windows Server 2008 and Windows Vista

To view the IPv6 routing table on a computer running Windows Server 2008 or Windows Vista, you can use the following commands at a command prompt:

- **netsh interface ipv6 show route**
- **route print**

The netsh interface ipv6 show route Command

The following is an example display of the **netsh interface ipv6 show route** command on a host computer running Windows Vista on a subnet with an advertising default router that is advertising the 2001:db8:21d0:3f48::/64 and fd5e:2aa9:b3e:3f48::/64 prefixes:

```
Publish  Type      Met  Prefix                         Idx  Gateway/Interface Name
-------  --------  ---  -----------------------        ---  -----------------------
No       Manual    256  ::/0                             8  fe80::69ee:7d26:3:fbec
No       Manual    256  ::1/128                          1  Loopback Pseudo-Interface 1
No       Manual    8    2001:db8:21d0:3f48::/64          8  Local Area Connection
No       Manual    256  2001:db8:21d0:3f48:1b9:88d1:cf98:fcaf/128
      8  Local Area Connection
No       Manual    256  2001:db8:21d0:3f48:b500:734b:fe5b:3945/128
      8  Local Area Connection
No       Manual    8    fd5e:2aa9:b3e:3f48::/64          8  Local Area Connection
No       Manual    256  fd5e:2aa9:b3e:3f48:1b9:88d1:cf98:fcaf/128
      8  Local Area Connection
No       Manual    256  fd5e:2aa9:b3e:3f48:b500:734b:fe5b:3945/128
```

```
  8   Local Area Connection
No        Manual   256   fe80::/64                        10   Local Area Connection* 9
No        Manual   256   fe80::/64                         8   Local Area Connection
No        Manual   256   fe80::100:7f:fffe/128            10   Local Area Connection* 9
No        Manual   256   fe80::5efe:10.0.0.2/128          11   Local Area Connection* 6
No        Manual   256   fe80::b500:734b:fe5b:3945/128     8   Local Area Connection
No        Manual   256   ff00::/8                          1   Loopback Pseudo-Interface 1
No        Manual   256   ff00::/8                         10   Local Area Connection* 9
No        Manual   256   ff00::/8                          8   Local Area Connection
```

The display of the IPv6 routing table for the **netsh interface ipv6 show route** command has the following columns:

- **Publish**   Whether the route is published (advertised in a Routing Advertisement message).

- **Type**   The origin of the route.

- **Met**   The preference of the route. The lowest metric is the most preferred route. The metric is used to select between multiple routes with the same prefix.

- **Prefix**   The address prefix for the route.

- **Idx**   The interface index for the route, indicating the interface over which packets matching the address prefix are reachable. You can view the interface indexes from the display of the **netsh interface ipv6 show** interface command.

- **Gateway/Interface Name**   Either the next-hop IPv6 address (for remote routes) or an interface name corresponding to the interface indicated in the Idx column (for directly attached routes).

Table 10-1 lists the routes in this example display and provides a description of each route.

Table 10-1   Example Routing Table Entries

Route (by prefix)	Description
::/0	Default route. The Gateway/Interface Name column contains the link-local address of the default router.
::1/128	Host route for the loopback address.
2001:db8:21d0:3f48::/64	Subnet prefix for the directly attached subnet.
2001:db8:21d0:3f48:1b9:88d1: cf98:fcaf/128	Host route for a global unicast address assigned to the Local Area Connection interface.
2001:db8:21d0:3f48:b500:734b: fe5b:3945/128	Host route for another global unicast address assigned to the Local Area Connection interface.
fd5e:2aa9:b3e:3f48::/64	Subnet prefix for the directly attached subnet.
fd5e:2aa9:b3e:3f48:1b9:88d1: cf98:fcaf/128	Host route for a unique local unicast address assigned to the Local Area Connection interface.
fd5e:2aa9:b3e:3f48:b500:734b: fe5b:3945/128	Host route for another unique local unicast address assigned to the Local Area Connection interface.
fe80::/64	Routes for the link-local address space.

Table 10-1   Example Routing Table Entries

Route (by prefix)	Description
fe80::100:7f:fffe/128	Host route for a link-local unicast address assigned to the Local Area Connection* 9 interface (Teredo).
fe80::5efe:10.0.0.2/128	Host route for a link-local unicast address assigned to the Local Area Connection* 6 interface (ISATAP).
fe80::b500:734b:fe5b:3945/128	Host route for a link-local unicast address assigned to the Local Area Connection interface.
ff00::/8	Routes for the multicast address space.

When determining the next-hop address from a route in the routing table, the following actions occur:

- If the Gateway/Interface Name column of the route table entry has an interface name, the destination is a neighbor and the next-hop address is set to the destination address of the IPv6 packet.

- If the Gateway/Interface Name column of the route table entry has an address (the address of a neighboring router), the destination is remote and the next-hop address is set to the address in the Gateway/Interface Name column.

In both cases, the next-hop interface is the interface in the Idx column of the route.

For example, when this IPv6 host sends a packet to 2001:db8:21d0:3f48:2aa:ff:fe90:4d3c, the longest matching route is the route for the directly attached subnet 2001:db8:21d0:3f48::/64. The next-hop address is set to the destination address of 2001:db8:21d0:3f48:dd48:ab34:d07c:3914 (the destination), and the next-hop interface is the interface that corresponds to interface index 8 (the Ethernet network adapter named Local Area Connection). When this IPv6 host sends traffic to 2001:db8:21d0:a957:2aa:ff:fe03:21a6, the longest matching route is the default route (::/0). The next-hop address is set to the router address of fe80::69ee:7d26:3:fbec, and the next-hop interface is the interface that corresponds to interface index 8 (Local Area Connection).

The route print Command

The following is the display of the **route print** command on the same host computer running Windows Vista with the IPv4 route table portion removed:

```
C:\Windows\system32>route print
===========================================================================
Interface List
  8 ...00 12 3f 17 e0 cf ...... Broadcom NetXtreme 57xx Gigabit Controller
  1 ........................... Software Loopback Interface 1
 11 ...00 00 00 00 00 00 00 e0  isatap.{17940FE6-D6C7-4AF3-8B79-8BC68D192EB4}
 10 ...02 00 54 55 4e 01 ...... Teredo Tunneling Pseudo-Interface
===========================================================================

IPv6 Route Table
```

```
================================================================================
Active Routes:
 If Metric Network Destination      Gateway
  8    286 ::/0                      fe80::69ee:7d26:3:fbec
  1    306 ::1/128                   On-link
  8     38 2001:db8:21d0:3f48::/64   On-link
  8    286 2001:db8:21d0:3f48:1b9:88d1:cf98:fcaf/128
                                     On-link
  8    286 2001:db8:21d0:3f48:b500:734b:fe5b:3945/128
                                     On-link
  8     38 fd5e:2aa9:b3e:3f48::/64   On-link
  8    286 fd5e:2aa9:b3e:3f48:1b9:88d1:cf98:fcaf/128
                                     On-link
  8    286 fd5e:2aa9:b3e:3f48:b500:734b:fe5b:3945/128
                                     On-link
  8    286 fe80::/64                 On-link
 11    296 fe80::5efe:10.0.0.2/128   On-link
  8    286 fe80::b500:734b:fe5b:3945/128
                                     On-link
  1    306 ff00::/8                  On-link
  8    286 ff00::/8                  On-link
================================================================================
Persistent Routes:
  None
```

The display of the IPv6 routing table for the **route print** command has the following columns:

- **If**   The interface index for the route. The interface indexes are listed in the Interface List portion of the **route print** display.

- **Metric**   The preference for the route. The lowest metric is the most preferred route. This is the metric used to select between multiple routes with the same prefix.

- **Network Destination**   The address prefix for the route.

- **Gateway**   A next-hop IPv6 address (for remote routes), or an indication that the destination is on-link (for directly attached routes).

Table 10-2 lists the routes in this example display and provides a description of each route.

Table 10-2   Example Routing Table Entries

Route (by prefix)	Description
::/0	Default route. The Gateway column has the link-local address of the default router.
::1/128	Host route for the loopback address.
2001:db8:21d0:3f48::/64	Subnet prefix for the directly attached subnet.
2001:db8:21d0:3f48:1b9:88d1: cf98:fcaf/128	Host route for a global unicast address assigned to the Local Area Connection interface.
2001:db8:21d0:3f48:b500:734b :fe5b:3945/128	Host route for another global unicast address assigned to the Local Area Connection interface.
fd5e:2aa9:b3e:3f48::/64	Subnet prefix for the directly attached subnet.

Table 10-2   **Example Routing Table Entries**

Route (by prefix)	Description
fd5e:2aa9:b3e:3f48:1b9:88d1: cf98:fcaf/128	Host route for a unique local unicast address assigned to the Local Area Connection interface.
fd5e:2aa9:b3e:3f48:b500:734b: fe5b:3945/128	Host route for another unique local unicast address assigned to the Local Area Connection interface.
fe80::/64	Route for the link-local address space.
fe80::5efe:10.0.0.2/128	Host route for a link-local unicast address assigned to the Local Area Connection* 6 interface (ISATAP).
fe80::b500:734b:fe5b:3945/128	Host route for a link-local unicast address assigned to the Local Area Connection interface.
ff00::/8	Routes for the multicast address space.

End-to-End IPv6 Delivery Process

The following sections describe the process of forwarding an IPv6 packet from the sending host, across one or more IPv6 routers, and its receipt at the final destination. This example assumes that the Hop-by-Hop Options, Destination Options, and Routing extension headers are not present.

IPv6 on the Sending Host

An IPv6 host uses the following algorithm when sending a packet to an arbitrary unicast destination address:

1. Set the Hop Limit field value to either a default or application-specified value.

2. Check the destination cache for an entry matching the destination address. For computers running Windows Server 2008 or Windows Vista, you can view the destination cache with the **netsh interface ipv6 show destinationcache** command.

3. If an entry matching the destination address is found in the destination cache, obtain the next-hop address and interface from the destination cache entry. Go to step 9.

4. If there is no source address for the packet, perform an unconstrained route lookup.

5. If there is a source address for the packet and strong host send behavior is enabled on the source interface, perform a constrained route lookup.

6. If there is a source address for the packet and strong host send behavior is disabled on the source interface, perform an unconstrained route lookup.

7. If there is a longest matching usable route, determine the next-hop interface and address used for forwarding the packet from the route.

   If there is not a longest matching usable route, indicate an error.

8. Update the destination cache.

9. Check the neighbor cache for an entry matching the next-hop address. For computers running Windows Server 2008 or Windows Vista, you can view the neighbor cache with the **netsh interface ipv6 show neighbors** command.

10. If an entry matching the next-hop address is found in the neighbor cache, obtain the link-layer address. Go to step 12.

11. If an entry matching the next-hop address is not found in the neighbor cache, use address resolution to obtain the link-layer address for the next-hop address and add an entry to the neighbor cache.

    If address resolution is not successful, indicate an error.

12. Send the packet using the link-layer address of the neighbor cache entry.

> **Note**   For unicast destination addresses that are assigned to the sending host, IPv6 skips steps 9 through 11.

Figure 10-1 shows the sending host process.

IPv6 on the Router

An IPv6 router uses the following algorithm when receiving and forwarding a packet to an arbitrary unicast or anycast destination:

1. Perform optional header error checks, such as ensuring that the Version field is set to 6 and that the source address is not the loopback address (::1) or a multicast address.

2. Verify whether the destination address in the IPv6 packet corresponds to an address assigned to a router interface.

    If so, process the IPv6 packet as the destination host. (See step 3 in the "IPv6 on the Destination Host" section in this chapter.)

3. Decrement the value of the Hop Limit field by 1.

    If the value of the Hop Limit field is less than 1, send an ICMPv6 Time Exceeded–Hop Limit Exceeded in Transit message to the sender and discard the packet.

4. If the value of the Hop Limit field is greater than 0, update the Hop Limit field in the IPv6 header of the packet.

5. Check the destination cache for an entry matching the destination address.

    If an entry matching the destination address is found in the destination cache, obtain the next-hop interface and address from the destination cache entry. Go to step 9.

6. Check the local IPv6 routing table, and select the longest matching usable route to the destination IPv6 address with the lowest metric.

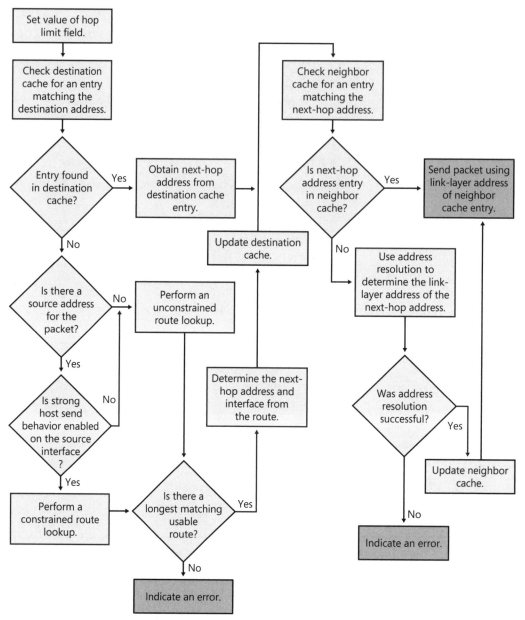

Figure 10-1   The sending host process

7. Based on the selected route, determine the next-hop interface and address used for forwarding the packet.

    If no route is found, send an ICMPv6 Destination Unreachable—No Route to Destination message to the sending host and discard the packet.

8. Update the destination cache.

9. If the interface on which the packet was received is the same as the interface on which the packet is being forwarded, the interface is a point-to-point link, and the Destination Address field matches a prefix assigned to the interface, send an ICMPv6 Destination Unreachable—Address Unreachable message to the sending host and discard the packet. This prevents the needless "ping-pong" forwarding of IPv6 packets between the two interfaces on a point-to-point link for a packet whose destination matches the prefix of the point-to-point link but does not match the address of either interface.

10. If the interface on which the packet was received is the same as the interface on which the packet is being forwarded, and the Source Address field matches a prefix assigned to the interface, send a Redirect message to the sending host.

11. Compare the link maximum transmission unit (MTU) of the next-hop interface to the size of the IPv6 packet being forwarded.

    If the link MTU is smaller than the packet size, send an ICMPv6 Packet Too Big message to the sending host and discard the packet.

12. Check the neighbor cache for an entry matching the next-hop address.

13. If an entry matching the next-hop address is found in the neighbor cache, obtain the link-layer address. Go to step 15.

14. If an entry matching the next-hop address is not found in the neighbor cache, use address resolution to obtain the link-layer address for the next-hop address and add an entry to the neighbor cache.

    If address resolution is not successful, send an ICMPv6 Destination Unreachable—Address Unreachable message to the sending host and discard the packet.

15. Send the packet with the link-layer address of the neighbor cache entry.

Figures 10-2 and 10-3 show the router forwarding process.

This entire process is repeated at each router in the path between the source and destination hosts.

IPv6 on the Destination Host

An IPv6 host uses the following algorithm when receiving an IPv6 packet:

1. Perform optional header error checks, such as ensuring that the Version field is set to 6 and that the source address is not the loopback address (::1) or a multicast address.

2. Verify whether the destination address in the IPv6 packet corresponds to an IPv6 address assigned to a local host interface.

    If the destination address is not assigned to a local host interface, silently discard the IPv6 packet.

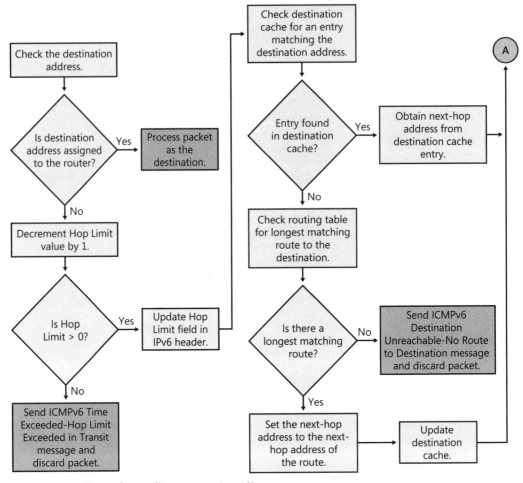

Figure 10-2   Router forwarding process (part 1)

3. If the strong host model for received packets is enabled, verify that the receiving interface is assigned the destination address in the IPv6 packet. If the destination address in the IPv6 packet is not assigned to the receiving interface, silently discard the packet.

    Computers running Windows Server 2008 or Windows Vista support the strong host model for received IPv6 packets by default. You can enable the weak host model for received IPv6 packets with the **netsh interface ipv6 set interface** *InterfaceNameOrIndex* **weakhostreceive=enabled** command.

4. Based on the Next Header field, process extension headers (if present).

5. Verify that the protocol for the value of the Next Header field exists.

    If the protocol does not exist, send an ICMPv6 Parameter Problem–Unrecognized Next Header Type Encountered message back to the sender and discard the packet.

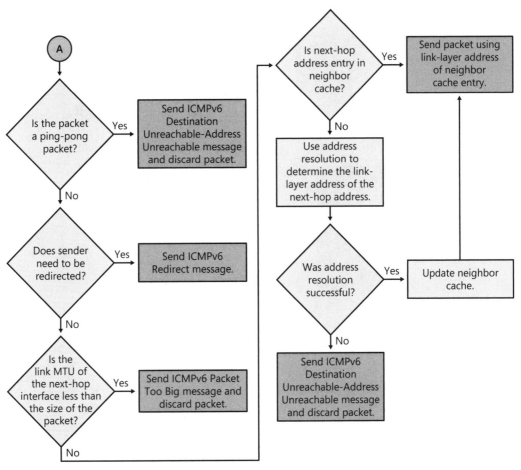

Figure 10-3   Router forwarding process (part 2)

6. If the upper-layer protocol data unit (PDU) is not a Transmission Control Protocol (TCP) segment or User Datagram Protocol (UDP) message, pass the upper-layer PDU to the appropriate protocol.

7. If the upper-layer PDU is a TCP segment or UDP message, check the destination port.

    If no application exists for the UDP port number, send an ICMPv6 Destination Unreachable–Port Unreachable message back to the sender and discard the packet. If no application exists for the TCP port number, send a TCP Connection Reset segment back to the sender and discard the packet.

8. If an application exists for the UDP or TCP destination port, process the contents of the TCP segment or UDP message.

Figure 10-4 shows the receiving host process.

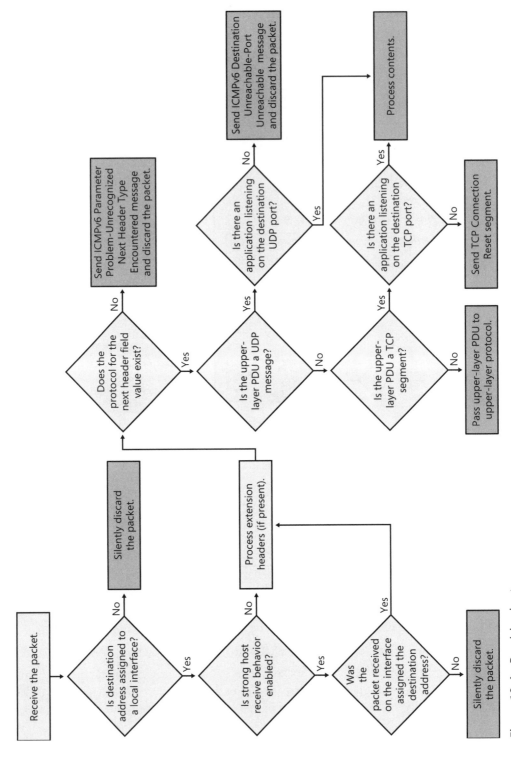

Figure 10-4 Receiving host process

IPv6 Routing Protocols

An IPv6 network consists of multiple IPv6 subnets interconnected by IPv6 routers. To provide reachability to any arbitrary location on the IPv6 network, routes must exist on sending hosts and routers to forward the traffic to the desired destination. These routes can either be general routes, such as a default route that summarizes all locations, or specific routes, such as subnet routes that summarize all locations on a specific subnet.

Hosts typically use directly attached subnet routes to reach neighboring nodes and a default route to reach all other locations. Routers typically use subnet routes to reach all locations within their site, and they use summarized routes to reach other sites or the Internet. Although the configuration of hosts with directly attached subnet routes and a default route is done automatically with a Router Advertisement message, configuration of routers is more complex. A router can have routes statically configured or dynamically maintained through the use of routing protocols.

Static routing is based on routing table entries that are manually configured and do not change with changing network topology. A router with manually configured routing tables is known as a *static router*. A network administrator, with knowledge of the network topology, manually builds and updates the routing table, entering all routes in the routing table. Static routers can work well for small networks, but they do not scale well to large or dynamically changing networks because they require manual administration.

Static routers are not fault tolerant. The lifetime of a manually configured static route is infinite, and therefore, static routers do not sense and recover from downed routers or downed links.

A computer running the IPv6 protocol for Windows Server 2008 and Windows Vista can be configured as a static IPv6 router.

Overview of Dynamic Routing

Dynamic routing is the automatic updating of routing table entries for changes in network topology. A router with dynamically configured routing tables is known as a *dynamic router*. The routing tables of dynamic routers are built and maintained automatically through ongoing communication between routers. This communication is facilitated by a routing protocol, which employs a series of periodic or on-demand messages containing routing information that is exchanged between routers. Except for their initial configuration, typical dynamic routers require little ongoing maintenance, and therefore can scale to larger networks. The ability to scale and recover from network faults makes dynamic routing the better choice for medium, large, and very large networks.

Dynamic routers use routing protocols to facilitate the ongoing communication and dynamic updating of routing tables. Routing protocols are used between routers and represent additional network traffic overhead on the network. This additional traffic can become an important factor in planning wide area network (WAN) link usage.

Some widely used routing protocols for IPv4 are Routing Information Protocol (RIP), Open Shortest Path First (OSPF), and Border Gateway Protocol (BGP).

An important element of a routing protocol implementation is its ability to sense and recover from network faults. How quickly it can recover is determined by the type of fault, how it is sensed, and how the routing information is propagated through the network. When all the routers on the network have the correct routing information in their routing tables, the network has converged. When convergence is achieved, the network is in a stable state and all routing occurs along optimal paths.

When a link or router fails, the network must reconfigure itself to reflect the new topology. Information in routing tables must be updated. Until the network reconverges, it is in an unstable state in which routing loops and black holes can occur. The time it takes for the network to reconverge is known as the *convergence time*. The convergence time varies based on the routing protocol and the type of failure (downed link or downed router).

Unlike IPv4, Routing and Remote Access in Windows Server 2008 does not support any IPv6 routing protocols.

Routing Protocol Technologies

Routing protocols are based either on a distance vector, link state, or path vector technology.

Distance Vector

Distance vector routing protocols propagate routing information in the form of an address prefix and its "distance" (hop count). Routers use distance vector-based routing protocols to periodically advertise the routes in their routing tables. Routing information exchanged between typical distance vector-based routers is unsynchronized and unacknowledged. The advantages of distance vector-based routing protocols include simplicity and ease of configuration. The disadvantages of distance vector-based routing protocols include relatively high network traffic, a long convergence time, and inability to scale to a large or very large network.

Link State

Routers using link state-based routing protocols exchange link state advertisements (LSAs) throughout the network to update routing tables. LSAs consist of a router's attached network prefixes and their assigned costs. Routers advertise LSAs upon startup and when changes in the network topology are detected. Link state updates are sent using unicast or multicast traffic rather than broadcasting. Link state routers build a database of link state advertisements and use the database to calculate the optimal routes to add to the routing table. Routing information exchanged between link state-based routers is synchronized and acknowledged.

The advantages of link state-based routing protocols are low network overhead, low convergence time, and the ability to scale to large and very large networks. The disadvantages of link state-based routing protocols are that they can be more complex and difficult to configure.

Path Vector

Routers use path vector–based routing protocols to exchange sequences of hop numbers—for example, autonomous system numbers—indicating the path for a route. An autonomous system is a portion of the network under the same administrative authority. Autonomous systems are assigned a unique, autonomous system identifier. Routing information exchanged between path vector–based routers is synchronized and acknowledged. The advantages of path vector–based routing protocols are low network overhead, low convergence time, and the ability to scale to very large networks containing multiple autonomous systems. The disadvantages of path vector–based routing protocols are that they can be complex and difficult to configure.

Routing Protocols for IPv6

As of the writing of this book, the following routing protocols are defined by the Internet Engineering Task Force (IETF) for IPv6:

- RIPng for IPv6
- OSPF for IPv6
- Integrated Intermediate System-to-Intermediate System (IS-IS) for IPv6
- BGP-4

RIPng for IPv6

RIP Next Generation (RIPng) is a distance vector routing protocol for IPv6 that is defined in RFC 2080. RIPng for IPv6 is an adaptation of the RIPv2 protocol—defined in RFC 1723—to advertise IPv6 network prefixes. RIPng for IPv6 has a simple packet structure and uses UDP port 521 to periodically advertise its routes, respond to requests for routes, and asynchronously advertise route changes.

RIPng for IPv6 has a maximum distance of 15, where 15 is the accumulated cost (hop count). Locations that are a distance of 16 or further are considered unreachable. RIPng for IPv6 is a simple routing protocol with a periodic route-advertising mechanism designed for use in small- to medium-sized IPv6 networks. RIPng for IPv6 does not scale well to a large or very large IPv6 network.

When a RIPng for IPv6 router is initialized, it announces the appropriate routes in its routing table on all interfaces. The RIPng for IPv6 router also sends a General Request message on all interfaces. All neighboring routers send the contents of their routing tables in response; those responses build the initial routing table. Learned routes are given a 3-minute lifetime (by default) before being removed from the IPv6 routing table by RIPng for IPv6.

After initialization, the RIPng for IPv6 router periodically announces (every 30 seconds, by default) the appropriate routes in its routing table for each interface. The exact set of routes being announced depends on whether the RIPng for IPv6 router is implementing split horizon (where routes are not announced over the interfaces on which they were learned) or split horizon with poison reverse (where routes are announced as unreachable over the interfaces on which they were learned).

Fault tolerance for RIP networks is based on the timeout of RIPng for IPv6-learned routes. If a change occurs in the network topology, RIPng for IPv6 routers can send a triggered update—a routing update, sent immediately—rather than waiting for a scheduled announcement.

For a detailed explanation of RIPng for IPv6, see RFC 2080.

OSPF for IPv6

OSPF for IPv6, also known as OSPFv3, is a link state routing protocol defined in RFC 2740. It is designed to be run as a routing protocol for a single autonomous system. OSPF for IPv6 is an adaptation of the OSPF routing protocol version 2 for IPv4 defined in RFC 2328. The OSPF cost of each router link is a unitless number that the network administrator assigns, and it can include delay, bandwidth, and monetary cost factors. The accumulated cost between network segments in an OSPF network must be less than 65,535. OSPF messages are sent as an upper-layer PDU using the next header value of 89.

OSPF for IPv6 has the following changes from OSPF version 2:

- The structure of OSPF packets has been modified to remove dependencies on IPv4 addressing.
- New LSAs are defined to carry IPv6 addresses and prefixes.
- OSPF runs over each link, rather than each subnet.
- The scope of the network for flooding LSAs is generalized.
- The OSPF protocol no longer provides authentication. Instead, OSPF relies on the Authentication header (AH) and Encapsulating Security Payload (ESP) header and trailer.

Each router has an LSA that describes its current state. The LSA of each OSPF for IPv6 router is efficiently propagated throughout the OSPF network through logical relationships between neighboring routers called *adjacencies*. When the propagation of all current router LSAs is complete, the OSPF network has converged.

Based on the collection of OSPF LSAs—known as the *link state database* (LSDB)—OSPF calculates the lowest-cost path to each route, and those paths become OSPF routes in the IPv6 routing table. To reduce the size of the LSDB, OSPF allows the creation of *areas*. An OSPF area is a grouping of contiguous network segments. In all OSPF networks, there is at least one area called the *backbone area*. OSPF areas allow the summarization or aggregation of routing information at the boundaries of an OSPF area. A router at the boundary of an OSPF area is known as an *area border router* (ABR).

For a detailed explanation of OSPF for IPv6, see RFC 2740.

Integrated IS-IS for IPv6

Integrated IS-IS, also known as *dual IS*, is a link state routing protocol very similar to OSPF that is defined in International Standards Organization (ISO) document 10589. IS-IS supports both IPv4 and Connectionless Network Protocol (CLNP), the Network layer of the Open Systems Interconnect (OSI) protocol suite. IS-IS allows two levels of hierarchical scaling, whereas OSPF allows only one (areas). Integrated IS-IS for IPv6 is described in the Internet draft titled "Routing IPv6 with IS-IS."

For a detailed explanation of Integrated IS-IS for IPv6, see ISO 10589 and the Internet draft titled "Routing IPv6 with IS-IS."

BGP-4

Border Gateway Protocol version 4 (BGP-4) is a path vector routing protocol defined in RFC 4271. Unlike RIPng for IPv6 and OSPF for IPv6, which are used within an autonomous system, BGP-4 is designed to exchange information between autonomous systems. BGP-4 routing information is used to create a logical path tree, which describes all the connections between autonomous systems. The path tree information is then used to create loop-free routes in the routing tables of BGP-4 routers. BGP-4 messages are sent using TCP port 179. BGP-4 is the primary interdomain protocol used to maintain routing tables on the IPv4 Internet.

BGP-4 has been defined to be independent of the address family for which routing information is being propagated. For IPv6, BGP-4 has been extended to support IPv6 address prefixes as described in RFCs 2545 and 4760. For a detailed explanation of BGP-4 for IPv6, see RFCs 4271, 2545, and 4760.

Static Routing with the IPv6 Protocol for Windows Server 2008 and Windows Vista

The IPv6 protocol for Windows Server 2008 and Windows Vista supports static routing. You can configure static IPv6 routing in the following ways:

- For computers running Windows Server 2008 or Windows Vista, with commands in the **netsh interface ipv6** context
- For computers running Windows Server 2008, with Routing and Remote Access

Configuring Static Routing with Netsh

To create a static IPv6 router with the Netsh tool, you must enable forwarding and advertising on the required interfaces. To enable forwarding and advertising on an interface, use the following command:

netsh interface ipv6 set interface [**interface=**]*InterfaceNameOrIndex* [**forwarding=**]enabled | disabled] [[**advertise=**]enabled | disabled]

By default, forwarding and advertising on all IPv6 interfaces are disabled.

For example, a computer named ROUTER1 running Windows Server 2008 is being configured as a router. ROUTER1 has three interfaces, named Local Area Connection, Local Area Connection 2, and Local Area Connection 3. The Local Area Connection and Local Area Connection 2 interfaces are connected to peripheral subnets. The Local Area Connection 3 interface is connected to a subnet containing a neighboring IPv6 router named ROUTER2. Figure 10-5 shows this example configuration.

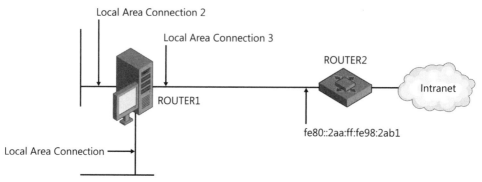

Figure 10-5 Example configuration

To enable forwarding and advertising over Local Area Connection and Local Area Connection 2 and forwarding over Local Area Connection 3, the commands to run on ROUTER1 are as follows:

```
netsh interface ipv6 set interface "Local Area Connection"
forwarding=enabled advertise=enabled
netsh interface ipv6 set interface "Local Area Connection 2"
forwarding=enabled advertise=enabled
netsh interface ipv6 set interface "Local Area Connection 3" forwarding=enabled
```

The Local Area Connection 3 interface is attached to a subnet that already contains ROUTER2, an advertising router.

After these commands are run, ROUTER1 sends Router Advertisement messages on the two peripheral subnets using the Local Area Connection and Local Area Connection 2 interfaces. However, the router advertisements do not contain any Prefix Information or Route Information options through which hosts on the attached subnets can automatically configure addresses and routes. To advertise Prefix Information or Route Information options, you must configure ROUTER1 to publish routes.

To add a route and configure it to be published, use the following command:

netsh interface ipv6 add route *IPv6Address/PrefixLength* [**interface=**]*InterfaceNameOrIndex* [[**nexthop=**]*IPv6Address*] [[**metric=**]*Integer*] [[**publish=**]**no**|**yes**|**immortal**]

By default, there is no next-hop address (the prefix is on-link), the route metric is automatically determined, and the route is not published.

For example, to configure ROUTER1 to publish the on-link subnet prefix 2001:db8:0:1::/64 on Local Area Connection and publish the on-link subnet prefix 2001:db8:0:2::/64 on Local Area Connection 2, the commands are as follows:

```
netsh interface ipv6 add route 2001:db8:0:1::/64 "Local Area Connection" publish=yes
netsh interface ipv6 add route 2001:db8:0:2::/64 "Local Area Connection 2" publish=yes
```

Routes that are configured to be published on an interface are advertised on that interface as Prefix Information options with the On-link flag set. If the on-link advertised route has a prefix length of 64, ROUTER2 sets the Autonomous flag in the Prefix Information option to allow hosts to create stateless addresses.

To provide hosts with reachability for directly attached subnets of the advertising routers, ROUTER1 includes the subnet prefixes that are configured to be published on other interfaces in the Router Information option in the Router Advertisement message. RFC 4191 describes the use of the Router Information option. The prefixes in Router Information options are added as static routes on the receiving hosts to make locations on other subnets that are directly attached to the advertising router reachable. For this example, ROUTER1 includes the 2001:db8:0:2::/64 prefix as a Router Information option in the router advertisement sent on Local Area Connection. Similarly, ROUTER1 includes the 2001:db8:0:1::/64 prefix as a Router Information option in the router advertisement sent on Local Area Connection 2.

For this configuration, ROUTER1 does not advertise itself as a default router. Hosts on the 2001:db8:0:1::/64 and 2001:db8:0:2::/64 subnets automatically configure addresses and add routes to their routing tables, but they do not automatically configure a default route (::/0). A computer running Windows Server 2008 or Windows Vista does not advertise itself as a default router unless there is a default route that is configured to be published.

To configure the router to be a default router for hosts on the 2001:db8:0:1::/64 and 2001:db8:0:2::/64 subnets, you must add a default route to the router and publish it. For example, the subnet of Local Area Connection 3 contains ROUTER2 with the link-local address of fe80::2aa:ff:fe98:2ab1. The following command on ROUTER1 adds a default route and publishes it:

```
netsh interface ipv6 add route ::/0 "Local Area Connection 3" nexthop=fe80::2aa:
ff:fe98:2ab1 publish=yes
```

After this command is run, ROUTER1 sends Router Advertisement messages on Local Area Connection and Local Area Connection 2 with the Router Lifetime field set to 65535, indicating that it is a default router with a maximum lifetime.

Additional Netsh Command Options to Configure IPv6 Router Behavior

The Netsh tool commands to configure IPv6 router behavior described so far in this chapter use only the minimum commands and options to enable forwarding and advertising behavior and to publish routes. This section describes the **netsh interface ipv6 set interface** and **netsh interface ipv6 add route** commands in more detail to configure advanced IPv6 router behavior.

The command to configure IPv6 router interfaces for forwarding and advertising router behavior with all of its options is the following:

netsh interface ipv6 set interface [**interface=**]*InterfaceNameOrIndex* [[**forwarding=**]**enabled**|**disabled**] [[**advertise=**]**enabled**|**disabled**] [[**mtu=**]*Integer*] [[**metric=**]**automatic**|*Integer*] [[**siteprefixlength=**]*Integer*] [[**basereachabletime=**]*Integer*] [[**retransmittime=**]*Integer*] [[**managedaddress=**]**enabled**|**disabled**] [[**otherstateful=**]**enabled**|**disabled**] [[**store=**]**active**|**persistent**]

Table 10-3 lists the command option, its default value, and a description.

Table 10-3   The netsh interface ipv6 set interface Command Options for Routing Behavior

Option	Default Value or Behavior	Description
forwarding	Disabled	Enables or disables forwarding for incoming packets on an interface.
advertise	Disabled	Enables or disables sending router advertisements on an interface.
mtu	MTU of the interface	Sets the maximum IPv6 packet size that can be sent on the interface and is the value of the MTU field in the MTU option of the Router Advertisement message.
metric	Automatic	Sets the metric for routes that use the interface.
basereachable	0	Sets the value of the Reachable Time field in the Router Advertisement message.
retransmittime	0	Sets the value of the Retransmission Timer field in the Router Advertisement message.
managedaddress	Disabled	Sets or clears the Managed Address Autoconfiguration flag in the Router Advertisement message.
otherstateful	Disabled	Sets or clears the Other Stateful Configuration flag in the Router Advertisement message.
store	Persistent	Specifies whether to store the configuration change so that it will be in effect when the computer is restarted.

There are no Netsh command options to specify the following:

- The Router Lifetime field in the Router Advertisement message. If the router is advertising itself as a default router, IPv6 sets the Router Lifetime to 65,635.

- The Default Router Preference field in the Router Advertisement message. IPv6 sets the Default Router Preference field to 0 for medium preference.

■ The Current Hop Limit field in the Router Advertisement message. IPv6 sets the Current Hop Limit field to 0, which indicates to the receiving hosts that the router is not specifying a value for the default hop limit.

The command to add a published route with all of its options is the following:

netsh interface ipv6 add route [**prefix=**]*IPv6Prefix/PrefixLength* [**interface=**]*InterfaceNameOrIndex* [[**nexthop=**]*IPv6Address*] [[**siteprefixlength=**]*Integer*] [[**publish=**]**no**|**yes**|**immortal**] [[**validlifetime=**]*Integer*|**infinite**] [[**preferredlifetime=**]*Integer*|**infinite**] [[**store=**]**active**|**persistent**]

Table 10-4 lists the command option, its default value or behavior, and a description.

Table 10-4   The netsh interface ipv6 add route Command Options for Advertised Routes

Option	Default Value or Behavior	Description
nexthop	None	Specifies the next-hop address for the route.
siteprefixlength	Not included in the Prefix Information option	Specifies the prefix length of the entire site for the advertised route, and sets the value of the Site Prefix Length field in the Prefix Information option.
Publish	No	Specifies whether the route will be included in Prefix Information or Route Information options in Router Advertisement messages. For the **immortal** option, the route is advertised with maximum valid and preferred lifetimes.
validlifetime	Maximum of 0xFFFFFFFF	Specifies the value of the Valid Lifetime field in the Prefix Information option.
preferredlifetime	Maximum of 0xFFFFFFFF	Specifies the value of the Preferred Lifetime field in the Prefix Information option.
Store	Persistent	Specifies whether to store the configuration change so that it will be in effect when the computer is restarted.

Configuring Static Routing with Routing and Remote Access

On a computer running Windows Server 2008, you can enable IPv6 routing and configure static IPv6 routes with the Routing and Remote Access snap-in.

To enable IPv6 routing, do the following:

1. In the console tree of the Routing and Remote Access snap-in, right-click the server name and then click Properties.

2. On the General tab, click IPv6 Router and then select either Local Area Network (LAN) Routing Only or LAN And Demand-Dial Routing.

3. Click OK.

To add a static IPv6 route, do the following:

1. In the console tree of the Routing and Remote Access snap-in, open IPv6.

2. Right-click Static Routes, and then click New Static Route.

3. In the IPv6 Static Route dialog box, select the interface and type the destination, prefix length, gateway (the next-hop IPv6 address), and metric for the static route. For demand-dial interfaces, you can also select the Use This Route To Initiate Demand-Dial Connections check box to initiate a demand-dial connection for traffic that matches the route. The following figure shows an example of the IPv6 Static Route dialog box:

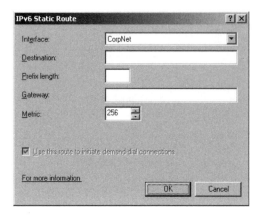

4. Click OK.

5. Repeat steps 2–4 for additional IPv6 static routes.

To modify an existing IPv6 static route in Routing and Remote Access, right-click the route in the details pane and then click Properties. To delete an existing IPv6 static route in Routing and Remote Access, right-click the route in the details pane and then click Delete.

Dead Gateway Detection

The TCP component of TCP/IP in Windows Server 2008 and Windows Vista uses dead gateway detection to detect the failure of the default router and to adjust the IPv6 routing table to use the next default router when there are multiple default routers configured. Dead gateway detection takes two forms:

■ By using Neighbor Unreachability Detection, the IPv6 host can determine that the neighboring default router is no longer reachable. If Neighbor Unreachability Detection determines that the next default router in the list is unreachable, dead gateway detection attempts to use the next default router in the list, returning to the first default router after cycling through the entire list.

- When a TCP segment for a TCP connection forwarded through the default router is retransmitted three times, dead gateway detection changes the destination cache entry for that remote IPv6 address to use the next default router in the list as its next-hop address. A *destination cache entry* is an entry in the destination cache, which stores the next-hop IPv6 address for a destination IPv6 address. When one-fourth of the TCP connections routed through the default router have had their destination cache entries adjusted to the next default router, dead gateway detection informs IPv6 to change the computer's default router to the one that the adjusted connections are now using. If TCP connections continue to fail, dead gateway detection attempts to use the next default router in the list, returning to the first default router after cycling through the entire list.

TCP/IP in Windows Server 2008 and Windows Vista also supports fail-back behavior for default router changes. The lack of fail-back support for default routers can cause throughput problems on a subnet containing two routers: a high-capacity primary router and a lower-capacity backup router. The hosts on the subnet have the high-capacity router as their first default router and the backup router as their second default router. If the high-capacity router has a temporary failure, hosts on the subnet will switch over to the backup router. When the high-capacity router becomes available again, none of the hosts on the network use it because they have switched to the backup router.

TCP/IP in Windows Server 2008 and Windows Vista performs fail-back for default router changes by periodically attempting to send TCP traffic through the previous router. If the TCP traffic sent through the previous router is successful, TCP/IP in Windows Server 2008 and Windows Vista switches the default router to the previous router.

In the example with the high-capacity router and backup router, if the neighboring high-capacity router becomes unavailable, the hosts on the subnet use Neighbor Unreachability Detection to switch their default routers to the backup router. The hosts then periodically attempt to send TCP traffic through the high-capacity router. When the high-capacity router becomes available and the hosts determine that TCP traffic sent through the high-capacity router is successful, the hosts switch their default router back to the high-capacity router.

Support for fail-back to primary default routers can provide faster throughput by sending traffic through the primary default router on the subnet.

References

The following references were cited in this chapter:

- RFC 1723 – "RIP Version 2"
- RFC 2080 – "RIPng for IPv6"
- RFC 2328 – "OSPF Version 2"
- RFC 2545 – "Use of BGP-4 Multiprotocol Extensions for IPv6 Inter-Domain Routing"

- RFC 2740 – "OSPF for IPv6"

- RFC 4191 – "Default Router Preferences and More-Specific Routes"

- RFC 4271 – "A Border Gateway Protocol 4 (BGP-4)"

- RFC 4760 – "Multiprotocol Extensions for BGP-4"

- Internet draft – "Routing IPv6 with IS-IS"

- ISO 10589 – "Intermediate system to Intermediate system intra-domain routing information exchange protocol for use in conjunction with the protocol for providing the connectionless-mode Network Service"

You can obtain these RFCs from the \RFCs_and_Drafts folder on the companion CD-ROM or from *http://www.ietf.org/rfc.html*.

Testing for Understanding

To test your understanding of IPv6 routing, answer the following questions. See Appendix D, "Testing for Understanding Answers," to check your answers.

1. How does IPv6 on a router determine the single route in the routing table to use when forwarding a packet? How is the process different for an IPv6 sending host?

2. Describe the conditions that would cause a router to send the following ICMPv6 error messages:

    ❑ ICMPv6 Packet Too Big

    ❑ ICMPv6 Destination Unreachable–Address Unreachable

    ❑ ICMPv6 Time Exceeded–Hop Limit Exceeded in Transit

    ❑ ICMPv6 Destination Unreachable–Port Unreachable

    ❑ ICMPv6 Destination Unreachable–No Route to Destination

    ❑ ICMPv6 Parameter Problem–Unrecognized IPv6 Option Encountered

3. A host running Windows Vista receives a Router Advertisement message from a router advertising itself as a default router with the link-local address of fe80::2aa:ff:fe45:a431:2c5d, and containing a Prefix Information option to autoconfigure an address with the prefix 2001:db8:0:952a::/64 and a Route Information option with the prefix 2001:db8:0:952c::/64. Fill in the expected entries for the host based on this Router Advertisement message in the following abbreviated routing table:

    ```
    Network Destination    Gateway
    -------------------    -------
    ```

4. Describe the differences between distance vector, link state, and path vector routing protocol technologies in terms of convergence time, ability to scale, ease of deployment, and appropriate use (intranet vs. Internet).

5. A static IPv6 router running Windows Server 2008 is configured with the following commands.

```
netsh interface ipv6 set interface "Local Area Connection" forwarding=enabled
 advertise=enabled
netsh interface ipv6 set interface "Local Area Connection 2" forwarding=enabled
 advertise=enabled
netsh interface ipv6 add route 2001:db8:0:1a4c::/64 "Local Area Connection"
 publish=yes
netsh interface ipv6 add route 2001:db8:0:90b5::/64 "Local Area Connection 2"
 publish=yes
```

With just these commands, will a host on the 2001:db8:0:90b5::/64 subnet have a default route? Why or why not? With just these commands, can a host on the 2001:db8:0:90b5::/64 subnet reach a host on the 2001:db8:0:1a4c::/64 subnet? If so, how?

Chapter 11
IPv6 Transition Technologies

At the end of this chapter, you should be able to do the following:

- List and describe the IPv4-to-IPv6 transition criteria.

- List and describe the different types of nodes.

- List and describe the use of each type of transition address.

- Describe the mechanisms for IPv4 and IPv6 coexistence.

- List and describe the types of tunneling configurations.

- Describe configured and automatic tunneling.

- Describe the purpose and configuration of the PortProxy component in Windows Server 2008 and Windows Vista.

Overview

Protocol transitions are not easy, and the transition from Internet Protocol version 4 (IPv4) to Internet Protocol version 6 (IPv6) is no exception. Protocol transitions are typically deployed by installing and configuring the new protocol on all nodes within the network and verifying that all host and router operations work successfully. Although this might be easily managed in a small or medium-sized organization, the challenge of making a rapid protocol transition in a large organization is very difficult. Additionally, given the scope of the Internet, rapid protocol transition from IPv4 to IPv6 of the total networking environment is an impossible task.

The designers of IPv6 recognized that the transition from IPv4 to IPv6 will take years and that there might be organizations or nodes within organizations that will continue to use IPv4 indefinitely. Therefore, although migration is the long-term goal, equal consideration must be given to the interim coexistence of IPv4 and IPv6 nodes.

The designers of IPv6 in the original "The Recommendation for the IP Next Generation Protocol" specification (RFC 1752) defined the following transition criteria:

- Existing IPv4 hosts can be upgraded at any time, independent of the upgrade of other hosts or routers.

- New hosts, using only IPv6, can be added at any time, without dependencies on other hosts or routing infrastructure.

- Existing IPv4 hosts, with IPv6 installed, can continue to use their IPv4 addresses and do not need additional addresses.

- Little preparation is required to either upgrade existing IPv4 nodes to IPv6 or deploy new IPv6 nodes.

The inherent lack of dependencies between IPv4 and IPv6 hosts, IPv4 routing infrastructure, and IPv6 routing infrastructure requires mechanisms that allow seamless coexistence.

Node Types

RFC 2893, "Transition Mechanisms for IPv6 Hosts and Routers," defines the following node types:

- **IPv4-only node**   Implements only IPv4 and is assigned only IPv4 addresses. This node does not support IPv6. Most hosts—such as client computers, server computers, and network-capable devices such as printers—and routers installed today are IPv4-only nodes.

- **IPv6-only node**   Implements only IPv6 and is assigned only IPv6 addresses. An IPv6-only node is only able to communicate with IPv6 nodes and IPv6-enabled applications. Although this type of node is not common today, it will become more prevalent as smaller devices such as cellular phones and handheld computing devices include only IPv6 stacks.

- **IPv6/IPv4 node**   Implements both IPv4 and IPv6 and is assigned both IPv4 and IPv6 addresses. Computers running Windows Server 2008 or Windows Vista are by default IPv6/IPv4 nodes.

- **IPv4 node**   Implements IPv4 and can send and receive IPv4 packets. An IPv4 node can be an IPv4-only node or an IPv6/IPv4 node.

- **IPv6 node**   Implements IPv6 and can send and receive IPv6 packets. An IPv6 node can be an IPv6-only node or an IPv6/IPv4 node.

For coexistence to occur, the largest number of IPv4 or IPv6 nodes can communicate using an IPv4 infrastructure, an IPv6 infrastructure, or an infrastructure that is a combination of IPv4 and IPv6. True migration is achieved when all IPv4 nodes are converted to IPv6-only nodes. However, for the foreseeable future, practical migration is achieved when as many IPv4-only nodes as possible are converted to IPv6/IPv4 nodes. IPv4-only nodes cannot communicate directly with IPv6-only nodes, but you can use an IPv4-to-IPv6 proxy or translation gateway. An example is the PortProxy component of the IPv6 protocol for Windows Server 2008 and Windows Vista. For more information, see the "PortProxy" section in this chapter.

IPv6 Transition Addresses

The following addresses are defined to aid in the transition of IPv4 to IPv6:

- **IPv4-compatible addresses**   The IPv4-compatible address, 0:0:0:0:0:0:w.x.y.z or ::w.x.y.z (where w.x.y.z is the dotted-decimal representation of a public IPv4 address), is used by IPv6/IPv4 nodes that are communicating with IPv6 over an IPv4-only infrastructure. When the IPv4-compatible address is used as an IPv6 destination, the IPv6 traffic is automatically encapsulated with an IPv4 header and sent to the destination over the IPv4-only infrastructure. However, the IPv4-compatible address has been deprecated and is not supported by the IPv6 protocol for Windows Server 2008 and Windows Vista. The IPv6 protocol for Windows XP and Windows Server 2003 supports IPv4-compatible addresses, but it is disabled by default. To enable the use of IPv4-compatible addresses, use the **netsh interface ipv6 set state v4compat=enabled** command.

- **IPv4-mapped addresses**   The IPv4-mapped address, 0:0:0:0:0:FFFF:w.x.y.z or ::FFFF:w.x.y.z, is used to internally represent an IPv4 node to an IPv6 node. The IPv4-mapped address is never used as a source or destination address of an IPv6 packet. The IPv6 protocol for Windows Server 2008 and Windows Vista supports IPv4-mapped addresses. The IPv6 protocol for Windows XP and Windows Server 2003 does not support IPv4-mapped addresses.

- **Intra-Site Automatic Tunnel Addressing Protocol (ISATAP) addresses**   Typical ISATAP addresses, defined in RFC 4214, are composed of a valid 64-bit unicast address prefix and the interface identifier ::0:5efe:w.x.y.z (where w.x.y.z is a private IPv4 address assigned to a node). An example of a link-local ISATAP address is fe80::5efe:192.168.4.92. ISATAP hosts assign ISATAP addresses to their ISATAP tunnel interfaces. ISATAP is supported by the IPv6 protocol for Windows Server 2008, Windows Vista, Windows Server 2003, and Windows XP. For more information about ISATAP, see Chapter 12, "ISATAP."

- **6to4 addresses**   6to4 addresses, defined in RFC 3056, are based on the prefix 2002:WWXX:YYZZ::/48 (in which WWXX:YYZZ is the colon hexadecimal representation of w.x.y.z, a public IPv4 address). 6to4 address prefixes are used to create global address prefixes for IPv6-capable sites on the IPv4 Internet and global addresses for IPv6 nodes within sites. An example of a 6to4 address is 2002:836b:1:25:2aa:ff:fe53:ba63. In this example, 836b:1 is the colon hexadecimal version of 131.107.0.1. 6to4 is supported by the IPv6 protocol for Windows Server 2008, Windows Vista, Windows Server 2003, and Windows XP. For more information, see Chapter 13, "6to4."

- **Teredo addresses**   Teredo addresses, defined in RFC 4380, are based on the prefix 2001::/32. Teredo address prefixes are used to create global IPv6 addresses for IPv6/IPv4 nodes that are connected to the IPv4 Internet, even when they are located behind network address translators (NATs). An example of a Teredo address is 2001::ce49:7601:2cad:dfff:7c94:fffe. Teredo is supported by the IPv6 protocol for Windows Server 2008, Windows Vista, Windows Server 2003 with Service Pack 1, and Windows XP with Service Pack 2. The 2001::/32 prefix is used by Teredo in Windows Vista and Windows Server 2008. Teredo in Windows XP and Windows Server 2003 initially used the 3ffe:831f::/32 prefix. Computers running Windows XP or Windows Server 2003 use the 2001::/32 Teredo prefix when updated with Microsoft Security Bulletin MS06-064. For more information, see Chapter 14, "Teredo."

Transition Mechanisms

To coexist with an IPv4 infrastructure and to provide eventual migration to an IPv6-only infrastructure, the IPv6 transition standards define the following mechanisms:

- Using both IPv4 and IPv6
- IPv6-over-IPv4 tunneling
- Domain Name System (DNS) infrastructure

Using Both IPv4 and IPv6

During the time that the routing infrastructure is being transitioned from IPv4-only, to IPv4 and IPv6, and finally to IPv6-only, nodes must be able to reach destinations using either IPv4 or IPv6. For example, during the transition, some server services will be reachable over IPv6. However, some services, which have not yet been updated to support both IPv4 and IPv6, are reachable only over IPv4. Therefore, hosts must be able to use both IPv4 and IPv6. To use both IPv4 and IPv6 Internet layers on the same node, IPv6/IPv4 nodes can have the following architectures:

- Dual IP layer architecture
- Dual stack architecture

Dual IP Layer Architecture

A dual IP layer architecture contains both IPv4 and IPv6 Internet layers with a single implementation of Transport layer protocols such as Transmission Control Protocol (TCP) and User Datagram Protocol (UDP). Figure 11-1 shows a dual IP layer architecture.

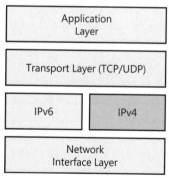

Figure 11-1 A dual IP layer architecture

The TCP/IP protocol in Windows Server 2008 and Windows Vista includes both IPv4 and IPv6 in a dual IP layer architecture as shown in Figure 11-1. A single Windows driver,

Tcpip.sys, contains implementations of both IPv4 and IPv6. A node running Windows Server 2008 or Windows Vista can create the following types of packets:

- IPv4 packets

- IPv6 packets

- IPv6-over-IPv4 packets

These are IPv6 packets that are encapsulated with an IPv4 header. For more information, see the "IPv6-over-IPv4 Tunneling" section in this chapter.

Figure 11-2 shows the types of packets with a dual IP layer architecture.

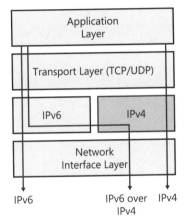

Figure 11-2   Types of packets with a dual IP layer architecture

In Windows Server 2008 and Windows Vista, the dual IP layer architecture also simplifies application programming by allowing a dual-stack socket, which can handle both IPv6 and IPv4 traffic. For Windows Server 2003 and Windows XP, an IPv6-capable application must open two separate sockets, one for IPv4 and one for IPv6.

Dual-Stack Architecture

A dual-stack architecture contains both IPv4 and IPv6 Internet layers, but they are within different protocol stacks that contain separate implementations of Transport layer protocols such as TCP and UDP. Figure 11-3 shows a dual-stack architecture.

Windows Server 2003 and Windows XP have a dual-stack architecture. The IPv4 protocol driver, Tcpip.sys, contains IPv4, TCP, and UDP (among other protocols). The IPv6 protocol driver, Tcpip6.sys, contains IPv6 and a separate implementation of TCP and UDP. With both IPv4 and IPv6 protocol stacks installed, a host running Windows Server 2003 or Windows XP can create the following types of packets:

- IPv4 packets

- IPv6 packets
- IPv6-over-IPv4 packets

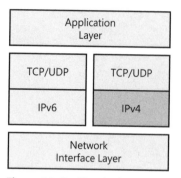

Figure 11-3   The dual-stack architecture

Figure 11-4 shows the types of packets with a dual-stack architecture.

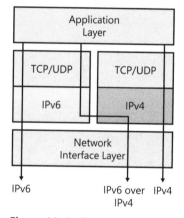

Figure 11-4   Types of packets with a dual-stack architecture

Although the IPv6 protocol for Windows Server 2003 and Windows XP is not a dual IP layer, it functions in the same way as a dual IP layer to provide functionality for IPv6 transition.

IPv6-over-IPv4 Tunneling

IPv6-over-IPv4 tunneling is the encapsulation of IPv6 packets with an IPv4 header so that IPv6 packets can be sent over an IPv4-only infrastructure. Within the IPv4 header

- The IPv4 Protocol field is set to 41 to indicate an encapsulated IPv6 packet.
- The Source and Destination fields are set to IPv4 addresses of the IPv6-over-IPv4 tunnel endpoints. The local tunnel endpoint is an IPv4 address assigned to the sender. The remote tunnel endpoint is an IPv4 address assigned to either the destination or an

intermediate router. The tunnel endpoints are either manually configured as part of the tunnel interface or are automatically derived based on the next-hop address for the destination IPv6 address and the tunnel interface.

Figure 11-5 shows IPv6-over-IPv4 tunneling.

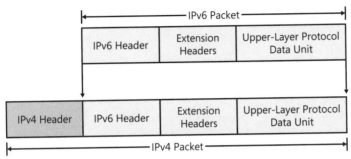

Figure 11-5   IPv6-over-IPv4 tunneling

Tunneled IPv6 traffic has the following issues:

- Firewalls and routers using packet filtering must be configured to allow IPv4 Protocol 41 traffic to be received and forwarded. Otherwise, the traffic will be silently discarded. Discarding IPv4 Protocol 41 traffic might be desired at an IPv4 Intranet edge router to prevent tunneled IPv6 traffic from leaving the intranet.

- Most NATs only translate TCP or UDP traffic or must have an installed NAT editor to handle the translation of other IPv4 protocols. Because IPv4 Protocol 41 translation is not a common feature of NATs, IPv4-encapsulated IPv6 traffic will not flow through typical NATs.

To IPv6, an IPv6-over-IPv4 tunnel is just another link-layer encapsulation, which treats an IPv4-only infrastructure as a link layer in much the same way as an Ethernet segment. Therefore, an entire IPv4-only infrastructure can be treated as a single logical IPv6 subnet and the IPv6-over-IPv4 tunnel acts as a single hop in a path between a source and destination.

For IPv6-over-IPv4 tunneling, the IPv6 path maximum transmission unit (PMTU) for the destination is typically 20 less than the IPv4 PMTU for the destination. However, if the IPv4 PMTU is not stored for each tunnel, there are instances in which the IPv4 packet will need to be fragmented at an intermediate IPv4 router. In this case, an IPv6-over-IPv4 tunneled packet must be sent with the Don't Fragment flag in the IPv4 header set to 0.

Note   IPv6-over-IPv4 tunneling describes only an encapsulation of IPv6 packets with an IPv4 header so that the resulting packet can traverse an IPv4-only infrastructure. Unlike tunneling for the Point-to-Point Tunneling Protocol (PPTP) and the Layer Two Tunneling Protocol (L2TP) virtual private network (VPN) protocols, there is no tunnel maintenance protocol that is used for tunnel setup, maintenance, or termination.

Network Monitor Capture

Here is an example of an Internet Control Message Protocol version 6 (ICMPv6) Echo Request message encapsulated with an IPv4 header as displayed by Network Monitor 3.1 (capture 11_01 in the \NetworkMonitorCaptures folder on the companion CD-ROM):

```
  Frame:
+ Ethernet: Etype = Internet IP (IPv4)
- Ipv4: Next Protocol = IPv6 over IPv4, Packet ID = 65372,
   Total IP Length = 100
  + Versions: IPv4, Internet Protocol; Header Length = 20
  + DifferentiatedServicesField: DSCP: 0, ECN: 0
    TotalLength: 100 (0x64)
    Identification: 65372 (0xFF5C)
  + FragmentFlags: 0 (0x0)
    TimeToLive: 128 (0x80)
    NextProtocol: IPv6 over IPv4, 41(0x29)
    Checksum: 60987 (0xEE3B)
    SourceAddress: 157.54.138.19
    DestinationAddress: 157.60.136.82
- Ipv6: Next Protocol = ICMPv6, Payload Length = 40
  + Versions: IPv6, Internet Protocol, DSCP 0
    PayloadLength: 40 (0x28)
    NextProtocol: ICMPv6, 58(0x3a)
    HopLimit: 128 (0x80)
    SourceAddress: FE80:0:0:0:0:5EFE:9D36:8A13
    DestinationAddress: FE80:0:0:0:0:5EFE:9D3C:8852
+ Icmpv6: Echo request, ID = 0x0, Seq = 0x11
```

Notice that the Protocol field in the IPv4 header indicates an IPv6 packet. In this example, the IPv6 packet is addressed to and from link-local ISATAP addresses to tunnel an ICMPv6 Echo Request message across an IPv4-only infrastructure.

DNS Infrastructure

You need a DNS infrastructure for successful coexistence because of the prevalent use of names rather than addresses to refer to network resources. For IPv6, resolving names to IPv6 addresses is highly desired because of the length and unfamiliar form of IPv6 addresses to most computer users. Upgrading the DNS infrastructure for IPv6 consists of populating the DNS servers with AAAA records for name-to-IPv6 address resolutions and with PTR records for IPv6 address-to-name resolutions. After a host obtains a set of addresses with a DNS name query, it must select which pairs of source and destination addresses to use for communication.

Address Records

The DNS infrastructure must contain the following resource records (populated either manually or dynamically) for the successful resolution of fully qualified domain names (FQDNs) to addresses:

- A records for IPv4-only and IPv6/IPv4 nodes
- AAAA records for IPv6-only and IPv6/IPv4 nodes

Pointer Records

The DNS infrastructure must contain the following resource records (populated either manually or dynamically) for the successful resolution of addresses to FQDNs:

- PTR records in the IN-ADDR.ARPA domain for IPv4-only and IPv6/IPv4 nodes
- PTR records in the IP6.ARPA domain for IPv6-only and IPv6/IPv4 nodes

Address Selection Rules

IPv6 hosts can be assigned multiple IPv6 addresses and can obtain multiple IPv6 addresses in a DNS name query. Based on these two sets of addresses, the IPv6 host must determine the best source address to use for each possible destination address and the list of destination addresses in order of preference. This is the purpose of source and destination address selection that is defined in RFC 3484.

The default address selection rules are determined by the prefix policy table, which you can view for the IPv6 protocol for Windows Server 2008 and Windows Vista with the **netsh interface ipv6 show prefixpolicies** command. You can modify the entries in the prefix policy table by using the **netsh interface ipv6 add|set|delete prefixpolicy** commands.

For more information about address selection and the prefix policy table, see Chapter 9, "IPv6 and Name Resolution."

Tunneling Configurations

RFC 2893 defines the following tunneling configurations to tunnel IPv6 traffic between IPv6/IPv4 nodes over an IPv4-only infrastructure:

- Router-to-router
- Host-to-router and router-to-host
- Host-to-host

Router-to-Router

In the router-to-router tunneling configuration, two IPv6/IPv4 routers connect two IPv6-enabled infrastructures over an IPv4-only infrastructure. The tunnel endpoints span a single hop in the path between the source and destination. Routes within each IPv6-enabled infrastructure point to the IPv6/IPv4 router on its edge. For each IPv6/IPv4 router, there is a tunnel interface representing the IPv6-over-IPv4 tunnel and routes that use the tunnel interface.

> **Note**   An *IPv6-enabled infrastructure* has IPv6 connectivity, either native or tunnel-based. An *IPv6-capable infrastructure* has native IPv6 connectivity.

Figure 11-6 shows router-to-router tunneling.

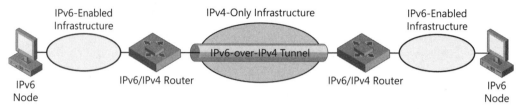

Figure 11-6   Router-to-router tunneling

Examples of this tunneling configuration include the following:

- An IPv6-only test lab that tunnels across an organization's IPv4-only infrastructure to reach the IPv6 Internet.

- Two IPv6-capable sites of an organization that tunnel across the IPv4 Internet.

- A 6to4 router that tunnels across the IPv4 Internet to reach another 6to4 router or a 6to4 relay router. For more information about 6to4, see Chapter 13.

Host-to-Router and Router-to-Host

In the host-to-router tunneling configuration, an IPv6/IPv4 host that resides within an IPv4-only infrastructure uses an IPv6-over-IPv4 tunnel to reach an IPv6/IPv4 router. The tunnel endpoints span the first hop in the path between the source and destination IPv6 nodes.

On the IPv6/IPv4 node, there is a tunnel interface representing the IPv6-over-IPv4 tunnel and one or more routes (typically a default route) that use the tunnel interface. The IPv6/IPv4 node tunnels the IPv6 packet based on the matching route, the tunnel interface, and the next-hop IPv6 address of the IPv6/IPv4 router.

In the router-to-host tunneling configuration, an IPv6/IPv4 router creates an IPv6-over-IPv4 tunnel across an IPv4 infrastructure to reach an IPv6/IPv4 node. The tunnel endpoints span the last hop in the path between the source and destination nodes.

On the IPv6/IPv4 router, there is a tunnel interface representing the IPv6-over-IPv4 tunnel and routes (typically a subnet route) that use the tunnel interface. The IPv6/IPv4 router tunnels the IPv6 packet based on the matching subnet route, the tunnel interface, and the destination IPv6 address of the IPv6/IPv4 node.

Figure 11-7 shows host-to-router tunneling (for traffic traveling on the IPv4-only infrastructure from Node A to Node B) and router-to-host tunneling (for traffic traveling from Node B to Node A).

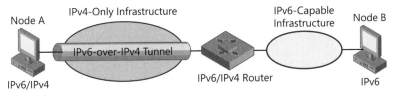

Figure 11-7   Host-to-router and router-to-host tunneling

Examples of host-to-router and router-to-host tunneling include the following:

- An IPv6/IPv4 host that tunnels across an organization's IPv4-only infrastructure to reach the IPv6 Internet (host-to-router tunneling).

- An ISATAP host that tunnels across the IPv4-only portion of the intranet to an ISATAP router to reach an IPv6-capable portion of the intranet (host-to-router tunneling).

- An ISATAP router that tunnels across the IPv4-only portion of the intranet to reach a destination ISATAP host (router-to-host tunneling).

Host-to-Host

In the host-to-host tunneling configuration, an IPv6/IPv4 node that resides within an IPv4-only infrastructure uses an IPv6-over-IPv4 tunnel to reach another IPv6/IPv4 node that resides within the same IPv4-only infrastructure. The tunnel endpoints span the entire path consisting of a single hop between the source and destination nodes.

Each IPv6/IPv4 node has an interface that represents the IPv6-over-IPv4 tunnel. A route is present to indicate that the destination node is on the same logical subnet defined by the IPv4-only infrastructure. Based on the sending interface, the on-link subnet route, and the destination address, the sending host tunnels the IPv6 traffic to the destination.

Figure 11-8 shows host-to-host tunneling.

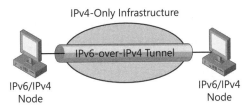

Figure 11-8   Host-to-host tunneling

Examples of host-to-host tunneling include the following:

- ISATAP hosts that tunnel traffic to each other across an organization's IPv4-only infrastructure.

- 6to4 host/routers that tunnel traffic to each other across the IPv4 Internet.

Types of Tunnels

RFC 2893 defines the following types of tunnels:

■ Configured

■ Automatic

Configured Tunnels

A configured tunnel requires manual configuration of the local and remote tunnel endpoints. In a configured tunnel, the IPv4 addresses of the remote tunnel endpoint are not embedded or encoded in the next-hop IPv6 address for the destination IPv6 address. Manually configured tunnels are typically used for router-to-router tunneling. The tunnel interface configuration, consisting of the IPv4 addresses of the local and remote tunnel endpoints, must be manually specified along with routes that use the tunnel interface. For example, you can use a manually configured tunnel to connect two IPv6-capable test lab networks across an IPv4-only intranet without using an IPv6 transition technology such as ISATAP.

To manually create configured tunnels for the IPv6 protocol for Windows Server 2008 and Windows Vista, use the following command:

netsh interface ipv6 add v6v4tunnel [interface=]Name **[localaddress=]**LocalIPv4Address **[remoteaddress=]**RemoteIPv4address

■ Name is the name of the new tunnel interface.

■ LocalIPv4Address is an IPv4 address assigned to the computer on which the command is run and corresponds to the local tunnel endpoint.

■ RemoteIPv4address is an IPv4 address of the remote tunnel endpoint.

You must create tunnel interfaces on the routers on both sides of the tunnel and add routes that use the tunnel interfaces.

For example, there are two IPv6 test lab subnets that are located in different parts of an intranet. Router 1 is connected to the IPv6 subnet of 2001:db8:0:1::/64 and has the IPv4 address of 131.107.47.121. Router 2 is connected to the IPv6 subnet of 2001:db8:0:2::/64 and has the IPv4 address of 157.54.9.211. Figure 11-9 shows the configuration.

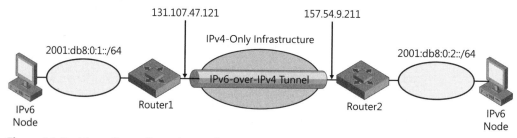

Figure 11-9   Manually configured tunneling example

To create a configured tunnel between Router 1 and Router 2, you would use the following commands on Router 1:

netsh interface ipv6 add v6v4tunnel TunnelTo2 131.107.47.121 157.54.9.211

netsh interface ipv6 add route 2001:db8:0:2::/64 TunnelTo2

Similarly, you would use the following commands at Router 2:

netsh interface ipv6 add v6v4tunnel TunnelTo1 157.54.9.211 131.107.47.121

netsh interface ipv6 add route 2001:db8:0:1::/64 TunnelTo1

Automatic Tunnels

An automatic tunnel is a tunnel that does not require manual configuration. Tunnel endpoints for automatic tunnels are determined by the use of routes, tunnel interfaces, and next-hop addresses for destination IPv6 addresses. The IPv6 protocol for Windows Server 2008 and Windows Vista supports the following automatic tunneling technologies:

- **ISATAP**   Used for unicast communication between IPv6/IPv4 hosts across an IPv4-only intranet. For more information, see Chapter 12.

- **6to4**   Used for unicast communication between IPv6/IPv4 hosts and IPv6-capable sites across the IPv4 Internet when 6to4 routers or 6to4 host/routers have public IPv4 addresses. For more information, see Chapter 13.

- **Teredo**   Used for unicast communication between IPv6/IPv4 hosts across the IPv4 Internet, even when they have private IPv4 addresses and are located behind NATs. For more information, see Chapter 14.

For automatic tunneling technologies in Windows Server 2008 and Windows Vista, the sending or forwarding node determines the IPv6-over-IPv4 tunnel endpoints from the following:

- The IPv4 address of the remote tunnel endpoint is embedded or encoded in the next-hop IPv6 address corresponding to the matching route for the destination IPv6 address.

- The IPv4 address of the local tunnel endpoint is determined by the best source IPv4 address to reach the destination IPv4 address (the remote tunnel endpoint).

PortProxy

To facilitate the communication between nodes or applications that cannot connect using a common Internet layer protocol (IPv4 or IPv6), the IPv6 protocol for Windows Server 2008 and Windows Vista provides PortProxy, a component that allows the proxying of the following traffic:

- **IPv4 to IPv4**   TCP traffic to an IPv4 address is proxied to TCP traffic at another IPv4 address.

- **IPv4 to IPv6**   TCP traffic to an IPv4 address is proxied to TCP traffic at an IPv6 address.

- **IPv6 to IPv6**   TCP traffic to an IPv6 address is proxied to TCP traffic at another IPv6 address.

- **IPv6 to IPv4**   TCP traffic to an IPv6 address is proxied to TCP traffic at an IPv4 address.

The most interesting and useful proxying for IPv6 transition is from IPv4 to IPv6 and from IPv6 to IPv4, which enables the following scenarios:

- **An IPv4-only node can indirectly access an IPv6-only node.**   In the IPv4 DNS infrastructure of the IPv4-only node, the name of the IPv6-only node resolves to an IPv4 address assigned to an interface of the PortProxy computer. This might require manual configuration of an A record in the DNS. When the PortProxy computer is configured to proxy IPv4 to IPv6, all TCP traffic sent by the IPv4-only node is proxied in a manner similar to Internet proxy servers: the IPv4-only node establishes a TCP connection with the PortProxy computer, and the PortProxy computer establishes a separate TCP connection with the IPv6-only node. The PortProxy computer transfers TCP connection data between the IPv4-only node and the IPv6-only node.

- **An IPv6-only node can access an IPv4-only node.**   In the IPv6 DNS infrastructure of the IPv6-only node, the name of the IPv4-only node resolves to an IPv6 address assigned to an interface of the PortProxy computer. This might require manual configuration of AAAA records in the DNS. When the PortProxy computer is configured to proxy IPv6 to IPv4, PortProxy proxies (translates) the TCP traffic sent between the IPv6-only node and the IPv4-only node.

- **An IPv6 node can access an IPv4-only service running on an IPv6/IPv4 node.**   In the IPv6 DNS infrastructure of the IPv6-only node, the name of the IPv6/IPv4 node resolves to an IPv6 address assigned to an interface of the PortProxy computer. When the PortProxy computer is configured to proxy from IPv6 to IPv4, PortProxy proxies the TCP traffic sent between the IPv6-only node and the IPv4-only service or application running on the PortProxy computer.

To configure the PortProxy component, use the **netsh interface portproxy add|set|delete v4tov4|v4tov6|v6tov4|v6tov6** commands.

The syntax for the **netsh interface portproxy add v6tov4** command is

netsh interface portproxy add v6tov4 [**listenport=**]*LPortNumber*|*LPortName* [[**connectaddress=**]*IPv4Address*|*IPv4HostName*] [[**connectport=**]*CPortNumber*|*CPortName*] [[**listenaddress=**]*IPv6Address*|*IPv6HostName*]

- *LPortNumber*|*LPortName* is the TCP port number or service name on which PortProxy is listening.

- *IPv6Address|IPv6HostName* is the IPv6 address or host name on which PortProxy is listening. (If it is unspecified, all IPv6 addresses assigned to the PortProxy computer are assumed.)

- *CPortNumber|CPortName* is the TCP port number or service name that PortProxy attempts to connect to. (If it is unspecified, the connect port is set to the same port as the listening port.)

- *IPv4Address|IPv4HostName* is the IPv4 address or host name that PortProxy attempts to connect to. (If it is unspecified, the loopback address is assumed.)

The syntax for the **netsh interface portproxy add v4tov6** command is

netsh interface portproxy add v4tov6 [listenport=]*LPortNumber|LPortName*
[[connectaddress=]*IPv6Address|IPv6HostName*] **[[connectport=]***CPortNumber|CPortName*]
[[listenaddress=]*IPv4Address|IPv4HostName*]

- *LPortNumber|LPortName* is the TCP port number or service name on which PortProxy is listening.

- *IPv4Address|IPv4HostName* is the IPv4 address or host name on which PortProxy is listening. (If it is unspecified, all IPv4 addresses assigned to the PortProxy computer are assumed.)

- *CPortNumber|CPortName* is the TCP port number or service name that PortProxy attempts to connect to. (If it is unspecified, the connect port is set to the same port as the listening port.)

- *IPv6Address|IPv6HostName* is the IPv6 address or host name that PortProxy attempts to connect to. (If it is unspecified, the loopback address is assumed.)

> **Note**   PortProxy works only for TCP traffic and for application-layer protocols that do not embed address or port information inside the TCP connection data. Unlike NATs, there are no equivalents to NAT editors for PortProxy. An example of a protocol that will not work across a PortProxy computer is File Transfer Protocol (FTP), which embeds IPv4 addresses when using the FTP Port command.

References

The following references were cited in this chapter:

- RFC 1752 – "The Recommendation for the IP Next Generation Protocol"

- RFC 2529 – "Transmission of IPv6 over IPv4 Domains without Explicit Tunnels"

- RFC 2893 – "Transition Mechanisms for IPv6 Hosts and Routers"

- RFC 3056 – "Connection of IPv6 Domains via IPv4 Clouds"

- RFC 3484 – "Default Address Selection for IPv6"

- RFC 4214 – "Intra-Site Automatic Tunnel Addressing Protocol (ISATAP)"

- RFC 4380 – "Teredo: Tunneling IPv6 over UDP through Network Address Translations (NATs)"

You can obtain these RFCs from the \RFCs_and_Drafts folder on the companion CD-ROM or from *http://www.ietf.org/rfc.html*.

Testing for Understanding

To test your understanding of IPv6 transition, answer the following questions. See Appendix D, "Testing for Understanding Answers," to check your answers.

1. Describe the difference between migration and coexistence.

2. How does an IPv4-only host communicate with an IPv6-only host?

3. What is an IPv4-mapped address used for?

4. Is the IPv6 protocol for Windows Server 2008 and Windows Vista a dual IP layer? Why or why not?

5. How are the source and destination addresses in the IPv4 header determined for IPv6-over-IPv4 tunnel traffic?

6. What is the Netsh command to enable the proxying of TCP connection data between an IPv6-only host and an IPv4-only service that is running on the PortProxy computer and listening on TCP port 32175?

7. Why might you have to manually add A or AAAA DNS records to help facilitate communication between IPv4-only nodes and IPv6-only nodes when using PortProxy?

Chapter 12
ISATAP

At the end of this chapter, you should be able to do the following:

- Define the address format, encapsulation, and intended use of the Intra-Site Automatic Tunnel Addressing Protocol (ISATAP) IPv6 transition technology.

- Describe how the IPv6 protocol in Windows Server 2008 and Windows Vista supports ISATAP as a host and router.

- List and describe the routes on ISATAP hosts, ISATAP routers, and IPv6 routers that make ISATAP-based communication possible.

- Describe how ISATAP communication works between ISATAP hosts and native IPv6 hosts on an intranet.

- Describe how to configure a computer running Windows Server 2008 or Windows Vista as an ISATAP router.

ISATAP Overview

ISATAP is an address assignment and host-to-host, host-to-router, and router-to-host automatic tunneling technology defined in RFC 4214 that provides unicast IPv6 connectivity between IPv6/IPv4 hosts across an IPv4 intranet. ISATAP hosts do not require any manual configuration, and they can create ISATAP addresses using standard IPv6 address autoconfiguration mechanisms.

ISATAP addresses have one of the two following formats:

64-bitUnicastPrefix:0:5EFE:w.x.y.z

64-bitUnicastPrefix:200:5EFE:w.x.y.z

The ISATAP address consists of the following:

- *64-bitUnicastPrefix* is any 64-bit unicast address prefix, including link-local, global, and unique local prefixes.

- ::0:5EFE:*w.x.y.z* and ::200:5EFE:*w.x.y.z* are the locally administered interface identifiers. For ::0:5EFE:*w.x.y.z*, *w.x.y.z* is a private unicast IPv4 address. For ::200:5EFE:*w.x.y.z*, *w.x.y.z* is a public unicast IPv4 address. The interface identifier (ID) portion of an ISATAP address contains an embedded IPv4 address that determines the destination IPv4 address in the encapsulating IPv4 header of ISATAP traffic.

There is a common misconception that before you can begin experimenting with IPv6 connectivity and application migration, you must deploy native IPv6 addressing and routing, which requires a detailed analysis of IPv6 addressing schemes, router updates and configuration, and a rollout schedule. Although this should eventually be done for intranets, ISATAP allows you to turn the IPv4-only portion of your intranet into a logical IPv6 subnet. Once this subnet is defined and assigned a global or unique local prefix, IPv6/IPv4 hosts that support ISATAP can use ISATAP-based addresses for IPv6 connectivity. ISATAP allows you to make your IPv4-only intranet IPv6-capable, without requiring modifications to your existing router infrastructure to support native IPv6 addressing and routing. With ISATAP, you can immediately begin experimenting with IPv6 connectivity and application migration.

ISATAP allows you to phase in the native IPv6 addressing and routing capability on your intranet in the following way:

- **Phase 1: IPv4-only intranet**   In this phase, your entire intranet can be a single, logical ISATAP subnet.

- **Phase 2: IPv4-only and IPv6-capable portions of your intranet**   In this phase, your intranet has an IPv4-only portion (the logical ISATAP subnet) and an IPv6-capable portion. The IPv6-capable portion of your intranet has been updated to support native IPv6 addressing and routing.

- **Phase 3: IPv6-capable intranet**   In this phase, your entire intranet supports both IPv4 and native IPv6 addressing and routing and ISATAP is no longer needed.

With ISATAP, you can have IPv6 connectivity between hosts and applications during the first two phases of the transition from an IPv4-only to an IPv6-capable intranet.

ISATAP Tunneling

ISATAP-based IPv6 traffic is tunneled or encapsulated with an IPv4 header, also known as IPv6-over-IPv4 traffic. For the details of IPv6-over-IPv4 traffic, see Chapter 11, "IPv6 Transition Technologies." This tunneling is automatically done by an ISATAP tunneling interface on the sending host or forwarding router. The ISATAP tunneling interface treats the entire IPv4-only portion of the intranet as a single link layer, in much the same way as Ethernet. In the case of ISATAP, the link-layer encapsulation is IPv4.

The IPv6 protocol for Windows Server 2008 and Windows Vista creates a separate ISATAP tunneling interface for each LAN interface that is installed in the computer that has a different DNS suffix. For example, if a computer running Windows Vista has two LAN interfaces and they are both attached to the same intranet and are assigned the same DNS suffix, there is only one ISATAP tunneling interface. If these two LAN interfaces are attached to two different networks with different DNS suffixes, there are two ISATAP tunneling interfaces. For computers running Windows Server 2008 or Windows Vista with Service Pack 1, the ISATAP tunnel interfaces are placed in a media disconnected state unless the name "ISATAP" can be resolved.

By default, the IPv6 protocol for Windows Vista with no service packs installed automatically configures link-local ISATAP addresses (FE80::5EFE:*w.x.y.z* or FE80::200:5EFE:*w.x.y.z*) on the ISATAP tunnel interfaces for the IPv4 addresses that are assigned to the corresponding LAN interface. The IPv6 protocol for Windows Server 2008 and Windows Vista with Service Pack 1 configures link-local ISATAP addresses (FE80::5EFE:*w.x.y.z* or FE80::200:5EFE:*w.x.y.z*) on ISATAP tunnel interfaces only if the name "ISATAP" can be resolved.

These link-local ISATAP addresses allow two hosts to communicate over an IPv4-only network without requiring additional global or unique local ISATAP addresses. You can determine the names and interface indexes of the ISATAP tunneling interfaces from the display of the **ipconfig /all** command.

All tunneling interfaces by default have an asterisk ("*") in their name, such as "Local Area Connection* 6". ISATAP tunneling interfaces have an asterisk in their name, "ISATAP" in their description, and are assigned a link-local ISATAP address. You can obtain the interface index for an ISATAP tunneling interface from the number after the percent sign ("%") in the link-local addresses assigned to the interface. For example, the interface index of the ISATAP tunneling interface with the address FE80::200:5EFE:131.107.9.221%10 is 10.

You can disable ISATAP by setting the HKEY_LOCAL_MACHINE\SYSTEM\CurrentControl-Set\Services\tcpip6\Parameters\DisabledComponents registry value to 0x4 (DWORD).

> **Note**   IPv6 for Windows Server 2003 and Windows XP created only a single ISATAP tunneling interface that was named "Automatic Tunneling Pseudo-Interface," with an interface index that was typically set to 2.

ISATAP Tunneling Example

Host A has a single LAN interface and is configured with the IPv4 address of 10.40.1.29. Host B has a single LAN interface and is configured with the IPv4 address of 192.168.41.30. IPv6 on Host A has the ISATAP address of FE80::5EFE:10.40.1.29 assigned to its ISATAP tunneling interface (named "Local Area Connection* 6" with the interface index 10) and Host B has the ISATAP address of FE80::5EFE:192.168.41.30 assigned to its ISATAP tunneling interface (named "Local Area Connection* 5" with the interface index 11). Figure 12-1 shows this example configuration.

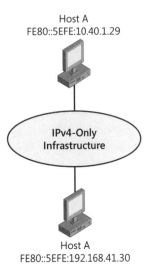

Host A
FE80::5EFE:10.40.1.29

IPv4-Only
Infrastructure

Host A
FE80::5EFE:192.168.41.30

Figure 12-1   An example ISATAP configuration

When Host A sends IPv6 traffic to Host B destined for Host B's link-local ISATAP address, the source and destination addresses for the IPv6 and IPv4 headers are as listed in Table 12-1.

Table 12-1   Example Link-Local ISATAP Addresses

Field	Value
IPv6 Source Address	FE80::5EFE:10.40.1.29
IPv6 Destination Address	FE80::5EFE:192.168.41.30
IPv4 Source Address	10.40.1.29
IPv4 Destination Address	192.168.41.30

To test connectivity between ISATAP hosts, you can use the Ping tool (subject to Windows Firewall exceptions for Internet Control Message Protocol for IPv6 [ICMPv6] traffic). For example, to ping Host B at its link-local ISATAP address from Host A, you would use the following command:

```
ping fe80::5efe:192.168.41.30%10
```

Because the destination of the ping command is a link-local address, you must use the %*ZoneID* as part of the destination address to specify the interface index of the interface from which traffic must be sent. In this case, "%10" specifies interface index 10, which is the interface index assigned to the ISATAP tunneling interface on Host A. The ISATAP tunneling interface uses its own link-local ISATAP address as a source IPv6 address. The ISATAP tunneling interface determines the destination IPv4 address of the encapsulating IPv4 header from the last 32 bits in the destination IPv6 address, which correspond to the embedded IPv4 address of Host B. For the source IPv4 address in the encapsulating IPv4 header, IPv4 on Host A determines the best source IPv4 address to use to reach the destination IPv4 address 192.168.41.30. In this case, Host A has only a single IPv4 address assigned, so IPv4 on Host A uses the source address of 10.40.1.29.

ISATAP Components

An ISATAP deployment consists of ISATAP hosts, ISATAP routers, and one or more logical ISATAP subnets. Figure 12-2 shows the components of an IPv4-capable intranet that is using ISATAP and a single ISATAP subnet.

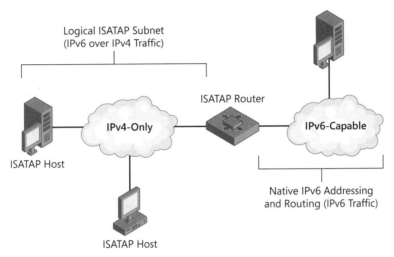

Figure 12-2   Components of ISATAP

The IPv4-only portion of the intranet is the ISATAP subnet. The IPv6-capable portion of the intranet has native IPv6 routers and addressing. Hosts on the IPv6-capable portion of the intranet are configured with global or unique local addresses on their LAN interfaces and do not need to use IPv4 encapsulation to communicate with each other using IPv6.

ISATAP hosts have an ISATAP tunneling interface and perform their own tunneling to other ISATAP hosts on the same ISATAP subnet (host-to-host tunneling) or to an ISATAP router (host-to-router tunneling). ISATAP hosts can use global, unique local, or link-local ISATAP addresses to communicate with each other. To communicate with other ISATAP hosts on the ISATAP subnet using their ISATAP global, unique local, or link-local addresses, ISATAP hosts tunnel their packets directly to each other. To communicate with IPv6 hosts on the IPv6-capable portion of the intranet using their native global or unique local addresses, ISATAP hosts tunnel their packets to an ISATAP router.

Note   Hosts running Windows Vista with no service packs on the IPv6-enabled portion of the intranet, by default, have ISATAP enabled and automatically configure link-local ISATAP addresses on their ISATAP tunneling interfaces. It is possible for these ISATAP hosts on the ISATAP subnet to communicate directly with native IPv6 hosts on the IPv6-capable portion of the intranet through host-to-host tunneling by using link-local ISATAP addresses. However, because link-local addresses are not registered in DNS, ISATAP hosts would have to manually specify the destination link-local ISATAP address and interface index to reach a host on the IPv6-capable portion of the intranet without first tunneling the traffic to the ISATAP router. This type of communication is not practical or commonly used and is not described further in this chapter.

To prevent the hosts on the IPv6-capable portion of the intranet from using ISATAP, you can disable ISATAP with the DisabledComponents registry value as previously described.

An ISATAP router is an IPv6 router with an ISATAP tunneling interface that does the following:

- Forwards packets between ISATAP hosts on ISATAP subnets and IPv6 hosts on IPv6-capable subnets.

- Advertises address prefixes to ISATAP hosts on the ISATAP subnet. ISATAP hosts use the advertised address prefixes to configure global or unique local ISATAP addresses.

- Acts as a default router for ISATAP hosts. When an ISATAP host receives a router advertisement from an ISATAP router that is advertising itself as a default router, the ISATAP host adds a default route (::/0) using the ISATAP tunneling interface with next-hop address set to the link-local ISATAP address of the ISATAP router. When ISATAP hosts send packets destined to locations beyond their ISATAP subnet, the packets are tunneled to the IPv4 address of the ISATAP router corresponding to the ISATAP router's interface on the ISATAP subnet. The ISATAP router then forwards the IPv6 packet to the appropriate next-hop on the IPv6-capable portion of the intranet.

An IPv6-capable portion of an intranet is optional, in which case the ISATAP router is only functioning as an advertising router and not a forwarding or default router. This is the case for an initial ISATAP deployment in which there are no IPv6-capable subnets.

Router Discovery for ISATAP Hosts

To receive a Router Advertisement message from the ISATAP router, the ISATAP host must send the ISATAP router a Router Solicitation message. On an Ethernet subnet, a native IPv6 host sends a multicast Router Solicitation message and the routers on the subnet respond with a multicast Router Advertisement message. Because ISATAP does not use IPv4 multicast traffic or require an IPv4 multicast-capable infrastructure, the ISATAP host must unicast the Router Solicitation message to the ISATAP router. To unicast the Router Solicitation message to the ISATAP router, the ISATAP host must first determine the unicast IPv4 address of the ISATAP router's interface on the ISATAP subnet.

For the IPv6 protocol for Windows Server 2008 and Windows Vista, an ISATAP host obtains the unicast IPv4 address of the ISATAP router through one of the following methods:

■ The successful resolution of the host name "ISATAP" to an IPv4 address

■ The **netsh interface isatap set router** command

Resolving the Name "ISATAP"

When the IPv6 protocol for Windows Server 2008 or Windows Vista starts, it attempts to resolve the host name "ISATAP" to an IPv4 address using normal Windows-based TCP/IP host name resolution techniques. If it is successful, the host unicasts an IPv4-encapsulated Router Solicitation message to the ISATAP router at the resolved address. The ISATAP router responds with an IPv4-encapsulated unicast Router Advertisement message that contains prefixes to use for autoconfiguration of additional ISATAP addresses and, optionally, indicates that the ISATAP router is a default router.

Normal Windows-based host name resolution techniques for resolving the name "ISATAP" include the following:

1. Checking the local host name.

2. Checking the DNS client resolver cache, which includes the entries in the Hosts file in the *%SystemRoot%*/system32\drivers\etc folder.

3. Forming a fully qualified domain name (FQDN), and sending a DNS name query. For example, if the computer is a member of the example.microsoft.com domain (and example.microsoft.com is the only domain name in the search list), the computer sends a DNS name query to resolve the FQDN isatap.example.microsoft.com.

4. Converting the host name "ISATAP" into the NetBIOS name **"ISATAP   <00>"** and checking the NetBIOS name cache.

5. Sending a NetBIOS name query for the NetBIOS name **"ISATAP   <00>"** to the configured Windows Internet Name Service (WINS) servers.

6. Sending NetBIOS name query broadcasts for the NetBIOS name **"ISATAP   <00>"** on the local IPv4 subnet.

7. Checking the Lmhosts file in the *SystemRoot*\system32\drivers\etc folder for an entry with the name "ISATAP".

To ensure that at least one of these attempts is successful, you can do one of the following:

■ If the ISATAP router is a computer running Windows Server 2008 or Windows Vista, name the computer "ISATAP" and it will automatically register the appropriate records in DNS and WINS.

- Manually create an address (A) record for the name "ISATAP" in the appropriate domains in DNS. For example, for the example.microsoft.com domain, create an A record for isatap.example.microsoft.com.

- Manually create a static WINS record in WINS for the NetBIOS name **"ISATAP <00>"**.

- Add the following entry to the Hosts file of the computers that need to resolve the name ISATAP:

  IPv4Address ISATAP

- Add the following entry to the Lmhosts file of the computers that need to resolve the name ISATAP:

  IPv4Address ISATAP

> **Note**   Computers running Windows XP with no service packs installed attempt to resolve the name "_ISATAP" to determine the IPv4 address of the ISATAP router.

Figure 12-3 shows how an ISATAP host obtains the IPv4 address of the ISATAP router through a DNS name query and performs router discovery with an ISATAP router.

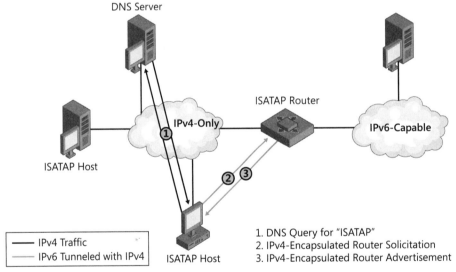

Figure 12-3   Performing router discovery with an ISATAP router

ISATAP hosts on the ISATAP subnet send their DNS name queries over IPv4, rather than IPv6, because the ISATAP hosts do not have native IPv6 connectivity. By default, an ISATAP host running Windows Server 2008 or Windows Vista will attempt to register global and unique local ISATAP addresses in DNS using DNS dynamic update.

Network Monitor Capture

Here is an example of the IPv4-encapsulated Router Solicitation message as displayed by Network Monitor 3.1 (frame 1 of capture 12_01 in the \NetworkMonitorCaptures folder on the companion CD-ROM):

```
Frame:
+ Ethernet: Etype = Internet IP (IPv4)
- Ipv4: Next Protocol = IPv6 over IPv4, Packet ID = 56, Total IP Length = 68
  + Versions: IPv4, Internet Protocol; Header Length = 20
  + DifferentiatedServicesField: DSCP: 0, ECN: 0
    TotalLength: 68 (0x44)
    Identification: 56 (0x38)
  + FragmentFlags: 0 (0x0)
    TimeToLive: 128 (0x80)
    NextProtocol: IPv6 over IPv4, 41(0x29)
    Checksum: 9815 (0x2657)
    SourceAddress: 10.0.0.2
    DestinationAddress: 10.0.0.1
- Ipv6: Next Protocol = ICMPv6, Payload Length = 8
  + Versions: IPv6, Internet Protocol, DSCP 0
    PayloadLength: 8 (0x8)
    NextProtocol: ICMPv6, 58(0x3a)
    HopLimit: 255 (0xFF)
    SourceAddress: FE80:0:0:0:0:5EFE:A00:2
    DestinationAddress: FE80:0:0:0:0:5EFE:A00:1
- Icmpv6: Router Solicitation
    MessageType: Router Solicitation, 133(0x85)
  - RouterSolicitation:
    Code: 0 (0x0)
    Checksum: 43963 (0xABBB)
    Reserved: 0 (0x0)
```

Notice that the IPv4 address of the ISATAP router is 10.0.0.1. Also note the use of the unicast ISATAP address of the ISATAP router as the IPv6 destination address in the IPv6 header.

Here is an example of the IPv4-encapsulated Router Advertisement message as displayed by Network Monitor 3.1 (in the \NetworkMonitorCaptures folder on the companion CD-ROM, frame 2 of capture 12_01):

```
Frame:
+ Ethernet: Etype = Internet IP (IPv4)
- Ipv4: Next Protocol = IPv6 over IPv4, Packet ID = 4011, Total IP Length = 148
  + Versions: IPv4, Internet Protocol; Header Length = 20
  + DifferentiatedServicesField: DSCP: 0, ECN: 0
    TotalLength: 148 (0x94)
    Identification: 4011 (0xFAB)
  + FragmentFlags: 0 (0x0)
    TimeToLive: 128 (0x80)
    NextProtocol: IPv6 over IPv4, 41(0x29)
    Checksum: 5780 (0x1694)
    SourceAddress: 10.0.0.1
    DestinationAddress: 10.0.0.2
```

```
- Ipv6: Next Protocol = ICMPv6, Payload Length = 88
  + Versions: IPv6, Internet Protocol, DSCP 0
    PayloadLength: 88 (0x58)
    NextProtocol: ICMPv6, 58(0x3a)
    HopLimit: 255 (0xFF)
    SourceAddress: FE80:0:0:0:0:5EFE:A00:1
    DestinationAddress: FE80:0:0:0:0:5EFE:A00:2
- Icmpv6: Router Advertisement
    MessageType: Router Advertisement, 134(0x86)
  - RouterAdvertisement:
    Code: 0 (0x0)
    Checksum: 46260 (0xB4B4)
    CurHopLimit: 0 (0x0)
  - RouterAdvertisementFlag:
    M:              (0.......) Not managed address configuration
    O:              (.0......) Not other stateful configuration
    A:              (..0.....) Not a Mobile IP Home Agent
    RouterPreference: (...00...) Medium,0(0x0)
    Reserved:       (.....000)
    RouterLifetime: 65535 (0xFFFF)
    ReachableTime: 0 (0x0)
    RetransTimer: 0 (0x0)
  - MTU:
    Type: MTU, 5(0x5)
    Length: 1, in unit of 8 octets
    Reserved: 0 (0x0)
    MTU: 1280 (0x500)
  - PrefixInformation:
    Type: Prefix Information, 3(0x3)
    Length: 4, in unit of 8 octets
    PrefixLength: 64 (0x40)
  - Flags: 192 (0xC0)
    L:    (1.......) On-Link determination allowed
    A:    (.1......) Autonomous address-configuration
    R:    (..0.....) Not router Address
    S:    (...0....) Not a site prefix
    P:    (....0...) Not a router prefix
    Rsv:  (.....000)
    ValidLifetime: 4294967295 (0xFFFFFFFF)
    PreferredLifetime: 4294967295 (0xFFFFFFFF)
    Reserved: 0 (0x0)
    Prefix: 2001:DB8:3C5A:21DA:0:0:0:0
  - PrefixInformation:
    Type: Prefix Information, 3(0x3)
    Length: 4, in unit of 8 octets
    PrefixLength: 64 (0x40)
  - Flags: 192 (0xC0)
    L:    (1.......) On-Link determination allowed
    A:    (.1......) Autonomous address-configuration
    R:    (..0.....) Not router Address
    S:    (...0....) Not a site prefix
    P:    (....0...) Not a router prefix
    Rsv:  (.....000)
    ValidLifetime: 4294967295 (0xFFFFFFFF)
    PreferredLifetime: 4294967295 (0xFFFFFFFF)
    Reserved: 0 (0x0)
    Prefix: FD31:2C00:8D33:21DA:0:0:0:0
```

Notice that the Router Advertisement message contains an MTU option setting the maximum transmission unit (MTU) over the tunnel interface to 1280 and two Prefix Information options—one for the global prefix 2001:DB8:3C5A:21DA::/64, and one for the unique local prefix FD31:2C00:8D33:21DA::/64.

Using the netsh interface isatap set router Command

Although automatic configuration of the IPv4 address of the ISATAP router through the reso- lution of the name "ISATAP" is the recommended method to use, you can manually configure the IPv4 address of the ISATAP router with the **netsh interface isatap set router** command. The syntax of this command is

netsh interface isatap set router *AddressOrName*

AddressOrName is the name or IPv4 address of the ISATAP router's interface on the ISATAP subnet. If you use a name, the name must be resolvable to the IPv4 address of the ISATAP router. An address is recommended over a name.

For example, if the ISATAP router's IPv4 address on the ISATAP subnet is 192.168.39.1, the command is

netsh interface isatap set router 192.168.39.1

> **Note**   Computers running Windows Server 2008 or Windows Vista support Netsh commands for configuring ISATAP behavior in both the **netsh interface isatap** and **netsh interface ipv6 isatap** contexts. Computers running Windows Server 2003 or Windows XP support only the **netsh interface ipv6 isatap** context. This chapter uses the ISATAP commands in the **netsh interface isatap** context.

ISATAP Addressing Example

Figure 12-4 shows an ISATAP addressing example.

In this configuration, the ISATAP router is advertising the global subnet prefix 2001:DB8:0:7::/64 to the ISATAP hosts on the ISATAP subnet. ISATAP Host A, configured with the IPv4 address 192.168.47.99, uses the subnet prefix advertised by the ISATAP router to automatically configure the global ISATAP address of 2001:DB8::7:0:5EFE:192.168.47.99. Host A attempts to register the IPv6 address record (AAAA) for the address 2001:DB8::7:0:5EFE:192.168.47.99 in DNS.

Similarly, ISATAP Host B uses the subnet prefix to automatically configure the global ISATAP address of 2001:DB8::7:200:5EFE:131.107.71.209. Host B attempts to register the IPv6 address record (AAAA) for the address 2001:DB8::7:200:5EFE:131.107.71.209 in DNS.

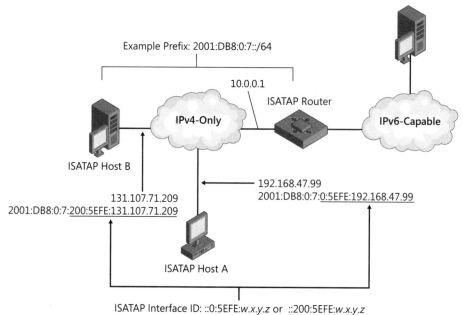

Figure 12-4 ISATAP addressing example

ISATAP Routing

Figure 12-5 shows the relevant routes for ISATAP communication for the example configuration shown in Figure 12-4.

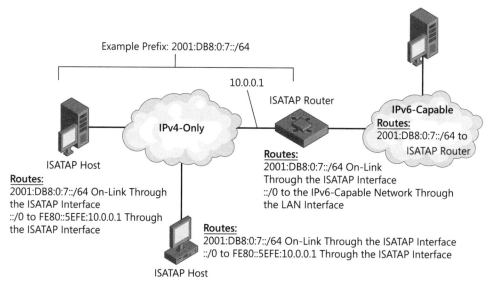

Figure 12-5 ISATAP routing example

ISATAP hosts use the following routes:

■ An on-link route for the ISATAP subnet prefix that uses the ISATAP tunneling interface. This route allows ISATAP hosts to perform host-to-host tunneling to reach other ISATAP hosts on the same ISATAP subnet. In the example configuration, this is the 2001:DB8:0:7::/64 route.

■ A default route with the next-hop address of the ISATAP router's link-local ISATAP address (FE80::5EFE:10.0.0.1) that uses the ISATAP tunneling interface. This route allows ISATAP hosts to perform host-to-router tunneling to reach the IPv6 hosts on the IPv6-capable portion of the intranet.

An ISATAP router uses the following routes:

■ An on-link route for the ISATAP subnet prefix that uses the ISATAP tunneling interface that is associated with the LAN interface that is connected to the ISATAP subnet. This route allows the ISATAP router to perform router-to-host tunneling to reach other ISATAP hosts on the ISATAP subnet. In the example configuration, this is the 2001:DB8:0:7::/64 route.

■ A default route that uses a LAN interface that is connected to the IPv6-capable portion of the intranet and has the next-hop address of a neighboring router (not shown in Figure 12-5). This route allows the ISATAP router to forward IPv6 traffic to destinations on the IPv6-capable portion of the intranet.

The routers of the IPv6-capable network use a route for the ISATAP subnet prefix that points back to the ISATAP router. This route allows the routers of the IPv6-capable network to forward traffic destined for the ISATAP hosts on the ISATAP subnet to the ISATAP router. In the example configuration, this is the 2001:DB8:0:7::/64 route.

ISATAP Communication Examples

The following sections describe how ISATAP communication works for the following types of communication:

■ An ISATAP host sends a packet to an ISATAP host on the same ISATAP subnet.

■ An ISATAP host sends a packet to an IPv6 host that is on an IPv6-capable subnet.

ISATAP Host to ISATAP Host

Figure 12-6 shows how an ISATAP host communicates with another ISATAP host on the same ISATAP subnet for the example configuration of Figure 12-4.

In this example, ISATAP Host A has resolved ISATAP Host B's global ISATAP address through a DNS name query and is sending ISATAP Host B a packet. When sending the packet, IPv6 on ISATAP Host A performs the IPv6 route determination process and finds that the closest matching route to the destination is the 2001:DB8:0:7::/64 route for the on-link ISATAP subnet. Because it is an on-link route, the next-hop IPv6 address for the packet is set to the destination address (2001:DB8::7:200:5EFE:131.107.71.209). IPv6 on ISATAP Host A hands the IPv6 packet and the next-hop address to the ISATAP tunneling interface for processing.

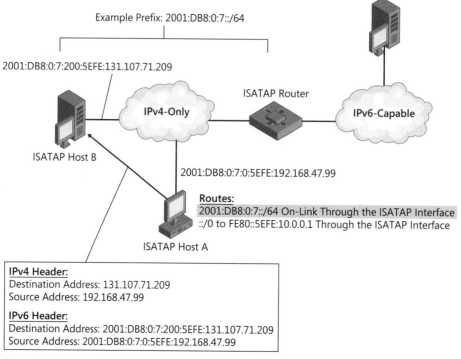

Figure 12-6 Example of ISATAP host to ISATAP host communication

The ISATAP tunneling interface sets the destination IPv4 address in the IPv4 header to the last 32 bits of the next-hop address, which in this case is ISATAP Host B's IPv4 address of 131.107.71.209. IPv4 on ISATAP Host A determines that the best source address to use is the IPv4 address assigned to ISATAP Host A (192.168.47.99), and then IPv4 sends the packet.

On ISATAP Host B, IPv4 processes the IPv4 header and, because the Protocol field is set to 41, it hands the encapsulated IPv6 packet to the IPv6 protocol for further processing.

ISATAP Host to IPv6 Host

When an ISATAP host sends a packet to an IPv6 host on the IPv6-capable network, the packet's journey has two parts:

- Part 1: From the ISATAP host to the ISATAP router
- Part 2: From the ISATAP router to the IPv6 host

Continuing our example configuration shown in Figure 12-4, ISATAP Host A sends to a destination that is not on the ISATAP subnet (IPv6 Host C at the destination 2001:DB8:0:12:2AA:FF:FE9A:21AC). IPv6 on ISATAP Host A performs the route determination process and finds that the closest matching route to the destination is the default route (::/0). The default route has a next-hop IPv6 address of FE80::5EFE:10.0.0.1, which is the link-local ISATAP address corresponding to the ISATAP router's interface on the ISATAP subnet. IPv6 on ISATAP Host A hands the IPv6 packet and the next-hop address to the ISATAP tunneling interface for processing.

The ISATAP tunneling interface sets the destination IPv4 address in the IPv4 header to the last 32 bits of the next-hop address, which in this case is the ISATAP router's IPv4 address of 10.0.0.1. IPv4 on ISATAP Host A determines that the best source address to use is the IPv4 address assigned to ISATAP Host A (192.168.47.99), and then IPv4 sends the packet. Figure 12-7 shows part 1 of the journey of the packet from ISATAP Host A to the ISATAP router.

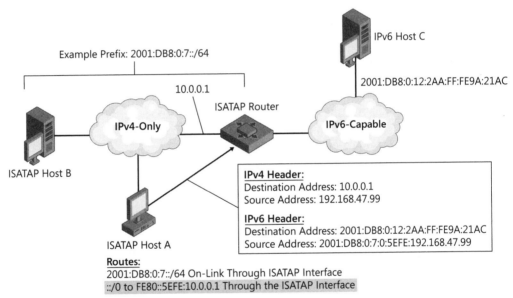

Figure 12-7   ISATAP host to IPv6 host communication–Part 1

On the ISATAP router, IPv4 processes the IPv4 header and, because the Protocol field is set to 41, it hands the IPv6 packet to IPv6 for processing. IPv6 on the ISATAP router performs the route determination process and finds that the closest matching route to the destination is the default route (::/0) (assuming that IPv6 Host C is not a neighboring node of the ISATAP router). The default route has a next-hop IPv6 address of a neighboring IPv6 router on the IPv6-capable network (not shown). The IPv6 packet and the next-hop address are handed to the appropriate LAN interface for processing. The IPv4 header is stripped off, and the IPv6 router forwards the IPv6 packet that was originally encapsulated by ISATAP Host A. The packet is forwarded by the native IPv6 routers of the IPv6-capable network to its destination. Figure 12-8 shows part 2 of the journey of the packet from the ISATAP router to IPv6 Host C.

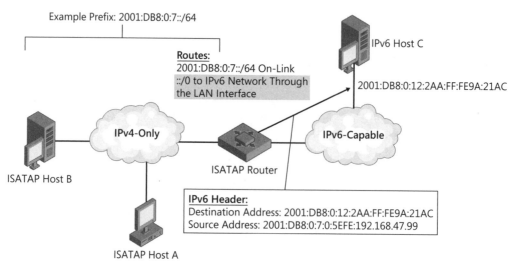

Figure 12-8   ISATAP host to IPv6 host communication–Part 2

Configuring an ISATAP Router

A computer running Windows Server 2008 or Windows Vista can be configured as an ISATAP router. Assuming that the router is already configured to forward IPv6 traffic on its LAN interfaces that are connected to the IPv6-capable portion of the intranet and has a default route that is configured to be published, the following additional commands need to be issued on the router:

- **netsh interface ipv6 set interface** *ISATAPInterfaceNameOrIndex* **forwarding=enabled advertise=enabled**

  This command enables forwarding and advertising on an ISATAP tunneling interface (*ISATAPInterfaceNameOrIndex*). Most ISATAP routers will have a single ISATAP interface. For ISATAP routers with multiple ISATAP tunneling interfaces, you must specify the ISATAP tunneling interface that is associated with the LAN interface that is connected to the ISATAP subnet. The correct ISATAP tunneling interface has the link-local ISATAP address based on the IPv4 address assigned to the LAN interface that is connected to the ISATAP subnet. For example, if the LAN interface that is connected to the ISATAP subnet has the IPv4 address 131.107.41.99, the correct ISATAP tunneling interface has the link-local ISATAP address FE80::200:5EFE:131.107.41.99 assigned.

- **netsh interface ipv6 add route** *Address/PrefixLength ISATAPInterfaceNameOrIndex* **publish=yes**

  This command adds a route and advertises a specific subnet prefix (*Address/Prefix-Length*) over the ISATAP tunneling interface specified in the previous command (*ISATAPInterfaceNameOrIndex*).

Use this command one or multiple times to advertise as many prefixes as required. For example, the ISATAP subnet might have both global and unique local subnet prefixes. All the prefixes configured using this command are included in the Router Advertisement message sent by the ISATAP router to the ISATAP host.

If the router is not named ISATAP or the name "ISATAP" cannot be resolved to the IPv4 address assigned to the router's interface on the ISATAP subnet, you also need to issue the **netsh interface isatap set router** *AddressOrName* command on the router.

For example, a computer running Windows Server 2008 that is a member of the example.microsoft.com domain has the following configuration:

- A LAN interface named "Local Area Connection" is attached to the ISATAP subnet and assigned the IPv4 address 10.0.91.211.

- A LAN interface named "Local Area Connection 2" is attached to the IPv6-capable network.

- The ISATAP tunneling interface that is associated with the "Local Area Connection" LAN interface is named "Local Area Connection* 7".

Additionally, the address prefix assigned to the ISATAP subnet is 2001:DB8:2A05:10::/64 and the computer uses a default router on the IPv6-capable network at the next-hop address of FE80::2AA:FF:FE98:2AB1. To configure this computer as an ISATAP advertising and forwarding router, run the following commands:

- **netsh interface isatap set router 10.0.91.211**

  This command activates the ISATAP tunneling interface on the router.

- **netsh interface ipv6 set interface "Local Area Connection 2" forwarding=enabled**

  This command enables IPv6 forwarding on the LAN interface connected to the IPv6-capable portion of the intranet.

- **netsh interface ipv6 add route ::/0 "Local Area Connection 2" nexthop=fe80::2aa:ff:fe98:2ab1 publish=yes**

  This command adds a default route pointing to a neighboring router on the IPv6-capable portion of the intranet. Because the default route is configured to be published, the computer will advertise itself as a default router.

- **netsh interface ipv6 set interface "Local Area Connection* 7" forwarding=enabled advertise=enabled**

  This command enables IPv6 forwarding and advertising on the ISATAP tunneling interface that is associated with the LAN interface that is connected to the ISATAP subnet.

- **netsh interface ipv6 add route 2001:db8:2a05:10::/64 "Local Area Connection* 7" publish=yes**

  This command adds a published route for the ISATAP subnet to the ISATAP tunneling interface.

The ISATAP router is now configured for forwarding and advertising, but the ISATAP hosts and the ISATAP router need to be able to resolve the name "ISATAP" to the IPv4 address 10.0.91.211. Therefore, the last step in this simplified example is to add the following example A record to DNS:

```
isatap.example.microsoft.com.    3600    A    IN    10.0.91.211
```

ISATAP hosts that are members of the example.microsoft.com domain will use an IPv4-based DNS name query to resolve the name "isatap.example.microsoft.com." and send an encapsulated Router Solicitation message to the ISATAP router at 10.0.91.211. The ISATAP router responds with an encapsulated Router Advertisement message from its link-local ISATAP address (FE80::5EFE:10.0.91.211) containing the following:

- The Router Lifetime field set to 65,535, indicating that the ISATAP router is a default router. Based on this field, the ISATAP hosts add a default route to their routing tables with the next-hop address of FE80::5EFE:10.0.91.211.

- A Prefix Information option containing the 2001:DB8:2A05:10::/64 prefix with the On-link and Autonomous flags set. Based on this option, the ISATAP hosts configure a global ISATAP address on their ISATAP tunneling interfaces, add a route to their routing tables for the on-link subnet prefix 2001:DB8:2A05:10::/64, and attempt to register their global ISATAP addresses in DNS using DNS dynamic update.

For information about deploying ISATAP in more complex configurations, see the Intra-site Automatic Tunnel Addressing Protocol Deployment Guide at *http://www.microsoft.com/ipv6*.

References

The following reference was cited in this chapter:

- RFC 4214 – "Intra-Site Automatic Tunnel Addressing Protocol (ISATAP)"

You can obtain this RFC from the \RFCs_and_Drafts folder on the companion CD-ROM or from *http://www.ietf.org/rfc.html*.

Testing for Understanding

To test your understanding of ISATAP, answer the following questions. See Appendix D, "Testing for Understanding Answers," to check your answers.

1. Describe the intended use of the ISATAP IPv6 transition technology.

2. How can you recognize an ISATAP address?

3. How are the source and destination addresses in the encapsulating IPv4 header determined for ISATAP traffic?

4. Define the required and optional roles of an ISATAP router.

5. List and describe the steps that a Windows Vista–based ISATAP host with a single LAN interface goes through to perform router discovery for its ISATAP tunneling interface.

6. To reach a native IPv6 host, IPv6 packets from an ISATAP host must traverse seven IPv4 routers on the ISATAP subnet and three native IPv6 routers on the IPv6-capable portion of the intranet. If the IPv6 packets were sent by the ISATAP host with a Hop Limit field of 128, what is the value of the Hop Limit field when the packets are received at the destination?

7. A network administrator needs to begin experimenting with IPv6 connectivity on their IPv4-only intranet. Describe how the network administrator can configure a computer running Windows Server 2008 as an ISATAP router to immediately turn the entire IPv4-only intranet into a logical IPv6 subnet. What other steps must be done?

Chapter 13
6to4

At the end of this chapter, you should be able to do the following:

■ Define the address format, encapsulation, and intended use of the 6to4 IPv6 transition technology.

■ Describe how the IPv6 protocol in Windows Server 2008 and Windows Vista supports 6to4 as a host, host/router, and router.

■ List and describe the routes on a 6to4 host, a 6to4 host/router, a 6to4 router, and the IPv6 routers on the IPv6 Internet that make 6to4-based communication possible.

■ Describe how 6to4-tunneled communication works between 6to4 hosts, 6to4 host/routers, 6to4 routers on the IPv4 Internet, and IPv6 hosts on the IPv6 Internet.

■ Describe how to manually configure a computer running Windows Server 2008 or Windows Vista as a 6to4 router.

6to4 Overview

6to4 is an address assignment and router-to-router, host-to-router, and router-to-host automatic tunneling technology defined in RFC 3056 that is used to provide unicast IPv6 connectivity between IPv6 sites and hosts across the IPv4 Internet. 6to4 treats the entire IPv4 Internet as a single link.

Figure 13-1 shows the structure of a 6to4 address.

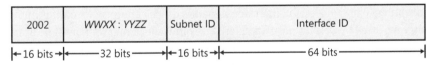

Figure 13-1   The structure of a 6to4 address

The 6to4 address consists of the following:

■ 2002::/16 is the address space reserved for 6to4.

■ WWXX:YYZZ is the colon hexadecimal representation of a public IPv4 address (*w.x.y.z*) assigned to a site or host on the IPv4 Internet. Public IPv4 addresses are directly reachable on the IPv4 Internet.

■ Subnet ID is used within the site of an organization to number individual subnets.

■ Interface ID identifies a node on a subnet within an organization.

There is a common misconception that before you can begin communicating between IPv6-enabled sites of an organization over a public network or connecting to public resources on the IPv6 Internet, you need a direct connection to the IPv6 Internet and a 48-bit global address prefix from an Internet service provider (ISP). Although this should eventually be done, 6to4 allows you to do the following:

- Create and use 48-bit global IPv6 address prefixes (2002:*WWXX:YYZZ*::/48) based on public IPv4 addresses that are assigned to your organization.

- Connect IPv6-capable portions of your intranet together by tunneling IPv6 traffic over the IPv4 Internet.

- Connect to IPv6-only resources on the IPv6 Internet.

6to4 allows you to assign global IPv6 addresses within your organization and to reach locations on the IPv6 Internet without requiring that you obtain a direct connection to the IPv6 Internet or an IPv6 global address prefix from an ISP.

6to4 Tunneling

6to4 traffic sent across the IPv4 Internet is tunneled or encapsulated with an IPv4 header, also known as IPv6-over-IPv4 traffic. For the details of IPv6-over-IPv4 traffic, see Chapter 11, "IPv6 Transition Technologies." This tunneling is automatically done by a 6to4 tunneling interface on the sending host or a forwarding router. The 6to4 tunneling interface treats the entire IPv4 Internet as a single link layer, in much the same way as Ethernet. In the case of 6to4, the link layer encapsulation is IPv4.

The IPv6 protocol for Windows Server 2008 and Windows Vista creates and enables a 6to4 tunneling interface when there are no other forms of IPv6 connectivity—that is, there are no router advertisements received from native IPv6 or Intra-Site Automatic Tunnel Addressing Protocol (ISATAP) routers—and there is a public IPv4 address assigned to one of the interfaces of the computer. The name of the interface depends on the computer's configuration. All tunneling interfaces by default have an asterisk (*) in their name, such as "Local Area Connection* 6". To determine the name of the 6to4 tunneling interface, display the TCP/IP configuration with the **ipconfig /all** command. The 6to4 tunneling interface has an asterisk in its name and has the description "Microsoft 6to4 Adapter" or "6TO4 Adapter."

The IPv6 protocol for Windows Server 2008 and Windows Vista automatically assigns the 6to4 tunneling interface the address 2002:*WWXX:YYZZ*::*WWXX:YYZZ*, in which *WWXX:YYZZ* is the colon hexadecimal notation of a public IPv4 address assigned to an interface of the computer. If there are multiple public IPv4 addresses, the 6to4 tunneling interface will be assigned multiple addresses of the form 2002:*WWXX:YYZZ*::*WWXX:YYZZ*. For example, for a computer running Windows Vista that is assigned the public IPv4 address 131.107.0.1, IPv6 assigns the address 2002:836B:1::836B:1 to the 6to4 tunneling interface. This special type of 6to4 address, which uses a Subnet ID of 0 and an interface ID of ::*WWXX:YYZZ*, is for used for Windows-based 6to4 routers or host/routers. For more information, see "6to4 Components" in this chapter.

To disable 6to4, set the HKEY_LOCAL_MACHINE\SYSTEM\CurrentControlSet\Services\ tcpip6\Parameters\DisabledComponents registry value to 0x2 (DWORD) and then restart the computer.

Note   IPv6 for Windows Server 2003 and Windows XP creates a 6to4 tunneling interface that was always named "6to4 Tunneling Pseudo-Interface."

6to4 Tunneling Example

Host A running Windows Vista has a single local area network (LAN) interface and is configured with the public IPv4 address of 131.107.0.1. Host B running Windows Vista has a single LAN interface and is configured with the IPv4 address of 157.54.0.1. IPv6 on Host A automatically configures the 6to4 address of 2002:836B:1::836B:1 on its 6to4 tunneling interface (named "Local Area Connection* 6"), and Host B automatically configures the 6to4 address of 2002:9D36:1::9D36:1 on its 6to4 tunneling interface (named "Local Area Connection* 5"). Both Host A and Host B are directly connected to the IPv4 Internet. Figure 13-2 shows this example configuration.

Host A
2001:836B:1::836B:1

IPv4 Internet

Host B
2002:9D36:1::9D36:1

Figure 13-2   An example 6to4 configuration

When Host A sends IPv6 traffic to Host B destined to Host B's 6to4 address, the source and destination addresses for the IPv6 and IPv4 headers are as listed in Table 13-1.

To test connectivity between 6to4 hosts, you can use the Ping tool (subject to Windows Firewall exceptions for Internet Control Message Protocol for IPv6 [ICMPv6] traffic). For example, to ping Host B at its 6to4 address from Host A, you use the following command:

```
ping 2002:9d36:1::9d36:1
```

Table 13-1 Example 6to4 Addresses

Field	Value
IPv6 Source Address	2002:836B:1::836B:1
IPv6 Destination Address	2002:9D36:1::9D36:1
IPv4 Source Address	131.107.0.1
IPv4 Destination Address	157.54.0.1

Because 6to4 addresses are always global, you do not need *%ZoneID* as part of the destination address.

The 6to4 tunneling interface uses its own 6to4 address as a source IPv6 address. The 6to4 tunneling interface determines the destination IPv4 address of the encapsulating IPv4 header from the second and third blocks of the destination IPv6 address (the first 32 bits after 2002::/16), which correspond to the embedded IPv4 address of Host B. For the source IPv4 address in the encapsulating IPv4 header, IPv4 on Host A determines the best source IPv4 address to use to reach the destination IPv4 address 157.54.0.1. In this case, Host A has only a single IPv4 address assigned, so IPv4 on Host A uses the source address of 131.107.0.1.

6to4 Components

A 6to4 deployment consists of 6to4 hosts, 6to4 routers, 6to4 host/routers, and 6to4 relays. Figure 13-3 shows the components of 6to4 and their placement on the IPv4 and IPv6 Internets.

The 6to4 components shown in Figure 13-3 are the following:

- **6to4 host** A native IPv6 host that is configured with at least one 6to4 address (a global address with the 2002::/16 prefix). 6to4 hosts do not require any additional support or manual configuration and can create 6to4 addresses using standard address autoconfiguration mechanisms. 6to4 hosts do not have a 6to4 tunneling interface and do not perform 6to4 tunneling.

- **6to4 router** An IPv6/IPv4 router that uses a 6to4 tunneling interface to forward 6to4-addressed traffic between the 6to4 hosts within a site and other 6to4 routers, 6to4 host/routers, or 6to4 relays across the IPv4 Internet. 6to4 routers might require manual configuration.

- **6to4 host/router** An IPv6/IPv4 host that uses a 6to4 tunneling interface to exchange 6to4-addressed traffic with other 6to4 host/routers, 6to4 routers, or 6to4 relays across the IPv4 Internet. Unlike a 6to4 router, a 6to4 host/router does not forward traffic for other 6to4 hosts. An example of a 6to4 host/router is a computer running Windows Vista that is directly connected to the Internet and has been assigned a public IPv4 address.

- **6to4 relay**   An IPv6/IPv4 router that forwards 6to4-addressed traffic between 6to4 routers and 6to4 host/routers on the IPv4 Internet and hosts on the IPv6 Internet. Microsoft has deployed a 6to4 relay on the IPv4 Internet, which is reachable by resolving the Domain Name System (DNS) name 6to4.ipv6.microsoft.com to an IPv4 address. RFC 3068 also defines an IPv4 anycast prefix for 6to4 relays.

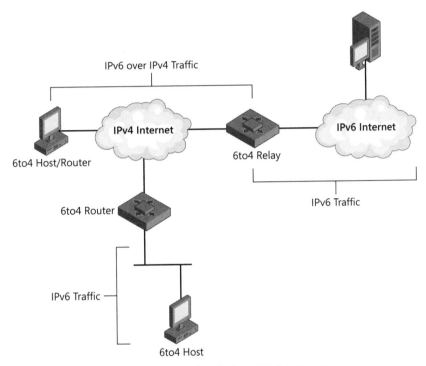

Figure 13-3   6to4 components on the IPv4 and IPv6 Internets

> **Note**   RFC 3056 uses the term "relay router" for the 6to4 relay. This chapter uses the term "6to4 relay" to better distinguish a 6to4 relay from other types of IPv6 transition relays between the IPv4 Internet and IPv6 Internet.

Both the 6to4 host/router and the intranet connected to the 6to4 router are 6to4 sites, which are hosts or networks connected to the IPv4 Internet that have their own unique 2002:*WWXX:YYZZ*::/48 prefix. For the 6to4 host/router the entire 6to4 site consists of a single computer. For the 6to4 router, the entire intranet is a 6to4 site, which can consist of up to 65,636 IPv6 subnets (using all possible combinations of the 16-bit Subnet ID). A 6to4 site can be created from every public IPv4 address.

Within a 6to4 site connected to the IPv4 Internet with a 6to4 router, IPv6 routers advertise 2002:*WWXX:YYZZ:SubnetID*::/64 prefixes so that 6to4 hosts can create an autoconfigured 6to4 address.

6to4 Addressing Example

Figure 13-4 shows an example of a 6to4 configuration.

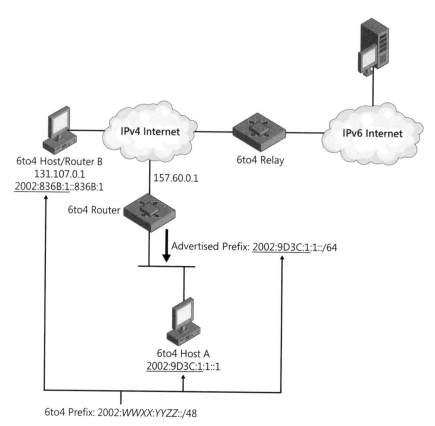

Figure 13-4 An example of a 6to4 configuration

The 6to4 router is directly connected to the Internet and has been assigned the public IPv4 address of 157.60.0.1. From this public IPv4 address, the intranet connected to the 6to4 router can use the 48-bit prefix 2002:9D3C:1::/48. (9D3C:1 is the colon hexadecimal notation for 157.60.0.1.) The 6to4 router advertises the 2002:9D3C:1:1::/64 prefix on the LAN interface connected to the single-subnet intranet. The *SubnetID* portion of the 64-bit prefix can be manually specified or automatically determined by the 6to4 router. IPv6 hosts on the intranet subnet configure an IPv6 address based on the 2002:9D3C:1:1::/64 prefix using standard IPv6 stateless address autoconfiguration. In this example, 6to4 Host A automatically configures the IPv6 address 2002:9D3C:1:1::1.

6to4 Host/router B is directly connected to the Internet and has been assigned the public IPv4 address of 131.107.0.1. The IPv6 protocol for Windows Server 2008 and Windows Vista automatically derives an address of the form 2002:*WWXX:YYZZ::WWXX:YYZZ*. Therefore,

6to4 Host/router B assigns itself the IPv6 address 2002:836B:1::836B:1. (836B:1 is the colon hexadecimal notation for 131.107.0.1.)

To determine the IPv4 address of the 6to4 relay on the IPv4 Internet, a 6to4 host/router or 6to4 router that is running Windows Server 2008 or Windows Vista by default automatically attempts to resolve the DNS name 6to4.ipv6.microsoft.com to an IPv4 address.

6to4 Routing

Figure 13-5 shows the relevant routes for 6to4 communication for the example configuration shown in Figure 13-4.

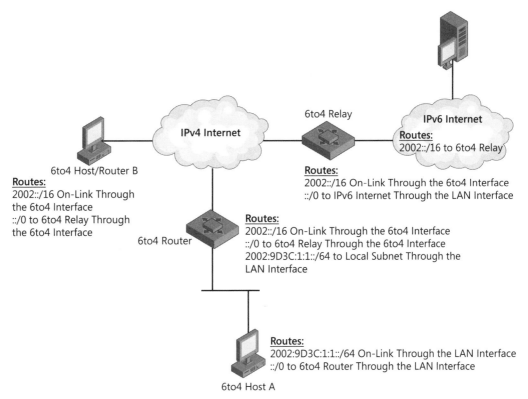

Figure 13-5   A 6to4 routing example

6to4 Host A uses the following routes:

■ An on-link route for the intranet subnet prefix that uses the LAN interface. In the example configuration, this is the 2002:9D3C:1:1::/64 route.

■ A default route that uses the LAN interface and has the next-hop address of the link-local address of the 6to4 router. This route allows 6to4 Host A to reach other 6to4 hosts, 6to4 host/routers, or locations on the IPv6 Internet.

The 6to4 router uses the following routes:

- An on-link route for the intranet subnet prefix that uses the LAN interface. This route allows the 6to4 router to forward traffic to and from 6to4 hosts on the intranet subnet. In the example configuration, this is the 2002:9D3C:1:1::/64 route.

- An on-link route for the 6to4 address prefix (2002::/16) that uses the 6to4 tunneling interface. This route allows the 6to4 router to perform router-to-router tunneling to reach other 6to4 routers and the 6to4 relay and router-to-host tunneling to reach 6to4 host/routers.

- A default route that uses the 6to4 tunneling interface and has the next-hop address of the 6to4 address of the 6to4 relay. This route allows the 6to4 router to forward IPv6 traffic to IPv6 destinations that are located on the IPv6 Internet.

The 6to4 relay uses the following routes:

- An on-link route for the 6to4 address prefix (2002::/16) that uses the 6to4 tunneling interface. This route allows the 6to4 relay to perform router-to-router tunneling to reach 6to4 routers and router-to-host tunneling to reach 6to4 host/routers.

- A default route that uses a LAN interface and has the next-hop address of a neighboring router on the IPv6 Internet (not shown). This route allows the 6to4 relay to forward IPv6 traffic to destinations that are located on the IPv6 Internet.

For 6to4 communication, the routers of the IPv6 Internet use a route for the 6to4 address prefix (2002::/16) that points back to the 6to4 relay. This route allows the routers of the IPv6 Internet to forward traffic destined for 6to4 hosts or 6to4 host/routers to the 6to4 relay.

6to4 Support in Windows Server 2008 and Windows Vista

The IPv6 protocol for Windows Server 2008 and Windows Vista provides support as a 6to4 host. The additional 6to4 component that is part of the IPv6 protocol for Windows Server 2008 and Windows Vista also provides support as a 6to4 host/router and a 6to4 router.

6to4 Host/Router Support

If there is a public IPv4 address assigned to an interface on the host and a global prefix is not received in a router advertisement, the 6to4 component of the IPv6 protocol automatically configures itself as a 6to4 host/router by doing the following:

- Assigns 6to4 addresses of the form 2002:*WWXX:YYZZ::WWXX:YYZZ* on the 6to4 tunneling interface for all public IPv4 addresses that are assigned to LAN interfaces on the computer.

- Creates an on-link 2002::/16 route using the 6to4 tunneling interface. All IPv6 traffic forwarded by this host/router to 6to4-addressed destinations is encapsulated with an IPv4 header.

■ Performs a DNS query for the name 6to4.ipv6.microsoft.com to obtain the IPv4 address of a 6to4 relay on the IPv4 Internet. You can also use the **netsh interface 6to4 set relay** command to specify the DNS name to query. If the query is successful, the 6to4 component adds a default route that uses the 6to4 tunneling interface and sets the next-hop address to the 6to4 address of the 6to4 relay (2002:*WWXX:YYZZ*::1).

As a 6to4 host/router, a computer running Windows Server 2008 or Windows Vista can reach other 6to4 host/routers on the IPv4 Internet, 6to4 hosts in other 6to4 sites on the IPv4 Internet, and locations on the IPv6 Internet.

> **Note** Computers running Windows Server 2008 or Windows Vista support Netsh commands for configuring 6to4 behavior in both the **netsh interface 6to4** and **netsh interface ipv6 6to4** contexts. Computers running Windows Server 2003 or Windows XP support only the **netsh interface ipv6 6to4** context. This chapter uses the 6to4 commands in the **netsh interface 6to4** context.

6to4 Router Support

Windows Server 2008 or Windows Vista supports both automated and manual configuration as a 6to4 router.

Automated 6to4 Router Configuration

The 6to4 component automatically configures a computer running Windows Server 2008 or Windows Vista as a 6to4 router when you enable Internet Connection Sharing (ICS) from the Sharing tab for the properties of a connection in the Network Connections folder. ICS provides IPv4 network address translation that allows a computer on single-subnet intranet to share its Internet connection with other computers. Small office/home office (SOHO) networks typically use ICS. The automated configuration of a 6to4 router provides global IPv6 connectivity for SOHO networks.

When ICS is enabled on an interface that is assigned a public IPv4 address, the 6to4 component automatically does the following:

■ Enables IPv6 forwarding on both the 6to4 tunneling and private interfaces.

The private interface is connected to a single-subnet intranet and uses private IPv4 addresses from the 192.168.0.0/24 prefix.

■ Determines a 64-bit IPv6 subnet prefix to advertise on the private intranet.

The 6to4 component derives the intranet subnet prefix from 2002:*WWXX:YYZZ: Inter faceIndex*::/64, in which *WWXX:YYZZ* is the colon hexadecimal notation of the public IPv4 address assigned to the public interface and *InterfaceIndex* is the interface index of the private interface.

- Determines the IPv4 address of a 6to4 relay.

  The 6to4 component queries the name 6to4.ipv6.microsoft.com for the IPv4 address of a 6to4 relay. If successfully resolved, it adds a default IPv6 route with the next-hop address of the 6to4 address of the 6to4 relay (2002:WWXX:YYZZ::1).

- Sends Router Advertisement messages on the private interface.

  The router advertisements contain the derived 6to4 subnet prefix for stateless address autoconfiguration and, if applicable, advertise the ICS computer as a default router.

For example, for an ICS computer using the public IPv4 address of 131.107.23.89 and whose private interface is assigned the interface index 5, the advertised subnet prefix is 2002:836B:1759:5::/64. (836B:1759 is the colon hexadecimal notation for 131.107.23.89.) Private hosts receiving this router advertisement create global addresses through normal stateless address autoconfiguration and add a 2002:836B:1759:5::/64 route for the local subnet and a default route with a next-hop address of the link-local address of the ICS computer's private interface. Private hosts can communicate with each other on the same subnet using the 2002:836B:1759:5::/64 route. For all other destinations to other 6to4 sites or the IPv6 Internet, private network hosts forward the IPv6 packets to the ICS computer using the default route.

For traffic to other 6to4 sites, the ICS computer uses its 2002::/16 route and encapsulates the IPv6 traffic with an IPv4 header to send it across the IPv4 Internet to another 6to4 router or 6to4 host/router. For all other IPv6 traffic, the ICS computer uses its default route and encapsulates the IPv6 traffic with an IPv4 header and sends it across the IPv4 Internet to the 6to4 relay.

> **Note**   The 6to4 component is not performing network address translation on the IPv6 packets being forwarded. ICS is providing network address translation services on IPv4 packets being forwarded to and from intranet hosts. The 6to4 component uses the ICS configuration to determine the public IPv4 address and the public interface.

Manual 6to4 Router Configuration

The automatic 6to4 router configuration based on ICS is designed for SOHO networks. For 6to4-based connectivity for larger, multi-subnet networks, you need to manually configure a 6to4 router on a computer connected to the IPv4 Internet. To manually configure a computer running Windows Server 2008 or Windows Vista as a 6to4 router, you must do the following:

- Ensure that the 6to4 router computer has a public address assigned to its IPv4 Internet interface and has not received a Router Advertisement message from either an IPv6 router on an attached subnet or an ISATAP router.

  If this is the case, the 6to4 component automatically creates a 6to4 tunneling interface, adds a 2002::/16 route to the routing table that uses the 6to4 tunneling interface, and adds a default route that uses the 6to4 tunneling interface and points to a 6to4 relay on the IPv4 Internet.

- Enable forwarding and advertising on the interfaces attached to your intranet (as needed). You can do this with the following command:

netsh interface ipv6 set interface *InterfaceNameOrIndex* **forwarding=enabled advertise=enabled**

- Enable the 6to4 service. You can do this with the following command:

netsh interface 6to4 set state enabled

- Enable forwarding on the 6to4 tunneling interface. You can do this with the following command:

netsh interface ipv6 set interface *InterfaceNameOrIndex* **forwarding=enabled**

- Add routes to make the locations on your intranet reachable. For example, add a route for the 48-bit 6to4 prefix of your 6to4 site to an interface attached to your intranet with the next-hop address of a neighboring IPv6 router. You can do this with the following command:

netsh interface ipv6 add route 2002:WWXX:YYZZ**::/48** *InterfaceNameOrIndex* *NextHopAddress*

For example, a computer running Windows Server 2008 has two LAN interfaces and the following configuration:

- Local Area Connection is attached to the IPv4 Internet and is assigned the public IPv4 address 131.107.0.1.

- Local Area Connection 2 is attached to the perimeter network.

- Local Area Connection* 5 is the name of the 6to4 tunneling interface.

An IPv6 router on the intranet forwards IPv6 traffic on behalf of the IPv6-capable intranet and advertises on the subnet containing the 6to4 router, which is assigned the Subnet ID 472A. The IPv6 router's link-local address on the subnet is FE80::2AA:FF:FE90:AC6B:21E0. Figure 13-6 shows this example configuration.

To configure this computer as a 6to4 router, run the following commands:

```
netsh interface ipv6 set interface "Local Area Connection 2" forwarding=enabled
netsh interface 6to4 set state enabled
netsh interface ipv6 set interface "Local Area Connection* 5" forwarding=enabled
netsh interface ipv6 add route 2002:836b:1:472a::/64 "Local Area Connection 2"
netsh interface ipv6 add route 2002:836b:1::/48 fe80::2aa:ff:fe90:ac6b:21e0
  "Local Area Connection 2"
```

For this example, the 2002:836B:1:472A::/64 route is added to make locations on the intranet subnet reachable and the 2002:836b:1::/48 route is added to make all of the locations on the IPv6-capable intranet reachable through the IPv6 router. The IPv6 router has a default route that points to the 6to4 router.

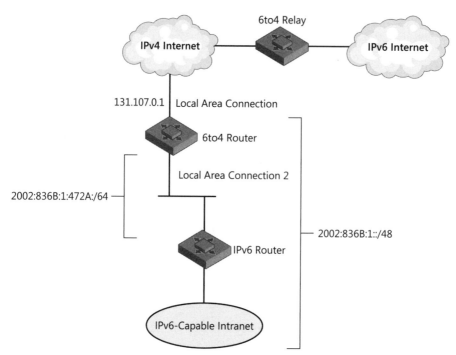

Figure 13-6   An example configuration for a manually configured 6to4 router

6to4 Communication Examples

This section describes the details of how 6to4 communication works on the example configuration shown in Figure 13-4 when a 6to4 host sends a packet to a 6to4 host/router and when a 6to4 host sends a packet to an IPv6 host on the IPv6 Internet.

6to4 Host to 6to4 Host/Router

In the example shown in Figure 13-4, 6to4 Host A wants to send a packet to 6to4 Host/router B. 6to4 Host A has determined 6to4 Host B's IPv6 address through a DNS name query or other method, such as the Windows Peer-to-Peer Networking platform's Peer Name Resolution Protocol (PNRP). The journey of the IPv6 packets from 6to4 Host A to 6to4 Host/router B has two parts:

- Part 1: From 6to4 Host A to the 6to4 router
- Part 2: From the 6to4 router to 6to4 Host/router B

In the first part of the journey, IPv6 on 6to4 Host A performs the route determination process and finds that the closest matching route to the destination is the default route. The default route has a next-hop address of the link-local address of the 6to4 router. 6to4 Host A performs normal IPv6 address resolution and sends the IPv6 packet to the 6to4 router. Figure 13-7 shows the delivery of the IPv6 packet to the 6to4 router.

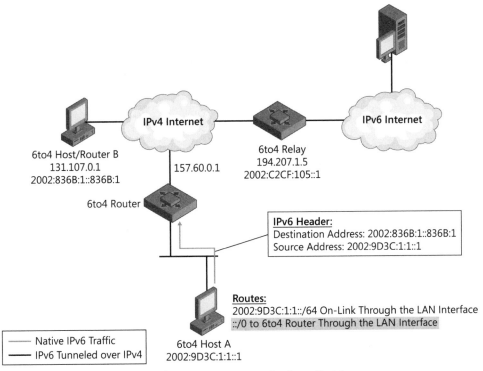

Figure 13-7   6to4 host to 6to4 host/router communication—Part 1

In the second part of the journey, IPv6 on the 6to4 router performs the route determination process and finds that the closest matching route to the destination is the 2002::/16 route. Because it is an on-link route, the next-hop IPv6 address is set to the destination (2002:836B:1::836B:1). The IPv6 packet and the next-hop address are handed to the 6to4 tunneling interface.

The 6to4 tunneling interface sets the destination IPv4 address in the IPv4 header to the 32 bits corresponding to the second and third blocks of the next-hop address, which in this case is 6to4 Host/router B's IPv4 address of 131.107.0.1. IPv4 on the 6to4 router determines that the best source address to use is the public IPv4 address assigned to the 6to4 router (157.60.0.1) and then sends the packet. Figure 13-8 shows the delivery of the IPv4-encapsulated IPv6 packet to 6to4 Host/router B.

On 6to4 Host/router B, IPv4 processes the IPv4 header. Because the Protocol field is set to 41, it hands the IPv6 packet to IPv6 for additional processing.

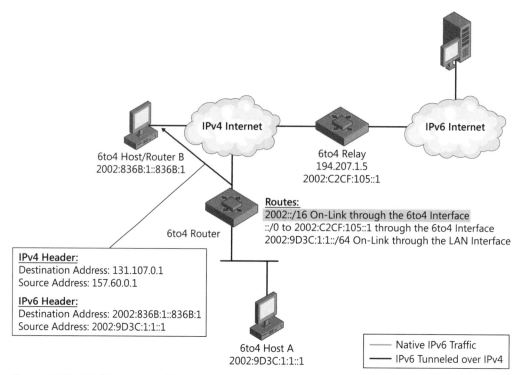

Figure 13-8   6to4 host to 6to4 host/router communication—Part 2

6to4 Host to IPv6 Host

When a 6to4 host sends an IPv6 packet to an IPv6 host on the IPv6 Internet, the packet's journey has three parts:

- Part 1: From the 6to4 host to the 6to4 router
- Part 2: From the 6to4 router to the 6to4 relay
- Part 3: From the 6to4 relay to the IPv6 host

In the first part of the journey, 6to4 Host A sends the IPv6 packet to the 6to4 router in the manner previously described in the "6to4 Host to 6to4 Host/Router" section of this chapter. Figure 13-9 shows the delivery of the IPv6 packet to the 6to4 router.

In the second part of the journey, IPv6 on the 6to4 router performs the route determination process and finds that the closest matching route to the destination is the default route. The next-hop IPv6 address is set to the 6to4 address of the 6to4 relay (2002:C2CF:105::1). The IPv6 packet and the next-hop address are handed to the 6to4 tunneling interface.

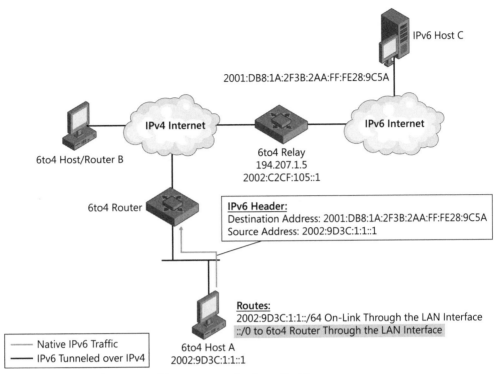

Figure 13-9   6to4 host to IPv6 host communication—Part 1

The 6to4 tunneling interface sets the destination IPv4 address in the IPv4 header to the 32 bits corresponding to the second and third blocks of the next-hop 6to4 address, which in this case is 6to4 relay's IPv4 address of 194.207.1.5. IPv4 on the 6to4 router determines that the best source address to use is the public IPv4 address assigned to the 6to4 router (157.60.0.1) and then sends the packet. Figure 13-10 shows the delivery of the IPv4-encapsulated IPv6 packet to the 6to4 relay.

In the third part of the journey, IPv4 on the 6to4 relay processes the IPv4 header. Because the Protocol field is set to 41, it hands the IPv6 packet to IPv6. IPv6 on the 6to4 relay performs the route determination process and finds that the closest matching route to the destination is the default route (::/0). The default route has a next-hop IPv6 address of the next IPv6 router on the IPv6 Internet (not shown in Figure 13-11). The IPv6 packet and the next-hop address are handed to the appropriate LAN interface for forwarding. Intermediate IPv6 routers forward the packet across the IPv6 Internet to its destination. Figure 13-11 shows the journey of the IPv6 packet from the 6to4 relay to IPv6 Host C.

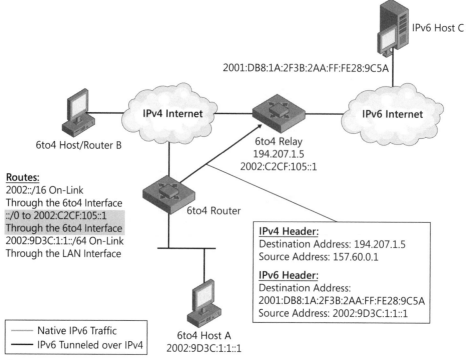

Figure 13-10 6to4 host to IPv6 host communication—Part 2

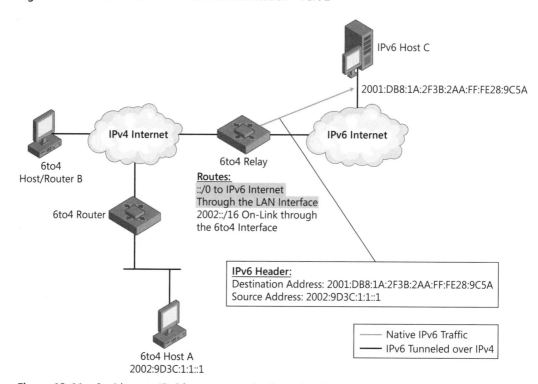

Figure 13-11 6to4 host to IPv6 host communication—Part 3

Network Monitor Capture

Here is an example of an IPv4-encapsulated ICMPv6 Echo Request message from a 6to4 host/router on the IPv4 Internet to a host on the IPv6 Internet as displayed by Network Monitor 3.1 (frame 1 of capture 13_01 in the \NetworkMonitorCaptures folder on the companion CD-ROM):

```
Frame:
+ Ethernet: Etype = Internet IP (IPv4)
- Ipv4: Next Protocol = IPv6 over IPv4, Packet ID = 2225, Total IP Length = 100
  + Versions: IPv4, Internet Protocol; Header Length = 20
  + DifferentiatedServicesField: DSCP: 0, ECN: 0
    TotalLength: 100 (0x64)
    Identification: 2225 (0x8B1)
  + FragmentFlags: 0 (0x0)
    TimeToLive: 128 (0x80)
    NextProtocol: IPv6 over IPv4, 41(0x29)
    Checksum: 42468 (0xA5E4)
    SourceAddress: 71.112.33.18
    DestinationAddress: 192.88.99.1
- Ipv6: Next Protocol = ICMPv6, Payload Length = 40
  + Versions: IPv6, Internet Protocol, DSCP 0
    PayloadLength: 40 (0x28)
    NextProtocol: ICMPv6, 58(0x3a)
    HopLimit: 128 (0x80)
    SourceAddress: 2002:4770:2112:0:0:0:4770:2112
    DestinationAddress: 2001:770:800:3:0:0:0:1
+ Icmpv6: Echo request, ID = 0x0, Seq = 0x3
```

In the IPv4 header, the packet is addressed from 71.112.33.18, the public IPv4 address of the 6to4 host/router, to 192.88.99.1, an address in the 6to4 Relay anycast prefix of 192.88.99.0/24 that is defined in RFC 3068. In the IPv6 header, the packet is addressed from the derived 6to4 address of the 6to4 host/router (2002:4770:2112:0:0:0:4770:2112, in which 4770:2112 is the colon hexadecimal notation of 71.112.33.18).

The following is the corresponding IPv4-encapsulated ICMPv6 Echo Reply message from the host on the IPv6 Internet as displayed by Network Monitor 3.1 (frame 2 of capture 13_01):

```
Frame:
+ Ethernet: Etype = Internet IP (IPv4)
- Ipv4: Next Protocol = IPv6 over IPv4, Packet ID = 44903, Total IP Length = 100
  + Versions: IPv4, Internet Protocol; Header Length = 20
  + DifferentiatedServicesField: DSCP: 0, ECN: 0
    TotalLength: 100 (0x64)
    Identification: 44903 (0xAF67)
  + FragmentFlags: 0 (0x0)
    TimeToLive: 244 (0xF4)
    NextProtocol: IPv6 over IPv4, 41(0x29)
    Checksum: 10848 (0x2A60)
    SourceAddress: 193.1.195.37
    DestinationAddress: 71.112.33.18
- Ipv6: Next Protocol = ICMPv6, Payload Length = 40
  + Versions: IPv6, Internet Protocol, DSCP 0
```

```
        PayloadLength: 40 (0x28)
        NextProtocol: ICMPv6, 58(0x3a)
        HopLimit: 61 (0x3D)
        SourceAddress: 2001:770:800:3:0:0:0:1
        DestinationAddress: 2002:4770:2112:0:0:0:4770:2112
+ Icmpv6: Echo reply, ID = 0x0, Seq = 0x3
```

Notice that in the IPv4 header, the packet is addressed from 193.1.195.37, which is the public address of the 6to4 relay on the IPv4 Internet.

Example of Using ISATAP and 6to4 Together

Figure 13-12 shows how both ISATAP and 6to4 can be used together to provide connectivity that would be difficult to achieve with IPv4. Two ISATAP hosts using 6to4 prefixes are communicating across the IPv4 Internet even though each site is using the 192.168.0.0/16 private address space internally.

> **Note**   The example configuration described in this section is deliberately simplified to show how you can use IPv6 transition technologies to achieve end-to-end IPv6 connectivity over a network infrastructure that does not support end-to-end IPv4 connectivity. This example configuration does not reflect real-world security considerations or configuration to protect the private traffic traveling across the IPv4 Internet or to prevent malicious Internet users from attacking intranet hosts, and it is not a desired or recommended configuration for a production network.

ISATAP Host A can reach 6to4 Router A and all other hosts within Site A using link-local ISATAP addresses. However, ISATAP Host A cannot reach any addresses outside Site A. As a 6to4 router, 6to4 Router A constructs the global prefix 2002:9D36:1:5::/64. (9D36:1 is the colon hexadecimal notation for 157.54.0.1, and 5 is the interface index of 6to4 Router A's intranet interface.) Router A then advertises it using a router advertisement on its intranet interface. However, ISATAP Host A is not on 6to4 Router A's subnet and will never create a global address based on this 6to4 prefix.

To configure ISATAP Host A to receive the router advertisement from 6to4 Router A, the network administrator for Site A has configured 6to4 Router A as an ISATAP router and added an A record to Site A's DNS infrastructure so that the name ISATAP is resolved to the IPv4 address of 192.168.204.1. Upon startup, the IPv6 protocol on Host A resolves the ISATAP name, automatically configures the link-local ISATAP address FE80::5EFE:192.168.12.9, and sends a Router Solicitation message containing the addresses listed in Table 13-2.

Upon receipt of the Router Solicitation message from ISATAP Host A, 6to4 Router A sends back a unicast Router Advertisement message advertising 6to4 Router A as a default router and with a Prefix Information option for the prefix 2002:9D36:1:2::/64. (9D36:1 is the colon hexadecimal notation for 157.54.0.1, and 2 is the interface index of 6to4 Router A's ISATAP tunneling interface.)

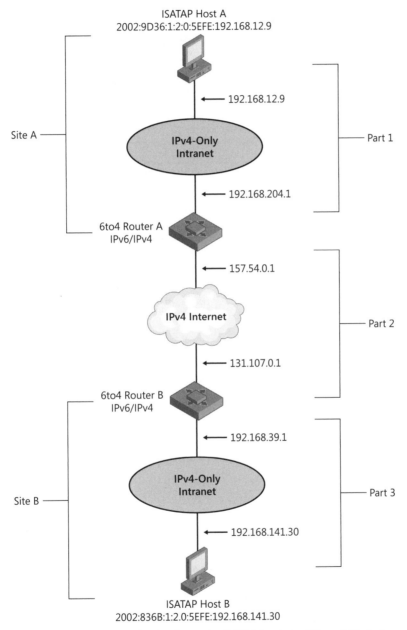

Figure 13-12   Communication between ISATAP hosts in different 6to4 sites

Table 13-2   Addresses in the Router Solicitation Message

Field	Value
IPv6 Source Address	FE80::5EFE:192.168.12.9
IPv6 Destination Address	FE80::5EFE:192.168.204.1
IPv4 Source Address	192.168.12.9
IPv4 Destination Address	192.168.204.1

The Router Advertisement contains the addresses listed in Table 13-3.

Table 13-3   Addresses in the Router Advertisement Message

Field	Value
IPv6 Source Address	FE80::5EFE:192.168.204.1
IPv6 Destination Address	FE80::5EFE:192.168.12.9
IPv4 Source Address	192.168.204.1
IPv4 Destination Address	192.168.12.9

Upon receipt of the Router Advertisement message, ISATAP Host A autoconfigures the address 2002:9D36:1:2:0:5EFE:192.168.12.9, a default route (::/0) with the next-hop address of FE80::5EFE:192.168.204.1 using its ISATAP tunneling interface, and a 2002:9D36:1:2::/64 route using its ISATAP tunneling interface.

Similarly, 6to4 Router B is configured as an ISATAP router and Site B has an appropriate A record in its DNS infrastructure so that ISATAP Host B autoconfigures the address 2002:836B:1:2:0:5EFE:192.168.141.30 (836B:1 is the colon hexadecimal notation for 131.107.0.1), a default route (::/0) with the next-hop address of FE80::5EFE:192.168.39.1 using its ISATAP tunneling interface, and a 2002:836B:1:2::/64 route using its ISATAP tunneling interface.

ISATAP Host A can now send a packet to ISATAP B. Let's examine the packet addressing in three parts (as shown in Figure 13-12) during its trip from ISATAP Host A to ISATAP Host B.

Part 1: From ISATAP Host A to 6to4 Router A

When ISATAP Host A sends the IPv6 packet, it uses the ::/0 route with the next-hop address of FE80::5EFE:192.168.204.1 and the ISATAP tunneling interface. The next-hop address for this packet is set to the link-local ISATAP address of 6to4 Router A (FE80::5EFE:192.168.204.1). The ISATAP tunneling interface tunnels the packet from the IPv4 address assigned to its intranet interface (192.168.12.9) to the embedded IPv4 address in the ISATAP interface ID of the next-hop address (192.168.204.1). The resulting addresses are listed in Table 13-4.

Table 13-4   **Addresses in Part 1**

Field	Value
IPv6 Source Address	2002:9D36:1:2:0:5EFE:192.168.12.9
IPv6 Destination Address	2002:836B:1:2:0:5EFE:192.168.141.30
IPv4 Source Address	192.168.12.9
IPv4 Destination Address	192.168.204.1

Part 2: From 6to4 Router A to 6to4 Router B

6to4 Router A receives the IPv4 packet and removes the IPv4 header. When 6to4 Router A forwards the IPv6 packet, it uses the 2002::/16 route with the 6to4 tunneling interface. The next-hop address for this packet is set to the destination address (2002:836B:1:2:0:5EFE: 192.168.141.30). The 6to4 tunneling interface tunnels the packet from the IPv4 address assigned to its Internet interface (157.54.0.1) to the embedded IPv4 address in the 6to4 prefix (836B:1) of the next-hop address (131.107.0.1). The resulting addresses are listed in Table 13-5.

Table 13-5   **Addresses in Part 2**

Field	Value
IPv6 Source Address	2002:9D36:1:2:0:5EFE:192.168.12.9
IPv6 Destination Address	2002:836B:1:2:0:5EFE:192.168.141.30
IPv4 Source Address	157.54.0.1
IPv4 Destination Address	131.107.0.1

Part 3: From 6to4 Router B to ISATAP Host B

6to4 Router B receives the IPv4 packet and removes the IPv4 header. When 6to4 Router B forwards the IPv6 packet, it uses the 2002:836B:1:2::/64 route with the ISATAP tunneling interface. The next-hop address for this packet is set to the destination address (2002:836B: 1:2:0:5EFE:192.168.141.30). The ISATAP tunneling interface tunnels the packet from the IPv4 address assigned to its intranet interface (192.168.39.1) to the embedded IPv4 address in the ISATAP interface ID of the next-hop IPv6 address (192.168.141.30). The resulting addresses are listed in Table 13-6.

Table 13-6   **Addresses in Part 3**

Field	Value
IPv6 Source Address	2002:9D36:1:2:0:5EFE:192.168.12.9
IPv6 Destination Address	2002:836B:1:2:0:5EFE:192.168.141.30
IPv4 Source Address	192.168.39.1
IPv4 Destination Address	192.168.141.30

References

The following references were cited in this chapter:

- RFC 3056 – "Connection of IPv6 Domains via IPv4 Clouds"
- RFC 3068 – "An Anycast Prefix for 6to4 Relay Routers"

You can obtain these RFCs from the \RFCs_and_Drafts folder on the companion CD-ROM or from *http://www.ietf.org/rfc.html.*

Testing for Understanding

To test your understanding of 6to4, answer the following questions. See Appendix D, "Testing for Understanding Answers," to check your answers.

1. Describe the intended use of the 6to4 IPv6 transition technology.

2. How can you recognize a 6to4 address?

3. How are the source and destination addresses in the encapsulating IPv4 header determined for 6to4-tunneled traffic?

4. To reach a native IPv6 host on the IPv6 Internet, IPv6 packets from a 6to4 host must traverse 3 native IPv6 routers on an intranet, 13 IPv4 routers on the IPv4 Internet, and 6 native IPv6 routers on the IPv6 Internet. If the IPv6 packets were sent by the 6to4 host with a Hop Limit field of 128, what is the value of the Hop Limit field when the packets are received at the destination?

5. A network administrator needs to begin experimenting with IPv6-only Web sites on the IPv6 Internet. Describe how the network administrator can configure a computer running Windows Server 2008 as a 6to4 router to immediately obtain connectivity to the IPv6 Internet.

Chapter 14

Teredo

At the end of this chapter, you should be able to do the following:

- Define the address format, encapsulation, and intended use of the Teredo IPv6 transition technology.

- Describe how the IPv6 protocol in Windows Server 2008 and Windows Vista supports Teredo as a Teredo client and a Teredo host-specific relay.

- List and describe the routes on Teredo clients, Teredo servers, Teredo relays, and IPv6 routers on the IPv6 Internet that make Teredo-based communication possible.

- Describe how Teredo clients perform automatic address configuration.

- Describe how Teredo clients on the same link, Teredo clients in different sites, Teredo host-specific relays, and IPv6 hosts on the IPv6 Internet initiate communication with each other.

Introduction to Teredo

Teredo is an address assignment and automatic tunneling technology defined in RFC 4380 that provides unicast IPv6 connectivity across the IPv4 Internet. 6to4 is an automatic tunneling technology described in Chapter 13, "6to4," that also provides unicast IPv6 connectivity across the IPv4 Internet. However, 6to4 works well when a 6to4 router exists at the edge of the site. The 6to4 router uses a public IPv4 address to construct the 6to4 prefix and acts as an IPv6 advertising and forwarding router. The 6to4 router encapsulates and decapsulates IPv6 traffic sent to and from site hosts.

6to4 relies on the configuration of a public IPv4 address and the implementation of 6to4 routing functionality in the edge device. Many small office/home office (SOHO) configurations use an IPv4 Network Address Translator (NAT) for Internet connectivity. For more information about how a NAT works, see Chapter 1, "Introduction to IPv6." In most NAT configurations, the device providing NAT functionality is not capable of acting as a 6to4 router. Even if 6to4 was universally supported in Internet edge devices, there are some Internet connectivity configurations that contain multiple levels of NATs. A 6to4-capable edge device cannot use 6to4 if it is not assigned a public IPv4 address.

Teredo addresses the issues related to the lack of 6to4 functionality in modern-day Internet edge devices and multilayered NAT configurations by tunneling IPv6 packets between hosts. In contrast, 6to4 tunnels IPv6 packets between the edge devices. Tunneling from the hosts presents another issue for NATs: IPv6 packets that are encapsulated with IPv4 have the Protocol field in the IPv4 header set to 41. Most NATs translate only Transmission Control

Protocol (TCP) or User Datagram Protocol (UDP) traffic and must either be manually config-ured to translate other protocols or have NAT editors installed that handle the translation. Because Protocol 41 translation is not a common feature of NATs, IPv4-encapsulated IPv6 traffic will not flow through typical NATs. Therefore, to allow IPv6 traffic to flow through one or multiple NATs, Teredo encapsulates the IPv6 packet as an IPv4 UDP message, containing both an IPv4 and UDP header. UDP messages can be translated by most NATs and can traverse multiple layers of NATs.

To summarize, Teredo is an IPv6 transition technology that allows automatic IPv6 tunneling between hosts that are located on the IPv4 Internet, even when those hosts are behind one or more IPv4 NATs. IPv6 traffic from Teredo clients can flow across NATs because it is sent as an IPv4 UDP message. If the NAT supports UDP port translation, the NAT supports Teredo (with the exception of symmetric NATs, described later in this chapter).

Benefits of Using Teredo

Teredo is a NAT traversal technology for IPv6 traffic. IPv6 traffic tunneled using Teredo can cross one or multiple NATs and allow a Teredo client to access other Teredo clients on the IPv4 Internet and hosts on the IPv6 Internet (through a Teredo relay). The ability to connect to other Teredo clients that are connected to the IPv4 Internet enables communication between applications that would otherwise have problems communicating over a NAT. With Teredo, IPv6-enabled applications can successfully communicate more frequently over the IPv4 Internet than IPv4-only applications.

Some types of IPv4-only server or peer applications have problems communicating when running on a computer that is behind a NAT. These types of applications either require manual configuration of the NAT (to allow unsolicited incoming traffic to the server or peer computer on the private network) or must provide their own solution for NAT traversal.

If the application is IPv6-capable, it can use Teredo, the NAT traversal solution for Windows. There is no need to either configure the NAT or modify the application to perform its own NAT traversal. Therefore, rather than spending development time modifying applications for a custom NAT traversal solution, application vendors should update their applications to be IPv6-capable.

Teredo Support in Microsoft Windows

Teredo is supported in the following versions of Microsoft Windows:

- Windows Server 2008
- Windows Vista
- Windows XP with Service Pack 2 (SP2)

■ Windows Server 2003 with Service Pack 1

■ Windows XP with Service Pack 1 (SP1) with the Advanced Networking Pack for Windows XP

All implementations of Teredo in Windows are based on RFC 4380.

In Windows Server 2008 and Windows Vista, the Teredo component might be enabled or disabled depending on the computer's configuration. When enabled, the Teredo component can be in the dormant or qualified states. For more information, see "The Teredo Client and Host-Specific Relay in Windows" later in this chapter.

In Windows Server 2008 or Windows Vista, any IPv6-capable application can use Teredo for incoming traffic by adding an inbound rule to the Windows Firewall for the application's traffic with edge traversal enabled. You can manually enable edge traversal with the Windows Firewall with Advanced Security snap-in, on the Advanced tab for the properties of an inbound rule. In Windows Server 2008 or Windows Vista, any IPv6-capable application can use Teredo for outgoing traffic if the outgoing traffic uses the Teredo tunneling interface as its next-hop interface.

Teredo and Protection from Unsolicited Incoming IPv6 Traffic

IPv6 traffic that is tunneled with Teredo is not subject to the IPv4 packet-filtering function of typical NATs. Although this might sound like Teredo is bypassing the NAT and allowing potentially malicious IPv6 traffic on private networks, consider the following:

■ Teredo does not change the behavior of NATs. Teredo clients create dynamic NAT translation table entries for their own Teredo traffic. The NAT forwards incoming Teredo traffic to the host that created the matching NAT translation table entry. The NAT will not forward Teredo traffic to computers on the private network that are not Teredo clients.

■ Teredo clients that use a host-based, stateful firewall that supports IPv6 traffic, such as Windows Firewall, are protected from unsolicited, unwanted, incoming IPv6 traffic. Windows Firewall is enabled by default for Windows XP with SP2, Windows Vista, and Windows Server 2008.

The combination of IPv6, Teredo, and a host-based, stateful, IPv6 firewall does not affect the packet-filtering function of the NAT for IPv4-based traffic and does not make your Windows-based computer more susceptible to attacks by malicious users and programs that use IPv6 traffic rather than IPv4 traffic.

Network Address Translators (NATs)

As described in Chapter 1, a NAT is an IPv4 router defined in RFC 1631 that can translate the IPv4 addresses and TCP/UDP port numbers of packets as they are forwarded. A NAT can map private addresses to a single or to multiple public IPv4 addresses.

NAT is a common solution for the following combination of requirements:

- You want to leverage the use of a single connection, rather than connecting multiple computers, to the Internet.

- You want to use private addressing.

- You want access to Internet resources without having to deploy a proxy server.

The mappings for private-to-public traffic are stored in a NAT translation table, which can contain the following types of entries:

- **Dynamic mappings**   Created when private network clients initiate communications. Dynamic mappings are removed from the NAT translation table after a specified amount of time, unless refreshed by traffic that corresponds to the NAT translation table entry.

- **Static mappings**   Configured manually so that communications initiated by Internet clients can be mapped to a specific private network address and port. Static mappings are needed when there are servers (for example, Web servers) or applications (for example, games) on the private network that you want to make available to computers that are connected to the Internet. Static mappings are not removed from the NAT translation table.

For outgoing traffic to the Internet, the NAT translation table maps the destination address in the packet from an internal address (the address assigned to a host on the private network) to an external address (the public IPv4 address assigned to the NAT's Internet interface) and the destination port number from an internal port number (the port number being used by the host on the private network) to an external port number (the port number assigned by the NAT).

For incoming traffic from the Internet, the NAT translation table maps the destination address in the packet from an external address to an internal address and the destination port number from an external port number to an internal port number.

The NAT forwards traffic from the Internet to the private network only if a mapping exists in the NAT translation table. In this way, the NAT provides a simple, stateful, packet-filtering function for the computers on the private network.

Types of NATs

The following types of NATs are defined:

- **Cone NATs**   A NAT in which the NAT translation table entry stores a mapping between an internal address and port number and an external address and port number. Once the NAT translation table entry is in place, inbound traffic to the external address and port number from any source address and port number is allowed and translated.

- **Restricted NATs**   A NAT in which the NAT translation table entry stores a mapping between an internal address and port number and an external address and port number, for either specific source addresses or a specific source address and port numbers. An inbound packet that matches the NAT translation table entry for the external destination address and port number from an unknown external address or port number is silently discarded.

- **Symmetric NATs**   A NAT that maps the same internal address and port number to different external addresses and ports, depending on the external destination address (for outbound traffic).

Teredo works well over cone and restricted NATs. Teredo in Windows Server 2008 and Windows Vista can work between Teredo clients if only one Teredo client is behind one or more symmetric NATs. For example, Teredo in Windows Server 2008 and Windows Vista will work if one of the peers is behind a symmetric NAT and the other is behind a cone or restricted NAT.

Teredo in Windows XP SP2, Windows XP SP1 with the Advanced Networking Pack for Windows XP, and Windows Server 2003 Service Pack 1 cannot work over symmetric NATs.

Teredo Components

The Teredo infrastructure consists of the following components:

- Teredo clients
- Teredo servers
- Teredo relays
- Teredo host-specific relays

Figure 14-1 shows the components of a Teredo infrastructure.

The following sections describe these components in detail.

Teredo Client

A Teredo client is an IPv6/IPv4 node that supports a Teredo tunneling interface through which packets are tunneled to either other Teredo clients or nodes on the IPv6 Internet (via a Teredo relay or Teredo host-specific relay). A Teredo client communicates with a Teredo server to obtain an address prefix from which a Teredo-based IPv6 address is configured or to help initiate communication with other Teredo clients or hosts on the IPv6 Internet.

Windows Server 2008, Windows Vista, Windows XP SP2, Windows XP SP1 with the Advanced Networking Pack for Windows XP, and Windows Server 2003 with Service Pack 1 include a Teredo client.

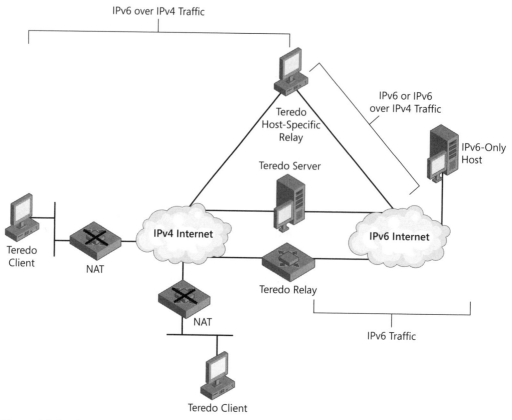

Figure 14-1   Components of the Teredo infrastructure

Teredo Server

A Teredo server is an IPv6/IPv4 node that is connected to both the IPv4 Internet and the IPv6 Internet, and it supports a Teredo tunneling interface over which packets are received. The general role of the Teredo server is to assist in the address configuration of Teredo clients and to facilitate the initial communication between Teredo clients and other Teredo clients or between Teredo clients and IPv6-only hosts. The Teredo server listens on UDP port 3544 for Teredo traffic.

For more information about the role of the Teredo server in facilitating initial communication, see the "Teredo Processes" section later in this chapter.

Windows Server 2008, Windows Vista, Windows XP SP2, Windows XP SP1 with the Advanced Networking Pack for Windows XP, and Windows Server 2003 with Service Pack 1 do not include Teredo server functionality. To facilitate communication between Windows-based Teredo client computers, Microsoft has deployed Teredo servers on the IPv4 Internet.

Teredo Relay

A Teredo relay is an IPv6/IPv4 router that can forward packets between Teredo clients on the IPv4 Internet (using a Teredo tunneling interface) and IPv6-only hosts on the IPv6 Internet. In some cases, the Teredo relay interacts with a Teredo server to help it facilitate initial communication between Teredo clients and IPv6-only hosts. The Teredo relay listens on UDP port 3544 for Teredo traffic.

For more information about the role of the Teredo relay in facilitating initial and ongoing communication between Teredo clients and IPv6-only hosts, see the "Teredo Processes" section later in this chapter.

Windows Server 2008, Windows Vista, Windows XP SP2, Windows XP SP1 with the Advanced Networking Pack for Windows XP, and Windows Server 2003 with Service Pack 1 do not include Teredo relay functionality. Microsoft does not plan to deploy any Teredo relays on the IPv4 Internet. Individual Internet service providers (ISPs) could deploy their own Teredo relays. The Windows-based Teredo client will work with a Teredo relay when sending traffic to an IPv6-only host on the IPv6 Internet. Teredo relays are not needed to communicate between Teredo clients and with Teredo host-specific relays.

Teredo Host-Specific Relay

Communication between Teredo clients and IPv6 hosts that are configured with a global address must go through a Teredo relay. This is required for IPv6-only hosts connected to the IPv6 Internet. However, when the IPv6 host is IPv6-capable and IPv4-capable and connected to both the IPv4 Internet and IPv6 Internet, communication should occur between the Teredo client and the IPv6 host over the IPv4 Internet, rather than having to traverse the IPv6 Internet and go through a Teredo relay.

A Teredo host-specific relay is an IPv6/IPv4 node that has an interface and connectivity to both the IPv4 Internet and the IPv6 Internet and can communicate directly with Teredo clients over the IPv4 Internet, without the need for an intermediate Teredo relay. The connectivity to the IPv4 Internet can be through a public IPv4 address or through a private IPv4 address and a neighboring NAT. The connectivity to the IPv6 Internet can be through a direct connection to the IPv6 Internet or through an IPv6 transition technology such as 6to4, where IPv6 packets are tunneled across the IPv4 Internet. The Teredo host-specific relay listens on UDP port 3544 for Teredo traffic.

Windows Server 2008, Windows Vista, Windows XP SP2, Windows XP SP1 with the Advanced Networking Pack for Windows XP, and Windows Server 2003 with Service Pack 1 include Teredo host-specific relay functionality, which is automatically enabled if the computer has a global address assigned. A global address can be assigned from a received Router Advertisement message from a native IPv6 router, an ISATAP router, or a 6to4 router. A global address can also be assigned when the computer configures itself as a 6to4 host/router.

Teredo host-specific relay functionality allows Teredo clients to efficiently communicate with Teredo-capable hosts that use 6to4, a non-6to4 global prefix, or ISATAP within organizations that use a global prefix for their addresses.

The Teredo Client and Host-Specific Relay in Windows

When enabled, the Teredo client in Windows Server 2008 and Windows Vista is in either a dormant or qualified state. In the dormant state, the Teredo client has an address, but this address is the previous Teredo address used by the Teredo client and might not be valid. In the dormant state, the Teredo client does not communicate with a Teredo server to automatically configure a current address or send periodic packets to maintain the NAT mapping for incoming Teredo traffic and verify that the current address is valid. In the qualified state, the Teredo client initiates address configuration and sends periodic packets to a Teredo server. By default, the Teredo client sends a packet to a Teredo server every 30 seconds. You can specify the interval between periodic packets with the **netsh interface teredo set state refreshinterval =***Seconds* command.

The Teredo client is normally in the dormant state. When an IPv6-capable application uses the Teredo tunneling interface for sending or receiving traffic, the Teredo client switches to the qualified state. If the Teredo tunneling interface is not used after one hour and there are no applications listening on the Teredo interface, the Teredo client switches back to the dormant state. The Teredo client uses dormant and qualified states to reduce unnecessary network traffic. The Teredo client performs Teredo address configuration and sends periodic packets to a Teredo server only when an IPv6 application is using the Teredo tunneling interface.

Table 14-1 lists whether the Teredo client and Teredo host-specific relay are enabled or disabled for the dormant and qualified states based on the IPv4 and IPv6 address configuration of the computer.

Table 14-1   Teredo Client and Host-Specific Relay

Computer Configuration	Teredo Client	Teredo Host-Specific Relay
Public IPv4 addresses only	Enabled for both dormant and qualified states	Enabled only for the qualified state
Private IPv4 addresses only	Enabled	Disabled
Private IPv4 addresses and 6to4 connectivity via a 6to4 router	Enabled for both dormant and qualified states	Enabled only for the qualified state
Global IPv6 addresses only	Disabled	Disabled
Private IPv4 addresses and global IPv6 addresses	Enabled for both dormant and qualified states	Enabled only for the qualified state
Public IPv4 addresses and global IPv6 addresses	Enabled for both dormant and qualified states	Enabled only for the qualified state

To configure the initial state of the Teredo client, use the **netsh interface teredo set state type=disabled|client|enterpriseclient|default** command. The Teredo client state types are the following:

- **disabled**   The Teredo client and host-specific relay are disabled.

- **client**   The Teredo component will detect if the computer is connected to a managed network that contains Active Directory domain service domain controllers of the domain to which the computer belongs. If the computer is connected to a managed network, the Teredo client is disabled. This is to prevent the Teredo client from traversing organization network firewalls. If the computer is not connected to a managed network, the Teredo client is enabled.

- **enterpriseclient**   The Teredo component will skip detection to determine if the computer is connected to a managed network and enable the Teredo client. This option will enable the Teredo client on a managed network and must be set by a user with administrator-level access to the computer.

- **default**   Sets the client state to its default option (**client**).

By default, the Teredo client is disabled when the computer is on a managed network. To enable the Teredo client on a managed network, use the **netsh interface teredo set state type=enterpriseclient** command.

By default, the Teredo client uses a dynamically assigned UDP port for incoming Teredo traffic. To configure the Teredo client to use a specific UDP port, use the **netsh interface teredo set state clientport=***PortNumber* command.

> **Note**   For computers running Windows XP with SP2, Windows XP with Service Pack 1 with the Advanced Networking Pack for Windows XP, or Windows Server 2003 with Service Pack 1, you use **netsh interface ipv6 set teredo** commands to configure the Teredo client.

Teredo Addresses

Teredo addresses have the format shown in Figure 14-2.

Teredo Prefix	Teredo Server IPv4 Address	Flags	Obscured External Port	Obscured External Address
◄——— 32 bits ———►	◄——— 32 bits ———►	◄— 16 bits —►	◄— 16 bits —►	◄——— 32 bits ———►

Figure 14-2   Teredo address format

A Teredo address consists of the following:

- **Teredo prefix**   The first 32 bits are for the Teredo prefix, which is the same for all Teredo addresses. The Teredo prefix defined in RFC 4380 is 2001::/32 and is the prefix used by Teredo in Windows Server 2008 and Windows Vista. Windows XP and Windows Server 2003 initially used the 3FFE:831F::/32 Teredo prefix. Computers running Windows XP or Windows Server 2003 will use the 2001::/32 Teredo prefix when updated with Microsoft Security Bulletin MS06-064.

- **Teredo server IPv4 address** The next 32 bits contain the IPv4 public address of the Teredo server that helped configure this Teredo address. For more information, see the "Initial Configuration for Teredo Clients" section later in this chapter.

- **Flags** The next 16 bits are reserved for Teredo flags. RFC 4380 defines the high-order bit as the Cone flag. The Cone flag is set when a Teredo client is behind a cone NAT. The determination of whether the NAT connected to the Internet is a cone NAT occurs during the Teredo client's initial configuration. For more information, see the "Initial Configuration for Teredo Clients" section later in this chapter. RFC 4380 defines the entire Flags field as C00000UG 00000000. Because the Flags field is part of the Interface ID field, the U bit is for the Universal/Local flag (set to 0) and the G bit is Individual/Group flag (set to 0). This is the use of the Flags field for Windows XP and Windows Server 2003–based Teredo clients.

Windows Server 2008 and Windows Vista–based Teredo clients always set the Cone flag to 1 and use unused bits within the Flags field to provide a level of protection from address scans by malicious users. For Windows Server 2008 and Windows Vista–based Teredo clients, the 16 bits within the Flags field consist of the following: CRAAAAUG AAAAAAAA. The R bit is reserved for future use (set to 0). The A bits are set to a 12-bit randomly generated number. By using a random number for the A bits, a malicious user who has determined the rest of the Teredo address by capturing the initial configuration exchange of packets between the Teredo client and Teredo server will have to try up to 4096 (2^{12}) different addresses to determine a Teredo client's address during an address scan.

- **Obscured external port** The next 16 bits store an obscured version of the external UDP port corresponding to all Teredo traffic for this Teredo client. When the Teredo client sends its initial packet to a Teredo server, the source UDP port of the packet is mapped by the NAT to a different, external UDP port. The Teredo client maintains this port mapping so that it remains in the NAT's translation table. Therefore, all Teredo traffic for the host uses the same external, mapped UDP port. The external UDP port is determined by the Teredo server from the source UDP port of the incoming initial packet sent by the Teredo client and sent back to the Teredo client.

The external port is obscured by XORing the external port with 0xFFFF. For example, the obscured version of the external port 5000 in hexadecimal format is EC77 (5000 = 0x1388, 0x1388 XOR 0xFFFF = 0xEC77). Some NATs attempt to translate the external port number to the internal port number when the external port number is within the payload. Obscuring the external port number prevents these types of NATs from translating the external port within the Teredo address.

■ **Obscured external address**   The last 32 bits store an obscured version of the external IPv4 address corresponding to all Teredo traffic for this Teredo client. Just like the external port, when the Teredo client sends its initial packet to a Teredo server, the source IPv4 address of the packet is mapped by the NAT to a different, external (public) address. The Teredo client maintains this address mapping so that it remains in the NAT's translation table. Therefore, all Teredo traffic for the host uses the same external, mapped, public IPv4 address. The external IPv4 address is determined by the Teredo server from the source IPv4 address of the incoming initial packet sent by the Teredo client and sent back to the Teredo client.

The external address is obscured by XORing the external address with 0xFFFFFFFF. For example, the obscured version of the public IPv4 address 131.107.0.1 in colon hexadecimal format is 7C94:FFFE (131.107.0.1 = 0x836B0001, 0x836B0001 XOR 0xFFFFFFFF = 0x7C94FFFE). Some NATs attempt to translate the external address to the internal address number when the external address is within the payload. Obscuring the external address prevents these types of NATs from translating the external address within the Teredo address.

Figure 14-3 shows an example Teredo configuration with two Teredo clients; one Teredo client is located behind a cone NAT (Teredo Client A), and one is located behind a restricted NAT (Teredo Client B).

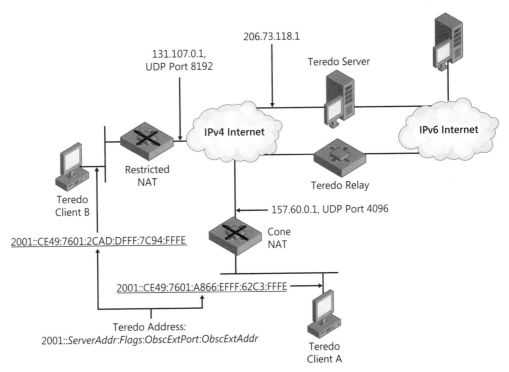

Figure 14-3   Teredo addressing example

Teredo Client A uses the following to construct its Teredo address:

- Its Teredo server is at the public IPv4 address of 206.73.118.1.

- It is behind a cone NAT.

- The external address and port for its Teredo traffic are 157.60.0.1, UDP port 4096.

Therefore, using the Teredo address format of 2001::*ServerAddr:Flags:ObscExtPort:ObscExtAddr*, Teredo Client A derives the address 2001::CE49:7601:A866:EFFF:62C3:FFFE. This is based on the following:

- 2001::/32 is the Teredo prefix.

- CE49:7601 is the colon hexadecimal version of 206.73.118.1.

- A866 is the Flags field in which the Cone flag is set to 1 (indicating that Teredo Client A is located behind a cone NAT); the R, U, and G flags are set to 0; and the remaining 12 bits are set to a random sequence (101001100110) to help prevent external address scans. For a Windows XP–based Teredo client without the Microsoft Security Bulletin MS06-064 installed, the Flags field would be set to 0x8000.

- EFFF is the obscured version of UDP port 4096.

- 62C3:FFFE is the obscured version of the public IPv4 address 157.60.0.1.

Teredo Client B uses the following to construct its Teredo address:

- Its Teredo server is at the public IPv4 address of 206.73.118.1.

- It is behind a restricted NAT.

- The external address and port for its Teredo traffic are 131.107.0.1, UDP port 8192.

Therefore, Teredo Client B derives the address 2001::CE49:7601:2CAD:DFFF:7C94:FFFE. This is based on the following:

- 2001::/32 is the Teredo prefix.

- CE49:7601 is the colon hexadecimal version of 206.73.118.1.

- 2CAD is the Flags field in which the Cone flag is set to 0 (indicating that Teredo Client B is located behind a restricted NAT); the R, U, and G flags are set to 0; and the remaining 12 bits are set to a random sequence (101110101101) to help prevent external address scans. For a Windows XP–based Teredo client without the Microsoft Security Bulletin MS06-064 installed, the Flags field would be set to 0x0.

- DFFF is the obscured version of UDP port 8192.

- 7C94:FFFE is the obscured version of the public IPv4 address 131.107.0.1.

Teredo addresses are assigned only to Teredo clients. Teredo servers, Teredo relays, and Teredo host-specific relays are not assigned a Teredo address.

Teredo Packet Formats

This section describes the following:

- Teredo data packet format
- Teredo bubble packets
- Teredo indicators

Teredo Data Packet Format

Figure 14-4 shows the format of Teredo data packets defined in RFC 4380.

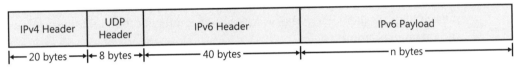

IPv4 Header	UDP Header	IPv6 Header	IPv6 Payload
←— 20 bytes —→	←- 8 bytes -→	←———— 40 bytes ————→	————————— n bytes ————————→

Figure 14-4   Teredo data packet format

A Teredo packet consists of the following:

- The IPv4 header contains the source and destination IPv4 addresses corresponding to the automatic tunnel endpoints and can be translated by a NAT.
- The UDP header contains source and destination UDP ports for Teredo traffic and can be translated by a NAT.
- The IPv6 header contains the source and destination IPv6 addresses, at least one of which is a Teredo address.
- The IPv6 payload contains zero or more IPv6 extension headers and the upper-layer protocol data unit (PDU) of the encapsulated IPv6 packet.

Teredo Bubble Packets

A Teredo bubble packet is typically sent to create or maintain a NAT mapping and consists of an IPv6 header with no IPv6 payload. Figure 14-5 shows the Teredo bubble packet.

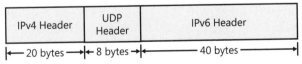

IPv4 Header	UDP Header	IPv6 Header
←— 20 bytes —→	←- 8 bytes -→	←———— 40 bytes ————→

Figure 14-5   Teredo bubble packet

In the IPv6 header, the Next Header field is set to 59, indicating that there is no payload present.

Teredo Indicators

Teredo uses two different indicators defined in RFC 4380—the Authentication and Origin indicators—which are headers that are used to contain authentication or address and port information.

Authentication Indicator

The Authentication indicator is used to protect the exchange of Router Solicitation and Router Advertisement messages between a Teredo client and a Teredo server. Both the Teredo client and the Teredo server are configured with a secret key, which is used to construct the authentication data in the Authentication indicator. The Authentication indicator is placed between the UDP header and the IPv6 packet. If both the Origin and Authentication indicators are present in the Router Advertisement message, the Authentication indicator is placed before the Origin indicator.

Figure 14-6 shows the structure of the Authentication indicator.

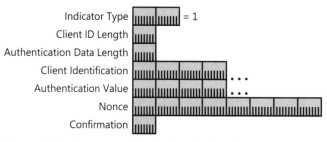

Figure 14-6   Structure of the Authentication indicator

The Authentication indicator contains the following fields:

- **Indicator Type**   This two-byte field specifies the type of indicator. For the Authentication indicator, it is set to 1. The Teredo client and the Teredo server can distinguish the Authentication indicator from the first two bytes of an IPv6 packet because the four high-order bits of an IPv6 packet are set to 0110 (6), which correspond to the Version field of the IPv6 header.

- **Client ID Length**   This one-byte field indicates the length of the Client Identification field.

- **Authentication Data Length**   This one-byte field indicates the length of the Authentication Value field.

- **Client Identification**   This variable-length field contains an identification string for the Teredo client.

- **Authentication Value**   This variable-length field contains the authentication value for this packet, calculated using the shared secret key.

- **Nonce**   This eight-byte field contains a random number, which is used to provide proof of a live exchange of packets and to prevent packet replay attacks.

- **Confirmation**   This one-byte field contains a value that indicates whether the Teredo client is using the correct secret key. In the Router Solicitation message, the Confirmation field is set to 0. In the Router Advertisement, the Confirmation field is set to either 0 if the secret key is correct or a non-zero value if it is not.

In Windows Server 2008, Windows Vista, Windows XP SP2, Windows XP SP1 with the Advanced Networking Pack for Windows XP, and Windows Server 2003 with Service Pack 1, Teredo does not use a client identifier or an authentication value, although the Authentication indicator is still present in the Router Advertisement and Router Solicitation messages. Figure 14-7 shows the format of the Authentication indicator when there is no client identifier or authentication value.

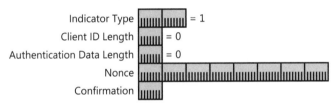

Indicator Type = 1
Client ID Length = 0
Authentication Data Length = 0
Nonce
Confirmation

Figure 14-7   Structure of the Authentication indicator when there is no client identifier or authentication value

Origin Indicator

The Origin indicator is used to indicate a public IPv4 address and UDP port number of a Teredo client, Teredo relay, or Teredo host-specific relay. An example of its use is when a Teredo server sends a router advertisement message in response to a Teredo client's router solicitation message. In this case, the Origin indicator contains the external (public) IPv4 address and UDP port number corresponding to the Teredo traffic of a Teredo client. For more information, see the "Initial Configuration for Teredo Clients" section in this chapter.

Like the Authentication indicator, the Origin indicator is placed between the UDP header and the IPv6 packet. Figure 14-8 shows the structure of the Origin indicator.

Indicator Type = 0
Obscured Origin Port Number
Obscured Origin Address

Figure 14-8   Structure of the Origin indicator

The Origin indicator contains the following fields:

■ **Indicator Type**   This two-byte field specifies the type of indicator. For the Origin indicator, it is set to 0. The Teredo client can distinguish the Origin indicator from the first two bytes of an IPv6 packet because the four high-order bits of an IPv6 packet are set to 0110 (6), which correspond to the Version field of the IPv6 header.

■ **Obscured Origin Port Number**   This two-byte field contains the obscured (XORed with 0xFFFF) external port corresponding to the Teredo traffic of a Teredo client, Teredo relay, or Teredo host-specific relay. To obtain the original port number, the receiver XORs the value of the Obscured Origin Port Number field with 0xFFFF.

■ **Obscured Origin Address**   This four-byte field contains the obscured (XORed with 0xFFFFFFFF) external IPv4 address corresponding to the Teredo traffic of a Teredo client, Teredo relay, or Teredo host-specific relay. To obtain the original address, the receiver XORs the value of the Obscured Origin Address field with 0xFFFFFFFF.

Figure 14-9 shows the three different types of packets that contain the Origin and Authentication indicators for the Windows-based Teredo client.

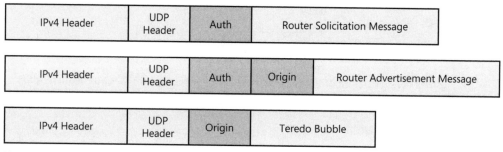

Figure 14-9   Types of packets containing the Authentication or Origin indicators

Teredo Routing

Figure 14-10 shows the routes that exist to enable reachability between Teredo hosts, Teredo servers, Teredo relays, Teredo host-specific relays, and IPv6-only hosts.

On the IPv6 Internet, 2001::/32 routes in the routing infrastructure are used to forward packets using the Teredo prefix to the nearest Teredo relay. Teredo servers, Teredo relays, and Teredo host-specific relays have a 2001::/32 route, which considers all addresses using the prefix as on-link using the Teredo tunneling interface. The Teredo tunneling interface is a logical interface that performs automatic IPv4 and UDP encapsulation for forwarded packets. Teredo servers, Teredo relays, and Teredo host-specific relays also have a default route (::/0) that points to the IPv6 Internet. Typically, this default route contains a next-hop IPv6 address of a neighboring router on the IPv6 Internet using a physical interface that is connected to the IPv6 Internet.

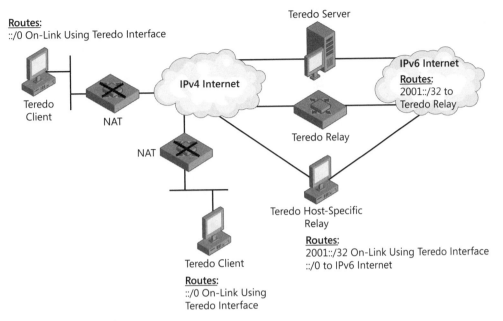

Figure 14-10   Teredo routes

Routing for the Teredo Client in Windows

The Teredo client in Windows Server 2008, Windows Vista, Windows XP with SP2, Windows XP with SP1 with the Advanced Networking Pack for Windows XP, and Windows Server 2003 with Service Pack 1 has an on-link default route (::/0) that uses the Teredo tunneling interface. When this default route is used, IPv6 sets the next-hop address to the destination address in the IPv6 packet and the next-hop interface to the Teredo tunneling interface.

When the Teredo tunneling interface forwards the packet, it distinguishes the following three cases:

1. The destination is a Teredo client on the same IPv4 link.

2. The destination is a Teredo client that is in another site.

3. The destination is a node on the IPv6 Internet.

On-Link Teredo Client Destinations

For packets destined for another Teredo client on the same link, the Teredo tunneling interface uses an exchange of bubble packets as the substitute for the address resolution process of Neighbor Discovery. The exchange of bubble packets assures Teredo clients that they can begin sending packets directly to each other. For more information, see the "Initial Communication Between Teredo Clients on the Same Link" section later in this chapter.

To determine whether a destination Teredo address corresponds to a Teredo client on the same link, a Teredo client checks its multicast bubble cache. Each Teredo client sends out multicast bubble packets on its IPv4 link to indicate its presence on the link. Each Teredo client receives the multicast bubble packets of other Teredo clients and adds their Teredo addresses and IPv4 addresses to the multicast bubble cache. Therefore, if the destination Teredo address is in the multicast bubble cache, the destination is an on-link neighbor.

Intersite Teredo Client Destinations

For packets destined for another Teredo client in a different site, the Teredo tunneling interface uses bubble packets as the substitute for the address resolution process of Neighbor Discovery when both Teredo clients are across restricted NATs. The exchange of bubble packets creates address and port-specific mappings in both restricted NATs so that the two Teredo clients can send packets directly to each other. For more information, see the "Initial Communication Between Teredo Clients in Different Sites" section later in this chapter.

IPv6 Internet Destinations

For packets destined for the IPv6 Internet, the Teredo tunneling interface uses ICMPv6 Echo Request and Echo Reply messages as substitutes for the address resolution process of Neighbor Discovery. An ICMPv6 Echo Request message is sent to the destination. The ICMP Echo Reply message that is returned contains the IPv4 address of the Teredo relay closest to the IPv6 host on the IPv6 Internet. For more information, see the "Initial Communication from a Teredo Client to a Teredo Host-Specific Relay" and "Initial Communication from a Teredo Client to an IPv6-Only Host" sections later in this chapter.

Teredo Processes

This section provides details on the set of Teredo packets exchanged to perform the following:

- Initial configuration for Teredo clients
- Maintaining the NAT mapping
- Initial communication between Teredo clients on the same link
- Initial communication between Teredo clients in different sites
- Initial communication from a Teredo client to a Teredo host-specific relay
- Initial communication from a Teredo host-specific relay to a Teredo client
- Initial communication from a Teredo client to an IPv6-only host
- Initial communication from an IPv6-only host to a Teredo client

All of these processes are supported by the Teredo client in Windows Server 2008, Windows Vista, Windows XP with SP2, Windows XP with SP1 with the Advanced Networking Pack for

Windows XP, and Windows Server 2003 with Service Pack 1 and are performed automatically, without requiring configuration or intervention from the user.

Initial Configuration for Teredo Clients

Initial configuration for Teredo clients is accomplished by sending a series of Router Solicitation messages to Teredo servers to determine a Teredo address and whether the client is behind a cone, restricted, or symmetric NAT. Figure 14-11 shows the initial configuration process defined in RFC 4380.

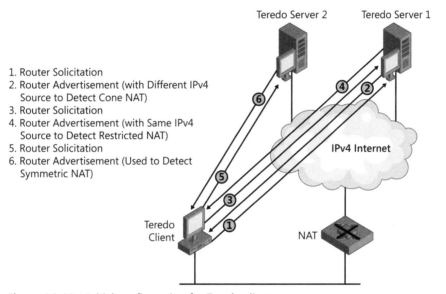

1. Router Solicitation
2. Router Advertisement (with Different IPv4 Source to Detect Cone NAT)
3. Router Solicitation
4. Router Advertisement (with Same IPv4 Source to Detect Restricted NAT)
5. Router Solicitation
6. Router Advertisement (Used to Detect Symmetric NAT)

Figure 14-11   Initial configuration for Teredo clients

This initial configuration for Teredo clients consists of the following process:

1. The Teredo client sends a Router Solicitation message to a preferred Teredo server (Teredo Server 1). The Teredo client sends the router solicitation from a link-local address for which the Cone flag is set.

2. Teredo Server 1 responds with a Router Advertisement message. Because the router solicitation had the Cone flag set, Teredo Server 1 sends the router advertisement from an alternate IPv4 address. If the Teredo client receives the router advertisement, it determines that it is behind a cone NAT.

3. If a router advertisement is not received, the Teredo client sends another router solicitation from a link-local address for which the Cone flag is not set.

4. Teredo Server 1 responds with a router advertisement. Because the router solicitation did not have the Cone flag set, Teredo Server 1 sends the router advertisement from the source IPv4 address corresponding to the destination IPv4 address of the router

solicitation. If the Teredo client receives the router advertisement, it determines that it is behind a restricted NAT.

5. To determine whether the Teredo client is behind a symmetric NAT, it sends another router advertisement to a secondary Teredo server (Teredo Server 2).

6. Teredo Server 2 responds with a router advertisement. The Teredo client compares the mapped addresses and UDP ports in the Origin indicators of the router advertisements received by both Teredo servers. If they are different, the NAT is mapping the same internal address and port number to different external addresses and port numbers. The Teredo client determines that the NAT is a symmetric NAT.

Based on the received router advertisement (step 2 or 4 in the previous process), the Teredo client constructs its Teredo address from the following:

- The first 64 bits are set to the value included in the Prefix Information option of the received router advertisement. The 64-bit prefix advertised by the Teredo server consists of the Teredo prefix (32 bits) and the IPv4 address of the Teredo server (32 bits).

- The next 16 bits are the Flags field.

- The next 16 bits are set to the obscured external UDP port number from the Origin indicator in the router advertisement.

- The last 32 bits are set to the obscured external IPv4 address from the Origin indicator in the router advertisement.

Teredo clients running Windows Server 2008 or Windows Vista skip the detection for cone NATs and attempt to detect a symmetric NAT by sending router solicitations to both its primary and secondary Teredo server and comparing the Origin indicators from the received router advertisements.

The Teredo client in Windows Server 2008, Windows Vista, Windows XP with SP2, Windows XP with SP1 with the Advanced Networking Pack for Windows XP, and Windows Server 2003 with Service Pack 1 automatically attempts to determine the IPv4 addresses of Teredo servers by resolving the name teredo.ipv6.microsoft.com. You can use the **netsh interface teredo set state servername**=*NameOrAddress* command to configure the DNS name or IPv4 address of a Teredo server.

Network Monitor Capture

Here is an example of a Teredo-encapsulated router advertisement from a Teredo client on the IPv4 Internet to a Teredo server as displayed by Network Monitor 3.1 (frame 1 of capture 14_01 in the \NetworkMonitorCaptures folder on the companion CD-ROM):

```
Frame:
+ Ethernet: Etype = Internet IP (IPv4)
- Ipv4: Next Protocol = UDP, Packet ID = 1967, Total IP Length = 105
  + Versions: IPv4, Internet Protocol; Header Length = 20
  + DifferentiatedServicesField: DSCP: 0, ECN: 0
```

```
    TotalLength: 105 (0x69)
    Identification: 1967 (0x7AF)
  + FragmentFlags: 0 (0x0)
    TimeToLive: 128 (0x80)
    NextProtocol: UDP, 17(0x11)
    Checksum: 42382 (0xA58E)
    SourceAddress: 71.112.33.18
    DestinationAddress: 65.54.227.142
- Udp: SrcPort = 1151, DstPort = Teredo Servers(3544), Length = 85
    SourcePort: 1151, 1151(0x47f)
    DestinationPort: Teredo Servers(3544), 3544(0xdd8)
    TotalLength: 85 (0x55)
    Checksum: 39434 (0x9A0A)
- Teredo: Tunneling IPv6 over UDP through NATs, No Authentication
  - AuthenticationHeader:
    AuthenticationIndicator: 1 (0x1)
    IDLen: 0 (0x0)
    AULen: 0 (0x0)
    NonceValue: 0x0
    Confirmation: The client's key is still valid, 0(0x0)
  - TunnelingIpv6: Next Protocol = ICMPv6, Payload Length = 24
  + Versions: IPv6, Internet Protocol, DSCP 0
    PayloadLength: 24 (0x18)
    NextProtocol: ICMPv6, 58(0x3a)
    HopLimit: 255 (0xFF)
    SourceAddress: FE80:0:0:0:8000:FFFF:FFFF:FFFD
    DestinationAddress: FF02:0:0:0:0:0:0:2
  - Icmpv6: Router Solicitation
    MessageType: Router Solicitation, 133(0x85)
  + RouterSolicitation:
  + SourceLinkLayerAddress:
```

In the IPv4 header, the packet is addressed from 71.112.33.18, the public IPv4 address of the Teredo client, to 65.54.227.142, the public IPv4 address of a Teredo server. The packet contains the Authentication indicator with no authentication information present. In the IPv6 header, the packet is addressed from a link-local address assigned to the Teredo tunneling interface to the link-local scope, all-routers multicast address.

The following is the corresponding Teredo-encapsulated router advertisement message from the Teredo server as displayed by Network Monitor 3.1 (frame 2 of capture 14_01):

```
  Frame:
+ Ethernet: Etype = Internet IP (IPv4)
- Ipv4: Next Protocol = UDP, Packet ID = 40784, Total IP Length = 137
  + Versions: IPv4, Internet Protocol; Header Length = 20
  + DifferentiatedServicesField: DSCP: 0, ECN: 0
    TotalLength: 137 (0x89)
    Identification: 40784 (0x9F50)
  + FragmentFlags: 0 (0x0)
    TimeToLive: 118 (0x76)
    NextProtocol: UDP, 17(0x11)
    Checksum: 6092 (0x17CC)
    SourceAddress: 65.54.227.143
    DestinationAddress: 71.112.33.18
```

```
- Udp: SrcPort = Teredo Servers(3544), DstPort = 1151, Length = 117
    SourcePort: Teredo Servers(3544), 3544(0xdd8)
    DestinationPort: 1151, 1151(0x47f)
    TotalLength: 117 (0x75)
    Checksum: 39734 (0x9B36)
- Teredo: Tunneling IPv6 over UDP through NATs, No Authentication,
  OriginAddress = 71.112.33.18, OriginPort = 1151
  - AuthenticationHeader:
    AuthenticationIndicator: 1 (0x1)
    IDLen: 0 (0x0)
    AULen: 0 (0x0)
    NonceValue: 0x0
    Confirmation: The client's key is still valid, 0(0x0)
  - OriginHeader:
    OriginIndicator: 0 (0x0)
    OriginPort: 1151 (0x047F)
    OriginIPv4Address: 71.112.33.18
  - TunnelingIpv6: Next Protocol = ICMPv6, Payload Length = 48
  + Versions: IPv6, Internet Protocol, DSCP 0
    PayloadLength: 48 (0x30)
    NextProtocol: ICMPv6, 58(0x3a)
    HopLimit: 255 (0xFF)
    SourceAddress: FE80:0:0:0:8000:F227:BEC9:1C71
    DestinationAddress: FE80:0:0:0:8000:FFFF:FFFF:FFFD
  - Icmpv6: Router Advertisement
    MessageType: Router Advertisement, 134(0x86)
  + RouterAdvertisement:
  - PrefixInformation:
    Type: Prefix Information, 3(0x3)
    Length: 4, in unit of 8 octets
    PrefixLength: 64 (0x40)
  - Flags: 64 (0x40)
    L:  (0.......) Not on-Link specification
    A:  (.1......) Autonomous address-configuration
    R:  (..0.....) Not router Address
    S:  (...0....) Not a site prefix
    P:  (....0...) Not a router prefix
    Rsv: (.....000)
    ValidLifetime: 4294967295 (0xFFFFFFFF)
    PreferredLifetime: 4294967295 (0xFFFFFFFF)
    Reserved: 0 (0x0)
    Prefix: 2001:0:4136:E38E:0:0:0:0
```

This packet contains the Authentication indicator and the Origin indicator. Because this Teredo client was not behind a NAT, the public IPv4 address and UDP port number in the Origin indicator is the same as the destination IPv4 address and UDP port of the packet. In the IPv6 header, the packet is addressed from a link-local address of the Teredo server to the link-local address of the Teredo client. The router advertisement contains a Prefix Information option for the prefix formed from the Teredo prefix and the colon hexadecimal representation of the Teredo server's public IPv4 address (65.54.227.143 is 4136:E38E).

Maintaining the NAT Mapping

Figure 14-12 shows how Teredo clients that are behind a NAT maintain the NAT mapping for Teredo traffic.

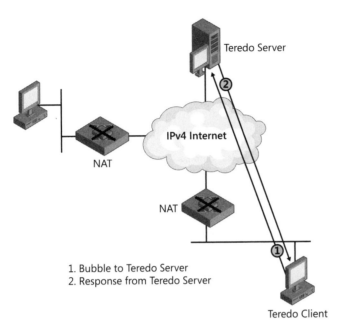

Figure 14-12   Maintaining the NAT mapping

On a periodic basis, Teredo clients send a single bubble packet to their Teredo server. The Teredo server discards the bubble packet and sends a response. The periodic bubble packet refreshes the IP address/UDP port mapping in the NAT's translation table. Otherwise, the mapping becomes stale and is removed. If the mapping is not present, all inbound Teredo traffic (for a cone NAT) or inbound Teredo traffic from the Teredo server (restricted NAT) to the Teredo client is silently discarded by the NAT. From the response, the Teredo client can determine if the external address and port number for its Teredo traffic have changed.

You can configure how often a Windows-based Teredo client refreshes its NAT mapping with the **netsh interface teredo set state refreshinterval**=*Seconds* command. The default refresh interval is 30 seconds.

Initial Communication Between Teredo Clients on the Same Link

Figure 14-13 shows the initial communication between Teredo clients on the same link.

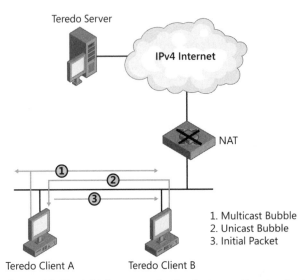

Figure 14-13   Initial communication between Teredo clients on the same link

To send an initial communication packet from Teredo Client A to Teredo Client B on the same link, the following process is used:

1.   Teredo Client A sends a bubble packet to the Teredo IPv4 Discovery Address of 224.0.0.253, a reserved IPv4 multicast address. In the IPv6 header of the bubble packet, the destination address is set to the link-local scope, all-nodes multicast address (FF02::1).

2.   Upon receipt of the multicast bubble packet from Teredo Client A, Teredo Client B determines the on-link IPv4 address of Teredo Client A and the UDP port used for Teredo traffic and sends a unicast bubble packet to Teredo Client A in response. Upon receipt of the unicast bubble packet from Teredo Client B, Teredo Client A determines the on-link IPv4 address of Teredo Client A and the UDP port used for Teredo traffic.

3.   Teredo Client A sends an initial communication packet to Teredo Client B.

Initial Communication Between Teredo Clients in Different Sites

Initial communication between Teredo clients in different sites depends on whether the sites are using cone NATs or restricted NATs.

Cone NAT

Figure 14-14 shows the initial communication between Teredo clients in different sites when both sites are using cone NATs.

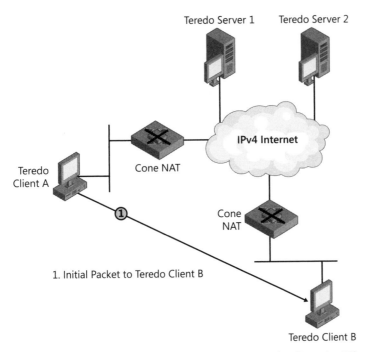

Figure 14-14   Initial communication between Teredo clients in different sites with cone NATs

When both Teredo clients are located behind cone NATs, the NAT translation table entry for Teredo traffic for each Teredo client allows traffic from any source IP address or source UDP port. Therefore, Teredo Client A can send packets directly to Teredo Client B without the use of bubble packets to establish additional NAT translation table entries.

Restricted NAT

Figure 14-15 shows the initial communication between Teredo clients in different sites when both sites are using restricted NATs.

To send an initial communication packet from Teredo Client A to Teredo Client B, the following process is used:

1. Teredo Client A sends a bubble packet directly to Teredo Client B. Because Teredo Client B is behind a restricted NAT, Teredo traffic from an arbitrary source IPv4 address and UDP port number is not allowed unless there is a source-specific NAT translation table entry. Assuming that there is none, the restricted NAT silently discards the bubble packet. However, when the restricted NAT for Teredo Client A forwarded the bubble packet, it created a source-specific NAT translation table entry that will allow future packets sent from Teredo Client B to be forwarded to Teredo Client A.

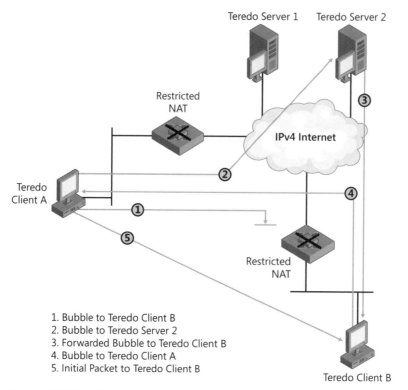

1. Bubble to Teredo Client B
2. Bubble to Teredo Server 2
3. Forwarded Bubble to Teredo Client B
4. Bubble to Teredo Client A
5. Initial Packet to Teredo Client B

Figure 14-15 Initial communication between Teredo clients in different sites with restricted NATs

2. Teredo Client A sends a bubble packet to Teredo Client B via Teredo Server 2 (Teredo Client B's Teredo server). The IPv4 destination address in the bubble is set to the IPv4 address of Teredo Server 2, which Teredo Client A determines from the third and fourth blocks of Teredo Client B's Teredo address.

3. Teredo Server 2 processes the packet, determines that the IPv6 destination address is for a Teredo client, and then forwards the bubble packet to Teredo Client B. The restricted NAT for Teredo Client B forwards the packet because there is an existing source-specific mapping for Teredo traffic from Teredo Server 2.

4. Teredo Client B responds to the bubble packet received from Teredo Client A with its own bubble packet sent directly to Teredo Client A. Because Teredo Client A's restricted NAT has a source-specific mapping for Teredo traffic from Teredo Client B (as established by the initial bubble packet sent from Teredo Client A in step 1), the bubble packet is forwarded to Teredo Client A.

5. Upon receipt of the bubble packet from Teredo Client B, Teredo Client A determines that source-specific NAT mappings exist for both NATs. Teredo Client A sends an initial communication packet directly to Teredo Client B.

Initial Communication from a Teredo Client to a Teredo Host-Specific Relay

Initial communication from a Teredo client to a Teredo host-specific relay depends on whether the Teredo client is behind a cone NAT or restricted NAT.

Cone NAT

Figure 14-16 shows the initial communication from a Teredo client to a Teredo host-specific relay when the Teredo client is located behind a cone NAT.

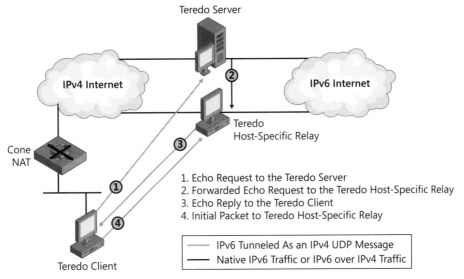

Figure 14-16   Initial communication from a Teredo client to a Teredo host-specific relay with a cone NAT

To send an initial communication packet from the Teredo client to the Teredo host-specific relay, the following process is used:

1. Teredo Client A sends an ICMPv6 Echo Request message to the Teredo host-specific relay via its own Teredo server.

2. The Teredo server receives the ICMPv6 Echo Request message and forwards it to the Teredo host-specific relay over the IPv6 Internet or tunneled over the IPv4 Internet.

3. The Teredo host-specific relay responds with an ICMPv6 Echo Reply message sent to Teredo Client A's Teredo address. Because the Teredo host-specific relay has a Teredo route (2001::/32) and a Teredo tunneling interface, the Teredo host-specific relay sends the packet directly to Teredo Client A.

4. After receiving the Echo Reply from the Teredo host-specific relay, the Teredo client sends an initial communication packet to the IPv4 address and UDP port of the Teredo host-specific relay.

All subsequent packets between the Teredo client and the Teredo host-specific relay are sent directly.

Restricted NAT

Figure 14-17 shows the initial communication from a Teredo client to a Teredo host-specific relay when the Teredo client is located behind a restricted NAT.

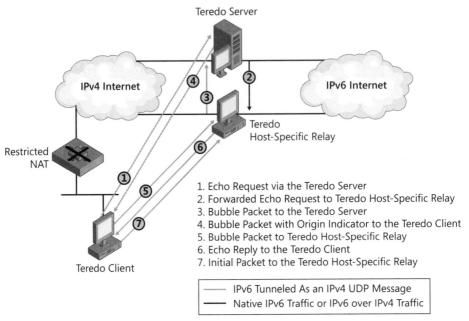

1. Echo Request via the Teredo Server
2. Forwarded Echo Request to Teredo Host-Specific Relay
3. Bubble Packet to the Teredo Server
4. Bubble Packet with Origin Indicator to the Teredo Client
5. Bubble Packet to Teredo Host-Specific Relay
6. Echo Reply to the Teredo Client
7. Initial Packet to the Teredo Host-Specific Relay

------- IPv6 Tunneled As an IPv4 UDP Message
——— Native IPv6 Traffic or IPv6 over IPv4 Traffic

Figure 14-17   Initial communication from a Teredo client to a Teredo host-specific relay with a restricted NAT

To send an initial communication packet from the Teredo client to the Teredo host-specific relay, the following process is used:

1. The Teredo client sends an ICMPv6 Echo Request message to the Teredo host-specific relay via its own Teredo server.

2. The Teredo server receives the ICMPv6 Echo Request message and forwards it to the Teredo host-specific relay over the IPv6 Internet or tunneled over the IPv4 Internet.

3. The Teredo host-specific relay determines that the Teredo client is behind a restricted NAT. If the Teredo relay were to send the ICMPv6 Echo Request message to the Teredo client, the NAT would silently discard it because there is no source-specific mapping for Teredo traffic from the Teredo host-specific relay. Therefore, the Teredo host-specific relay sends a bubble packet to the Teredo client via the Teredo server over the IPv4 Internet.

4. The Teredo server receives the bubble packet from the Teredo host-specific relay. The Teredo server forwards the bubble packet to the Teredo client, with an Origin indicator that contains the IPv4 address and UDP port number of the Teredo host-specific relay. Because a source-specific mapping for Teredo traffic from the Teredo server exists in the NAT, the bubble packet is forwarded to the Teredo client.

5. The Teredo client determines the IPv4 address and UDP port of the Teredo host-specific relay from the Origin indicator of the received bubble packet. To establish a source-specific mapping for Teredo traffic from the Teredo host-specific relay, the Teredo client sends a bubble packet to the Teredo host-specific relay.

6. Based on the receipt of the bubble packet from the Teredo client that corresponds to a packet that is queued for forwarding (the ICMPv6 Echo Reply message), the Teredo host-specific relay determines that a source-specific NAT mapping now exists in the restricted NAT of the Teredo client. The Teredo host-specific relay forwards the ICMPv6 Echo Reply message to the Teredo client.

7. An initial communication packet is sent from the Teredo client to the IPv4 address and UDP port of the Teredo host-specific relay.

All subsequent packets between the Teredo client and the Teredo host-specific relay are sent directly.

Initial Communication from a Teredo Host-Specific Relay to a Teredo Client

Initial communication from a Teredo host-specific relay to a Teredo client depends on whether the Teredo client is behind a cone NAT or restricted NAT.

Cone NAT

Figure 14-18 shows the initial communication from a Teredo host-specific relay to a Teredo client when the Teredo client is located behind a cone NAT.

To send an initial communication packet from the Teredo host-specific relay to the Teredo client, the Teredo host-specific relay determines that the Teredo client is behind a cone NAT. Therefore, it sends the initial communication packet directly to the Teredo client.

To ensure that the IPv6 address of the initial communication packet has not been spoofed and corresponds to the Teredo host-specific relay, the Teredo client performs an ICMPv6 Echo Request/Echo Reply message exchange with the Teredo host-specific relay using steps 1 through 3 of the "Initial Communication from a Teredo Client to a Teredo Host-Specific Relay" (for a cone NAT) section of this chapter. After this exchange is complete, the Teredo client sends the response to the initial communication packet to the Teredo host-specific relay.

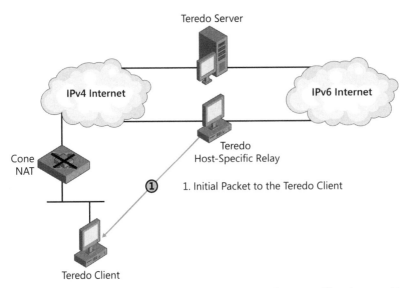

Figure 14-18 Initial communication from a Teredo host-specific relay to a Teredo client with a cone NAT

Restricted NAT

Figure 14-19 shows the initial communication from a Teredo host-specific relay to a Teredo client when the Teredo client is located behind a restricted NAT.

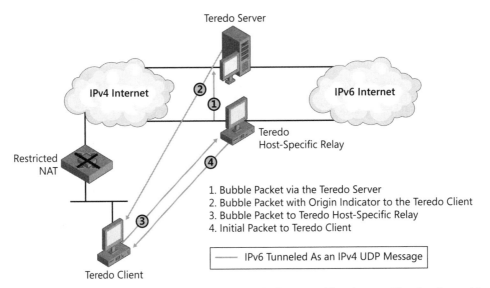

Figure 14-19 Initial communication from a Teredo host-specific relay to a Teredo client with a restricted NAT

To send an initial communication packet from the Teredo host-specific relay to the Teredo client, the following process is used:

1. The Teredo host-specific relay sends a bubble packet to the Teredo client via the Teredo server over the IPv4 Internet.

2. The Teredo server receives the bubble packet from the Teredo host-specific relay. The Teredo server forwards the bubble to the Teredo client, with an Origin indicator that contains the IPv4 address and UDP port number of the Teredo host-specific relay. Because a source-specific mapping for Teredo traffic from the Teredo server exists in the NAT, the bubble packet is forwarded to the Teredo client.

3. The Teredo client determines the IPv4 address and UDP port of the Teredo host-specific relay from the Origin indicator of the received bubble packet. To establish a source-specific mapping for Teredo traffic from the Teredo relay, the Teredo client sends a bubble packet to the Teredo host-specific relay.

4. Based on the receipt of the bubble packet that corresponds to a packet that is queued for forwarding (the packet from the Teredo host-specific relay), the Teredo host-specific relay determines that a source-specific NAT mapping now exists in the restricted NAT of the Teredo client. The Teredo host-specific relay sends the initial communication packet to the Teredo client.

To ensure that the IPv6 address of the initial communication packet has not been spoofed and corresponds to the Teredo host-specific relay, the Teredo client performs an ICMPv6 Echo Request/Echo Reply message exchange with the Teredo host-specific relay using steps 1 through 6 of the "Initial Communication from a Teredo Client to a Teredo Host-Specific Relay" (for a restricted NAT) section of this chapter. After this exchange is complete, the Teredo client sends the response to the initial communication packet to the Teredo host-specific relay.

Initial Communication from a Teredo Client to an IPv6-Only Host

Initial communication from a Teredo client to an IPv6-only host depends on whether the Teredo client is behind a cone NAT or restricted NAT.

Cone NAT

Figure 14-20 shows the initial communication from a Teredo client to an IPv6-only host when the Teredo client is located behind a cone NAT.

To send an initial communication packet from Teredo client to the IPv6-only host, the following process is used:

1. To send an initial communication packet to the IPv6-only host, the Teredo client must first determine the IPv4 address and UDP port of the Teredo relay that is nearest to the IPv6-only host. The Teredo client sends an ICMPv6 Echo Request message to the IPv6-only host via its own Teredo server.

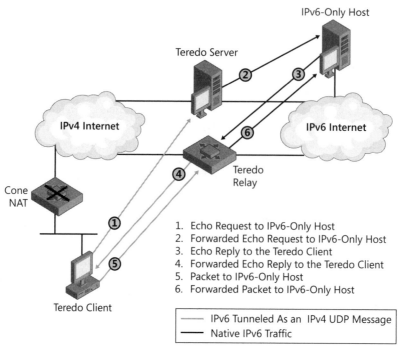

Figure 14-20   Initial communication from a Teredo client to an IPv6-only host with a cone NAT

2. The Teredo server receives the ICMPv6 Echo Request message and forwards it to the IPv6-only host over the IPv6 Internet.

3. The IPv6-only host responds with an ICMPv6 Echo Reply sent to Teredo Client A's Teredo address. Because of the routing infrastructure of the IPv6 Internet, the Teredo addressed packet is forwarded to the nearest Teredo relay.

4. The Teredo relay encapsulates the ICMPv6 Echo Reply message and sends it directly to the Teredo client. Because the NAT is a cone NAT, the packet from the Teredo relay is forwarded to the Teredo client.

5. The Teredo client determines the IPv4 address of the Teredo relay closest to the IPv6-only host from the source IPv4 address and UDP port of the ICMPv6 Echo Reply message. An initial communication packet is sent from the Teredo client to the IPv4 address and UDP port of the Teredo relay.

6. The Teredo relay removes the IPv4 and UDP headers and forwards the packet to the IPv6-only host.

All subsequent packets sent between the Teredo client and the IPv6-only host take this path via the Teredo relay.

Restricted NAT

Figure 14-21 shows the initial communication from a Teredo client to an IPv6-only host when the Teredo client is located behind a restricted NAT.

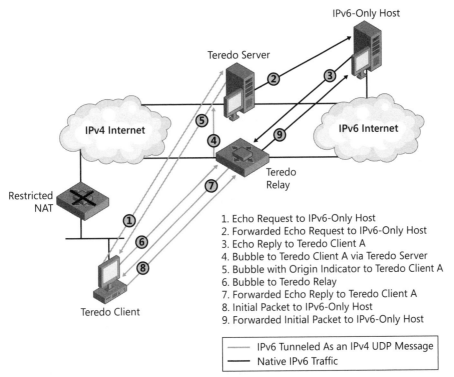

1. Echo Request to IPv6-Only Host
2. Forwarded Echo Request to IPv6-Only Host
3. Echo Reply to Teredo Client A
4. Bubble to Teredo Client A via Teredo Server
5. Bubble with Origin Indicator to Teredo Client A
6. Bubble to Teredo Relay
7. Forwarded Echo Reply to Teredo Client A
8. Initial Packet to IPv6-Only Host
9. Forwarded Initial Packet to IPv6-Only Host

.... IPv6 Tunneled As an IPv4 UDP Message
——— Native IPv6 Traffic

Figure 14-21 Initial communication from a Teredo client to an IPv6-only host with a restricted NAT

To send an initial communication packet from the Teredo client to the IPv6-only host, the following process is used:

1. To send an initial communication packet to the IPv6-only host, the Teredo client must first determine the IPv4 address of the Teredo relay that is nearest to the IPv6-only host. Teredo Client A sends an ICMPv6 Echo Request message to the IPv6-only host via its own Teredo server.

2. The Teredo server receives the ICMPv6 Echo Request message and forwards it to the IPv6-only host over the IPv6 Internet.

3. The IPv6-only host responds with an ICMPv6 Echo Reply sent to Teredo Client A's Teredo address. Because of the routing infrastructure of the IPv6 Internet, the Teredo addressed packet is forwarded to the nearest Teredo relay.

4. The Teredo relay determines that the Teredo client is behind a restricted NAT. If the Teredo relay were to send the ICMPv6 Echo Request message to the Teredo client, the

NAT would silently discard it because there is no source-specific mapping for Teredo traffic from the Teredo relay. Therefore, the Teredo relay sends a bubble packet to the Teredo client via the Teredo server over the IPv4 Internet.

5. The Teredo server receives the bubble packet from the Teredo relay. The Teredo server forwards the bubble packet to the Teredo client, with an Origin indicator that contains the IPv4 address and UDP port number of the Teredo relay. Because a source-specific mapping for Teredo traffic from the Teredo server exists in the NAT, the bubble packet is forwarded to the Teredo client.

6. The Teredo client determines the IPv4 address of the Teredo relay closest to the IPv6-only host from the Origin indicator of the received bubble packet. To establish a source-specific mapping for Teredo traffic from the Teredo relay, the Teredo client sends a bubble packet to the Teredo relay.

7. Based on the receipt of the bubble packet that corresponds to a packet that is queued for forwarding (the ICMPv6 Echo Reply message), the Teredo relay determines that a source-specific NAT mapping now exists in the restricted NAT of the Teredo client. The Teredo relay forwards the ICMPv6 Echo Reply message to the Teredo client.

8. An initial communication packet is sent from the Teredo client to the IPv4 address and UDP port of the Teredo relay.

9. The Teredo relay removes the IPv4 and UDP headers and forwards the packet to the IPv6-only host.

All subsequent packets sent between the Teredo client and the IPv6-only host takes this path via the Teredo relay.

Initial Communication from an IPv6-Only Host to a Teredo Client

Initial communication from an IPv6-only host to a Teredo client depends on whether the Teredo client is behind a cone NAT or restricted NAT.

Cone NAT

Figure 14-22 shows the initial communication from an IPv6-only host to a Teredo client when the Teredo client is located behind a cone NAT.

To send an initial communication packet from the IPv6-only host to the Teredo client, the following process is used:

1. The IPv6-only host sends an initial communication packet to the Teredo client. Because of the routing infrastructure of the IPv6 Internet, the Teredo-addressed packet is forwarded to the nearest Teredo relay.

2. The Teredo relay determines that the Teredo client is behind a cone NAT. Therefore, it forwards the packet from the IPv6-only host, encapsulated with IPv4 and UDP headers, to the Teredo client.

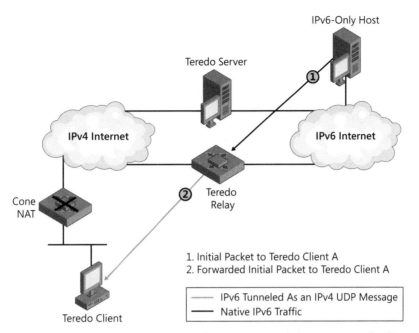

Figure 14-22   Initial communication from an IPv6-only host to a Teredo client with a cone NAT

Upon receipt of this packet, the Teredo client stores the IPv4 address and UDP port corresponding to the Teredo relay so that response packets can be forwarded to the Teredo relay, which receives them, removes the IPv4 and UDP headers, and forwards the IPv6 packet to the IPv6-only host.

To ensure that the IPv6 address of the initial communication packet has not been spoofed and corresponds to the IPv6-only host, the Teredo client performs an ICMPv6 Echo Request/ Echo Reply message exchange with the IPv6-only host using steps 1 through 4 of the "Initial Communication from a Teredo Client to an IPv6-Only Host" (for a cone NAT) section of this chapter. After this exchange is complete, the Teredo client sends the response to the initial communication packet to the IPv6-only host.

Restricted NAT

Figure 14-23 shows the initial communication from an IPv6-only host to a Teredo client when the Teredo client is located behind a restricted NAT.

To send an initial communication packet from the IPv6-only host to the Teredo client, the following process is used:

1. The IPv6-only host sends a packet to the Teredo client. Because of the routing infrastructure of the IPv6 Internet, the Teredo-addressed packet is forwarded to the nearest Teredo relay.

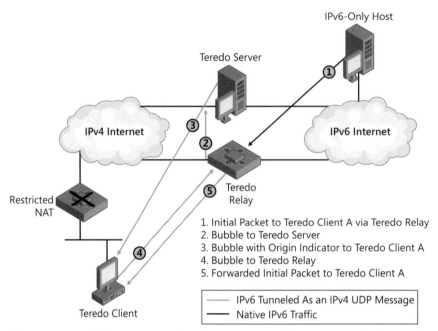

Figure 14-23   Initial communication from an IPv6-only host to a Teredo client with a restricted NAT

2. The Teredo relay determines that the Teredo client is behind a restricted NAT. If the Teredo relay were to send the packet to the Teredo client, the NAT would silently discard it because there is no source-specific mapping for Teredo traffic from the Teredo relay. Therefore, the Teredo relay sends a bubble packet to the Teredo client via the Teredo server over the IPv4 Internet.

3. The Teredo server receives the bubble packet from the Teredo relay. The Teredo server forwards the bubble to the Teredo client, with an Origin indicator that contains the IPv4 address and UDP port number of the Teredo relay. Because a source-specific mapping for Teredo traffic from the Teredo server exists in the NAT, the bubble packet is forwarded to the Teredo client.

4. The Teredo client determines the IPv4 address of the Teredo relay closest to the IPv6-only host from the Origin indicator of the received bubble packet. To establish a source-specific mapping for Teredo traffic from the Teredo relay, the Teredo client sends a bubble packet to the Teredo relay.

5. Based on the receipt of the bubble packet that corresponds to a packet that is queued for forwarding (the packet from the IPv6-only host), the Teredo relay determines that a source-specific NAT mapping now exists in the restricted NAT of the Teredo client. The Teredo relay forwards the packet to the Teredo client.

To ensure that the IPv6 address of the initial communication packet has not been spoofed and corresponds to the IPv6-only host, the Teredo client performs an ICMPv6 Echo Request/Echo

Reply message exchange with the IPv6-only host using steps 1 through 7 of the "Initial Communication from a Teredo Client to an IPv6-Only Host" (for a restricted NAT) section of this chapter. After this exchange is complete, the Teredo client sends the response to the initial communication packet to the IPv6-only host.

References

The following references were cited in this chapter:

- RFC 1631 – "The IP Network Address Translator (NAT)"
- RFC 4380 – "Teredo: Tunneling IPv6 over UDP through Network Address Translations (NATs)"

You can obtain these RFCs from the \RFCs_and_Drafts folder on the companion CD-ROM or from *http://www.ietf.org/rfc.html*.

Testing for Understanding

To test your understanding of Teredo, answer the following questions. See Appendix D, "Testing for Understanding Answers," to check your answers.

1. Describe the intended use of the Teredo IPv6 transition technology.

2. How can you recognize a Teredo address?

3. How are the source and destination addresses in the encapsulating IPv4 header determined for Teredo-tunneled traffic to another Teredo client?

4. Why are portions of the Teredo address obscured?

5. What is the difference between a Teredo relay and a Teredo host-specific relay?

6. A Teredo client has the address 2001::62C3:1B8D:346B:EBC9:7C94:EA26. Is this client behind a cone NAT or a restricted NAT? What is the public IPv4 address of its Teredo server? What are the external IPv4 address and UDP port number for this Teredo client's Teredo traffic?

7. How does a Teredo client determine the external IPv4 address and UDP port number for its traffic during the Teredo address configuration process?

8. Initial communication between two Teredo clients in different sites when both Teredo clients are behind restricted NATs requires four more packets than when both Teredo clients are behind cone NATs. What is the purpose of these four additional packets?

9. How does a Teredo client determine the public IPv4 address of the Teredo relay when initiating communication to a host on the IPv6 Internet?

Chapter 15
IPv6 Security Considerations

At the end of this chapter, you should be able to do the following:

- Describe how to prevent unauthorized hosts from obtaining automatic Internet Protocol version 6 (IPv6) configuration.
- Describe how to provide protection for IPv6 packets.
- Describe how to protect IPv6 hosts from address and port scanning attacks.
- Describe how to control what traffic is exchanged with the Internet.

IPv6 Security Considerations

Before deploying IPv6 you should be aware of the following aspects of security for IPv6 traffic:

- Authorization for automatically assigned addresses and configurations
- Protection of IPv6 packets
- Host protection from scanning and attacks
- Control of what traffic is exchanged with the Internet

The following sections describe each of these aspects of security and provide recommendations and best practices for computers running Windows Server 2008 or Windows Vista.

Authorization for Automatically Assigned Addresses and Configurations

After gaining access to an intranet, any computer can obtain a valid IPv6 address configuration through stateless or stateful address autoconfiguration and begin communicating on the network. IPv6 hosts can use the following methods to obtain an address configuration:

- Neighbor Discovery (ND) with an exchange of Router Solicitation and Router Advertisement messages, as defined in RFC 4861
- Dynamic Host Configuration Protocol for IPv6 (DHCPv6), as defined in RFC 3315

For more information about ND and DHCPv6, see Chapter 8, "Address Autoconfiguration."

For ND-based IPv6 configuration, SEcure Neighbor Discovery (SEND) (defined in RFC 3971) can provide protection for Router Solicitation and Router Advertisement messages. SEND can also provide protection for Neighbor Solicitation and Neighbor Advertisement message exchanges for address resolution or neighbor unreachability detection. This provides protection against ND-based denial of service (DoS) attacks by nodes with manually config-ured IPv6 addresses, which are not derived from an exchange of Router Solicitation and Router Advertisement messages. In contrast, there is no protection against Address Resolution Protocol (ARP) DoS attacks for IPv4. However, IPv6 in Windows Server 2008 and Windows Vista does not support SEND.

RFC 3118 defines a method to authenticate message exchanges for stateful address configura-tion with DHCPv6. IPv6 in Windows Server 2008 and Windows Vista supports DHCPv6 but does not support RFC 3118.

Another configuration consideration is that IPv6 hosts can configure additional routes based on received Router Advertisement messages. A malicious node could configure IPv6 hosts with improper routes and disrupt IPv6-based network connectivity. IPv6 nodes that support RFC 4191 can detect unreachable routes and prevent them from being added to the IPv6 routing table. IPv6 in Windows Server 2008 and Windows Vista supports RFC 4191.

Recommendations

To prevent unauthorized computers from communicating on intranets, the recommendation is that you use IEEE 802.1X authentication to authenticate all computers that are connecting to your network with wired or wireless connections. With IEEE 802.1X–based authentication at the link layer, computers cannot send any network traffic until they have authenticated themselves to a switch or wireless access point. Only after a successful IEEE 802.1X authenti-cation can an IPv6 host use address autoconfiguration protocols such as ND or DHCPv6 to obtain an automatically assigned IPv6 address configuration.

In Windows Server 2008 and Windows Vista, the Network Access Protection (NAP) platform provides additional protection for 802.1X-authenticated connections by requiring that com-puters meet system health requirements before obtaining a connection that allows unlimited access to the intranet. For more information about NAP, see *http://www.microsoft.com/nap*.

Protection of IPv6 Packets

To help protect IPv6 packets from tampering (data modification) and interpretation (passive capturing) by intermediate or neighboring nodes, IPv6 packets can be protected with Internet Protocol security (IPsec). IPsec uses cryptographic security services to provide tampering protection, spoofing protection, and optional encryption for IP packets. IPsec is defined in RFCs 4301, 4302, and 4303 for both IPv4 and IPv6 traffic.

Windows Server 2008 and Windows Vista provide full support for IPsec for both IPv4 and IPv6 with negotiation of security associations using Internet Key Exchange (IKE) or Authen-ticated IP (AuthIP), automatic determination of cryptographic keys, and a graphical user interface to configure IPsec policy settings. You can configure IPsec policy settings as part of Computer Configuration Group Policy and easily propagate IPsec policy settings throughout an organization that uses Active Directory domain services.

Recommendations

Use the Windows Firewall with Advanced Security snap-in to configure connection security rules to protect IPv6 traffic on your intranet with IPsec. The NAP platform provides additional protection for IPsec-protected communications by requiring that computers meet system health requirements before they can authenticate as an IPsec peer and communicate with protected intranet resources.

Host Protection from Scanning and Attacks

Hosts can be scanned and attacked by malicious software (malware), such as viruses or worms, even when connected to an intranet. During a scan, an attacker attempts to determine the address of a host (an address scan) and the set of Transmission Control Protocol (TCP) and User Datagram Protocol (UDP) ports being listened to by the host (a port scan). An attacker then attempts to access the services and resources of the host or compromise its security.

Address Scanning

With IPv6, the scanning of a subnet for valid unicast IPv6 addresses is made much more difficult by the large number of possible addresses. On an IPv6 subnet, unicast IPv6 addresses use 64 bits for the interface ID portion of the address. Therefore, an attacker must theoretically scan up to 2^{64} possible addresses. In contrast, on an IPv4 subnet, an attacker must typically scan less than 2^{10} possible IPv4 addresses.

A permanent interface ID can be derived in a number of ways. The two most common ways are randomly derived or derived from the Extended Unique Identifier (EUI)-64 address of the network adapter. For local area network (LAN) interfaces, the EUI-64 address can be determined from the 48-bit IEEE 802 address assigned to the network adapter, also known as the media access control (MAC) address. In MAC addresses, the first 24 bits are a company ID that is assigned to the network adapter manufacturer and the last 24 bits are an extension ID that is assigned to an individual network adapter. Because of the way in which EUI-based interface IDs are created from MAC addresses and because the company IDs of widely used network adapters are well known, 40 bits of the 64-bit interface ID can be easily determined. Therefore, it is still possible to perform an address scan on an IPv6 subnet by scanning up to 2^{24} possible combinations of interface IDs. IPv6 for Windows Server 2008 and Windows Vista can use EUI-64–based interface IDs for link-local, unique local, and public addresses, but this is disabled by default permanent.

Randomly derived permanent interface IDs mitigate the risk of address scans by requiring scans of up to 2^{64} possible interface IDs. IPv6 for Windows Server 2008 and Windows Vista by default uses randomly derived permanent interface IDs for link-local, unique local, and public addresses.

For more information about IPv6 address behavior in Windows Server 2008 and Windows Vista, see Chapter 3, "IPv6 Addressing."

Port Scanning

To prevent a port scan, hosts should use a host-based stateful firewall. Host-based stateful firewalls silently discard all incoming traffic that does not correspond to either traffic sent in response to a request of the computer (solicited traffic) or unsolicited traffic that has been specified as allowed (excepted traffic). A host-based stateful firewall will not prevent an attacker from determining open ports on a host if those ports are being used for active communication or the ports correspond to a service being offered by the host. For example, the host-based firewall on a Web server host must have an exception for Hypertext Transfer Protocol (HTTP) traffic at TCP port 80. An attacker will be able to determine that the host is listening on TCP port 80 even though the host-based firewall is enabled.

Windows Server 2008 and Windows Vista include Windows Firewall, a host-based stateful firewall for both IPv4 and IPv6 traffic, which is enabled by default.

Recommendations

To help prevent address scans, use the default behavior of IPv6 for Windows Server 2008 and Windows Vista to randomly derive the 64-bit permanent interface ID for link-local, unique local, and public addresses.

To help prevent port scans, use Windows Firewall or another host-based stateful firewall that supports IPv6 traffic. You can centrally configure Windows Firewall for exceptions and other behavior through Computer Configuration Group Policy in an Active Directory environment.

Control of What Traffic Is Exchanged with the Internet

To prevent unwanted traffic from the Internet, organizations typically deploy edge firewalls, proxies, and intrusion detection systems (IDSs). These security devices attempt to ensure that an attacker's traffic from the Internet cannot penetrate to the intranet, such as when a host on the intranet is compromised by malware and becomes reachable by attackers on the Internet. Because not all of these security devices are currently IPv6-capable, there are additional security risks for IPv6 traffic.

For example, an edge firewall or proxy device that is not aware of IPv6 or IPv6 tunneled traffic could pass that traffic to and from the Internet, creating a conduit for attacks from the Internet. However, to exchange tunneled IPv6 packets with hosts on the IPv4 Internet, the edge device must forward IPv4-based UDP traffic or IPv4 protocol 41 packets to and from the Internet. Otherwise, the traffic for current IPv6 automatic tunneling technologies, such as the Intra-Site Automatic Tunnel Addressing Protocol (ISATAP) or Teredo, will not be able to traverse IPv4 edge firewalls to the Internet.

As another example, an IDS that has been configured to detect the traffic associated with common attacks and malicious behavior for IPv4 might not be able to detect similar traffic when it is sent over IPv6. For example, an IDS might be capable of analyzing all network traffic with the EtherType of 0x800 or 0x806, corresponding to IPv4 and ARP traffic. However, the IDS might not be capable of analyzing all network traffic with the EtherType of 0x86DD, corresponding to IPv6 traffic. Additionally, an IDS might not be capable of analyzing IPv4 Protocol 41 traffic, corresponding to IPv4-encapsulated IPv6 traffic. IDSs will be updated over time to inspect IPv6 native and tunneled traffic.

Recommendations

To prevent unwanted and unauthorized IPv6 traffic from the Internet, you can do the following:

- Upgrade your edge firewall, proxy, and IDS to include IPv6 and tunneled IPv6 functionality.

- If your intranet computers must communicate with hosts on the IPv6 Internet, upgrade your edge firewall between your intranet and the IPv6 Internet to support stateful IPv6 firewalling.

- For IPv6-over-IPv4 tunneled traffic from intranet hosts to Internet hosts, configure your IPv4-based edge firewall to drop all IPv4 protocol 41 packets on its intranet interface.

- For IPv6-over-IPv4 tunneled traffic from Internet hosts to intranet hosts, configure your IPv4-based edge firewall to drop all IPv4 protocol 41 packets on its Internet interface. An exception is when you are using 6to4. The 6to4 router must be able to receive IPv6-over-IPv4 tunneled traffic from the Internet.

- For Teredo traffic from intranet hosts to Internet hosts, configure your IPv4-based edge firewall to silently discard all IPv4 traffic with the source or destination UDP port of 3544 on the interface attached to the intranet.

- For Teredo traffic from Internet hosts to intranet hosts, configure your IPv4-based edge firewall to silently discard all IPv4 traffic with the source or destination UDP port of 3544 on the interface attached to the Internet.

- Deploy ISATAP correctly on your intranet so that default route traffic is never forwarded to the IPv4 Internet. Default route traffic from ISATAP hosts on the IPv4 portion of your network should be forwarded to an ISATAP router, which is connected to both the IPv4 and IPv6-capable portions of your intranet. The default route on the ISATAP router should point to the IPv6-capable portion of your intranet.

- If your ISATAP router and edge firewall is the same device, ensure that the device's default route for IPv6 traffic points to the IPv6-capable portion of your network, not to the IPv4 Internet.

- If your ISATAP router and edge firewall are different devices, configure your IPv4-based edge firewall to silently discard all IPv4 traffic with the IPv4 Protocol field set to 41 on the interface attached to the intranet. This will prevent IPv4 Internet connectivity to ISATAP hosts on the intranet.

- If the ISATAP hosts on your intranet must communicate with hosts on the IPv6 Internet, upgrade your edge firewall between your intranet and the IPv6 Internet to support stateful IPv6 firewalling.

For more information about 6to4, see Chapter 13, "6to4." For more information about ISATAP, see Chapter 12, "ISATAP." For more information about Teredo, see Chapter 14, "Teredo."

Summary

When deploying IPv6 on your network, you should be aware of the following security considerations: authorization for automatically assigned addresses and configurations, protection of IP packets, host protection from scanning and attacks, and control of what traffic is exchanged with the Internet.

References

The following references were cited in this chapter:

- RFC 3118 – "Authentication for DHCP Messages"
- RFC 3315 – "Dynamic Host Configuration Protocol for IPv6 (DHCPv6)"
- RFC 3971 – "SEcure Neighbor Discovery (SEND)"
- RFC 4191 – "Default Router Preferences and More-Specific Routes"
- RFC 4301 – "Security Architecture for the Internet Protocol"
- RFC 4302 – "IP Authentication Header"
- RFC 4303 – "IP Encapsulating Security Payload (ESP)"
- RFC 4861 – "Neighbor Discovery for IP Version 6 (IPv6)"

You can obtain these RFCs from the \RFCs_and_Drafts folder on the companion CD-ROM or from *http://www.ietf.org/rfc.html*.

Testing for Understanding

To test your understanding of IPv6 security considerations, answer the following questions. See Appendix D, "Testing for Understanding Answers," to check your answers.

1. Without support for SEND or DHCP message authentication, what can you do to help prevent unauthorized intranet hosts from obtaining an IPv6 address and configuration?

2. Why are IPv6 addresses with EUI-64-based interface IDs more vulnerable to address scans than addresses with randomly derived interface IDs?

3. Will a port scan be able to detect a server service on a host even when a host-based stateful firewall is running?

4. What is the recommended configuration for exchanging IPv6 traffic between an intranet and the IPv6 Internet?

Chapter 16
Deploying IPv6

At the end of this chapter, you should be able to do the following:

- Describe the major planning issues for deploying IPv6 on an existing IPv4-only intranet for platform and application support, connectivity, name resolution, security, and prioritized delivery.

- List and describe the major steps to deploying IPv6 connectivity on an IPv4-only intranet.

Introduction

Chapters 1 through 15 describe IPv6 from the protocol definition, protocol operation, and security perspectives. Although much of this information is well known by IPv6 experts, few enterprise networks have the experience of deploying IPv6 on a large scale. This chapter describes the planning issues and the major steps for deployment of IPv6 connectivity on an existing IPv4-based intranet. The result of an IPv6 deployment is an IPv6-capable intranet that supports both IPv4 and native IPv6 traffic.

 Note This chapter does not describe how to convert an IPv4-only intranet to an IPv6-only intranet. Because much of the Internet still uses IPv4 and many users are dependent on IPv4-based network resources, most intranets will use a combination of IPv4 and IPv6 for the foreseeable future.

Planning for IPv6 Deployment

When deploying IPv6, you should consider the following in your planning:

- Platform support for IPv6
- Application support for IPv6
- Unicast IPv6 addressing
- Tunnel-based IPv6 connectivity
- Native IPv6 connectivity
- Name resolution with DNS
- DHCPv6

- Host-based security and IPv6 traffic
- Prioritized delivery for IPv6 traffic

Platform Support for IPv6

Microsoft has supplied a production-quality IPv6 protocol in the following versions of Windows for personal computers:

- Windows Server 2008
- Windows Vista
- Windows Server 2003
- Windows XP with Service Pack 1 or later

As described in Chapter 2, "IPv6 Protocol for Windows Server 2008 and Windows Vista," almost all of the included applications in Windows Server 2008 and Windows Vista will work over IPv6. Windows Server 2008 and Windows Vista are the recommended versions of Windows for an IPv6 deployment because of the widespread application use for authentication (Active Directory) and user (Internet Information Services) services.

Windows Server 2003 and Windows XP with Service Pack 1 or later provide an IPv6 protocol, but they have limited support for IPv6 operation in included applications. For example, Windows Server 2003 and Windows XP with Service Pack 1 or later components do not support Active Directory operations over IPv6. Therefore, if you deploy IPv6 on an intranet that consists of computers running Windows Server 2003 or Windows XP with Service Pack 1 or later, there will not be a lot of IPv6 traffic because not many built-in applications in these operating systems support IPv6.

However, an intranet with computers running only Windows Server 2008 or Windows Vista is not a prerequisite for IPv6 deployment. For example, if your intranet consists of hosts running Windows Server 2003 or Windows XP, you can deploy IPv6 connectivity and name resolution infrastructure and begin updating your applications for IPv6 support now. As you deploy Windows Vista, Windows Server 2008, and updated applications on hosts across your intranet, the amount of IPv6 traffic on your intranet will gradually increase.

Application Support for IPv6

Although almost all the applications in Windows Server 2008 and Windows Vista support operation over IPv6, whether third-party applications and custom applications developed for use by your organization support operation over IPv6 depends on the application programming interfaces (APIs) that they use for network operations. For applications that use IP protocol–independent APIs, such as Microsoft Remote Procedure Call (RPC) or the .NET Framework, no modification is needed for operation over IPv6.

Applications that use IP protocol-dependent APIs such as Windows Sockets (Winsock) might need to be updated to support operation over IPv6. For example, a Winsock application might use the older *Gethostbyname()* function, which is an IPv4 protocol–specific function that returns only IPv4 addresses. This application must be modified to use the new *Getaddrinfo()* function, which returns both IPv4 and IPv6 addresses.

For the details of Winsock support for IPv6, see Appendix B, "Windows Sockets Changes for IPv6."

Unicast IPv6 Addressing

Just as for your IPv4 infrastructure, you must decide on a unicast IPv6 addressing plan for your intranet, even if you are initially using tunnel-based IPv6 connectivity. You must determine how to number the individual subnets of your organization. Subnet addressing for IPv6 is actually easier than IPv4, due to the 64-bit prefix length for LAN subnets and the relative abundance of address space for organizations.

You can implement a flat addressing scheme that does not use route summarization, in which each subnet prefix becomes a separate route in the routing tables of your native IPv6 routers. Alternately, you can configure your routing infrastructure so that unicast address prefixes are summarized by routers at suitable boundaries. For unicast addresses for your subnets, you can use global addresses and unique local addresses.

Global addresses require a global address prefix. Most organizations can obtain a global address prefix from their Internet service providers (ISPs). A large enterprise or an organization that is providing IPv6 connectivity for other organizations should obtain a suitable global prefix from a regional Internet registry, such as the American Registry for Internet Numbers (ARIN) at *http://www.arin.net*. A global address implies reachability from any location on the IPv6 Internet, although actual reachability between an IPv6 Internet location and an intranet location can be restricted by the edge firewalls of an organization or by not advertising the global prefix outside the organization's intranet.

For unique local addresses, you must create a 40-bit random hexadecimal number which, when combined with the prefix FC00::/8 or FD00::/8, becomes a 48-bit unique local prefix for your organization. See RFC 4193 for information about how to create a random number for the Global ID portion of your unique local prefixes. If your organization has multiple sites, you can create a 48-bit unique local prefix for each site. A unique local address prefix is not designed to be reachable from the IPv6 Internet—your edge routers should not be advertising your unique local prefix to other routers on the IPv6 Internet. The use of unique local address prefixes is optional.

When determining the boundaries of IPv6 subnets, consider the following:

- You can define your subnet boundaries to be the same as your IPv4 subnet boundaries. This is the easiest approach to take because there are already IPv4 routers at your IPv4 subnet boundaries and they just need to be configured or updated to act as IPv6 routers. In this configuration, every local area network (LAN) subnet will have an IPv4 subnet prefix and one or multiple IPv6 subnet prefixes.

■ Because IPv6 subnets can contain many more hosts than IPv4 subnets, you can use your switching and router infrastructure to define larger subnets for IPv6 traffic. For example, a single IPv6 subnet might span four IPv4 subnets. However, this requires additional planning and configuration and the support on your switches and routers to define the boundaries of LAN subnets on a per-protocol basis.

For more information, see the Internet draft titled "IPv6 Unicast Address Assignment Considerations."

Tunnel-Based IPv6 Connectivity

If you are not ready to deploy native IPv6 connectivity across your entire intranet, you can deploy a tunnel-based IPv6 transition technology and eventually migrate from a tunnel-based infrastructure to a native infrastructure. Windows Server 2008 and Windows Vista support the following tunneling technologies and methods:

■ Intra-Site Automatic Tunnel Addressing Protocol (ISATAP)

■ 6to4

■ Teredo

■ Manually configured tunnels

ISATAP

ISATAP provides unicast connectivity for IPv6/IPv4 hosts on an intranet. Unlike 6to4 and Teredo, ISATAP is specifically designed for host-to-host tunneling on an intranet and is the recommended IPv6 transition technology to migrate an IPv4-only intranet to an IPv6-capable intranet. ISATAP is well suited to most intranets because it can be used with both private and public IPv4 addresses. The staged migration of an IPv4-only intranet to an IPv6-capable intranet can occur in the following phases:

1. Starting with an IPv4-only intranet, deploy ISATAP to provide tunnel-based IPv6 connectivity between the ISATAP hosts on the intranet.

2. Begin converting your IPv4-only subnets to IPv6-capable subnets. The IPv6/IPv4 hosts on these subnets will have both native IPv6 addresses and ISATAP addresses, and they can communicate with native IPv6 hosts using native IPv6 connectivity and ISATAP hosts with ISATAP connectivity.

3. When all of your intranet subnets are IPv6-capable, disable ISATAP. All of your IPv6/IPv4 hosts will now use native IPv6 connectivity.

ISATAP allows you to deploy IPv6 on an existing IPv4 intranet without requiring the immediate upgrade or configuration of any of your routers. With ISATAP, IPv4-only applications can continue to use IPv4 while newer IPv6-capable applications can be developed, tested, and deployed. The traffic of both types of applications share a single common IPv4 infrastructure.

ISATAP does not support IPv6 multicast traffic. Therefore, as you begin to convert IPv4-only subnets to native IPv6-capable subnets, those subnets might have IPv6 multicast support. However, all the ISATAP hosts on the IPv4-only portion of your intranet will not be able to use IPv6 multicast traffic. For example, some organizations use multicast traffic for streaming media of live presentations. During the transition between an IPv4-only to IPv6-capable intranet, multicast traffic sent over IPv6 will not reach the ISATAP hosts on the IPv4-only portion of the intranet. Therefore, you should send your multicast traffic over IPv4 until your entire intranet is IPv6-capable.

ISATAP is described in Chapter 12, "ISATAP."

6to4

6to4 provides unicast connectivity for IPv6/IPv4 hosts or IPv6 sites and connectivity to the IPv6 Internet across the IPv4 Internet. As implemented in Windows, 6to4 is best suited for small office/home office networks that use the Internet Connection Sharing (ICS) feature and for individual computers that connect to the IPv4 Internet with a public IPv4 address.

For intranets, 6to4 can provide a 48-bit global prefix for each site that has a public IPv4 address and connectivity to the IPv6 Internet across the IPv4 Internet. However, for connectivity between IPv6-enabled sites of an organization across the Internet, 6to4 does not provide any protection for the IPv4-encapsulated IPv6 packets. To protect 6to4-based traffic between sites across the IPv4 Internet, you can manually configure 6to4 routing and use Internet Protocol security (IPsec) policies to protect all IPv4 protocol 41 traffic between the public IPv4 addresses of your 6to4 routers. Alternately, you can use Routing and Remote Access and configure site-to-site virtual private network (VPN) connections to route IPv6 packets between the sites of an organization across the IPv4 or IPv6 Internets.

6to4 is described in Chapter 13, "6to4."

Teredo

Teredo provides unicast connectivity across the IPv4 Internet between IPv6/IPv4 hosts, even when they are located behind IPv4 Network Address Translators (NATs). With a Teredo relay, Teredo also provides connectivity to the IPv6 Internet across the IPv4 Internet. As implemented in Windows, Teredo is designed for individual computers that connect to the IPv4 Internet and is not a suitable technology for tunneling between IPv6/IPv4 hosts on an intranet.

Teredo is described in Chapter 14, "Teredo."

Manually Configured Tunnels

You can also manually configure tunnels between IPv6-capable routers. Configured tunnels are static tunnels that rely on routes in the IPv6 routing table to forward traffic through the tunnel. Routers on each end of the tunnel must be configured with a tunneling interface and an appropriate set of routes. You can use configured tunnels to do the following:

- **Connect IPv6 islands on an intranet**   For example, if you have different portions of your intranet that are not contiguous but are IPv6-capable, you can connect them with configured tunnels.

- **Connect to the IPv6 Internet across the IPv4 Internet**   Rather than using an ISP with native IPv6 connectivity, you can also connect to the IPv6 Internet through an ISP that offers tunneled connectivity to the IPv6 Internet. In this case, you configure an edge router of your organization with a configured tunnel to the ISP's router.

Manual tunnel configuration is described in Chapter 11, "IPv6 Transition Technologies."

Disabling Tunneling Technologies

If you decide not to use tunnel-based IPv6 connectivity and you want to disable all the automatic tunneling technologies for computers running Windows Server 2008 or Windows Vista, you can create and set the HKEY_LOCAL_MACHINE\SYSTEM\CurrentControlSet\Services\tcpip6\Parameters\DisabledComponents registry value to 1 (DWORD type). *DisabledComponents* does not exist by default and must be manually created with the Registry Editor tool (Regedit.exe). Setting *DisabledComponents* to 1 disables all ISATAP, 6to4, and Teredo interfaces.

Because the *DisabledComponents* registry value applies only to computers running Windows Server 2008 and Windows Vista, an intranet containing computers running Windows Server 2003 or Windows XP with Service Pack 1 or later can still use ISATAP, 6to4, or Teredo. To prevent IPv6 tunneled traffic for ISATAP, 6to4, or Teredo from being forwarded across your intranet, you can configure your routers to silently discard the following types of traffic:

- IPv6 protocol 41 (ISATAP and 6to4 traffic)
- Source or destination UDP port 3544 (Teredo traffic)

To prevent IPv6 tunneled traffic for ISATAP, 6to4, or Teredo from being forwarded between your intranet and hosts on the IPv4 Internet, configure your edge routers to silently discard these types of traffic.

As an alternative to the *DisabledComponents* registry value, you can disable 6to4 and Teredo by creating records in your internal Domain Name System (DNS) that resolve the names 6to4.ipv6.microsoft.com and teredo.ipv6.microsoft.com to unreachable addresses. If the 6to4 and Teredo components cannot successfully contact the servers at their resolved addresses, the 6to4 and Teredo tunneling interfaces will be disabled.

To prevent a host from using DNS dynamic update to create an A record with the name ISATAP, manually create ISATAP A records in your DNS domains with an unreachable IPv4 address. ISATAP hosts running Windows Server 2003 or Windows XP with Service Pack 1 or later will use the ISATAP A record to attempt to contact the ISATAP router. However, because no reply will be received, these ISATAP hosts will not have a global or unique local IPv6 address for ISATAP connectivity.

For computers running Windows Server 2008 or Windows Vista, you can also prevent ISATAP, 6to4, and Teredo traffic by configuring inbound and outbound rules in the Windows Firewall with Advanced Security snap-in. For example, you can enable the default outbound rule named Core Networking – Teredo (UDP-Out) and the default inbound rule named Core Networking – Teredo (UDP-In).

Native IPv6 Connectivity

Native IPv6 connectivity consists of the following capabilities:

- Unicast routing (required)
- Multicast routing (optional)

Unicast Routing

Native unicast IPv6 connectivity depends on the capability of your current routers. Many modern routers already support unicast IPv6 routing and just need to be configured to perform IPv6 forwarding and the advertising of subnet prefixes. For medium to large intranets, IPv6-capable routers also need to be configured with an IPv6 routing protocol to provide dynamic routing updates for the IPv6 subnets and address prefixes of the intranet. See Chapter 10, "IPv6 Routing," for a discussion of IPv6 routing protocols. Older routers that are not IPv6-capable need to be upgraded or replaced.

A small intranet can use static IPv6 routing, but extra configuration is required to ensure that all locations on the intranet are reachable by all of the IPv6 routers. A computer running Windows Server 2008 or Windows Vista can act as a static IPv6 router.

Multicast Routing

Multicast support is required in IPv6 for neighboring node interactions on a subnet, such as address resolution and router discovery. However, forwarding of non-link-local multicast IPv6 traffic between IPv6 subnets is optional. Enabling multicast forwarding and routing on your intranet can depend on whether you are already using multicast traffic over IPv4 and eventually want to use multicast traffic over IPv6.

Native multicast IPv6 support also depends on the capability of your current set of routers. Many modern routers already support IPv4 multicast routing. However, you need to verify that your routers also support IPv6 multicast forwarding and a multicast routing protocol. Older routers that are not IPv6 multicast-capable need to be upgraded or replaced.

Name Resolution with DNS

For your internal DNS to provide the same level of service for IPv6-related information as it does for IPv4-related information, you need to ensure that your DNS infrastructure supports the following:

- AAAA records for IPv6 addresses
- DNS dynamic updates so that IPv6 hosts can automatically register AAAA records

Optionally, you can investigate whether your applications require PTR records. If so, ensure that your DNS infrastructure supports the following:

- PTR records in the IP6.ARPA reverse domain
- DNS dynamic updates so that IPv6 hosts can automatically register PTR records

Additionally, because Windows hosts can send their IPv6 traffic over IPv4 or IPv6, you can investigate whether you want to configure your DNS servers and Windows hosts for DNS operation over IPv6.

DHCPv6

Because the IPv6/IPv4 hosts on your intranet, whether they are located on the IPv4-only or IPv6-capable portion, will continue to use IPv4 and Dynamic Host Configuration Protocol (DHCP) to obtain configuration settings such as the IPv4 addresses of your DNS servers or the DNS name suffix for your organization, the use of DHCP for IPv6 (DHCPv6) is optional. For example, you might want to use DHCPv6 so that your hosts use stateful IPv6 addresses that can be monitored and managed or because you want to configure your IPv6 hosts on the IPv6-capable portion of your intranet so that they perform their DNS operations over IPv6.

If you use DHCPv6, consider the following:

- You can use DHCPv6 on IPv6-capable subnets only when the routing path between the DHCPv6 relay agent on the subnet and the DHCPv6 server supports the forwarding of IPv6 traffic.

- You must determine whether the IPv6 hosts on the IPv6-capable portion of your intranet will use a combination of stateless and stateful addresses, or just stateful addresses.

- You must be able to configure your IPv6 routers to advertise the Managed Address Configuration (M) and Other Stateful Configuration (O) flags with the appropriate values.

- You must configure a DHCPv6 relay agent for each IPv6 subnet and configure the relay agent with the IPv6 addresses of your DHCPv6 servers. Ensure that your routers support a DHCPv6 relay agent. The Routing and Remote Access service in Windows Server 2008 includes a DHCPv6 relay agent.

■ You must determine the location and configuration of your DHCPv6 servers. You might be able to use the same server computers that are being used for DHCP. For example, the DHCP Server service in Windows Server 2008 can be configured for both DHCP operation and for DHCPv6 stateless or stateful operation.

Host-Based Security and IPv6 Traffic

As described in Chapter 15, "IPv6 Security Considerations," providing security for IPv6 traffic for IPv6 hosts running Windows Server 2008 or Windows Vista consists of the following:

■ Protection of IPv6 packets

■ Host protection from scanning and attacks

■ Control of what traffic is exchanged with the Internet

For cryptographic protection of IPv6 traffic, use IPsec. In Windows Server 2008 and Windows Vista, you can use the Windows Firewall with Advanced Security snap-in to configure connection security rules to specify IPsec protection for all types or specific types of native IPv6 traffic. You can also use connection security rules to protect IPv4-tunneled IPv6 traffic.

To control what types of IPv6 traffic, either tunneled or native, are allowed to travel within your intranet, you can use the following:

■ **Router-based firewalls**   Verify that your routers can perform IPv4 packet filtering (for tunneled IPv6 traffic) based on the IPv4 Protocol field and IPv6 packet filtering (for native IPv6 traffic).

■ **Host-based firewalls**   Use the built-in Windows Firewall for Windows Server 2008 and Windows Vista or an alternative that can be configured for inbound and outbound IPv4 packet filtering (for tunneled IPv6 traffic) and IPv6 packet filtering (for native IPv6 traffic).

To control what types of IPv6 traffic, either tunneled or native, are allowed to travel between your intranet and the IPv4 or IPv6 Internet, consider the following:

■ Edge routers connected to the IPv4 Internet must support the filtering of IPv4 protocol 41 and UDP port 3544 traffic.

■ Edge routers connected to the IPv6 Internet must support filtering of IPv6 traffic.

Additionally, investigate whether your intrusion detection systems (IDSs) include support for analyzing both native IPv6 and tunneled IPv6 traffic.

Prioritized Delivery for IPv6 Traffic

IPv6 supports prioritized delivery of IPv6 traffic through the Traffic Class and Flow Label fields. The Traffic Class field, also known as the Differentiated Services (DS) field, contains the Differentiated Services Code Point (DSCP) field, which can instruct routers to handle packets with different levels of priority. This is also referred to as Quality of Service (QoS).

QoS support in Windows Server 2008 and Windows Vista allows you to prioritize or manage the sending rate for outgoing network traffic based on the following conditions:

- Sending application
- Source or destination IPv6 addresses
- Protocol (TCP, UDP, or both)
- Source or destination ports (TCP or UDP)

QoS policies are applied to a user or computer account as part of a Group Policy object (GPO) that is linked to an Active Directory container such as a domain, site, or organizational unit (OU). As part of Group Policy, QoS policies in Windows Server 2008 and Windows Vista leverage your existing Active Directory management infrastructure.

To define the priority of traffic, you can configure a QoS policy to mark outbound network traffic with a specific DSCP. This DSCP value allows routers to determine which queue they should place the packet in and what traffic-shaping behavior should be applied. For example, the IT department can configure routers to place packets into a high-priority, best effort, or lower-than-best effort queue based on specific DSCP values. Therefore, mission-critical network traffic gets high priority and is not delayed by other lower-priority traffic. For example, to give higher priority to time-dependent Voice over IP (VoIP) traffic, a QoS policy can specify the DSCP value of 46 for the VoIP application, allowing routers to place those packets in a low-latency queue.

To use DSCP values for QoS, your routers must support DSCP marking and prioritized delivery for native IPv6 traffic.

Deploying IPv6

The deployment of IPv6 connectivity on your IPv4 intranet can consist of the following steps:

- Set up an IPv6 test network.
- Begin application migration.
- Configure DNS infrastructure to support AAAA records and dynamic updates.
- Deploy a tunneled IPv6 infrastructure with ISATAP.
- Upgrade IPv4-only hosts to IPv6/IPv4 hosts.
- Begin deploying a native IPv6 infrastructure.
- Connect portions of your intranet over the IPv4 Internet.
- Connect portions of your intranet over the IPv6 Internet.

Set Up an IPv6 Test Network

When deploying any new networking technology, it is vital to gain hands-on experience with the technology and see it working. For IPv6, you should create an IPv6 test network that allows you to test both tunneled and native IPv6 connectivity, routing, name resolution, and applications and services.

Appendix E, "Setting Up an IPv6 Test Lab," describes how to create an IPv6 test network consisting of five computers and three subnets. The instructions tell you how to do the following:

- Create functioning IPv4 connectivity.
- Configure ISATAP-based tunneled IPv6 connectivity.
- Configure native IPv6 connectivity.
- Use name resolution for IPv6 addresses.
- Configure an IPv6-only infrastructure.

Begin Application Migration

Application migration, the updating of your applications to support IPv6, is not a prerequisite of an IPv6 deployment. You can deploy IPv6 connectivity without migrating your applications. You can also migrate your applications without deploying IPv6 connectivity. This chapter describes how these two independent projects can be done in parallel, so that while you are deploying IPv6 connectivity, your applications are being updated to take advantage of the new connectivity.

To migrate the applications used on your intranet for IPv6 support, you must do the following:

- Inventory your applications.
- Scope the work, and schedule application migration.

Inventory Your Applications

Before you begin to migrate your applications, you must first account for and categorize all of the applications that run over your network. For each application, you should determine the following:

- Where did the application come from?

  Was the application purchased from an independent software vendor (ISV), or did the IT staff of your organization develop it?

- Does the application already support IPv6?

  For applications that have been purchased, contact the ISV to determine whether the version of the application that you are using supports IPv6 and has been tested in an IPv6-only environment.

For applications that have been developed by your IT department, determine the APIs that the application uses. Applications that exclusively use APIs that have already been IPv6-enabled might not need to be modified. You can use the Checkv4.exe tool from the Microsoft Windows Software Development Kit (SDK) released for Windows Vista to quickly scan the application code for IPv4-specific Winsock API calls.

■ How critical is the application to your organization?

Some applications are more important to the operation of your organization than others. Try to rank your applications in order of importance.

■ How easy is the application to modify?

For applications that have been developed by your IT department, determine the ability to modify the application to support IPv6. Some older applications are harder to maintain because either the source code is not easily available or the IT department does not have the experience or expertise to maintain the application.

When categorizing your applications, you might determine that some applications cannot be migrated or do not need to be migrated. For example, older legacy applications for which the source code is not available cannot be migrated. In these cases, you can use a port translation or proxy solution to allow access to IPv4-only resources from IPv6-only nodes or applications. An example of a port proxy solution is the PortProxy service in Windows Server 2008 and Windows Vista. For more information, see Chapter 11.

For new applications, use the following guidelines to ensure IPv6 support:

■ For applications being purchased from an ISV, verify that the application has been tested in an IPv6-only environment.

■ For applications that are being developed by your IT department, instruct them to do the following:

❑ Use Windows APIs that are not dependent on IPv4 or IPv6. For example, use managed code, APIs that are already IPv6-enabled (such as RPC and the .NET Framework), or the new Winsock functions such as *Getaddrinfo()* and *Getnameinfo()*. For more information, see the "IPv6 Guide for Windows Sockets Applications" at *http://go.microsoft.com/fwlink/?LinkID=87735*.

❑ Ensure that the application does not use any user interface elements that are IPv4-specific, such as those used for IPv4 addresses and subnet masks.

❑ Ensure that the application does not have internal IPv4 dependencies, such as the storage of 32-bit IPv4 addresses or subnet masks.

Scope the Work and Schedule Application Migration

For applications developed by your IT department, determine how much work is required to migrate each application. For applications that use Windows Sockets, you can use the Checkv4.exe tool to display a set of suggested changes. Checkv4.exe scans your application code for IPv4-specific functions and provides advice about how to change those functions to be independent of IPv4 or IPv6. Checkv4.exe does not scan for other IPv4 dependencies in your code, such as user interface controls or storage for IPv4 addresses and subnet masks. Therefore, use Checkv4.exe as one source of information to scope the changes required for an application.

After you have determined the work required for each application, compare that with how difficult it will be to make those changes and the importance of your application to your organization. Based on your requirements, you can determine the order in which you will migrate your applications and can schedule IPv6 migration into the next update of your applications.

After each application has been migrated, you can optionally verify that it works properly over IPv6 by testing its operation on an IPv6-only network. You can use the instructions in Appendix E to create an IPv6-only network.

Configure DNS Infrastructure to Support AAAA Records and Dynamic Updates

Update, upgrade, or configure your DNS servers to support IPv6 AAAA records and DNS dynamic updates for AAAA records in the appropriate domains. DNS servers that are running Windows Server 2008 or Windows Server 2003 already support AAAA records and DNS dynamic updates for AAAA records.

Optionally, if PTR records are required by your applications, update, upgrade, or configure your DNS servers to support IPv6 PTR records and DNS dynamic updates for PTR records in the IP6.ARPA reverse domain. DNS servers that are running Windows Server 2008 or Windows Server 2003 already support IPv6 PTR records and DNS dynamic updates for PTR records in the IP6.ARPA domain.

If you want your DNS traffic sent over IPv6 rather than IPv4, update, upgrade, or configure your DNS servers to support operation over IPv6. DNS servers that are running Windows Server 2008 support DNS operation over IPv6 by default. For DNS servers running Windows Server 2003, you must enable DNS operation over IPv6 with the **dnscmd /config /EnableIPv6 1** command.

Deploy a Tunneled IPv6 Infrastructure with ISATAP

To allow IPv6/IPv4 hosts to communicate without a native IPv6 routing infrastructure, deploy an ISATAP infrastructure consisting of ISATAP logical subnet prefixes, the appropriate number of ISATAP routers (at least one for each logical ISATAP subnet), and DNS A records for the name "ISATAP" in the appropriate domains so that Windows-based ISATAP hosts can determine the location of ISATAP routers. To ensure that Windows Server 2008–based DNS servers can resolve the ISATAP name for ISATAP hosts, use the Registry Editor (Regedit.exe) to remove the ISATAP entry from the HKEY_LOCAL_MACHINE\System\CurrentControlSet\Services\DNS\Parameters\GlobalQueryBlockList registry value on the DNS servers.

For more information about configuring a computer running Windows Server 2008 or Windows Vista as an ISATAP router, see Chapter 12. For the details of deploying an ISATAP infrastructure, see the Intra-site Automatic Tunnel Addressing Protocol Deployment Guide at *http://www.microsoft.com/ipv6.*

Upgrade IPv4-Only Hosts to IPv6/IPv4 Hosts

Intranet hosts must be upgraded to use a dual IP layer or dual IP stack architecture and a DNS resolver that can process DNS query results containing both IPv4 and IPv6 addresses. For hosts running Windows Server 2003 or Windows XP with Service Pack 1 or later, you can do one of the following:

- Install the Microsoft TCP/IP version 6 protocol component from the Network Connections folder or from a command prompt with the **netsh interface ipv6 install** command.

- Upgrade computers running Windows XP with Service Pack 1 or later with Windows Vista. Upgrade computers running Windows Server 2003 with Windows Server 2008.

As described in the "Platform Support for IPv6" section earlier in this chapter, IPv6/IPv4 hosts running Windows Server 2003 or Windows XP have limited built-in network application support for IPv6.

With an ISATAP infrastructure in place, Windows-based IPv6/IPv4 hosts will determine the IPv4 address of the appropriate ISATAP router, automatically configure global or unique local ISATAP addresses based on the advertised prefixes, and register those addresses in DNS. They can then begin communicating with other ISATAP hosts.

Begin Deploying a Native IPv6 Infrastructure

Determining when to begin deploying a native IPv6 infrastructure depends on when your IT department is ready to begin handling operation and management of a dual IPv4 and IPv6 network and when you want to begin using IPv6 native traffic for your applications. You can measure where and when to deploy IPv6 capability on portions of your intranet by analyzing ISATAP-encapsulated traffic patterns and usage.

For unicast IPv6 traffic, see the documentation for your routers for information about how to do the following:

- Enable IPv6 unicast forwarding.

- Enable IPv6 unicast advertising.

- Configure route prefixes for each native IPv6 subnet.

- Enable and configure your chosen IPv6 unicast routing protocol.

To use a computer running Windows Server 2008 or Windows Vista as a static unicast IPv6 router, use commands in the **netsh interface ipv6** context to enable unicast forwarding and advertising and configure route prefixes for each native IPv6 subnet and other routes as needed to provide the appropriate IPv6 connectivity. For more information, see Chapter 10.

For multicast IPv6 traffic, see the documentation for your routers for information about how to do the following:

- Enable IPv6 multicast forwarding.
- Enable and configure your chosen IPv6 multicast routing protocol.

As IPv4-only routers are configured to also support native IPv6 traffic, there will be portions of your network that are IPv4-only and portions that are IPv6-capable. Coordinate the rollout of IPv6 capability with your ISATAP deployment so that when a portion of your network that is served by an ISATAP router is converted, the ISATAP router can be removed. For example, if there is a site of your organization that uses its own ISATAP router and the entire site is converted to be IPv6-capable, remove the A record for that ISATAP router and then remove the ISATAP router. IPv6/IPv4 hosts in the site will no longer use ISATAP and will use IPv6 native traffic exclusively.

During the rollout of IPv6 capability across your network, the following types of communications exist:

- Communication between IPv6 hosts on the IPv6-capable portion of your intranet is native IPv6 traffic that flows across IPv6-capable routers.
- Communication between ISATAP hosts on the ISATAP-deployed portions of your intranet is tunneled IPv6 traffic that either is sent directly between ISATAP hosts (when the hosts are on the same ISATAP logical subnet) or flows through one or more ISATAP routers (when the hosts are on different ISATAP logical subnets).
- Communication between IPv6 hosts on the IPv6-capable portion of your intranet and an ISATAP host is native IPv6 traffic on the IPv6-capable portion of your intranet and tunneled IPv6 traffic on the ISATAP-deployed portions of your intranet.

For infrastructure servers running Windows Server 2008, such as DNS or DHCPv6 servers, disable randomized interface identifiers (IDs) with the **netsh interface ipv6 set global randomizeidentifiers=disabled** command. With randomized interface IDs enabled, Windows Server 2008 generates a new randomized interface ID each time Windows Server 2008 is installed, which can create incorrect AAAA entries in DNS. With randomized interface IDs disabled, Windows Server 2008 uses Extended Unique Identifier (EUI)-64-based interface IDs, which remain the same if Windows Server 2008 is reinstalled.

Coincident with the rollout of native unicast IPv6 capability on your intranet is the optional rollout of DHCPv6. To deploy a DHCPv6 infrastructure, you must do the following:

- Set up DHCPv6 servers, and configure them with IPv6 configuration settings and, if needed, IPv6 subnet prefixes.

- Set up a DHCPv6 relay agent for each IPv6 subnet, and configure them with the IPv6 addresses of your DHCPv6 servers. For your routers, update or upgrade the routers as needed and configure the DHCPv6 relay agent. You can also use a computer running Windows Server 2008 and Routing and Remote Access as a DHCPv6 relay agent.

- Configure your IPv6 routers to advertise the M and O flags with the appropriate values, depending on whether you are using DHCPv6 stateless or stateful modes of operation.

Computers running Windows Server 2008 or Windows Vista require no additional configuration as DHCPv6 clients. They perform DHCPv6 stateless or stateful operation based on the M and O flags in received router advertisements.

Connect Portions of Your Intranet over the IPv4 Internet

To connect different portions of your intranet across the IPv4 Internet, you can configure the following:

- 6to4 with IPsec protection of 6to4-tunneled traffic
- Site-to-site virtual private network (VPN) connections

6to4 with IPsec Protection of 6to4-tunneled Traffic

As described in the "Tunnel-Based IPv6 Connectivity" section earlier in this chapter, 6to4 provides automatic tunneling of IPv6 packets between 6to4 sites and the IPv6 Internet across the IPv4 Internet, but it does not provide any protection of those packets. 6to4-tunneled private traffic sent unprotected across the IPv6 Internet can be easily interpreted by malicious intermediate hosts. If you must use 6to4, protect the 6to4-tunneled traffic between organization sites with IPsec and encryption.

For 6to4 routers running Windows Server 2008 or Windows Vista, you must configure connection security rules or IPsec policies for protocol 41 traffic between the IPv4 addresses of your 6to4 routers. For 6to4 routers that are not running Windows Server 2008 or Windows Vista, see the router documentation for information about how to configure the equivalent IPsec protection.

Site-to-Site VPN Connections

The preferred method to send private intranet data across the IPv4 intranet is with a site-to-site VPN connection between site edge routers. The site-to-site VPN connection provides encapsulation and encryption for intranet packets. If your edge routers are running Windows Server 2008, you can send the following types of traffic over the site-to-site VPN connection:

- **Tunneled IPv6 traffic**   You can send tunneled IPv6 traffic over a site-to-site VPN connection that uses the Point-to-Point Tunneling Protocol (PPTP) or Layer Two Tunneling Protocol with IPsec (L2TP/IPsec). You can also use edge routers running Windows Server 2003.

- **Native IPv6 traffic**   You can send native IPv6 traffic over a site-to-site VPN connection that uses L2TP/IPsec. Edge routers running Windows Server 2003 do not support the forwarding of native IPv6 traffic over a site-to-site VPN connection.

For the details of creating a site-to-site VPN connection with PPTP or L2TP/IPsec, see *Windows Server 2008 Networking and Network Access Protection (NAP)* by Joseph Davies and Tony Northrup (Microsoft Press, 2008).

If your edge routers are not running Windows Server 2008 or Windows Server 2003, see the router documentation for information about how they support IPv6 tunneled or IPv6 native traffic over site-to-site VPN connections.

Connect Portions of Your Intranet over the IPv6 Internet

To connect different portions of your intranet across the IPv6 Internet, you can also use site-to-site VPN connections. If your edge routers are running Windows Server 2008, you can send native IPv6 traffic over a site-to-site VPN connection that uses L2TP/IPsec. Edge routers running Windows Server 2003 do not support the forwarding of native IPv6 traffic over a site-to-site VPN connection.

For the details of creating a site-to-site VPN connection with L2TP/IPsec, see the *Windows Server 2008 Networking and Network Access Protection (NAP)* book from Microsoft Press.

If your edge routers are not running Windows Server 2008, see the router documentation for information about how they support IPv6 native traffic over site-to-site VPN connections.

Summary

It is possible to deploy IPv6 connectivity on your IPv4-only intranet today with minimal cost and investment. Before you start this process, consider the following:

- **Security**   Ensure that your edge routers and firewalls can block IPv6 traffic for the initial deployment. Ensure that packet inspection and tunneling technologies can be enabled later on your edge routers and firewalls.

- **DNS infrastructure support**   Ensure that your DNS servers can store AAAA records and support DNS dynamic updates for AAAA records.

- **Device and applications support for IPv6**   Determine which devices, such as computers and routers, and applications support IPv6.

- **Whether to use tunnel-based, native IPv6 connectivity, or both**   Determine how your computers will communicate using IPv6.

- **Prioritized delivery for native IPv6 traffic**   Optionally, determine your routers' support for prioritized delivery of native IPv6 traffic.

When deploying IPv6 on your IPv4-only intranet, first set up an IPv6 test network to gain hands-on experience. Then begin to inventory your applications and plan for the migration of your applications that currently use only IPv4. Configure your DNS infrastructure to support IPv6 AAAA and PTR records and dynamic updates. If you want to start with tunnel-based IPv6 connectivity, deploy an ISATAP infrastructure. Begin upgrading or configuring your IPv4-only hosts to become IPv6/IPv4 hosts. Begin deploying a native IPv6 infrastructure. Eventually, the native IPv6 infrastructure will encompass your entire intranet and you can disable ISATAP. Optionally, you can create protected connections between the sites of your organization across the IPv4 or IPv6 Internet.

References

The following references were cited in this chapter:

- RFC 4193 – "Unique Local IPv6 Unicast Addresses"
- Internet Draft – "IPv6 Unicast Address Assignment Considerations"

You can obtain this RFC and this Internet draft from the \RFCs_and_Drafts folder on the companion CD-ROM or from *http://www.ietf.org/rfc.html* and *http://www.ietf.org/ html.charters/v6ops-charter.html*.

Testing for Understanding

To test your understanding of an IPv6 deployment, answer the following questions. See Appendix D, "Testing for Understanding Answers," to check your answers.

1. What is the value of deploying IPv6 on an intranet for which most of the hosts run Windows Server 2003 or Windows XP with Service Pack 2?

2. What types of applications must be migrated for IPv6 support and why? Do they need to be migrated before you begin deploying IPv6?

3. How do you determine the boundaries of IPv6 subnets?

4. Why is ISATAP the automatic tunneling technology supplied with Windows that is most suitable for intranet deployment?

5. A user on an ISATAP host calls her help desk because she is unable to receive a live media presentation that is being multicast over IPv6. What is the most likely problem and its solution?

6. Why is DHCPv6 an optional and technically unnecessary technology to deploy on an intranet that is using both IPv4 and IPv6?

7. Two different sites of an organization's intranet have deployed a native IPv6 routing infrastructure serving their individual sites. How would you connect these two IPv6-capable portions of the intranet together across an IPv4-only infrastructure?

Appendix A
Link-Layer Support for IPv6

This appendix describes the link-layer encapsulation for Internet Protocol version 6 (IPv6) packets for common local area network (LAN) and wide area network (WAN) technologies and describes how IPv6 packets are encapsulated when sent across an IPv4 infrastructure.

Basic Structure of IPv6 Packets

On LAN and WAN media, IPv6 packets exist as link-layer frames. Figure A-1 shows the basic structure of IPv6 packets sent over LAN and WAN media.

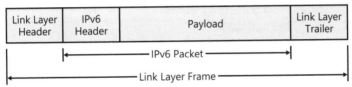

Figure A-1   Basic structure of IPv6 packets sent on LAN and WAN media

The structure of IPv6 packets sent on LAN and WAN media consists of the following:

- **A link-layer header and trailer**   The encapsulation placed on the IPv6 packet at the link layer is composed of a link-layer header and trailer.

- **An IPv6 header**   This is the new IPv6 header. For more information, see Chapter 4, "The IPv6 Header."

- **Payload**   The payload of the IPv6 packet includes zero or more IPv6 extension headers and the upper-layer protocol data unit (PDU). For more information, see Chapter 4.

LAN Media

To successfully troubleshoot IPv6 problems on a LAN, it is important to understand LAN encapsulations. Commonly used LAN technologies include Ethernet and IEEE 802.11. Older and less commonly used LAN technologies include Token Ring and Fiber Distributed Data Interface (FDDI). In some technologies (such as Ethernet), multiple encapsulations might exist. In each of these technologies, the IPv6 packet needs to be delimited, addressed, and identified as an IPv6 packet.

IPv6 in Windows Server 2008 and Windows Vista supports IPv6 packets over the following LAN media:

- Ethernet (RFC 2464)
- Token Ring (RFC 2470)

- FDDI (RFC 2467)

- IEEE 802.11

The IPv6 protocol for Windows Server 2008 and Windows Vista also supports the sending and receiving of IPv6 packets over any LAN interface that registers itself with the Network Device Interface Specification (NDIS) layer as an 802.3 media type. This media type includes Ethernet, phone line, power line, and other technologies.

Ethernet: Ethernet II

When sent over an Ethernet network, IPv6 packets use either Ethernet II or IEEE 802.3 Sub-Network Access Protocol (SNAP) encapsulation. IPv6 encapsulation for Ethernet links is described in RFC 2464. Figure A-2 shows Ethernet II encapsulation of IPv6 packets.

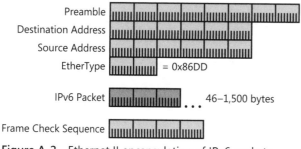

Figure A-2   Ethernet II encapsulation of IPv6 packets

The fields in the Ethernet header and trailer are the following:

- **Preamble**   The Preamble field is used to synchronize the receiver and indicate the start of the Ethernet frame. The size of this field is 64 bits.

- **Destination Address**   The Destination Address field contains the media access control (MAC) address of the destination Ethernet node. The size of this field is 48 bits.

- **Source Address**   The Source Address field contains the MAC address of the sending Ethernet node. The size of this field is 48 bits.

- **EtherType**   The EtherType field indicates the upper-layer protocol of the Ethernet payload. The size of this field is 16 bits. The EtherType field is set to 0x86DD for IPv6 packets. In contrast, the EtherType field is set to 0x800 for IPv4 packets.

- **Frame Check Sequence**   The value of this field is a checksum that is used to check for bit-level errors in the Ethernet frame. The checksum value is computed by the sending Ethernet node and verified by the receiving Ethernet node. The size of this field is 32 bits.

IPv6 packets sent using Ethernet II encapsulation have a maximum size of 1500 bytes and a minimum size of 46 bytes. IPv6 packets under 46 bytes in length are padded to

46 bytes to preserve the Ethernet minimum frame size of 64 bytes (not including the Preamble field).

Network Monitor Capture

Here is an example of Ethernet II encapsulation as displayed by Network Monitor 3.1 (capture AppA_01 in the \NetworkMonitorCaptures folder on the companion CD-ROM):

```
    Frame:
- Ethernet: Etype = IPv6
  + DestinationAddress: 3333FF 52F9D8
  + SourceAddress: 00B0D0234733
    EthernetType: IPv6, 34525(0x86dd)
+ Ipv6: Next Protocol = ICMPv6, Payload Length = 32
+ Icmpv6: Multicast Listener Report
```

Notice that Network Monitor 3.1 does not display the Preamble and Frame Check Sequence fields.

Ethernet: IEEE 802.3 SNAP

The IEEE 802.3 SNAP encapsulation uses a SNAP header to encapsulate the IPv6 packet so that it can be sent on an IEEE 802.3-compliant network. IEEE 802.3 SNAP encapsulation consists of an IEEE 802.3 header, an IEEE 802.2 Logical Link Control (LLC) header, a SNAP header, and an IEEE 802.3 trailer. Figure A-3 shows Ethernet IEEE 802.3 SNAP encapsulation of IPv6 packets.

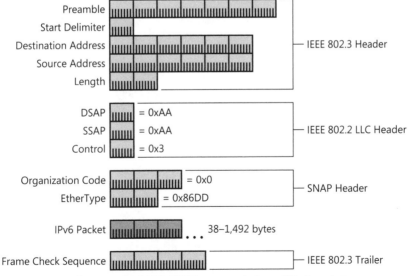

Figure A-3   Ethernet IEEE 802.3 SNAP encapsulation of IPv6 packets

The fields in the IEEE 802.3 SNAP encapsulation are the following:

- **Preamble**   The Preamble field is used to synchronize the receiver. The size of this field is 56 bits.

- **Start Delimiter**   The Start Delimiter field indicates the start of the Ethernet frame. The size of this field is 8 bits.

- **Destination Address**   The Destination Address field contains the MAC address of the destination Ethernet node. The size of this field is 48 bits.

- **Source Address**   The Source Address field contains the MAC address of the sending Ethernet node. The size of this field is 48 bits.

- **Length**   The Length field specifies the number of bytes in the IEEE 802.3 payload. This includes the IEEE 802.2 header and the SNAP header. The size of this field is 16 bits.

- **Destination Service Access Point (DSAP)**   The DSAP field indicates the upper-layer protocol of the payload for the destination. For SNAP-encapsulated payloads, the DSAP is set to the defined value of 0xAA. The size of this field is 8 bits.

- **Source Service Access Point (SSAP)**   The SSAP field indicates the upper-layer protocol of the payload for the sender. For SNAP-encapsulated payloads, the SSAP is set to the defined value of 0xAA. The size of this field is 8 bits.

- **Control**   For SNAP-encapsulated payloads, the Control field is set to the defined value of 0x3, indicating that the 802.2 frame is an unnumbered frame. The size of this field is 8 bits.

- **Organization Code**   The Organization Code field indicates the ID of the organization that defines the values in the 16-bit field that follows the Organization Code field. For SNAP encapsulation, the Organization Code field is set to 0, indicating the Internet Engineering Task Force (IETF), which administers the values of the EtherType field. The size of this field is 24 bits.

- **EtherType**   The EtherType field indicates the upper-layer protocol of the payload. The size of this field is 16 bits. The EtherType field is set to 0x86DD for IPv6 packets.

- **Frame Check Sequence**   The value of this field is a checksum that is used to check for bit-level errors in the Ethernet frame. The checksum value is computed by the sending Ethernet node and verified by the receiving Ethernet node. The size of this field is 32 bits.

IPv6 packets sent using an IEEE 802.3 SNAP frame have a maximum size of 1492 bytes and a minimum size of 38 bytes. IPv6 packets under 38 bytes in length are padded to 38 bytes to preserve the Ethernet minimum frame size of 64 bytes (not including the Preamble and Start Delimiter fields).

Token Ring: IEEE 802.5 SNAP

When sent over a Token Ring network, IPv6 packets use the IEEE 802.5 SNAP encapsulation. IPv6 encapsulation for Token Ring links is described in RFC 2470. Figure A-4 shows IEEE 802.5 SNAP encapsulation of IPv6 packets.

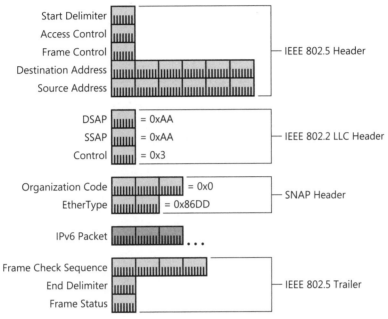

Figure A-4   IEEE 802.5 SNAP encapsulation of IPv6 packets

The fields in the IEEE 802.5 SNAP encapsulation are the following:

- **Start Delimiter**   The Start Delimiter field indicates the start of the Token Ring frame. The size of this field is 8 bits.

- **Access Control**   The Access Control field indicates the frame type (token or data frame), the frame's priority, the frame's reservation level, and whether the frame has passed the ring monitor station. The size of this field is 8 bits.

- **Frame Control**   The Frame Control field indicates whether the frame is a data frame or a Token Ring management frame and, if it is a Token Ring management frame, the specific type. The size of this field is 8 bits.

- **Destination Address**   The Destination Address field contains the MAC address of the destination Token Ring node. The size of this field is 48 bits.

- **Source Address**   The Source Address field contains the MAC address of the sending Token Ring node. The size of this field is 48 bits.

- **DSAP** The DSAP field indicates the upper-layer protocol of the payload for the destination. For SNAP-encapsulated payloads, the DSAP is set to the defined value of 0xAA. The size of this field is 8 bits.

- **SSAP** The SSAP field indicates the upper-layer protocol of the payload for the sender. For SNAP-encapsulated payloads, the SSAP is set to the defined value of 0xAA. The size of this field is 8 bits.

- **Control** For SNAP-encapsulated payloads, the Control field is set to the defined value of 0x3, indicating that the 802.2 frame is an unnumbered frame. The size of this field is 8 bits.

- **Organization Code** The Organization Code field indicates the ID of the organization that defines the values in the 16-bit field that follows the Organization Code field. For SNAP encapsulation, the Organization Code field is set to 0, indicating the IETF, which administers the values of the EtherType field. The size of this field is 24 bits.

- **EtherType** The EtherType field indicates the upper-layer protocol of the payload. The size of this field is 16 bits. The EtherType field is set to 0x86DD for IPv6 packets.

- **Frame Check Sequence** The value of this field is a checksum that is used to check for bit-level errors in the Token Ring frame. The checksum value is computed by the sending Token Ring node and verified by the receiving Token Ring node. The size of this field is 32 bits.

- **End Delimiter** The End Delimiter field indicates the end of the Token Ring frame. The size of this field is 8 bits.

- **Frame Status** The Frame Status field indicates whether or not the destination address was recognized and whether or not the frame was copied. The size of this field is 8 bits.

IPv6 packets sent using Token Ring have a variety of maximum transmission units (MTUs), depending on the maximum amount of time that a Token Ring node can hold the token. This amount can vary based on the data rate and the number of nodes on the ring. For more information, see RFC 2470.

FDDI

FDDI also uses the SNAP encapsulation. IPv6 encapsulation for FDDI links is described in RFC 2467. Figure A-5 shows FDDI encapsulation of IPv6 packets.

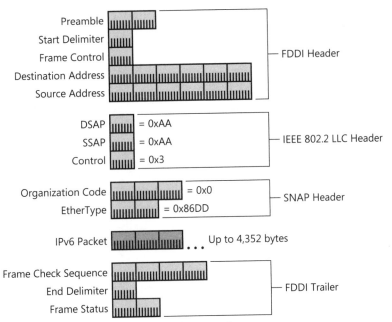

Figure A-5   FDDI encapsulation of IPv6 packets

The fields in the FDDI encapsulation are the following:

■ **Preamble**   The Preamble field is used to synchronize the receiver. The size of this field is 16 bits.

■ **Start Delimiter**   The Start Delimiter field indicates the start of the FDDI frame. The size of this field is 8 bits.

■ **Frame Control**   The Frame Control field indicates the frame class, the size of the source and destination addresses, and the frame type (token or data frame). The size of this field is 8 bits.

■ **Destination Address**   The Destination Address field contains the MAC address of the destination FDDI node. The size of this field is 48 bits.

■ **Source Address**   The Source Address field contains the MAC address of the sending FDDI node. The size of this field is 48 bits.

■ **DSAP**   The DSAP field indicates the upper-layer protocol of the payload for the destination. For SNAP-encapsulated payloads, the DSAP is set to the defined value of 0xAA. The size of this field is 8 bits.

■ **SSAP**   The SSAP field indicates the upper-layer protocol of the payload for the sender. For SNAP-encapsulated payloads, the SSAP is set to the defined value of 0xAA. The size of this field is 8 bits.

- **Control**   For SNAP-encapsulated payloads, the Control field is set to the defined value of 0x3, indicating that the 802.2 frame is an unnumbered frame. The size of this field is 8 bits.

- **Organization Code**   The Organization Code field indicates the ID of the organization that defines the values in the 16-bit field that follows the Organization Code field. For SNAP encapsulation, the Organization Code field is set to 0, indicating the IETF, which administers the values of the EtherType field. The size of this field is 24 bits.

- **EtherType**   The EtherType field indicates the upper-layer protocol of the payload. The size of this field is 16 bits. The EtherType field is set to 0x86DD for IPv6 packets.

- **Frame Check Sequence**   The value of this field is a checksum that is used to check for bit-level errors in the FDDI frame. The checksum value is computed by the sending FDDI node and verified by the receiving FDDI node. The size of this field is 32 bits.

- **End Delimiter**   The End Delimiter field indicates the end of the FDDI frame. The size of this field is 8 bits.

- **Frame Status**   The Frame Status field indicates whether or not the destination address was recognized, whether or not the frame was copied, and whether or not the Frame Check Sequence field is valid. The size of this field is 16 bits.

FDDI allows an MTU of 4352 bytes for IPv6 packets. The IPv6 MTU is derived from the 4500-byte maximum payload for FDDI, less 22 bytes for FDDI MAC overhead, 8 bytes for the SNAP header, and 118 bytes that are reserved for future MAC header uses. All IPv6 packets are transmitted as asynchronous LLC frames using unrestricted tokens.

IEEE 802.11

The IEEE 802.11 standard for wireless LAN networks also uses the SNAP encapsulation. Figure A-6 shows IEEE 802.11 encapsulation for IPv6 packets that are sent between wireless nodes or between a wireless node and a wireless access point (AP) (rather than between wireless APs).

Figure A-6 shows an unencrypted 802.11 frame.

The fields in the IEEE 802.11 encapsulation are the following:

- **Frame Control**   A 16-bit field that contains control information that defines the type of frame and how to process the frame. For more information, see the "Frame Control Field" section later in this appendix.

- **Duration/ID Field**   A 16-bit field that is used to indicate the duration of time in microseconds needed to transmit the frame and the acknowledgment.

- **Address 1**   A 48-bit field that contains either the destination MAC address of a wireless node (when sent by a wireless node to another wireless node or sent by the wireless AP to the wireless node) or the Service Set Identifier (SSID) (when sent by a wireless node to a wireless AP).

- **Address 2**   A 48-bit field that contains either the MAC address of the sending node (when sent to another wireless node or sent to the wireless AP) or the SSID (when sent by the wireless AP to a wireless node).

- **Address 3**   A 48-bit field that contains the SSID for frames sent to another wireless node in ad hoc mode, the source address for frames sent from the wireless AP to a wireless node, or the destination address for frames sent from a wireless node to the wireless AP.

- **Sequence Control**   A 16-bit field that contains a 4-bit Fragment Number field and a 12-bit Sequence Number field that, when used together, allow the receiver to discard duplicate frames. When a frame is fragmented, the Fragment Number field is used to indicate the number of the fragment. Otherwise, the Fragment Number field is set to 0. The Sequence Number field indicates the number of the frame starting at 0, incrementing to 4095, and then starting again at 0. All fragments of a frame have the same sequence number.

- **Frame Check Sequence**   A 32-bit checksum that uses the same algorithm as Ethernet to provide a bit-level integrity check of all fields in the IEEE 802.11 frame, from the Frame Control field to the Payload field.

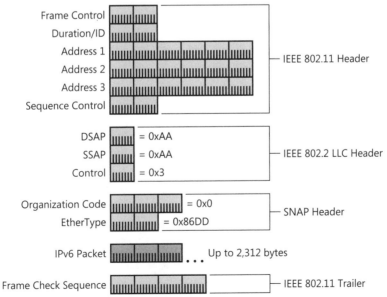

Figure A-6   IEEE 802.11 encapsulation of IPv6 packets

An IPv6 packet for an IEEE 802.11 frame can have a maximum size of 2312 bytes.

If the payload of a data frame is encrypted with Wired Equivalent Privacy (WEP), the IPv6 packet is preceded by a plaintext 32-bit field containing an Initialization Vector (IV) field and followed with an encrypted 32-bit Integrity Check Value (ICV) field, lowering the maximum IPv6 packet size to 2304 bytes.

If the payload of a data frame is encrypted with Wi-Fi Protected Access (WPA) and the Temporal Key Integrity Protocol (TKIP), the IPv6 packet is preceded by a plaintext 64-bit field containing the IV and followed with an encrypted 64-bit Message Integrity Code (MIC) and 32-bit ICV field, lowering the maximum IPv6 packet size to 2292 bytes.

If the payload of a data frame is encrypted with Wi-Fi Protected Access 2 (WPA2) and the Advanced Encryption Standard (AES), the IPv6 packet is preceded by a plaintext 64-bit field containing the Packet Number field and followed with an encrypted 64-bit Message Integrity Code (MIC), lowering the maximum IPv6 packet size to 2296 bytes.

Frame Control Field

Figure A-7 shows the Frame Control field in the IEEE 802.11 header.

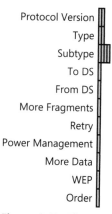

Figure A-7   The Frame Control field in the IEEE 802.11 header

The Frame Control field contains the following subfields:

- **Protocol Version**   A 2-bit field that indicates the version of the 802.11 protocol used to construct the frame. This field is set to 0 for the current version of IEEE 802.11. If the Protocol Version field is set to a value that is not supported by the receiving wireless node, the frame is silently discarded.

- **Type**   A 2-bit field that indicates the type of IEEE 802.11 frame. There are three defined values: 00 for management frames, 01 for control frames, and 10 for data frames. The value of 11 is currently reserved.

- **Subtype**   A 4-bit field that indicates the specific type of management, control, or data frame.

- **To DS**   A 1-bit flag that indicates (when set to 1) that the frame is destined for the distribution system (DS), which is the wired network that connects wireless APs and provides access to wired network nodes. Only wireless nodes that are operating in infrastructure mode set this flag.

- **From DS**   A 1-bit flag that indicates (when set to 1) that the frame is originating from the wired network. This flag is set by the wireless AP only when forwarding a frame to a wireless node operating in infrastructure mode.

- **More Fragments**   A 1-bit flag that indicates (when set to 1) that there are more fragments of the frame for which this frame is also a fragment. If the frame is not fragmented or is the last fragment of a fragmented frame, the More Fragments flag is set to 0.

- **Retry**   A 1-bit flag that indicates (when set to 1) that this frame is a retransmission of a previously transmitted frame.

- **Power Management**   A 1-bit flag that indicates (when set to 1) that the transmitting wireless node is operating in a power-saving mode.

- **More Data**   A 1-bit flag that indicates (when set to 1) that the wireless AP has at least one frame buffered to send to the wireless node.

- **WEP**   A 1-bit flag that indicates (when set to 1) that the payload is encrypted.

- **Order**   A 1-bit flag that indicates (when set to 1) that the frames must be processed in order.

WAN Media

To successfully troubleshoot IPv6 problems in a wide area network, it is important to understand WAN encapsulations. WAN technologies encompass point-to-point technologies—for example, analog phone lines, Integrated Services Digital Network (ISDN), T-Carrier, and Switched-56—and packet-switched technologies—for example, X.25, Frame Relay, and Asynchronous Transfer Mode (ATM). In each of these technologies, the packet needs to be delimited, addressed, and identified as an IPv6 packet.

Current RFCs exist for sending IPv6 packets over the following WAN media:

- Point-to-Point Protocol (PPP) (RFC 5072)

- X.25 (RFC 1356)

- Frame Relay (RFC 2590)

- ATM (RFC 2492)

 Note   There is no specific RFC for IPv6 packets over an X.25 link; however, RFC 1356 describes how any packet is sent over an X.25 link.

Windows Server 2008 and Windows Vista support IPv6 over PPP and Frame Relay links.

PPP

PPP, described in RFC 1661, is a standardized serial line encapsulation method that can be used over asynchronous serial lines—such as analog phone lines—and over synchronous serial lines—such as T-Carrier, ISDN, or Synchronous Optical Network (SONET). PPP is a family of protocols that describe the following:

- A multiprotocol encapsulation method.

- A Link Control Protocol (LCP) for establishing, configuring, and testing the data-link connection.

- A family of Network Control Protocols (NCPs) for establishing and configuring different network-layer protocols. RFC 5072 describes the IPv6 Control Protocol (IPV6CP), which is the NCP for configuring the IPv6 protocol over a PPP link.

Only the encapsulation method is described here.

PPP encapsulation uses a variant of the ISO High-Level Data Link Control (HDLC) protocol as described in RFC 1662. IPv6 encapsulation for PPP links is described in RFC 5072. Figure A-8 shows PPP encapsulation of IPv6 packets.

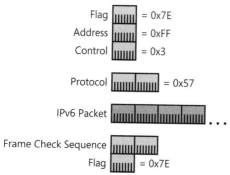

Figure A-8   PPP with HDLC framing encapsulation of IPv6 packets

The fields in the PPP header and trailer are the following:

- **Flag**   The Flag field indicates the start and end of a PPP frame and is set to 0x7E. In consecutive PPP frames, only a single Flag character is used to mark both the end of a PPP frame and the beginning of the next PPP frame. The size of this field is 8 bits.

- **Address**   The Address field is used in HDLC environments to address the frame to a destination node. On a point-to-point link, the destination node does not need to be addressed. Therefore, for PPP, the Address field is set to 0xFF, which is the broadcast address. The size of this field is 8 bits. Typically, PPP peers suppress the use of this field.

- **Control**   The Control field is used in HDLC environments for data-link layer sequencing and acknowledgments. For PPP, the Control field is set to 0x3 to indicate an unnumbered information (UI) frame. The size of this field is 8 bits. Typically, PPP peers suppress the use of this field.

- **Protocol**   The Protocol field identifies the protocol of the PPP payload. The Protocol field is set to 0x57 to indicate an IPv6 packet. In contrast, the Protocol field is set to 0x21 to indicate an IPv4 packet. The size of this field is 16 bits. Although defined as a 16-bit field, typically the Protocol field size is compressed to 8 bits.

- **Frame Check Sequence**   The Frame Check Sequence field stores a checksum value that is used to check for bit-level errors in the PPP frame. The size of this field is 16 bits.

The MTU for a PPP connection—called the Maximum Receive Unit (MRU)—is negotiated by using LCP. The default MRU is 1500 octets. If negotiated lower, a PPP host must still have the ability to receive 1500-octet frames in the case of link synchronization failure.

X.25

X.25 was developed in the 1970s to provide dumb terminals with WAN connectivity across public data networks (PDNs). However, because of its flexibility and reliability, X.25 has emerged as an international standard for sending data across PDNs.

X.25 is a connection-oriented interface to a packet-switched network (PSN). It provides error checking with guaranteed delivery of packets over the PSN by using either switched virtual circuits (SVCs) or permanent virtual circuits (PVCs). Because of its reliability and guaranteed delivery, X.25 works effectively for applications that require reliable transmission.

A router can connect via a Packet Assembler/Disassembler (PAD) to the X.25 network. The PAD is responsible for breaking down messages into packets and addressing them appropriately. The connection between the router and the PAD, the operations at the PAD, and the connection from the PAD to the carrier office is defined by the X.28, X.3, and X.29 specifications.

The X.25 specification maps to layers 1 through 3 of the Open Systems Interconnect (OSI) model. However, the X.25 specification was developed before the OSI model, so layer names are slightly different. The Physical layer is called X.21 and specifies the electrical and physical interface. The Data Link layer is the Link Access Procedure-Balanced (LAPB) protocol, which takes care of frame composition, flow control, and error checking at the Link Access layer. The Packet layer corresponds to the Network layer and is responsible for the setup and addressing of the virtual circuit.

When IPv6 packets are encapsulated for transmission on X.25 networks, they are wrapped with two sets of headers that correspond to the X.25 Network and Data Link layers. The X.25 Network layer uses the Packet Layer Protocol (PLP). The X.25 Data Link layer uses LAPB, which is the same HDLC format as PPP.

Figure A-9 shows X.25 encapsulation of IPv6 packets.

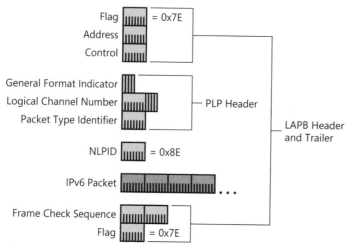

Figure A-9   X.25 encapsulation of IPv6 packets

The fields in the PLP header are the following:

- **General Format Indicator**   The General Format Indicator (GFI) indicates X.25 control information. The size of this field is 4 bits.

- **Logical Channel Number**   The Logical Channel Number (LCN) field indicates the virtual circuit over which the packet is sent. When an X.25 virtual circuit is created, an X.25 LCN is assigned to that virtual circuit so that data can be addressed to the proper destination. The size of this field is 12 bits, allowing a maximum of 4095 simultaneous connections. (LCN 0 is used for X.25 signaling.)

- **Packet Type Identifier**   The Packet Type Identifier field indicates the type of X.25 packet (X.25 signaling messages vs. X.25 user data). The size of this field is 8 bits.

The fields in the LAPB header and trailer are the following:

- **Flag**   The Flag field indicates the start and end of the X.25 frame and is fixed at 0x7E. The size of this field is 8 bits.

- **Address**   The Address field is used to specify X.25 commands and responses. The size of this field is 8 bits.

- **Control**   The Control field is used to indicate sequencing and acknowledgments for reliable data transfer. The size of this field is 8 bits.

- **Frame Check Sequence**   The value of this field is a checksum used to check for bit-level errors in the LAPB frame. The size of this field is 16 bits.

To identify the X.25 payload being encapsulated, X.25 packets use the Network Layer Protocol Identifier (NLPID) field. The size of this field is 8 bits. For IPv6 packets, the NLPID is set to 0x8E. For IPv4 packets, the NLPID is set to 0xCC.

IPv6 packets sent over X.25 links have a default MTU size of 1280 bytes, unless negotiated higher by the sender and receiver. Most X.25 networks have a maximum X.25 packet size of 256 or 512 bytes. In this case, X.25 fragmentation is used to send the 1280-byte IPv6 packets across the X.25 network.

Frame Relay

Frame Relay was originally conceived as a protocol for use over ISDN interfaces. Because Frame Relay could be applied outside the realm of ISDN, it was developed as an independent protocol. Frame Relay is a Data Link layer protocol that is much faster than X.25 because it is more streamlined and does not provide error correction and flow control.

Within the Frame Relay PDN, Frame Relay switching implements statistical multiplexing instead of time division multiplexing. With statistical multiplexing, circuits can be used from devices that are not currently using their allocated circuits. This makes real-time networks that are "bursty" in nature ideal candidates for Frame Relay.

The Local Management Interface (LMI) manages the link. LMI is responsible for establishing a link and monitoring PVCs. Because modern digital links are less susceptible to errors, Frame Relay employs only a checksum to detect a corrupted frame and does not include an error-correction mechanism. Frame Relay also relies on upper protocols for flow control over the link.

IPv6 packets sent over a Frame Relay network are encapsulated in a header and trailer that are also derived from the ISO HDLC protocol and have a similar structure to the PPP encapsulation. IPv6 packet behavior and encapsulation for Frame Relay links are described in RFCs 2491 and 2590. Figure A-10 shows Frame Relay encapsulation of IPv6 packets.

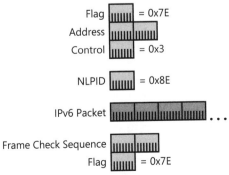

Figure A-10   Frame Relay encapsulation of IPv6 packets

The fields in the Frame Relay header and trailer are the following:

- **Flag**   The Flag field indicates the start and end of the Frame Relay frame and is fixed at 0x7E. The size of this field is 8 bits.

- **Address**   The Address field contains both the Data Link Connection Identifier (DLCI) that identifies the virtual circuit over which the frame is sent and congestion flags. Frame Relay standards allow for an Address field of variable size, but most implementations use a size of 16 bits.

- **Control**   The Control field is set to 0x3 to indicate a UI frame. The size of this field is 8 bits.

- **Frame Check Sequence**   The Frame Check Sequence (FCS) field stores a checksum value that is used to check for bit-level errors in the Frame Relay frame. The size of this field is 16 bits.

Like X.25, Frame Relay uses the NLPID field to identify the encapsulated payload. For IPv6 packets, the NLPID is set to 0x8E. For IPv4 packets, the NLPID is set to 0xCC.

MTUs for Frame Relay links vary according to the Frame Relay provider. As specified in RFC 2590, Frame Relay links have a maximum frame size of at least 1600 bytes. Therefore, the default IPv6 MTU for Frame Relay links that use a 16-bit Address field is 1592.

ATM: Null Encapsulation

ATM technology is based on the development of Broadband Integrated Services Digital Network (B-ISDN) for the high-speed transfer of voice, video, and data through PDNs. ATM is a connection-oriented nonguaranteed delivery service. ATM scales very well to LANs and WANs and can be used in a private network as well as a public data network.

ATM is different from Frame Relay in that, instead of sending messages that have frames of variable size, all messages are segmented and sent as equally sized cells. Each cell consists of a 5-byte header and a 48-byte payload. By making all messages the same size, switching is optimized and the need to buffer messages of varying sizes is eliminated. With these improvements, ATM is capable of reaching speeds from 64 kilobits per seconds (Kbps) to 76 gigabits per second (Gbps), depending upon the underlying physical layer.

Because it is an asynchronous mechanism, ATM differs from synchronous transfer mode methods, in which time-division multiplexing (TDM) techniques are employed to pre-assign devices to time slots. TDM is inefficient relative to ATM because with TDM the station can transmit only at a specified time, even though all the other time slots are empty. With ATM, a station can send cells whenever necessary.

Relative to IPv6, ATM functions as a link layer. ATM itself has its own set of layers that define the following:

- How ATM cells are sent over several different physical mediums, such as SONET and Digital Service (DS)-3.

- How connections are established and cells are passed through the ATM network.

- How the data of higher-level protocols, such as IPv4 and IPv6, are segmented and reassembled using 48-byte segments suitable for transmission over an ATM network. This layer is known as the ATM Adaptation layer.

IPv6 packets sent over an ATM network have an MTU of 9180 bytes and are encapsulated by using ATM Adaptation Layer 5 (AAL5). AAL5 encapsulation consists of an AAL5 trailer added to the end of the IPv6 packet. The resulting data block (called the AAL5 PDU) is then segmented into 48-byte segments that become the payloads for 53-byte ATM cells.

IPv6 encapsulation for ATM links is described in RFC 2492. Figure A-11 shows ATM null encapsulation of IPv6 packets.

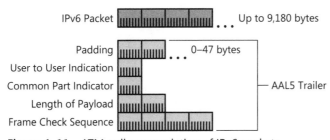

Figure A-11   ATM null encapsulation of IPv6 packets

The fields in the AAL5 trailer are the following:

- **Padding**   The Padding field is added to the IPv6 packet so that the AAL5 PDU is an integral number of 48-byte segments. The size of this field varies from 0 to 47 bytes.

- **User to User Indication**   The User to User Indication field is used to transfer information between AAL5 nodes. The size of this field is 8 bits.

- **Common Part Indicator**   The Common Part Indicator field is used for alignment purposes so that the unpadded portion of the AAL5 trailer is on an 8-byte boundary. The size of this field is 8 bits.

- **Length of Payload**   The Length of Payload field specifies the length in bytes of the IPv6 packet so that the receiver can discard the Padding field. The size of this field is 16 bits.

- **Frame Check Sequence**   The Frame Check Sequence field stores a checksum value that is used to check for bit-level errors in the AAL5 PDU. The size of this field is 32 bits. AAL5 uses the same CRC-32 algorithm as 802.x networks such as Ethernet and Token Ring.

Before being sent on the ATM network, the AAL5 PDU is segmented by the ATM Segmentation and Reassembly (SAR) sublayer into 48-byte units. These units become the ATM payloads for a stream of ATM cells. When the last 48-byte segment is sent, a bit in the Payload Type field of the ATM header is set to 1 to indicate the last cell in the AAL5 PDU.

When the last cell is received, the receiver uses the Frame Check Sequence field to check the validity of the bits in the AAL5 PDU. The receiver then uses the Length of Payload field to discard any padding. The AAL5 trailer is stripped, and the originally transmitted IPv6 packet is then passed to the IPv6 protocol for processing. If a single ATM cell for the AAL5 PDU is dropped from the network, the entire IPv6 packet must be resent.

ATM: SNAP Encapsulation

The ATM null encapsulation can be used when only the IPv6 protocol is operating over a given ATM virtual circuit. Multiple protocols operating over the same ATM virtual circuit require a protocol identifier so that the receiver can determine the protocol being sent and pass the resulting data to the appropriate protocol parsing or routing routine. This capability is especially important for multiprotocol routers.

To add a protocol identifier to the AAL5 PDU, an IEEE 802.x SNAP header is added. It contains the EtherType (set to 0x86DD) that identifies the payload as an IPv6 packet. As part of the virtual channel connection (VCC) negotiation process between two ATM endpoints, an agreement is reached on whether a single protocol is to be used (in which case the SNAP header is not required) or multiple protocols are to be used (in which case a SNAP header is required).

Figure A-12 shows ATM SNAP encapsulation of IPv6 packets.

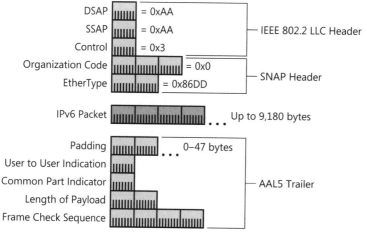

Figure A-12   ATM SNAP encapsulation of IPv6 packets

For information on the fields in the IEEE 802.2 LLC and SNAP headers, see the section "Ethernet: IEEE 802.3 SNAP" in this appendix.

IPv6 over IPv4

IPv6-over-IPv4 tunneling is the encapsulation of IPv6 packets with an IPv4 header so that IPv6 packets can be sent over an IPv4 infrastructure. Figure A-13 shows IPv4 encapsulation of IPv6 packets.

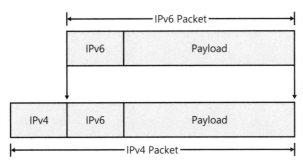

Figure A-13   IPv4 encapsulation of IPv6 packets

Within the IPv4 header is the following:

- The IPv4 Protocol field is set to 41 to indicate an encapsulated IPv6 packet.

- The Source and Destination fields are set to the IPv4 addresses of the tunnel endpoints. The tunnel endpoints are either manually configured as part of the tunnel interface or are automatically determined from the IPv4 address of the sending interface and the next-hop address for the destination address in the IPv6 header.

For IPv6-over-IPv4 tunneling, the IPv6 path MTU for the destination is typically 20 less than the IPv4 path MTU for the destination (to a minimum of 1280 bytes between the tunnel endpoints). However, if the IPv4 path MTU is not stored for each tunnel, there are instances in which the IPv4 packet will need to be fragmented at an intermediate router. In this case, the IPv6-over-IPv4 tunneled packet must be sent with the Don't Fragment flag in the IPv4 header set to 0.

References

The following references were cited in this appendix:

- RFC 1356 – "Multiprotocol Interconnect on X.25 and ISDN in the Packet Mode"

- RFC 1661 – "The Point to Point Protocol (PPP)"

- RFC 1662 – "PPP in HDLC-like Framing"

- RFC 2464 – "Transmission of IPv6 Packets over Ethernet Networks"
- RFC 2467 – "Transmission of IPv6 Packets over FDDI Networks"
- RFC 2470 – "Transmission of IPv6 Packets over Token Ring Networks"
- RFC 2491 – "IPv6 over Non-Broadcast Multiple Access (NBMA) Networks"
- RFC 2492 – "IPv6 over ATM Networks"
- RFC 2590 – "Transmission of IPv6 Packets over Frame Relay Networks Specification"
- RFC 5072 – "IP Version 6 over PPP"

You can obtain these RFCs from the \RFCs_and_Drafts folder on the companion CD-ROM or from *http://www.ietf.org/rfc.html.*

Appendix B
Windows Sockets Changes for IPv6

This appendix includes information on changes that have been made to the Windows Sockets application programming interface (API) to support Internet Protocol version 6 (IPv6) applications, and it provides examples of how and when to use these changes in an application. The following topics are described:

- Added constants
- Address data structures
- Wildcard addresses
- Core sockets functions
- Name-to-address translation
- Address-to-name translation
- Address conversion functions
- Socket options
- New macros

Changes to Windows Sockets for IPv6 are defined in RFCs 3493 and 3542.

Additional details about how to modify applications so that they can use both IPv4 and IPv6 can be found in the "IPv6 Guide for Windows Sockets Applications" article at *http://go. microsoft.com/fwlink/?LinkID=87735*.

For additional information, see the "Developer Resources" section of the Microsoft IPv6 Web site at *http://www.microsoft.com/ipv6*.

Added Constants

A new address family name for IPv6 is required so that the address structure can be correctly identified and parsed. Similarly, a new protocol family name (with the same value as the address family name) must be defined so that a socket is created using the appropriate protocol. The address family name and protocol family name constants for IPv6 are the following:

- AF_INET6
- PF_INET6

Address Data Structures

The term *sockets* defines a protocol-specific data structure that holds elements of a socket address. For IPv4, this structure is *sockaddr_in*. *Sockets* also defines a protocol-independent structure (*sockaddr*) for the protocol-specific structures to be cast into. The identifying field (the address family) in the protocol-specific structure overlays the family field in the generic structure. Because IPv6 addresses are different than IPv4 addresses, a new protocol-specific structure for IPv6 is required.

The data structures *sockaddr* and *sockaddr_in* are the same size, which could lead you into making incorrect assumptions about the size of their related address structures. The IPv6 address structure, *sockaddr_in6*, is larger by necessity. For example, the *sockaddr* structure cannot be used to allocate storage for *sockaddr_in6*.

in6_addr

```
struct in6_addr {
    union {
        u_char Byte[16];
        ushort Word[8];
        } u;
};
```

The socket address structure contains information above and beyond the address for the socket. One portion of the structure, however, needs to be the address. In IPv4's address structure, this address is contained in *in_addr*. A larger structure, *in6_addr*, has been defined to hold the larger IPv6 address.

sockaddr_in6

In addition to the larger address size, there are other members that must be represented in the socket address structure for IPv6. Although the IPv4 *sockaddr_in* structure has unused space, it is not enough to contain this additional information. The *sockaddr_in6* structure is used to contain an IPv6 address.

```
struct sockaddr_in6 {
    sa_family_t     sin6_family;
    in_port_t       sin6_port;
    uint32_t        sin6_flowinfo;
    struct in6_addr sin6_addr;
    uint32_t        sin6_scope_id;
};
```

In addition to the family, port, and address information, this structure contains *sin6_flowinfo* and *sin6_scope_id* members. *sin6_flowinfo* contains the traffic class and the flow label from and for the IPv6 header. *sin6_scope_id* contains the scope ID, which is used to identify a set of interfaces that are appropriate for the address carried in the address field.

sockaddr_storage

As mentioned earlier, *sockaddr* and *sockaddr_in6* have different sizes. Because of this, *struct sockaddr* cannot be used to allocate storage and then be cast to a *sockaddr_in6* pointer. If static allocation of storage for *sockaddr_in6* (or even *sockaddr_in*) structures is needed, *struct sockaddr_storage* should be used. Here is an example:

```
struct sockaddr_storage newaddr;
...
msgsock = accept(listen_socket,(struct sockaddr*) &newaddr, &newaddrlen);
```

In addition to being large enough to accommodate all known protocol-specific socket address structures (including *sockaddr_in6*), *sockaddr_storage* is aligned at an appropriate boundary so that protocol-specific socket address data-structure pointers can be cast to it. This enables it to access fields without experiencing alignment problems.

Wildcard Addresses

To allow the protocol implementation to choose the source address for a connection or datagram with IPv4, a constant of INADDR_ANY (the wildcard address) is used as the address in the *bind()* call.

The IPv6 address type (*in6_addr*) is a structure. A constant cannot be used in an assignment for this variable, but one can be used to initialize the structure. Thus, we end up with two possible ways to provide the wildcard address.

The global variable, *in6addr_any*, can be used in an assignment—for example:

```
sin6.sin6_addr = in6addr_any;
```

Or the constant, IN6ADDR_ANY_INIT, can be used to initialize the address structure (at declaration time only)—for example:

```
struct in6_addr anyaddr = IN6ADDR_ANY_INIT;
```

in6addr_loopback and **IN6ADDR_LOOPBACK_INIT**

Similarly, the INADDR_LOOPBACK constant is used in IPv4 *connect()*, *send()*, and *WSASendMsg()* calls to communicate with services that reside on the local node. For IPv6 loopback, a global variable (*in6addr_loopback*) is used for assignment and a constant (IN6ADDR_LOOPBACK_INIT) is used for initialization at declaration time.

Note   The IPv4 INADDR_*XXX* constants were defined in host-byte order. The IPv6 equivalents are defined in network-byte order.

Core Sockets Functions

An address is passed in core sockets functions as an opaque address pointer and length. Because of this, changes need not be made to these core sockets functions for IPv6. The application developer needs simply to supply the appropriate IPv6 address structure and family constants.

Sockets functions that pass addresses are the following:

- *bind()*
- *connect()*
- *WSASendMsg()*
- *sendto()*

Sockets functions that return addresses are the following:

- *accept()*
- *recvfrom()*
- *WSARecvMsg()*
- *getpeername()*
- *getsockname()*

Name-to-Address Translation

To resolve a host name to one or more IP addresses in IPv4, the application might use *gethostbyname()*. This API does not allow the caller to specify anything about the types of addresses wanted, and the structure contains only enough space to store an IPv4 address. To address these issues, there is a new API named *getaddrinfo()*. This API is protocol-independent and can be used for both IPv4 and IPv6 name-to-address resolutions. The return from this call is in the form of *addrinfo* structures that can subsequently be used to both open and use a socket.

The function prototype for *getaddrinfo()* is the following:

```
int getaddrinfo(
    IN const char FAR *nodename,
    IN const char FAR *servname,
    IN const struct addrinfo FAR *hints,
    OUT struct addrinfo FAR *FAR *res
    );
struct addrinfo {
    int ai_flags;
    int ai_family;
    int ai_socktype;
    int ai_protocol;
```

```
     size_t ai_addrlen;
     char *ai_canonname;
     struct sockaddr *ai_addr;
struct addrinfo *ai_next;
};
```

As arguments, either a node name or service name (or both) are provided. The node name can (optionally) be a numeric address string, and the service name can (optionally) be a decimal port number. An *addrinfo* structure can be provided (optionally) to provide hints for the type of socket that the caller supports. The *addrinfo* structure pointed to by this hints parameter can specify a preferred socket type, family and protocol, and the following flags:

- **AI_PASSIVE**   This flag indicates that the caller plans to use the returned address structure in a *bind()* call when set or in a *connect()* call when not set. Setting the node name to NULL has additional meaning depending on this flag. If the node name in the hints is NULL and this flag is set, the returned addresses will be wildcard addresses. If the node name in the hints is NULL and this flag is not set, the returned addresses will be loopback addresses.

- **AI_CANONNAME**   The AI_CANONNAME flag indicates (when set) that the first *addrinfo* structure returned should contain a null-terminated string that contains the canonical name of the node name in the *ai_canonname* member.

- **AI_NUMERICHOST**   This flag indicates that the node name in the call is a numeric address string.

- **AI_NUMERICSRV**   This flag indicates that the node name in the call is a service name string.

- **AI_V4MAPPED**   If the address family specified is AF_INET6, the caller will accept IPv4-mapped IPv6 addresses. Windows Server 2008 and Windows Vista do not support the use of this flag.

- **AI_ALL**   This flag is used with the AI_V4MAPPED flag to indicate that the caller wants all addresses, both true IPv6 addresses and IPv4-mapped IPv6 addresses. The address family specified must be AF_INET6. Windows Server 2008 and Windows Vista do not support the use of this flag.

- **AI_ADDRCONFIG**   The AI_ADDRCONFIG flag controls whether the query requests AAAA DNS records or A records, based on the locally configured source addresses. AAAA records are queried only if the node has at least one IPv6 source address. A records are queried only if the node has at least one IPv4 source address.

A pointer to a linked list of *addrinfo* structures is returned. The order of the addresses is in decreasing order of desirability.

The *addrinfo* structures (and structures contained as members within those structures) are dynamically allocated and must be released by calling *freeaddrinfo()* with a pointer to the linked list of *addrinfo* structures.

The function prototype for *freeaddrinfo()* is the following:

```
void freeaddrinfo(
  struct addrinfo FAR *ai
);
```

Address-to-Name Translation

A reverse lookup can be performed by using another new sockets function, *getnameinfo()*. To use this API, a socket address structure is provided. The function prototype for *getnameinfo()* is the following:

```
int getnameinfo(
    IN const struct sockaddr FAR *sa,
    IN socklen_t salen,
    OUT char FAR *host,
    IN size_t hostlen,
    OUT char FAR *serv,
    IN size_t servlen,
    IN int flags
    );
```

It contains the address and port in question. This can be either an IPv4 or IPv6 socket address structure because the length is also provided.

Additionally, buffers are provided to receive the node name and service name associated with that address, and the flags field can be used to change the default behavior of the API. The lengths of these buffers are provided in the call, and constants are defined (NI_MAXHOST, NI_MAXSERV) to aid the application in allocating buffers of the maximum size required.

The flags adjust the behavior as follows:

- **NI_NOFQDN**   Setting the NI_NOFQDN flag results in returning only the node name (not the fully qualified domain name, or FQDN) for local hosts.
- **NI_NUMERICHOST**   Setting this flag results in returning the numeric form of the host's address instead of its name.
- **NI_NAMEREQD**   Setting the NI_NAMEREQD flag results in returning an error if the name cannot be located.
- **NI_NUMERICSERV**   Setting NI_NUMERICSERV results in returning the numeric port number instead of the service name.
- **NI_DGRAM**   Setting this flag specifies that the service is a datagram service, causing a search for a User Datagram Protocol (UDP) service–instead of a Transmission Control Protocol (TCP) service.

Using *getaddrinfo*

Here is an example of a client application using *getaddrinfo()* to connect to a specific server:

```
{/* Client Side...*/}
if (getaddrinfo(service_name, port, NULL, &ai) != 0) {/* Error Handling */}

conn_socket = socket(ai->ai_family, ai->ai_socktype,ai->ai_protocol);
if (conn_socket <0 ) {/* Error Handling */}

if (connect(conn_socket,ai->ai_addr,ai->ai_addrlen) == SOCKET_ERROR)
{/* Error Handling */}

freeaddrinfo(ai);
```

Here is an example of the corresponding server application using *getaddrinfo()* to resolve the address information for the socket creation and bind calls:

```
{/* Server Side... */}
hints.ai_family = AF_INET6;
hints.ai_socktype = SOCK_STREAM;
hints.ai_flags = AI_NUMERICHOST | AI_PASSIVE;

retval = getaddrinfo(interface, port, &hints, &ai);
if (retval != 0) {/* Error Handling */}

listen_socket = socket(ai->ai_family, ai->ai_socktype, ai->ai_protocol);
if (listen_socket == INVALID_SOCKET){/* Error Handling */}

if (bind(listen_socket,ai->ai_addr,ai->ai_addrlen )== SOCKET_ERROR)
{/* Error Handling */}

freeaddrinfo(ai);
```

The *interface* parameter in this call could be NULL, or it could be set to a numeric string.

Address Conversion Functions

The *inet_addr()* and *inet_ntoa()* functions are provided to convert IPv4 addresses between binary and text formats. The Internet Engineering Task Force (IETF) defined similar functions—*inet_pton()* and *inet_ntop()*—to convert both IPv4 and IPv6 addresses. These functions contain an additional address family argument to make them protocol-independent.

Because *getaddrinfo()* and *getnameinfo()* provide the same functionality, Windows Server 2008 and Windows Vista do not support the *inet_pton()* and *inet_ntop()* functions.

Socket Options

A new socket option level, IPPROTO_IPV6, has been defined for IPv6-specific socket options. Although an application can send multicast UDP packets by specifying a multicast address in *sendto()*, most of the new socket options currently defined for IPv6 are intended to adjust multicast behavior. New socket options are the following:

- **IPV6_MULTICAST_IF**   This option sets the default interface to use for outgoing multicast traffic to the interface indicated by the index specified in the argument. (A 0 indicates that the system chooses the interface.)

- **IPV6_MULTICAST_HOPS**   This option sets the hop limit for outgoing multicast packets based on the argument. Valid values are either 0 to 255 inclusive or −1 (to use the system default).

- **IPV6_MULTICAST_LOOP**   This option controls whether outgoing multicast packets addressed to a group, of which the interface is a member, is looped back.

For reception of multicast traffic, new options are defined to join and leave multicast groups. These options take an argument of an *ipv6_mreq* structure:

```
struct ipv6_mreq {
    struct in6_addr ipv6mr_multiaddr;
    unsigned int ipv6mr_interface;
};
```

This structure contains the multicast address of the group to be joined or left, and an interface index to use for this join or leave.

Following is a list of new multicast socket options:

- **IPV6_JOIN_GROUP**   This option is used to join the specified multicast group on the interface indicated. (A 0 indicates that the system chooses the interface.)

- **IPV6_LEAVE_GROUP**   The IPV6_LEAVE_GROUP option is used to leave the specified group on the interface indicated.

In addition, another socket option, IPV6_UNICAST_HOPS, is defined to control the hop limit for outgoing unicast packets.

New Macros

The additions to Windows Sockets that support IPv6 include the following set of macros to test addresses and determine whether they are special IPv6 addresses:

- IN6_IS_ADDR_UNSPECIFIED

- IN6_IS_ADDR_LOOPBACK

- IN6_IS_ADDR_MULTICAST

- IN6_IS_ADDR_LINKLOCAL

- IN6_IS_ADDR_SITELOCAL

- IN6_IS_ADDR_V4MAPPED

- IN6_IS_ADDR_V4COMPAT

- IN6_IS_ADDR_MC_NODELOCAL

- IN6_IS_ADDR_MC_LINKLOCAL

- IN6_IS_ADDR_MC_SITELOCAL

- IN6_IS_ADDR_MC_ORGLOCAL

- IN6_IS_ADDR_MC_GLOBAL

The first seven macros in the preceding list return a true value if the address is of the specified type. The last five test the scope of a multicast address, returning a true value if the address is a multicast address of the specified scope and returning a false value if the address is either not a multicast address or is not of the specified scope.

The IN6_IS_ADDR_V4MAPPED macro can be used to determine whether the destination address for a socket is an IPv4 node.

References

The following references were cited in this chapter:

- RFC 3493 – "Basic Socket Interface Extensions for IPv6"
- RFC 3542 – "Advanced Sockets Application Program Interface (API) for IPv6"

You can obtain these RFCs from the \RFCs_and_Drafts folder on the companion CD-ROM or from *http://www.ietf.org/rfc.html*.

Appendix C
IPv6 RFC Index

This appendix contains tables of Internet Engineering Task Force (IETF) Requests for Comments (RFCs) and Internet drafts for the IPv6 protocol and related technologies that were available at the time of the publication of this book, arranged by function. All of these RFCs and Internet drafts are provided in the \RFCs_and_Drafts folder on the companion CD-ROM.

General

Table C-1   IPv6 General RFCs

RFC #	Category	Title
1752	Standards Track	The Recommendation for the IP Next Generation Protocol
1924	Informational	A Compact Representation of IPv6 Addresses
4001	Standards Track	Textual Conventions for Internet Network Addresses
4294	Informational	IPv6 Node Requirements

Addressing

Table C-2   IPv6 Addressing RFCs and Internet Drafts

RFC #	Category	Title
1881	Informational	IPv6 Address Allocation Management
1887	Informational	An Architecture for IPv6 Unicast Address Allocation
2375	Informational	IPv6 Multicast Address Assignments
2526	Standards Track	Reserved IPv6 Subnet Anycast Addresses
3315	Standards Track	Dynamic Host Configuration Protocol for IPv6 (DHCPv6)
3587	Informational	IPv6 Global Unicast Address Format
3633	Standards Track	IPv6 Prefix Options for DHCP version 6
3646	Standards Track	DNS Configuration Options for DHCPv6
3736	Standards Track	Stateless DHCP Service for IPv6
3879	Standards Track	Deprecating Site Local Addresses
4007	Standards Track	IP version 6 Scoped Address Architecture

Table C-2 IPv6 Addressing RFCs and Internet Drafts

RFC #	Category	Title
4193	Standards Track	Unique Local IPv6 Unicast Addresses
4291	Standards Track	IP Version 6 Addressing Architecture
4941	Standards Track	Privacy Extensions for Stateless Address Autoconfiguration in IPv6
	Internet draft	IPv6 Unicast Address Assignment Considerations

Applications

Table C-3 IPv6 Applications RFCs

RFC #	Category	Title
1886	Standards Track	DNS Extensions to support IP version 6
2428	Standards Track	FTP Extensions for IPv6 and NATs
2874	Standards Track	DNS Extensions to Support IPv6 Address Aggregation and Renumbering
3596	Standards Track	DNS Extensions to Support IP Version 6
3986	Standards Track	Uniform Resource Identifier (URI): Generic Syntax
4620	Experimental	IPv6 Node Information Queries
4795	Informational	Link-Local Multicast Name Resolution (LLMNR)

Sockets API

Table C-4 IPv6 Sockets API RFCs

RFC #	Category	Title
3493	Informational	Basic Socket Interface Extensions for IPv6
3542	Informational	Advanced Sockets Application Program Interface (API) for IPv6

Transport Layer

Table C-5 IPv6 Transport Layer RFCs

RFC #	Category	Title
4022	Standards Track	IP Version 6 Management Information Base for the Transmission Control Protocol
4113	Standards Track	IP Version 6 Management Information Base for the User Datagram Protocol

Internet Layer

Table C-6   IPv6 Internet Layer RFCs and Internet Drafts

RFC #	Category	Title
1981	Standards Track	Path MTU Discovery for IP version 6
2460	Standards Track	Internet Protocol, Version 6 (IPv6) Specification
2474	Standards Track	Definition of the Differentiated Services Field (DS Field) in the IPv4 and IPv6 Headers
2675	Standards Track	IPv6 Jumbograms
2710	Standards Track	Multicast Listener Discovery (MLD) for IPv6
2711	Standards Track	IPv6 Router Alert Option
3019	Standards Track	IP Version 6 Management Information Base for the Multicast Listener Discovery Protocol
3122	Standards Track	Extensions to IPv6 Neighbor Discovery for Inverse Discovery Specification
3168	Standards Track	The Addition of Explicit Congestion Notification (ECN) to IP
3484	Standards Track	Default Address Selection for IPv6
3697	Standards Track	IPv6 Flow Label Specification
3775	Standards Track	Mobility Support in IPv6
3776	Standards Track	Using IPsec to Protect Mobile IPv6 Signaling Between Mobile Nodes and Home Agents
3810	Standards Track	Multicast Listener Discovery Version 2 (MLDv2) for IPv6
4191	Standards Track	Default Router Preferences and More Specific Routes
4293	Standards Track	Management Information Base for the Internet Protocol (IP)
4311	Standards Track	IPv6 Host-to-Router Load Sharing
4429	Standards Track	Optimistic Duplicate Address Detection (DAD) for IPv6
4443	Standards Track	Internet Control Message Protocol (ICMPv6) for the Internet Protocol Version 6 (IPv6) Specification
4861	Standards Track	Neighbor Discovery for IP Version 6 (IPv6)
4862	Standards Track	IPv6 Stateless Address Autoconfiguration
	Internet draft	Deprecation of Type 0 Routing Headers in IPv6

Network Layer Security

Table C-7   IPv6 Network Layer Security RFCs

RFC #	Category	Title
4301	Standards Track	Security Architecture for the Internet Protocol
4302	Standards Track	IP Authentication Header
4303	Standards Track	IP Encapsulating Security Payload (ESP)

Link Layer

Table C-8   IPv6 Link Layer RFCs and Internet Drafts

RFC #	Category	Title
2464	Standards Track	Transmission of IPv6 Packets over Ethernet Networks
2467	Standards Track	Transmission of IPv6 Packets over FDDI Networks
2470	Standards Track	Transmission of IPv6 Packets over Token Ring Networks
2473	Standards Track	Generic Packet Tunneling in IPv6 Specification
2491	Standards Track	IPv6 over Non-Broadcast Multiple Access (NBMA) networks
2492	Standards Track	IPv6 over ATM Networks
2497	Standards Track	Transmission of IPv6 Packets over ARCnet Networks
2507	Standards Track	IP Header Compression
2508	Standards Track	Compressing IP/UDP/RTP Headers for Low-Speed Serial Links
2590	Standards Track	Transmission of IPv6 Packets over Frame Relay Networks Specification
3146	Standards Track	Transmission of IPv6 Packets over IEEE 1394 Networks
3544	Standards Track	IP Header Compression over PPP
5072	Standards Track	IP Version 6 over PPP

Routing

Table C-9   IPv6 Routing RFCs

RFC #	Category	Title
2080	Standards Track	RIPng for IPv6
2185	Informational	Routing Aspects of IPv6 Transition
2545	Standards Track	Use of BGP-4 Multiprotocol Extensions for IPv6 Inter-Domain Routing
2740	Standards Track	OSPF for IPv6
2894	Standards Track	Router Renumbering for IPv6
4760	Standards Track	Multiprotocol Extensions for BGP-4
	Internet draft	Routing IPv6 with IS-IS

IPv6 Transition Technologies

Table C-10   IPv6 Transition Technologies RFCs

RFC #	Category	Title
3053	Informational	IPv6 Tunnel Broker
3056	Standards Track	Connection of IPv6 Domains via IPv4 Clouds
4213	Standards Track	Transition Mechanisms for IPv6 Hosts and Routers
4214	Experimental	Intra-Site Automatic Tunnel Addressing Protocol (ISATAP)
4380	Standards Track	Teredo: Tunneling IPv6 over UDP through Network Address Translations (NATs)

For the latest list of RFCs and Internet drafts describing IPv6, see the IETF IPv6 Working Group at *http://www.ietf.org/html.charters/OLD/ipv6-charter.html* and the IETF IPv6 Operations Working Group at *http://www.ietf.org/html.charters/v6ops-charter.html*.

For additional RFCs, see the IETF Request for Comments Web page at *http://www.ietf.org/rfc.html*.

Appendix D
Testing for Understanding Answers

This appendix contains the answers to the "Testing for Understanding" sections of Chapters 1 through 16.

Chapter 1: Introduction to IPv6

1. What are the problems with IPv4 on today's Internet?

   ❑ Internet Protocol version 4 (IPv4) has a rapidly depleting public address space.

   ❑ The configuration of IPv4 could be simpler.

   ❑ Security at the Internet Protocol (IP) level should be required so that applications can count on standardized Internet layer security services.

   ❑ IPv4 has limited support for prioritized delivery.

2. How does IPv6 solve these problems?

   The 128-bit address length of Internet Protocol version 6 (IPv6) allows for a large public address space.

   IPv6 provides automatic configuration, even without the use of a stateful address configuration protocol such as the Dynamic Host Configuration Protocol for IPv6 (DHCPv6).

   Support for Internet Protocol security (IPsec) headers is an IPv6 implementation requirement.

   There is better support for prioritized delivery using the Traffic Class and Flow Label fields.

3. How does IPv6 provide better prioritized delivery support?

   IPv6 uses a combination of the Traffic Class field, to define a specific type of service, and the Flow Label field, to indicate that the packet requires special handling, even when the payload is encrypted.

4. Describe at least three ways in which IPv6 is more efficient than IPv4.

   IPv6 addresses are hierarchical and summarizable, which can lead to smaller routing tables.

   The IPv6 address space removes the need for Network Address Translators (NATs), making end-to-end communication faster because no address discovery or translation is needed.

The IPv6 header is designed for minimal overhead and optimal processing speed at intermediate routers.

IPv6 Neighbor Discovery (ND) replaces the broadcast-based Address Resolution Protocol (ARP) with unicast and multicast ND messages. Common neighbor operations such as address resolution involve very few nodes.

IPv6 hosts are self-configuring and do not require a DHCPv6 server to discover addresses and other configuration information, reducing host startup times.

5. Explain how NATs prevent peer-to-peer applications from working properly.

Because each peer behind a NAT is represented by two addresses (a public address and a private address), peers cannot connect without manually configuring the NAT or relay address information about each other without making the peer-to-peer application NAT-aware.

6. What are the key technical benefits of deploying IPv6 now?

You will be able to take advantage of a much larger address space.

You can get public IPv6 address space in areas of the world that have few available public IPv4 addresses.

IPv6 restores true end-to-end communication without intermediate translation. Peer-to-peer applications can now connect without compensating for one or more NATs between peers.

IPv6 forwarding is more efficient and is address-scope aware.

7. What are the key business benefits of deploying IPv6 now?

IPv6 guarantees the future growth of the Internet by providing enough public addresses for the foreseeable future that can be allocated based on regional connectivity needs.

IPv6 simplifies connectivity by creating a single, global addressing scheme and removing disjoint address spaces.

IPv6 eliminates the need for public address conservation technologies such as NATs and their inherent complications for end-to-end connectivity.

IPv6 requires support for IPsec headers, defining a single standard to provide end-to-end protection of IPv6 packets across intranets or the IPv6 Internet.

Chapter 2: IPv6 Protocol for Windows Server 2008 and Windows Vista

1. List and describe the features of the IPv6 protocol for IPv6 transition.

Intra-Site Automatic Tunnel Addressing Protocol (ISATAP) allows IPv6/IPv4 hosts on an IPv4-only portion of an intranet to use unicast IPv6 traffic to communicate with each other and with native IPv6 nodes on an IPv6-capable portion of the intranet.

6to4 allows a host and a site to use unicast IPv6 traffic to communicate with each other across the IPv4 Internet and with native IPv6 nodes on the IPv6 Internet.

Teredo allows IPv6/IPv4 hosts on the IPv4 Internet to use unicast IPv6 traffic to communicate with each other and with nodes on the IPv6 Internet, even when the IPv6/IPv4 hosts are behind a NAT.

PortProxy functions as a Transmission Control Protocol (TCP) proxy to facilitate the communication between nodes or applications that cannot connect using a common Internet layer protocol (IPv4 or IPv6).

2. What are the two ways to configure the IPv6 protocol for Windows Server 2008 and Windows Vista?

   For most hosts, no configuration is required because stateless address autoconfiguration automatically configures addresses, routes, and other settings. To manually configure the IPv6 protocol for Windows Server 2008 and Windows Vista, use the properties of the Internet Protocol version 6 (TCP/IPv6) component in the Network Connections folder or at the Windows command prompt with commands in the **netsh interface ipv6** context.

3. A network administrator wants to disable all 6to4 and Teredo tunnel interfaces for computers running Windows Server 2008 or Windows Vista. What is the correct value of the *DisabledComponents* registry value?

   To disable 6to4 and Teredo interfaces, you must set bits 1 and 3 to 1, forming the binary number 00001010, or 0xA. Therefore, set *DisabledComponents* to 0xA.

4. Describe the purpose of Link-Local Multicast Name Resolution (LLMNR) and when it is used as the primary method for name resolution for IPv6 addresses.

   LLMNR allows IPv6 hosts on a subnet to resolve each other's names through an exchange of a multicast query and unicast response messages. LLMNR is the primary method of name resolution when a Domain Name System (DNS) server is not available, such as on an ad hoc wireless network.

5. Under what circumstances will an IPv6 router running Windows Server 2008 or Windows Vista advertise itself as a default router?

   By default, an IPv6 router running Windows Server 2008 or Windows Vista advertises itself as a default router only if it has a default route that is configured to be published.

6. List how the common TCP/IP troubleshooting tools have been enhanced to support IPv6 in Windows Server 2008 and Windows Vista.

   Ipconfig.exe displays both IPv4 and IPv6 configurations.

   Route.exe displays and allows modifications to both IPv4 and IPv6 routing tables.

   Ping.exe uses both Internet Control Message Protocol for IPv4 (ICMPv4) Echo and Internet Control Message Protocol for IPv6 (ICMPv6) Echo Request messages and supports additional options for IPv6.

Tracert.exe uses both ICMPv4 Echo and ICMPv6 Echo Request messages and supports additional options for IPv6.

Pathping.exe uses both ICMPv4 Echo and ICMPv6 Echo Request messages and supports additional options for IPv6.

Netstat.exe now displays the IPv6 routing table and information about the IPv6, ICMPv6, TCP over IPv6, and User Datagram Protocol (UDP) over IPv6 protocols.

7. What do the asterisks in the default interface names in the display of the Ipconfig.exe tool indicate?

The asterisks in the default names of the interfaces indicate that the interface is a tunneling interface (ISATAP, 6to4, Teredo), rather than the loopback interface or a local area network (LAN) interface.

8. Which Netsh command displays the interface indexes that correspond to IPv6 interfaces?

netsh interface ipv6 show interface

Chapter 3: IPv6 Addressing

1. Why is the IPv6 address length 128 bits?

The IPv6 address length is 128 bits so that it can be divided into hierarchical routing domains that reflect the topology of the modern-day Internet. For unicast IPv6 addresses, 64 bits for the subnet prefix allows for multiple levels of hierarchy and flexibility in designing hierarchical addressing and routing between the backbone of the IPv6 Internet and the individual subnets within an organization's site. The 64 bits of interface identifier (ID) accommodate the mapping of current and future link-layer media access control (MAC) addresses.

2. Express FEC0:0000:0000:0001:02AA:0000:0000:0007A more efficiently.

FEC0::1:2AA:0:0:7A or FEC0:0:0:1:2AA::7A. However, by convention, when there are multiple equal-length blocks of zeros that can be compressed, the leftmost block is compressed. Therefore, the correct compressed address is FEC0::1:2AA:0:0:7A.

3. How many blocks and bits are expressed by "::" in the addresses 2001:DB8::2AA:9FF:FE56:24DC and FF02::2?

In 2001:DB8::2AA:9FF:FE56:24DC, :: expresses 2 blocks (8 − 6) and 32 bits (2 × 16).

In FF02::2, :: expresses 6 blocks (8 − 2) and 96 bits (6 × 16).

4. Describe the difference between unicast, multicast, and anycast addresses in terms of a host sending packets to zero or more interfaces.

A sending host uses a unicast address to send packets to a single interface (within the scope of the unicast address).

A sending host uses a multicast address to send packets to zero or more interfaces belonging to the multicast group (within the scope of the multicast address).

A sending host uses an anycast address to send packets to a single nearest interface belonging to the set of interfaces using the anycast address (within the scope of the any-cast address).

5. Why are no broadcast addresses defined for IPv6?

All IPv4 broadcast addresses are replaced with IPv6 multicast addresses.

6. Define the structure, including field sizes, of the global unicast address.

- ❏ **001:**   Fixed portion of the global unicast address. The size of this field is 3 bits.

- ❏ **Global Routing Prefix:**   Indicates the global routing prefix for a specific organization's site. The size of this field is 45 bits. The combination of the three fixed bits and the 45-bit Global Routing Prefix is used to create a 48-bit site prefix, which is assigned to an individual site of an organization.

- ❏ **Subnet ID:**   Indicates an individual subnet within an organization's site. The size of this field is 16 bits.

- ❏ **Interface ID:**   Indicates the interface on a specific subnet. The size of this field is 64 bits.

7. Define the scope for each of the different types of unicast addresses.

- ❏ **Global:**   The IPv6 Internet

- ❏ **Link-local:**   A single link

- ❏ **Unique local:**   Designed to be scoped by routing topology for an organization network

- ❏ **Site-local:**   The site of an organization network

8. Explain how global and unique local addressing can share the same subnetting infra-structure within an organization.

The global address and unique local address share the same structure beyond the first 48 bits of the address. In global addresses, the Subnet ID field identifies the subnet within an organization. For unique local addresses, the Subnet ID field performs the same function. Because of this, you can create a subnetting infrastructure to number individual subnets with subnet IDs that can be used for both unique local and global unicast addresses.

9. Define the structure, including field sizes, of the multicast address.

- ❏ **11111111:**   Fixed portion of the multicast address. The size of this field is 8 bits.

- ❏ **Flags:**   Indicates flags set on the multicast address. The size of this field is 4 bits.

- ❏ **Scope:**   Indicates the scope of the IPv6 network for which the multicast traffic is intended to be delivered. The size of this field is 4 bits.

- ❏ **Group ID:**   Identifies the multicast group and is unique within the scope. The size of this field is 112 bits.

10. Explain how the solicited-node multicast address acts as a pseudo-unicast address.

    Because the last 24 bits of the solicited-node multicast address are either based on the manufacturer ID portion of an IEEE 802 address or is randomly derived, the chances of two nodes on the same link having the same solicited-node multicast address is small. Therefore, because there is typically only one listener on a subnet for a given solicited-node multicast address, it is almost like using a unicast address.

11. How do routers know the nearest location of an anycast group member?

    Routers within the routing domain of the anycast address have host routes that provide information about the location of the nearest anycast group member. Routers outside the routing domain of the anycast address have a summary route that provides information about the location of the routing domain of the anycast address.

12. Perform a 4-bit subnetting on the unique local prefix FD1A:39C1:4BC2:3D80::/57.

    The result is the following subnetted network prefixes:

    1 - FD1A:39C1:4BC2:3D80::/61

    2 - FD1A:39C1:4BC2:3D88::/61

    3 - FD1A:39C1:4BC2:3D90::/61

    4 - FD1A:39C1:4BC2:3D98::/61

    5 - FD1A:39C1:4BC2:3DA0::/61

    6 - FD1A:39C1:4BC2:3DA8::/61

    7 - FD1A:39C1:4BC2:3DB0::/61

    8 - FD1A:39C1:4BC2:3DB8::/61

    9 - FD1A:39C1:4BC2:3DC0::/61

    10 - FD1A:39C1:4BC2:3DC8::/61

    11 - FD1A:39C1:4BC2:3DD0::/61

    12 - FD1A:39C1:4BC2:3DD8::/61

    13 - FD1A:39C1:4BC2:3DE0::/61

    14 - FD1A:39C1:4BC2:3DE8::/61

    15 - FD1A:39C1:4BC2:3DF0::/61

    16 - FD1A:39C1:4BC2:3DF8::/61

13. What is the EUI-64–based IPv6 interface identifier for the universally administered, unicast IEEE 802 address of 0C-1C-09-A8-F9-CE? What is the corresponding link-local address? What is the corresponding solicited-node multicast address?

    Interface ID: ::E1C:9FF:FEA8:F9CE

Link-local address: FE80::E1C:9FF:FEA8:F9CE

Solicited-node multicast address: FF02::1:FFA8:F9CE

14. What is the IPv6 interface identifier for the locally administered, unicast EUI-64 address of 02-00-00-00-00-00-00-09? What is the corresponding link-local address?

Interface ID: ::9

Link-local address: FE80::9

15. For each type of address shown in the following table, identify how the address begins in colon hexadecimal notation.

Type of Address	Begins with...
Link-local unicast address	FE80
Site-local unicast address	FEC, FED, FEE, FEF
Unique local unicast address	FC or FD
Global address (as defined by RFC 3587)	2 or 3
Multicast address	FF
Link-local scope multicast address	FF02 or FF12
Site-local scope multicast address	FF05 or FF15
Solicited-node multicast address	FF02::1:FF
IPv4-mapped address	::FFFF:
6to4 address	2002:
Teredo address	2001::

Chapter 4: The IPv6 Header

1. Why does the IPv6 header not include a checksum?

In IPv6, the link layer performs bit-level error detection for the entire IPv6 packet.

2. What is the IPv6 equivalent to the Internet Header Length (IHL) field in the IPv4 header?

There is no equivalent. The IPv6 header is always a fixed size of 40 bytes.

3. How does the combination of the Traffic Class and Flow Label fields provide better support for prioritized traffic delivery?

The Traffic Class field is equivalent to the IPv4 Type of Service field and contains the Differentiated Services Code Point (DSCP) value to indicate non-default delivery service. The Flow Label field allows the flow—the series of packets between a source and destination with a non-zero flow label—to be identified by intermediate routers for non-default handling without relying on upper-layer protocol stream identifiers such as TCP or UDP ports (which might be encrypted with IPsec).

4. Which extension headers are fragmentable and why? Which extension headers are not fragmentable and why?

   Fragmentable:

   Authentication header—Needed only by final destination

   ESP header and trailer—Needed only by final destination

   Destination Options header (for final destination)—Needed only by final destination

   Not fragmentable:

   Hop-by-Hop Options header—Needed by every intermediate router

   Destination Options header (for intermediate destinations)—Might be needed by intermediate destinations

   Routing header—Might be needed by intermediate destinations

   Fragment header—Not present prior to fragmentation

5. Describe a situation that results in an IPv6 packet that contains a Fragment header in which the Fragment Offset field is set to 0 and the More Fragments flag is not set to 1.

   IPv6 packets sent to IPv4 destinations that undergo IPv6-to-IPv4 header translation might receive a path maximum transmission unit (PMTU) update of less than 1280 bytes. In this case, the sending host sends IPv6 packets with a Fragment header and a smaller payload size of 1272 bytes. In the Fragment header, the Fragment Offset field is set to 0 and the More Fragments flag is not set to 1. The Fragment header is included so that the IPv6-to-IPv4 translator can use the Identification field in the Fragment header to perform IPv4 fragmentation to reach the IPv4 destination.

6. Describe how the new upper-layer checksum calculation affects transport layer protocols such as TCP and UDP.

   TCP and UDP implementations must be updated to perform the checksum calculation that includes the new IPv6 pseudo-header when sending or receiving data over IPv6.

7. If the minimum MTU for IPv6 packets is 1280 bytes, how are 1280-byte packets sent on a link that supports only 512-byte frames?

   The link layer must provide a fragmentation and reassembly scheme that is independent of and transparent to IPv6.

Chapter 5: ICMPv6

1. How do you distinguish ICMPv6 error messages from ICMPv6 informational messages?

   The value of the Type field for error messages is in the range 0 to 127. (The high-order bit is set to 0.) The value of the Type field for informational messages is in the range 128 to 255. (The high-order bit is set to 1.)

2. Which fields of the Echo Request message are echoed in the Echo Reply message?

   Identifier, Sequence Number, Data

3. For a maximum-sized IPv6 packet with a Fragment extension header sent on an Ethernet link, how many bytes of the original payload are returned in an ICMPv6 Destination Unreachable message?

   1184 bytes (1280 – 40 byte IPv6 header – 8 byte ICMPv6 header – 40 byte IPv6 header – 8 byte Fragment header)

4. How can you tell whether a returned packet was discarded by a firewall that is enforcing network policy or a router that could not resolve the link-layer address of the destination?

   If the Code field in the ICMPv6 Destination Unreachable message is set to 1, the packet was discarded by a firewall that is enforcing network policy. If the Code field is set to 3, a router could not resolve the link-layer address of the destination.

5. Why is the MTU field in the ICMPv6 Packet Too Big message 4 bytes long when the Next Hop MTU field in the ICMPv4 Destination Unreachable-Fragmentation Needed and DF Set message is only 2 bytes long?

   The maximum IPv4 packet size is 65,535 bytes, a number that can be expressed with 16 bits. To support IPv6 jumbograms, 32 bits are needed to express the MTU of the link.

6. Why isn't the ICMPv6 Parameter Problem–Unrecognized Option message sent when the two high-order bits of an option's Option Type field are set to either 00 (binary) or 01 (binary)?

   If the two high-order bits in the Option Type field are set to 00, the option is ignored. If the two high-order bits in the Option Type field are set to 01, the packet is silently discarded.

7. Based on the IPv6 design requirement to minimize processing at IPv6 routers, why is there no equivalent to the ICMPv4 Source Quench message in IPv6?

   A Source Quench message is sent to inform a sending host to lower its transmission rate when the router is congested. To minimize the processing of the router, the router should devote its processing and resources to clearing the congestion, and not creating and sending Source Quench messages.

Chapter 6: Neighbor Discovery

1. List the IPv4 facilities that are replaced by the IPv6 ND protocol.

   ARP, Gratuitous ARP, ICMP Router Discovery, Redirect

2. List the capabilities of the IPv6 ND protocol that are not present in IPv4.

Neighbor unreachability detection; ability to advertise changes in link-layer addresses and the node's role on the network; ability to advertise configuration parameters, address prefixes, and routes.

3. List the five different ND messages and the options that can be included with them.

   ❏ **Router Solicitation:** Source Link-Layer Address option

   ❏ **Router Advertisement:** Source Link-Layer Address, Prefix Information, MTU, Advertisement Interval, Home Agent Information, and Route Information options

   ❏ **Neighbor Solicitation:** Source Link-Layer Address option

   ❏ **Neighbor Advertisement:** Target Link-Layer Address option

   ❏ **Redirect:** Redirected Header and Target Link-Layer Address options

4. Describe the interpretation of the Length field in ND options.

   The Length field is the number of 8-byte blocks in the entire Neighbor Discovery option.

5. What is the value of the Length field for a maximum-sized Redirected Header option (assuming no IPv6 extension headers are present)?

   [1280 − 40 (IPv6 header) − 40 (ICMPv6 Redirect message header)]/8 = 150

6. Describe how you would use the MTU option to provide seamless connectivity between Ethernet nodes and Asynchronous Transfer Mode (ATM) nodes on a transparently bridged link.

   Set the MTU option on the router to advertise a 1500-byte link maximum transmission unit (MTU) so that the ATM nodes do not send 9180-byte IPv6 packets.

7. Why is the Source Link-Layer Address option not included in the Neighbor Solicitation message sent during duplicate address detection?

   It is not included because the reply must be multicast to all nodes on the link, rather than unicast to the sender of the Neighbor Solicitation message.

8. Describe the configuration parameters and their corresponding fields sent in the Router Advertisement message (not including options). Describe the configuration parameters and their corresponding fields sent in the Prefix Information option.

   Router Advertisement message:

   ❏ Default value of the Hop Limit field: Current Hop Limit

   ❏ Whether to use a stateful address configuration protocol to obtain addresses or other configuration information: Managed Address Configuration (M) flag, Other Stateful Configuration (O) flag

   ❏ Whether the advertising router is capable of acting as a home agent: Home Agent flag

- ❑ The default router preference level of the advertising router: Default Router Preference

- ❑ Whether the advertising router is a default router, and for how long: Router Lifetime

- ❑ The value of the reachable time for neighbor unreachability detection: Reachable Time

- ❑ The time interval between successive Neighbor Solicitation messages: Retransmission Timer

Prefix Information option:

- ❑ The prefix: Prefix Length, Prefix

- ❑ Whether the advertised prefix is on-link: On-link flag

- ❑ Whether to create a stateless address based on the prefix: Autonomous flag

- ❑ Whether the Prefix field contains the address of the Home Agent: Router Address flag

- ❑ Whether to update the site prefix table with a site prefix: Site Prefix flag, Site Prefix Length

- ❑ The valid lifetime of the stateless address: Valid Lifetime

- ❑ The preferred lifetime of the stateless address: Preferred Lifetime

9. Under what circumstances is an unsolicited Neighbor Advertisement message sent?

   An unsolicited Neighbor Advertisement message is sent in response to a duplicate address detection Neighbor Solicitation and when either the link-layer address or the role of the node changes.

10. What are the differences in address resolution and duplicate address detection node behavior for anycast addresses?

    In Neighbor Advertisement messages, the Override flag is always set to 0. Duplicate address detection is not performed for anycast addresses.

11. Why is the response to a duplicate address detection sent as multicast? Who sends the response, the offending or defending node?

    The response is multicast because the sender of the Neighbor Solicitation message cannot receive unicast packets at the duplicated IPv6 address. The defending node always sends the response.

12. Why is the value of the Hop Limit field set to 255 for all ND messages?

    The value is set to 255 to prevent ND-based attacks from being launched from off-link nodes. The Hop Limit field for all traffic of an off-link node is always less than 255.

13. Describe the purpose of each of the host data structures described in RFC 2461.

   - **Destination cache:** Maps a destination address to a next-hop address, and stores the PMTU to the destination

   - **Neighbor cache:** Maps a next-hop address to a link-layer address, and stores the state of the entry for neighbor unreachability detection

   - **Prefix list:** Stores all the on-link prefixes

   - **Default router list:** Stores all the routers that advertised themselves as default routers

14. What field in the Redirect message contains the next-hop address of the better router to use for packets addressed to a specific destination? Describe how the contents of that field are used to update the conceptual host data structures for subsequent data sent to the destination.

   The Target Address field. The Target Address field updates the Next-Hop Address field of the destination cache entry corresponding to the Destination Address field on the host that receives the Redirect message.

15. Under what circumstances does a router send a Router Advertisement?

   Pseudo-periodically—the interval between unsolicited advertisements is randomized to reduce synchronization issues when there are multiple advertising routers on a link— and in response to a Router Solicitation message.

16. For Host A and Host B on the same link, why is the exchange of a Neighbor Solicitation message (sent by Host A to Host B) and a Neighbor Advertisement message (sent by Host B to Host A) not considered by Host B as proof that Host A is reachable?

   Host B receives no confirmation that Host A received and processed the Neighbor Advertisement sent by Host B.

Chapter 7: Multicast Listener Discovery and MLD Version 2

1. Why is the IPv6 Router Alert option used in the Hop-by-Hop Options header for Multicast Listener Discovery (MLD) and MLDv2 messages?

   The IPv6 Router Alert option is used to ensure that routers process MLD and MLDv2 messages that are sent to multicast addresses on which the router is not listening.

2. Which addresses are used as the source address in MLD and MLDv2 messages?

   The Source Address field is set to the link-local address of the interface on which the message is being sent. If a Multicast Listener Report message is for a solicited-node multicast address corresponding to a unicast address for which duplicate address detection has not been completed, the source address is set to the unspecified address (::).

3. Which addresses are used as the IPv6 destination address in MLD and MLDv2 messages?

   ❏ **MLD Multicast Listener Query:**   For the general query, the Destination Address field is set to the link-local scope all-nodes multicast address (FF02::1). For the multicast-address-specific query, the Destination Address field is set to the specific multicast address being queried.

   ❏ **MLD Multicast Listener Report:**   The specific multicast address being reported.

   ❏ **MLD Multicast Listener Done:**   The link-local scope all-routers multicast address (FF02::2).

   ❏ **MLDv2 Multicast Listener Query:**   For the general query, the Destination Address field is set to the link-local scope all-nodes multicast address (FF02::1). For the multicast-address-specific and multicast-address-and-source-specific queries, the Destination Address field is set to the specific multicast address being queried.

   ❏ **MLDv2 Multicast Listener Report:**   The All MLDv2-Capable Routers address (FF02::16).

4. How do you distinguish a general query from a multicast-address-specific query in the Multicast Listener Query message?

   In the general query, the Destination Address field in the IPv6 header is set to the link-local scope all-nodes multicast address (FF02::1) and the Multicast Address field in the message is set to the unspecified address (::). In the multicast-address-specific query, the Destination Address field in the IPv6 header and the Multicast Address field in the message are set to the specific address being queried.

5. How do you distinguish a multicast-address-specific query from a multicast-address-and-source-specific query in the MLDv2 Multicast Listener Query message?

   The multicast-address-and-source-specific query contains a list of multicast sources and the multicast-address-specific query does not.

6. For which multicast addresses are Multicast Listener Report messages never sent?

   The only multicast addresses that are not reported are the link-local scope all-nodes multicast address (FF02::1), and all multicast addresses with a scope of 0 (reserved) or 1 (interface-local).

7. In which MLD message is the value of the Maximum Response Delay field significant?

   MLD Multicast Listener Query (both general and multicast-address-specific)

8. Describe the use of the Multicast Address field for each MLD and MLDv2 message.

   ❏ **MLD or MLDv2 Multicast Listener Query:**   Requests reporting for all multicast addresses (except excluded ones) or for a specified multicast address

❑ **MLD or MLDv2 Multicast Listener Report:**   Reports group membership for the specified multicast address

❑ **MLD Multicast Listener Done:**   Reports that there might not be any more members on the subnet for the specified multicast address

Chapter 8: Address Autoconfiguration

1. List and describe the states of an IPv6 autoconfigured address.

   ❑ Tentative: The address is in the process of being verified as unique.

   ❑ Valid: The address can be used for sending and receiving unicast traffic.

      ● Preferred: The address is valid, and it can be used for unlimited communication.

      ● Deprecated: The address is valid, but its use is discouraged for new communication.

   ❑ Invalid: The address can no longer be used to send or receive unicast traffic.

2. What is the formula for calculating the amount of time an autoconfigured address remains in the deprecated state?

   Valid Lifetime – Preferred Lifetime

3. How does a router obtain addresses other than link-local addresses?

   It obtains them through manual configuration.

4. According to RFC 4862, what addresses are autoconfigured for LAN interfaces on hosts when duplicate address detection for the EUI-64–derived link-local address fails? What is the behavior for the IPv6 protocol for Windows Server 2008 and Windows Vista?

   No addresses are autoconfigured in this case.

   If the link-local address is a duplicate, the IPv6 protocol for Windows Server 2008 and Windows Vista can continue with the receipt of a multicast Router Advertisement message containing non-link-local prefixes and automatically configure non-link-local addresses.

5. A host computer is running Windows Vista and is assigned the IPv4 address 172.30.90.65 on its single LAN interface. IPv6 on this computer starts up and receives a Router Advertisement message on its LAN interface that contains both a unique local prefix (FD0D:3A41:21D:29D8::/64) and a global prefix (2001:DB8:A3:29D8::/64), and both M and O flags are set to 0. List and describe the autoconfigured addresses for all the interfaces on this host.

   ❑ **LAN interface:**   FE80::[random permanent interface ID], FD0D:3A41:21D:29D8:[random permanent interface ID], 2001:DB8:A3:29D8:[random permanent interface ID], FD0D:3A41:21D:29D8:[random temporary interface ID], 2001:DB8:A3:29D8: [random temporary interface ID]

❑ **ISATAP tunneling interface:**   FE80::5EFE:172.30.90.65

❑ **Loopback Interface:**   ::1, FE80::1

6. Describe the difference between IPv6 stateful and stateless autoconfiguration. Describe the difference between DHCPv6 stateful and stateless operation.

IPv6 stateless autoconfiguration is done through the router discovery process and the receipt of a Router Advertisement message containing address prefixes, routes, and other settings. IPv6 stateful autoconfiguration is done through an address configuration protocol such as DHCPv6.

DHCPv6 stateful operation is when a DHCPv6 client requests IPv6 address configuration information in addition to other configuration settings. DHCPv6 stateless operation is when a DHCPv6 client requests only configuration settings.

7. List all the different ways that an IPv6 host running Windows Vista can be configured with IPv6 addresses.

Stateless address autoconfiguration

DHCPv6 stateful operation

Manual configuration through the properties of the Internet Protocol version 6 (TCP/IPv6) component in the Network Connections folder or at the Windows command prompt with commands in the **netsh interface ipv6** context

Chapter 9: IPv6 and Name Resolution

1. Why is the DNS record for IPv6 name resolution named the "AAAA" record?

It is named the "AAAA" record because 128-bit IPv6 addresses are four times longer than 32-bit IPv4 addresses, which use a host (A) record.

2. A host computer running Windows Vista is assigned the IPv4 address 172.30.90.65 on its single LAN interface. IPv6 on this computer receives a Router Advertisement message on its ISATAP tunneling interface that contains both a unique local prefix (FD3A:47A1:2CB9:C140::/64) and a global prefix (2001:DB8:A3:C140::/64). List the IPv6 addresses for the AAAA records registered with DNS by this host.

FD3A:47A1:2CB9:C140::5EFE:172.30.90.65, 2001:DB8:A3:C140::5EFE:172.30 .90.65

3. Describe the importance of address selection rules for a node running both IPv4 and IPv6 that is using a DNS infrastructure containing both A and AAAA records.

Source and destination address selection determine the best source address to use with a destination address and the preference order for possible destination addresses. With a standard method to select source and destination addresses, applications do not need to include their own address selection algorithms, reducing the development burden on IPv6-capable applications.

4. Describe how LLMNR messages are the same as and different from DNS messages.

Same: LLMNR messages use Name Query Request and Name Query Response messages in a similar format as the corresponding DNS message.

Different: LLMNR messages can be multicast (DNS messages are unicast). LLMNR messages use a different port than DNS messages. LLMNR messages are exchanged by hosts. (DNS messages are between a DNS client and a DNS server.)

Chapter 10: IPv6 Routing

1. How does IPv6 on a router determine the single route in the routing table to use when forwarding a packet? How is the process different for an IPv6 sending host?

Based on the list of matching routes, the route that has the largest prefix length is chosen. If there are multiple longest matching routes, the router uses the lowest metric to select the best route. If there are multiple longest matching routes with the lowest metric, IPv6 can choose which routing table entry to use.

An IPv6 host first determines the source address and source interface. IPv6 on the host then performs either a constrained (for strong host, only routes with a next-hop interface of the source interface are considered) or unconstrained (for weak host, all routes are considered) route lookup to determine the closest matching route.

2. Describe the conditions that would cause a router to send the following ICMPv6 error messages.

❏ **ICMPv6 Packet Too Big**   The IPv6 MTU of the forwarding interface is lower than the size of the IPv6 packet being forwarded.

❏ **ICMPv6 Destination Unreachable–Address Unreachable**   The neighboring destination node does not respond to Neighbor Solicitation messages being sent to resolve its link-layer address. Or the packet is a ping-pong packet (a packet being sent to a destination address that does not exist on a point-to-point link).

❏ **ICMPv6 Time Exceeded–Hop Limit Exceeded in Transit**   The Hop Limit field for a packet is less than 1 after decrementing it.

❏ **ICMPv6 Destination Unreachable–Port Unreachable**   There is no application on the router listening on the UDP destination port (for packets sent to an address assigned to a router interface).

❏ **ICMPv6 Destination Unreachable–No Route to Destination**   There is no matching route in the IPv6 routing table.

❏ **ICMPv6 Parameter Problem–Unrecognized IPv6 Option Encountered**   The router processed an unrecognized option within a Hop-by-Hop Options or Destination Options (for intermediate destinations) extension header, and the two high-order bits of the Option Type field were set to either 10 or 11.

3. A host running Windows Vista receives a Router Advertisement message from a router advertising itself as a default router with the link-local address of fe80::2aa:ff:fe45:a431:2c5d, and containing a Prefix Information option to autoconfigure an address with the prefix 2001:db8:0:952a::/64 and a Route Information option with the prefix 2001:db8:0:952c::/64. Fill in the expected entries for the host based on this Router Advertisement message in the following abbreviated routing table.

```
Network Destination        Gateway
-----------------------    -------------
::/0                       fe80::2aa:ff:fe45:a431:2c5d
2001:db8:0:952a::/64       on-link
2001:db8:0:952c::/64       fe80::2aa:ff:fe45:a431:2c5d
```

4. Describe the differences between distance vector, link state, and path vector routing protocol technologies in terms of convergence time, ability to scale, ease of deployment, and appropriate use (intranet vs. Internet).

   ❑ **Distance vector:** High convergence time; does not scale to large or very large networks; very easy to deploy; appropriate for use within a small intranet

   ❑ **Link state:** Low convergence time; scales to large networks; more difficult to deploy; appropriate for use within an intranet consisting of a single autonomous system

   ❑ **Path vector:** Low convergence time; scales to very large networks; difficult to deploy; appropriate for use between autonomous systems on the Internet

5. A static IPv6 router running Windows Server 2008 is configured with the following commands.

   netsh interface ipv6 set interface "Local Area Connection" forwarding=enabled advertise=enabled
   netsh interface ipv6 set interface "Local Area Connection 2" forwarding=enabled advertise=enabled
   netsh interface ipv6 add route 2001:db8:0:1a4c::/64
   "Local Area Connection" publish=yes
   netsh interface ipv6 add route 2001:db8:0:90b5::/64
   "Local Area Connection 2" publish=yes

   With just these commands, will a host on the 2001:db8:0:90b5::/64 subnet have a default route? Why or why not? With just these commands, can a host on the 2001:db8:0:90b5::/64 subnet reach a host on the 2001:db8:0:1a4c::/64 subnet? If so, how?

   No. For a static router running the IPv6 protocol for Windows Server 2008 or Windows Vista to advertise itself as a default router, it must have a default route that is configured to be published. For example, the command

   netsh interface ipv6 add route ::/0 "Local Area Connection 2"
   FE80::2AA:FF:FE19:9B84 publish=yes

   would add a publishable default route.

Yes. The IPv6 router running Windows Server 2008 will include the 2001:db8:0:1a4c::/64 prefix in a Route Information option for the Router Advertisement sent on the 2001:db8:0:90b5::/64 subnet. Hosts on the 2001:db8:0:90b5::/64 subnet add a route to their local IPv6 routing table for the 2001:db8:0:1a4c::/64 prefix.

Chapter 11: IPv6 Transition Technologies

1. Describe the difference between migration and coexistence.

   Migration is the equipping and configuration of all nodes to replace one protocol (IPv4) with another (IPv6). Coexistence is allowing both types of protocols to maintain connectivity—an advantage while migration is occurring.

2. How does an IPv4-only host communicate with an IPv6-only host?

   It communicates by using an Application or Transport layer gateway or proxy that translates or proxies IPv4 traffic to IPv6 traffic, and vice versa. The PortProxy component of the IPv6 protocol for Windows Server 2008 and Windows Vista is an example of a Transport layer proxy.

3. What is an IPv4-mapped address used for?

   An IPv4-mapped address is used by an IPv6 implementation to internally represent IPv4-only hosts and IPv4 addresses.

4. Is the IPv6 protocol for Windows Server 2008 and Windows Vista a dual IP layer? Why or why not?

   Yes. The IPv6 protocol for Windows Server 2008 and Windows Vista includes single implementations of TCP and UDP that operate over both IPv4 and IPv6.

5. How are the source and destination addresses in the IPv4 header determined for IPv6-over-IPv4 tunnel traffic?

   For configured tunneling, the source and destination IPv4 addresses are determined from the manually configured tunnel endpoints.

   For automatic tunneling, the destination IPv4 address is derived from the next-hop address for the packet, which contains an embedded IPv4 address that is determined by the tunneling interface. The source address is the best source address to use to reach the already determined destination IPv4 address.

6. What is the Netsh command to enable the proxying of TCP connection data between an IPv6-only host and an IPv4-only service that is running on the PortProxy computer and listening on TCP port 32175?

   netsh interface portproxy add v6tov4 listenport=32175 connectport=32175

7. Why might you have to manually add A or AAAA DNS records to help facilitate communication between IPv4-only nodes and IPv6-only nodes when using PortProxy?

   For communication initiated by the IPv4-only node, the name of the IPv6-only node must resolve to an IPv4 address that is assigned to an interface of the PortProxy computer. This might require the addition of an A record. For communication initiated by the IPv6-only node, the name of the IPv4-only node must resolve to an IPv6 address assigned to an interface of the PortProxy computer. This might require the addition of an AAAA record.

Chapter 12: ISATAP

1. Describe the intended use of the ISATAP IPv6 transition technology.

   ISATAP is intended to provide unicast IPv6 connectivity between IPv6/IPv4 hosts across an IPv4 intranet.

2. How can you recognize an ISATAP address?

   You can recognize an ISATAP address from the "5efe" in the sixth block of the address and the dotted decimal notation of an IPv4 address in the seventh and eighth blocks of the address.

3. How are the source and destination addresses in the encapsulating IPv4 header determined for ISATAP traffic?

   The ISATAP tunneling interface determines the destination IPv4 address from the last 32-bits of the next-hop address corresponding to the destination ISATAP address of the packet. The source address is the best source address to use to reach the already determined destination IPv4 address.

4. Define the required and optional roles of an ISATAP router.

   ❑ **Required:**   An ISATAP router must advertise one or more address prefixes that are assigned to the logical ISATAP subnet.

   ❑ **Optional:**   An ISATAP router can forward IPv6 packets between the logical ISATAP subnet and other IPv6 subnets.

5. List and describe the steps that a Windows Vista–based ISATAP host with a single LAN interface goes through to perform router discovery for its ISATAP tunneling interface.

   Step 1. The IPv6 component in Windows Vista creates ISATAP tunneling interfaces as needed and assigns link-local ISATAP addresses to them.

   Step 2. The IPv6 component in Windows Vista attempts to resolve the name ISATAP to an IPv4 address using built-in name resolution techniques.

Step 3. When the name ISATAP is resolved to an IPv4 address, IPv6 sends an IPv4-encapsulated Router Solicitation message to the ISATAP router.

Step 4. When the IPv6 component in Windows Vista receives the Router Advertisement message, it configures additional ISATAP addresses and routes based on the message contents.

In Windows Server 2008 and Windows Vista with SP1, the steps are in the order 2, 1, 3, 4.

6. To reach a native IPv6 host, IPv6 packets from an ISATAP host must traverse 7 IPv4 routers on the ISATAP subnet and 3 native IPv6 routers on the IPv6-capable portion of the intranet. If the IPv6 packets were sent by the ISATAP host with a Hop Limit field of 128, what is the value of the Hop Limit field when the packets arrive at the destination?

124 (1 for the ISATAP router and 3 more for the native IPv6 routers)

7. A network administrator needs to begin experimenting with IPv6 connectivity on his company's IPv4-only intranet. Describe how the network administrator can configure a computer running Windows Server 2008 as an ISATAP router to immediately turn the entire IPv4-only intranet into a logical IPv6 subnet.

Use the following commands to enable advertising on the ISATAP interface and advertise an address prefix for the logical ISATAP subnet:

netsh interface ipv6 set interface *ISATAPInterfaceNameOrIndex* **advertise=enabled**

netsh interface ipv6 add route *Address/PrefixLength ISATAPInterfaceNameOrIndex* **publish=yes**

Then add A records to the appropriate DNS domains to resolve the name ISATAP to the IPv4 address of the computer running Windows Server 2008.

Chapter 13: 6to4

1. Describe the intended use of the 6to4 IPv6 transition technology.

6to4 is intended to provide unicast IPv6 connectivity between IPv6/IPv4 hosts in IPv6-capable sites across the IPv4 intranet and to provide connectivity to the IPv6 Internet.

2. How can you recognize a 6to4 address?

6to4 addresses begin with 2002.

3. How are the source and destination addresses in the encapsulating IPv4 header determined for 6to4-tunneled traffic?

The 6to4 tunneling interface determines the destination IPv4 address from the second and third blocks of the next-hop address corresponding to the destination 6to4 address of the packet. The source address is the best source address to use to reach the already determined destination IPv4 address.

4. To reach a native IPv6 host on the IPv6 Internet, IPv6 packets from a 6to4 host must traverse 3 native IPv6 routers on an intranet, 13 IPv4 routers on the IPv4 Internet, and 6 native IPv6 routers on the IPv6 Internet. If the IPv6 packets were sent by the 6to4 host with a Hop Limit field of 128, what is the value of the Hop Limit field when the packets are received at the destination?

   118 (1 for the IPv4 Internet and 9 more for the native IPv6 routers on the intranet and the IPv6 Internet)

5. A network administrator needs to begin experimenting with IPv6-only Web sites on the IPv6 Internet. Describe how the network administrator can configure a computer running Windows Server 2008 as a 6to4 router to immediately obtain connectivity to the IPv6 Internet.

   Configure the computer running Windows Server 2008 with a public IPv4 address, and enable Internet Connection Sharing on the Internet interface.

Chapter 14: Teredo

1. Describe the intended use of the Teredo IPv6 transition technology.

   Teredo is intended to provide unicast IPv6 connectivity between IPv6/IPv4 hosts that are connected to the IPv4 intranet and to provide connectivity to the IPv6 Internet.

2. How can you recognize a Teredo address?

   A Teredo address begins with 2001::.

3. How are the source and destination addresses in the encapsulating IPv4 header determined for Teredo-tunneled traffic to another Teredo client?

   The Teredo tunneling interface determines the destination IPv4 address from the last 32 bits of the next-hop address corresponding to the destination address of the packet. The source address is the best source address to use to reach the already determined destination IPv4 address.

4. Why are portions of the Teredo address obscured?

   To prevent "smart" NATs from translating the internal and external address and port numbers of traffic that the NAT forwards.

5. What is the difference between a Teredo relay and a Teredo host-specific relay?

   A Teredo relay is an IPv6/IPv4 router that can forward packets between Teredo clients on the IPv4 Internet and IPv6 hosts on the IPv6 Internet. A Teredo host-specific relay is an IPv6/IPv4 node that has an interface and connectivity to both the IPv4 Internet and the IPv6 Internet and can communicate directly with Teredo clients over the IPv4 Internet, without the need for an intermediate Teredo relay.

6. A Teredo client has the address 2001::62C3:1B8D:346B:EBC9:7C94:EA26. Is this client behind a cone NAT or a restricted NAT? What is the public IPv4 address of its Teredo server? What is the external IPv4 address and UDP port number for this Teredo client's Teredo traffic?

    This client is behind a restricted NAT. (The Cone flag is set to 0 in fifth block.)

    The public IPv4 address of the Teredo server is 98.195.27.141 (decimal representation of 62C3:1B8D).

    The external IPv4 address for this Teredo client's Teredo traffic is 131.107.21.217 (dotted decimal representation of 7C94:EA26 XOR FFFF:FFFF).

    The external UDP port for this Teredo client's Teredo traffic is 5174 (decimal representation of EBC9 XOR FFFF).

7. How does a Teredo client determine the external IPv4 address and UDP port number for its traffic during the Teredo address configuration process?

    The incoming Router Advertisement message to the Teredo client from the Teredo server includes the Origin indicator, which contains the external IPv4 address and UDP port number of the Router Solicitation message that the Teredo server received from the Teredo client.

8. Initial communication between two Teredo clients in different sites when both Teredo clients are behind restricted NATs requires four more packets than when both Teredo clients are behind cone NATs. What is the purpose of these four additional packets?

    The four additional packets create the source-specific NAT mappings that are needed by the restricted NATs to forward incoming traffic to the Teredo clients.

9. How does a Teredo client determine the public IPv4 address of the Teredo relay when initiating communication to a host on the IPv6 Internet?

    From the Echo Reply message forwarded to the Teredo client by the Teredo relay.

Chapter 15: IPv6 Security Considerations

1. Without support for SEcure Neighbor Discovery (SEND) or DHCP message authentication, what can you do to help prevent unauthorized intranet hosts from obtaining an IPv6 address and configuration?

    Use IEEE 802.1X authentication for all computers that are connecting to your network with wired or wireless connections.

2. Why are IPv6 addresses with EUI-64–based interface IDs more vulnerable to address scans than addresses with randomly derived interface IDs?

    Because with EUI-64–based interface IDs, the first 24 bits are the well-known manufacturer IDs of network adapter vendors and the next 16 bits are set to FF-FE. Therefore,

40 bits of an interface ID can be determined and address scans must scan up to 2^{24} combinations for each manufacturer ID. With randomly derived interface IDs, none of the bits of an interface ID can be determined and address scans must scan up to 2^{64} combinations.

3. Will a port scan be able to detect a server service on a host even when a host-based stateful firewall is running?

Yes. To allow unsolicited incoming traffic, a server service on the host must instruct the host-based firewall to open the port.

4. What is the recommended configuration for exchanging IPv6 traffic between an intranet and the IPv6 Internet?

Upgrade your edge firewall between your intranet and the IPv6 Internet to support stateful IPv6 firewalling.

Chapter 16: Deploying IPv6

1. What is the value of deploying IPv6 on an intranet for which most of the hosts run Windows Server 2003 or Windows XP with Service Pack 2?

Even though many of the built-in applications and services in Windows Server 2003 and Windows XP with Service Pack 2 do not operate over IPv6, you can gain valuable experience in deploying IPv6 connectivity and name resolution and can begin migrating and testing your custom applications to support IPv6.

2. What types of applications must be migrated for IPv6 support and why? Do they need to be migrated before you begin deploying IPv6?

The types of applications that must be migrated are those that use IPv4-specific application programming interfaces (APIs) and have IPv4-specific code for IPv4 addresses and subnet masks.

No. You can begin migrating them to operate over either IPv4 or IPv6 before you deploy IPv6.

3. How do you determine the boundaries of IPv6 subnets?

You can define your subnet boundaries to be the same as your IPv4 subnet boundaries. Alternately, you can use your switching and router infrastructure to define larger subnets for IPv6 traffic.

4. Why is ISATAP the automatic tunneling technology supplied with Windows that is most suitable for intranet deployment?

ISATAP was specifically designed as a host-to-host and host-to-router tunneling technology for connectivity across an IPv4-only intranet, rather than across the IPv4 Internet.

5. A user on an ISATAP host calls her help desk because she is unable to receive a live media presentation that is being multicast over IPv6. What is the most likely problem and its solution?

   ISATAP does not support IPv6 multicast. To solve this problem, send the live media presentation over IPv4.

6. Why is DHCPv6 an optional and technically unnecessary technology to deploy on an intranet that is using both IPv4 and IPv6?

   IPv6/IPv4 nodes can continue to use DHCP to obtain additional configuration settings, such as the addresses of DNS servers and DNS domain names. IPv6 hosts can be configured with address prefixes and default gateways with stateless address autoconfiguration.

7. Two different sites of an organization's intranet have deployed a native IPv6 routing infrastructure serving their individual sites. How would you connect these two IPv6-capable portions of the intranet together across an IPv4-only infrastructure?

   You can use a manually configured tunnel between two IPv6 routers in the two sites.

Appendix E
Setting Up an IPv6 Test Lab

This appendix provides information about how you can use five computers to create a test lab to configure and test the IPv6 protocol for Windows Server 2008 and Windows Vista. These instructions are designed to guide you through a set of tasks that transform a test lab network from an IPv4-only infrastructure, to a mixed IPv4-only and IPv6-capable infrastructure, to an IPv6-only infrastructure. Beyond the set of tasks, these instructions allow you to create a functioning IPv6-capable network. You can use this network to learn about and experiment with IPv6 features and functionality and to aid in developing applications for IPv6 or modifying existing applications to work over both IPv4 and IPv6.

IPv6 Test Lab Setup

The infrastructure for the IPv6 test lab network consists of five computers performing the following services:

- A computer running Windows Server 2008 that is used as a Domain Name System (DNS) server. This computer is named DNS1.

- A computer running Windows Vista that is used as a client. This computer is named CLIENT1.

- A computer running Windows Vista that is used as a router. This computer is named ROUTER1.

- A computer running Windows Vista that is used as a router. This computer is named ROUTER2.

- A computer running Windows Vista that is used as a client. This computer is named CLIENT2.

Figure E-1 shows the configuration of the IPv6 test lab.

There are three subnets:

- Subnet 1 uses the IPv4 subnet prefix of 10.0.1.0/24 and IPv6 subnet prefix of 2001:DB8:0:1::/64.

- Subnet 2 uses the IPv4 subnet prefix of 10.0.2.0/24 and IPv6 subnet prefix of 2001:DB8:0:2::/64.

- Subnet 3 uses the IPv4 subnet prefix of 10.0.3.0/24 and IPv6 subnet prefix of 2001:DB8:0:3::/64.

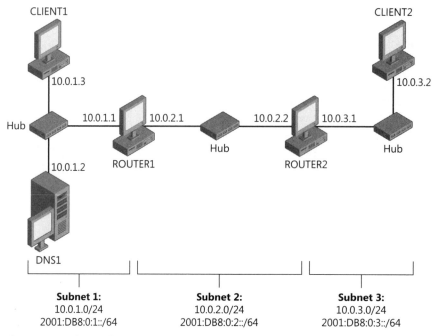

Figure E-1   The configuration of the IPv6 test lab

All of the computers on each subnet are connected to a separate common hub or Layer 2 switch. The two router computers, ROUTER1 and ROUTER2, have two network adapters installed.

For the IPv4 configuration, each computer is configured manually with the appropriate IPv4 address, subnet mask, default gateway, and DNS server IPv4 address. Dynamic Host Configuration Protocol (DHCP) and Windows Internet Name Service (WINS) servers are not used. For the IPv6 configuration, link-local addresses are used initially.

The following sections describe how each of the computers in the test lab is configured. To reconstruct this test lab, please configure the computers in the order presented.

Microsoft Virtual PC 2007 allows you to create the computer lab used in this document using only one physical computer. After the virtual lab is configured, you can switch between the five virtual computers needed for this lab with the click of a button. For more information, see *http://www.microsoft.com/virtualpc*.

Note   The following instructions are for configuring an IPv6 test lab using a minimum number of computers. Individual computers are needed to separate the services provided on the network and to clearly show the desired functionality. You can use any member of the Windows Server 2008 family for DNS1 and any version of Windows Vista or Windows Server 2008 for the other computers. This configuration is not designed to reflect best practices or a desired or recommended configuration for a production network. The configuration, including addresses and all other configuration parameters, is designed to work on a separate test lab network.

DNS1

DNS1 is a computer running Windows Server 2008. It is providing DNS server services for the testlab.microsoft.com DNS domain. To configure DNS1, perform the following steps:

1. Install Windows Server 2008 as a stand-alone server. Set the Administrator password.

2. After restarting, log on as Administrator.

3. From the Network Connections folder, configure the Internet Protocol Version 4 (TCP/IPv4) protocol for the Local Area Connection with the IPv4 address of 10.0.1.2, the subnet mask of 255.255.255.0, and a default gateway of 10.0.1.1.

4. From Initial Configuration Tasks, disable the Windows Firewall.

5. From Initial Configuration Tasks, add the DNS Server role.

6. From the DNS snap-in, create a forward lookup zone named "testlab.microsoft.com" as a primary zone that allows both nonsecure and secure dynamic updates.

> **Note**   The domain name testlab.microsoft.com is used here for example purposes only. You can use any domain name in your test lab configuration.

CLIENT1

CLIENT1 is a computer running Windows Vista that is being used as a client. To configure CLIENT1, perform the following steps:

1. On CLIENT1, install Windows Vista as a workgroup computer. Set the Administrator password.

2. After restarting, log on as Administrator.

3. From the Network Connections folder, configure the Internet Protocol Version 4 (TCP/IPv4) protocol for the Local Area Connection with the following:

   ❑ An IPv4 address of 10.0.1.3, the subnet mask of 255.255.255.0, and a default gateway of 10.0.1.1

   ❑ A DNS server IPv4 address of 10.0.1.2

   ❑ The connection-specific suffix is "testlab.microsoft.com", and specify to use the connection's DNS suffix in DNS registration.

4. From Control Panel-Windows Firewall, disable the Windows Firewall.

ROUTER1

ROUTER1 is a computer running Windows Vista that is being used as a router between Subnet 1 and Subnet 2. To configure ROUTER1, perform the following steps:

1. On ROUTER1, install Windows Vista as a workgroup computer. Set the Administrator password.

2. After restarting, log on as Administrator.

3. From the Network Connections folder, rename the local area network (LAN) connection connected to Subnet 1 to "Subnet 1 Connection" and rename the LAN connection connected to Subnet 2 to "Subnet 2 Connection."

4. For Subnet 1 Connection, configure the Internet Protocol Version 4 (TCP/IPv4) protocol with the following:

   ❑ An IPv4 address of 10.0.1.1, the subnet mask of 255.255.255.0, and the DNS server IPv4 address of 10.0.1.2

   ❑ The connection-specific suffix for the connection is "testlab.microsoft.com", and specify to use the connection's DNS suffix in DNS registration.

5. For Subnet 2 Connection, configure the Internet Protocol Version 4 (TCP/IPv4) protocol with the following:

   ❑ An IPv4 address of 10.0.2.1, the subnet mask of 255.255.255.0, and a default gateway of 10.0.2.2

   ❑ The connection-specific suffix for the connection is "testlab.microsoft.com", and specify to use the connection's DNS suffix in DNS registration.

6. From Control Panel-Windows Firewall, disable the Windows Firewall.

7. Run the registry editor (Regedit.exe), and set the HKEY_LOCAL_ MACHINE\SYSTEM\CurrentControlSet\Services\Tcpip\Parameters\IPEnableRouter registry value to 1. This enables IPv4 routing between Subnet 1 and Subnet 2.

8. Restart ROUTER1.

ROUTER2

ROUTER2 is a computer running Windows Vista that is being used as a router between Subnet 2 and Subnet 3. To configure ROUTER2, perform the following steps:

1. On ROUTER2, install Windows Vista as a workgroup computer. Set the Administrator password.

2. After restarting, log on as Administrator.

3. From the Network Connections folder, rename the LAN connection connected to Subnet 2 to "Subnet 2 Connection" and rename the LAN connection connected to Subnet 3 to "Subnet 3 Connection."

4. For Subnet 2 Connection, configure the Internet Protocol Version 4 (TCP/IPv4) protocol with the following:

   ❑ An IPv4 address of 10.0.2.2, the subnet mask of 255.255.255.0, a default gateway of 10.0.2.1, and the DNS server IPv4 address of 10.0.1.2

   ❑ The connection-specific suffix for the connection is "testlab.microsoft.com", and specify to use the connection's DNS suffix in DNS registration.

5. For Subnet 3 Connection, configure the Internet Protocol Version 4 (TCP/IPv4) protocol with the following:

   ❑ An IPv4 address of 10.0.3.1, and the subnet mask of 255.255.255.0

   ❑ The connection-specific suffix for the connection is "testlab.microsoft.com", and specify to use the connection's DNS suffix in DNS registration.

6. From Control Panel-Windows Firewall, disable the Windows Firewall.

7. Run the registry editor (Regedit.exe), and set the HKEY_LOCAL_ MACHINE\SYSTEM\CurrentControlSet\Services\Tcpip\Parameters\IPEnableRouter registry value to 1. This enables IPv4 routing between Subnet 2 and Subnet 3.

8. Restart ROUTER2.

CLIENT2

CLIENT2 is a computer running Windows Vista that is being used as a client. To configure CLIENT2, perform the following steps:

1. On CLIENT2, install Windows Vista as a workgroup computer. Set the Administrator password.

2. After restarting, log on as Administrator.

3. From the Network Connections folder, configure the Internet Protocol Version 4 (TCP/IPv4) protocol for the Local Area Connection with the following:

   ❑ An IPv4 address of 10.0.3.2, the subnet mask of 255.255.255.0, a default gateway of 10.0.3.1, and the DNS server IPv4 address of 10.0.1.2

   ❑ The connection-specific suffix for the connection is "testlab.microsoft.com", and specify to use the connection's DNS suffix in DNS registration.

4. From Control Panel-Windows Firewall, disable the Windows Firewall.

5. Verify the integrity of the IPv4 routing infrastructure with the following command:

   ping 10.0.1.3

This tests whether IPv4 packets can be forwarded between CLIENT2 on Subnet 3 and CLIENT1 on Subnet 1.

At this point in the test lab configuration, there is an IPv4-only routing infrastructure. IPv4 traffic can be sent and received by any node on the test lab network. All the nodes have IPv6 installed, but there is no native IPv6 routing or autoconfiguration of global or unique local address prefixes. Therefore, IPv6 nodes can communicate only with each other if they are connected to the same subnet and can use only link-local addresses. For example, CLIENT1 can use link-local addresses to communicate with DNS1 and ROUTER1, but it cannot use link-local addresses to communicate with ROUTER2 or CLIENT2.

IPv6 Test Lab Tasks

The following sections are designed to take you through the common IPv6 tasks and configurations to transform the IPv4-only test lab network to an IPv6-only test lab network:

- Performing link-local pings
- Enabling native IPv6 connectivity on Subnet 1
- Configuring ISATAP
- Configuring native IPv6 connectivity for all subnets
- Using name resolution
- Configuring an IPv6-only routing infrastructure

The last step is optional because most intranets in the near future will not be IPv6-only networks, but IPv6-capable networks that support both IPv4 and native IPv6 connectivity. However, you might need an IPv6-only test network to test IPv6-capable applications.

Performing Link-Local Pings

To ping a node using link-local addresses and view the entries created in the neighbor cache, complete the following steps:

1. On ROUTER1, type the **netsh interface ipv6 show address** command to obtain the link-local address of the interface named Subnet 1 Connection.

2. On CLIENT1, type the **netsh interface ipv6 show address** command to obtain the link-local address and interface index of the interface named Local Area Connection.

3. On CLIENT1, type the following command to ping the link-local address of ROUTER1's interface on Subnet 1:

   ping *ROUTER1LinkLocalAddress%InterfaceIndex*

   InterfaceIndex is the interface index of the interface named Local Area Connection obtained in step 2.

For example, if the link-local address of ROUTER1's interface on Subnet 1 is fe80::b500:734b:fe5b:3945 and the interface index for the Local Area Connection interface on CLIENT1 is 7, the command is

ping fe80::b500:734b:fe5b:3945%7

4. On CLIENT1, type the **netsh interface ipv6 show neighbors** command to view the entry in the CLIENT1 neighbor cache for ROUTER1. You should see an entry for ROUTER1's link-local address.

5. On CLIENT1, type the **netsh interface ipv6 show route** command to view the entries in the CLIENT1 routing table.

Enabling Native IPv6 Connectivity on Subnet 1

To enable native IPv6 connectivity on Subnet 1, complete the following steps:

1. On ROUTER1, type the following commands:

    netsh interface ipv6 set interface "Subnet 1 Connection" advertise=enabled forwarding=enabled

    netsh interface ipv6 add route 2001:db8:0:1::/64 "Subnet 1 Connection" publish=yes

    netsh interface ipv6 add route ::/0 "Subnet 2 Connection" fe80::1 publish=yes

    These commands configure ROUTER1 to advertise the 2001:DB8:0:1::/64 prefix on Subnet 1 and itself as a default IPv6 router. The FE80::1 address is a temporary next-hop IPv6 address for ROUTER1.

2. On ROUTER1, type the **netsh interface ipv6 show address** command to obtain the public address assigned to the interface named Subnet 1 Connection.

3. On CLIENT1, type the **netsh interface ipv6 show address** command to obtain the public address assigned to the interface named Local Area Connection.

4. On CLIENT1, type the following command to ping the public address of ROUTER1's interface on Subnet 1:

    ping *ROUTER1PublicAddress*

    For example, if the public address of ROUTER1's interface on Subnet 1 is 2001:db8::1:b500:734b:fe5b:3945, the command is

    ping 2001:db8::1:b500:734b:fe5b:3945

At this point in the test lab configuration, there is an IPv4 routing infrastructure throughout the network and Subnet 1 has native IPv6 connectivity. CLIENT1 can use IPv6 addresses based on the 2001:DB8:0:1::/64 global address prefix and native IPv6 traffic to communicate with DNS1 and ROUTER1, but it still cannot use IPv6 to communicate with ROUTER2 or CLIENT2. To enable IPv6 connectivity to ROUTER2 and CLIENT2 without enabling native IPv6 routing and advertising on Subnet 2 and Subnet 3, our next task is to configure ROUTER1 as an Intra-Site Automatic Tunnel Addressing Protocol (ISATAP) router.

Configuring ISATAP

In this task, we configure ROUTER1 as an ISATAP router so that IPv6 hosts on the IPv4-only portion of the test lab network (Subnet 2 and Subnet 3) can communicate with IPv6 hosts on the native IPv6 portion of the test lab network (Subnet 1). To configure the test lab network to use ISATAP, do the following:

1. On ROUTER1, type the **netsh interface isatap set router 10.0.2.1** command, and then the **netsh interface ipv6 show address** command to obtain the interface index of the ISATAP interface that is assigned the link-local address FE80::5EFE:10.0.2.1.

2. On ROUTER1, enable forwarding and advertising on the ISATAP interface, using the following commands:

   netsh interface ipv6 set interface *ISATAPInterfaceIndex* **forwarding=enabled advertise=enabled**

   ISATAPInterfaceIndex is the interface index obtained in step 1.

   This command configures ROUTER1 as an advertising ISATAP router for the logical ISATAP subnet consisting of Subnet 2 and Subnet 3.

3. On ROUTER1, add a route for the subnet prefix of the logical ISATAP subnet to the ISATAP interface and configure it to be published with the following command:

   netsh interface ipv6 add route 2001:db8:0:99::/64 *ISATAPInterfaceIndex* **publish=yes**

   This command configures ROUTER1 to advertise the 2001:DB8:0:99::/64 route to ISATAP hosts on the logical ISATAP subnet.

4. On DNS1, use the Registry Editor (Regedit.exe) to remove the ISATAP entry from the HKEY_LOCAL_MACHINE\System\CurrentControlSet\Services\DNS\Parameters\GlobalQueryBlockList registry value.

5. Use the DNS snap-in to restart the DNS Server service on DNS1.

6. Use the DNS snap-in to add a host (A) resource record named "ISATAP" to the testlab.microsoft.com forward lookup zone for the IPv4 address of 10.0.2.1.

7. On CLIENT1, type the **netsh interface ipv6 show address** command to obtain the public address assigned to the interface named Local Area Connection.

8. From the Network Connections folder on CLIENT2, disable and then enable the Local Area Connection. This renews CLIENT2's configuration to determine the ISATAP router

IPv4 address of 10.0.2.1 and obtain an ISATAP address with the global prefix of 2001:DB8:0:99::/64.

9. Ping CLIENT1 from CLIENT2. On CLIENT2, type the following command:

   ping *CLIENT1PublicAddress*

   CLIENT1PublicAddress is the public address of CLIENT1 obtained in step 7.

   This ping command should succeed because IPv6 connectivity using ISATAP now exists between CLIENT2 and CLIENT1. On the logical ISATAP subnet between CLIENT2 and ROUTER1, the IPv6 traffic is encapsulated as IPv4 packets.

At this point in the test lab configuration, there is an IPv4 routing infrastructure throughout the network. For IPv6 traffic, Subnet 1 has native IPv6 connectivity and Subnet 2 and Subnet 3 are a logical ISATAP subnet. CLIENT1 can communicate with DNS1 and ROUTER1 with native IPv6 traffic and communicate with ROUTER2 or CLIENT2 with encapsulated IPv6 traffic. In the next task, we will remove ISATAP and configure native IPv6 connectivity for all three subnets.

Configuring Native IPv6 Connectivity for All Subnets

To configure native IPv6 connectivity for all the subnets of the test lab network, complete the following steps:

1. On DNS1, type the **netsh interface ipv6 show address** command to obtain the public address assigned to the Local Area Connection interface.

2. On DNS1, use the DNS snap-in to remove the address (A) resource record named "ISATAP" from the testlab.microsoft.com forward lookup zone.

3. On ROUTER1, type the **netsh interface ipv6 show address** command to obtain the interface index of the ISATAP interface that is assigned the link-local address FE80::5EFE:10.0.2.1 and the link-local address of the interface named Subnet 2 Connection.

4. On ROUTER1, type the following commands:

   netsh interface isatap set router default

   netsh interface ipv6 set interface *ISATAPInterfaceIndex* **forwarding=disabled advertise=disabled**

   netsh interface ipv6 delete route 2001:db8:0:99::/64 *ISATAPInterfaceIndex*

   netsh interface ipv6 add dnsserver "Subnet 2 Connection" *DNS1IPv6Address*

   ISATAPInterfaceIndex is the interface index of the ISATAP interface obtained in step 3. *DNS1IPv6Address* is the public address of DNS1 obtained in step 1.

5. On ROUTER2, type the **netsh interface ipv6 show address** command to obtain the link-local address of the interface named Subnet 2 Connection.

6. On ROUTER1, type the following commands:

   netsh interface ipv6 set interface "Subnet 2 Connection" forwarding=enabled advertise=enabled

   netsh interface ipv6 add route 2001:db8:0:2::/64 "Subnet 2 Connection" publish=yes

   netsh interface ipv6 delete route ::/0 "Subnet 2 Connection"

   netsh interface ipv6 add route ::/0 "Subnet 2 Connection" *ROUTER2AddressOnSubnet2* **publish=yes**

   netsh interface ipv6 add dnsserver "Subnet 1 Connection" *DNS1IPv6Address*

   ROUTER2AddressOnSubnet2 is the link-local address assigned to ROUTER2's Subnet 2 Connection obtained in step 5.

7. On ROUTER2, type the following commands:

   netsh interface ipv6 set interface "Subnet 2 Connection" forwarding=enabled advertise=enabled

   netsh interface ipv6 set interface "Subnet 3 Connection" forwarding=enabled advertise=enabled

   netsh interface ipv6 add route 2001:db8:0:2::/64 "Subnet 2 Connection" publish=yes

   netsh interface ipv6 add route 2001:db8:0:3::/64 "Subnet 3 Connection" publish=yes

   netsh interface ipv6 add route ::/0 "Subnet 2 Connection" *ROUTER1AddressOnSubnet2* **publish=yes**

   ROUTER1AddressOnSubnet2 is the link-local address assigned to ROUTER1's Subnet 2 Connection obtained in step 3.

8. On CLIENT1, run the **netsh interface ipv6 add dnsserver "Local Area Connection"** *DNS1IPv6Address* command.

9. From the Network Connections folder on CLIENT1, disable and then enable the Local Area Connection. This renews CLIENT1's configuration.

10. On CLIENT1, type the **netsh interface ipv6 show route** command to view the new routes for 2001:DB8:0:1::/64, 2001:DB8:0:2::/64, and ::/0.

    As described in Chapter 10, "IPv6 Routing," the IPv6 protocol for Windows Server 2008 and Windows Vista advertises off-link prefixes using the Route Information option in Router Advertisement messages. These prefixes become routes in the routing table of the receiving host.

11. On CLIENT2, run the **netsh interface ipv6 add dnsserver "Local Area Connection"** *DNS1IPv6Address* command.

12. From the Network Connections folder on CLIENT2, disable and then enable the Local Area Connection. This renews CLIENT2's configuration.

13. On CLIENT2, type the **netsh interface ipv6 show address** command to view the new addresses that are based on the global prefix of 2001:DB8:0:3::/64.

14. On CLIENT2, type the **netsh interface ipv6 show route** command to view new routes for 2001:DB8:0:2::/64, 2001:DB8:0:3::/64, and ::/0.

15. On CLIENT1, type the following command to ping CLIENT2's public address:

    ping *CLIENT2PublicAddress*

    On CLIENT1, type the following command to trace the route between CLIENT1 and CLIENT2:

    tracert -d *CLIENT2PublicAddress*

    In the Tracert.exe tool display, you should see the link-local address of the Subnet 1 Connection of ROUTER1 and the link-local address of the Subnet 2 Connection of ROUTER2.

16. On ROUTER1, type the **netsh interface ipv6 show neighbors** command to view the entries in the ROUTER1 neighbor cache for CLIENT1 and ROUTER2. Type the **netsh interface ipv6 show destinationcache** command to view the entries in the ROUTER1 destination cache for CLIENT1 and CLIENT2.

Using Name Resolution

To test the use of DNS and the local Hosts file to resolve names to IPv6 addresses, complete the following steps:

1. On DNS1, use the DNS snap-in to view the A and AAAA records in the testlab.microsoft.com forward lookup zone that were dynamically registered by the computers in the test lab. Verify that an AAAA record for CLIENT2 exists.

2. If an AAAA record for CLIENT2 does not exist, create a host resource record for CLIENT2 with the DNS name client2.testlab.microsoft.com for its public IPv6 address.

    For example, if CLIENT2's public address is 2001:db8::3:3cec:bf16:505:eae6, create an AAAA resource record in the testlab.microsoft.com forward lookup zone for the following:

    Name: **client2**

    IP address: **2001:db8::3:3cec:bf16:505:eae6**

3. On CLIENT1, type the following command:

    ping client2.testlab.microsoft.com

    The name client2.testlab.microsoft.com is resolved to its public address by sending a DNS query to DNS1.

4. On CLIENT2, create the following entry in the Hosts file (located in the *%SystemRoot%*\System32\Drivers\Etc folder):

`Client1PublicAddress     c1`

For example, if CLIENT1's public address is 2001:db8::1:dd48:ab34:d07c:3914, the entry in the Hosts file is

`2001:db8::1:dd48:ab34:d07c:3914     c1`

5. On CLIENT2, type the following command:

ping c1

The name c1 is resolved to CLIENT1's public address by using the local Hosts file.

Configuring an IPv6-Only Routing Infrastructure

To configure a routing infrastructure so that all test lab nodes are reachable only by using IPv6 traffic, complete the following steps:

1. On DNS1, type the **netsh interface ipv4 uninstall** command. Restart DNS1.

2. On CLIENT1, type the **netsh interface ipv4 uninstall** command. Restart CLIENT1.

3. On ROUTER1, type the **netsh interface ipv4 uninstall** command. Restart ROUTER1.

4. On ROUTER2, type the **netsh interface ipv4 uninstall** command. Restart ROUTER2.

5. On CLIENT2, type the **netsh interface ipv4 uninstall** command. Restart CLIENT2.

At this point in the test lab configuration, there is only an IPv6 routing infrastructure throughout the test lab network. IPv4-based connectivity is not supported. You can now begin testing IPv6-only connectivity and functionality for Windows-based services and for your applications that have been modified to support both IPv4 and IPv6.

 Note   To reinstall IPv4 support, use the **netsh interface ipv4 install** command and restart the computer.

Some examples of tasks that you can do to continue your testing and evaluation of IPv6 connectivity for Windows-based services are the following:

- Make DNS1 an Active Directory domain controller for the testlab.microsoft.com domain.

- Join CLIENT1 and CLIENT2 to the testlab.microsoft.com domain, and test Active Directory domain operations.

- Make DNS1 a Web server, and test HTTP traffic over IPv6 from CLIENT1 and CLIENT2.

Appendix F
Mobile IPv6

This appendix describes how Mobile Internet Protocol version 6 (IPv6), defined in RFC 3775, allows an IPv6 node to change its location on an IPv6 network and still maintain existing connections. Connection maintenance for mobile nodes is not done by modifying Transport layer protocols, but by handling the changes of addresses at the Internet layer using Mobile IPv6 messages, options, and processes that ensure the correct delivery of data regardless of the mobile node's location.

Overview

Mobile IPv6 allows an IPv6 node to be mobile—to arbitrarily change its location on an IPv6 network—and still maintain existing connections. When an IPv6 node changes its location, it might also change its link. When an IPv6 node changes its link, its IPv6 address might also change in order to maintain connectivity. There are mechanisms to allow for the changes in addresses when moving to a different link, such as stateful and stateless address autoconfiguration for IPv6. However, when the address changes, the existing connections of the mobile node that are using the address assigned from the previously connected link cannot be maintained and are ungracefully terminated.

The key benefit of Mobile IPv6 is that even though the mobile node changes locations and addresses, the existing connections through which the mobile node is communicating are maintained. To accomplish this, connections to mobile nodes are made with a specific address that is always assigned to the mobile node, and through which the mobile node is always reachable. Mobile IPv6 provides Transport layer connection survivability when a node moves from one link to another by performing address maintenance for mobile nodes at the Internet layer.

Mobile IPv6 Components

Figure F-1 shows the components of Mobile IPv6.

The components of Mobile IPv6 are the following:

- **Home link**   The link that is assigned the home subnet prefix, from which the mobile node obtains its home address. The home agent resides on the home link.

- **Home address**   An address assigned to the mobile node when it is attached to the home link and through which the mobile node is always reachable, regardless of its location on an IPv6 network. If the mobile node is attached to the home link, Mobile IPv6 processes are not used and communication occurs normally. If the mobile node is away from home (not attached to the home link), packets addressed to the mobile node's home address are intercepted by the home agent and tunneled to the mobile node's current location on an IPv6 network. Because the mobile node is always assigned the home address, it is always logically connected to the home link.

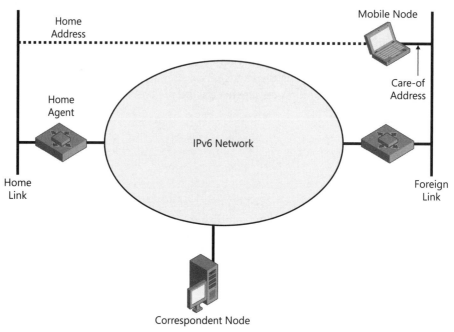

Figure F-1   Components of Mobile IPv6

- **Home agent**   A router on the home link that maintains registrations of mobile nodes that are away from home and the different addresses that they are currently using. If the mobile node is away from home, it registers its current address with the home agent, which tunnels data sent to the mobile node's home address to the mobile node's current address on an IPv6 network and forwards tunneled data sent by the mobile node.

  Although the figures in this appendix show the home agent as the router connecting the home link to an IPv6 network, the home agent does not have to serve this function. The home agent can also be a node on the home link that does not perform any forwarding when the mobile node is at home.

- **Mobile node**   An IPv6 node that can change links, and therefore addresses, and maintain reachability using its home address. A mobile node has awareness of its home address and the global address for the link to which it is attached (known as the *care-of address*), and it indicates its home address/care-of address mapping to the home agent and Mobile IPv6–capable nodes with which it is communicating.

- **Foreign link**   A link that is not the mobile node's home link.

- **Care-of address** An address used by a mobile node while it is attached to a foreign link. For stateless address configuration, the care-of address is a combination of the foreign subnet prefix and an interface ID determined by the mobile node. A mobile node can be assigned multiple care-of addresses; however, only one care-of address is registered as the primary care-of address with the mobile node's home agent. The association of a home address with a care-of address for a mobile node is known as a *binding*. Correspondent nodes and home agents keep information on bindings in a binding cache.

- **Correspondent node** An IPv6 node that communicates with a mobile node. A correspondent node does not have to be Mobile IPv6–capable. If the correspondent node is Mobile IPv6–capable, it can also be a mobile node that is away from home.

> **Note** The drawings in this appendix assume some sort of IPv6 network over which Mobile IPv6 messages or data is sent. This IPv6 network can be the IPv6 Internet, an IPv6-capable portion of a private intranet, or a public or private IPv4 infrastructure when using an IPv6 transition technology.

Mobile IPv6 Transport Layer Transparency

To achieve Transport layer transparency for the home address while the mobile node is assigned a care-of address, Mobile IPv6–capable nodes use the following:

- When a mobile node that is away from home sends data to a correspondent node, it sends the packets from its care-of address and includes the mobile node's home address in a Home Address option in a Destination Options extension header. When the correspondent node receives the packet, it logically replaces the source address of the packet (the care-of address) with the home address stored in the Home Address option.

- When a Mobile IPv6–capable correspondent node sends data to a mobile node that is away from home, it sends the packets to the care-of address and includes a Type 2 Routing extension header containing a single address, the mobile node's home address. When the mobile node receives the packet, it processes the Type 2 Routing header and logically replaces the destination address of the packet (the care-of address) with the home address from the Type 2 Routing header.

If a correspondent node is not Mobile IPv6–capable, packets sent between the correspondent node and the mobile node that is away from home are exchanged via the home agent. The correspondent node sends packets to the mobile node's home address. These packets are intercepted by the home agent and tunneled to the mobile node's care-of address. The mobile node tunnels packets destined for the correspondent node to the home agent, which forwards them to the correspondent node. This indirect method of delivery, known as *bidirectional tunneling*, although inefficient, allows communication between mobile nodes that are away from home and correspondent nodes that are not Mobile IPv6–capable.

Mobile IPv6 Messages and Options

Mobile IPv6 requires the use of the following messages and message options:

- A new Mobility extension header with a set of Mobile IPv6 messages
- A set of mobility options to include in mobility messages
- A new Home Address option for the Destination Options header
- A new Type 2 Routing header
- New Internet Control Message Protocol for IPv6 (ICMPv6) messages to discover the set of home agents and to obtain the prefix of the home link
- Changes to router discovery messages and options, and additional Neighbor Discovery options

Mobility Header and Messages

To facilitate the sending of messages between mobile nodes, correspondent nodes, and home agents for the purposes of managing the set of bindings between home addresses and care-of addresses, the Internet Engineering Task Force (IETF) has defined a new Mobility extension header. This new header can contain one of several defined mobility messages to perform specific functions. Some mobility messages can contain one or more options.

Mobility Header

The new Mobility extension header is dedicated to carrying mobility messages and has the structure shown in Figure F-2. Setting the previous header's Next Header field to the value of 135 identifies the Mobility extension header.

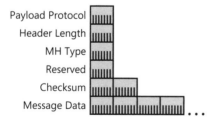

Figure F-2 Structure of the Mobility extension header

Within the Mobility extension header, you will find the following settings:

- The Payload Protocol field, equivalent to the Next Header field in the IPv6 header, is always set to the value of 59 to indicate that the Mobility header is the last header in the packet.
- The MH Type field identifies the specific type of mobility message.
- The Message Data field contains a mobility message.

The following types of mobility messages are defined:

- **Binding Refresh Request**   Sent by a correspondent node or home agent to request the current binding from a mobile node. If a mobile node receives a binding refresh request, it responds with a binding update. A correspondent node sends a binding refresh request when a binding cache entry is in active use and the lifetime of the binding cache entry approaches expiration. A home agent sends a binding refresh request when the lifetime of its binding cache entry approaches expiration.

- **Home Test Init (HoTI)**   Sent by the mobile node during the Return Routability procedure to test the indirect path from a mobile node to a correspondent node via the home agent. For more information, see the "Return Routability Procedure" section of this appendix.

- **Care-of Test Init (CoTI)**   Sent by the mobile node during the Return Routability procedure to test the direct path from a mobile node to a correspondent node.

- **Home Test (HoT)**   Sent by the correspondent node during the Return Routability procedure to respond to the HoTI message.

- **Care-of Test (CoT)**   Sent by the correspondent node during the Return Routability procedure to respond to the CoTI message.

- **Binding Update**   Sent by a Mobile IPv6 node that is away from home to update another node with its new care-of address. The Binding Update option is used for the following:

  - To update the home agent with a new primary care-of address. This is known as a home registration binding update. The home agent uses the home address in the Home Address option and the care-of address in an Alternate Care-of Address mobility option to update its Home Address/Primary Care-of Address binding cache entry for the mobile node.

  - To update a Mobile IPv6–capable correspondent node with which the mobile node is actively communicating with a binding that maps the home address of the mobile node to its care-of address. This is known as a *correspondent registration binding update*. The correspondent node uses the home address in the Home Address option and the source address of the packet to update its Home Address/Care-of Address binding cache entry for the mobile node.

- **Binding Acknowledgement**   Sent by a home agent or a correspondent node to acknowledge the receipt of a Binding Update message. Included in the binding acknowledgement is an indication of how long the node will cache the binding. For home agents, this lifetime indicates how long the home agent will be in service as the home agent for the mobile node. To refresh the binding, either the mobile node sends a new binding update or the correspondent nodes and home agent send Binding Refresh Request messages. The binding acknowledgement also includes an indication of how often the mobile node should send binding updates.

- **Binding Error**   Sent by a correspondent node to report errors in a binding update.

Mobility messages can contain mobility message options. RFC 3775 defines the following options:

- **Pad1 Option**   Used to insert a single byte of padding

- **PadN Option**   Used to insert 2 or more bytes of padding

- **Binding Refresh Advice Option**   Used in a Binding Acknowledgement sent from a home agent to indicate how long before the mobile node should send a new home registration

- **Alternate Care-of Address Option**   Used to indicate the care-of address in the Binding Update message

- **Nonce Indices Option**   Used to indicate information needed to determine binding keys

- **Binding Authorization Data Option**   Used to contain cryptographic information from which the receiver can verify that the binding message originated from a node with which a Return Routability procedure has occurred

Type 2 Routing Header

Mobile IPv6–capable correspondent nodes use a new Type 2 Routing header when sending a packet directly to a mobile node that is away from home to indicate the mobile node's home address. Correspondent nodes set the Destination Address field in the IPv6 header to the mobile node's care-of address when performing direct delivery.

Figure F-3 shows the structure of the new Type 2 Routing header.

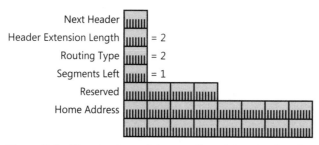

Figure F-3   The structure of the new Type 2 Routing header

During the processing of a packet with a Type 2 Routing header, the mobile node replaces the Destination Address field with the value in the Home Address field. The Home Address field in the Type 2 Routing header is the actual destination address of the mobile node to which the packet has been sent. (The care-of address stored in the Destination Address field of the IPv6 header is merely an intermediate delivery address.)

The Type 2 Routing header is different from the Type 0 Routing header defined in RFC 2460 in that it can store only a single address and is specified for use only with Mobile IPv6. The

Type 0 Routing header can store multiple addresses and is processed by routers for generalized source routing. Using a different routing type allows firewalls to treat source-routed packets differently from packets sent directly by Mobile IPv6–capable correspondent nodes to mobile nodes that are away from home.

Home Address Option for the Destination Options Header

The Home Address option in the Destination Options extension header is used to indicate the home address of the mobile node. It is included in binding updates sent to home agents and packets sent directly to Mobile IPv6–capable correspondent nodes by a mobile node when it is away from home when a binding exists. When a mobile node sends a packet, the source address in the IPv6 header is set to the care-of address. If the source address in the IPv6 header were set to the home address, the router on the foreign link might discard the packet because the source address does not match the prefix of the link on which the mobile node is located. To help minimize Internet attacks in which the source address of attack packets is spoofed with an address that is not assigned to the attacking computer, peripheral routers can implement ingress filtering and silently discard packets that do not have topologically correct source addresses. Ingress in this instance is defined relative to the Internet for packets entering the Internet, rather than packets entering an intranet from the Internet.

Figure F-4 shows the structure of the Home Address destination option.

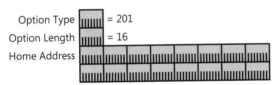

Figure F-4   The structure of Home Address destination option

By using the care-of address as the source address in the packet (a topologically correct address on the foreign link) and including the Home Address destination option, the router on the foreign link forwards the packet to its destination. When the packet is received at the destination, the correspondent node processes the Destination Options header and logically replaces the source address of the packet with the address in the Home Address option before passing the payload to the upper-layer protocol. To the upper-layer protocol, the packet was sent from the home address.

In contrast to the Home Address field in the Type 2 Routing header, the Home Address field in the Home Address destination option is the actual source address of the mobile node from which the packet was sent. (The care-of address stored in the Source Address of the IPv6 header is merely an intermediate address.)

The Home Address option is also included with the binding update so that the home address for the binding is indicated to the receiving node.

ICMPv6 Messages for Mobile IPv6

The mobile node uses the following ICMPv6 messages for dynamic home agent address and home subnet prefix discovery:

- Home Agent Address Discovery Request
- Home Agent Address Discovery Reply
- Mobile Prefix Solicitation
- Mobile Prefix Advertisement

Dynamic home agent address discovery is a process by which the mobile node dynamically discovers the global address of a home agent on the home link. This process is needed only if the mobile node is not already configured with the address of its home agent or if the current home agent becomes unavailable.

Home subnet prefix discovery is the process by which a mobile node dynamically discovers the address prefix of its home link. This process is needed only when a mobile node's home address is about to enter the invalid state.

Home Agent Address Discovery Request

The mobile node uses the ICMPv6 Home Agent Address Discovery Request message to begin dynamic home agent address discovery. The ICMPv6 Home Agent Address Discovery Request message is sent to the Mobile IPv6 Home-Agents anycast address that is described in RFC 2526. The Mobile IPv6 Home-Agents anycast is composed of the 64-bit home subnet prefix and the interface ID of ::FEFF:FFFF:FFFF:FFFE. All home agents are automatically configured with this anycast address. The home agent that is topologically closest to the mobile node receives the request message.

Figure F-5 shows the structure of the ICMPv6 Home Agent Address Discovery Request message.

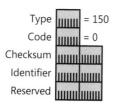

Figure F-5   The structure of ICMPv6 Home Agent Address Discovery Request message

In the Home Agent Address Discovery Request message, the Type field is set to 150 and the Code field is set to 0. Following the Checksum field is a 16-bit Identifier field. The value of the Identifier field is chosen by the sending node, and it is copied to the Identifier field of the Home Agent Address Discovery Reply message to match a reply with its request. Following the Identifier field is a 16-bit Reserved field that is set to 0 by the sender.

The Home Agent Address Discovery Request message is sent with the source address in the IPv6 header set to the mobile node's care-of address.

Home Agent Address Discovery Reply

The home agent uses the ICMPv6 Home Agent Address Discovery Reply message to complete the dynamic home agent address discovery process by informing the mobile node of the addresses of the home agents on the mobile node's home link.

Figure F-6 shows the structure of the ICMPv6 Home Agent Address Discovery Reply message.

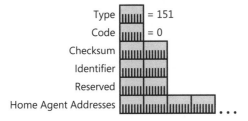

Figure F-6   The structure of the ICMPv6 Home Agent Address Discovery Reply message

In the Home Agent Address Discovery Reply message, the Type field is set to 151 and the Code field is set to 0. Following the Checksum field is a 16-bit Identifier field. The value of the Identifier field is set to the same value as the Identifier field of the received Home Agent Address Discovery Request message. Following the Identifier field is a 16-bit Reserved field that is set to 0 by the sender, and one or more 128-bit Home Agent Address fields. The Home Agent Address fields contain the global addresses of home agents on the home link in preference order (highest preference first).

The Home Agent Address Discovery Reply message is sent with the source address in the IPv6 header set to the global address of the answering home agent, and with the destination address set to the mobile node's care-of address. A Type 2 Routing extension header is not included.

Mobile Prefix Solicitation

A mobile node uses the ICMPv6 Mobile Prefix Solicitation message to obtain its home subnet prefix while it is away from home. The response to the ICMPv6 Mobile Prefix Solicitation message is an ICMPv6 Mobile Prefix Advertisement message from the home agent, which contains the home subnet prefix and other configuration information by which the mobile node can update or refresh its home address.

Figure F-7 shows the structure of the ICMPv6 Mobile Prefix Solicitation message.

The Identifier field is set by the mobile node and used to match a sent Mobile Prefix Solicitation message with its corresponding Mobile Prefix Advertisement message.

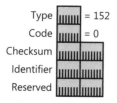

Figure F-7   The structure of the ICMPv6 Mobile Prefix Solicitation message

Mobile Prefix Advertisement

The home agent uses the ICMPv6 Mobile Prefix Advertisement message to advertise the home subnet prefix and other configuration options to mobile nodes that are away from home, either unsolicited or in response to a received ICMPv6 Mobile Prefix Solicitation message

Figure F-8 shows the structure of the ICMPv6 Mobile Prefix Advertisement message.

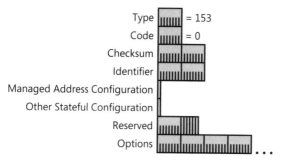

Figure F-8   The structure of the ICMPv6 Mobile Prefix Advertisement message

The Identifier field is set to the value of the Identifier field of a received Mobile Prefix Solicitation message. The Managed Address Configuration, Other Stateful Configuration, and Options fields are the same as the corresponding fields of the Router Advertisement message as defined in RFC 4861, except that RFC 3775 defines the use of the Mobile IPv6–modified Prefix Information option, described in the next section.

Modifications to Neighbor Discovery Messages and Options

Mobile IPv6 defines the following changes to Neighbor Discovery (ND) messages and options:

- Modified Router Advertisement message
- Modified Prefix Information option
- New Advertisement Interval option
- New Home Agent Information option

Modifications to the Router Advertisement Message

Mobile IPv6 defines an additional flag in the Router Advertisement message to help facilitate home agent discovery by the home agents on a home link. The new flag, known as the Home Agent (H) flag, indicates whether the advertising router is capable of being a home agent. Each of the home agents on the home link sets this flag when it sends its router advertisements, and each home agent receives each router advertisement. Therefore, each home agent can compile the list of possible home agents.

Figure F-9 shows the structure of the modified Router Advertisement message.

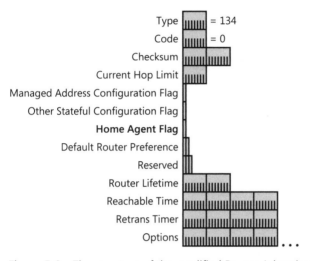

Type = 134
Code = 0
Checksum
Current Hop Limit
Managed Address Configuration Flag
Other Stateful Configuration Flag
Home Agent Flag
Default Router Preference
Reserved
Router Lifetime
Reachable Time
Retrans Timer
Options

Figure F-9   The structure of the modified Router Advertisement message

Additionally, Mobile IPv6 allows a router advertisement to be sent more frequently than every three seconds, as specified in RFC 4861. By sending router advertisements more frequently, mobile nodes can use a newly received router advertisement to detect movement to a foreign link more quickly. Recommended values for the pseudo-periodic router advertisement process for routers that might provide connectivity for mobile IPv6 nodes are a minimum of 0.03 seconds and a maximum of 0.07 seconds.

Modified Prefix Information Option

To indicate the global address of the advertising router, Mobile IPv6 defines an additional flag and a redefined use of the Prefix field in the Prefix Information option.

Figure F-10 shows the structure of the modified Prefix Information option.

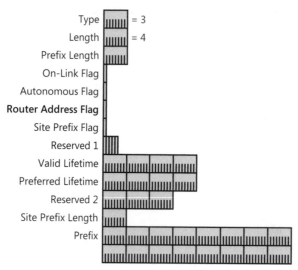

Figure F-10   The structure of the modified Prefix Information option

According to RFC 4861, router advertisements are sent from the link-local address. However, the global address for a home agent must be indicated in the router advertisement it sends so that each home agent can compile a list of home agents. Mobile IPv6 defines the Router Address (R) flag in the Prefix Information option. When set to 1, the R flag indicates to the receiver that the Prefix field contains the global address of the advertising router. In the originally defined Prefix field, the high-order bits corresponding to the value of the Prefix Length field are set to the appropriate values for the advertised prefix and the bits beyond the indicated prefix length are set to 0. With this new definition, the Prefix Length field is advertised in the same way, only the Prefix field contains the entire 128-bit global address of the advertising router.

Advertisement Interval Option

The Advertisement Interval option is sent in Router Advertisement messages to specify how often the router sends unsolicited multicast router advertisements. A mobile node that receives a router advertisement with the Advertisement Interval option can use the advertisement interval to detect whether it has moved to another link.

Figure F-11 shows the structure of the Advertisement Interval option.

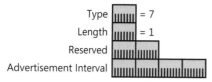

Figure F-11   The structure of the Advertisement Interval option

The Advertisement Interval option contains a 32-bit field that indicates the maximum number of milliseconds between consecutive unsolicited multicast Router Advertisement messages sent by the router using the pseudo-periodic advertising scheme described in section 6.2.4 of RFC 4861.

Home Agent Information Option

The Home Agent Information option is sent in Router Advertisement messages sent by a home agent to specify the home agent's configuration. Figure F-12 shows the structure of the Home Agent Information option.

Type   = 8
Length   = 1
Reserved
Home Agent Preference
Home Agent Lifetime

Figure F-12   The structure of the Home Agent Information option

Included in the Home Agent Information option are the home agent preference (a number indicating a preference level for the advertising router to be a home agent) and the home agent lifetime (how long the home agent is acting as a home agent).

The home agents on a home link use the home agent preference values to order the list of home agents that are sent to the mobile node during home agent address discovery.

Mobile IPv6 Data Structures

The following data structures are needed to facilitate the processes of Mobile IPv6:

- Binding cache
- Binding update list
- Home agents list

Binding Cache

The binding cache is a table maintained by each correspondent node and home agent that contains the current bindings for mobile nodes. Each binding cache entry contains the following information:

- The home address for the mobile node
- The care-of address for the mobile node
- The lifetime of the binding cache entry

The lifetime is obtained from a Lifetime field of the last Binding Update message that was received for this cache entry.

- A flag indicating whether the binding is a home registration

  This flag is set to 1 only for the binding cache entries on home agents.

- The time that the last binding request was sent

The actual implementation details for the binding cache are not specified, as long as the external behavior is consistent with RFC 3775. For example, you can either maintain a separate binding cache or combine the binding cache with the destination cache. If you have a separate binding cache, you can either check it before you check the destination cache or have a pointer from the destination cache entry to the corresponding binding cache entry.

In any case, the information in the binding cache takes precedence over the information in the destination cache. For mobile destinations that are away from home, packets should be sent to the mobile node's home address by way of its care-of address. If packets are sent directly to the home address while the mobile node is away from home, the home agent must intercept the packets and tunnel them to the mobile node, lowering the efficiency and performance of the communication between the correspondent node and the mobile node.

For a separate binding cache, each binding cache entry stores the home address, its current care-of address, and a pointer to the entry in the destination cache for the care-of address. A destination cache entry for a home address of a mobile node that is away from home has a pointer to an entry in the binding cache. The entry in the binding cache maps the home address to its care-of address and indicates the entry in the destination cache for the care-of address. The care-of address destination cache entry stores the next-hop address and interface for the care-of address.

For more information about how a node sends a packet in a Mobile IPv6 environment, see the "Mobile IPv6 Host Sending Algorithm" section in this appendix.

Binding Update List

The binding update list is maintained by a mobile node to record the most recent binding updates sent for the home agent and correspondent nodes. A binding update list entry contains the following information:

- The address of the node to which the binding update was sent
- The home address for the binding update
- The care-of address sent in the last binding update
- The value of the Lifetime field in the binding update
- The remaining lifetime of the binding

The initial value is the value of the Lifetime field in the binding update. When the lifetime expires, the entry is deleted from the binding update list.

- The maximum value of the Sequence Number field sent in previous binding updates

- The time that the last binding update was sent

- An indication of whether a retransmission is needed for binding updates sent with the Acknowledge flag set to 1 and when the retransmission is to be sent

- A flag indicating that no future binding updates need to be sent

    This flag is set to 1 when the mobile node receives an ICMPv6 Parameter Problem-Unrecognized Next Header Type Encountered message in response to a Return Routability message or a binding update.

Home Agents List

Home agents maintain the home agents list and record information about each router from which a Router Advertisement message was received on the home link with the Home Agent (H) flag set to 1. Home agents maintain the home agents list so that they can send the list of home agents to a requesting mobile node away from home during home agent address discovery.

A home agents list entry contains the following information:

- The link-local address of the router on the link, obtained from the source address of the received Router Advertisement message

- The global address or addresses of the home agent, obtained from the Prefix field in the Prefix Information options in the Router Advertisement message with the Router Address (R) flag set to 1

- The remaining lifetime of this entry

    The initial lifetime is obtained from either the Home Agent Lifetime field in the Home Agent Information option or the Router Lifetime field in the Router Advertisement message. When the lifetime expires, the entry is deleted from the home agents list.

- The preference for the home agent, obtained from the Home Agent Preference field in the Home Agent Information option

    If the router advertisement does not contain a Home Agent Information option, the preference is set to 0. Based on the definition of the Home Agent Preference field, 0 is a medium priority level. A mobile node uses the preference value to select the home agent. A home agent uses the preference value to order by preference value the list of home agents returned to a mobile node during home agent address discovery. When the mobile node receives the list of home agents, it chooses the first home agent in the list.

Correspondent Registration

There are two ways in which mobile nodes that are away from home can communicate with correspondent nodes:

- **Directly**   If the correspondent node is Mobile IPv6–capable, data can be sent directly between the mobile node and the correspondent node. The mobile node sends data directly to the correspondent node using the correspondent node's address and includes the Home Address destination option to indicate its home address. The correspondent node sends data directly to the mobile node's care-of address and includes the Type 2 Routing header to indicate the mobile node's home address. The direct method of data delivery is referred to in RFC 3775 as *route optimization.*

- **Indirectly**   If the correspondent node is not Mobile IPv6–capable or the registration of the binding for the mobile node with the correspondent node that is Mobile IPv6–capable has not yet been completed, data can be sent indirectly between the mobile node and the correspondent node via the home agent.

  For traffic from the mobile node to the correspondent node, packets are tunneled to the home agent. The mobile node encapsulates the IPv6 packet sent from the mobile node's home address and to the correspondent node's address with an additional IPv6 header, the source address of the mobile node's care-of address, and the destination address of the home agent's global address. After receiving the packet, the home agent strips the outer IPv6 header and forwards the original IPv6 packet to the correspondent node.

  For traffic from the correspondent node to the mobile node, the correspondent node sends the packet to the mobile node's home address. When the home agent intercepts the packet, it is encapsulated with an additional IPv6 header containing the source address of the home agent's address, and the destination address of the mobile node's care-of address.

  Indirect delivery via the home agent, although inefficient, allows communication between mobile nodes and correspondent nodes that are not Mobile IPv6–capable.

  The indirect method of data delivery is referred to in RFC 3775 as *bidirectional tunneling.*

For direct delivery to occur, the correspondent node with which the mobile node is communicating must be Mobile IPv6–capable and must have a binding cache entry that maps the mobile node's home address to its care-of address. Correspondent nodes that receive packets that contain a Home Address option in a Destination Options header must have a corresponding binding cache entry; otherwise, the packet is silently discarded. This behavior provides some protection against malicious users or programs that attempt to impersonate mobile nodes that are away from home.

The process of creating a binding cache entry on the correspondent node and a binding update list entry on the mobile node is known as *correspondent registration* and consists of the following:

- **Return Routability procedure**   The Return Routability procedure establishes proof to the correspondent node that the mobile node is reachable at both its home address (using the indirect path) and its care-of address (using the direct path). It also determines tokens that are used to derive a binding management key, which is used to calculate authorization data values for binding messages.

- **Binding Update and Binding Acknowledgement message exchange**   The Binding Update and Binding Acknowledgement message exchange uses the binding management key to prove that the messages were sent from the nodes that participated in the Return Routability procedure. For the binding update, the correspondent node verifies the included authorization data, updates its binding cache with an entry for the mobile node, and typically returns a Binding Acknowledgement message, which also contains authorization data calculated using the binding management key.

The result of the correspondent registration is the following:

- On the mobile node, there is an entry in its binding update list for the correspondent node.
- On the correspondent node, there is an entry in its binding cache for the mobile node.

The binding management key can be used for subsequent binding maintenance as long as the mobile node's home address or care-of address does not change. When they do, the Return Routability procedure is performed again to ensure that the mobile node is reachable at its new addresses.

Return Routability Procedure

Figure F-13 shows the Return Routability procedure.

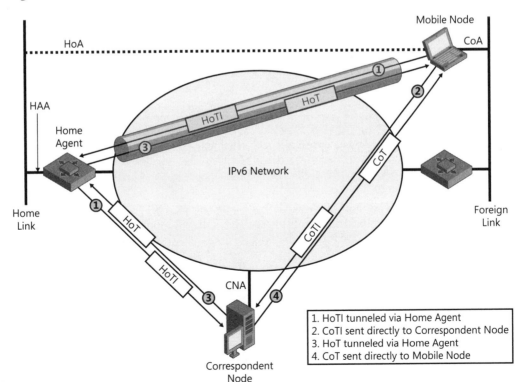

Figure F-13   The Return Routability procedure

The full Return Routability process is the following:

1. The mobile node sends a Home Test Init (HoTI) message indirectly to the correspondent node, tunneling the message through the home agent.

2. The mobile node sends a Care-of Test Init (CoTI) message directly to the correspondent node.

3. The correspondent node sends a Home Test (HoT) message in response to the HoTI message (sent indirectly to the mobile node via the home agent).

4. The correspondent node sends a Care-of Test (CoT) message in response to the CoTI message (sent directly to the mobile node).

The correspondent node responds to the HoTI and CoTI messages as they arrive, independently of each other. The messages can arrive in any order. The correspondent node does not store any state information after responding to the HoTI or CoTI message.

The HoT message is sent to the mobile node's home address. To provide security for the HoTI and HoT messages in the path from the home agent to the mobile node, the home agent can use Internet Protocol security (IPsec) Encapsulating Security Payload (ESP) tunnel mode to provide data confidentiality, data origin authentication, and data integrity for the HoT message.

For information about how IPsec and ESP are used to protect Mobile IPv6 traffic, see RFC 3776.

From the tokens in the HoT and CoT messages, the mobile node can derive a binding management key. From information in the Binding Update message, the correspondent node can derive the same binding management key and use it to verify authentication data stored in the Binding Update message.

Note   The Return Routability procedure is designed to verify that the mobile node is reachable at both its home address and its care-of address. The home address must be verified to prevent spoofing of binding updates. The care-of address must be verified to protect against denial-of-service attacks in which the correspondent node is tricked to flood a false care-of address with packets.

The binding management key is derived from two separate token values: one value in the HoT message, and one in the CoT message. The purpose of the HoT message is to verify that the mobile node is reachable at its home address. An attacker can learn the home address token in the HoT message only if it has access to the path from the correspondent node to the home agent. The purpose of the CoT message, on the other hand, is to verify that the mobile node is reachable at the care-of address. To learn the care-of address token in the CoT message, the attacker must have access to either the care-of address or the path from the correspondent node to the mobile node. If an attacker cannot capture both tokens, it cannot calculate the binding management key.

Detecting Correspondent Nodes That Are Not Mobile IPv6–Capable

If a correspondent node is not Mobile IPv6–capable, it will not recognize mobility messages, specifically the HoTI and CoTI messages sent by the mobile node that use the new Mobility header. Because the correspondent node does not recognize the new Mobility header, it responds with an ICMPv6 Bad Parameter-Unrecognized Next Header Type Encountered (ICMPv6 Type 4, Code 1) message. Upon receipt of the ICMPv6 message, the mobile node records the correspondent node's lack of support for Mobile IPv6 in its corresponding entry in the binding update list. Subsequent packets sent to the correspondent node are always tunneled via the home agent. Depending on the Mobile IPv6 implementation, the mobile node might periodically retry the Return Routability procedure to test for the correspondent node's current support for Mobile IPv6.

Mobile IPv6 Message Exchanges

Before understanding the various processes used for Mobile IPv6, it is important to understand the different sets of messages and data exchanged between mobile nodes and correspondent nodes and between mobile nodes and home agents. This section examines the following types of Mobile IPv6 message exchanges:

- Data between a mobile node and a correspondent node
- Binding maintenance
- Home Agent Discovery
- Mobile Prefix Discovery

Data Between a Mobile Node and a Correspondent Node

Data between a mobile node that is away from home and a correspondent node can be sent in the following ways:

- Indirect delivery via Home Agent because there is no binding (bidirectional tunneling)
- Direct delivery because there is a binding (route optimization)

Indirect Delivery via the Home Agent

When a correspondent node either does not yet have a binding for the mobile node (correspondent registration is in progress) or does not support Mobile IPv6, it sends packets to the mobile node using only its home address. These data packets are forwarded to the home address of the mobile node.

Figure F-14 shows the correspondent node sending data packets to a mobile node that is away from home via indirect delivery.

> **Note**   In Figure F-14 and subsequent figures, *CNA* is the correspondent node's address, *CoA* is the mobile node's care-of address, *HoA* is the mobile node's home address, and *HAA* is the home agent's global address.

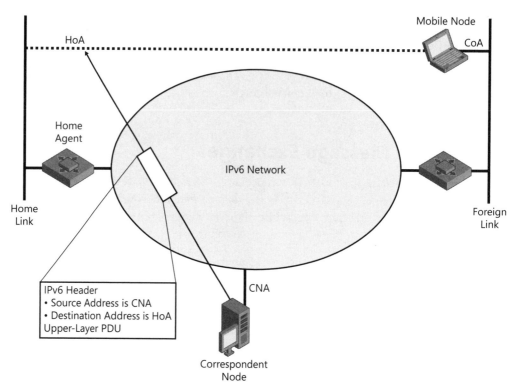

Figure F-14   Data packets sent by a correspondent node to the mobile node's home address

These packets contain the following:

- **IPv6 header**   In the IPv6 header, the source address is the correspondent node address and the destination address is the mobile node's home address. Because a binding cache entry does not exist, the correspondent node sends the packet as if the mobile node were physically attached to the home link.

- **Upper layer PDU**   The upper-layer PDU contains the Application layer data sent from the correspondent node to the mobile node.

When the home agent intercepts a packet sent to a mobile node's home address, it tunnels the packet to the mobile node using the form shown in Figure F-15.

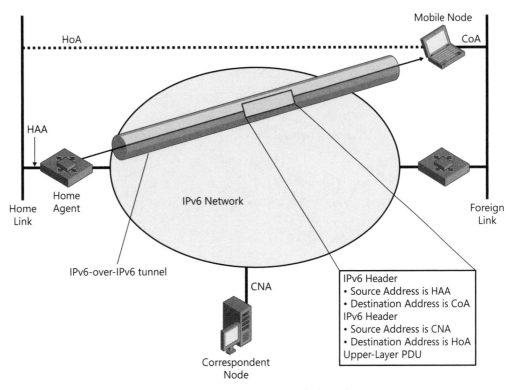

Figure F-15   Intercepted packet tunneled to a mobile node by its home agent

These packets contain the following:

- **IPv6 header (outer)**   In the outer IPv6 header, the source address is the home agent's address on the home link and the destination address is the mobile node's care-of address.

- **IPv6 header (inner)**   In the inner IPv6 header, the source address is the correspondent node's address and the destination address is the mobile node's home address.

- **Upper-layer PDU**   The upper-layer protocol data unit (PDU) contains the Application layer data sent from the correspondent node to the mobile node at its home address. From the Application layer perspective, the data was addressed from the correspondent node address to the home address.

Optionally, the home agent can protect the packet by using IPsec ESP. In this case, an ESP header is placed between the outer IPv6 header and the inner IPv6 header (not shown in Figure F-15).

When the correspondent registration process is not yet complete or the correspondent node is not Mobile IPv6–capable, the mobile node that is away from home sends packets to the correspondent node by tunneling them to the home agent, as shown in Figure F-16.

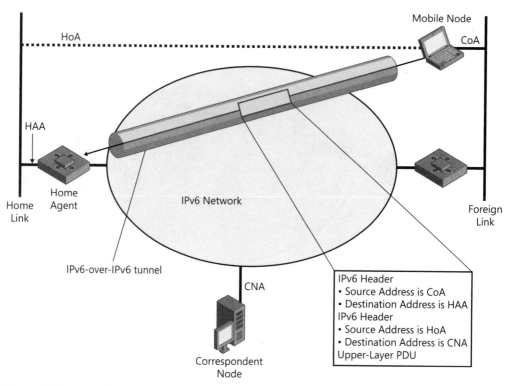

Figure F-16 Tunneled packets to a home agent

These packets contain the following:

- **IPv6 header (outer)**   In the outer IPv6 header, the source address is the mobile node's care-of address and the destination address is the home agent's address on the home link.

- **IPv6 header (inner)**   In the inner IPv6 header, the source address is the mobile node's home address and the destination address is the correspondent node's address.

- **Upper-layer PDU**   The upper-layer PDU contains the Application layer data sent from the mobile node to the correspondent node.

Optionally, the mobile node can protect the packet by using IPsec ESP. In this case, an ESP header is placed between the outer IPv6 header and the inner IPv6 header (not shown in Figure F-16).

The home agent forwards tunneled data packets from a mobile node that is away from home to a correspondent node using the form shown in Figure F-17.

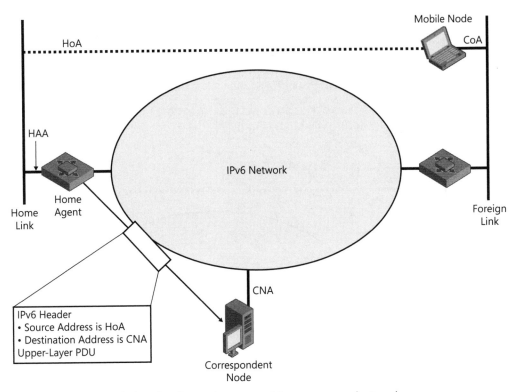

Figure F-17   Forwarded packet from a home agent to a correspondent node

These packets contain the following:

- **IPv6 header**   The source address is the mobile node's home address and the destination address is the correspondent node's address.

- **Upper-layer PDU**   The upper-layer PDU contains the Application layer data sent from the mobile node to the correspondent node.

Direct Delivery

When the mobile node is away from home, it can choose to send data either from its home address using Mobile IPv6 or from its care-of address without using Mobile IPv6, based on the following:

- For Transport layer connection data (such as Transmission Control Protocol [TCP] sessions) that is long-term and being sent to a correspondent node with which it has completed correspondent registration, the mobile node sends the data from its home address and includes the Home Address option.

■ For short-term communication that does not require a logical connection, such as the exchange of Domain Name System (DNS) Name Query Request and Name Query Response messages for DNS name resolution, the mobile node can send data from its care-of address and not use a Home Address option. In this case, the mobile node is sending and receiving packets normally from its care-of address.

Figure F-18 shows data packets sent directly from the mobile node to the correspondent node when the mobile node has a binding update list entry for the correspondent node's address.

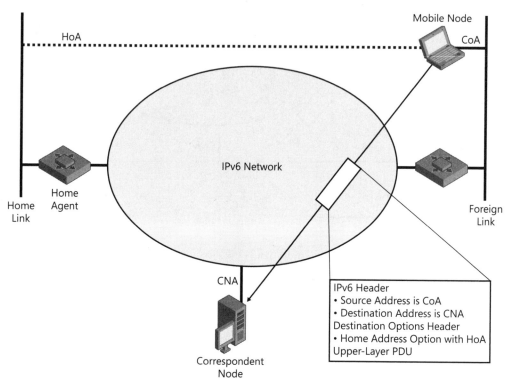

Figure F-18   Data sent from the mobile node to the correspondent node

These packets contain the following:

■ **IPv6 header**   In the IPv6 header, the source address is the mobile node's care-of address and the destination address is the correspondent node's address. By using the care-of address rather than the home address, ingress filtering by the foreign-link router does not prevent the packet from being forwarded.

■ **Destination Options header**   In the Destination Options extension header, the Home Address option contains the home address of the mobile node. When the correspondent node processes the Home Address option, it replaces the source address of the packet with the home address.

■ **Upper-layer PDU**   The upper-layer (PDU contains the Application layer data sent from the mobile node to the correspondent node. From the Application layer perspective, the data was addressed from the home address to the correspondent node address.

Note   The drawings in this appendix assume that the data packets being sent by the mobile node and the correspondent node do not contain additional IPv6 extension headers.

If the correspondent node is also a mobile node that is away from home, the destination address in the IPv6 header is set to the correspondent node's care-of address and the packet includes a Type 2 Routing header with the correspondent node's home address. The Type 2 Routing header is placed before the Destination Options header. This is not shown in Figure F-18.

Figure F-19 shows the form of data packets sent from the correspondent node to the mobile node when the correspondent node has a binding cache entry for the mobile node's home address.

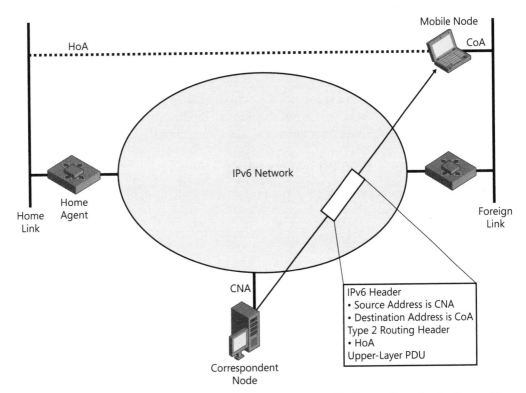

Figure F-19   Data sent from the correspondent node when a binding cache entry for the mobile node is present

These packets contain the following:

- **IPv6 header**   In the IPv6 header, the source address is the correspondent node's address and the destination address is the mobile node's care-of address. By using the care-of address rather than the home address, the packet is delivered to the mobile node's current location on an IPv6 network.

- **Type 2 Routing header**   In the Type 2 Routing header, the Home Address field is set to the mobile node's home address. When the mobile node receives the packet, it removes the Type 2 Routing header and replaces the care-of address with the home address as the destination address in the IPv6 header. When the packet is passed to the upper-layer protocol, it appears to have been addressed to the mobile node's home address.

- **Upper-layer PDU**   The upper-layer PDU contains the Application layer data sent from the correspondent node to the mobile node. From the Application layer perspective, the data was addressed from the correspondent node address to the home address.

If the correspondent node is also a mobile node that is away from home, the source address in the IPv6 header is set to the correspondent node's care-of address and the packet includes a Destination Options header with the Home Address option containing the correspondent node's home address. The Destination Options header is placed after the Type 2 Routing header. This is not shown in Figure F-19.

Binding Maintenance

Bindings with the home agent and the correspondent node must be created, refreshed, and when the mobile node returns home, removed. Bindings must be maintained with the home agent and with correspondent nodes.

Home-Agent Binding Maintenance

Figure F-20 shows Binding Update messages sent from the mobile node to the home agent for home registration.

The packets contain the following:

- **IPv6 header**   In the IPv6 header, the source address is the mobile node's care-of address and the destination address is the home agent's address. By using the care-of address rather than the home address, ingress filtering by the foreign-link router does not prevent the packet from being forwarded.

- **Destination Options header**   The Destination Options extension header contains the Home Address option. By including the Home Address option, the home address for the binding is indicated to be the home agent.

- **ESP header**   An IPsec ESP header is used to provide data integrity protection, data origin authentication, data confidentiality, and replay protection for the Binding Update message.

- **Mobility header**   The Mobility header contains the Binding Update message with the Home Registration flag set to 1, indicating that the sender is requesting that the receiver be the home agent for the mobile node. The Acknowledgement flag is also set to 1 to request a binding acknowledgement from the home agent.

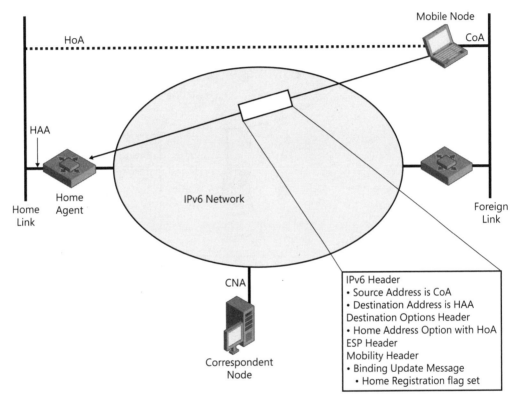

Figure F-20   Binding updates sent from the mobile node to the home agent

Binding maintenance messages sent from the home agent to the mobile node are either binding acknowledgments or binding refresh requests and are shown in Figure F-21.

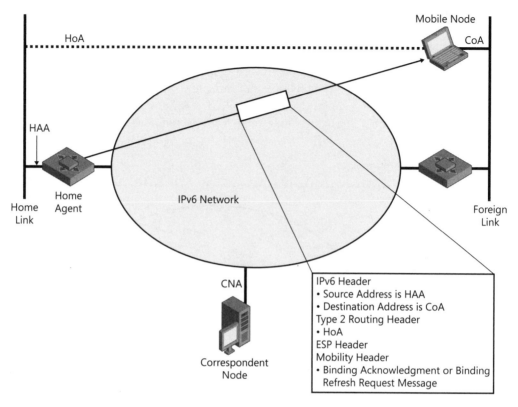

Figure F-21   Binding maintenance packets sent from the home agent to the mobile node

These packets contain the following:

- **IPv6 header**   In the IPv6 header, the source address is the home agent's address and the destination address is the mobile node's care-of address.

- **Type 2 Routing header**   The Type 2 Routing header contains the mobile node's home address. The mobile node removes the Type 2 Routing header and logically replaces the care-of address with the home address as the destination in the IPv6 header.

- **ESP header**   An ESP header is used to provide data integrity protection, data origin authentication, replay protection, and data confidentiality for the binding acknowledgments or binding refresh requests.

- **Mobility header**   The Mobility header contains either a Binding Acknowledgement message (sent in response to a binding update) or a Binding Refresh Request message.

Correspondent Node Binding Maintenance

Figure F-22 shows Binding Update messages sent from the mobile node to the correspondent node as part of correspondent registration.

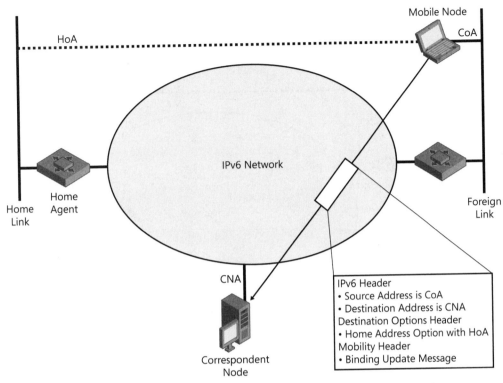

Figure F-22   Binding updates sent from the mobile node to the correspondent node

These packets contain the following:

- **IPv6 header**   In the IPv6 header, the source address is the mobile node's care-of address and the destination address is the correspondent node's address. By using the care-of address rather than the home address, ingress filtering by the foreign link router does not prevent the packet from being forwarded.

- **Destination Options header**   The Destination Options extension header contains the Home Address option. By including the Home Address option, the home address for the binding is indicated to be the correspondent node.

- **Mobility header**   The Mobility header contains the Binding Update message, which contains the cryptographic proof that the mobile node has knowledge of the binding management key derived from the Return Routability procedure performed with the correspondent node.

If the correspondent node is also a mobile node that is away from home, the destination address in the IPv6 header is set to the correspondent node's care-of address and the packet includes a Type 2 Routing header with the correspondent node's home address. The Type 2 Routing header is placed before the Destination Options header. This is not shown in Figure F-22.

Binding maintenance messages sent from the correspondent node to the mobile node are either binding acknowledgments or binding refresh requests and are shown in Figure F-23.

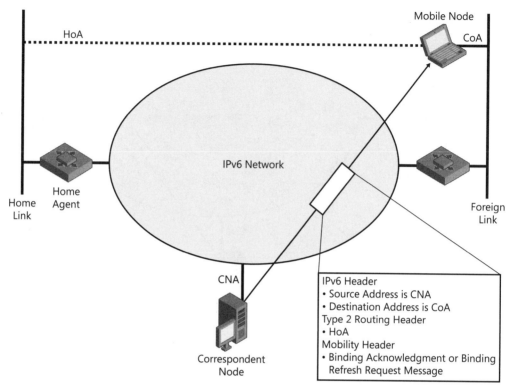

Figure F-23   Binding maintenance packets sent from the correspondent node to the mobile node

These packets contain the following:

- **IPv6 header**   In the IPv6 header, the source address is the correspondent node's address and the destination address is the mobile node's care-of address.

- **Type 2 Routing header**   In the Type 2 Routing header, the Home Address field is set to the mobile node's home address. When the mobile node receives the packet, it removes the Type 2 Routing header and replaces the care-of address with the home address as the destination address in the IPv6 header.

- **Mobility header**   The Mobility header contains either a Binding Acknowledgement message (if a received binding request had the Acknowledgement flag set to 1) or a Binding Refresh Request message.

If the correspondent node is also a mobile node that is away from home, the source address in the IPv6 header is set to the correspondent node's care-of address and the packet includes a Destination Options header with a Home Address option containing the correspondent node's home address. The Destination Options header is placed after the Type 2 Routing header. This is not shown in Figure F-23.

Home Agent Discovery

When the mobile node sends an ICMPv6 Home Agent Address Discovery Request message, it has the form shown in Figure F-24.

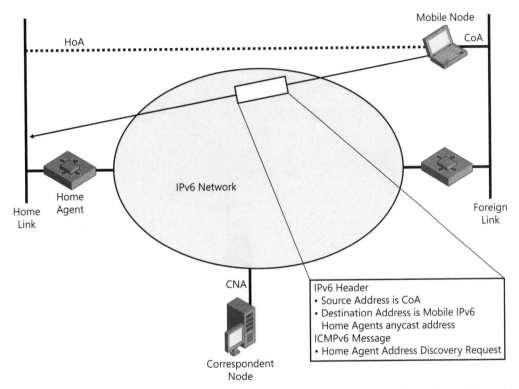

Figure F-24   ICMPv6 Home Agent Address Discovery Request message sent from the mobile node

These packets contain the following:

■ **IPv6 header**   In the IPv6 header, the source address is the care-of address of the mobile node and the destination address is the Mobile IPv6 Home Agents anycast address corresponding to the home link prefix.

■ **ICMPv6 Home Agent Address Discovery Request message**   The mobile node uses the ICMPv6 Home Agent Address Discovery Request message to query the home link for a list of home agents. For more information, see the "ICMPv6 Messages for Mobile IPv6" section in this appendix.

When the home agent sends an ICMPv6 Home Agent Address Discovery Reply message in response to an ICMPv6 Home Agent Address Discovery Request message, it has the form shown in Figure F-25.

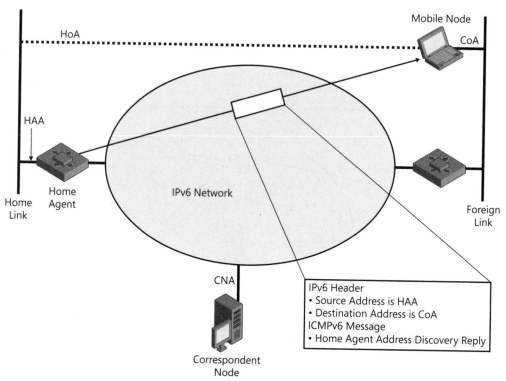

Figure F-25 ICMPv6 Home Agent Address Discovery Reply message sent from the home agent

These packets contain the following:

- **IPv6 header** In the IPv6 header, the source address is the home agent's address and the destination address is the mobile node's care-of address.

- **ICMPv6 Home Agent Address Discovery Reply message** The ICMPv6 Home Agent Address Discovery Reply message contains the list of home agents on the home link in order of preference. For more information, see the "ICMPv6 Messages for Mobile IPv6" section in this appendix.

Mobile Prefix Discovery

When the mobile node sends an ICMPv6 Mobile Prefix Solicitation message, it has the form shown in Figure F-26.

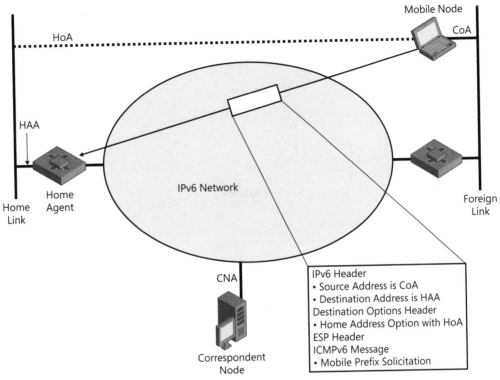

Figure F-26   ICMPv6 Mobile Prefix Solicitation message sent from the mobile node

These packets contain the following:

- **IPv6 header**   In the IPv6 header, the source address is the care-of address of the mobile node and the destination address is the home agent's global address on the home link.

- **Destination Options header**   The Destination Options extension header contains the Home Address option. By including the Home Address option, the home address for the binding is indicated to the home agent.

- **ESP header**   An ESP header is used to provide data confidentiality, data integrity protection, data origin authentication, and replay protection for the ICMPv6 Mobile Prefix Solicitation message.

- **ICMPv6 Mobile Prefix Solicitation message**   The mobile node uses the ICMPv6 Mobile Prefix Solicitation message to query its home agent for the current home subnet prefix. For more information, see the "ICMPv6 Messages for Mobile IPv6" section in this appendix.

When the home agent sends an ICMPv6 Mobile Prefix Advertisement message in response to a Mobile Prefix Solicitation message or periodically to refresh the mobile node's home address, it has the form shown in Figure F-27.

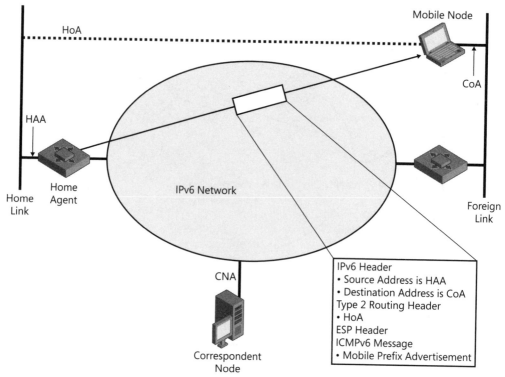

Figure F-27   ICMPv6 Mobile Prefix Advertisement message sent from the mobile node

These packets contain the following:

- **IPv6 header**   In the IPv6 header, the source address is the home agent's global address on the home link and the destination address is the mobile node's care-of address.

- **Type 2 Routing header**   The Type 2 Routing header contains the mobile node's home address. The mobile node removes the Type 2 Routing header and logically replaces the care-of address with the home address as the destination in the IPv6 header.

- **ESP header**   An ESP header is used to provide data confidentiality, data integrity protection, data origin authentication, and replay protection for the ICMPv6 Mobile Prefix Advertisement message.

- **ICMPv6 Mobile Prefix Advertisement message**   The ICMPv6 Mobile Prefix Solicitation message contains the current home subnet prefix. For more information, see the "ICMPv6 Messages for Mobile IPv6" section in this appendix.

Mobile IPv6 Processes

Mobile IPv6 provides a method for a mobile node to determine it is on its home link and message exchanges for the following processes:

- Moving from the home link to a foreign link

- Moving from a foreign link to another foreign link

- Returning home

Additionally, the sending host and receiving host processes are modified to include special processing for mobility support.

 Note   This section assumes that the correspondent node is not a mobile node that is away from home.

Attaching to the Home Link

The method used by a mobile node to determine that it is attached to the home link is not defined in RFC 3775. Once a mobile node determines that it is connected to its home link, it can store the home subnet prefix, home address, and global address of its home agent. The following are methods for configuring home-link parameters:

- **Manual configuration**   In the simplest case, the home subnet prefix, home address, and address of the home agent are manually configured, typically through a keyboard-based command, and are permanent until manually changed. These implementations do not support the dynamic discovery of home agents or changes in the home subnet prefix.

- **Pseudo-automatic configuration**   For pseudo-automatic configuration, when an IPv6 node is attached to a link, the user has the option (typically through a button in the user interface of the operating system) to indicate to the IPv6 protocol that the node is now connected to the home link. Based on this indication, the IPv6 protocol stores the home subnet link prefix and home address and listens for additional router advertisements containing the Home Agent (H) flag set to 1. The home agent is the router advertising itself with home agent capabilities and has the highest preference level. Once the address is determined, the IPv6 protocol stores the address of the home agent. These implementations might or might not support the dynamic discovery of home agents or changes in the home subnet prefix.

- **Automatic configuration**   With automatic configuration, the IPv6 node is always listening for router advertisements with the H flag set to 1. Based on additional protocol or operating system parameters, the IPv6 node determines that the IPv6 node is potentially on its home link. Next, it chooses the most preferred home agent and attempts to establish a security relationship with it. If the security relationship with the home agent fails, the IPv6 node must not be on its home link. If the security relationship succeeds, the IPv6 node is on its home link and stores its home subnet prefix, its home address, and the address of its home agent. These implementations might or might not support the dynamic discovery of home agents or changes in the home subnet prefix.

Moving from the Home Link to a Foreign Link

When the mobile node is at home, it autoconfigures its home address through the receipt of a router advertisement, and communication with other nodes occurs normally without the use of Mobile IPv6 functionality.

Attaching to the Foreign Link

When the mobile node attaches to the foreign link, it must perform the following functions:

- Receive a new care-of address.
- Discover a home agent on the home link (if needed).
- Register the primary care-of address with the selected home agent on the home link.

When the mobile node attaches to the foreign link, the following occurs:

1. The mobile node sends a multicast Router Solicitation message on the foreign link. The mobile node might send a router solicitation either because the link layer indicated a media change or because the node received a router advertisement that contains a new prefix. Depending on the Mobile IPv6 implementation, the mobile node sends a router solicitation either from its link-local address (assuming that the link-local address of the mobile node is most likely unique on the foreign link) or from the unspecified address (::) (assuming that the link-local address of the mobile node might not be unique on the foreign link).

2. All routers on the foreign link reply with a Router Advertisement message. Depending on the source address of the Router Solicitation message, the reply is either unicast (because the Router Solicitation was sent from a link-local address) or multicast (because the router solicitation was sent from the unspecified address). Figure F-28 shows the router advertisement being unicast to the mobile node. The stateless autoconfiguration and registration of solicited node multicast addresses on the foreign link introduces some latency in the process of obtaining a valid care-of address.

   From the receipt of the Router Advertisement message or messages, the mobile node determines that it has connected to a foreign link because the router advertisements contain new network prefixes. The mobile node forms care-of addresses from the advertised prefixes, verifies their uniqueness by using duplicate address detection, and joins the corresponding solicited node multicast groups (not shown in Figure F-28).

3. If the mobile node is already configured with the address of its home agent, go to step 5. If not, to determine the address of a home agent on the mobile node's home link, the mobile node uses the home agent discovery process.

   Mobile nodes do not maintain a list of home agents while connected to the home link. To automatically discover the home agents on the home link, it is sufficient for the mobile node to learn its home subnet prefix. When the mobile node that uses automatic configuration of home agents leaves its home link and moves to the first foreign link, it sends an ICMPv6 Home Agent Address Discovery Request message to the Mobile IPv6 Home Agents anycast address formed from the home subnet prefix.

4. A home agent on the home link that is using the Mobile IPv6 Home Agents anycast address corresponding to the home subnet prefix and is topologically closest to the mobile node receives the ICMPv6 Home Agent Address Discovery Request message. Next, it sends back an ICMPv6 Home Agent Address Discovery Reply message containing the entries in the home agent's home agent list in preference order.

    Upon receipt of the ICMPv6 Home Agent Address Discovery Reply message, the mobile node selects the first home agent in the list as its home agent.

5. Before the binding update is sent, an IPsec security association (SA) must be created between the mobile node and the home agent. If the mobile node and the home agent support the use of Internet Key Exchange (IKE) for Mobile IPv6, an IKE negotiation takes place to create SAs for the ESP protection of packets sent between the mobile node and the home agent. The IKE negotiation is not shown in Figure F-28.

    If the mobile node and the home agent support the sending of binding updates without IPsec protection or the manual configuration of an IPsec SA, this step is skipped.

6. To register the primary care-of address with the home agent, the mobile node sends the home agent a binding update. In the binding update, the Home Registration and Acknowledgement flags are set to 1.

7. The home agent receives the binding update and updates its binding cache. To intercept packets destined for the mobile node's home address while the mobile node is away from home, the home agent performs duplicate address detection and proxy ND for the mobile node by answering neighbor solicitations on behalf of the mobile node. Depending on the implementation, the home agent might immediately send an unsolicited multicast Neighbor Advertisement message as if it were the mobile node or respond only to multicast neighbor solicitations for the mobile node's home address. The duplicate address detection and proxy ND introduces an additional latency in the home registration process.

    In the first case, to ensure that the nodes on the home link are updated with the new link-layer address of the home agent's interface on the home link, the home agent sends an unsolicited multicast Neighbor Advertisement message to the link-local scope all-nodes multicast address (FF02::1) with the Override (O) flag set to 1. Additionally, the home agent joins the multicast group for the solicited node multicast address corresponding to the mobile node's home address, and it registers interest in receiving link-layer multicast frames to the multicast MAC address corresponding to the solicited node multicast address. This is shown in Figure F-28.

    In the second case, the home agent does not send an unsolicited multicast Neighbor Advertisement message. However, the home agent does join the multicast group for the solicited node multicast address corresponding to the mobile node's home address, and it registers interest in receiving link-layer multicast frames to the multicast MAC address corresponding to the solicited node multicast address. If a node on the home link was communicating with the mobile node while it was at home, neighbor unreachability detection eventually causes the home node to send three unicast neighbor solicitations (while in the PROBE state) and then send a multicast neighbor solicitation. The home agent answers the multicast neighbor solicitation on behalf of the mobile node. This is not shown in Figure F-28.

If the mobile node has set the Link-Local Address Compatibility (L) flag in the binding update to 1, the home agent also performs duplicate address detection and proxy ND for the link-local address associated with the interface identifier (the last 64 bits) of the mobile node's home address.

8. Because the binding update has the A flag set to 1, the home agent responds with a binding acknowledgement.

Figure F-28 shows this process.

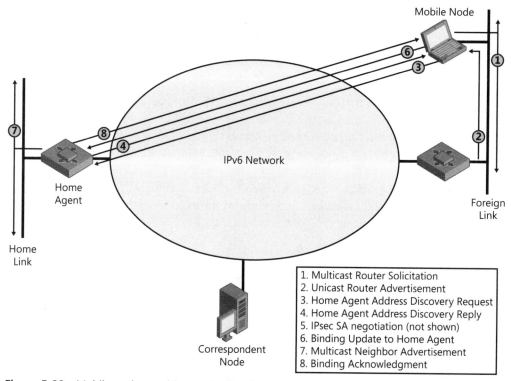

Figure F-28   Mobile node attaching to the first foreign link

Because there are no entries in the binding update list, the mobile node does not send a binding update to all the nodes with which the mobile node was communicating when connected to the home link. The mobile node relies on subsequent data sent on existing connections or the receipt of traffic tunneled via the home agent to initiate correspondent registration with correspondent nodes.

Mobile Node Initiates Communication with a New Correspondent Node

When a mobile node initiates communication with a new correspondent node (a node for which no binding exists), it must perform a correspondent registration, which consists of the Return Routability procedure and the exchange of Binding Update and Binding Acknowledgement messages. Although this process must occur for any kind of communication using the home address that is initiated by a mobile node that is away from home, the following example is for a TCP connection.

When a mobile node that is away from home initiates a new TCP connection with a correspondent node, the following occurs:

1. The mobile node begins the TCP connection by sending the initial TCP SYN (synchronize) segment to the correspondent node, tunneled via the home agent. Subsequent TCP handshake segments and the initial data communication between the mobile node and the correspondent node are sent using bidirectional tunneling until the correspondent registration is complete. (See step 5.) This is done so that the application that is attempting to communicate does not have to wait until the correspondent registration is complete before it can begin communicating.

2. The mobile node adds an entry for the correspondent node to its binding update list and performs the Return Routability procedure with the correspondent node to determine the binding management key for binding management (not shown in Figure F-29).

3. The mobile node sends a Binding Update message to the correspondent node with the Acknowledgement flag set to 1.

4. The correspondent node updates its binding cache and sends a Binding Acknowledgement message back to the mobile node.

5. After the correspondent registration is complete, subsequent TCP segments on the connection are sent directly between the mobile node and the correspondent node.

Figure F-29 shows this process.

If the mobile node is resuming communication on an existing TCP connection, the TCP segments of the continuing communication are bidirectionally tunneled until the correspondent registration is complete.

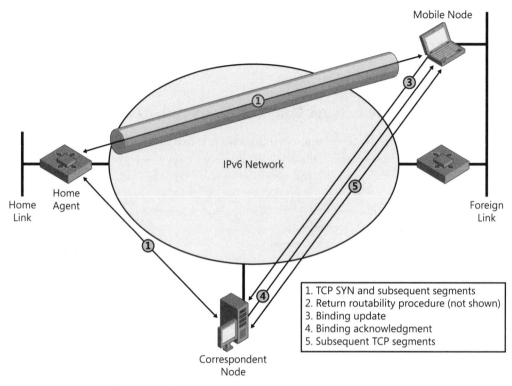

Figure F-29 A mobile node initiating a new TCP connection with a new correspondent node

After correspondent registration is complete, data between the correspondent node and the mobile node is sent as follows:

- Data from the mobile node is sent from the mobile node's care-of address to the correspondent node's address and includes the Home Address option in the Destination Options header.

- Data from the correspondent node is sent to the mobile node's care-of address and includes a Type 2 Routing header containing the mobile node's home address.

Note If the mobile node is multihomed, it is possible for the mobile node to register different care-of addresses with different correspondent nodes. Which care-of address is chosen depends on the source address selection algorithm. The mobile node chooses the care-of address that is matched in scope and is topologically closest to the correspondent node.

A New Correspondent Node Communicates with a Mobile Node

When a new correspondent node either resumes communication or initiates communication with a mobile node using the mobile node's home address and the mobile node is away from home, the following occurs:

1. The correspondent node begins the TCP connection by sending the initial TCP SYN segment to the mobile node, tunneled via the home agent. Subsequent TCP handshake segments and the initial data communication between the correspondent node and the mobile node are sent using bidirectional tunneling until the correspondent registration is complete. (See step 5.) This is done so that the application that is attempting to communicate does not have to wait until the correspondent registration is complete before it can begin communicating.

2. The mobile node adds an entry for the correspondent node to its binding update list and initiates the Return Routability procedure (not shown in Figure F-30).

3. After the Return Routability procedure is complete, the mobile node sends the correspondent node a Binding Update message with the A flag set to 1.

4. Upon receipt of the Binding Update message, the correspondent node updates its binding cache and sends back a Binding Acknowledgement message.

5. After the correspondent registration is complete, subsequent TCP segments on the connection are sent directly between the mobile node and the correspondent node.

Because the TCP connection creation occurs separately from the correspondent registration, the subsequent segments in the TCP handshake (the SYN Acknowledge [ACK] and ACK segments) and the ensuing application data sent over the TCP connection are bidirectionally tunneled until the correspondent registration is complete.

Figure F-30 shows this process.

After this process is complete, data between the correspondent node and the mobile node is sent as follows:

- Data from the mobile node is sent from the care-of address to the correspondent node's address and includes the Home Address option in the Destination Options header.

- Data from the correspondent node is sent to the mobile node's care-of address and includes a Type 2 Routing header containing the mobile node's home address.

If the upper-layer session is idle and no packets are sent for a while, the binding cache entry might expire. When the communication resumes, the same process is performed starting from step 1.

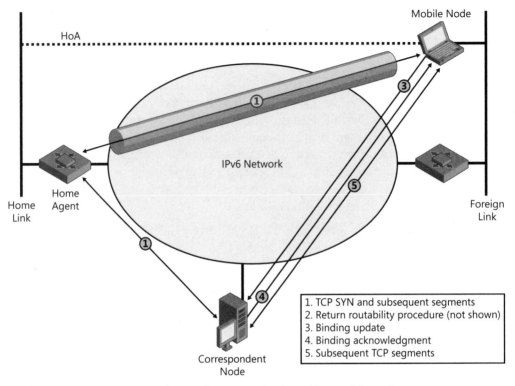

Figure F-30   A new correspondent node communicating with a mobile node

A Node on the Home Link Communicates with the Mobile Node

When a node on the home link either resumes or initiates communication with a mobile node using the mobile node's home address and the mobile node is away from home, the following occurs (example assumes a new TCP connection):

1. The node on the home link sends a multicast Neighbor Solicitation message to the solicited node multicast address corresponding to the mobile node's home address.

2. The home agent is acting as an ND proxy for the mobile node. It has registered the solicited node multicast address corresponding to the mobile node's home address as a multicast address to which it is listening. The home agent receives the neighbor solicitation and sends a unicast neighbor advertisement containing the home agent's link-layer address.

3. The initial TCP SYN segment and subsequent TCP segments are sent between the node on the home link and the home agent using each other's link-layer address.

4. The TCP segments are tunneled to and from the mobile node. The bidirectional tunneling of TCP segments continues until the correspondent registration is complete. (See step 5.)

5. Upon receipt of the initial tunneled TCP SYN segment from the home agent, the mobile node performs a Return Routability procedure with the node on the home link (not shown in Figure F-31).

6. The mobile node sends the node on the home link a Binding Update message.

7. The node on the home link sends a Binding Acknowledgement message.

8. After the correspondent registration is complete, subsequent TCP segments on the connection are sent directly between the mobile node and the node on the home link.

Figure F-31 shows this process.

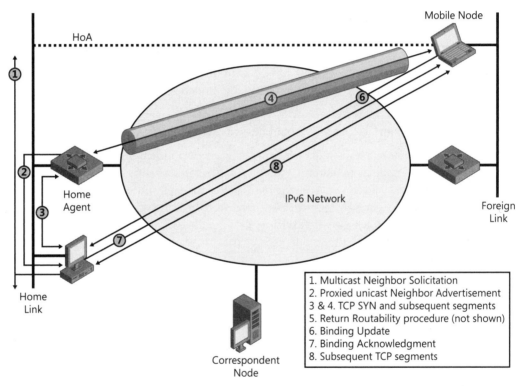

1. Multicast Neighbor Solicitation
2. Proxied unicast Neighbor Advertisement
3 & 4. TCP SYN and subsequent segments
5. Return Routability procedure (not shown)
6. Binding Update
7. Binding Acknowledgment
8. Subsequent TCP segments

Figure F-31   A node on the home link communicating with the mobile node

As previously described in "A New Correspondent Node Communicates with a Mobile Node," because the TCP connection creation occurs separately from the correspondent registration, the subsequent segments in the TCP handshake (the SYN ACK and ACK segments) and the ensuing application data sent over the TCP connection are sent indirectly via the home agent until the correspondent registration is complete.

This same process of intercepting a packet for the mobile node (steps 1 through 3) is also used when a packet addressed to the mobile node's home address is delivered to the home link by a router that is not the mobile node's home agent.

Mobile Node Changes Its Home Address

To refresh a home address that is approaching the end of its valid lifetime or to receive a new home address following a change in the home subnet prefix, the following process is used:

1. The mobile node sends an ICMPv6 Home Prefix Solicitation message to the home agent.

2. The home agent sends back an ICMPv6 Home Prefix Advertisement message.

   Upon receipt of the Home Prefix Advertisement message, the mobile node examines the Prefix Information option. If there is no change in the home subnet prefix and therefore no change in the home address, the mobile node refreshes the valid and preferred lifetimes of the stateless home address and this process ends.

   If there is a change in the home subnet prefix, the mobile node must refresh the bindings at the home agent and all the correspondent nodes in its binding update list.

3. To register the new home address with the home agent, the mobile node sends the home agent a binding update. In the binding update, the Home Registration and Acknowledgement flags are set to 1.

4. The home agent sends a binding acknowledgement.

5. The mobile node must perform a new correspondent registration with each correspondent node in its binding update list. Therefore, a Return Routability procedure is performed (not shown in Figure F-32) with each correspondent node in the binding update list. Because only the path associated with the home address has changed, only the HoTI and HoT messages are exchanged.

6. After the Return Routability procedure is successful, the mobile node sends a binding update to each correspondent node.

7. Upon the receipt of the binding update, the correspondent node updates its binding cache and sends a binding acknowledgment.

Figure F-32 shows this process.

Moving to a New Foreign Link

When the mobile node attaches to a new foreign link after being attached to another foreign link, it must perform the following functions:

- Receive a new care-of address.
- Register the new care-of address with its home agent.
- Send binding updates to all correspondent nodes.

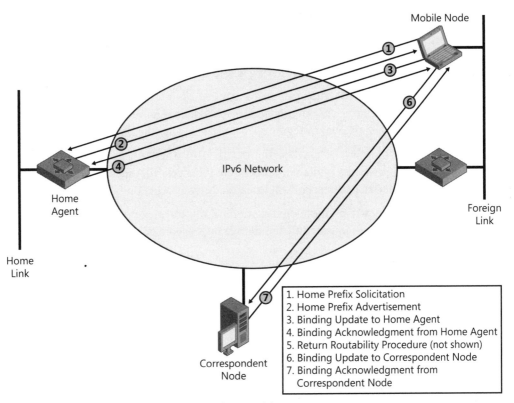

Figure F-32   A mobile node changing its home address

When the mobile node attaches to the new foreign link, the following occurs:

1. The mobile node sends a multicast Router Solicitation message on the new foreign link. Depending on the Mobile IPv6 implementation, the mobile node sends the router solicitation either from its link-local address (assuming that the link-local address of the mobile node is most likely unique on the new foreign link) or from the unspecified address (::) (assuming that the link-local address of the mobile node might not be unique on the new foreign link).

2. All routers on the new foreign link reply with a Router Advertisement message. Depending on the source address of the Router Solicitation message, the reply is either unicast (because the router solicitation was sent from a link-local address) or multicast (because the router solicitation was sent from the unspecified address). Figure F-33 shows the Router Advertisement message being unicast to the mobile node.

    From the receipt of the Router Advertisement message or messages, the mobile node forms a care-of address or addresses, verifies their uniqueness by using duplicate address detection, and joins the corresponding solicited node multicast groups (not shown in Figure F-33).

3. To register the new primary care-of address with the home agent, the mobile node sends the home agent a binding update. In the binding update, the Home Registration and Acknowledgement flags are set to 1.

4. The home agent sends a binding acknowledgement.

5. The mobile node must perform a new correspondent registration with each correspondent node in its binding update list. Therefore, a Return Routability procedure is performed (not shown in Figure F-33). Because only the path to the care-of address has changed, only the exchange of CoTI and CoT messages is performed.

6. After the Return Routability procedure is successful, the mobile node sends a binding update to the correspondent node.

7. Upon the receipt of the binding update, the correspondent node updates its binding cache and, if requested by the mobile node, sends a binding acknowledgment.

Figure F-33 shows this process.

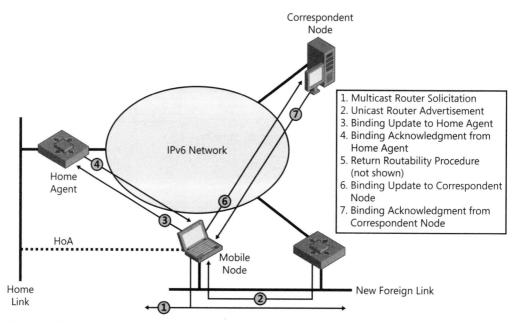

Figure F-33 A mobile node attaching to a new foreign link

If the binding update sent by the mobile node to a correspondent node is dropped from the network, the correspondent node continues to send packets to the mobile node's previous care-of address based on the contents of its now outdated binding cache entry. The packets are forwarded to the previous foreign link and the router on the previous foreign link attempts to deliver them. If the previous foreign link router still considers the mobile node reachable on the previous foreign link, packets are forwarded to the mobile node's link-layer address.

Because the mobile node is no longer attached to the previous foreign link, the packets are dropped.

The methods for correcting this error condition are the following:

- The mobile node, after not receiving a binding acknowledgment from the correspondent node, retransmits a binding update. The correspondent node receives the retransmitted binding update, and its binding cache is updated with the mobile node's new care-of address.

- The previous foreign link router uses neighbor unreachability detection to determine that the mobile node is no longer attached to the previous foreign link. For a point-to-point link such as a wireless connection, the unreachability of the mobile node is indicated immediately by the lack of a wireless signal from the mobile node. For a broadcast link such as an Ethernet segment, the entry in the previous foreign link router's neighbor cache goes through the REACHABLE, STALE, DELAY, and PROBE states. After the neighbor cache entry for the mobile node is removed, attempts to deliver to the mobile node's previous care-of address are unsuccessful and the previous foreign link router sends an ICMPv6 Destination Unreachable-Address Unreachable message to the correspondent node. Upon receiving this message, the correspondent node removes the entry for the mobile node from its binding cache and communication resumes as described in the "A New Correspondent Node Communicates with a Mobile Node" section of this appendix.

- All binding cache entries have a finite lifetime as determined by the Lifetime field of the last received binding update and the correspondent node's local policy. After the lifetime expires, the binding cache entry is removed and communication resumes as described in the "A New Correspondent Node Communicates with a Mobile Node" section of this appendix. Alternately, the correspondent node can send a binding refresh request before the binding cache entry expires. When there is no response to the binding refresh request, the correspondent node removes the entry from the binding cache.

Returning Home

When the mobile node attaches to its home link after being away from home, it must perform the following functions:

- Send a binding update to the home agent to delete the binding for the mobile node.

- Inform home link nodes that the correct link-layer address for the home address is now the mobile node's link-layer address.

- Send binding updates to all correspondent nodes to delete the binding for the mobile node.

When the mobile node returns home (reattaches to its home link), the following occurs:

1. The mobile node sends a multicast Router Solicitation message on the home link. The mobile node might send a router solicitation either because the link layer indicated a media change or because the node received a router advertisement that contains a new prefix. Depending on the Mobile IPv6 implementation, the mobile node sends a router solicitation either from its link-local address (assuming that the link-local address of the mobile node is most likely unique on the new link) or from the unspecified address (::) (assuming that the link-local address of the mobile node might not be unique on the new link).

2. All routers on the home link reply with a Router Advertisement message. Depending on the source address of the Router Solicitation message, the reply is either unicast (because the router solicitation was sent from a link-local address) or multicast (because the router solicitation was sent from the unspecified address). Figure F-34 shows the Router Advertisement message being unicast to the mobile node.

   Because the router advertisement contains the address prefix that matches its home address prefix, the mobile node determines that it is attached to its home link. Depending on the Mobile IPv6 implementation, the mobile node might or might not perform duplicate address detection for its home address because the home agent is acting as an ND proxy for the mobile node and defending the use of the mobile node's home address. If the mobile node does perform duplicate address detection, it must ignore the Neighbor Advertisement message sent from the home agent.

3. To remove the binding cache entry from the home agent, the mobile node sends the home agent a binding update with the care-of address set to the mobile node's home address and with the Home Registration and Acknowledge flags set to 1.

   If multiple router advertisements are received, the mobile node can determine which router is its home agent from the router advertisement with the Prefix Information option that contains the home agent's global address in the Prefix field.

   The mobile node determines the home agent's link-layer address from the Link-Layer Address field in the Source Link-Layer Address option in the router advertisement sent by the home agent. If the Source Link-Layer Address option is not included, the mobile node can determine the link-layer address of the home agent using address resolution because the global address of the home agent is known.

4. Upon receipt of the binding update, the home agent removes the entry for the mobile node from its binding cache, stops defending the use of the mobile node's home address on the home link, and responds with a binding acknowledgement. This is shown in Figure F-34. Additionally, the home agent leaves the multicast group for the solicited node multicast address corresponding to the mobile node's home address and stops listening for link-layer multicast frames addressed to the multicast MAC address corresponding to the solicited node multicast address.

5. After receiving the binding acknowledgement from the home agent, the mobile node must inform nodes on the home link that the link-layer address for the home address has changed to the link-layer address of the mobile node. It sends an unsolicited multicast Neighbor Advertisement message to the link-local scope all-nodes multicast address (FF02::1) with the Override (O) flag set to 1.

   The mobile node also joins the multicast group for the solicited node multicast address corresponding to the mobile node's home address and registers interest in receiving link-layer multicast frames to the multicast MAC address corresponding to the solicited node multicast address (not shown in Figure F-34).

6. Before sending a binding update to each correspondent node to delete the binding for the mobile node, the mobile node performs a Return Routability procedure (not shown in Figure F-34). Because the home address and the mobile node's new address are the same, it is sufficient to exchange only the HoTI and HoT messages. The CoTI and CoT messages are not sent when the mobile node returns home.

7. The mobile node sends a binding update to each correspondent node with the care-of address set to the mobile node's home address.

8. Upon receipt of the binding update, the correspondent nodes remove the entry for the mobile node in their binding cache and send a binding acknowledgment.

Figure F-34 shows this process.

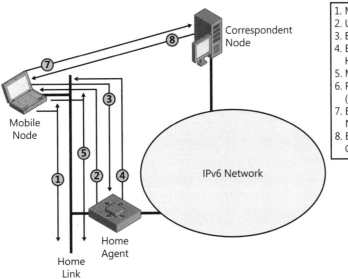

Figure F-34   A mobile node returning home

Mobile IPv6 Host Sending Algorithm

The IPv6 host sending algorithm is described in Chapter 6, "Neighbor Discovery." However, the description in Chapter 6 does not include Mobile IPv6 functionality for the sending or receiving hosts. A Mobile IPv6 node can be both a mobile node and correspondent node at the same time. Therefore, the host sending algorithm for a Mobile IPv6 node must take into account the following:

- **If the sending host is away from home**   If so, the sending host must set the source address of the IPv6 header to the sending host's care-of address and include the Destination Options header with the Home Address option set to the node's home address.

- **If the receiving node is away from home**   If so, the sending host must set the destination address of the IPv6 header to the receiving node's care-of address and include a Type 2 Routing header with the Home Address field set to the receiving node's home address.

The sending host must also determine if the receiving node has already been determined to be Mobile IPv6–capable, and if not, whether or not a correspondent registration has already been initiated.

A Mobile IPv6 host uses the following algorithm when sending a unicast or anycast packet to an arbitrary destination:

1. Check the destination cache for an entry matching the destination address.

2. If an entry matching the destination address is not found in the destination cache, go to step 13.

3. If an entry matching the destination address is found in the destination cache, check for a pointer to an entry in the binding cache. (This algorithm assumes the use of separate destination and binding caches.) This pointer will be present if the destination is a mobile node away from home.

4. If there is a pointer to an entry in the binding cache, set the destination address in the IPv6 header to the destination node's care-of address and inserts a Type 2 Routing header that includes the destination node's home address. The binding cache entry for the home address contains a pointer to the destination cache entry for the care-of address, from which the sending host obtains the next-hop address and interface for the care-of address.

5. If there is no pointer to an entry in the binding cache, obtain the next-hop address and interface from the destination cache entry.

6. If the packet is tunneled to the home agent, go to step 16.

7.   If the sending host is a mobile node that is at home, go to step 16.

8.   If the sending host is a mobile node away from home, it checks its binding update list for an entry matching the destination.

9.   If an entry is found, set the source address in the IPv6 header to the sending host's care-of address and insert a Destination Options header that includes the Home Address option containing the sending host's home address. Go to step 16.

10. If an entry is not found, check whether the destination has been determined to be Mobile IPv6–capable. If the destination is not Mobile IPv6–capable, go to step 12.

11. If the sending host has not yet determined whether the destination is Mobile IPv6–capable (the assumption is that it is capable until determined otherwise), it checks whether a correspondent registration has already been initiated with the destination, and if not, it initiates one.

12. Set the source address to the home address and the destination address to the correspondent node's address, and then encapsulate the packet with an IPv6 header from the care-of address to the home agent's address. Go to step 1.

13. Check the local IPv6 routing table for the longest matching route with the lowest metric to the destination address. If there are multiple longest matching routes with the lowest metric, IPv6 chooses a route to use.

14. Based on the chosen route, determine the next-hop interface and address used for forwarding the packet.

15. Update the destination cache.

16. Check the neighbor cache for an entry matching the next-hop address.

17. If an entry matching the next-hop address is found in the neighbor cache, obtain the link-layer address.

18. If an entry matching the next-hop address is not found in the neighbor cache, use address resolution to obtain the link-layer address for the next-hop address.

     If address resolution is not successful, indicate an error.

19. Send the packet by using the link-layer address of the neighbor cache entry.

Figure F-35 shows the Mobile IPv6 host sending algorithm.

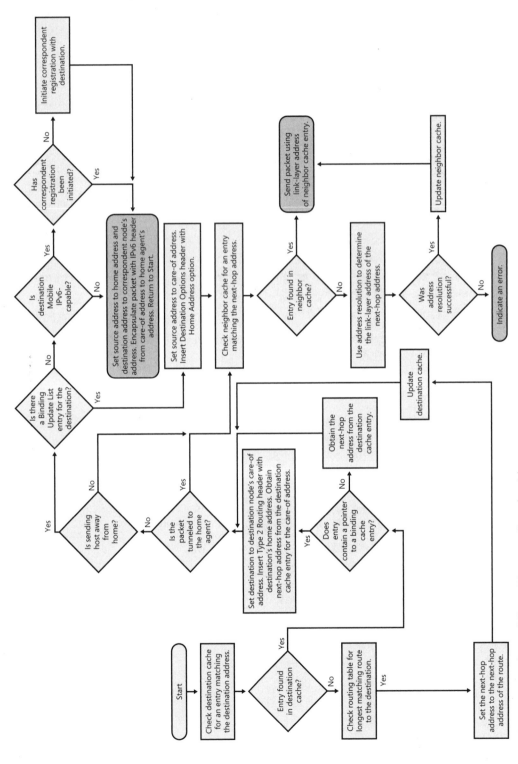

Figure F-35 The Mobile IPv6 host sending algorithm

Mobile IPv6 Host Receiving Algorithm

A Mobile IPv6 node can be both a mobile node and correspondent node at the same time. Therefore, the host receiving algorithm for a Mobile IPv6 node must take into account the following:

- **If the receiving node is away from home**   If so, the receiving node processes the Type 2 Routing header in the IPv6 packet and logically sets the destination address of the IPv6 header to the value of the Home Address field in the Type 2 Routing header.

- **If the sending host is away from home**   If so, the receiving node processes the Destination Options header and logically sets the source address of the IPv6 packet to the home address contained in the Home Address option.

Additionally, a receiving Mobile IPv6 host must recognize a packet tunneled from its home agent in order to determine when to initiate a correspondent registration to a new correspondent node.

A Mobile IPv6 host uses the following algorithm when receiving a unicast or anycast packet from an arbitrary source:

1. Verify whether the destination address in the IPv6 packet corresponds to an IPv6 address assigned to a local host interface.

   If the destination address is not assigned to a local host interface, silently discard the IPv6 packet.

2. Check to see if there is a Type 2 Routing header present. If so, process it and set the destination address of the IPv6 packet to the value of the Home Address field in the Type 2 Routing header.

3. Check to see if the packet was tunneled from the home agent. If the packet was not tunneled from the home agent, go to step 8.

4. If the packet is a Home Test (HoT) message, process its contents.

5. If the packet is not a HoT message, check to see whether the sender has been determined to be Mobile IPv6–capable. If the sender is not Mobile IPv6–capable, go to step 7.

6. If the sender has not been determined to be Mobile IPv6–capable (the assumption is that it is capable until determined otherwise), it checks whether a correspondent registration has already been initiated with the sender, and if not, the receiver initiates one.

7. Strip the outer IPv6 header (in which the destination address is set to the receiving node's care-of address and the source address is set to the home agent), and then process and remove the ESP header and trailer, if present.

8. Check to see if there is a Destination Options header with a Home Address option. If so, logically set the source address of the IPv6 packet to the home address in the Home Address option.

9. Based on the Next Header field, process extension headers (if present) and pass the upper-layer PDU to the appropriate upper-layer protocol.

   If the protocol does not exist, send an ICMPv6 Parameter Problem-Unrecognized Next Header Type Encountered message back to the sender and discard the packet.

10. If the upper-layer PDU is not a TCP segment or UDP message, pass the upper-layer PDU to the appropriate protocol.

11. If the upper-layer PDU is a TCP segment or UDP message, check the destination port.

    If no application exists for the UDP port number, send an ICMPv6 Destination Unreachable-Port Unreachable message back to the sender and discard the packet. If no application exists for the TCP port number, send a TCP Connection Reset segment back to the sender and discard the packet.

12. If an application exists for the UDP or TCP destination port, process the contents of the TCP segment or UDP message.

Figure F-36 shows the Mobile IPv6 host receiving algorithm.

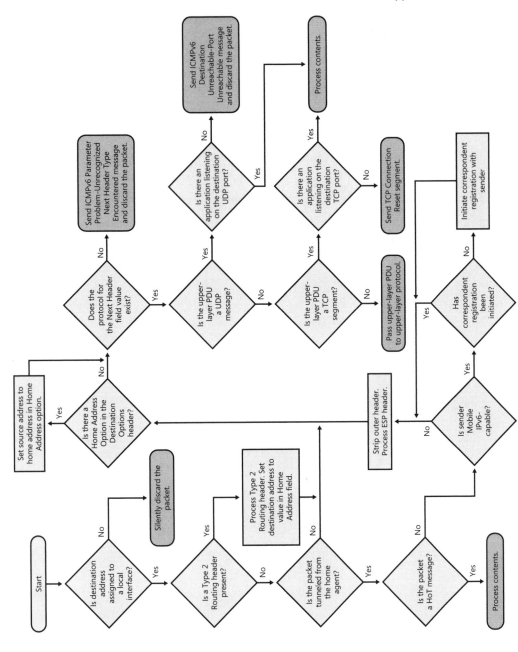

Figure F-36   The Mobile IPv6 host receiving algorithm

References

The following references were cited in this appendix:

- RFC 2460 – "Internet Protocol, Version 6 (IPv6) Specification"
- RFC 2526 – "Reserved IPv6 Subnet Anycast Addresses"
- RFC 3775 – "Mobility Support in IPv6"
- RFC 3776 – "Using IPsec to Protect Mobile IPv6 Signaling Between Mobile Nodes and Home Agents"
- RFC 4861 – "Neighbor Discovery for IP Version 6 (IPv6)"

You can obtain these RFCs from the \RFCs_and_Drafts folder on the companion CD-ROM or from *http://www.ietf.org/rfc.html*.

Appendix G
IPv6 Reference Tables

This appendix contains a series of summary reference tables for Internet Protocol version 6 (IPv6).

Table G-1   Defined Values for the Scope Field for IPv6 Multicast Addresses

Scope Field Value	Scope
0	Reserved
1	Interface-local scope
2	Link-local scope
3	Reserved
4	Admin-local scope
5	Site-local scope
8	Organization-local scope
E	Global scope
F	Reserved

In RFC 4291, all other values of the Scope field are unassigned.

Table G-2   Typical Values of the Next Header Field in the IPv6 Header

Value (Decimal)	Header
0	Hop-by-Hop Options header
6	Transmission Control Protocol (TCP)
17	User Datagram Protocol (UDP)
41	Encapsulated IPv6 header
43	Routing header
44	Fragment header
50	Encapsulating Security Payload header
51	Authentication header
58	Internet Control Message Protocol for IPv6 (ICMPv6)
59	No next header
60	Destination Options header

For a current list, see *http://www.iana.org/assignments/protocol-numbers*.

Table G-3 Option Types for Hop-by-Hop Options and Destination Options Headers

Option Type	Option and Where It Is Used	Alignment Requirement
0	Pad1 option: Hop-by-Hop Options and Destination Options headers	None
1	PadN option: Hop-by-Hop Options and Destination Options headers	None
194 (0xC2)	Jumbo Payload option: Hop-by-Hop Options header	$4n + 2$
5	Router Alert option: Hop-by-Hop Options header	$2n + 0$
201 (0xC9)	Home Address option: Destination Options header	$8n + 6$

For a current list, see *http://www.iana.org/assignments/ipv6-parameters*.

Table G-4 IPv6 Maximum Transmission Units (MTUs) for Common LAN and WAN Technologies

LAN or WAN Technology	IPv6 MTU
Ethernet (Ethernet II encapsulation)	1,500
Ethernet (IEEE 802.3 SubNetwork Access Protocol [SNAP] encapsulation)	1,492
IEEE 802.11	2,312
Token Ring	Varies
Fiber Distributed Data Interface (FDDI)	4,352
Attached Resource Computer Network (ARCNet)	9,072
Point-to-Point Protocol (PPP)	1,500
X.25	1,280
Frame Relay	1,592
Asynchronous Transfer Mode (ATM) (Null or SNAP encapsulation)	9,180

Table G-5 ICMPv6 Messages

ICMPv6 Type	Message	Chapter for Details
1	Destination Unreachable	5
2	Packet Too Big	5
3	Time Exceeded	5
4	Parameter Problem	5
128	Echo Request	5

Table G-5   ICMPv6 Messages

ICMPv6 Type	Message	Chapter for Details
129	Echo Reply	5
130	Multicast Listener Query	7
131	Multicast Listener Report	7
132	Multicast Listener Done	7
133	Router Solicitation	6
134	Router Advertisement	6
135	Neighbor Solicitation	6
136	Neighbor Advertisement	6
137	Redirect	6
143	Multicast Listener Discovery (MLD) Version 2 Multicast Listener Report	7
144	Home Agent Address Discovery Request	Appendix F
145	Home Agent Address Discovery Reply	Appendix F
146	Mobile Prefix Solicitation	Appendix F
147	Mobile Prefix Advertisement	Appendix F

For a complete and current list, see *http://www.iana.org/assignments/icmpv6-parameters.*

Table G-6   ICMPv6 Destination Unreachable Messages

Code Field Value	Description
0 - No Route to Destination	No route matching the destination was found in the routing table.
1 - Communication with Destination Administratively Prohibited	The communication with the destination is prohibited by administrative policy. This message is typically sent when the packet is discarded by a firewall.
2 - Beyond Scope of Source Address	The destination is beyond the scope of the source address. A router sends this message when the packet is forwarded by using an interface that is not within the scoped zone of the source address.
3 - Address Unreachable	The destination address is unreachable. This message is typically sent because of an inability to resolve the destination's link-layer address.
4 - Port Unreachable	The destination port was unreachable. This message is typically sent when an IPv6 packet containing a UDP message arrived at the destination but there were no applications listening on the destination UDP port.

Table G-6   ICMPv6 Destination Unreachable Messages

Code Field Value	Description
5 - Source Address Failed Ingress/Egress Policy	The packet with this source address is not allowed because of inbound (ingress) or outbound (egress) packet filtering policies.
6 - Reject Route to Destination	The packet matched a reject route and was discarded. A reject route is an address prefix configured on a router for traffic that the router must immediately discard.

For a complete and current list, see *http://www.iana.org/assignments/icmpv6-parameters.*

Table G-7   ICMPv6 Parameter Problem Messages

Code Field Value	Description
0 - Erroneous Header Field Encountered	An error in a field within the IPv6 header or an extension header was encountered.
1 - Unrecognized Next Header Type Encountered	An unrecognized Next Header field value was encountered. This message is equivalent to the ICMPv4 Destination Unreachable-Protocol Unreachable message.
2 - Unrecognized IPv6 Option Encountered	An unrecognized IPv6 option was encountered.

For a complete and current list, see *http://www.iana.org/assignments/icmpv6-parameters.*

Table G-8   IPv6 Neighbor Discovery Option Types

Type	Option Name	Source Document
1	Source Link-Layer Address	RFC 4861
2	Target Link-Layer Address	RFC 4861
3	Prefix Information	RFC 4861
4	Redirected Header	RFC 4861
5	MTU	RFC 4861
7	Advertisement Interval	RFC 3775
8	Home Agent Information	RFC 3775
24	Route Information	RFC 4191

For a complete and current list, see *http://www.iana.org/assignments/icmpv6-parameters.*

Table G-9   Neighbor Discovery Messages and the Options That Might Be Included

Neighbor Discovery (ND) Message	ND Options That Might Be Included
Router Solicitation	Source Link-Layer Address option: Informs the router of the link-layer address of the host for the unicast Router Advertisement response.
Router Advertisement	■ Source Link-Layer Address option: Informs the receiving host or hosts of the link-layer address of the router. ■ Prefix Information option or options: Informs the receiving host or hosts of on-link prefixes and whether to autoconfigure stateless addresses. ■ MTU option: Informs the receiving host or hosts of the IPv6 MTU of the link. ■ Advertisement Interval option: Informs the receiving host how often the router (the home agent) is sending unsolicited multicast router advertisements. ■ Home Agent Information option: Advertises the home agent's preference and lifetime. ■ Route Information option or options: Informs the receiving host or hosts of specific routes to add to a local routing table.
Neighbor Solicitation	Source Link-Layer Address option: Informs the receiving node of the link-layer address of the sender.
Neighbor Advertisement	Target Link-Layer Address option: Informs the receiving node or nodes of the link-layer address corresponding to the Target Address field.
Redirect	■ Redirected Header option: Includes all or a portion of the packet that was redirected. ■ Target Link-Layer Address option: Informs the receiving node or nodes of the link-layer address corresponding to the Target Address field.

Glossary

.NET Framework The programming model of the .NET platform for building, deploying, and running Extensible Markup Language (XML) Web services and applications.

6to4 An IPv6 transition technology that is used to provide unicast IPv6 connectivity between IPv6 sites and hosts across the IPv4 Internet. 6to4 uses a public IPv4 address to construct a global IPv6 address prefix.

6to4 address An address of the type 2002:*WWXX:YYZZ*:[*Subnet ID*]: [*Interface ID*], where *WWXX:YYZZ* is the colon hexadecimal representation of *w.x.y.z* (a public IPv4 address), which is used to represent a node for the 6to4 transition technology.

6to4 host An IPv6 host that is configured with at least one 6to4 address (a global address with the 2002::/16 prefix). 6to4 hosts do not require manual configuration and create 6to4 addresses by using standard address autoconfiguration mechanisms.

6to4 host/router A computer running Windows Server 2008 or Windows Vista that is connected directly to the Internet and uses 6to4 to connect to other 6to4 host/routers or other 6to4 sites and hosts on the IPv6 Internet.

6to4 relay An IPv6/IPv4 router that forwards 6to4-addressed traffic between 6to4 routers on the Internet and hosts on the IPv6 Internet. It is also known as a 6to4 relay router.

6to4 relay router *See* 6to4 relay.

6to4 router An IPv6/IPv4 router that supports the use of a 6to4 tunnel interface and is typically used to forward 6to4-addressed traffic between the 6to4 hosts within a site and other 6to4 routers or 6to4 relays on the IPv4 Internet.

A

AAAA record The Domain Name System (DNS) resource record type that is used to resolve a fully qualified domain name to an IPv6 address.

AAL5 *See* ATM Adaptation Layer 5.

AH *See* Authentication header.

address An identifier that is assigned at the IPv6 layer to an interface or set of interfaces and can be used as the source or destination of IPv6 packets.

address autoconfiguration The process of automatically configuring IPv6 addresses on an interface. *See also* stateless address autoconfiguration and stateful address autoconfiguration.

address prefix The portion of an address that is fixed and used to determine a subnet prefix, a route, or an address range.

address resolution The process of resolving the link-layer address for a next-hop IPv6 address on a link.

address selection rules The address selection logic that is needed to decide which pair of addresses to use for communication.

anonymous address *See* temporary address.

anycast address An address assigned from the unicast address space that identifies multiple interfaces and is used for one-to-one-of-many delivery. With the appropriate routing topology, packets addressed to an anycast address are delivered to a single interface—the nearest interface that is identified by the address.

APIPA *See* Automatic Private IP Addressing.

Asynchronous Transfer Mode A cell-based packet-switching technology that supports both isochronous (time-dependent) and non-isochronous data types.

ATM *See* Asynchronous Transfer Mode.

ATM Adaptation Layer 5 The Asynchronous Transfer Mode (ATM) adaptation layer designed for local area network (LAN) traffic and used to encapsulate IPv6 packets when they are sent across an ATM link.

Authentication header An IPv6 extension header that provides data origin authentication, data integrity, and antireplay services for the entire IPv6 packet, excluding changeable fields in the IPv6 header and extension headers.

Automatic Private IP Addressing The automatic configuration of an IPv4 address in the 169.254.0.0/16 range and the subnet mask of 255.255.0.0 when an interface is configured for automatic configuration and a Dynamic Host Configuration Protocol (DHCP) server is not available.

automatic tunnel An IPv6-over-IPv4 tunnel in which the tunnel endpoints are determined by the use of logical tunnel interfaces, routes, and destination IPv6 addresses.

B

binding acknowledgement A message that is used by correspondent nodes and home agents to confirm that a binding update was received and to indicate error conditions, if any.

binding cache A table maintained by a correspondent node that maps the home address of mobile nodes that are away from home to their current care-of address.

binding request A message that is used by correspondent nodes and home agents to request a binding update from a mobile node that is away from home.

binding update A message that is used by a mobile node to update correspondent nodes and its home agent with its new care-of address.

binding update list A list maintained by a mobile node that is away from home to record the most recent binding updates sent for the home agent and correspondent nodes.

C

care-of address A global address used by a mobile node while it is connected to a foreign link.

CNA *See* correspondent node address.

CoA *See* care-of address.

colon hexadecimal notation The notation used to express IPv6 addresses. The 128-bit address is divided into eight 16-bit blocks. Each block is expressed as a hexadecimal number, and adjacent blocks are delimited with colons. Within each block, leading zeros are suppressed. An example of an IPv6 unicast address in colon hexadecimal notation is 2001:DB8:2A1D:48C:2AA: 3CFF:FE21:81F9.

compatibility addresses IPv6 addresses that are used when sending IPv6 traffic over an IPv4 infrastructure. Examples of compatibility addresses are 6to4 addresses and Intra-Site Automatic Tunnel Addressing Protocol (ISATAP) addresses.

configured tunnel An IPv6-over-IPv4 tunnel in which the tunnel endpoints are determined by manual configuration.

correspondent node A node that is capable of communicating with a mobile node when it is away from home.

correspondent node address The global address assigned to a correspondent node when it is communicating with a mobile node that is away from home.

critical router loop The set of instructions that must be executed by a router to forward a packet.

D

DAD   *See* duplicate address detection.

default route   The route with the prefix ::/0. The default route matches all destinations and is the route used to determine the next-hop address if there are no other matching routes.

default router list   A list maintained by a host that lists all the routers from which a router advertisement was received with the Router Lifetime field set to a nonzero value.

defending node   The node that is assigned a valid address set to a duplicate address being detected.

DELAY state   The state of the neighbor cache entry after it was in the STALE state and a packet is sent. The DELAY state is used to wait for an upper-layer protocol to provide an indication that the neighbor is still reachable.

deprecated state   The state of an autoconfig-ured address in which the address is valid but its use is discouraged for new communication.

destination cache   A table maintained by IPv6 nodes that maps a destination address to a next-hop address and stores the path maximum transmission unit (MTU).

Destination Options header   An IPv6 exten-sion header that contains packet delivery parameters for either intermediate destinations or the final destination.

DHCP   *See* Dynamic Host Configuration Protocol.

DHCPv6   *See* Dynamic Host Configuration Protocol for IPv6.

DHCPv6 stateful   A Dynamic Host Configura-tion Protocol for IPv6 (DHCPv6) operating mode in which a DHCPv6 server assigns stateful addresses to IPv6 hosts.

DHCPv6 stateless   A Dynamic Host Configura-tion Protocol for IPv6 (DHCPv6) operating mode in which a DHCPv6 server provides stateless configuration settings but does not assign stateful addresses to IPv6 hosts.

distance vector   A routing protocol technol-ogy that propagates routing information in the form of a network prefix and its "distance" (hop count).

DNS   *See* Domain Name System.

Domain Name System   A hierarchical namespace and protocol used for storing and querying name and address informa-tion.

double colon   The practice of compressing a single contiguous series of zero blocks of an IPv6 address to a double colon symbol (::). For example, the multicast address FF02:0:0:0:0:0:0:2 is expressed as FF02::2. If there are two series of zero blocks of the same highest length, by convention the leftmost block is expressed as "::".

dual IP layer   The architecture of an IPv6/IPv4 node in which a single implementation of Transport layer protocols such as Transmis-sion Control Protocol (TCP) and User Datagram Protocol (UDP) operate over separate implementations of IPv4 and IPv6.

dual stack architecture   The architecture of an IPv6/IPv4 node that consists of two separate protocol stacks—one for IPv4 and one for IPv6—and each stack has its own implemen-tation of the Transport layer protocols (Transmission Control Protocol [TCP] and User Datagram Protocol [UDP]).

duplicate address detection   The process of using a Neighbor Solicitation message to confirm that a tentative address is not already assigned to an interface on the link.

Dynamic Host Configuration Protocol   A stateful address configuration protocol that provides an IPv4 address and other configuration parameters.

Dynamic Host Configuration Protocol for IPv6   A stateful address configuration protocol that can provide IPv6 hosts with a stateful IPv6 address and other configuration parameters.

E

Encapsulating Security Payload An IPv6 extension header and trailer that provides data origin authentication, data integrity, data confidentiality, and antireplay services for the payload encapsulated by the Encapsulating Security Payload (ESP) header and trailer.

ESP *See* Encapsulating Security Payload.

EUI *See* Extended Unique Identifier.

EUI-64 address A 64-bit link-layer address that can be used as a basis for an IPv6 interface identifier.

Extended Unique Identifier Link-layer addresses defined by the Institute of Electrical and Electronics Engineers (IEEE).

extension headers Headers placed between the IPv6 header and the upper-layer protocol data unit that provide IPv6 with additional capabilities.

F

FDDI *See* Fiber Distributed Data Interface.

Fiber Distributed Data Interface A desktop and backbone local area network (LAN) technology specified by the American National Standards Institute (ANSI) that uses token-passing media access control and optical fiber, and that operates at the bit rate of 100 Mbps.

flow A series of packets exchanged between a source and a destination that requires special handling by intermediate IPv6 routers, as identified by the source and destination addresses and a non-zero value of the Flow Label field in the IPv6 header.

foreign link A link that is not the mobile node's home link. A foreign link is identified by a foreign link prefix.

foreign link prefix The global address prefix assigned to a foreign link and used by a mobile node to obtain a care-of address.

fragment A portion of an original IPv6 payload sent by a host. Fragments contain a Fragment header.

fragmentation The process of dividing an IPv6 payload into fragments by the sending host so that all the fragments are appropriately sized for the path maximum transmission unit (MTU) to the destination.

Fragment header An IPv6 extension header that contains reassembly information for use by the receiving node.

frame relay A virtual circuit-based wide area network (WAN) technology designed to forward local area network (LAN) data.

G

gateway An IPv4 term for a router. IPv6 does not use the term "gateway" for a router.

global address Global addresses are equivalent to public IPv4 addresses and are globally routable and reachable on the IPv6 portion of the Internet.

Group ID The last 112 bits of an IPv6 multicast address, which identifies the multicast group.

H

HA *See* home address.

HAA *See* home agent address.

home address An address assigned to the mobile node when it is attached to the home link and through which the mobile node is always reachable, regardless of its location on the IPv6 Internet.

home agent A router on the home link that maintains an awareness of the mobile nodes of its home link that are away from home and the care-of addresses that they are currently using. If the mobile node is on the home link, the home agent acts as an IPv6 router, forwarding packets addressed to the mobile node. If the mobile node is away from home, the home agent tunnels data sent to the mobile node's home address to the mobile node's current location on the IPv6 Internet.

home agent address The global address of the home agent's interface on the home link.

Home Agent Address Discovery   A mobile IPv6 process in which a mobile node that is away from home discovers the list of home agents on its home link.

home agents list   A table maintained by home agents that contains the list of routers on the home link that can act as a home agent.

home link   The link that is assigned the home subnet prefix. The mobile node uses the home subnet prefix to create a home address.

Hop-by-Hop Options header   An IPv6 extension header that contains options that must be processed by every intermediate router and the destination.

host   A node that cannot forward IPv6 packets not explicitly addressed to itself (a non-router). A host is typically the source and a destination of IPv6 traffic and it silently discards traffic received that is not explicitly addressed to itself.

host group   The set of nodes listening for multicast traffic on a specific multicast address.

host route   A route to a specific IPv6 address. Host routes allow routing to occur on a per-IPv6 address basis. For host routes, the route prefix is a specific IPv6 address with a 128-bit prefix length.

Hosts file   A text file that is used to store name-to-address mappings. For computers running Windows Server 2008 or Windows Vista, the Hosts file is stored in the *%SystemRoot%*/System32\Drivers\Etc folder.

host-to-host tunneling   IPv6-over-IPv4 tunneling where the tunnel endpoints are two hosts. For example, an IPv6/IPv4 node that resides within an IPv4 infrastructure creates an IPv6-over-IPv4 tunnel to reach another host that resides within the same IPv4 infrastructure.

host-to-router tunneling   IPv6-over-IPv4 tunneling where the tunnel begins at a sending host and ends at an IPv6/IPv4 router. For example, an IPv6/IPv4 node that resides within an IPv4 infrastructure creates an IPv6-over-IPv4 tunnel to reach an IPv6/IPv4 router.

I

ICMPv6   *See* Internet Control Message Protocol for IPv6.

IEEE 802 address   A 48-bit link-layer address defined by the Institute of Electrical and Electronics Engineers (IEEE). Ethernet, Token Ring, and IEEE 802.11 network adapters use IEEE 802 addresses.

IEEE 802.3 Sub-Network Access Protocol (SNAP) encapsulation   The encapsulation used when IPv6 packets are sent over an Institute of Electrical and Electronics Engineers (IEEE) 802.3-compliant Ethernet link.

IEEE 802.5 Sub-Network Access Protocol (SNAP) encapsulation   The encapsulation used when IPv6 packets are sent over a Token Ring link.

IEEE EUI-64 address   *See* EUI-64 address.

INCOMPLETE state   The state of a neighbor cache entry in which a neighbor solicitation has been sent and no response has been received.

interface   The representation of a physical or logical attachment of a node to a link. An example of a physical interface is a network adapter. An example of a logical interface is a tunnel interface that is used to send IPv6 packets across an IPv4 network by encapsulating the IPv6 packet inside an IPv4 header.

interface ID   The last 64 bits of an IPv6 unicast or anycast address.

Internet Control Message Protocol for IPv6   A protocol that provides error messages for IPv6 packet routing and delivery and informational messages for diagnostics, Neighbor Discovery, Multicast Listener Discovery, and Mobile IPv6.

Internet Protocol Helper   An application programming interface (API) that assists in the administration of the network configuration of the local computer. You can use Internet Protocol Helper (IP Helper) to programmatically retrieve information about the network configuration of the local computer and to modify that configuration. IP Helper also provides notification mechanisms to ensure that an application is notified when certain aspects of the network configuration change on the local computer.

Internet Protocol security   A framework of open standards for ensuring private, secure communications at the Internet layer, through the use of cryptographic security services. Internet Protocol security (IPsec) supports network-level peer authentication, data origin authentication, data integrity, data confidentiality (encryption), and replay protection.

Intra-Site Automatic Tunnel Addressing Protocol   A transition technology that is used to provide unicast IPv6 connectivity between IPv6 hosts across anIPv4 intranet. Intra-Site Automatic Tunnel Addressing Protocol (ISATAP) derives an interface ID based on the IPv4 address (public or private) assigned to a host. The ISATAP-derived interface ID is used for automatic tunneling across an IPv4 infrastructure.

invalid state   The state of an autoconfigured address in which it can no longer be used to send or receive unicast traffic. An address enters the invalid state after the valid lifetime expires.

IP Helper   *See* Internet Protocol Helper.

IP6.ARPA   The Domain Name System (DNS) domain created for IPv6 reverse queries. Also called pointer queries, reverse queries determine a host name based on the address.

IPsec   *See* Internet Protocol security.

IPv4-compatible address   An address of the form 0:0:0:0:0:0:*w.x.y.z* or ::*w.x.y.z*, in which *w.x.y.z* is the dotted decimal representation of a public IPv4 address. For example, ::131.107.89.42 is an IPv4-compatible address. IPv4-compatible addresses have been deprecated.

IPv4-mapped address   An address of the form 0:0:0:0:0:FFFF:*w.x.y.z* or ::FFFF:*w.x.y.z*, in which w.x.y.z is an IPv4 address. IPv4-mapped addresses are used to represent an IPv4-only node to an IPv6 node.

IPv4 node   A node that implements IPv4. It can send and receive IPv4 packets. It can be an IPv4-only node or an IPv6/IPv4 node.

IPv4-only node   A node that implements only IPv4 (and is assigned only IPv4 addresses). This node does not support IPv6. Most hosts and routers installed today are IPv4-only nodes.

IPv6 Control Protocol   A Network Control Protocol (NCP) for configuring the IPv6 protocol over a Point-to-Point Protocol (PPP) link.

IPV6CP   *See* IPv6 Control Protocol.

IPv6 host address record   *See* AAAA record.

IPv6 in IPv4   *See* IPv6-over-IPv4 tunneling.

IPv6/IPv4 node   A node that has an implementation of both IPv4 and IPv6.

IPv6 MTU   The maximum-sized IP packet that can be sent on a link. (*MTU* stands for maximum transmission unit.)

IPv6 node   A node that implements IPv6. (It can send and receive IPv6 packets.) An IPv6 node can be an IPv6-only node or an IPv6/IPv4 node.

IPv6-only node   A node that implements only IPv6 (and is assigned only IPv6 addresses). It is able to communicate with IPv6 nodes and applications only.

IPv6-over-IPv4 tunneling   The encapsulation of IPv6 packets with an IPv4 header so that IPv6 traffic can be sent across an IPv4 infrastructure. In the IPv4 header, the Protocol field is set to 41.

IPv6 route table   *See* IPv6 routing table.

IPv6 routing table   The set of routes used to determine the next-hop address and interface for IPv6 traffic sent by a host or forwarded by a router.

ISATAP   *See* Intra-Site Automatic Tunnel Addressing Protocol.

ISATAP address   An address of the type [*64-bit prefix*]:0:5EFE:*w.x.y.z*, where *w.x.y.z* is a private IPv4 address, or [*64-bit prefix*]: 200:5EFE:*w.x.y.z*, where *w.x.y.z* is a public IPv4 address, that is assigned to an Intra-Site Automatic Tunnel Addressing Protocol (ISATAP) host.

ISATAP host   A host that is assigned an Intra-Site Automatic Tunnel Addressing Protocol (ISATAP) address.

ISATAP name   The name that is resolved by computers running Windows Server 2008 or Windows Vista to automatically discover the IPv4 address of the Intra-Site Automatic Tunnel Addressing Protocol (ISATAP) router.

ISATAP router   An IPv6/IPv4 router that responds to tunneled router solicitations from Intra-Site Automatic Tunnel Addressing Protocol (ISATAP) hosts and forwards traffic between ISATAP hosts and nodes on another IPv6 subnet or network.

J

join latency   The time between when a new member of a multicast group on a subnet that does not contain any group members sends a Multicast Listener Report message and when multicast packets for that multicast group are sent on the subnet.

jumbogram   An IPv6 packet that has a payload larger than 65,535 bytes. Jumbograms are indicated by setting the Payload Length field in the IPv6 header to 0 and including a Jumbo Payload option in the Hop-by-Hop Options header.

Jumbo Payload option   An option in the Hop-by-Hop Options header that indicates the size of a jumbogram.

L

LAN segment   A portion of a link consisting of a single medium that is bounded by bridges or Layer 2 switches.

leave latency   The time between when the last member of the multicast group on a subnet sends a Multicast Listener Done message and when multicast packets for that multicast group are no longer sent on the subnet.

link   One or more local area network (LAN) segments bounded by routers.

link MTU   The maximum transmission unit (MTU)—the number of bytes in the largest IPv6 packet—that can be sent on a link. Because the maximum frame size includes the link-layer medium headers and trailers, the link MTU is not the same as the maximum frame size of the link. The link MTU is the same as the maximum payload size of the link-layer technology.

link state   A routing protocol technology that exchanges routing information consisting of a router's attached network prefixes and their assigned costs. Link state information is advertised upon startup and when changes in the network topology are detected.

link-local address   A local-use address identified by the prefix FE80::/64, whose scope is the local link. Nodes use link-local addresses to communicate with neighboring nodes on the same link. Link-local addresses are equivalent to Automatic Private IP Addressing (APIPA) IPv4 addresses.

Link-Local Multicast Name Resolution   A protocol that resolves the names of neighboring computers for networks that do not have a Domain Name System (DNS) server.

LLMNR   *See* Link-Local Multicast Name Resolution.

local-use address   An IPv6 unicast address that is not reachable on the IPv6 Internet. Local-use addresses include link-local and site-local addresses.

longest matching route   The algorithm used by the route determination process to select the routes in the routing table that most closely match the destination address of the packet being sent or forwarded.

loopback address   The IPv6 address of ::1 that is assigned to the loopback interface.

loopback interface   An internal interface created so that a node can send packets to itself.

M

MAC   *See* media access control, MAC address.

MAC address The link-layer address for typical local area network (LAN) technologies, such as Ethernet, Token Ring, and 802.11. It is also known as the physical address, the hardware address, or the network adapter address.

maximum transmission unit The largest protocol data unit that can be sent. Maximum transmission units (MTUs) are defined at the link layer (maximum frame sizes) and at the Internet layer (maximum IPv6 packet sizes).

media access control An Institute of Electrical and Electronics Engineers (IEEE)-defined sublayer of the ISO Data Link layer, whose responsibilities include framing and managing access to the media.

MLD *See* Multicast Listener Discovery.

MLDv2 *See* Multicast Listener Discovery version 2.

Mobile IPv6 A set of messages and processes that allow an IPv6 node to arbitrarily change its location on the IPv6 Internet and still maintain existing connections.

mobile node An IPv6 node that can change links, and therefore addresses, and maintain reachability using its home address. A mobile node has awareness of its home address and care-of address, and it indicates its home address/care-of address mapping to the home agent and IPv6 nodes with which it is communicating.

MTU *See* maximum transmission unit.

multicast address An address that identifies zero or multiple interfaces and is used for one-to-many delivery. With the appropriate multicast routing topology, packets addressed to a multicast address are delivered to all interfaces identified by the address.

multicast group The set of hosts listening on a specific multicast address.

Multicast Listener Discovery A set of ICMPv6 messages used by hosts and routers to manage multicast group membership on a subnet.

Multicast Listener Discovery version 2 Like Multicast Listener Discovery (MLD), a set of ICMPv6 messages used by hosts and routers to manage multicast group membership on a subnet. A Multicast Listener Discovery version 2 (MLDv2)-capable host can register interest in receiving IPv6 multicast traffic from only specific source addresses (an include list) or from any source except specific source addresses (an exclude list).

N

name resolution The process of resolving a name to an address. For IPv6, name resolution resolves a host name or fully qualified domain name (FQDN) to an IPv6 address.

NAT *See* Network Address Translator.

NBMA *See* non-broadcast multiple access link.

ND *See* Neighbor Discovery.

neighbor A node connected to the same link.

neighbor cache A cache maintained by every IPv6 node that stores the on-link IPv6 address of a neighbor, its corresponding link-layer address, and an indication of the neighbor's reachability state. The neighbor cache is equivalent to the Address Resolution Protocol (ARP) cache in IPv4.

Neighbor Discovery A set of ICMPv6 messages and processes that determine relationships between neighboring nodes. Neighbor Discovery (ND) replaces Address Resolution Protocol (ARP), Internet Control Message Protocol (ICMP) router discovery, and the ICMP Redirect message used in IPv4. ND also provides neighbor unreachability detection.

Neighbor Discovery options Options in Neighbor Discovery messages that indicate link-layer addresses, prefix information, maximum transmission unit (MTU), redirect, routes, and Mobile IPv6 configuration information.

neighbor unreachability detection The Neighbor Discovery process, also known as NUD, that determines whether the IPv6 layer of a neighbor is no longer receiving packets. The reachability state of each neighbor with which a node is communicating is stored in the node's neighbor cache.

network   Two or more subnets connected by routers. Another term for network is internetwork.

Network Address Translator   An IPv4 router that translates addresses and ports when forwarding packets between a privately addressed network and the Internet.

network segment   *See* subnet.

next-hop determination   The process of determining the next-hop address and interface for sending or forwarding a packet based on the contents of the routing table.

node   For IPv6, any device that runs an implementation of IPv6, which includes both routers and hosts.

NO ENTRY EXISTS state   The state of a neighbor cache entry before it is added to the neighbor cache.

non-broadcast multiple access link   A link-layer technology that supports a link with more than two nodes but with no facility to broadcast a single packet to multiple locations. For example, X.25, frame relay, and Asynchronous Transfer Mode (ATM) are non-broadcast multiple access (NBMA) network types.

NUD   *See* neighbor unreachability detection.

O

offending node   The node that is performing duplicate address detection for an address that is already in use on the subnet.

P

packet   The protocol data unit (PDU) that exists at the Internet layer. For IPv6, a packet is composed of an IPv6 header and a payload.

parameter discovery   A Neighbor Discovery process that enables hosts to discover configuration parameters, including the link maximum transmission unit (MTU) and the default hop limit for outgoing packets.

path MTU   The maximum-sized IPv6 packet that can be sent without using host fragmentation between a source and destination over a path in an IPv6 network. The path maximum transmission unit (PMTU) is the smallest link MTU of all the links in the path.

Path MTU Discovery   The use of the ICMPv6 Packet Too Big message to discover the highest IPv6 maximum transmission unit (MTU) for all links between two hosts.

path vector   A routing protocol technology that exchanges sequences of hop information indicating the path for a route. For example, Border Gateway Protocol (BGP)-4 exchanges sequences of autonomous system numbers. An autonomous system is a portion of the network under the same administrative authority.

PDU   *See* protocol data unit.

PMTU   *See* path MTU.

pointer records   *See* PTR records.

Point-to-Point Protocol   A standardized point-to-point network encapsulation method that provides frame delimitation, protocol identification, and bit-level integrity services. It is often referred to as PPP.

PortProxy   A component of IPv6 for Windows Server 2008 and Windows Vista that enables Transmission Control Protocol (TCP) proxying to facilitate the communication between nodes or applications that cannot connect using a common Internet layer protocol (IPv4 or IPv6).

PPP   *See* Point-to-Point Protocol.

preferred lifetime   The amount of time in which a unicast address configured through stateless address autoconfiguration remains in the preferred state. The preferred lifetime is indicated by the Preferred Lifetime field in the Prefix Information option in a Router Advertisement message.

preferred state   The state of an autoconfigured address for which the address is valid and its uniqueness has been verified, and can be used for unlimited communications.

prefix   *See* address prefix.

prefix discovery   A Neighbor Discovery process by which hosts discover the network prefixes for local link destinations and for stateless address configuration.

prefix length notation   The practice of expressing network prefixes as *address prefix/prefix-length*, in which *prefix-length* is the number of high-order bits in the address prefix that are fixed.

prefix list   A list of link prefixes maintained by each host. Each entry in the prefix list defines a range of IPv6 addresses for destinations that are directly reachable (neighbors).

PROBE state   The state of a neighbor cache entry that was in the STALE and DELAY states for which reachability confirmation is in progress.

protocol data unit   The entity that exists at any layer of a layered network architecture. The protocol data unit of layer *n* becomes the payload of layer *n*-1 (a lower layer).

pseudo-header   A temporary header constructed for the purposes of calculating a checksum to associate the IPv6 header with its payload. For IPv6, a new pseudo-header format is used for the ICMPv6, Transmission Control Protocol (TCP), and User Datagram Protocol (UDP) checksum calculations.

pseudo-periodic   Occurring at intervals for which the interval between successive events is not constant. For example, router advertisements sent by IPv6 routers occur pseudo-periodically; the next interval for advertising is chosen randomly between a maximum and minimum value.

PTR records   Domain Name System (DNS) resource records that resolve an address to a name.

public address   A global address with a permanent interface ID.

Q

quad-A record   *See* AAAA record.

R

REACHABLE state   The state of an entry in the neighbor cache for which reachability has been confirmed by receipt of a solicited unicast Neighbor Advertisement message.

reassembly   The process of reconstructing the original payload from a series of fragments.

redirect   The Neighbor Discovery process of informing a host of a better first-hop IPv6 address to reach a destination.

remote procedure call   An application programming interface (API) that is used for creating distributed client/server programs. The remote procedure call (RPC) run-time stubs and libraries manage most of the details relating to network protocols and communication. RPC functions are used to forward application function calls to a remote system across the network.

route cache   *See* destination cache.

route determination process   The process of determining which single route in the routing table to use for forwarding a packet.

route table   *See* IPv6 routing table.

router   A node that can forward packets not explicitly addressed to itself. On an IPv6 network, a router also typically advertises its presence and host configuration information.

router advertisement   A Neighbor Discovery message sent by a router either pseudo-periodically or in response to a Router Solicitation message. Router advertisements typically contain at least one Prefix Information option, from which hosts create stateless autoconfigured unicast IPv6 addresses.

router discovery   A Neighbor Discovery process in which a host discovers the local routers on an attached link.

router-to-host tunneling   IPv6-over-IPv4 tunneling in which the tunnel begins at a forwarding router and ends at an IPv6/IPv4 host. For example, an IPv6/IPv4 router creates an IPv6-over-IPv4 tunnel to reach an IPv6/IPv4 host that resides within an IPv4 infrastructure.

router-to-router tunneling IPv6-over-IPv4 tunneling in which the tunnel begins at a forwarding router and ends at an IPv6/IPv4 router. For example, an IPv6/IPv4 router on the edge of an IPv4-only network creates an IPv6-over-IPv4 tunnel to reach another IPv6/IPv4 router.

Routing header An IPv6 extension header that is used to perform source routing over an IPv6 network. A source route is a list of intermediate destinations for the packet to travel to on its path to the final destination.

routing loop A condition on a network in which traffic is forwarded in a loop, never reaching its destination.

routing protocols A series of periodic or on-demand messages containing routing information that is exchanged between dynamic routers.

routing table *See* IPv6 routing table.

RPC *See* remote procedure call.

S

scope For IPv6 addresses, the scope is the region of the network over which the traffic is intended to propagate.

scope ID *See* zone ID.

site-local address A local-use address identified by the prefix FEC0::/10. The scope of a site-local address is the site. Site-local addresses are equivalent to the IPv4 private address space. Site-local addresses are not reachable from other sites, and routers must not forward site-local traffic outside the site. Site-local addresses have been deprecated.

site prefix Typically, a 48-bit prefix that is used to indicate all the addresses in the site. Site prefixes are stored in a local site prefix table, which is used to confine traffic to the site.

solicited-node address A multicast address used by nodes for the address resolution process. The solicited-node address is constructed from the prefix FF02::1:FF00:0/104 and the last 24 bits of a unicast IPv6 address. The solicited-node address acts as a pseudo-unicast address for very efficient address resolution on IPv6 links.

STALE state The state of a neighbor cache entry for which the reachable time (the duration since the last reachability confirmation was received) has elapsed. The neighbor cache entry goes into the STALE state after the value (milliseconds) in the Reachable Time field in the Router Advertisement message (or a host default value) elapses, and it remains in this state until a packet is sent to the neighbor.

stateful address autoconfiguration The use of a stateful address configuration protocol, such as DHCPv6, to configure IPv6 addresses and configuration parameters.

stateless address autoconfiguration The use of Neighbor Discovery Router Advertisement messages to configure IPv6 addresses and configuration parameters.

static routing The use of manually configured routes in the routing tables of routers.

subnet For IPv6, one or more links that use the same 64-bit IPv6 address prefix. Another term for subnet is network segment.

subnet route For IPv6, a route with a 64-bit prefix that indicates a specific IPv6 subnet.

subnet-router anycast address The anycast address [*64-bit prefix*]:: that is assigned to router interfaces.

T

temporary address An address that uses a randomly derived temporary interface ID. Temporary addresses change over time, making it more difficult to track someone's Internet usage based on his or her IPv6 address.

tentative address A unicast address whose uniqueness has not yet been verified.

tentative state The state of an autoconfigured address in which uniqueness has not yet been verified.

Teredo   An IPv6 transition technology that is used to provide unicast IPv6 connectivity between IPv6 hosts across the IPv4 Internet, even when the hosts are located behind IPv4 Network Address Translators (NATs).

Teredo address   An address from the prefix 2001::/16 that is assigned to a Teredo client.

Teredo client   An IPv6/IPv4 node that can communicate with other Teredo clients or nodes on the IPv6 Internet using a Teredo relay or Teredo host-specific relay.

Teredo host-specific relay   An IPv6/IPv4 node that has connectivity to both the IPv4 Internet and the IPv6 Internet and can communicate directly with Teredo clients over the IPv4 Internet, without the need for an intermediate Teredo relay.

Teredo relay   An IPv6/IPv4 router that can forward packets between Teredo clients on the IPv4 Internet and IPv6 hosts on the IPv6 Internet.

Teredo server   An IPv6/IPv4 node that is connected to both the IPv4 Internet and the IPv6 Internet that assists in the address configuration of Teredo clients. It facilitates the initial communication between Teredo clients and other Teredo clients or between Teredo clients and IPv6-only hosts.

U

unicast address   An address that identifies a single interface within the scope of the type of address and is used for one-to-one delivery. The scope of an address is the region of the IPv6 network over which the address is unique. With the appropriate unicast routing topology, packets addressed to a unicast address are delivered to a single interface.

unique local address   IPv6 unicast addresses with the prefix FC00::/7 that can be used within organization sites and are not reachable on the IPv6 Internet.

unspecified address   The address 0:0:0:0:0:0:0:0 (or ::) that is used to indicate the absence of an address. It is equivalent to the IPv4 unspecified address of 0.0.0.0.

The unspecified address is typically used as a source address for packets attempting to verify the uniqueness of a tentative address.

upper-layer checksum   The checksum calculation performed by Internet Control Message Protocol for IPv6 (ICMPv6), Transmission Control Protocol (TCP), and User Datagram Protocol (UDP) that incorporates the new IPv6 pseudo-header.

upper-layer protocol   A protocol above IPv6 that uses IPv6 as its transport. Examples include Internet Control Message Protocol for IPv6 (ICMPv6) and Transport layer protocols such as Transmission Control Protocol (TCP) and User Datagram Protocol (UDP) (but not Application layer protocols such as File Transfer Protocol [FTP] and Domain Name System [DNS], which use TCP and UDP as their transport).

V

valid lifetime   The amount of time in which a unicast address configured through stateless address autoconfiguration remains in the valid state, which includes both the preferred and deprecated states. The valid lifetime is indicated by the Valid Lifetime field in the Prefix Information option sent in a Router Advertisement message.

valid state   The state of an autoconfigured address for which the address can be used for sending and receiving unicast traffic. The valid state includes both the preferred and deprecated states.

W

Win32 Internet Extensions   An application programming interface (API) used for creating an Internet client application. An Internet client application is a program that accesses information from a network data source (server) by using Internet protocols such as File Transfer Protocol (FTP) or Hypertext Transfer Protocol (HTTP).

Windows Sockets   A Windows application programming interface (API) based on

Berkeley Sockets that applications use to access the network services of Transmission Control Protocol/Internet Protocol (TCP/IP), IPv6, and other protocols.

WinInet   *See* Win32 Internet Extensions.

WinSock   *See* Windows Sockets.

X

X.25   A virtual circuit-based, packet-switching wide area network (WAN) technology originally designed in the 1970s to provide a reliable, connection-oriented service for local area network (LAN) traffic.

Z

zone ID   An integer that specifies the zone of the destination for IPv6 traffic. In the Ping, Tracert, and Pathping commands, the syntax for specifying a zone ID is *IPv6Address%ZoneID*. Unless manually configured otherwise, the *ZoneID* value for link-local addresses is equal to the interface index. For site-local addresses, *ZoneID* is equal to the site number. If multiple sites are not being used, a zone ID for site-local addresses is not required. The *ZoneID* parameter is not needed when the destination is a global address.

Index

About the Author

Joseph Davies is a technical writer for the Microsoft Corporation. He has been a writer and instructor of TCP/IP, networking, and security topics since 1992. He started writing as a courseware developer for Microsoft Corporate Support group and then moved into the Windows group to write product help and resource kit content on networking and security technologies. Since 2001, he has been writing white papers, TechNet articles, Web sites, and Microsoft Press books for the Windows networking technology teams. He is the author of TechNet's monthly The Cable Guy column (*http://www.microsoft.com/technet/community/columns/cableguy/default.mspx*), now appearing in TechNet Magazine.

Joseph is co-author of *Windows Server 2008 Networking and Network Access Protection (NAP)* (2008), *Deploying Virtual Private Networks with Microsoft Windows Server 2003* (2004), *Microsoft Windows Server 2003 TCP/IP Protocols and Services Technical Reference* (2003), and *Microsoft Windows 2000 TCP/IP Protocols and Services Technical Reference* (2000), all from Microsoft Press. He is author of *Understanding IPv6,* Second Edition (Microsoft Press, 2008), *Windows Server 2008 TCP/IP Protocols and Services* (Microsoft Press, 2008), *TCP/IP Fundamentals for Microsoft Windows* (TechNet, 2006), *Deploying Secure 802.11 Wireless Networks with Microsoft Windows* (Microsoft Press, 2004), and *Understanding IPv6* (Microsoft Press, 2003), which won the Puget Sound Society for Technical Communication (STC) Best of Show and International STC Distinguished Awards.

Windows Server 2008 Resource Kit—
Your Definitive Resource!

**Windows Server® 2008
Resource Kit**

Microsoft® MVPs with
Microsoft Windows Server Team

ISBN 9780735623613

Your definitive reference for deployment and operations—from the experts who
know the technology best. Get in-depth technical information on Active Directory®,
Windows PowerShell™ scripting, advanced administration, networking and network
access protection, security administration, IIS, and other critical topics—plus an
essential toolkit of resources on CD.

Also available as single volumes

**Windows Server 2008
Security Resource Kit**

Jesper M. Johansson et al. with
Microsoft Security Team

ISBN 9780735625044

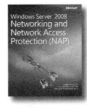

**Windows Server 2008
Networking and Network
Access Protection (NAP)**

Joseph Davies, Tony Northrup,
Microsoft Networking Team

ISBN 9780735624221

**Windows Server 2008
Active Directory Resource Kit**

Stan Reimer et al. with
Microsoft Active Directory Team

ISBN 9780735625150

**Windows® Administration
Resource Kit: Productivity
Solutions for IT Professionals**

Dan Holme

ISBN 9780735624313

**Windows Powershell
Scripting Guide**

Ed Wilson

ISBN 9780735622791

**Internet Information
Services (IIS) 7.0
Resource Kit**

Mike Volodarsky et al. with
Microsoft IIS Team

ISBN 9780735624412

See our complete line of books at: **microsoft.com/mspress**

Microsoft Press® products are sold worldwide wherever quality computer books are sold.
For more information, contact your bookseller, computer retailer, software reseller, or local
Microsoft Sales Office, or visit our Web site at microsoft.com/mspress. To locate a source near you,
or to order directly, call 1-800-MSPRESS in the United States. (In Canada call 1-800-268-2222).

Windows Server 2008—
Resources for Administrators

Windows Server® 2008 Administrator's Companion

Charlie Russel and Sharon Crawford

ISBN 9780735625051

Your comprehensive, one-volume guide to deployment, administration, and support. Delve into core system capabilities and administration topics, including Active Directory®, security issues, disaster planning/recovery, interoperability, IIS 7.0, virtualization, clustering, and performance tuning.

Windows Server 2008 Administrator's Pocket Consultant

William R. Stanek

ISBN 9780735624375

Portable and precise—with the focused information you need for administering server roles, Active Directory, user/group accounts, rights and permissions, file-system management, TCP/IP, DHCP, DNS, printers, network performance, backup, and restoration.

Windows Server 2008 Resource Kit

Microsoft MVPs with Windows Server Team

ISBN 9780735623613

Six volumes! Your definitive resource for deployment and operations—from the experts who know the technology best. Get in-depth technical information on Active Directory, Windows PowerShell™ scripting, advanced administration, networking and network access protection, security administration, IIS, and more—plus an essential toolkit of resources on CD.

Internet Information Services (IIS) 7.0 Administrator's Pocket Consultant

William R. Stanek

ISBN 9780735623644

This pocket-sized guide delivers immediate answers for administering IIS 7.0. Topics include customizing installation; configuration and XML schema; application management; user access and security; Web sites, directories, and content; and performance, backup, and recovery.

Windows PowerShell Step by Step

Ed Wilson

ISBN 9780735623958

Teach yourself the fundamentals of the Windows PowerShell command-line interface and scripting language—one step at a time. Learn to use *cmdlets* and write scripts to manage users, groups, and computers; configure network components; administer Microsoft® Exchange Server 2007; and more. Includes 100+ sample scripts.

Additional Resources for IT Professionals

Windows Server 2008 Virtualization Resource Kit

Robert Larson and Janique Carbone

ISBN 9780735625174

Windows® Administration Resource Kit: Productivity Solutions for IT Professionals

Dan Holme

ISBN 9780735624313

Internet Information Services (IIS) 7.0 Resource Kit

Mike Volodarsky et al. with Microsoft IIS Team

ISBN 9780735624412

Windows Server 2008 Security Resource Kit

Jesper M. Johansson, MVPs, Microsoft Security Team

ISBN 9780735625044

See our complete line of books at: **microsoft.com/mspress**

Microsoft Press® products are sold worldwide wherever quality computer books are sold. For more information, contact your bookseller, computer retailer, software reseller, or local Microsoft Sales Office, or visit our Web site at microsoft.com/mspress. To locate a source near you, or to order directly, call 1-800-MSPRESS in the United States. (In Canada call 1-800-268-2222).

Get Certified—Windows Server 2008

Ace your preparation for the skills measured by the Microsoft® certification exams—and on the job. With 2-in-1 *Self-Paced Training Kits*, you get an official exam-prep guide + practice tests. Work at your own pace through lessons and real-world case scenarios that cover the exam objectives. Then, assess your skills using practice tests with multiple testing modes—and get a customized learning plan based on your results.

EXAMS 70-640, 70-642, 70-646

MCITP Self-Paced Training Kit:
Server Administrator
Core Requirements

ISBN 9780735625082

**EXAMS 70-640, 70-642,
70-643, 70-647**

MCITP Self-Paced Training Kit:
Enterprise Administrator
Core Requirements

ISBN 9780735625723

EXAM 70-640

MCTS Self-Paced Training Kit:
Configuring
Windows Server® 2008
Active Directory®
Dan Holme, Tony Northrup
ISBN 9780735625136

EXAM 70-647

MCITP Self-Paced Training Kit:
Windows® Enterprise
Administration
Chris McCain, Ted Malone, John Policelli
of Grandmasters
ISBN 9780735625099

EXAM 70-642

MCTS Self-Paced Training Kit:
Configuring
Windows Server 2008
Network Infrastructure
J.C. Mackin, Tony Northrup
ISBN 9780735625129

EXAM 70-643

MCTS Self-Paced Training Kit:
Configuring
Windows Server 2008
Applications Infrastructure
J.C. Mackin, Anil Desai
ISBN 9780735625112

Additional Resources for IT Professionals

**Windows Server 2008
Administrator's Pocket Consultant**
William R. Stanek
ISBN 9780735624375

**Windows Server 2008
Administrator's Companion**
Charlie Russel, Sharon Crawford
ISBN 9780735625051

**Windows Server 2008
Resource Kit**
Microsoft MVPs with Windows Server Team
ISBN 9780735623613

EXAM 70-646

MCITP Self-Paced Training Kit:
Windows Server Administration
Ian McLean, Orin Thomas
ISBN 9780735625105

For complete information on Microsoft certifications, visit: **microsoft.com/learning**.
And see our complete line of books at: **microsoft.com/mspres**

What do you think of this book?

We want to hear from you!

Do you have a few minutes to participate in a brief online survey?

Microsoft is interested in hearing your feedback so we can continually improve our books and learning resources for you.

To participate in our survey, please visit:

www.microsoft.com/learning/booksurvey/

...and enter this book's ISBN-10 or ISBN-13 number (located above barcode on back cover*). As a thank-you to survey participants in the United States and Canada, each month we'll randomly select five respondents to win one of five $100 gift certificates from a leading online merchant. At the conclusion of the survey, you can enter the drawing by providing your e-mail address, which will be used for prize notification only.

Thanks in advance for your input. Your opinion counts!

*Where to find the ISBN on back cover

ISBN-13: 000-0-0000-0000-0
ISBN-10: 0-0000-0000-0

Example only. Each book has unique ISBN.

Microsoft®
Press

No purchase necessary. Void where prohibited. Open only to residents of the 50 United States (includes District of Columbia) and Canada (void in Quebec). For official rules and entry dates see:

www.microsoft.com/learning/booksurvey/

System Requirements

To use this book's companion CD-ROM, you need a computer equipped with the following minimum configuration:

- Windows Server 2008, Windows Vista, Windows Server 2003, or Windows XP
- 1 GHz 32-bit (x86) or 64-bit (x64) processor
- 1 GB of system memory
- A hard disk partition with at least 1 GB of available space
- Support for DirectX 9 graphics and 32 MB of graphics memory
- Appropriate video monitor
- Keyboard
- Mouse or other pointing device
- CD-ROM drive

To view the online version of this book, you will need the Adobe Systems, Inc. Reader. See *http://www.adobe.com* for information about disk space requirements for the Adobe Reader.

To install Microsoft Network Monitor 3.1 from *http://go.microsoft.com/fwlink/?LinkID=92844* or a link on the companion CD-ROM, you need the following additional minimum configuration:

- A hard disk partition with approximately 25 MB of free disk space

To install the Microsoft PowerPoint Viewer from *http://go.microsoft.com/fwlink/?LinkID=59771* you need the following additional minimum configuration:

- A hard disk partition with approximately 4 MB of free disk space